THE ROYAL NAVY IN EASTERN WATERS

The
Royal Navy
in Eastern Waters

Linchpin of Victory 1935–1942

Andrew Boyd

Foreword by N A M Rodger

To all those in the Royal Navy who planned and fought to secure Britain's position in the East in this period. They deserve better memory.

Copyright © Andrew Boyd 2017

First published in Great Britain in 2017 by
Seaforth Publishing,
An imprint of Pen & Sword Books Ltd,
47 Church Street,
Barnsley S70 2AS

www.seaforthpublishing.com

British Library Cataloguing in Publication Data
A catalogue record for this book is available from the British Library

ISBN 978 1 4738 9248 4 (HARDBACK)
ISBN 978 1 4738 9250 7 (EPUB)
ISBN 978 1 4738 9249 1 (KINDLE)

Typeset and designed by MATS Typesetters, Leigh on Sea, Essex
Printed and bound in Great Britain by CPI Group (UK) Ltd, Croydon, CR0 4YY

Contents

List of Tables and Maps   vi
List of Illustrations   vii
Foreword by Professor N A M Rodger   viii
Acknowledgements   ix
Abbreviations   xi
Introduction   xiv

Part I Preparing for Two-Hemisphere War
1 The Royal Navy 1935–39: The Right Navy for the Right War   3
2 The Naval Defence of the Eastern Empire 1935–40: Managing
   Competing Risks   55

Part II Existential War in the West
3 Securing Eastern Empire War Potential after the Fall of France   119
4 The American Relationship, ABC-1 and the Resurrection of an
   Eastern Fleet   175

Part III July 1941: The Road to Disaster in the East
5 Royal Navy Readiness for a War with Japan in Mid-1941:
   Intelligence and Capability   225
6 Summer and Autumn 1941: Reinforcement and Deterrence   271
7 The Deployment of Force Z and its Consequences: Inevitable
   Disaster?   310

Part IV An Inescapable Commitment: The Indian Ocean in 1942
8 The Defence of the Indian Ocean in 1942   355

Conclusion   400
Annex: Warships Completed by Principal Naval Powers 1930–1942   410
Notes   416
Bibliography   501
Index   528

List of Tables and Maps

Tables
1 Warships commissioned by the main naval powers
   January 1922–December 1934   13
2 Proposed DRC fleet and actual orders compared   28
3 Royal Navy expansion options 1938–1942   30
4 Royal Navy strength at 31 March 1942 – proposed and achieved   32
5 Royal Navy ships commissioned compared with the three
   Axis powers 1 January 1935 – 31 December 1942   35
6 United States naval forces in the Atlantic 1940–1941   198
7 United States and Royal Navy forces in the Pacific and Asiatic
   theatres 1940–1941   200
8 British Empire target naval strength   255
A Total warship completions by the principal naval powers
   across the period 1930–1942   412
B Warship completion by the principal naval powers presented
   on an annual basis 1930–1942   413

Maps
1 The eastern theatre in the late 1930s   xiii
2 Eastern Fleet waiting area off Ceylon 2–4 April 1942   371
3 Comparative tracks of Eastern Fleet and IJN task force off Ceylon
   5–6 April 1942   375
4 Detour by IJN Carrier Division Two 1500–1800 on 5 April 1942   376

List of Illustrations

The plate section is between pages 298 and 299

Admiral of the Fleet Sir Ernle Chatfield
Admiral of the Fleet Sir Roger Backhouse
Admiral Sir Reginald Plunkett-Ernle-Erle-Drax
Vice Admiral Sir Tom Phillips
Admiral of the Fleet Sir Dudley Pound
Rear Admiral Roger Bellairs
Admiral Sir Andrew Cunningham
The launch of the battleship *Prince of Wales*
Illustrious on her building slip at the Vickers-Armstrong yard
Illustrious and *Indomitable* in the Buccleuch Dock, Barrow
Prime Minister Winston Churchill on the quarterdeck of *Prince of Wales*
Key figures involved in eastern theatre planning at a meeting in 1942
The arrival of *Prince of Wales* in Singapore
Vice Admiral Sir Geoffrey Layton and Captain Douglas Doig in Singapore
Vice Admiral Sir James Somerville, commander of Force H
The battlecruiser *Renown* and fleet carrier *Ark Royal*
Hermione, *Edinburgh* and *Euryalus* manoeuvring astern of *Sheffield*
Rear Admiral Kelly Turner in conversation with Admiral Sir Dudley Pound
The battlecruiser *Repulse* in 1941
Prince of Wales leaving Singapore
Martlet of 888 Squadron flying over Somerville's flagship *Warspite*
Fairey Albacore torpedo bombers on the flight deck of *Indomitable*
A Martlet being conveyed to the flight deck on *Illustrious*
Vice Admiral Chuichi Nagumo
The Japanese aircraft carrier *Akagi*
IJN aircraft carrier *Hiryu* running speed trials
Illustrious, *Formidable* and *Warspite* in the Indian Ocean, 1942
The IJN task force in the Indian Ocean during Operation C
Zuikaku preparing to launch the strike on Colombo, 1942
The flight deck of *Illustrious* during Eastern Fleet exercises in the Indian Ocean

Foreword

There are a great many books about the British part in the Second World War, but there are not that many original interpretations. It is historians, not generals, who are obsessed with re-fighting the battles of the last war, and always along the same lines. History has been unkind to Churchill, in spite of his having written it himself, because later generations of historians have concentrated on trying to undermine his reputation, but their fixation on personality, rather than policy, leaves his central role unchallenged – and not only his. Far too many discussions of strategy and policy in the Second World War are still framed in the terms first defined by the memoirs of the leading participants, and by defensive post-war writings designed to safeguard the reputations of particular countries or services. Writers who are aware of what was happening in countries beyond their own are distressingly rare, and Britain and America still tend to produce histories divided by a common language. More than seventy years after it ended, it is still hard to find dispassionate studies, free of emotional commitment, with a grasp of grand strategy broad enough to embrace what was truly a world war.

The bookshelves crack under the weight of books about forgotten fleets and forgotten armies, but here is one which easily escapes the limits of the cliché. This is indeed a book which fills in a very big void in most histories of the Second World War at sea: the gap between the Pacific and the Mediterranean. Viewed from distant capitals, in the manner of the famous *New Yorker* cover, the Indian Ocean shrinks to the remote margins of the Pacific or the Middle East. Occasional disasters like the loss of the *Prince of Wales* and the *Repulse* still attract passing attention, but it is hard to recover from the existing literature any overall understanding of the strategic importance of this vast area. Andrew Boyd's achievement here is to show how the Indian Ocean was inseparably connected to the Pacific and China Seas in one direction, and the Middle East and Mediterranean in the other. More than that, he traces a coherent British grand strategy which embraced all these seas, moving ships and fleets frequently between them as threats and opportunities developed. Though some serious mistakes were made, his analysis gives us a more creditable as well as a more credible and detailed picture of British strategy-making, and in the process absolves Churchill of the blame usually thrown on him for the sinking of Force Z. This is a book which ought to startle the many comfortable ideas which have been dozing too long in their armchairs.

N A M Rodger

Acknowledgements

L ike all authors I owe thanks to numerous people who have helped me in writing this book. Without the support and encouragement of the University of Buckingham, who offered me a research fellowship, I would not have undertaken a DPhil at my stage in life and nor would I have decided to explore this topic. I am especially grateful here to Professor John Adamson, Professor Saul David, Professor Gwythian Prins and Dr Graham Stewart. I could not have had better mentors in the writing of history. I must also thank John Adamson for explaining to me in trenchant terms that writing a book is a very different exercise to writing a doctoral thesis!

Professor Nicholas Rodger not only kindly wrote the foreword, but gave me vital assurance that the themes explored in this book deserved attention and that my arguments were well grounded.

All historians stand on the shoulders of their predecessors. No historian can study the Royal Navy in the Second World War without acknowledging a debt to Stephen Roskill and in the case of the eastern theatre also to Arthur Marder. I have drawn hugely on their work, although inevitably I do not endorse all their judgements and conclusions. I have also much valued the work and insights of Christopher Bell, John Ferris, Joe Maiolo, Norman Friedman, Paul Haggie, who provided a rare copy of his original DPhil thesis, and Ian Cowman. The last deserves special mention because he was the first historian to investigate the Admiralty's offensive planning in the autumn of 1941 which features significantly in Chapters 6 and 7. His early and tragic death sadly cut short his research.

I could not have written this book without the outstanding service provided by the holders of relevant archives. I am especially indebted to The National Archives at Kew, the Churchill Archives Centre at Cambridge, the British Library, the National Maritime Museum and, for access to the papers of Professor Arthur Marder, the University of California. I am also grateful to the Japan Centre for Asian Historical Studies and the Military Archives of the National Institute of Defence Studies of Japan for permission to quote from their records and to reproduce the track of the Japanese aircraft carrier *Hiryu* in Map 4. I also thank Sabine Skae of the Barrow Dock Museum for finding me the photographs of the aircraft carrier *Illustrious* under construction.

I owe special thanks to Julian Mannering at Seaforth Publishing. The publishing process is mysterious and daunting to a new author. From our first contact, Julian has been a patient and understanding guide to this new world and his support has been faultless in every way. I also thank Stephanie Rudgard-Redsell for her excellent and sensitive editing.

Many others have provided me with advice and constructive criticism or acted as independent readers. In particular I am grateful to Andy Taylor, Julian Bene and Adrian Gossage.

The most important person of all has been my wife Ginette. She has not only put up with my 'Eastern Waters' obsession over the last five years, but has provided constant encouragement and support and, not least, the benefit of her fine editorial judgement.

Lastly, I remember my father, John Ronald Boyd, who died fifty years ago, but first sparked my interest in naval history.

Abbreviations

ABC-1 American British Staff Conference No 1
ACNS Assistant Chief of Naval Staff
ADB American-Dutch-British
AMWIS Air Ministry Weekly Intelligence Survey
ASV Air to Surface Vessel Search Radar
CAS Chief of Air Staff
CIGS Chief of the Imperial General Staff
C-in-C Commander in Chief
CNO Chief of Naval Operations in the US Navy
COS Chiefs of Staff
DRC Defence Requirements Committee
DCNS Deputy Chief of Naval Staff
D of P Director of Plans
DMI Director of Military Intelligence
DNI Director of Naval Intelligence
EF Royal Navy Eastern Fleet
FAA Fleet Air Arm
FEA Far East Appreciation
FECB Far East Combined Bureau
Force G Royal Navy task force comprising battleship HMS *Prince of Wales*
    and escorts
Force H Royal Navy task force established mid-1940 to guard western
    Mediterranean
Force Z Royal Navy task force renamed from Force G on 8 December,
    comprising the battleship HMS *Prince of Wales*, battlecruiser HMS *Repulse*
    and escorts
FSL First Sea Lord and Chief of Naval Staff
GC&CS Government Code & Cypher School
IJN Imperial Japanese Navy
IJNAF Imperial Japanese Naval Air Force
IJAAF Imperial Japanese Army Air Force
JIC Joint Intelligence Committee
JPC Joint Planning Committee
JPS Joint Planning Staff
JN 25 Japanese Navy cypher
KGV *King George V*-class battleships

NEI Netherlands East Indies
NID Naval Intelligence Division
OIC Operational Intelligence Centre
PM Prime Minister
'R'-class *Royal Sovereign*-class battleships
RAF Royal Air Force
RN Royal Navy
SIS Secret Intelligence Service
USN US Navy
VCNS Vice Chief of Naval Staff
WIR Weekly Intelligence Report

Additional abbreviations used in references
ADM Admiralty
AIR Air Ministry
AT Admiralty Telegram
CAB Cabinet Office
CCA Churchill College Archives, Cambridge
FO Foreign Office
IWM Imperial War Museum
JM Japanese Monograph
NMM National Maritime Museum, Greenwich
PREM Premier
TNA The National Archives
UCI University of California Irvine Libraries
WO War Office

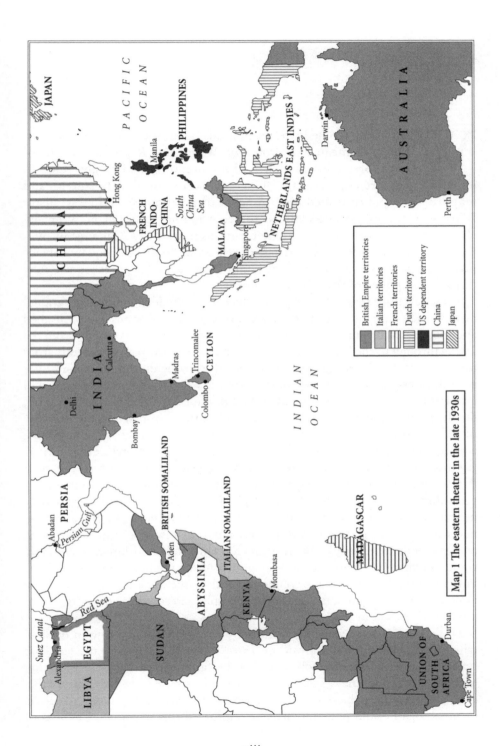

Map 1 The eastern theatre in the late 1930s

| British Empire territories |
| Italian territories |
| French territories |
| Dutch territory |
| US dependent territory |
| China |
| Japan |

Introduction

When I told people I was writing this book, the usual reaction was: 'Oh, you mean the *Prince of Wales* and *Repulse*, the fall of Singapore, and all that.' The more informed might refer to imperial over-stretch, arrogant underestimation of the Japanese, and inappropriate political meddling in naval dispositions by Prime Minister Winston Churchill. Some claimed to see a gloomy parallel between my chosen topic and Britain's recent interventions in Iraq and Afghanistan. Was there not a classic British pattern here of reluctance to make adequate defence provision, a conservative military establishment unable to recognise new threats, and poor political risk assessment?

These reactions reflect assumptions which are embedded in popular national memory. They are influenced by the way professional historians have described and interpreted Britain's effort to secure the eastern part of its empire from the 1920s through to the Second World War. The story conveyed consistently from the first post-1945 writings onward is one of strategic illusion in the interwar period, catastrophic defeat and moral collapse when the Japanese attacked in late 1941, irrelevance as the focus shifted to the Pacific theatre in 1942, and, finally, partial redemption from a successful Burma campaign in the last year of the war. British defeats in the East are explained primarily as the inevitable consequence of resource weakness and imperial over-stretch, especially as regards naval power.[1] Over-stretch, it is suggested, led Britain to pursue a flawed pre-war policy to secure Britain's Far East possessions not with a permanent military presence, but by deploying a naval fleet to Singapore only in time of crisis, the 'Singapore strategy'. The prevailing view insists that Britain never had the naval resources to protect a two-hemisphere empire, let alone meet a simultaneous triple threat from Germany, Italy and Japan. It certainly could not counter Japan once it was fighting for its life in Europe in 1940/41. Furthermore, the Royal Navy compounded resource weakness by persistently underestimating its Japanese opponent and failing to recognise the potential of modern air power at sea.[2]

This picture sat conveniently with the view of Britain as being in decline, which became fashionable from the 1960s.[3] Rapid collapse in the Far East reflected imperial over-stretch, but also the failings of a backward-looking military leadership and a sclerotic defence industrial base which was unable adequately to meet the demands of modern warfare. Other themes such as racial arrogance and poor intelligence reinforced this narrative. The loss of

Singapore and the other Far East territories therefore came to symbolise a wider failure of imperial will and capacity. Meanwhile, the defeats suffered by the Royal Navy in the East surely signalled the end of its claim to be the pre-eminent maritime power, on which the security of the British Empire rested.[4] In future, Australia and New Zealand would have to look to the United States for protection. There is also widespread agreement that while Britain's early war with Japan ended in ignominy, this ultimately had little impact on the overall global struggle against the Axis. Britain's role in the East was essentially irrelevant to the Allied cause, whatever the blow to imperial standing. The consensus is that both Japan's own fate, and that of the countries she conquered, was determined solely by American power in what was primarily a Pacific-based conflict.[5]

Even a brief look at British government records from the mid-1930s through to the first half of the war exposes problems with this still predominant narrative. From 1935 onward, the government's commitment of resources and the Royal Navy's planning for a future two-hemisphere war was remarkably ambitious. The challenges in dealing with three widely dispersed enemies in the short term were certainly viewed as formidable, but there was no lack of will to invest in the long-term naval defence of the empire in the East. Nor did the pace and quality of naval output from 1935 to 1942 easily fit with the traditional picture of a sclerotic, unresponsive shipbuilding industry. In early 1942, in response to the new Japanese threat, the Royal Navy deployed a larger fleet to the Indian Ocean than it had to any other war theatre previously. It intended to have three-quarters of its major vessels in the eastern theatre by the middle of the year. British decision-makers at the time did not, therefore, see the Indian Ocean as just a sideshow compared to the Atlantic and Mediterranean. On the contrary, they saw its security as critical to the successful conduct of the war. As the Joint Planning Committee emphasised, the consequences of failing to hold the Indian Ocean, including the loss of Persian oil, the Persian supply route to Russia, the whole position in the Middle East, India and, potentially, Australia and New Zealand, were 'incalculable'. For a while, such a scenario seemed entirely possible. Yet this aspect of the war has received surprisingly little attention.

Despite its numerous commitments elsewhere, and its heavy recent losses, the Royal Navy had the capacity, the resilience and determination to find considerable resources to protect this theatre. There is a discrepancy here between the established portrayal of the naval defence of Britain's empire in the East as a story of strategic illusion, weakness, and then irrelevance, and the much more positive reality of Royal Navy policy, planning and execution displayed in the official record. Many historians have gone to great lengths to explain why, faced with growing threats in Europe, Britain would never be able to send a fleet to the East. Few acknowledge that when it really mattered, Britain did send one, after all. To argue that commitments in the Atlantic and Mediterranean rendered naval defeat in the East inevitable is to oversimplify.

The records reveal another important challenge to the prevailing historical view. This concerns the portrayal of the debate and decisions over British naval reinforcement to the Far East in the autumn of 1941, which led to the deployment of the battleship *Prince of Wales* and battlecruiser *Repulse*, later known as Force Z. The subsequent loss of this force to the aircraft of an 'upstart Asian power' was traumatic at the time. But it has also been frequently presented as a fitting symbol for the wider collapse of British imperial and naval power. Starting with the British official history of the naval war published in 1954, responsibility for this disaster has been pinned firmly on Churchill.[6] He stands accused not only of pursuing an unrealistic goal of political deterrence in pushing for a modern battleship to be deployed direct to Singapore, but of brushing aside professional naval advice. This interpretation ignores substantial and unambiguous Admiralty and Cabinet Office records demonstrating that the naval staff shifted in September that year from their previous cautious defensive strategy in the Indian Ocean to the concept of a forward offensive strategy based on Singapore and, potentially, Manila. This offensive strategy is the direct opposite of that traditionally ascribed to the Admiralty. It was the Admiralty, not the prime minister, who wanted a Royal Navy battle-fleet in Singapore in the immediate run-up to war in late 1941. Their intent to conduct offensive operations with inadequate forces broke with previous policy, and showed reckless disregard for the risks.

This further striking discrepancy between established history and the official records raises important questions. First, why has this shift to a forward strategy, which the Admiralty certainly saw as important at the time, received so little attention?[7] There are fascinating issues of reliability and integrity here. While some historians have undoubtedly adopted a rather partisan position in telling this story, key contemporary naval witnesses were highly selective in their subsequent testimony during and after the war. Secondly, what caused the shift? The documents record that it took place, but do not adequately explain why. It can, however, be understood by looking at how Far East naval policy evolved across the whole of 1941, rather than concentrating on the well-known debate over naval reinforcement conducted between the prime minister and First Sea Lord in August that year. In particular, it is important to recognise the impact of developments in other war theatres and, crucially, how American attitudes influenced British strategic thinking during 1940/41. Finally, how much does this issue matter? Did it affect the fate of Force Z and subsequent events? More important, given the symbolism which has become attached to the whole Force Z story, if the facts are fundamentally different, is there a requirement to reconsider the whole way the Singapore strategy and the naval defence of the empire in the East has been presented?

The contemporary British records also reveal two wider problems with the way the naval defence of the empire in the East has traditionally been described and interpreted. The first concerns the part played by the Mediterranean and Middle East in British strategic thinking. An important theme in the established Far East narrative, which reinforces the traditional 'over-stretch' argument, is that Britain sacrificed the Far East in 1941 to concentrate its military effort in the Mediterranean and Middle East. It is often suggested that this choice was discretionary, and reflected prime ministerial prejudice, rather than careful strategic calculation. However, the way British leaders themselves perceived the balance of risk between Middle and Far East theatres at the time, the influence of pre-war thinking, and how and why priorities changed after the Japanese attack, is rarely properly addressed. Indeed, despite thousands of books written on the Middle East and Mediterranean campaigns in the Second World War, the rationale offered in most historical accounts for Britain's overall investment here prior to 1942 remains opaque.[8] That is largely due to the tendency of both critics and advocates of Britain's Mediterranean strategy to treat the theatre in isolation, and to view it through the optic of developments in the second half of the war. Critics see the Mediterranean as a commitment largely irrelevant to the successful prosecution of the war, with costs disproportionate to benefits.[9] Advocates emphasise the need to protect oil resources and empire communications, as well as the need to engage the main enemy somewhere, but struggle to explain why these factors were important when they present them within a narrow Middle East focus.

There was a key shift underway in how British leaders thought about the defence of the empire in the East, starting in the winter of 1938/39. They began to recognise that, faced with three potential Axis enemies and limited British resources, the essential objectives in the East were to protect the inner core, comprising Australasia and India, and also the communications across the Indian Ocean. Singapore was still seen as essential to secure the eastern perimeter of this core, but interests north of Singapore were ultimately dispensable. At the same time, there was growing awareness that controlling the eastern Mediterranean was essential too. This was not to protect a highway to the East, since the Admiralty expected the Mediterranean to be closed to through traffic in war. It was rather to protect the western boundary of the eastern core, and to shield the vital resources of the Middle East – above all, its oil.

What British strategy was reaching towards here, hesitantly at first, but with ever sharper definition under the pressure of events, was the concept of a single interdependent space under British control, an 'eastern empire', extending from Egypt, through the Middle East and Indian Ocean, to Australasia. By mid-

1941 Britain not only viewed the eastern empire in exactly this way, but recognised that to survive as an effective fighting power itself, and to ensure the survival of its new Russian ally, it needed the resources and strategic leverage of this wider space. It was an important force multiplier, giving Britain oil and other important raw materials, and vital additional human resources. Equally important, by controlling this wide eastern space, Britain denied its resources and opportunities to the Axis.

As this vision of a single 'eastern empire' space evolved from early 1939, the Royal Navy became the primary means for safeguarding it from the existential threats facing it at both ends. It therefore had to find a way of balancing its limited resources between the two ends from this time. This concept of a wider eastern empire, ultimately secured by ensuring command of the eastern Mediterranean and Indian Ocean, is different from the established historical view. This has defined Britain's empire in the East, and the role of the Royal Navy in securing it, in narrow terms. It has focused almost entirely on the specific problem of the defence of the Far East territories against Japan: above all, Singapore and its naval base. In reality, by 1939 Britain's leaders recognised that the use of naval power to defend British territories and interests in the East was more than protecting Singapore. Managing competing risks to east and west and across the Indian Ocean required a more flexible response. Events would demonstrate that the fate of Singapore and ability to deploy a fleet to the eastern theatre were different things.

The second structural problem with the traditional narrative concerns the role played by the United States. Most accounts of Royal Navy policy and performance during the approach to the Far East war, especially the issues surrounding naval reinforcement in the autumn of 1941, imply Britain was making decisions in isolation. They make only passing reference to American influence on Royal Navy plans for managing the naval risk from Japan. Yet American attitudes were, in reality, fundamental to the evolution of British strategy. As soon as France fell, Britain recognised it would be unable to provide any naval forces to counter Japanese intervention unless it withdrew from the eastern Mediterranean, which would now seriously undermine its ability to continue the war. It hoped therefore to enlist the United States to guard the eastern boundary of the eastern empire. The subsequent difficulty the two powers experienced in reaching any agreement on Far East naval defence during 1940/41 can only be understood by recognising the primacy they both gave to Atlantic security. Equally, explaining the despatch of British naval reinforcements to the Far East in autumn 1941 requires understanding of the compromise agreement reached at the ABC-1 staff talks the previous March. Here, the US Navy assumed certain Royal Navy responsibilities in the Atlantic, in order to release Royal Navy forces for a new Eastern Fleet. Meanwhile, the ambitious American plans initiated in autumn 1941 to reinforce the Philippines with air power to contain Japan have been largely ignored in accounts of Britain's war in the East. Yet American actions here gave the emerging Allied policy of deterrence and containment more credibility than has so far been recognised, even if, as this book shows, the measures proved too late and too ill co-ordinated to be effective.

In addition to these problems with the way the Royal Navy's role in the East has been described and interpreted, there are striking gaps in historical coverage. There is a large body of work addressing the Singapore strategy, and numerous books have addressed the origins and loss of Force Z. However, the former is heavily focused on the period before the fall of France, while the latter tend to begin with the debate between the prime minister and Admiralty in August 1941. There has been surprisingly little analysis of Royal Navy policy and planning in the eastern Mediterranean in the late 1930s, and how it sought to balance interests here with those in the Far East.[10] The same applies to the important debates over the trade-offs between these two theatres during 1941. There are several authoritative studies of Anglo-American naval relations through the 1930s and up to the ABC-1 staff talks, but then almost a void from March 1941 until late 1942.[11]

There is, of course, a huge literature addressing the performance of the Royal Navy in the Second World War. A similarly large literature examines the Pacific war from the vantage point of the US Navy and Imperial Japanese Navy (IJN).[12] However, with the notable exception of the Force Z story, only a tiny proportion of this historical coverage deals specifically with the Royal Navy's performance in the eastern war. Historians have generally tackled Royal Navy strategy and operations in the East after the loss of Force Z within more general studies of either the Royal Navy or the war with Japan. Only one historian, Arthur Marder, has attempted a comprehensive picture of the Royal Navy's engagement with Japan from build-up to war through to the final operations in the Pacific in 1945.[13] Marder apart, the period between the loss of Force Z in late 1941 and the build-up to the Pacific deployment in late 1944 has been barely touched outside the general histories.[14] This includes the critical importance of Indian Ocean communications during 1942 in sustaining Britain's whole position in the war at that time, and the implications of the IJN incursion against Ceylon in April that year.[15] It is striking that important issues such as the role of Persian oil and the Persian supply route to Russia are barely mentioned, in even the best general histories of the war.[16] A further gap is the limited biographical coverage of the Royal Navy officers who were most influential in policy and operations relating to the eastern empire in the period covered by this book.[17] Only Admiral Sir Andrew Cunningham has been relatively well served.[18]

The starting point for this book, therefore, is that the established view of Britain's eastern naval strategy from the late 1930s is not satisfactory. It provides a one-dimensional account of the Royal Navy's effort to counter a specific threat from Japan when, from 1938, the naval defence of the eastern empire was becoming a much more complex set of competing challenges. The story of how the Royal Navy identified and met those challenges amply deserves new scrutiny. It certainly involves much more than a catalogue of Britain's failings as a fading imperial and maritime power. The Royal Navy of 1939 was stronger, and its rearmament programme more effective, than mainstream accounts of its interwar history imply. Britain did not pursue a single rigid strategy based on sending a fleet to Singapore to meet an attack by Japan. It adjusted its defence plans and dispositions to the evolving threats. The fall of France made its position in the East much more difficult, but also brought home to Britain that it must secure the whole space from Egypt to Australasia if it was successfully to prosecute the war.

The importance of the war potential of this wider eastern empire and the role of the Royal Navy in securing it is the central theme of this book. With American help, the Royal Navy had to find a way of countering the existential threats to this empire war potential from both east and west. In meeting these threats, the campaigns it fought in the Mediterranean and Indian Ocean were both essential and interdependent, and they indirectly influenced the Atlantic outcome too. In a global war for survival, securing the overall war potential of this eastern empire space and denying it to the Axis powers ultimately mattered more than holding any specific territory, even Singapore. This is the measure against which Royal Navy performance in the East should be judged.

The book is in four parts:

Part 1 re-examines the strengths and weaknesses of the Royal Navy as it faced the prospect of war in two hemispheres in the late 1930s. It assesses the suitability of the rearmament programme for the war it would actually fight from 1939 to 1942, and its overall operational effectiveness compared to its three potential Axis enemies. It then examines how British strategy to maintain adequate security through naval power for the core territories of the eastern empire evolved between 1935 and the fall of France in 1940 against the looming Triple Axis threat. It explains why this strategy was more flexible and realistic, and better directed at what would prove the critical points in the first half of the war, than previously accepted.

Part 2 describes how, following the fall of France in mid-1940, Britain tried to establish a limited defensive screen against Japanese intervention in the Far East, while it concentrated on the existential threat to the United Kingdom homeland from Germany and securing the eastern Mediterranean and Middle

East. It explains why Britain's investment in the Middle East and the Royal Navy commitment to the eastern Mediterranean from 1940 to 1942 was essential to effective prosecution of the war. This part then shows how promises of US Navy support in the Atlantic and exaggerated expectations of American deterrent power against Japan encouraged Britain's war leadership to believe it could simultaneously maintain a forward defence strategy in the Middle and Far East theatres, opening the way to strategic failure.

Part 3 assesses British perceptions of the threat posed by Japan in mid-1941 and the naval resources available for Far East reinforcement in the second half of the year. It shows how reinforcement plans evolved through the summer and autumn, how the Admiralty came to embrace their reckless forward deployment policy north of Singapore, and how this led inexorably to the loss of Force Z.

Part 4 examines why the entry of Japan into the war demonstrated that control of the Indian Ocean was critical not just for Britain, but also the wider Allied cause – ranking, indeed, second only to the Atlantic lifeline in importance. It assesses whether the hastily gathered Eastern Fleet guarding Ceylon was really the helpless bystander popularly portrayed. It then reviews whether the Royal Navy could generate sufficient power during the rest of 1942 to defend the Indian Ocean theatre against any naval force Japan was likely to deploy.

The 1935 start date for the book marks the time when the threats posed by a resurgent Germany, an increasingly hostile Japan, and unpredictable Italy, moved from theoretical to real. The end of 1942 is an appropriate finishing point because, as the final chapter explains, it marks the end of any credible threat from the Axis to the core eastern empire through either the Indian Ocean or the Middle East.

PART I

Preparing for Two-Hemisphere War

1

The Royal Navy 1935–39:
The Right Navy for the Right War

For fifty years after the Second World War, the standard portrayal of the Royal Navy in the interwar period was one of decline and decay modified by a late (and from the political perspective reluctant) spurt of rearmament. Outside a few specialist works, this picture remains dominant.[1] This prevailing view stresses not only the rapid decline in size of the Royal Navy, both absolute and relative, from its zenith in 1919, but a failure of the Royal Navy leadership to learn the lessons of the First World War and especially to address the implications of air and submarine power. Thus the Royal Navy at the start of the 1930s has been described as 'technologically obsolescent, truncated by treaty, no longer a war hardened fighting service, but once again a kind of fashionable yacht club more apt for elegant displays of ship handling and Royal Tours of the Empire than for battle'.[2] Such language may be florid and overstated, but it captures the popular picture of the interwar Royal Navy. This portrays a service fixated on fighting another Jutland and, at best, technically and tactically conservative, if not backward, compared to its US Navy and Imperial Japanese Navy (IJN) peers.[3] There is a fascinating example recently highlighted which contributed to this image. This is the endless repetition of the claim first made by Stephen Roskill, the official naval historian of the Second World War, that 'not one exercise in the protection of a slow moving mercantile convoy against sea or air attack took place during the period 1919–1939'. This 'seeming extraordinary assertion' has been taken as fact ever since.[4] The claim is wrong, and one of many enduring myths.[5]

This chapter shows that the Royal Navy of the late 1930s was a stronger, more innovative, and more ambitious force than even the most revisionist views have so far suggested. It begins by examining the state of the Royal Navy, with its inherited strengths and weaknesses, in 1935. This is the chosen starting point for this book for three reasons. First, as already noted, it marks the moment when the risks to Britain's maritime security from a resurgent Germany in Europe and from Japan in the Far East became real. By the end

3

of that year, a third potential enemy, Italy, was in view as well. Secondly, it marks the beginning of a naval rearmament programme, designed to address the new risks, but also deficiencies in naval investment accumulated since the late 1920s. Finally, it marks the time when the naval limitation structures which had been in place since the Washington Treaty of 1922 began to break down. From this 1935 starting point, the chapter examines the Royal Navy's response to the emerging threats to Britain's naval security. It scrutinises the Royal Navy rearmament programme, the industrial capacity to support it, what it hoped to achieve, whether its goals were realistic, and how well it met Royal Navy requirements for the war it ultimately had to fight from 1939 through to the end of 1942. The final section assesses Royal Navy strengths and weaknesses by 1939 and its overall operational effectiveness then, compared to its future enemies. The evolution of Royal Navy strategy and planning during this period for a global war against three potential enemies is addressed in the next chapter.

1919–1935: Underlying strength and resilience
At the start of 1935, the Royal Navy remained the largest navy in the world, whether judged by total warship tonnage or by numbers of major warships.[6] Leaving aside the US Navy, where there was broad parity, it had a significant margin over any other single naval power, at least in quantity, in every category of major warship except submarines, where Japan and France had larger numbers. It had the three largest and arguably most powerful capital ships in the world. These were the battlecruiser *Hood* completed in 1920, the largest and fastest capital ship until the completion of the *Bismarck* in late 1940, and *Nelson* and *Rodney*, the extra capital ships permitted to the Royal Navy under the 1922 Washington Treaty. The two *Nelsons* completed in 1927 had a design more modern than any contemporary.[7] The Royal Navy also possessed a network of global bases that made it the only navy genuinely deployable on a worldwide basis, though until the Singapore base was complete (which was still some years away), there were no dockyards capable of heavy repair east of Suez and the Cape, which would constrain any long-term fleet deployment in the Far East.[8]

For the first fifteen years after the end of the First World War, there were certainly no immediate risks to the maritime security of the British Empire and, arguably, no credible risks at all. Despite naval rivalry and some economic tensions, war with the United States was inconceivable. Germany was effectively disarmed and other European powers were friendly. Japan, with the third largest navy in the world, posed a theoretical threat to British interests and territories in the Far East, but until the early 1930s it was hard to see how serious conflict would develop in practice. Against this background, the size

4

and composition of the post-war Royal Navy through to 1935 was shaped by three factors. These were: the strength inherited at the end of the war and the historic experience and assumptions that had created and sustained that strength; subsequent political judgement on the size of navy appropriate to a global empire dependent on secure global maritime communications; and an international environment that, until the early 1930s, favoured measures promoting peace and disarmament.

The key issue for the British political leadership, contemplating naval policy for a post-war world without obvious security risks, was whether to sustain the historical status of a Royal Navy stronger than all other powers, risking a ruinous competition with a US Navy set on parity. Their decision, which reflected a broad political consensus, and reluctant acceptance from the Royal Navy leadership, was to adopt a 'one-power standard'. This standard, first defined in 1921 and confirmed by the Cabinet in 1925, required that 'our fleet, wherever situated, should be equal to the fleet of any other nation wherever situated'. The US Navy, as the next largest after the Royal Navy, became the new standard against which Royal Navy strength was assessed. The British naval staff accepted this formula because it granted them a virtual 'two-power standard' over Japan, the only credible threat to British interests in the Far East, and France as the largest European naval power.[9] The Royal Navy therefore acquiesced in broad parity with the US Navy from 1921. This parity was underpinned by the Washington Naval Limitations Treaty negotiated at the end of that year. The Washington Treaty text contains no direct reference to parity, but British government willingness to concede this was crucial in making the treaty possible. It is worth noting, however, that although the limits established for capital ships came close to parity, the Royal Navy came away with a slight advantage in both permitted tonnage (about 6 per cent greater) and numbers (twenty versus eighteen). The US Navy calculated at the end of 1922 that the Royal Navy had come away from Washington with a much greater superiority, perhaps 30 per cent, in the effective fighting strength of its capital ship fleet.[10]

The one-power standard was interpreted flexibly. It was a target, not a precise measure. The Royal Navy leadership always stressed that Britain had 'absolute' naval requirements, notably the security of empire communications, which dictated Royal Navy strength in addition to the 'comparative' require-ments relative to other powers. British stakeholders generally accepted, therefore, that the Royal Navy could not slavishly copy the US Navy, or accept parity across all categories of warship. This flexibility of interpretation was inevitably used by the Admiralty to push for larger investment and by the Treasury to rein it in.[11] As the Director of Plans, Captain Tom Phillips, stated in 1937 – 'The term "One Power Naval Standard" is extremely vague and means different things to different people'.[12] The commitment of successive governments to the one-power standard through the 1920s and the Great Depression 1929–31 reflected the consensus that the continued security and wellbeing of the empire rested on the perception by both friends and potential enemies that Britain intended to remain the dominant maritime power. It was also due to the success of the Admiralty in portraying Japan as a plausible future opponent, and using this as a focus to frame plans, budgets and political debate in a practical way.[13]

The concept of a one-power standard suited British needs well enough during the 1920s, when other European navies were in decline and the international situation was benign. It also suited the Royal Navy which, through skilful negotiation with the Treasury, won rather more investment than parity strictly required and, arguably, ended the decade with its superiority over the US Navy enhanced. However, by the early 1930s, as the risk of naval conflict with Japan became more credible, the argument used to set the standard of strength shifted. By 1932 the Cabinet had effectively recognised, though not formally agreed to fund, a modified standard proposed by the Admiralty.[14] This recognised that security in Europe might be threatened while most of the Royal Navy was fighting a Far East war with Japan. It therefore stated that 'we should be able to retain in European waters a "deterrent force" to prevent our vital home terminal areas being commanded by the strongest European naval power while we took up a defensive position in the Far East and brought home the necessary units for home defence'. The growth of the French and Italian navies initially drove this change, more than concern over Germany. It clearly fell short, at this stage, of a two-power standard, excluding the United States. It was a move in this direction, but still a limited and achievable objective.[15] The change enabled the Royal Navy to bid for more resources, but it had little practical effect on Royal Navy funding before fiscal year 1935.[16]

The application of the one-power standard defined against the United States, and the subsequent two-power standard excluding the United States, were complicated by the interwar naval limitation treaties. These set internationally agreed limits on naval strength, both quantitative and qualitative, and also defined relative strengths between the naval powers. The treaties confirmed the general concept of British and United States parity, but did not initiate it. They rather endorsed a comparative balance that the two parties had already agreed for their own reasons. The treaties, therefore, allowed Britain to pursue a one-power standard up to the ceiling set for the US Navy but, with some exceptions, not to exceed it. The treaties also constrained the flexibility with which Britain interpreted the one-power standard, by setting common limits on certain warship categories that did not suit Britain's particular needs. While the treaties set upper limits, they naturally did not define minimum levels of strength. Britain invariably built up to her permitted limits while, during the period 1925–35, the US Navy often failed to do so. The Washington Treaty allowed the Royal Navy to build two new battleships as soon as it wished, but there was no requirement to commence construction immediately, or indeed at all. Nor was it obvious that the Royal Navy would be in a position of immediate inferiority without them for some years to come. In the event, the Royal Navy got immediate political backing for the ships and laid the two *Nelson*s down within ten months of the treaty. The Royal Navy also laid down fifteen heavy cruisers between 1924 and 1928, compared with just eight by the US Navy. The ambitions of the US Navy leadership to achieve parity with the Royal Navy never received the necessary political and financial backing in this period. The Royal Navy therefore retained an advantage in major surface units well into the 1930s and, as already noted, was still some 10 per cent larger than the US Navy in 1935.[17]

The Royal Navy in 1919 contained a huge number of warships which were less than five years old, in all categories completed or laid down during the war. Those laid down later in the war were often of innovative design, reflecting war experience. They included the battlecruiser *Hood*, arguably the world's first 'fast battleship', larger and faster than any contemporary, with protection superior to the *Queen Elizabeth*-class battleships until their reconstruction in the late 1930s, and the 'V'- and 'W'-class destroyers, the most advanced of their day. These destroyers set the standard for most navies through to the early 1930s. They had geared turbine machinery, were well armed and the best sea-boats of their size anywhere. Over one hundred ships of these classes were ordered, with sixty-seven completed between 1917 and 1924. Fifty-eight remained on the strength as second-line destroyers earmarked for convoy escort in 1939. Twenty were converted to specialist anti-aircraft escorts between 1938 and early 1941, and a further twenty-one to long-range Atlantic escorts during the first half of the war.[18] The Royal Navy completed twenty-nine cruisers and seventy-nine destroyers from mid-1917 onward, seventeen and thirty-one of these, respectively, after the war. Apart from *Hood*, completed in 1920, sixteen capital ships had been completed during the war and were four years old or less. All these vessels had a normal lifespan remaining of at least fifteen to twenty years.[19] Early replacement was hard to justify in threat terms, but the Admiralty recognised that without steady investment it faced a block obsolescence problem later.

The Royal Navy, therefore, had a very modern core through the 1920s, enhanced by the two new battleships, *Rodney* and *Nelson*, and the substantial number of County-class heavy cruisers completed at the end of the decade under the Washington Treaty terms.[20] However, by the 1930s, this core was

7

ageing. Two-thirds of the cruisers and destroyers, and almost all the capital units, in the Royal Navy fleet at the start of 1935 derived from wartime investment. Given treaty limitations and economic stringency, implementing a programme through the 1930s that combined modernisation with increased strength to meet new threats was certainly challenging. However, the political and economic limitations were overcome through a mixture of good foresight, shrewd political management, and some luck, and the Royal Navy achieved sufficient of the right capabilities at the right time to protect Britain's most critical maritime interests through the first and most dangerous half of the coming war.

In reviewing the factors that determined the strength of the Royal Navy in the 1920s and into the early 1930s, the 'ten-year rule' requires mention. This has gained some notoriety for those seeking reasons for Britain's apparent lack of preparedness for the Second World War. The 'rule' was effectively Treasury guidance to the three armed services that, in preparing annual estimates, they should assume no major war for ten years. The rule was theoretically in force for much of the period from 1919 to 1932, when it formally lapsed. It moved forward on a rolling basis, so that the ten years started again each year. The concept was not, however, applied in a consistent fashion, nor did the Treasury always get Cabinet backing when it tried to use it to restrain specific investment projects. In the 1920s the benign international environment made the rule a reasonable assumption and it was perhaps even defensible in assessing the outlook for Europe as late as 1932. It is best seen as a further weapon for the Treasury negotiating hand, especially against the Royal Navy as the biggest spender on major capital items. It is doubtful that it had much practical effect, compared to the other factors already discussed, in determining the frontline strength of the Royal Navy.[21] If the Treasury had been fully successful in applying the rule, then logically the *Nelson* battleships would have been postponed and the County-class cruiser programme emasculated. It did have an impact on support services, war stores and reserves, and, above all, on the progress of the Singapore base. To that extent, it impeded the Royal Navy's global mobility as well as its immediate readiness for war.[22]

Despite the limitations imposed by the ten-year rule, British maritime power remained considerable at the start of 1935. The Royal Navy maintained the largest force of warships. The quality of Royal Navy personnel and fighting doctrine was high. Weaponry and equipment in most areas was at least competitive. British shipbuilding and naval support industries had lost significant capacity since the mid-1920s, but were still the largest in the world.[23] These continuing strengths nevertheless concealed potential weaknesses. There is a good argument that the provisions of the Treaty of London in 1930, the second major naval limitations treaty, were especially ill-suited to British interests and weakened the Royal Navy more than any other naval power. Although the Royal Navy's immediate strength slipped only marginally, by limiting new build the treaty exacerbated the problem of block obsolescence facing the Royal Navy in the mid-1930s.[24] Meanwhile, the combination of a much reduced naval building programme resulting from the treaty, together with the impact of the 1929–31 depression, weakened the naval industries, reducing capacity by around half between 1929 and 1936.[25] Finally, this combination of obsolescence and reduced industrial capacity hit the Royal Navy just as potential enemies were growing significantly in strength. While at the end of the 1920s the Royal Navy could handle any combination of likely threats with ease, by the mid-1930s Germany and Italy were building sufficient new and competitive warships to stretch the Royal Navy if she had to counter a serious threat in Europe as well as fighting Japan in the Far East.[26] While the Royal Navy could rearm once free of treaty obligations and pursue a new two-power standard excluding the US Navy, the capacity cuts in British industry meant it could not do so quickly.[27]

In explaining these weaknesses, there is an obvious point that needs emphasis, namely that political support for naval investment in this period was inevitably shaped by perceptions of the existing risks to British Empire security. Those who argue that Royal Navy strength was allowed to decline to a dangerous level tend to view the first half of the 1930s through the optic of hindsight – their knowledge of what happened in the second half. They imply political and naval leaders should have anticipated future risks at a point when these were not reasonably foreseeable. Given the time lag involved in most naval investment, a more substantial modernisation and replacement programme to have better capability in place by 1935 would have required decisions in 1929–31. At that time there was still no credible naval threat to Britain from European powers, while that from Japan remained theoretical, dictated by her position as the world's third naval power, rather than any immediate evidence of hostile intent. By the late 1920s Britain could no longer sensibly calibrate its navy and industry to existing threats. Britain's leadership must either continue supporting a much larger navy than it needed, or allow it to get smaller. In the context of the Great Depression and the continuing absence of any foreseeable challenge to British sea power, some reduction was inevitable.[28]

At the political level, American attitudes and developments were also influential. For all the aggressive talk in United States naval circles of achieving parity with the Royal Navy, it proved impossible to win political support in Washington for even a modest replacement programme in the 1920s, let alone for an increase up to Washington Treaty limits. The US Navy had completed only two post-treaty warships by the end of 1929, the two heavy cruisers of the

Pensacola class. A further eight heavy cruisers joined the fleet by the end of 1933, by which time the Royal Navy had completed fifteen. No US Navy destroyers were laid down until 1934.[29] Only with the arrival of the Roosevelt administration in 1933 would significant investment start. From the vantage point of 1930, if the United States was not spending, why should Britain not also accept reductions?

The key issues for the British political leadership, as they weighed the balance of advantage in the London Treaty negotiations, were whether to insist on retaining the 1931 start on capital ship replacement envisaged at Washington, and a global cruiser force sufficient for all contingencies, or to accept reductions that would effectively freeze the status quo with the United States and Japan, but at the price of a reduced margin of superiority in Europe. Given the lead the Royal Navy had retained through the 1920s, despite supposed adherence to a one-power standard, and the new investment it had only recently received with the *Nelson*s and County-class cruisers, it is not surprising that in a still benign international environment, Britain opted for the latter.[30]

Comparative expenditure between the Royal Navy and US Navy across the interwar period requires further comment. Looking across the ten fiscal years 1925–34, the headline figures suggest that US Navy expenditure was about 26.5 per cent greater than the Royal Navy during this period.[31] It is frequently argued that this discrepancy, which continued through the later 1930s, demonstrated low investment and under-resourcing for the Royal Navy. However, there is convincing evidence that United States naval production costs were far higher than those of the United Kingdom, generally by a factor of as much as two to three. Indeed, this cost difference seems to have persisted through the coming war. Some of this higher cost in the United States reflected higher quality equipment, engineering standards and, not least, habitability. It appears the British shipbuilding industry, contrary to popular belief, was also more efficient.[32] Taking the quality differential into account, it seems the US Navy had to spend at least 50 per cent more on the production and support of its ships through this period than the Royal Navy.

Some of the higher US Navy expenditure also reflected higher average US Navy manpower, which exceeded that of the Royal Navy by about 17 per cent across these years. This is largely explained by the US Navy's much larger air arm. By 1936, the US Navy had 15,000 personnel in its air arm, operating nearly one thousand aircraft. Royal Navy personnel numbers here were about one thousand, although comparisons quickly become difficult because of the British dual-control system at this time and the resulting Royal Air Force contribution to personnel and aircraft, together with its responsibility for shore-based maritime support. Dominion expenditure and manpower, which for practical purposes came under the strategic direction of the Royal Navy, and supported ships which were included in Royal Navy strength, should also be added to the Royal Navy for a true comparison. Admiralty figures suggest the combined contribution from Australia, New Zealand and Canada to empire naval defence was about £6.7 million per year and 6,500 personnel by 1935, representing, therefore, about 10 per cent of Royal Navy expenditure.[33] When these two factors are taken into account, it appears non-air investment and running costs were not very different between the two navies, but that still left the Royal Navy with a substantial benefit from its lower production costs. This explains why it could sustain a surface fleet some 10 per cent larger than the US Navy through the 1930s, despite the headline budget difference. It also meant, of course, that the British taxpayer got rather better value for money.

Headline figures confirm that the Royal Navy's comparative strength and resource base did reduce markedly in the middle decade of the interwar period. However important qualifications are required when judging its standing in 1935. First, the impact of the financial reductions from fiscal year 1930 onward was modest. The drop in expenditure over the five fiscal years 1930–34 compared to 1925–29 was 8.6 per cent. However, the earlier period included the exceptional expenditure on the new battleships *Rodney* and *Nelson*, whose combined cost was £13 million.[34] If this is removed, the reduction was around 6.8 per cent and much of this was accounted for in a fall of manpower of about 10 per cent between the two periods, which was largely due to decommissioning five old capital ships, following the London Treaty.[35] Reductions are always painful, but this fall is modest compared to other drops in defence expenditure in periods of perceived low risk during the twentieth century. In terms of GDP, the fall in naval expenditure here was about 0.1 per cent from 1.35 per cent average in the late 1920s to 1.25 per cent in the early 1930s. Naval expenditure in this period was just under half of all United Kingdom defence expenditure. By contrast, overall United Kingdom defence expenditure fell by 1.0 per cent GDP from 1990–97, following the end of the Cold War, and by a further 0.5 per cent over the next ten years to 2007.[36]

The impact of these financial cuts on effective fighting strength over the period 1930–35 was also modest. It is claimed that the London Treaty 'gutted' Royal Navy power in capital ships by reducing numbers from sixteen to eighteen available in the 1920s to eleven or twelve in the mid to late 1930s.[37] In strict numerical terms, this reduction was correct, but the five retired ships of the pre-First World War *King George V* and *Iron Duke* classes were old, slow (burning a coal/oil mix), under-gunned and under-armoured, compared to later foreign rivals. They had little military value for fighting the IJN, but were manpower-intensive and increasingly costly to maintain. Indeed, the deletion of these vessels alone arguably covered most of the 1930–35

11

manpower reduction. Robert Craigie, the chief Foreign Office negotiator for the London Treaty, reminded the Admiralty in 1934 that the five capital ships retired had to be scrapped anyway by 1936 under the original Washington Treaty terms. Given the benign international environment, advancing this a few years posed no serious security risk and saved £4 million.[38] Meanwhile, Royal Navy manpower had returned to the level of the late 1920s as early as fiscal year 1936.

It is, nevertheless, still true that the continuing bar on building new capital ships and the tonnage limitation on aircraft carriers, under the London Treaty, presented the Royal Navy with a block obsolescence problem for these categories in the late 1930s. If the original Washington terms for restarting capital ship build had held at London, then Britain was permitted to lay down one or two ships per year, with a total of eight allowed by the end of fiscal year 1935. The Royal Navy could have had eight more modern ships by 1939, but would probably not then have undertaken any reconstructions of its existing ships, so the net increase in actual fighting strength must allow for this. If eight new ships were appearing from 1935, it is also unlikely five more ships would have been laid down (as the *King George V*s were) in fiscal years 1936 and 1937, so perhaps further reducing net availability in 1941. The upshot is that a steady investment programme from 1931 would certainly have given the Royal Navy more modern or modernised capital ships in 1941, but the difference between possible numbers compared to historical reality might have been rather less than often claimed. Whether such an increase would have proved a good use of resources, or was what the Royal Navy really needed in 1941, is another debate.

The problem of block obsolescence applied equally to Japan, which was the Royal Navy's primary naval threat, and to the US Navy. The IJN solution was the *Yamato* super-battleship, of which they planned to build five, although the third was not scheduled for completion until 1945 and the others even later. The programme was already stretching Japan industrially by late 1941. By 1945, eight out of ten pre-*Yamato* ships would be thirty years old and militarily useless. By contrast, in 1938, the Royal Navy planned to have ten new ships by 1944 and to lay down at least one more per year from fiscal year 1940. Most battleship specialists doubt the *Yamato*s had much advantage over the Royal Navy *Lion*s in practical battle conditions. Royal Navy confidence that it could always out-build Japan was justified.[39] France and Italy enjoyed some freedom to build new capital units, but their construction only proceeded slowly, and war with France was anyway unlikely. The French *Dunkerque*-class battlecruisers were laid down in 1932, but did not complete until 1938. The Italian *Vittorio Veneto* was laid down in 1934, but did not complete until 1940. The first two German warships which count as capital ships,

Scharnhorst and *Gneisenau*, were not laid down until mid-1935.

The London Treaty also severely curtailed the Royal Navy's cruiser allocation, at a time when revisionist naval powers were starting to invest heavily in this category. Over the five years 1930–34, the three future Axis enemies completed a combined total of nineteen cruisers (eleven heavy[40] and eight light) and the US Navy thirteen (all heavy), while the Royal Navy completed only six (with two heavy). However, the Royal Navy had invested significantly in cruisers during the 1920s (completing a total of twenty-one with thirteen heavy), and had a further thirteen under construction during 1935 (including five heavy *Southampton* class[41]).[42] By the time these thirteen were complete at the end of 1937, the Royal Navy was steadily reducing the cruiser deficit, even before its main rearmament programme kicked in. It would lay down a further twenty-four cruisers before the outbreak of war, far more than the combined total of its Axis enemies. The Royal Navy also made an important investment in minor war vessels in the lean period of the early 1930s, which is rarely mentioned.[43] Over the five years 1930–34, it completed forty-three modern destroyers (the first laid down since 1919), sixteen assorted anti-submarine vessels and twenty submarines. The three future Axis enemies completed a combined total of thirty-seven destroyers in this period, no dedicated anti-submarine vessels and only sixteen submarines. Strikingly, the US Navy completed only three destroyers and four submarines. The Royal Navy also had as many destroyers building as the combined Axis group in 1935, and would continue to match them.[44] Only in submarines would it rapidly lose ground as German production began.

Table 1, which sets out the new warships commissioned by the main naval powers between January 1922 and December 1934, illustrates many of the points made in this chapter. The start date is chosen because wartime construction and adjustments were broadly complete by this time, and it also coincides with the signing of the Washington Treaty.

Table 1 Warships commissioned by the main naval powers January 1922–December 1934

	Britain	*US*	*France*	*Germany*	*Italy*	*Japan*
Capital ships	2	0	0	0	0	0
Aircraft carriers	4	3	1	0	0	4
Heavy cruisers	15	15	7	2	7	12
Light cruisers	11	10	5	5	6	10
Destroyers	45	5	50	12	49	63
Submarines	33	41	60	0	47	49

Sources: See under Table A.
Notes: The heavy cruisers listed for Germany are the pocket battleships *Deutschland* and *Admiral Scheer*. The Admiralty considered three of these to be equivalent to one capital ship. British heavy cruisers include two built for Australia.

Assuming Britain was not going to renounce its treaty obligations (and whatever the shortcomings of the treaty structure in specific areas, objective analysis suggests they brought her more benefit than loss overall[45]), where might more money have been spent if there had been political willingness to support a somewhat higher level of naval funding in the five years after 1929? Net expenditure on the Royal Navy in fiscal year 1929 was £56 million. This was somewhat less than the average for the period 1925–29, but more than in fiscal years 1923 and 1924. From 1929 it dropped to a low point of £50.2 million in fiscal year 1932, before rising again to £56.6 million in 1934, the last year before serious rearmament began. If 1929 levels of funding had been sustained for the next five years, the Royal Navy would have had an extra £16.5 million, representing about 6 per cent of total expenditure from 1929–34. Full modernisation of two battleships would have cost an additional £4 million, six additional cruisers, perhaps £12 million, and an additional aircraft carrier about £3.75 million.[46]

There are perhaps four obvious candidates for this extra investment. More capital ships could have been modernised: specifically the long refits of *Barham* (1930–33), and *Royal Oak*, *Malaya* and *Repulse* (1933–36) could have been exploited to increase the range of their guns. This involved turret modifications to raise the elevation of the 15in guns from twenty to thirty degrees. This increased maximum range from 23,000yds (21,000m) to 32,000yds (29,000m) using the new streamlined 6crh shell introduced in 1938. Twelve US Navy capital ships and all IJN capital ships received increased elevation in the late 1920s and 1930s. The Royal Navy only implemented this for four ships, *Warspite*, *Valiant*, *Queen Elizabeth* and *Renown* in the late 1930s. In addition, *Hood* and the two *Nelson*s had all been built with high-elevation guns. *Malaya* and *Repulse* could also have been reconstructed to the same standard as *Warspite*, which was in refit at the same time. Her modernisation involved a virtual rebuild with new engines, boilers, armour, anti-aircraft armament, and new fire control, as well as the increased elevation for her main armament 15in guns. Subsequent modernisations for *Valiant*, *Queen Elizabeth* and *Renown* were even more comprehensive.[47] At over £3 million, they cost about 45 per cent of the predicted cost of a new capital ship, but provided perhaps 70 per cent of the capability of a new ship.[48] Had war not broken out in 1939, the Admiralty also planned comprehensive reconstructions of *Hood*, and possibly *Barham*, beginning in 1940, and significant upgrades were also planned at this time for the two *Nelson*s.

It is often argued that the Royal Navy implemented far fewer capital ship modernisations than the IJN (all ten ships) or the US Navy (ten out of fifteen).[49] Admiralty figures in early 1937 indicate that the US Navy actually spent just under twice the Royal Navy total on capital ship refit and modernisation between 1922 and March 1937.[50] However, the US Navy undertook no further major modernisations after this time, while the Royal Navy had three commencing, at a total cost of some £10.5 million. This suggests that by 1940, when their last reconstruction finished, the Royal Navy had spent rather more across the whole interwar period 1922–39. A fair assessment is that the four Royal Navy reconstructions implemented from 1934 to 1940 were more comprehensive than any of those done by the IJN or US Navy, while two other Royal Navy ships (*Royal Oak* and *Malaya*) received partial modernisations comparable to the early upgrades carried out by the IJN and US Navy on their ships. Furthermore, in 1940–42, some of the unmodernised Royal Navy battleships had their gun range extended by fitting them for 'supercharge' firing. This increased range not through increased elevation, but by increasing the power of the discharge. At the maximum elevation of twenty degrees, gun range increased from 23,734yds (21,702m) to about 26,000yds (23,800m) with the pre-1939 4crh ammunition and 28,732yds (26,272m) with the new 6crh ammunition. *Barham* was the first battleship equipped for supercharge firing during the first half of 1940.[51] *Repulse* was modified to take 6crh supercharge shells (twenty rounds per gun) by end June 1941.[52] *Malaya*, *Resolution* and *Royal Sovereign* were also modified during their refits in the course of 1941.[53]

Apart from additional capital ship modernisation, war stores, infrastructure and support services could have been better maintained and upgraded where appropriate, including earlier completion of the Singapore base. More money could have gone on air power, both accelerating the carrier replacement programme and building up overall Fleet Air Arm strength. Finally, more investment could have been made in anti-submarine warfare, upgrading older destroyers and purchasing Asdic anti-submarine detection sets to facilitate rapid expansion in wartime.[54]

More and earlier modernisation of capital ships would have enhanced Royal Navy fighting strength and reduced the level of risk in the late 1930s, when the Royal Navy had three ships absent from the frontline simultaneously for reconstruction. However, Admiralty papers suggest that earlier investment here would have meant that plans to reconstruct *Valiant*, certainly, and *Queen Elizabeth*, possibly, would have been shelved.[55] By taking place later, the reconstructions of *Valiant* and *Queen Elizabeth* were more comprehensive, making them more valuable units. Overall, therefore, the real impact of an earlier modernisation programme on operational capability in 1940/41 would have been limited.[56] The stores and support shortfall was broadly rectified from 1934–39 under the deficiencies programme associated with rearmament. There is no guarantee that doing this earlier would have released funds for other purposes. The same argument applies to anti-submarine warfare, where Admiralty strategy was to create a core capability to facilitate rapid expansion in wartime. As discussed later, the effort here over the five years 1934–39 was proportionate to the threat as it appeared at that time.

By contrast, better and more consistent investment in naval air power from 1930 would certainly have significantly enhanced the effectiveness of the Royal Navy from 1939. If carriers had been laid down annually from 1932–35 (instead of the single *Ark Royal* laid down in 1935), this would have transformed Royal Navy carrier capability in the first years of the war.[57] However, it is important to recognise that the first generation of Royal Navy carriers, converted from battlecruisers, were only completed gradually through the 1920s and only reached critical mass at the very end of the decade. *Eagle*, converted from the Chilean battleship *Almirante Cochrane*, was completed in 1923, *Furious* in 1925, *Courageous* in 1928 and *Glorious* in 1929. The commissioning rate for these Royal Navy first-generation carriers was no slower than in the US Navy or IJN. The US Navy only commissioned the *Lexington* and *Saratoga* conversions in late 1927 and the IJN commissioned *Akagi* and *Kaga* in 1927 and 1928 respectively. All these were comparable in size and capability to the Royal Navy ships at this time. There was thus no overseas experience or incentive for the Royal Navy to start investing in a completely new carrier-building programme. In addition, by 1929, with four large carriers, the Royal Navy had twice as many as the US Navy and IJN. Replacing them almost immediately with new carriers was hard to justify.

Furthermore, the experience of the next few years was important to determine future carrier design, and undoubtedly ensured the comparative success of *Ark Royal* when she arrived in 1938. *Ark Royal*, as the first purpose-built Royal Navy fleet carrier, was almost an exact contemporary of the first purpose-built US Navy fleet carrier *Yorktown*. Although the latter commissioned a year ahead, the two were comparable in most respects. The IJN's first purpose-built fleet carrier *Soryu* also commissioned in 1937 although, at 16,000 tons, she was significantly smaller than *Ark Royal* and *Yorktown*. All three navies were thus pursuing a broadly similar path of carrier development. Investing earlier might have led the Royal Navy to a wrong turn, as taken by the US Navy and IJN who invested in light carriers, *Ranger* and *Ryujo* respectively, in the early 1930s. Finally, the scope for upgrading and increasing the size of the Royal Navy air arm in order to make such a carrier force effective was constrained in the early 1930s by the politics of dual control with the Royal Air Force. This might well have prevented earlier carrier investment translating into a proportionate increase in fighting capability, including appropriate aircraft. Restoring Royal Navy control, finally achieved with the Inskip report of 1937, was almost certainly not achievable in the economic environment of the early 1930s, and needed the accumulated experience of carrier air operations in the years after 1930 to enable the Royal Navy to win the argument.[58]

Overall, it is doubtful therefore, given treaty constraints, that more money spent in the first half of the 1930s would have made a decisive difference to Royal Navy performance in the coming war, given the course it took, and the assets that later proved most relevant, and nor, for practical purposes, to its comparative standing in 1935.

It has still been argued that, by 1935, only in the best of cases could Britain fight an effective war in the Pacific against Japan, while retaining a defensive force in Europe, and that it would be hard pressed to win a simultaneous war against any two naval powers.[59] This was certainly the thrust of the Chiefs of Staff 1933 Annual Review, which suggested virtually the whole frontline Royal Navy would now be required to ensure an adequate margin over the IJN fleet and secure empire communications. However, it painted a worst-case picture of the balance of forces and was partly drafted to make the case for additional resources. It overstated the strength the IJN could deploy under any practical scenario at this time, and took no account of the logistic challenges an IJN fleet would face contesting the South China Sea some 3000 miles from Japan.[60]

The strength of potential enemies in Europe also remained limited. The German navy at the beginning of 1935 comprised two pocket battleships, six light cruisers, a handful of coastal escort vessels, and no submarines. It was little more than a nuisance force capable of a limited raiding campaign on Britain's trade. This would remain the case for some years yet. The Italians had gathered a more impressive navy, at least on paper, but their battle-fleet was tiny and heavily outgunned by Royal Navy ships and they had no carriers. While they might disrupt Britain's communications through the Mediterranean, they posed little threat to the United Kingdom home base. Under any likely scenario, the Royal Navy could still deal comfortably with either of these opponents and simultaneously deploy a competitive defensive force in the Far East, if needed.[61] This was indeed the Admiralty assessment a year later in mid-1936, when it argued that two Royal Navy battlecruisers were sufficient to deal with the German surface threat until the arrival of their first true capital ships, *Scharnhorst* and *Gneisenau*, expected in mid-1938. In making this judgement, it is essential to recognise that, for the Admiralty, a 'competitive fleet' was not 'designed to seize control of the Sea of Japan but rather to provide a defensive "fleet in being" so that before Japan could attack our main imperial interests she would have first to defeat our fleet under disadvantageous conditions'.[62]

The overwhelming comparative advantage the Royal Navy enjoyed in the 1920s had certainly eroded by 1935 although, as Table 1 demonstrates, by less than often suggested.[63] Nevertheless, a better judgement of its relative standing in 1935 is that, excluding the United States and France, it retained a broad two-power equivalence. It had enough construction already underway within existing treaty limits to sustain this equivalence for the next two years. It had also prioritised its scarce resources in the first half of the decade on exactly the types of warship, modern destroyers, general-purpose cruisers, and a fleet carrier, that would prove most relevant in the coming war.[64] There was sufficient strength here to ensure the Royal Navy remained adequate to protect Britain's vital maritime interests, so long as the government and Royal Navy leadership made the right choices in the coming years.

The problem of block obsolescence, while certainly valid for capital units (ie battleships and carriers), is also overstated if extended to the Royal Navy as a whole. By the outbreak of the European war in September 1939, two-thirds of the cruiser and destroyer force was less than twelve years old and one-third was less than five years old. Two of the battleships were under twelve years old, while three others had just completed rebuilds providing capability close to modern design, and a new fleet carrier had joined the strength. Most of this 1939 strength comprised units begun before the main rearmament effort started in fiscal year 1936. In addition, one new battleship, one rebuilt battleship, two fleet carriers, seven cruisers, eight destroyers, ten escort destroyers and some fifty escort vessels were within twelve months of completion.[65]

The damage done to naval industries by the reduced orders for major warships from 1929 to 1934 can also be exaggerated.[66] These industries were more resilient and effective in restoring capacity than is often suggested.[67] Their success is evident in their delivery record. The tonnage of major warships laid down in fiscal year 1937 at 201,900 was only exceeded in 1909 when it was 219,540. Over the three fiscal years 1936–38, total tonnage was 533,900 compared to 405,930 for the years 1911–13 at the height of the pre-First World War naval race.[68] Britain laid down the extraordinary total of nine capital units in the single calendar year 1937, five *King George V*-class battleships of 35,000 tons and four *Illustrious*-class fleet carriers of 23,000 tons. This was a far greater scale of complex armoured vessels than anything attempted in a single year before 1914. Seven were complete by the end of 1941, and at least one more would have been, if work had not been suspended for six months in 1940 to release resources for escort vessels.

It is customary to emphasise the difficulty Britain faced in resurrecting the specialised resources for battleship construction and the consequent delay in completing the *King George V*s. In fact, *King George V* herself was completed in just less than four years, *Prince of Wales* just over, and *Duke of York* in four and a half. Despite the disruptions of wartime, the *King George V* battleships were also completed faster than anticipated at the last pre-war progress review in August 1939.

Dates for Completion

Ship	August 1939 estimate	Actual achieved
King George V	Jan 1941	Oct 1940
Prince of Wales	Aug 1941	Mar 1941
Duke of York	Jan 1942	Oct 1941
Anson	Feb 1942	Jun 1942
Howe	Aug 1942	Aug 1942

The first three ships gained between three and five months on the August 1939 target dates, and the last two much the same when allowance is made for a six-month halt in construction during 1940.[69] This record compares well with five years (1922–27) for the two *Nelson*s, when British warship building was still apparently at the height of its powers. US Navy battleships contemporary to the *King George V*s, such as the *North Carolina*s, were completed quicker, in about three years, but did not suffer the disruption of a wartime environment. In tendering for the first two *Lion*s on 31 January 1939, the two winning companies, Vickers-Armstrong and Cammell Laird, both offered a forty-two-month delivery and in July, despite news of slippage in the production schedule for the main armament, the former still expected to complete *Lion* in February 1943, ie four years.[70]

Over the same five calendar years 1937–41, Britain produced, that is laid down and completed, thirteen cruisers, forty-one fleet destroyers, forty-four escort destroyers, 128 anti-submarine corvettes, and forty-five submarines. The final eighteen months of this productive effort took place against a background of severe disruption from bombing and diversion of resources to repair war-damaged vessels. Warship tonnage in hand and tonnage launched tripled in just three years between December 1936 and December 1939.[71]

Year	Tonnage in hand	Tonnage launched
1936 (Dec)	375,740	90,260
1937 (Dec)	547,014	92,090
1938 (Dec)	544,000	60,980
1939 (Sep)	904,500	256,730

The tonnage in hand on the outbreak of war was equal to 75 per cent of the overall tonnage of the 1935 Royal Navy.

A report from the Controller, Rear Admiral Bruce Fraser, to the First Sea Lord, dated 3 February 1940, underlines the strength of the production record compared with the previous war, and the resilience of the shipbuilding industry. The plan was to complete 440,000 tons and 530,000 tons of warships respectively in the first two years of the present war. This compared with outcomes of 340,000 tons and 500,000 tons for the first two years of the previous war. In addition, merchant shipping output was planned to rise from a pre-war average of 0.75 million tons per annum to a war target of 1.5 million tons per annum. By contrast, in the last war, a pre-war average of 1.5 million tons had dropped to a wartime average of 0.6 million tons.[72] The actual figures achieved for warships were 263,000 tons in 1940 and 437,000 tons in 1941, which exceeded total Axis output in both years. United States output was only 52,600 tons in 1940 and 219,000 tons in 1941.[73] Merchant ship output from British yards was 798,648 tons in 1940, 1,133,243 tons in 1941, and peaked at 1,267,882 tons in 1942.[74] These outcomes were some way short of the Controller's targets, but the overall shipbuilding effort over the first two full years of the Second World War (1940/41) still compared favourably with the first two full years of the previous war (1915/16). Warship output was down by 140,000 tons on the First World War, but merchant ship output was up by 250,000 tons. This 1940/41 record must also be weighed against the considerable resources committed to repairing damaged ships (much greater than in 1915–16) and the disruption to British yards from air attack, which was not a factor in the earlier war, and which the controller could not easily estimate in February 1940. Indeed, it is striking that merchant ship output over the four war years 1940–43 was almost identical to the four years 1915–18, when British shipbuilding capacity was supposedly at its peak. By any standard, this Second World War performance did not reflect a moribund and ineffective industry.

1935: New risks, rearmament and expansion

If the Royal Navy still enjoyed just sufficient comparative advantage at the start of 1935 to meet its 1932 modified standard, what new threats did the Royal Navy leadership now see to the maritime security on which the British Empire depended? How confident were they that British naval advantage could be maintained? The deliberations of the Defence Requirements Committee (DRC) during 1934 and 1935 provide the most authoritative answer to these questions. The government established the DRC at the end of 1933 in response to the Chiefs of Staff 1933 Annual Review. In doing so, it formally acknowledged that Britain faced potential new security risks from Japan and Germany. It accepted the chiefs of staff advice that these risks might require additional defence resources and directed the DRC to identify key deficiencies.

It also instructed the DRC to make no provision for defence expenditure aimed specifically at countering attack from the United States, France or Italy. The DRC was chaired by the secretary to the Committee of Imperial Defence, Sir Maurice Hankey. The other members were the three chiefs of staff, and the permanent secretaries of the Foreign Office and Treasury, respectively Sir Robert Vansittart and Sir Warren Fisher.[75]

The need to consider two potential enemies in widely divergent theatres posed obvious difficulties in managing the distribution and rapid redeployment of forces. From the naval perspective, as the chiefs of staff stated, 'the ability of the "one power standard" to satisfy our strategic needs is dependent on a sufficient margin between the strength of the power on which the standard is calculated and the strength of the next strongest power'. By the end of 1933, the margin over the next power, Japan, increasingly hostile and set on naval expansion, looked insufficient when set alongside the future naval potential of a resurgent Germany.[76] The chiefs' 1933 review accordingly emphasised that defence resources were now dangerously out of step with potential commitments. The central figure in preparing and presenting their case to the government was the new First Sea Lord, Admiral of the Fleet Sir Ernle Chatfield.

Chatfield was First Sea Lord and chairman of the chiefs of staff for almost six years from January 1933 to August 1938 and subsequently held the political post of Minister of Defence Co-ordination from January 1939 until May 1940. He was perhaps the finest peacetime First Sea Lord the Royal Navy ever had, variously described as an 'outstanding naval leader and administrator', who left the Royal Navy 'a daunting legacy' in materiel, strategy, finance and personnel,[77] and 'as well matched to prevailing circumstances as Jacky Fisher and far more sound'.[78] He was a man of commanding presence, but his formidable intellect, presentational skills and political astuteness also placed him head and shoulders above his other military colleagues. He was thus a dominant influence in shaping Britain's overall strategic response to the new threats which emerged through the 1930s, and perhaps the decisive voice on the Far East. For the Royal Navy itself, he restored morale in the wake of the Invergordon mutiny, directed an effective and balanced rearmament programme, and championed the capabilities and fighting qualities then ably exploited by fleet commanders in 1939–45.[79] Perhaps no senior naval officer had faced peacetime challenges comparable to those confronting Chatfield when he took office but, by the time he departed in 1938, he had prepared his service exceptionally well for its ultimate test.[80]

The DRC began with a narrow mandate, but its role expanded steadily through 1934 and 1935 as the scale of German rearmament became apparent, and the British response shifted from a limited programme to address deficiencies towards a comprehensive programme of modernisation and expansion for all three services. It became the 'arena' in which British strategic foreign policy 'was threshed out among competing interests', and it largely determined the path of strategic defence policy up to 1939.[81] The DRC was clear from the start that while Britain faced no imminent military threat in 1934, Germany was the 'ultimate enemy', the only country that might pose an existential risk to the United Kingdom homeland, and therefore the main focus for long-term defence planning. It also accepted that, for the present, the defence of British possessions and interests in the Far East remained the primary naval commitment, but the objective here was restoring credible deterrence, 'showing a tooth' to draw Japan into a more constructive relationship.

Effective deterrence meant restoring the global mobility of the fleet eroded by the ten-year rule, enhancing the Fleet Air Arm, and modernising capital ships to ensure the existing fleet remained competitive with the IJN. The DRC recognised that, at the end of 1933, the Royal Navy was already inferior to the IJN in carrier-borne air strength. The naval programme proposed in its first report was intended to restore equality by 1939. In the event, the Fleet Air Arm contribution would fall well short of the 1940 target of 402 frontline aircraft deployable from carriers, and the IJN had meanwhile moved further ahead.

The DRC initially judged that a five-year programme to make good current deficiencies and equip the Royal Navy adequately for a Far East war would cover the German naval threat as well.[82] However, by autumn 1935, there was a DRC consensus, reflected in their report at the end of that year, that the Royal Navy must be strong enough to fight a simultaneous war in the Far East and Europe. This meant moving to a 'New Standard of Naval Strength', effectively a two-power standard measured against Germany and Japan. The naval recommendations in this DRC Third Report, and especially the concept of the New Standard, would underpin Royal Navy policy, planning and procurement for the remainder of the decade.[83]

Britain's national security policy and strategy from 1935 to the outbreak of the European war in 1939 is traditionally described under two themes, 'appeasement' and 'rearmament', with the two invariably addressed separately. The Admiralty, unlike the other two services, was a key player in one strand of appeasement, the use of judicious concessions to reduce, or at least bring within manageable limits, the number of enemies the Royal Navy would face. Rearmament is a handy umbrella term, but for all three services, and especially the Royal Navy, it had three distinct elements: modernisation, expansion and repositioning, or redeployment. Recognising these three elements is important because while they inevitably overlapped, they involved different challenges, as the DRC acknowledged during its debates through 1934 and 1935.

Modernisation meant updating and adapting existing force levels, either through replacement or upgrading, to fit them for a defence environment which in the late 1930s was changing very fast. Obvious challenges for the Royal Navy were the impact of modern air and submarine power at sea, and also recognising the opportunities and limitations of new electronic sensors such as radar and the Asdic anti-submarine detection system. Repositioning was about how Britain redistributed its defence resources to meet first two and then three enemies in three distinct theatres. For the Royal Navy, the initial challenge was to balance its strength between Europe and the Far East, but in 1938 decision-makers increasingly saw a need to choose between the Far East and eastern Mediterranean.

Much has been written on Royal Navy policy and strategy between 1935 and 1940, and the more specific story of naval rearmament, but there remain important questions that have either not been adequately addressed or not covered at all.[84] Did the Admiralty make a reasonable assessment of the future naval risks to the empire in 1935, and did it promote the right priorities within the DRC? Were Admiralty goals, assumptions and calculations for the New Standard of naval strength which emerged from the DRC process in 1936 reasonable? Were the defined goals ever achievable in any reasonable timescale? How does the Royal Navy rearmament record look if New Standard targets are adjusted to reflect the real rate of Axis build, as opposed to what the Admiralty in 1936 thought they might build? Did the New Standard reflect adequate understanding of the modern air and submarine threat and the likely impact of new technology? How close did Royal Navy rearmament over fiscal years 1935–39 get to the New Standard? Where would this investment have placed the Royal Navy compared to the Axis in 1942 without war losses? How well did the final 1935–39 rearmament programme equip the Royal Navy for the war? Could it have made better choices? Did the Royal Navy sacrifice investment in anti-submarine warfare to its big capital programmes? Did it recognise and understand the trade-offs here?

There is an argument that by 1934, the Royal Navy leadership, above all Chatfield as incoming First Sea Lord, anticipated a new naval arms race in which Britain would struggle to compete if it had to modernise and expand simultaneously. Such a race would be driven primarily by Germany and Japan, but could be exacerbated by programmes adopted by France, Italy and the United States. Given the limitations on British naval building capacity by the mid-1930s, the challenge was to ensure such a race did not fatally compromise Britain's maritime security. For Chatfield, success meant building a new two-power standard fleet, able both to beat the Japanese and simultaneously to defend Britain against the largest fleet in Europe. To achieve this in an affordable way, mutually destructive competition would be prevented, or at least dampened down by a new naval treaty framework. Diplomacy would buy time, first for the Royal Navy to complete the capital ship replacement programme delayed by the 1930 London Treaty, build up the Fleet Air Arm and cruiser force, and then from 1939/40 to expand towards a two-power standard, to be reached in 1943/44. This thinking, it is suggested, explains the Admiralty's support for the 1935 Anglo-German Naval Agreement (AGNA) which granted Germany the right to a fleet 35 per cent of the size of the Royal Navy, and its promotion of qualitative rather than quantitative limits at the new London Treaty negotiations which began the same year.[85]

There is little doubt that, for the Admiralty, the attraction of the AGNA was indeed the cap on German naval strength at a level that the Royal Navy could counter, while retaining sufficient capacity to conduct a defensive Far East war at the same time.[86] A crucial element of reassurance here was that the Admiralty judged correctly that Germany would anyway be unable to reach a 35 per cent target before 1942.[87] They also probably saw the AGNA as a means to encourage Germany towards a conventional fleet structure and naval strategy, and away from an asymmetric 'freak navy' directed at a trade war, which the Royal Navy judged was more dangerous. Meanwhile, Chatfield saw a wider treaty framework based on qualitative limits as a means of discouraging an expensive one-upmanship competition, and promoting naval strengths based on genuine national security needs.

However, it is doubtful that as early as 1934 the Admiralty, or at least Chatfield, had a clear goal for achieving Royal Navy supremacy based on a new two-power standard, and then embarked on a comprehensive and consistent strategy to achieve this. Chatfield may have harboured this as a private ideal, but there are no official papers which give such a concept formal status, or show how it was to be achieved prior to the completion of the DRC Third Report at the end of 1935. The detailed work on the New Standard proposed by the DRC was done by the naval staff in the summer and autumn of 1936, and the final paper did not reach the Committee of Imperial Defence until April 1937.[88] It is true that the New Standard projections aimed at 1942 and beyond for Britain to achieve an adequate balance with its potential enemies, but this did not mean the possibility of earlier conflict with Germany was ruled out. Not only was the DRC naval rearmament programme heavily front-loaded, but it maintained in practice a careful balance between capital units and support forces. The evidence does not support an argument that Chatfield and the naval staff deliberately courted risk by pursuing long-term investment, especially in capital units, at the expense of short-term improvements in trade defence and anti-submarine warfare. What is evident is a more pragmatic and flexible strategy to build up Royal Navy strength as quickly as possible to meet first two, and then three, emerging threats, within the bounds of what was politically and financially feasible and within available capacity. The period of risk that worried the Admiralty was not 1939-42, but the two years prior to 1939, when three capital ships would be in rebuild, and before any benefits of rearmament could take effect.

The deliberations of successive DRC meetings through the summer and autumn of 1935 certainly argue against Chatfield having a preconceived vision for a two-power Royal Navy. In July he was more concerned by unforeseen naval commitments arising from British obligations under the League of Nations, and the new problems associated with Italy, than with Germany.[89] On 10 October, when presenting the naval requirements to the DRC, Chatfield stated that the dual risk posed by Germany and Japan demanded increased Royal Navy strength (as opposed to modernisation), but he was not yet advocating this because it could not be delivered quickly. It was Hankey as chairman and, surprisingly, Fisher from the Treasury who insisted present Royal Navy strength was insufficient.[90] The key meeting was on 18 October. Hankey proposed that the Royal Navy should be strong enough to deal with Germany and Japan, and that 'extra insurance' was needed to secure the empire. Fisher agreed that present strength was unsatisfactory, and the Cabinet should be told that the United Kingdom homeland was being held at the expense of the empire perimeter. Royal Navy strength should match the combined total of Germany and Japan. Chatfield insisted that resource and technical constraints would prevent expansion before 1942. The fleet must be rebuilt before it could get bigger. Other powers were in a similar position. He doubted the comparative balance would change much in the interim.

Pressed by Hankey, Chatfield admitted that, given anticipated German strength, the Royal Navy would struggle to find adequate resources for a defensive war in the Far East in 1939 and would have to rely on superior fighting efficiency. If the DRC were now to advocate a two-power standard, he proposed this should:

(i) Enable us to place a Fleet in the Far East adequate to act on the defensive and protect our interests in that part of the globe.
(ii) Leave in Home Waters a force able to meet a war with Germany at the same time.

A formula based on combined numbers was not sufficient, since a margin must be added for refits and the ability of the enemy to choose their selected moment to strike. The committee concluded that the Royal Navy should be strong enough for 'simultaneous war', but it could not expand before replacement, and that the Admiralty should investigate a New Standard formula, including options for accelerating a building programme.[91]

Chatfield's New Standard formula was a logical evolution of the 1932 Standard formula, but he clearly also wanted flexibility in the way the standard was interpreted. His insistence that combined numbers were not necessarily sufficient was reflected in the final version of the DRC Third Report. The first clause for the proposed New Standard now became: 'Enable us to place a Fleet in the Far East fully adequate to act on the defensive and serve as a strong deterrent against any threat to our interests in that part of the globe.' The terms 'defensive' and 'deterrent' are significant. There is no suggestion of a force sufficient to destroy Japan. This was a limited and achievable objective. 'Leave' in the second clause became 'maintain in all circumstances'. However, by placing the Far East commitment first, Chatfield implied that, for the Admiralty, Japan remained the primary enemy. Given that the DRC were clear that Germany was not only the 'ultimate' enemy, but rapidly becoming the most imminent threat, it would have been logical to insist the order was reversed.

This is not a minor matter of drafting. The DRC Third Report posed important questions about Britain's real naval priorities, and therefore future Royal Navy strength and composition. Placing Germany first would potentially affect the distribution of forces (emphasising superiority rather than a necessary minimum after the Far East was addressed), and also their composition. It might have encouraged an earlier shift towards investment directed at trade and anti-submarine warfare. Putting the Far East second would have underlined the 'defensive' role of the fleet there, and stimulated more discussion about what that really meant. A defensive force, and certainly a 'deterrent', could presumably be somewhat smaller in capital units than the IJN? Chatfield had therefore chosen a measure for Royal Navy strength that was risk-driven, rather than the traditional measure based on comparison with other naval powers. He did not, however, encourage his staff to explore the full logic of a risk-based strategy. For the remainder of his tenure, he and his staff defaulted to programmes and plans based on comparative strength, even when the arrival of Italy in the Axis camp reduced the size of the force that could credibly be sent east.

While the DRC Third Report recommended adoption of the New Standard, its implementation required the Admiralty to prepare detailed requirements and the Cabinet then to approve them. Meanwhile, the naval programme initially put forward was a modernisation and replacement programme over the five fiscal years 1936 to 1941. This was designed to provide a fleet able to meet the original 1932 standard by mid-1942. It became known as the DRC Fleet.

It is important here to understand what the distinction between the 1932 Standard and the proposed New Standard as strategic goals meant in practical terms. This is less straightforward than the customary translation of 'one-power' compared to 'two-power' standard suggests. By 1936, the only 'European power' likely to threaten 'home terminals' under the 1932 formula was Germany. This formula therefore required the Royal Navy to hold off a surprise German attack for long enough to bring back the bulk of the fleet if it had deployed to the Far East to deal with Japan. A defensive screen only would then be left in the East while the fleet refocused on Germany. In theory, therefore, the difference amounted to main war plus defensive screen (1932 Standard) compared with simultaneous two-theatre war (New Standard). However, Chatfield's New Standard envisaged that the simultaneous war in the Far East would also be conducted within a defensive framework, so the difference was less stark than it appeared. The 'defensive' strategy envisaged for the Far East translated into a willingness to accept significant inferiority of numbers compared to the IJN. In late summer 1938 the Director of Plans, Captain Tom Phillips, anticipated that with likely reductions to the New Standard target, then in order to guarantee an adequate margin over Germany, the Royal Navy would deploy 25 per cent fewer capital ships and 50 per cent fewer carriers than the maximum likely IJN strength. There would be a similar shortfall in cruisers and minor war vessels.[92]

Following submission of the DRC Third Report, the DRC Fleet was quickly approved. However, both the ministerial subcommittee on defence policy and requirements and the Cabinet consistently deferred any decision on the New Standard presented to them in final form by the Admiralty in May 1937. They did approve a substantial acceleration of the DRC Fleet, virtually telescoping seven years' planned investment into three.[93] The results are shown in Table 2. Over the three fiscal years 1936 to 1938, the Royal Navy ordered five large armoured carriers instead of the three originally planned under the DRC programme (at least one of which was to be 'of smaller type'), twenty-one cruisers for fifteen, and double the number of destroyers and submarines. This new investment was accompanied by three capital ship reconstructions, extensive modernisation of one older carrier Furious and seven older cruisers converted into anti-aircraft ships. The latter were seven of the ten light cruisers in the Ceres and Capetown classes. Some of these were among the earliest ships to receive RDF (later known as radar). Overall, this was not only a much larger building programme than Chatfield had told the DRC was feasible at the end of 1935, but it was also much more balanced than he had originally proposed. The extra carriers and, above all, destroyers proved critical in late 1941.

Table 2 Proposed DRC Fleet and actual orders compared

Type	1936		1937		1938		1939		Completions 1941	
	P	A	P	A	P	A	P	A	P	A
Battleships	2	2	3	3	2	2	0	2	5	3
Aircraft carriers	1	2	1	2	1	1	1	1+(1)	3	4
Cruisers	5	7	5	7	5	7	5	0	15	16
Destroyers	9	18	0	16	9	0	0	16	18	50
Destroyer escorts	0	0	0	0	0	0	0	20	0	20
ASW corvettes	6	4	6	2	6	0	6	60	24	66
Submarines	3	10	3	7	3	3	3	0	12	20

P = Planned under DRC
A = Achieved

Sources: DRC Third Report and those under Table A.

Notes:
(i)   1939 orders are those placed up to 1 September 1939 and do not include the war emergency programmes.
(ii)   Completions 1941 is units completed by the end of that fiscal year, ie 31 March 1942, which was the target of the original five-year DRC programme proposed in 1936. The 'planned' completions are inevitably an estimate based on a reasonable calculation of when planned (as opposed to actual) orders might have been completed.
(iii) The battleships ordered in 1936 and 1937 were the five *King George V*s. The last two were not completed until the summer of 1942, six months beyond the original DRC plan. This reflected periods of suspension in 1940 for more pressing war work. The ships ordered in 1938 and 1939 were the four *Lion* class. Only two had been laid down by the outbreak of war when work was suspended. All were later cancelled in favour of other priorities.
(iv)   The DRC programme originally envisaged an order of one carrier per year from 1936–39 with 'some of a smaller type'. The six carriers actually ordered were all large armoured fleet carriers of the *Illustrious* class. The additional carrier shown in parenthesis for 1939 is the maintenance carrier *Unicorn*, which was comparable in many respects to a light carrier.
(v)   The original DRC programme did not envisage a separate category of destroyer escorts, so none were planned.
(vi)   The category 'ASW corvettes' includes both dedicated anti-submarine warfare (ASW) sloops ordered in 1936/37 and the new category of escort corvette ordered in 1939. The original DRC programme envisaged orders of five to six sloops per year, but did not specify a role. Fourteen large minesweeping sloops were ordered in this period in addition to those units shown.

The Admiralty's ultimate New Standard target can be seen in Table 3 below at Column C, with the DRC Fleet for comparison at Column B. The New Standard total was built up from the comparative strength requirements set out in the columns at A. The prediction of German strength assumed they would build to the maximum permitted under the AGNA by 1942. IJN strength was based on known building and what was judged achievable by 1942, following Japanese withdrawal from the 1936 London Treaty.[94] As Germany could threaten the United Kingdom homeland, the New Standard allocated the Royal Navy a margin of superiority here, while in the Far East it was willing to accept some inferiority, given that war here would be fought within Chatfield's defensive framework. Under the original 1937 New Standard, this willingness to accept inferiority applied to carriers, as discussed later in the chapter, and minor war vessels, but not capital ships.

As Table 3 demonstrates, the New Standard was a formula based on predicted comparative numerical strengths with some simple risk-weighting adjustment. Judged within these terms, the proposed Royal Navy strength had logic, but was perhaps generous. In the event, the Admiralty seriously overestimated future German and IJN force levels for capital ships and, in the case of Germany, for cruisers and destroyers too. Their combined order and build rates fell well short of those of the Royal Navy. In the period between February 1936, which established the Royal Navy rearmament baseline, and the outbreak of the European war in September 1939, the actual combined orders for Germany and Japan were four battleships, four fleet carriers, and nine cruisers.[95] In presenting the New Standard case, the Admiralty suggested possible modifications if some diplomatic understanding could be reached to reduce the risk from either Germany or Japan. It did not, however, think creatively about how the New Standard strategic goal might be achieved with fewer resources if diplomatic rapprochement was not feasible. There was, for example, the possibility of discouraging Japan from attacking British interests by deploying a quality deterrent force smaller than that required for a full-scale defensive war.

By the time the Minister for Defence Co-ordination, Sir Thomas Inskip, reviewed naval expenditure in July 1938, overall pressures on the defence budget and the need to find additional resources for the army and Royal Air Force against a fast deteriorating situation in Europe, made the prospects for formal Cabinet endorsement of the New Standard strength bleak. Inskip recognised that the Admiralty deserved clarity, but doubted a long-term programme for a simultaneous naval war on the scale proposed was either feasible or appropriate, given the pressing need to meet an imminent German threat. Inskip was anyway aware that, as Table 3 Column D demonstrates, there was now little difference in practice between the maximum attainable strength in 1942 under a New Standard programme, and that achieved by now capping further investment in major units and focusing effort on escort vessels that could be completed quickly. Because the outbreak of war a year later did

Table 3 Royal Navy expansion options 1938–42

	A Strategical Requirements								B	C	D	
	Home			East			Trade					
	Germany	Britain	Difference	Japan	Britain	Difference	British Requirements	Minimum British Total Requirements in 1942	DRC Fleet	Proposed New Standard	Maximum British Total Attainable in 1942	British Strength in 1942 under DRC Proposals
Capital ships	4 + 3*	8	+3	12	13	+1		21	15	20	20†	15
Aircraft carriers	3	4	+1	8	4	-4	5	13	8 + 4 aircraft depot ships	14	13	10
Cruisers‡	16	20	+4	38	25	-13	45	90	70	98	68	64
Destroyer flotillas‡	7	8	+1	16	7	-9	6	21	16	21	18	16
Submarines	68	50	-18	70	23	-47	-	73	55	73	68	55

* 3 *Deutschlands* count as 1 capital ships.

† More battleships will be building but not completed.

‡ Figures in column D exclude ships to be converted to AA ships.

All figures include vessels provided by the Dominions. Escort vessels, patrol vessel and auxiliary vessels, etc, are not included.

Source: CP 170 (38), Naval Expenditure, dated 12 July 1938, CAB 24/278, TNA.

indeed bring this result, with the effective disappearance of the New Standard, there is a tendency to dismiss it as always unaffordable and unachievable in any reasonable timescale, even if it dictated the pace of building for a while. The decision never to endorse the New Standard is then used to underline the sheer impossibility of conducting a viable Singapore strategy at least after the mid-1930s, and confirmation that Britain ultimately lacked the will and resources adequately to defend its Far East interests.[96]

This interpretation underestimates the scale and effectiveness of naval investment from 1935, the strength this then made available in 1941/42, and the government's commitment to maintaining a global naval capability. This commitment is illustrated in Table 4, which compares the actual strength the Royal Navy would have achieved at 31 March 1942 without war losses, compared to the various building targets considered by the Admiralty in mid-1938. In considering Table 4, it is useful to compare the projected cost of a New Standard navy with the actual expenditure authorised for the Royal Navy up to autumn 1938. In April 1937 the Admiralty Board acknowledged that the building programmes in fiscal years 1936 and 1937 met those required for the New Standard. It also calculated that the 'stabilised cost' of a New Standard navy, once achieved, was £97 million per annum at current prices. The final budget authorised for the Royal Navy under peacetime conditions was the £410 million agreed by the Cabinet in July 1938 to cover the three fiscal years 1939 to 1941. At this point, the Cabinet was willing to provide, therefore, an extra £40 million per annum above the 1937 New Standard stabilised cost to maintain the momentum of new build and expansion: £40 million was two-thirds of the total naval estimates as recently as fiscal year 1935, and the current Royal Navy 'steady state' costs were still well below £97 million.[97]

Table 4 shows that the real building programme (Column E) missed the Admiralty's maximum attainable target for 1942 as estimated in 1938 (Column A) in two categories, battleships and carriers, but all other targets were equalled or significantly surpassed, while there was also a huge invest-ment in anti-submarine vessels not envisaged in the peacetime programme. The battleship target was only missed by six months, so in effect a two-year delay in the 1938 and 1939 programme carriers was traded for the extra destroyers and anti-submarine vessels. In September 1939, the naval staff had expected these two carriers, *Implacable* and *Indefatigable*, the fifth and sixth of the *Illustrious* class, to be commissioned in October 1941 and June 1942 respectively. The suspension meant they were delayed until mid-1944. Their availability in 1942 would have made a significant contribution to the Royal Navy's global commitments and made the Royal Navy the strongest carrier power until late 1943.[98]

Table 4 Royal Navy strength at 31 March 1942 – proposed and achieved

Type	A Maximum British total attainable in 1942	B British strength in 1942 under DRC	C Original New Standard	D Adjusted New Standard	E Total Royal Navy completions actually achieved in 1942
Battleships	20	15	20	20	18
Aircraft carriers	13	10	14	11	10
Cruisers	68	64	98	88	67
Destroyers (flotillas)	18	16	21	18	20
Destroyer escorts	–	–	–	–	52
ASW corvettes	–	–	–	–	134+75
Submarines	68	55	73	73	89

Notes:
(i) Columns A, B and C are lifted directly from the Admiralty figures in Columns C and D of Table 3.
(ii) Figures at Column D adjust the New Standard by taking real as opposed to hypothetical German strength in 1942 and then adjusting the Admiralty's required superiority margin as illustrated in Table 3.
(iii) Column E is total Royal Navy (including Dominion) strength achieved at 31 March 1942, incorporating new build from rearmament and war emergency programmes but without subtracting any war losses. The extra seventy-five corvettes were built in Canada but everything else in British yards. It represents therefore a measure of what British naval industry could achieve.
(iv) The carrier figures omit the training carrier *Argus*. The figure of thirteen carriers in Column A is assumed to include the maintenance carrier *Unicorn*.

In fairness, it should be noted that there was an additional trade-off made here to provide adequate anti-submarine warfare capacity. This was the suspension and later cancellation of the four *Lion*-class battleships. The first two were laid down in July 1939 and would have commissioned in mid-1943. The table also shows that if the original 1937 New Standard target (Column C) is adjusted to reflect the real German building programme for surface vessels (as opposed to the 35 per cent ratio assumed by the Admiralty in 1938), as shown in Column D, then, with the exception of cruisers, the Royal Navy was close to this also in 1942. By mid-1944, the original date for the New Standard, the Royal Navy would complete two more fleet carriers and a further thirteen cruisers, as well as numerous minor war vessels.

There is a danger in taking such a statistical exercise too far, and especially comparing wartime rates of building with peacetime programmes. However, Table 4 underlines two important points. It demonstrates first, the scale of building the British naval industry could deliver before the impact of United

States lend-lease took effect. This confirms its resilience and shows that the traditional picture of the damage done by the recession in the early 1930s is too bleak. Secondly, it demonstrates that the New Standard navy, capable of a two-hemisphere war, was not only a more feasible proposition than traditionally accepted, but was in many respects achieved.

Furthermore, despite Inskip's doubts in July 1938, the New Standard rate of investment proceeded right up to the outbreak of war. Two battleships and a carrier were ordered[99] in the first five months of fiscal year 1939 and plans for a further fast-build battleship using spare gun mountings were well advanced. This additional battleship would eventually become *Vanguard*, laid down in October 1941. She is first mentioned in an Admiralty paper dated 3 March 1939. This proposed building a modified *Lion* using spare 15in turrets and guns to facilitate faster (and cheaper) construction. The paper is of wider interest because it considered the balance of battle-fleets for a two-hemisphere war in mid-1944. Two *Lions*, five *King George Vs* and three battlecruisers would be needed to counter a German fleet estimated then at five new battleships, two *Scharnhorsts* and three pocket battleships, giving the Royal Navy a superiority of two. In the Far East, two *Lions*, two *Nelsons*, five *Queen Elizabeths* and three 'R' class would face the existing IJN fleet of ten, along with four new-build battleships and perhaps two new battlecruisers, giving a Royal Navy deficit of four. *Vanguard* was designed to counter the expected new battlecruisers.[100]

Admiralty planning papers for early 1939 not only confirm the continuing commitment to a two-hemisphere navy but also that, if war had not intervened, this goal would have achieved credibility as early as 1942. Director Naval Air Division illustrated this in his proposed distribution of aircraft carriers in 1942 under different war scenarios. For a 'Far Eastern War', the carriers *Formidable*, *Illustrious*, and *Victorious* (each with thirty-three aircraft) would be based at home, with *Furious* in a training role. *Ark Royal* (sixty aircraft), *Indomitable* (forty-five), *Implacable* and *Indefatigable* (each with forty-eight aircraft), and *Glorious* (twenty-four) would be at Singapore, with *Courageous* (twenty-four) in the Indian Ocean. Nine battleships and thirteen cruisers would be with the Home Fleet; twelve battleships and fifteen cruisers in the Far East. Another scenario for an 'Axis War' involving Italy gave priority to the Home and Mediterranean theatres with only one carrier allocated to Singapore.[101]

Indeed, if war had not broken out in 1939, then by fiscal year 1940 the Royal Navy would have achieved sufficient lead in major war vessels to reduce to a rate of one battleship and one carrier per year. It appears that the Admiralty's initial shopping list for the three fiscal years 1939–41, after the budget of £410 million was agreed for this period in July 1938, was four battleships, three carriers, twelve cruisers, three destroyer flotillas, twelve submarines and eight escort vessels.[102] This fits the 'modified' New Standard building programme produced by Director of Plans in early 1938 and was probably achievable within the allocated budget had war not intervened. It also implied a steady-state build rate of one battleship and one fleet carrier per year.[103]

Table 4 also underlines that heavy investment in capital ships and carriers did not come at the expense of investment in trade protection and anti-submarine warfare.[104] It is true that investment in specialist anti-submarine warfare vessels did not begin until 1939, but the new fleet destroyers had anti-submarine capability too and, overall, the Royal Navy programme was far better balanced across different capabilities than its Axis competitors. It has been argued that in pursuing a 'balanced fleet' with its interwar investment, the Royal Navy 'spent less on battleships than other navies' and, in consequence, 'an acute shortage of fast modern battleships was the major constraint on British naval strategy for most of the war'. In reality, expenditure on Royal Navy new-build battleships (the *Nelson*s 1922–27) and the *King George V*s (1937–39) easily surpassed that by other powers up to September 1939, and the Royal Navy spent as much, if not more, than the US Navy and IJN on reconstructions. More modern or modernised battleships would certainly have been useful and the Royal Navy, of course, planned to keep building them. However, it is hard to identify real scenarios in the Second World War where the benefit of extra fast battleships would have justified the price of fewer carriers, cruisers, destroyers and, above all, Atlantic escorts. The demands of war surely demonstrated that, within its available budget and shipbuilding resources, the Royal Navy achieved a better balance of investment in the late 1930s than others.[105]

Another way to assess the effectiveness of the Royal Navy building programme from 1935 to 1942 is to compare Royal Navy output in this period with that of its three Axis enemies as in Table 5.

This table demonstrates that over the rearmament period, the first phase of the European war and the first year of the Far East war, the Royal Navy broadly matched the combined Axis total for capital units, cruisers and fleet destroyers. The Royal Navy completed fewer battleships, where it started with a large advantage, but double the number of light cruisers, thus recovering the shortfall here from the early 1930s. Given that the Royal Navy entered this period as the largest navy in the world, and its primary enemy, Germany, entered it with no significant navy at all, Royal Navy rearmament did well in equipping Britain for a potential two-hemisphere naval war. Delivery of the major new Royal Navy fleet units was heavily weighted to the period 1940–42 but, for large units, that was true for the Axis also. This delivery weighting explains why, as the next chapter shows, the Admiralty would constantly stress the period 1938–40 as a window of vulnerability. It needed the output available from 1940 onward to deal with more than one enemy with confidence.

Table 5 Royal Navy ships commissioned compared with the three Axis powers 1 January 1935–31 December 1942

Type	Britain	Germany	Japan	Italy	Axis Total
Battleships	5	2	2	3	7
Battlecruisers	0	2	0	0	2
Aircraft carriers	5	0	6	0	6
Heavy cruisers	10	4	6	0	10
Light cruisers	27	1	4	7	12
Fleet destroyers	117	37	51	22	110
Destroyer escorts	82	0	4	36	40
ASW frigates	13+2	0	0	0	0
ASW corvettes	165+88	0	0	0	0
Submarines	89	551	48	82	681

Sources: See under Table A.

Notes:

(i)   Royal Navy totals include ships built for the Dominions.
(ii) German heavy cruisers include the final pocket battleship *Admiral Graf Spee* and three *Hipper* class.
(iii) Royal Navy destroyers do not include requisitions at the outbreak of war or the fifty US destroyers acquired in 1940 in the destroyers for bases deal.
(iv) The + figures under Royal Navy frigates and corvettes are units built in Canada.

The most striking difference between Royal Navy and Axis figures is the dramatic rise in Royal Navy investment in anti-submarine capability, destroyer escorts and other anti-submarine vessels from 1939 onward, and the corresponding rise in German U-boat production. For both countries, this was a major change in the balance of naval investment. For the Royal Navy it meant a decision to delay or suspend all major capital units of the 1938 and 1939 programmes in the winter of 1939/40. These comprised four *Lion*-class battleships and the fifth and sixth *Illustrious*-class carriers, *Implacable* and *Indefatigable*. The benefit is evident in the output figures for anti-submarine vessels, some 315 delivered over the three years 1940–42 (not including the fifty US Navy destroyers provided in 1940).

This shift to anti-submarine production preceded the German shift to U-boats by about a year and meant that, from mid-1940 to end 1941, Britain was producing at least one anti-submarine escort for every U-boat produced, and they were operational at sea more quickly. German U-boat strength, which was fifty-seven vessels in September 1939, did not increase at all in the first twelve months of the war. Indeed, operational availability almost halved by September 1940, dropping from about forty-eight vessels to around twenty-five. Only fifty submarines were built in 1940, compared to 199 in 1941, and 237 in 1942.[106] The Royal Navy commissioned some seventy-eight escort destroyers and corvettes in 1940, and 164 in 1941. The fifty destroyers acquired from the US Navy in August 1940 also began to join the frontline in early 1941. At the end of that year, total German U-boat strength had reached 245, but the number ready for operational deployment was still only eighty-eight. By contrast, the number of escorts deployed under British control had reached 370.[107]

Britain, therefore, had roughly four escorts operational for every U-boat at the point the United States entered the war. This lead arguably proved decisive in enabling the Royal Navy to counter the advantage the Germans gained through access to French bases after the fall of France.[108] It is, nevertheless, striking that the Royal Navy could make this shift to anti-submarine investment, while still broadly matching the combined outputs for Axis fleet units. It is also important to emphasise that United States support to naval construction in the period to end 1942 was limited, and less significant than that of Canada, which produced about 25 per cent of anti-submarine vessels. United States support was, of course, still vital in meeting the rapid growth in German U-boat production from mid-1942. The Annex provides more detailed analysis on warship output by the main naval powers for the whole period 1930–42.

The fighting effectiveness of the Royal Navy in 1939

In assessing comparative Royal Navy strength, the emphasis has been mainly on quantitative comparisons. However, comparative strength also depended on wider measures of capability, the comparative quality of ship classes, weapons systems, personnel and doctrine. These do not permit easy measurement and are consequently harder to judge. In building ships, Royal Navy designers usually aimed for a good balance of characteristics on a given displacement, ie armament, protection, speed, endurance, sea-keeping, and reliability, and generally achieved this. Other navies often emphasised particular characteristics at the expense of others. US Navy battleships pre-1937 prioritised protection at the expense of speed. IJN heavy cruisers were powerfully armed, but suffered hull stress and stability problems. IJN and German destroyers had powerful gun armament, but were poorly equipped for anti-submarine work. In general, with the obvious exception of the two IJN *Yamato* battleships, it is hard to find examples where Royal Navy warships laid down after 1930 were significantly inferior to their foreign equivalents. This is true whether judged on paper specification or, more important, comparative performance in battle during the war.[109]

Specialist comparative design studies have generally rated the Royal Navy well below the US Navy for quality of machinery, operational availability, reliability and maintainability, but ahead of most others in these areas. The Royal Navy scores very high for sea-keeping, but low for habitability, particularly compared to the US Navy. Royal Navy weapons were, with few exceptions, at least competitive, although there were too many different gun calibres, and destroyers lacked a satisfactory high-angle weapon. No Royal Navy weapon in use in 1939 suffered performance failures comparable to the torpedo problems experienced by both US Navy and German submarines. Royal Navy armour was the best in the world by the late 1930s and about 25 per cent more effective for given weight than that of the US Navy. Royal Navy surface fire-control systems were excellent, but it lagged behind the US Navy, Germany, and possibly the IJN too, in anti-aircraft fire-control technology. In the development and exploitation of modern electronic sensors, radar, Asdic, and high-frequency (HF) intercept, the Royal Navy was well ahead of everyone else in 1939.[110]

Attention has traditionally focused on four main areas of weakness in the Royal Navy of 1939, which it is claimed reflected both general neglect throughout the interwar period and insufficient attention during the specific period of rearmament. These were:

- Excessive preoccupation with the classic battle-fleet engagement, ie re-fighting Jutland, which took insufficient account of how naval war was changing;
- Failure adequately to recognise the implications of air power at sea and to create an effective carrier capability;
- Over-reliance on anti-aircraft gunnery to protect the fleet, compromised further by an ineffective high-altitude control system;
- Failure to draw the right lessons from the German U-boat campaign in 1917/18, leaving the Royal Navy ill-prepared for a new submarine campaign against British shipping.[111]

Underpinning all these perceived weaknesses is the wider charge that the Royal Navy was hampered by a conservative mindset and a lack of innovation in recognising and addressing the challenges of future naval warfare.[112]

The most frequent and persistent charge against the interwar Royal Navy is that it remained gripped by the concept of large-scale action between battle-fleets as the decisive arbiter in achieving maritime control.[113] The argument runs that sterile fixation on re-fighting Jutland stifled innovation, drew limited investment away from the new areas of naval warfare, and therefore exacerbated the other weaknesses highlighted above. It is certainly true that throughout the interwar period, the Royal Navy continued to see the battleship as the decisive factor in naval warfare. However, so did all the other naval powers, and the offensive power of the carrier, so evident in 1942, was far from clear in the late 1930s. However, for the Royal Navy, it is wrong to suggest that continued emphasis on the battleship meant conservatism. Indeed, there is a convincing case that financial stringency, far from imprisoning the service in the past, was a spur to new tactical thinking.[114] The Royal Navy was well aware of the threat posed by IJN capital-ship modernisation and their focus on long-range fire.[115] With only limited funds for its own modernisation programme, it countered by exploring tactics for short-range action and night-fighting. Using aircraft to destroy enemy spotters and disrupt the enemy with torpedo attacks was a vital part of achieving the desired short-range solution.

Meanwhile, under a succession of innovative commanders during the 1930s, night-fighting became standard in the Mediterranean Fleet. Cunningham emphasised this in a revealing passage in his autobiography, which described a 1934 exercise where the Mediterranean Fleet was tasked to intercept the Home Fleet simulating an IJN force escorting a convoy. It ended with the Mediterranean Fleet conducting a night attack. He stated:

> Bold and masterly tactics not only put an end to the exercise; but settled once and for all the much debated question as to whether or not British heavy ships could and should engage in night action against corresponding enemy units. At Jutland, night action was deliberately avoided. From now on it was an accepted principle that a highly trained and well-handled fleet had nothing to lose and much to gain by fighting at night.

His subsequent victory at Matapan admirably confirmed this.[116] These developments were accompanied by important organisational and cultural changes which promoted initiative, flexibility and rapid response.[117] By the late 1930s the Royal Navy was not expecting to fight in a traditional Jutland-style battle line manoeuvred rigidly by a single commander but, rather, in small divisional units able quickly to exploit opportunities offered by the enemy. It was also exploring the idea of the task force with its own integrated air component.

This picture of the evolution of Royal Navy battle-fleet tactics is confirmed in the major fleet exercises of the interwar period. However, a study of these exercises demonstrates that many wider problems and opportunities were being actively explored, besides new ways of handling a battle-fleet.[118] Three themes stand out: the relevance of many of the exercise scenarios to the war the Royal Navy would fight from 1939; a growing culture of initiative and innovation, a forerunner of the modern concept of 'mission command';[119] and the recognition that naval warfare now took place in a multi-threat environment requiring an integrated 'all arms' response.

The significant role played by carrier operations in these exercises from the mid-1920s onward, and the importance senior officers attached to this, is noteworthy. One of the earliest examples of an exercise involving carrier strike is Exercise MU conducted in the Mediterranean in August 1925 to explore an opposed transit through the Malacca Strait to relieve Singapore. The 'IJN carrier' carried out a very successful torpedo attack, which was judged to have damaged three Royal Navy battleships.[120] This focus on carrier operations is particularly striking, given that the number of aircraft deployed was always comparatively small, and multi-carrier operations were only possible after 1930.[121] The use of submarines for reporting and shadowing was also investigated as, of course, was the defensive potential offered by Asdic. But, again, it is noteworthy that as early as 1929, important lessons were being learnt about anti-submarine search involving aircraft and Asdic-equipped destroyers working together.[122] The exercises certainly show 'divisional tactics' in operation, but they also show the origins of the integrated task force with a carrier and battlecruiser working together and anticipating the future Force H concept.[123] The pattern of exercises through the 1930s demonstrates that most, if not all, senior Royal Navy officers fully recognised the potential role of air power, both as facilitator of naval objectives and as a threat. There were few aspects of this potential left unexplored.[124]

The interwar exercise programme demonstrates that the Royal Navy did recognise the importance of air power and thought about it deeply. Nevertheless, this increasing 'air-mindedness' must be reconciled with a still predominant belief that by the mid-1930s the Royal Navy was falling behind both the IJN and US Navy in carrier warfare and never really caught up.[125] As already noted, the Royal Navy was behind in the number of aircraft deployed in its carriers, and well aware of this. It would barely reduce the shortfall over the rest of the decade. A major review of the Fleet Air Arm prepared for the Admiralty Board on 30 November 1938 shows that Fleet Air Arm frontline carrier air strength was expected to be only 168 torpedo strike reconnaissance (TSR) aircraft and seventy-five fighters on 1 August 1939, rising to 295 TSR and 110 fighters by 1 April 1942. The paper (optimistically) expected the Fleet Air Arm to be close to IJN carrier capable air strength by 1942, but acknowledged it would be still well short of the anticipated combined Japanese and German total.[126]

This numerical weakness is invariably linked with a growing disparity in aircraft quality, although comparisons here are often less straightforward than they suggest, and too often ignore the actual timescales within which aircraft were introduced.[127] In particular, there is a tendency to project IJN aircraft superiority in late 1941 back into the 1930s. The Kate Type 97 B5N2 torpedo bomber did not start to reach the frontline until 1939 and the Zero fighter and Val Type 99 D3A1 dive-bomber until well into 1940. Until their arrival, the difference in individual aircraft capability between the Royal Navy and the IJN was not significant, although the IJN still had the advantage of numbers. The same argument broadly applies to comparisons with the US Navy. Royal Navy torpedo bombers, if judged as an overall weapon system, were superior to those of the US Navy until late 1942. The Wildcat, the standard US Navy fighter of 1942, was developed initially for the Royal Navy, which deployed it first.[128] The US Navy Dauntless dive-bomber was certainly superior to any contemporary Royal Navy bombing aircraft, but again did not arrive until 1940.

Any comparison between the Fleet Air Arm and the IJN and US Navy air arms must also recognise two linked factors that made the context in which British naval air power developed fundamentally different from the other two. First, Britain had in the Royal Air Force an independent air force with responsibility for all land-based air power, including that projected over the sea. It inevitably dominated air policy, strategy and procurement. Secondly, as mentioned earlier, until 1937 the Royal Air Force and Royal Navy had shared responsibility for the carrier fleet under a cumbersome dual-control system.[129] By 1939 the Royal Navy had regained full control of the Fleet Air Arm, but it remained dependent on the Air Ministry for procurement and, inevitably, lacked air expertise in many key areas, especially at senior levels of command.[130]

Several powerful arguments have been advanced to explain how the dominant role of the Royal Air Force weakened the Fleet Air Arm. First, that it encouraged the Royal Navy to view air power as 'ancillary', an aid to traditional capability, rather than a weapon in its own right.[131] The Royal Navy therefore lacked the visionary leadership that could think 'air strategy', as opposed to 'fleet tactics'.[132] This argument plays to the view that the interwar Royal Navy was an essentially conservative force. Secondly, it meant the Royal Navy air constituency lacked the bureaucratic muscle needed to make a decisive case for seaborne air power and to ensure that it was adequately resourced and supported.[133] In consequence, it was poorly placed to compete for resources with the Royal Air Force. It was less able to manage the design and procurement of the advanced monoplane fighters and strike aircraft becoming available in the late 1930s and necessary to provide an air fleet comparable to the IJN. There is some truth in this, but the picture is more complex. As Chapter 5 will show, a more decisive factor was, arguably, the extreme crisis Britain faced with the collapse of France in 1940. This forced an urgent reassessment of aircraft production priorities to the detriment of the next generation of Fleet Air Arm aircraft. A third argument is that 'dual control' promoted a conservative approach to aircraft handling and operational management, with the result that Royal Navy carriers operated fewer aircraft, did so less efficiently, and were slow to explore new ideas and technical innovations.

While there is no doubt the policy of dual control did hamper the development of the Fleet Air Arm, the claim that, at least by the mid-1930s, the Royal Navy leadership lacked a strategic vision for the place of air power in naval warfare, compared to the IJN and US Navy, is unconvincing. It fails to take account of Royal Navy investigation of multi-carrier operations, air strikes on enemy fleets in harbour, the threat posed by shore-based air power on Mediterranean transit, and the impact of air power, offensive and defensive, on the protection of trade. The Royal Navy concluded that multi-carrier operations would be a key theme in future naval warfare as early as 1930.[134] It led to the creation of the role of Rear Admiral Aircraft Carriers in 1931.[135] The Admiralty instructions to the first holder of the post, Rear Admiral Reginald Henderson, in June 1931 stated that he was 'to study and prepare a common doctrine for the tactical employment of the Fleet Air Arm'. Commanders-in-Chief Atlantic and Mediterranean should collaborate to provide him with the opportunity 'to operate the combined aircraft carriers of both fleets'.[136] Henderson did, indeed, conduct extensive research into multi-carrier operations. This led to a complete operational doctrine, with special procedures for flying off, forming up, and co-ordinating squadrons from different carriers. Separate exercises to investigate air defence from 1932 to 1934 led Henderson to consider the merits of carrier specialisation in particular roles.[137]

Critics of the Royal Navy approach to air power in the late 1930s also credit the IJN and US Navy at this time with strategic thinking that only matured much later. Apart from having a much larger embarked force, it is not evident that IJN thinking was further advanced than the Royal Navy at this stage. Nor was the IJN leadership any more committed to the carrier over the capital ship.[138] Emerging US Navy air doctrine in the late 1930s was thoughtful and ambitious, but again it is not evident that US Navy thinking on the use of carriers, or the growing influence of land-based air power at sea, was ahead of the Royal Navy. A key contributor to US Navy thinking in the late 1930s was Captain Richmond Kelly Turner in his role as Head of Strategy at the US Naval War College from 1935–38. He features in later chapters of this book in his subsequent appointment as US Navy Director of Plans.[139]

The central role of carriers for the Royal Navy by the mid-1930s, as a vital component of a modern fleet, is powerfully demonstrated in the planning papers for the rearmament programme.[140] These developed a well-argued and realistic case for the air power required to combat Japan and Germany and to secure empire communications. They show that by mid-1936 the naval staff were committed to completing a force of eight new fleet carriers by 1943, with five of the existing older carriers retained for trade protection. The eight planned fleet carriers included *Ark Royal*, already under construction in 1936 and completed in 1938. However, the Director of Plans, Captain Tom Phillips, recognised that there were too many uncertainties beyond 1939 to settle on a final size for the carrier fleet. It was the building rate that mattered.[141]

The planned rate was equal to the new battleship programme and the carriers would be delivered more quickly. By 1936 the Admiralty was planning a total of nine new battleships, the five *King George V*s and four *Lion*s, though many details of the latter, not least armament, had yet to be decided. The first *Lion*s under the fiscal year 1938 programme were not expected until 1943. By contrast, as late as March 1939 the Admiralty still hoped to have seven new carriers in commission by mid-1942, namely *Ark Royal* and six *Illustrious* class.[142] The size of this carrier programme was unequivocally dictated by the need to prepare for simultaneous two-hemisphere war, including the possibility of a simultaneous attack on trade. The attention the naval staff gave to the employment of carriers for trade protection is striking, and was not mirrored in any other navy. The staff recognised that carriers could potentially search large areas of sea more effectively than cruisers for enemy raiders. Deployment of carriers would make it possible to reduce cruiser numbers, though more exercises were needed to test this.[143]

Three points must be stressed regarding the planning of the carrier force for the Far East. First, the assessment of IJN carrier strength and its rate of growth were broadly accurate for this date. The only error was to underestimate the displacement of the new carriers *Soryu* (1937) and *Hiryu* (1939), which the Admiralty put at 10,000 tons against the real figure of 16,000 tons. The Royal Navy was well aware that IJN carrier air strength was significantly larger than its own and would remain so for some while. Phillips, as Director of Plans, assessed IJN ship-borne air strength in 1936 at 287 aircraft, estimated to rise to 397 in 1939. Royal Navy Fleet Air Arm air strength was 176 in 1937, estimated to reach 248 in 1939, 356 in 1940 and 500 in 1942.[144] The Royal Navy also knew IJN carriers had a much larger aircraft complement. Phillips estimated IJN carrier *Ryujo* could carry one aircraft for every 240 tons, whereas *Illustrious* would be one per 640 tons.[145] Secondly, the Royal Navy carrier requirement for simultaneous war in two hemispheres assumed that the Far East war would be fought on the defensive. The requirement was an adequate counter to IJN air capability, not to equal it. Finally, Royal Navy calculations took account of differences in carrier design philosophy which,

Phillips argued, made simple numerical comparisons misleading. The new Royal Navy carriers would be armoured. This meant a 50 per cent reduction in aircraft capacity, but made the carriers much less vulnerable to bombing or shelling. The IJN carriers had more aircraft, but would not be able to manage their large air complements with the same efficiency and flexibility as the Royal Navy, while lack of protection made them potentially vulnerable to a single hit.[146]

Tom Phillips, who oversaw the planning of the new carrier programme, plays a central role throughout this book. He was Director of Plans from August 1935 until April 1938[147] and was Chatfield's chief assistant in designing the naval rearmament programme and winning political and financial support for it. Following barely a year in an operational command with the Home Fleet, he then returned to the Admiralty in the rank of rear admiral as Deputy Chief of Naval Staff (DCNS) at the special request of the incoming First Sea Lord, Admiral of the Fleet Sir Dudley Pound. He was Pound's deputy[148] for the first two years of the war, before becoming commander-in-chief of the newly created Eastern Fleet in October 1941 and dying with the *Prince of Wales* six weeks later.[149] He was, therefore, the dominant single figure in planning for a Far East war over the whole period 1935–42.

Phillips has been presented as a hatchet man for Pound, who encouraged the latter's centralising tendencies, and as a desk-bound 'staff officer' who did not understand the realities of modern naval warfare and was therefore ill-suited to senior operational command. Above all, he has been typecast as a stubborn traditionalist who dismissed the air threat to capital ships and was thus directly responsible for the loss of Force Z in December 1941. The latter charge is now generally acknowledged to be unfair, and the planning of the new carrier programme demonstrates that Phillips grasped the importance of air power at an intellectual level, and was equally well sighted on IJN carrier capability. A recent biographical sketch of Phillips also portrays a much warmer, caring and thoughtful personality than previously implied.[150] This book will show that Phillips certainly bears a share of the responsibility for Royal Navy failures in the East, albeit not quite in the way popularly suggested. But his failings here must be weighed against two enormous achievements for which he has never received adequate credit, and for which his country is in his debt. These were his major role in designing and driving through a rearmament programme that served the Royal Navy well in the coming war. And then his central role as Deputy Chief of Naval Staff, subsequently changed to Vice Chief of Naval Staff (VCNS), in creating and implementing the strategy that enabled the Royal Navy not only to survive against considerable odds in the first critical defensive phase of the war, but to make significant gains too. He deserves better memory.

This carrier programme envisaged by Phillips in 1936 was substantially executed. By mid-1939, only one of the planned new eight fleet carriers, *Ark Royal*, was complete, but another six were building and the first two of these, *Illustrious* and *Formidable*, would commission the following year, with another two, *Victorious* and *Indomitable*, in 1941.[151] When the outbreak of war forced the Admiralty to delay major warships to release resources for escort construction they sacrificed the battleship programme first. Leaving the eighth planned carrier aside, had war not intervened, the Royal Navy would have had seven new fleet carriers by mid-1942 (six by end 1941), four large older carriers, earmarked for trade protection but capable of a fleet role, plus the old light carrier *Hermes* and the new 'maintenance carrier' *Unicorn*. This was not only close to the ultimate New Standard target, but a far more substantial investment in air power assets than either the IJN or US Navy made at this time. Even with war losses and delays in construction, the 1936 vision gave the Royal Navy a vital margin at the most critical moment of the war in early 1942. The Admiralty was able to deploy three *Illustrious*-class carriers to the Indian Ocean in early 1942, only one less than the plan prepared by Phillips in 1936.

In planning its future carrier programme, the Royal Navy made two linked bets about the future evolution of air power at sea which, with the benefit of hindsight, proved wrong. Exercises conducted through the early 1930s suggested that fighter defence mounted from a carrier against any substantial air attack, whether sea- or land-based would be ineffective and inefficient because it was impossible to provide sufficient warning to get the fighters to the right place.[152] This led to the judgement that defence against air attack should rely primarily on armour and anti-aircraft gun power, both for individual carriers and the wider fleet. It also led to the decision that future Fleet Air Arm fighters should be optimised for reconnaissance and long-range escort, which meant a two-seater aircraft. These were rational decisions in 1936, but by 1940 the scale and quality of attacking aircraft began to outweigh the benefits of carrier armour, while the arrival of radar transformed the prospects for defence by fighters. The result was that the Fleet Air Arm did not have a competitive single-seat fighter to defend the fleet.

Furthermore, the aircraft capacity of its carriers was reduced to achieve the increased protection. The value of deck armour and the trade-off with aircraft capacity is a complex issue. On the one hand, deck armour was probably less important to survival in many cases than other design factors, such as the isolation of hangars from the hull spaces. On the other, the capacity loss was not as great as formal specifications and Phillips's 1936 calculations suggest.[153] The last three *Illustrious* class were redesigned with extra hangar space, raising capacity to around fifty aircraft. The use of deck parking and outriggers meant that all six ships were eventually able to operate around sixty aircraft, and *Indefatigable* and *Implacable* up to eighty.[154] The largest IJN carriers could operate in excess of seventy aircraft but, apart from the Pearl Harbor attack, rarely deployed more than fifty-five.

The Royal Navy's critics link these 'wrong turns' with poor aircraft procurement decisions. Those decisions are held up as further evidence that the Royal Navy lagged behind the IJN and US Navy in carrier development.[155] The picture is again more complicated. All three carrier navies were struggling to come to terms with the interaction of fast-changing technology and ideas on how best to exploit it. Developments included dramatic improvements in engine power and radical new ideas in aerodynamics and the arrival of radio homing, very high frequency (VHF) communications, identification friend or foe (IFF), and radar. All three naval air forces had to assess how naval air war would evolve against these developments, and all were to an extent constrained by the initial choices they made.[156]

The armoured carrier ultimately had design limitations. However, it proved valuable while radar-directed fighter defence was still developing in 1940/41 and, later, against the special problem posed by Japanese suicide bombers in the Pacific. At Okinawa in 1945 Royal Navy armoured carriers brushed aside suicide attacks that crippled the new US Navy *Essex*-class carriers.[157] The US Navy were so impressed with the design of *Illustrious*, when she was under repair in the United States in 1941, that they too diverted down the armour path with their *Midway*-class carriers.[158]

The Royal Navy requirement for an observer in its fighters reflected its emphasis on quality reconnaissance and navigation, where it proved superior to the IJN and US Navy.[159] The Royal Navy did make some poor aircraft choices, but its shortcomings here are often exaggerated by comparing Royal Navy aircraft of 1939 with IJN aircraft of late 1941. The Fleet Air Arm frontline was much smaller than the IJN and US Navy in 1939, as the Royal Navy was acutely aware, but the capability of aircraft in all three navies at that time was similar. The Fleet Air Arm was growing fast and, had war not intervened, the aircraft in the pipeline, or potentially available, would have kept its capability competitive.[160] In the event, the stresses of war meant that Fleet Air Arm procurement suffered badly in 1940/41. The reasons for this are explored in Chapter 5.

Overall, there is a powerful case that the Royal Navy attitude to air power in the late 1930s, far from being too conservative, was too innovative too early. Properly understood, its record at this time, strategically, operationally, and technically, was impressive. The Admiralty's 1936 carrier programme was ambitious and visionary, and in advance of other powers, but the Royal Navy suffered because it had to rearm on the basis of 1936, not 1940, technology.

It was ironic that the Royal Navy, which was alone in practising multi-carrier operations in the 1930s, was unable to do so in wartime because of the sheer range of its commitments.[161]

The popular criticism that the Royal Navy both underestimated and neglected the modern air threat extends to its approach to anti-aircraft gunnery between the wars. It is claimed that it had unrealistic expectations regarding the effectiveness of anti-aircraft firepower, and that it made poor equipment choices. It is argued that the Admiralty made a fatal mistake in the late 1920s by adopting an anti-aircraft fire-control system based on estimation rather than measurement of target movement.[162] It is further argued that the resulting Royal Navy high-altitude control system (HACS) was not only conceptually flawed, but reflected cultural resistance in the Admiralty to scientific and technical advice, a tendency to ignore unwelcome evidence, and a backward British industry unable to design and produce a tachymetric system like the US, Japanese and German navies.

In simple terms, a tachymetric system computes a target solution direct from measured data inputs, as opposed to estimates. The primary US Navy anti-aircraft fire-control system, the Mark 37, introduced from 1940, was a true tachymetric system, and is generally considered the most effective anti-aircraft system of the Second World War.[163] The Royal Navy, therefore, entered the war 'firing at enemy aircraft with the hopeful wildness of aim of a tyro shot trying to bring down fast flying grouse'.[164] An alternative, more sophisticated, view suggests that financial stringency caused the Royal Navy to set over-ambitious requirements in a bid to maximise the return on its investment. This caused delay, complications and unreliability. As a result, although there was a huge increase in the anti-aircraft firepower mounted in Royal Navy warships of all types during the rearmament period, fire-control deficiencies made its overall anti-aircraft capability less effective than it would otherwise have been.[165]

There are important qualifications here. The charge that the Admiralty was resistant to technical advice or operational analysis in dealing with the air threat is easily countered. The Royal Navy's technical analysis of the aerial threat undertaken in 1931 by its Anti-Aircraft Gunnery Committee was 'exemplary, exhibiting innovative methodology and achieving a standard of operational research which would have been difficult to better decades later'. However, the Admiralty believed that the problem of air attack was capable of a once-for-all solution. It failed to anticipate sufficiently how the threat would evolve over the next decade and viewed the problem in rather limited operational scenarios.[166] The claim that British industry was incapable of providing a tachymetric system is not convincing since it did so for the army, and the Admiralty fire-control table for surface targets, introduced in the late

1920s, was also essentially a tachymetric system.[167] It seems that the initial choice of HACS was because it could be introduced relatively quickly and, importantly, because there were doubts that a tachymetric system would be fast enough or sufficiently reliable in producing the effective target solution. Chatfield, who was always focused on the air threat, certainly recognised the desirability of a tachymetric system. However, following poor results in a Home Fleet anti-aircraft exercise in 1937, he noted that although a tachymetric solution had been recommended during studies of the anti-aircraft problem in both 1921 and 1931, trials had so far been disappointing.[168]

There is also a tendency to compare the HACS of 1939 with US systems deployed in 1942. Although the US Navy Mark 37 began development in 1936, it first went to sea in 1940 and was only widely deployed from late 1941. At the Battle of Midway in June 1942, only *Hornet*, the most modern of the three US Navy carriers, had the Mark 37, while *Yorktown* and *Enterprise* had the more basic Mark 33. HACS, meanwhile, was a constantly evolving system. It incorporated analogue computers, remote power control, and some tachymetric inputs in 1940, and radar ranging and blind-fire capability, the first in any navy, from early 1941.[169] The new battleship *Prince of Wales* had no less than nine anti-aircraft fire-control radars in 1941. Nevertheless, despite these improvements, most specialist assessments have indeed judged HACS to be inferior to the US Mark 37 and this was the Royal Navy's professional view when it could compare the two systems in late 1941 and 1942. It was then able to make a detailed assessment of the Mark 37 system, combined with the US 5in/38 Mark 12 guns, installed in the cruiser *Delhi* during refit in the United States late in 1941. The Royal Navy was sufficiently impressed to order a further eighty-two systems, which could not be delivered, given US Navy demand following the outbreak of war.[170]

However, the difference in performance between the latest HACS and the latest US Mark 37 system in 1942, under real combat conditions, was less than the Royal Navy believed, and certainly not enough to justify the savage strictures often levelled at HACS.[171] From the admittedly incomplete statistics available, whether for naval anti-aircraft claims over the war as a whole, or from individual engagements, it is hard to demonstrate that the Mark 37 consistently provided a decisive advantage over HACS. The US Navy claimed 246 aircraft shot down by anti-aircraft fire in 1942, with sixty down to the Mark 37/5in gun combination at expenditure of 252 'rounds per bird'. This was the best hit rate ever achieved by the Mark 37 system without variable time (VT) proximity fuse ammunition. Expenditure of 500–1000 rounds to destroy an aircraft was more normal and was probably close to the HACS rate. The 1942 5in figure of sixty compared with eighty-two accounted for by the 20mm Oerlikon, which had no remote tracking and was also used by the Royal

Navy.[172] It is often suggested that the shortcomings of HACS contributed to the loss of *Prince of Wales* and *Repulse* in December 1941. The evidence does not support this. *Prince of Wales* damaged five out of eight IJN aircraft in the initial high-level bombing attack for 108 rounds fired, despite unfavourable manoeuvres by Admiral Phillips. Similarly, five of eight aircraft were hit in the last attack by just six operational 5.25in guns while the ship was sinking.[173]

The Admiralty acknowledged as early as July 1940 that the results of long-range anti-aircraft fire under combat conditions had proved disappointing compared to pre-war expectations. Analysis of enemy aircraft losses to date showed that anti-aircraft fire had accounted for only a small proportion of known enemy losses, for considerable ammunition expenditure – although it did have a useful deterrent effect. It assessed that the poor performance was probably due to a mix of: lack of practice firing, lack of tachymetric control, range-taking inaccuracies, and poor calibration facilities. Naval anti-aircraft fire could not alone protect a fleet anchorage, naval base or convoy from high-altitude bombing. By contrast, while close range and barrage fire could not cope adequately with dive-bombers, a sufficiently powerful battery, well handled, gave considerable protection to individual ships against other types of air attack.[174]

The reality is that no Second World War-vintage anti-aircraft fire-control system was reliably able to deliver the pinpoint tracking required to bring down a fast manoeuvring target with limited salvoes from a limited number of guns. In 1941, without the proximity fuse, even shore-based guns with tachymetric control, and optimum conditions, needed 3000 rounds per kill. To put the naval anti-aircraft problem in perspective, a Second World War attack aircraft, moving at say 240 knots, would be in the effective engagement envelope for heavy anti-aircraft guns for just one minute, the time to travel 8000yds. If the maximum likely rate of fire was twenty rounds per minute, the ten guns in a battleship broadside would get off 200 rounds, well below the average kill rate estimated by the US Navy for just one aircraft. The battleship could expect multiple attackers.[175] Two things that did have a significant effect were the introduction of the VT proximity fuse from late 1942 and the sheer number of guns available, especially of small-calibre rapid fire. US Navy statistics suggest VT ammunition improved the 5in gun kill rate by a factor of two to three. However, the massed ranks of rapid-fire, close-range 40mm and 20mm guns were always far more effective.[176]

The Royal Navy certainly made some poor weapon choices and had too many different gun calibres. From the 1930s through most of the Second World War, the Royal Navy persisted with 4in, 4.5in, two different 4.7in, and 5.25in anti-aircraft weapons, each with several variants. The US Navy, by comparison, standardised almost totally on the 5in. Many Royal Navy destroyer guns at the start of the Second World War, although supposedly dual-purpose, could not elevate above 40 degrees, quite inadequate for anti-aircraft fire against dive-bombers, which proved the primary threat to the Royal Navy in the first years of the war. The modern 5.25in was too slow in both movement and rate of fire. The Royal Navy is also criticised for being slow to adopt the Bofors 40mm and Oerlikon 20mm to replace the 2pdr multi-barrel pom-pom dating from the 1920s. However, the Oerlikon was being widely introduced from 1939.

Despite these limitations, what is most important is that in 1939, and through to late 1942, the Royal Navy was far ahead of other navies in the scale and quality of anti-aircraft gun outfit allocated to its major warships, especially new construction ships and rebuilds. For example, the capital ship rebuilds *Renown* and *Valiant*, completed in 1939, mounted twenty 4.5in primary anti-aircraft armament, thirty-two (4 x 8) 2pdrs (approximately 40mm), and sixteen 0.5in (4 x 4). The latest US Navy modernised battleships had eight 5in, four 3in, and just eight 0.5in machine guns. Even the new-build *North Carolina* on completion in mid-1941 after two years of European war, mounted only four by four 1.1in and twelve 0.5in machine guns, in addition to her main secondary armament of twenty 5in. By 1941 this was a pitifully light anti-aircraft armament for any major warship, let alone a brand-new battleship. The IJN *Yamato*, despite her great size, was no better armed when completed in late 1941 than *North Carolina*. Instead of a modern, dual-purpose secondary armament, she maintained an old-fashioned split between surface and anti-aircraft guns. For long-range anti-aircraft, she had twelve 5in, just over half the battery of *North Carolina*, and a light armament of twenty-four 25mm and four 13mm. By 1941 *Valiant* had added a further twenty-four 20mm Oerlikons and a comprehensive anti-aircraft radar suite to her 1939 armament. This comparison further underlines the comparative quality of the Royal Navy capital ship reconstructions.[177] The improvement in anti-aircraft outfit was not confined to new-build and modernised vessels. A statement on naval deficiencies prepared for the Committee of Imperial Defence in October 1938 reported that anti-aircraft rearmament had been completed for nine battleships, one carrier, ten heavy cruisers, six light cruisers and five anti-aircraft cruisers by that time. The programme had extended to most remaining major units by the outbreak of war.[178]

By 1939 the Royal Navy was also implementing new tactical dispositions to counter the air threat, based on the concept of a layered defence comprising an outer ring of destroyers or other light units to provide surface warning, with an inner ring of cruisers to provide long-range anti-aircraft fire. This defensive screen would deploy long-range fire to harass aircraft when first sighted; high-altitude fire to harass bombers at the point of release; and close-range 'barrage' fire. In addition, it had introduced the air defence officer to control and co-ordinate anti-aircraft fire, and ensure it was prioritised against the right targets. Here, too, its thinking was ahead of its competitors.[179]

The availability of a US-style tachymetric system would undoubtedly have improved some aspects of Royal Navy anti-aircraft fire control, but given Pacific experience in 1942, its overall impact against the Luftwaffe in the Mediterranean would have been less than is often suggested. If anti-aircraft success in the Second World War for practical purposes still depended on the 'barrage' and the 'hosepipe', then HACS was quite a good system for directing this. Royal Navy anti-aircraft firepower would prove grossly inadequate for the scale of land-based air attack it faced in the Mediterranean in 1940/41, but by 1939 it was still vastly better equipped for air defence than its contemporaries. Not only did its warships mount more powerful anti-aircraft batteries than any other navy, but it alone had made provision to protect merchant ships. However, when war experience demonstrated that even this greater anti-aircraft armament was insufficient, it created a particular problem for the Royal Navy. Because its designers had already maximised anti-aircraft armament, they had little margin to accommodate the weight of further increases.[180]

The final area of perceived weakness, inadequate commitment to anti-submarine warfare, is important for three reasons. First, it illuminates the quality of the Royal Navy's risk assessment, its priorities, and its capacity to innovate. Secondly, it is important to establish how far Chatfield and the naval staff deliberately compromised anti-submarine investment in the period 1935–38 for the sake of building capital units. Was the pursuit of the two-hemisphere navy bought at the cost of heavy losses and near defeat in the Battle of the Atlantic in 1940–42? Finally, to what extent did the IJN submarine threat influence Royal Navy anti-submarine capability?

There remains a widespread consensus that the discovery and deployment of Asdic in the early 1920s caused the Royal Navy to be grossly complacent about a future submarine threat until almost too late. It is suggested that an embedded belief that Asdic had mastered the submarine threat fed general disinterest in anti-submarine warfare. There was thus little new thinking about the problem, no new tactical development, no relevant exercises, no effective planning for the introduction of convoy, and inadequate investment in appropriate anti-submarine vessels.[181] The popular portrayal is of an interwar Royal Navy 'which, having developed Asdic, was content to ignore ASW and concentrate on cocktail parties and battle-fleet exercises'. When faced with a new attack on Atlantic trade, the Royal Navy 'is found blowing the dust off 1918 documents, learning how to do it all over again, and doing extra-ordinarily well in the circumstances.'[182]

The Royal Navy did not rest on its laurels with the discovery of Asdic. There were steady technical improvements throughout the interwar period. More importantly, Asdic was incorporated in a wider anti-submarine warfare system. A new anti-submarine warfare (ASW) branch was set up, new tactics were thoroughly explored and tested, and new ships and weapons evaluated. From the mid-1920s, the Japanese threat was important to anti-submarine warfare development because it gave the Royal Navy a specific scenario to explore: namely, the defence of the battle-fleet from submarine attack in contested waters.

There were also regular convoy exercises with multiple escorts and multiple attacking submarines. Early exercises invariably had a Far East scenario in mind, but in the mid-1930s the focus shifted to Europe and the Mediterranean. Some of these anticipated future U-boat wolf-pack tactics to a remarkable degree. Contrary to popular myth, the Royal Navy did not fail to spot the threat of night attack by surfaced submarines, and highlighted this in its convoy instructions drafted as early as 1934. However, it saw no effective way of countering this problem prior to the advent of radar.[183] Overall, the Royal Navy correctly predicted both German intent at the strategic level for execution of a trade war, and the methods they would adopt at the tactical level.[184]

The idea that the Royal Navy neglected the possibility of a new German submarine offensive has nevertheless been powerfully promoted. The Admiralty's 'most serious failure of judgement' between the wars was that 'with eyes focused on the battle-fleet, it ducked until too late the enormous problems of setting up a convoy system'.[185] The best single counter to this view is the Joint Planning Committee paper on the protection of seaborne trade produced for the chiefs of staff at the end of 1936.[186]

The Joint Planning Committee, which features frequently in this book, was a subcommittee of the chiefs of staff. As a formal committee, it comprised the Director of Plans in the naval staff and his equivalent in the army and air staffs. The three directors held the rank of captain, colonel and group captain respectively. They were prestigious posts and most directors went on to hold senior positions at the level of commander-in-chief or chief of staff. As 'joint planners', they addressed problems and questions set by the chiefs of staff that were best tackled on a tri-service basis. They produced 'joint' memoranda, 'joint papers' and, at the most strategic level, major 'appreciations'. These were researched and drafted by officers drawn from the single-service planning staff under each director, who for specific tasks therefore became the 'joint planning staff'. By 1935, the joint planning system was well established. Through the late 1930s, and then through the war, it provided Britain with an integrated strategic planning function that was not matched in any other country. From 1936 the same model was applied to strategic intelligence with the establishment of the Joint Intelligence Committee. This brought together the service directors of intelligence with a senior representative from the Foreign Office and the chief of the Secret Intelligence Service (SIS).

The 1936 paper on the protection of trade examined the worst-case scenario for an all-out German offensive against British trade in 1939. The estimate for the scale of attack was accurate, and the assessment of how it would be applied prescient. The paper assumed the German navy would comprise, by 1939, one battleship, two battlecruisers, three pocket battleships, one carrier, three 8in cruisers, six 6in cruisers, twenty-eight large destroyers, and sixty-six submarines. Twenty-four of the submarines would be small coastal type and the rest ocean-capable, which would allow about ten on station at one time. In the event, the battleship and one of the 8in cruisers were not ready until early 1941. The carrier was never completed. Only fifty-seven submarines were available in September 1939, of which thirty were the small coastal type the Admiralty anticipated. The force would barely increase over the first year of war.

Contrary to frequent claims, the paper demonstrates that the Admiralty was not fixated solely on the surface-raider threat, though it rightly took this into account. It fully anticipated early resort to unrestricted submarine warfare but also correctly emphasised the likelihood of an air offensive against ports and coastal shipping. The commitment to countering the submarine and air threat through convoy was unequivocal, and the paper addressed convoy routes, organisation and resources in detail. Its calculations for the escort requirement were proportionate to the scale of threat it anticipated. The paper gave a figure of 107 naval escorts, made up from seven flotillas of the over-age destroyers, thirty assorted sloops, ten patrol vessels, and seven anti-aircraft cruisers. This was not unreasonable to counter an assumed sustainable attack force of ten U-boats confined to the continental shelf. It also assumed a significant Royal Air Force contribution to reconnaissance, anti-U-boat patrol and fighter protection.

The Joint Planning Committee produced an updated paper a year later, which reviewed the threat to trade not only from a war with Germany, but also the scenarios of a war with Japan, and then a simultaneous war with both.[187] The paper judged, quite reasonably, that simple geography dictated that Japan could not exert decisive pressure through an attack on trade in the way Germany could, nor, given the huge distances involved, could she easily sustain submarines in the Indian Ocean. The United States reaction to unrestricted trade war would also be a factor. The paper was frank about the need to give overriding priority to dealing with the German threat in the event of simultaneous war and it recognised that it might only be possible to adopt a limited defensive holding operation in the Far East for quite some while. However, it is important to underline that these papers refer to the situation in

1939 and not 1942 onward, when the New Standard building programme would have better equipped the Royal Navy for a two-hemisphere war.

In reviewing how well the Royal Navy assessed the risks of a future German attack on Atlantic trade, the key development that the Admiralty did not and, arguably, could not reasonably predict was the fall of France. Royal Navy plans to counter the U-boat threat focused on United Kingdom coastal waters and the immediate Atlantic approaches. A sustained mid-Atlantic campaign was not regarded as feasible by submarines operating from Germany or Holland, given the long, dangerous transit. The Planning Committee paper confirms that the Admiralty expected submarine attack to be mainly confined to what it defined as the Home Waters area. This was an elongated circle extending from the Norwegian coast at Stavanger, passing just north of the Shetlands, to Rockall, then out to longitude 15° W, before swinging back to the coast just south of Brest. The pattern of U-boat operations in the first nine months of the war demonstrates that this was indeed a reasonable assumption.[188] It was German access to the Biscay ports that fundamentally changed the problem of trade defence.[189]

The Admiralty never regarded it as financially possible or militarily sensible to maintain in peacetime anti-submarine forces sufficient to counter a full-scale trade war on the British Empire. They envisaged, rather, the establishment in peace of a skeletal anti-submarine warfare organisation capable of rapid expansion. This included developing designs for anti-submarine vessels, and identifying production capacity, so that ships could be mass-produced quickly in wartime. Although there was steady evolution of anti-submarine sloops throughout the interwar period, and a small programme for these was included under the DRC Fleet, these were built to naval, not merchant, specifications, so could not be mass-produced quickly. The Flower-class corvette, based on the Southern Pride whale-catcher, is often presented as a hasty, last-minute Admiralty response to a requirement it had failed to anticipate. The design is also criticised as inappropriate to the demands of the mid-Atlantic. In reality, the Flower class fitted exactly the concept of identifying in peace a prototype suitable for mass production in war. Highlighting their limitations for the mid-Atlantic ignores the point that Admiralty planning prior to 1940 did not anticipate losing France: whether this assumption was reasonable is discussed further at the beginning of Chapter 3.

The best balanced and most forward-looking navy
The Royal Navy of 1939 was stronger, more capable, more innovative, and more ambitious in its strategic goals than the mainstream accounts of its interwar history have so far accepted. Despite the constraints imposed by the naval treaties and the damage wrought by the Great Depression, Britannia did

not let the trident slip in this period. The Royal Navy remained the largest navy backed by the largest naval industry and, given the scale of its rearmament programme from 1935, was well placed to sustain this position for the foreseeable future.[190] More important, the Royal Navy's rate of investment was broadly matching that of the combined Axis navies, and its strategic goal for 1942 of fighting an offensive war in Europe, while holding a defensive position in the East, seemed achievable in resource terms.

The Royal Navy was not the conservative service so often portrayed. It was fully alert to the risks and opportunities posed by air and submarine warfare. It was a powerful innovator in both these areas and in exploiting modern detection systems and communications. The Royal Navy had weaknesses and did not get everything right but, overall, the naval investment put in place from 1935 onward was both far-sighted and substantial, set against the risks visible at the time. It had also achieved a better balance across the different areas of naval capability than its enemies, including those most relevant to the coming war. Events would demonstrate that it had created sufficient margin to cope with the loss of the French ally in 1940 and, later, to hold the Indian Ocean against the Japanese in the worst of circumstances in 1942.

2

The Naval Defence of the
Eastern Empire 1935–40:
Managing Competing Risks

The previous chapter assessed the state of the Royal Navy in 1939 and its capacity to conduct simultaneous war in two theatres. This chapter now examines how Royal Navy strategy and plans for managing the naval risks to the eastern British Empire evolved in the face of the emerging 'triple threat' over the period 1935–40. It begins with the threat from Japan in the Far East in 1935, which the chiefs of staff judged the primary risk to the British Empire at that time. It then examines how established plans to counter the perceived threat from Japan through naval power evolved in the face of the growing threat from Germany to the British homeland and Atlantic, and from Italy in the Mediterranean. It assesses how far, and why, the Royal Navy prioritised its commitment to the eastern Mediterranean over the Far East from late 1938, and whether this represented a de facto strategic withdrawal of the Royal Navy from its Far East commitment or a deliberate strategic choice to concentrate scarce resources on protecting an inner core of the eastern empire from threats at both ends. The chapter ends in mid-1940 with the fall of France. This was a strategic shock not anticipated pre-war, requiring a fundamental reappraisal of naval priorities discussed in Chapter 3 onward.

The most likely enemy: planning to fight Japan in 1935
Throughout the interwar period, Britain's strategy for protecting its interests and territories in the Far East rested on three assumptions. First, that the primary security risk to the empire in this theatre was a conflict with Japan that translated into an attack on British trade and possessions. Secondly, geography and distance dictated that, with the important exception of the concessions[1] in China, successful Japanese action against Britain could only be prosecuted and sustained by sea. Finally, it followed that the only effective counter to Japanese action was to deploy sufficient naval power to assert maritime control and

ultimately coerce Japan into a satisfactory settlement. The evolution of this strategy through the 1920s and 1930s, and its endless scrutiny since, has a theological flavour reminiscent of cold war deterrence theory. For financial and logistical reasons, Britain was not prepared to station some two-thirds of Royal Navy strength permanently in the East as a deterrent to a putative Japanese attack, which until the mid-1930s was hypothetical. Chatfield summarised the arguments here at the Imperial Conference in June 1937. To be credible and effective, the Far East fleet must match that of Japan, which would reduce the home-based fleet to a small size. It would be hard to sell such a policy to the British public who paid for the fleet. Two-thirds or more of Royal Navy personnel would be on foreign service terms, presenting an almost impossible financial and administrative challenge. Finally, Japan might view a permanent British fleet in the East as a hostile act, complicating Britain's ability to resolve differences by diplomatic means.[2] Deterrence therefore rested on assurance that a fleet could and would be sent when required. Assurance required a suitable base in the theatre to support a major fleet, and Singapore was selected.[3] It also required a vast array of plans to mobilise the major part of the Royal Navy in a crisis and despatch it to the East. This became the 'Singapore strategy'.

Critics of the Singapore strategy argued that Britain always lacked the naval resources to counter enemies at home and simultaneously to deploy a credible fleet to the Far East able to overcome the world's third naval power. They invariably quoted Admiral Herbert Richmond, who suggested in 1925 that the strategy rested on 'the illusion that a Two Hemisphere Empire could be defended by a One Hemisphere Navy'.[4] For the critics, therefore, the adoption of the one-power standard of naval strength for the Royal Navy, described in the previous chapter, as well as the logistical challenge of supporting a fleet on the far side of the world, rendered the strategy fatally flawed from the outset.[5]

There have been some powerful rebuttals of the critics' case.[6] The Royal Navy's policy and planning for handling a conflict with Japan across the interwar period is not easily reduced to a single Singapore strategy. Too much attention has arguably focused on the size of Royal Navy fleet to be deployed and its passage out to Singapore, and too little on the strategic outcome the Admiralty hoped to achieve. Critics have often portrayed a 'sort of naval Schlieffen plan', when reality was more flexible. Admiralty planners were never fixated on fighting another 'Jutland', but anticipated a strategy of economic coercion designed to bring Japan to acceptable terms. They considered a range of options, depending on available Royal Navy resources and the evolving strategic context, both globally and within the Far East theatre. The Singapore strategy was therefore not always flawed. Britain had sufficient naval superiority in the 1920s to deploy a large fleet in the Far East, and still dominate European waters. Such deployment became more difficult with the emergence of the triple threat from the Axis powers in the late 1930s, but was only compromised by the fall of France in 1940, an event that could not reasonably be anticipated. By the mid-1930s, the real question facing British planners dealing with the Far East threat was whether they could generate sufficient forces for an offensive strategy, or only enough for a defensive one. British naval strength could still allow a defensive posture in Europe and the Far East simultaneously. With a reliable ally (France or the United States), it might even be possible to take the offensive in one theatre.[7]

This alternative interpretation of eastern naval strategy, which is consistent with that established in Chapter 1, deserves more recognition. It has yet to spark much support. There are further points to consider. The first is clarity in defining Britain's interests in the Far East. How did British decision-makers see these? Did they view some as vital and others more discretionary, not worth the risk of fundamental conflict? How did interests translate into an 'offensive' or 'defensive' strategy; indeed, what did these terms, embraced not least by Chatfield, really mean? A second is the relationship between the Mediterranean and, ultimately, the hostility of Italy, and the Far East problem. Was the hostility of Italy viewed by decision-makers as another call on scarce military resources, which reduced capacity available for the Far East? Or did it change the strategic framework for defending the empire in a more substantial way? Another issue is whether a more flexible interpretation of Admiralty policy in the 1930s understates the logistical challenge and opportunity costs faced by Royal Navy planners in deploying a fleet, and imposing the anticipated economic coercion strategy over a considerable period. Was this ever credible once Germany could threaten home terminals, as she could from 1935?

An authoritative picture of how the Royal Navy leadership and chiefs of staff saw the risk[8] posed by Japan and the means available to counter it at the beginning of 1935 can be gleaned from three papers circulated at that time to the Committee of Imperial Defence. The first is a Foreign Office memorandum on the Far East prepared in mid-March to support a chiefs of staff briefing for Dominion prime ministers. This saw Japanese ambition to achieve a dominant position in China as the key feature in the Far East landscape. Japan's goal might clash with the interests of Britain and the United States and provoke conflict, but the Foreign Office judged this risk manageable. Japan's immediate focus was the consolidation of her position in Manchuria, and she would avoid action that left her exposed to Russia. Britain should not impair relations with the United States or China for the sake of Japan, but could be conciliatory towards her. Britain should recognise Japan's reasonable economic interests, but avoid taking sides in disputes involving other parties, where possible. The Foreign Office did not think Japan yet posed a threat southward towards the oil and rubber supplies of the East Indies. She would calculate that the risks here outweighed the gains, although the balance could change if Britain became preoccupied in Europe, Russia was compliant, or the United States threatened Japan's access to oil.[9] This was a good assessment of actual Japanese attitudes and priorities which would remain valid until mid-1940.[10]

The second paper is the Admiralty response of early April. This judged the Foreign Office view complacent. Japan was building up her forces and intended to dominate China, and perhaps other regions too, confident that she could prevent others from interfering. She recognised British weakness in the East and would therefore override British interests in China and elsewhere whenever she judged she could get away with it. Distractions in Europe would only encourage her further. Britain's position in the Far East theatre could therefore 'become delicate' at any moment.[11]

This exchange would have informed the third paper, the Chiefs of Staff 1935 Annual Review, drafted during March and April.[12] This confirmed three main priorities for imperial defence: defence of possessions and interests in the Far East; European commitments; and the defence of India against the Soviet Union. It emphasised that from the naval perspective, 'the defence of our interests and possessions in the Far East is the greatest and most immediate of our commitments'. The naval responsibilities were 'the provision and operation in emergency of a main fleet in the Far East sufficient to meet the Japanese fleet at Japan's selected moment' and under cover of this fleet, protection of sea communications with the Dominions, India and the colonial empire. Meeting this responsibility required the use of bases in Singapore and, ideally, Hong Kong. The review emphasised that Japan was building up its strength rapidly with modernisation of its battle-fleet almost complete and significant investment in air power. Royal Navy modernisation was lagging, making 1936 potentially a dangerous year.

The 1935 review emphasised that war policy in the Far East must be 'defensive'. This recognised growing Japanese strength and the difficulty the Royal Navy would now have generating sufficient forces to pursue a successful coercion strategy. Earlier assessments by the chiefs of staff were frank about the challenges posed by Far East deployment. In their 1932 review, which followed the Japanese attack on Manchuria, and a potential threat therefore to British interests in China, they stated:

We possess only light naval forces in the Far East; the fuel supplies required for the passage of the main fleet to the East and for its mobility after arrival are in jeopardy; and the bases at Singapore and Hong Kong, essential to the maintenance of a fleet of capital ships on arrival are not in a defensible condition. The whole of our territory in the Far East, as well as the coastline of India and the Dominions and our vast trade and shipping lies open to attack.[13]

A year later they judged the risks were unchanged and there had been no progress in addressing deficiencies.[14] In their 1933 review, the chiefs underlined the growing strength of the IJN, including its air power, and the scale of Royal Navy force required to 'meet the IJN at her selected moment'. The Royal Navy would need all its immediately available capital ship and carrier force and most of its available cruisers, now reduced to fifty under the 1930 Treaty of London, although a reduction in the IJN capital ship force provided some comfort until its capital ship modernisation programme was completed in 1937.

The chiefs emphasised not only the growth of Japanese air power, but also that their equipment and training were 'approaching European standard'.[15] Several papers at the turn of 1933 considered how this air power might be applied and the British resources needed to counter it. Some of the thinking here, notably the possibility of surprise dawn strikes by carrier aircraft on bases like Singapore, was far-sighted.[16] The Royal Navy's poor state of preparedness to match growing IJN strength at this time was underlined in exchanges between Chatfield and the new Commander-in-Chief China, Admiral Sir Frederick Dreyer. Dreyer was scathing about Far East war-readiness. There were no effective war plans and the China Squadron was in a poor state. Chatfield agreed the Royal Navy was currently poorly prepared for a Far East war, but correcting deficiencies would take time. While not complacent, he doubted aggressive action by either Japan or Germany was imminent, which would give the Royal Navy time to rebuild its capability. The first phase of the Singapore defences had been approved and should complete in 1936.[17] Meanwhile, the 1934 Chiefs of Staff Review recorded further enhancements to Japanese strength. Seven out of nine IJN capital ships would be modernised by 1936. Imperial Japanese Naval Air Force (IJNAF) strength was now 675 aircraft compared to 279 in 1932, and was expected to reach 1000 by 1940. Strength in active personnel was above the Royal Navy and fleet manoeuvres were following a higher tempo.[18]

From 1933 onward, the chiefs of staff underlined that despatching an adequate fleet to the East would leave limited naval forces at home. Their 1935 review went further. Given the increase in IJN strength, a one-power standard for the Royal Navy was no longer satisfactory. 'The existing margin is only sufficient on the supposition that France will not be our enemy in Europe and we are not without allies'. Nevertheless, the chiefs judged that so long as France was an ally, and there was sufficient warning time to mobilise ships in refit, then it would still be possible to provide adequate naval security against Germany for the 'next three to four years', while 'defending against Japanese aggression' in the Far East.[19] On a more positive note, the 1935 review reported significant improvements to the Singapore defences.[20]

The Chiefs of Staff 1935 Review did not explain what their 'defensive policy' meant in practice, although a separate chiefs of staff memorandum at the end of 1934 did provide some insight into how Britain would conduct a Far East war at this time. The arrival of the fleet in Singapore would ensure adequate maritime security to the west across the Indian Ocean and south towards Australasia. It should also enable the Royal Navy to exert some control over the South China Sea, while the IJN was likely to control the area north of Formosa, leaving the space between these areas in dispute. If the IJN avoided a fleet action, the Royal Navy would harass Japan's sea communications and apply economic pressure to bring her to terms, though it recognised this could take considerable time, and decisive success was unlikely without active support from the United States and China.[21]

The ability of the Royal Navy to generate adequate forces to meet an emergency in the Far East, if one had occurred in the autumn of 1935, is illuminated by examining the deployments made against Italy during the Abyssinian crisis over the winter 1935/36. That autumn, Royal Navy planners had to produce sufficient forces in the Mediterranean to achieve an effective economic coercion strategy against Italy, even if Britain was the only power prepared to act. The Italian navy was significantly smaller than the IJN in capital ship strength (four compared to nine) and had no aircraft carriers, but its strength in cruisers and light forces was substantial, at least on paper, amounting to about 75 per cent of IJN strength in these categories.[22] Furthermore, Italy's central position in the Mediterranean made the application of British naval power in the face of Italian land-based air power challenging. There were some striking similarities to the Far East problem, both in planning an economic blockade strategy and in finding adequate support and forward operating bases for the fleet to execute it. The Royal Navy also had to consider the security of the United Kingdom homeland against Germany while the bulk of the Royal Navy was in the Mediterranean, although retrieving some or all of the fleet from here was an easier proposition than getting it back from the Far East. The Royal Navy originally envisaged a total Mediterranean commitment of ten capital ships, three aircraft carriers, fourteen cruisers and fifty-four destroyers but, without full mobilisation (ruled out on political and diplomatic grounds), manpower limitations reduced this force by three capital ships and one carrier.[23]

The following spring, the German occupation of the Rhineland raised the possibility of war with Germany while the bulk of the navy was still in the Mediterranean, effectively putting the 1932 standard to the test. The chiefs of staff initially reported that the minimum acceptable requirements for a naval war against Germany could only be met by withdrawing forces from the Mediterranean and jeopardising strategic goals against Italy. Risking war without withdrawal would be 'thoroughly dangerous'. They stated that the only naval forces immediately available in home waters were one 6in cruiser, seventeen destroyers, and nine submarines, although this force could be increased substantially by full mobilisation. Three battleships, one carrier, ten cruisers and fifteen destroyers could then be added to the 'immediate' forces within fourteen days, without affecting Mediterranean strength.[24]

A subsequent more detailed appraisal by the joint planning staff identified the total forces the Royal Navy could immediately generate on mobilisation for a war with Germany, together with their global distribution.[25] Not surprisingly, it demonstrated that the combined Royal Navy forces in the home and Mediterranean theatres vastly outnumbered Germany's forces, and the planning staff concluded there was no prospect of Germany winning a war at sea. The combined total for the home- and Mediterranean-based forces comprised eight battleships, two battlecruisers, three carriers, seven heavy cruisers, eight modern 6in cruisers, fourteen other light cruisers, ten destroyer flotillas and nineteen submarines. Only ten capital ships were available, because *Warspite* was being reconstructed, *Malaya*, *Royal Oak* and *Repulse* were in two-year extended refits, and one other was in short refit.

Although the paper did not say so, it also showed that on mobilisation there were enough Royal Navy forces in the two theatres comfortably to match both Germany and Italy, even without throwing the significant French forces into the balance.[26] By looking at these April 1936 estimates for Royal Navy force generation, the maximum force deployable for a Far East war at this time, in the absence of a requirement against Italy, can be estimated. It would have comprised most of the forces deployed in the Mediterranean for the Abyssinian crisis, together with the existing China Fleet. This came to seven capital ships, three carriers, ten heavy cruisers, twenty light cruisers, eight destroyer flotillas and twenty-five submarines. This left about three capital ships, one carrier, three heavy cruisers, three light cruisers, three destroyer flotillas and ten submarines in home waters to counter Germany. This figure was well short of the chiefs of staff 1933 estimate for the force required to meet the IJN, but broadly equated to the realistic maximum strength the IJN could generate for a war with Britain at this time.[27] It also compared well with the projected Royal Navy forces required for a defensive Far East war set out in the New Standard papers drafted by the naval staff in the autumn of 1936.[28] It would be sufficient for the 'defensive war' postulated in the Chiefs of Staff 1935 Review.

The picture here, drawn from a wide range of chiefs of staff and Admiralty papers, leads to several key conclusions. For the first half of the 1930s, Britain's military leadership assumed that a Far East war would be triggered by Japanese action against British interests in China, which were essentially commercial. Hong Kong was an obvious exception, being British owned or leased territory. There were also British troops based in Shanghai and Tientsin (a single battalion in each).[29] What followed would initially, therefore, be a trade war, conducted primarily at sea, where each side sought to inflict enough damage to persuade the other to desist. The Joint Planning Committee indeed stated in 1937: 'If war occurs, the basic cause is likely to be the conflict between Japanese policy and British interests in the Far East. We therefore assume that our object is to bring such pressure on Japan as to force her to desist from her policy.'[30]

Such a war might be limited in both scale and geography, but the Royal Navy anticipated wider attacks on British shipping, and possibly coastal raids towards Australasia and the Indian Ocean. It also expected Japan to inhibit British reinforcement through seaborne attacks on Hong Kong and Singapore, and possibly sabotage of the Suez Canal.[31] The minimum British 'defensive' objective was clearly to protect empire territory and the key empire trade and communication routes. In meeting this objective, the Singapore naval base was 'the pivot of our whole naval strategic position in the Far East', and until provided with adequate defences, would be 'liable to capture or destruction by coup de main' before the main fleet could arrive, while its recapture would be a 'major operation of the greatest difficulty'.[32] Assuming Singapore was held, the 1936 force was sufficient to protect Malaya and secure the sea routes to the south and west. It would also offer a reasonable chance of relieving Hong Kong.[33]

British planning for a Far East war never contemplated direct attack on Japan itself. Chatfield dismissed this as 'out of the question' in 1937.[34] Therefore, although none of the military planning documents say so explicitly, the difference between a 'defensive' war and an 'offensive' war was essentially twofold. First, an offensive strategy was the only way to secure the British stake in China. Since British planners acknowledged the IJN would exert control north of Formosa, Britain could not protect or recover its concessions in China without either inflicting a major defeat on the IJN fleet, or strangling Japanese trade until it was obliged to sue for peace. Secondly, an offensive strategy was the only way of bringing a war to a successful conclusion, rather than acquiescing in a stalemate which might include the loss of Hong Kong. The Royal Navy could not credibly generate the scale of force required over a sustained period to conduct an offensive war after 1930, and certainly not once it needed a substantial deterrent force against Germany in home waters, as opposed to minimum protection of home terminals. The China interest was not therefore defensible by military means.[35] This was the private view Chatfield expressed to Sir Warren Fisher, the Treasury Permanent Secretary, in mid-1934. The most Britain could hope for in the East was to have a sufficient navy to go there in emergency, not to threaten Japan, but to prevent her threatening Australia and India. Chatfield did not think Britain could ever prevent Japan dominating China, but he felt it should be possible to secure Britain's commercial interests through diplomacy.[36]

This raises the question of why the chiefs of staff and, above all, the Admiralty, devoted so much effort through the 1930s to planning for a war to protect China interests – particularly when they acknowledged implicitly, if not always explicitly, that they could not defend them. There is no simple answer to this. Britain's economic stake in China was substantial, and undoubtedly viewed as more important at that time than through the perspective of historical hindsight. It represented 6 per cent of Britain's overseas investment, was a key export market, and home to influential trading enterprises operating across the whole Far East region.[37] Britain was also a key stakeholder in the various international agreements that regulated external interests in China and the protection of China's rights under the League of Nations.

Perhaps more influential for those charged with empire security was the perception by 1936 of a 'domino effect', whereby successful Japanese control over northern China would feed wider ambitions to expand southward, and ultimately threaten Malaya and beyond. Japan would exploit any British weakness to further its aims. The Indian Army general staff judged Japan's immediate aim was to dominate China, especially the north, for economic and military reasons. This would then provide a base to attack Russia or move south. Ultimately, Japan aspired to long-term control of eastern Asia and the southern Pacific.[38] The chiefs of staff endorsed this view.[39] The perceived Japanese threat embraced non-British territories such as the Netherlands East Indies and Thailand that were judged vital to Britain's security and assured by British sea power.[40] However, this was all supposition. It did not reflect any evidence of Japanese intent because at this time, and indeed until 1940, no coherent intent to seize territories or interests south of China by force existed.[41] Nevertheless, it meant that the British stake in China was perceived as strategic as well as economic. China was the empire's first line of defence.[42]

Two other factors influenced Britain's view of the strategic status of China. First, Hong Kong was located geographically in China, but was British Crown territory. The chiefs of staff and Admiralty were obliged therefore to plan for its defence, and no British government could lightly contemplate its loss. The second factor was that in a conflict triggered by Japanese aggression in China, Britain would not necessarily be fighting alone. Hostile action by Japan would threaten American assets as well, and Britain and the United States shared a wider interest in containing Japanese ambition. Britain invariably found American policy in the Far East unpredictable and unreliable, but American naval support in executing an aggressive trade blockade was at least possible.

The rise of the Axis: contemplating war on three fronts

The previous chapter described how, in late 1935, the DRC argued that naval rearmament must be based on the needs of a two-hemisphere war, but failed to win formal Cabinet endorsement for this. During 1936, while the Admiralty developed proposals for a New Standard navy, the combination of perceived Japanese ambition, accelerating German rearmament, and the disruptive behaviour of Italy with its potential threat to Britain's position in the Mediterranean, all increased concerns about Britain's ability to cope with the global risks to empire security. Chatfield told Hankey privately at the beginning of 1937 that imperial security policy was 'drifting', while Britain's continued commitment to collective security under the League of Nations exposed her to unlimited liability.[43] He was doubtful it was possible to safeguard the empire if Britain became involved in simultaneous war east and west. This was 'something we have never done before' and 'should not contemplate'. Rearmament would provide deterrence and, after 1942, enable Britain to negotiate from a position of strength. Meanwhile, for the next five years, it was important to reduce the risk of conflict through judicious concessions. Empire responsibilities precluded Britain from taking risks in Europe.[44]

At chiefs of staff level, the growing security risks to the empire were addressed in two important papers prepared in the first half of 1937 for the Imperial Conference in June.[45] These were an overall review of imperial defence[46] and a more specific paper focused on the Far East.[47] The former doubled as the Chiefs of Staff Annual Review and comprised a major stocktaking of the empire's military liabilities and assets shared with Dominion governments. The Admiralty insisted on adding a naval appendix to the main review. This provided an overview of the empire's naval forces, current and planned, available to secure the sea communications of the empire against seaborne attack. It was intended to help the Dominions plan their individual naval contributions within a common framework. It was notable for its emphasis on trade defence and the scale of Royal Navy investment in anti-aircraft and anti-submarine capability.[48] The other chiefs were reluctant to have this appendix, but Chatfield insisted that a similar paper had been presented at previous conferences, and the Royal Navy had special responsibility for securing imperial communications and guiding the contributions of the individual Dominions.[49] The Far East appreciation was a wide-ranging review of the specific risks in the Far East and present strategy for countering them. It was a stocktake of the Singapore strategy in mid-1937.

At the Imperial Conference itself, the First Lord, Sir Samuel Hoare, in a statement designed to confront scepticism from Australia and New Zealand, insisted that the security of the empire continued to depend on Royal Navy ability to control sea communications anywhere in the world. He gave an unambiguous assurance to send a fleet to the Far East if necessary. This statement, in the presence of Prime Minister Stanley Baldwin, was the most authoritative commitment made at the conference, though it was subsequently confirmed and amplified by Chatfield and drew on the chiefs of staff papers already shared.[50] In February 1939 Prime Minster Neville Chamberlain would acknowledge this assurance as 'categorical and unqualified'.[51]

Chatfield, as chairman of the chiefs of staff, subsequently summarised Britain's strategy for a 'Pacific war' to Dominion representatives on 1 June.[52] In contemplating such a war, Britain faced two problems: two enemies separated by 10,000 miles with Italy lying between them, resentful, ambitious and able to do damage, and secondly, the prospect that the United Kingdom could be drawn into a European conflict not of its choosing. The latter was the scenario where Britain felt obliged to support France in a war with Germany triggered by events in eastern Europe and where no direct British interests were involved.[53] Chatfield saw two compensating advantages: the Anglo-German Naval Agreement which capped German naval strength; and the co-operation and resources of the Dominions and India. He confirmed that imperial defence had four primary tasks: defence of the United Kingdom homeland without which the empire would disintegrate; security of the Mediterranean; protection of Dominions and colonies; and security of imperial communications. However, he also underlined the conclusion of the chiefs' review that no risks associated with the Mediterranean could interfere with the despatch of a fleet to the Far East. There was an odd juxtaposition here. On the one hand, Chatfield highlighted the importance of the Mediterranean, but, on the other, insisted it would be sacrificed if necessary for the Far East. Britain might conceivably have to give up naval control in the Mediterranean and lose Malta and Cyprus, but that need not imply loss of Britain's whole position in the Middle East, since forces could be deployed and supported there via the Indian Ocean. The Mediterranean could always be recovered, but the Far East, once lost, could not.[54]

These statements were intended to convey, and were certainly interpreted by Australian and New Zealand representatives, as an unambiguous commitment to despatch a full competitive fleet in the event of any Japanese attack. Hoare had already given his even more direct pledge at the start of the conference. 'We believe that the very existence of the British Commonwealth of Nations as now constituted rests on our ability to send our fleet to the Far East should the need arise.'[55]

Chatfield then emphasised the differences between a European war and Pacific war. The former required a major contribution from all three armed services, while the latter would be predominantly a naval war. It did not require an army or air commitment on a national scale. In Europe, economic pressure

65

would contribute to the strategic outcome, but in the Pacific, economic pressure was the only means to victory, since invasion of Japan was inconceivable. This would be war fought at long distance with only part of the empire affected. Chatfield accepted that exerting economic pressure against Japan would take time, and decisive results were unlikely inside two years. But the expansion of Japan's overseas trade had rendered her vulnerable, and the more she invested in her military, the more dependent she became on imports.

Finally, Chatfield addressed the problems posed by two-hemisphere war. If Britain was already involved in a war with Germany, there would be two consequences for Far East strategy. First, the deployment of a fleet adequate to match Japan might be considerably delayed. It would be essential, therefore, to reinforce Singapore with extra troops and supplies as soon as war broke out with Germany, to ensure the base could hold out in the face of delay. Secondly, the scale of fleet would only be sufficient for a defensive strategy. These were important caveats which Chatfield appeared to have forgotten, or at least chose to play down in subsequent debates over Far East reinforcement with his successor, Admiral Sir Roger Backhouse, in early 1939. Economic pressure would remain the key lever under a defensive strategy, but its effect would be much slower.

Chatfield also highlighted here the capital ship modernisation programme, which would remove three ships from Royal Navy strength over the period 1937–39. If the Royal Navy was to retain adequate strength against Germany, it would therefore have little margin over the IJN capital ship force and at times would be inferior.[56] The Royal Navy believed it was more efficient than the IJN and could still win with inferior forces, but it was prudent to base calculations on numerical strength. Numbers also influenced deterrence. If the Royal Navy did have inferior forces, 'we must feel our way carefully at first and judge the efficiency of the Japanese by their conduct in cruiser and destroyer operations in the early stages of a war'. The Royal Navy could then better gauge what risk was acceptable.

Chatfield's belief that the Royal Navy was more 'efficient' than the IJN has inevitably encouraged the view that the Royal Navy consistently under-estimated the IJN. However, in planning for a Far East war in the 1930s, the Royal Navy always preferred numerical superiority over the IJN and always calculated the numerical balance through simple 'bean-counting' where one Japanese warship equated to one Royal Navy warship. Many Royal Navy decision-makers (including Chatfield here) thought, or at least hoped, the IJN threat would be more manageable than bean-counting implied. This was not necessarily unreasonable. Navies are not equally effective. The Royal Navy did enjoy ingrained self-belief that it was superior to all other navies (a belief consistently justified in regard to the German and Italian navies in the Second

World War). In the Far East it was contemplating a defensive war with the support of a fortified base and shore air support, while the IJN until 1940 would have very long and vulnerable lines of communication.[57]

A chiefs of staff memorandum issued shortly before Chatfield's briefing amplifies how the Royal Navy would address the risk posed by Japan in the first phase of a simultaneous war at this time.[58] It emphasised that the security of the eastern half of the empire depended on the early establishment of a fleet at Singapore. At a minimum, this fleet must be adequate to act on the defensive and serve as a strong deterrent. This language 'act on the defensive' and 'serve as a strong deterrent' was lifted direct from the definition of New Standard in the DRC Third Report. It was used increasingly from 1937, as the prospect of producing a fleet to match that of Japan became more difficult. The phrases clearly implied, and were certainly used to suggest, something less than a competitive fleet. Neither the size nor goals of such a defensive force were initially defined. Backhouse, Chatfield's successor as First Sea Lord, would focus on exactly this point in March 1939.[59] The memorandum emphasised that the time needed to deploy the fleet depended on the nature of the war. In a single-handed war, or if war with Japan came first, the fleet would be deployed within twenty-eight to seventy days. If war broke out simultaneously with Germany and Japan, deployment might need to await mobilisation of reserves and full force generation, which could take three to six months. If war with Germany came first, force generation would be complete, but redistribution of forces might be complex, extending the seventy-day target. The intervention of Italy would impose further complications, but it was a cardinal principle that the Far East took priority over the Mediterranean.

Meanwhile, Japanese action would depend on their perceived priorities and commitments. IJN deployment of two capital units in the Indian Ocean, together with cruisers, light forces and submarines was a reasonable assumption. Their role would be to attack British reinforcements, raid bases and destroy fuel stocks. In the worst case, this force might be deployed prior to formal hostilities. Pending arrival of the main Royal Navy Eastern Fleet, the only Royal Navy force available to counter an incursion into the Indian Ocean was the small East Indies squadron, possibly reinforced by units from the China station squadron. Protection of trade and troop convoys would therefore depend heavily on evasive routes. This underlined the need to reinforce Singapore with planned extra troops and supplies as soon as war broke out with Germany, and in advance of Japanese intervention.

Three fundamental conclusions can be drawn from this collection of papers and Chatfield's presentation at the Imperial Conference. The first is the extent to which British strategy at this time was shaped by the need to protect the empire as a whole, rather than a narrow focus on the security of the United

Kingdom homeland.[60] This is an obvious point not always sufficiently emphasised. The second is formal recognition by the chiefs of staff that Britain and its Allies might now face a global war against three enemies, Germany, Japan and Italy, which meant Britain must address risks in three different theatres. The third is the chiefs' view that in a global war, the priorities would be security of imperial communications, the security of the United Kingdom homeland against Germany, and the security of Far East interests against Japan. For the chiefs, the security of the United Kingdom and security of Singapore were the two 'keystones' on which survival of the 'British Commonwealth of Nations' rested. The defeat of the United Kingdom homeland 'would destroy the whole structure of the Commonwealth', while 'the security of Australia, New Zealand and India hinges on the retention of Singapore as a base for the British Fleet'.[61] No losses in the Mediterranean would be as serious as the surrender of British sea power in the Far East, which would leave the whole eastern empire exposed.

The chiefs were clear that the primary and most immediate threat to the United Kingdom homeland was German air attack, while in the Far East, as Chatfield emphasised, the threat was essentially naval. They also, however, recognised that, 'strategically', the future of the United Kingdom homeland and the empire were linked with France. If Germany crushed France, it would dominate all of western Europe and generate power that would render the situation very difficult for Britain.[62] Against this background, the chiefs took some comfort from the fact that none of the three potential enemies intended direct action against the British Empire in the immediate future, and Japan and Italy were only likely to move if Britain was already at war with Germany. For Japan, this was an accurate assessment.[63] In the meantime, rearmament had been initiated on a large scale primarily as insurance against Germany, but also to enable the Royal Navy to provide an adequate fleet to meet liabilities in the East, while leaving sufficient forces in home waters to neutralise Germany.[64]

Despite the growing global risks Britain faced, the Imperial Conference papers display coherence and confidence that belies any view that Far East defence was now increasingly hopeless. The supporting argument for the strength of fleet that could be deployed to the East in the period 1937–40, and the options for its use, was credible in the prevailing circumstances. The chiefs of staff were not willing, no doubt for political reasons, formally to admit the defence of Hong Kong was impossible, but the new Far East appreciation left little doubt this was their true assessment. They certainly saw little chance of recovering the territory once lost. Indeed by the summer of 1938, the chiefs had accepted that it was not possible to provide a protected naval base here, guaranteed to be available in war, without disproportionate investment. They therefore advocated a more limited holding investment to symbolise continuing

British commitment to the territory, and to buy time.[65] The appreciation also acknowledged that operations north of Singapore with the forces available before 1940 would be limited at best, even in a single-handed war, and probably confined to protecting the coast of Malaya. The appreciation, not unreasonably, judged that in a strictly defensive war, the Royal Navy could still cut Japanese trade with Southeast Asia and Europe and damage their trans-Pacific trade as well, while keeping British trade losses, other than China, to a minimum. It accepted, however, that in a full global war with both Germany and Japan, the scope for achieving serious economic pressure on Japan would lapse from lack of resources.

There were weaknesses in the chiefs of staff assessment. The figures in the Far East appreciation designed to demonstrate it was possible to provide a competitive fleet in the East, while maintaining a deterrent force against Germany, were optimistic as regards realistic force generation and political feasibility. This would be demonstrated when crises arose in the Far East at the end of 1937 and in mid-1939. These figures had to compensate for the absence of three capital ships, *Renown*, *Valiant* and *Queen Elizabeth*, under reconstruction from mid-1937 to mid-1939. They were therefore constructed to demonstrate how the Royal Navy could still produce a credible capital ship force over this period of 'maximum vulnerability', when for two years only twelve ships would be available.

- Summer 1937 – spring 1938: ten ships, leaving two battlecruisers at home to counter three German pocket battleships.
- Spring 1938 – summer 1939: eight ships, leaving two battlecruisers and two *Queen Elizabeth*-class battleships at home to counter three pocket battleships and two *Scharnhorst*s.
- Summer 1939 – late 1940: ten ships leaving three battlecruisers and two *Nelson*s at home to counter three pocket battleships, two *Scharnhorst*s and two *Bismarck*s.

The figures were optimistic on three counts. They suggested the rebuilds would be completed more quickly than experience with *Warspite* suggested was possible. They took no account of ships absent in short refits of up to six months. Most important, they understated the scale of force needed to contain the German fleet. Countering three pocket battleships with two battlecruisers was just about credible in military terms, if hard to sell politically. However, Chatfield's successor would judge in late 1938 that a minimum of six ships, including all three fast battlecruisers, were needed to counter three pocket battleships and two *Scharnhorst*s. As a result, with the rebuilds running late, the Admiralty would struggle to project a force of even seven ships in the summer of 1939.[66] A related point, hardly addressed in any of the planning papers throughout the 1930s, let alone once the triple threat was a reality, was the difficulty of keeping some two-thirds of the Royal Navy in the Far East theatre for an indefinite period, while sustaining economic coercion.

There were also two more fundamental problems. The first was the failure adequately to address the scenario of Far East deployment when war was already underway with Germany. This was, after all, when the chiefs judged a Japanese move was most likely. In his briefing to Dominion representatives on 1 June, Chatfield had implied both a considerable delay in deployment under this scenario, and that the scale of fleet would only be sufficient for a defensive strategy. These caveats were distinctly ambiguous. Did 'considerable delay' compromise the assurance that Singapore could hold out until relieved? Since strategy was now assumed to be defensive even in a single-handed war, what did a reduced scale imply? Buried in Part I of the Far East appreciation, under the heading 'If war breaks out when we, allied with France, are already at war with Germany', was more explicit, and for Australia and New Zealand, more alarming language:

> While the strength of the Fleet to be sent to the Far East can only be decided in the light of the conditions at the time, we cannot base our plans on any other assumption than that it will be unable to undertake operations forward of the Singapore area.
>
> We cannot accurately forecast the delay which might occur before we could despatch a Fleet to the Far East since it must depend on the naval and political situation *at the time.*

This language was close to that used by Vice Admiral Sir Andrew Cunningham as Deputy Chief of Naval Staff in a submission to the Committee of Imperial Defence almost exactly two years later, and which is often regarded as final confirmation that the traditional Singapore strategy was no longer feasible. A second problem was the failure to recognise that there were potential assets and risks in the Mediterranean and Middle East that might rival those in the Far East. This problem would loom ever larger over the coming year.

It is nevertheless important to keep in perspective the emerging question-marks over the size of fleet that could be sent to the East in a simultaneous war, as perceived in 1937. Those who see confirmation here that the Singapore strategy was an illusion, and that the Royal Navy already faced impossible over-stretch, overstate the case. The chiefs of staff and Admiralty were not saying that a fleet could not be sent, but that it would take more time to build it up, and that its ultimate strength in global war might be significantly inferior to the maximum IJN fleet. That would certainly rule out major Royal Navy operations north of Singapore, but it would still be reasonable to anticipate reinforcing and holding Singapore and the Malay Barrier, even with a much reduced force, given that the IJN would face long lines of communication and could need to consider Russian and American intervention.

From the vantage point of 1937, two other points should be kept in mind. First, the Admiralty viewed the two years from 1937 to 1939 as a temporary window of vulnerability in managing the problem of simultaneous two-hemisphere war. From 1940, it expected the fruits of the rearmament programme significantly to ease the pressures on the Royal Navy. Secondly, the permanent Royal Navy forces based east of Suez in 1937 were larger than the entire German navy of that time and, if employed boldly, could alone tie down significant IJN strength. Indeed, the Royal Navy could not only harass, and perhaps severely degrade, any Japanese invasion convoy heading south, but also deploy the asymmetric 'freak navy' tactics, which it so feared from the German navy in Europe, to harry the IJN.

In June 1937 the Royal Navy China Squadron comprised one carrier, four 8in heavy cruisers, two old 6in light cruisers, eleven destroyers, fifteen submarines and one minelayer. The East Indies, Africa and Australasia squadrons could add a further three 8in cruisers, four modern 6in cruisers, three old 6in cruisers and three destroyers.[67] The major units in the German Navy at this time comprised three pocket battleships and six 6in cruisers. The seven 8in cruisers available to the Royal Navy in the Far East were broadly equivalent to the three pocket battleships. An officer serving in the Far East-based 4th Submarine Flotilla from 1937 to 1939 provided a detailed account of the capability of the China Squadron and how it would have countered an IJN offensive in this period. His account included a 'war game' portrayal of what would have happened if Japan had immediately opened hostilities in September 1939. It demonstrated how the 4th Submarine Flotilla could inflict decisive damage on any Japanese invasion convoy heading south.[68] In October 1938 Backhouse, who had just taken over as First Sea Lord, took a similar view. He told Commander-in-Chief China, Vice Admiral Sir Percy Noble, that the Japanese would not relish running the gauntlet of the 4th Submarine Flotilla in any putative attack on Singapore.[69]

The caveats expressed in the Far East appreciation on the scale and speed of deployment in a global war nevertheless exposed an unfortunate circularity in Britain's Far East naval strategy, which it failed to address right up to the fall of Singapore in 1942. The modern definition of 'strategy' comprises 'ends, ways and means'.[70] There should be a desired overall goal, or end state, the route or ways to achieve this from the starting point, and the resources to enable the transition. This framework is helpful in illuminating the attitude of decision-makers in 1937 and later critiques of British strategy. The minimum end state sought by the chiefs of staff was the prevention of any serious Japanese attack on Malaya, India, Australasia, and the trade and communications between them. The maximum end state was to convince Japan to renounce any action against any British interest anywhere in the Far East theatre. For the minimum end state, the importance of India and Australasia to the empire in the 1930s was self-evident. Malaya mattered because it was a valuable economic asset, and because it contained Singapore and the naval base on which Far East defence depended. Other goals within a maximum end state, such as holding Hong Kong, and protecting commercial interests in China, might be desirable, but were effectively discretionary.

The chosen 'way' to achieve the minimum end state was by establishing control of the southern part of the South China Sea and all sea areas to the south and west of this. The 'way' towards the maximum end state was then to extend sea control steadily northwards. The primary 'means' to achieve sea control was a 'fleet' which decision-makers judged must be broadly equal to the IJN in capital units and required a base at Singapore to operate effectively. The circularity lay in the fact that, in 1937, and for long afterwards, the Admiralty argued that the 'means' (ie, a 'fleet') depended on the availability of Singapore, so the security of the base became an end in itself. The means therefore heavily influenced the inclusion of 'protecting Malaya' as an essential goal in the minimum end state. This in turn required control of the southern part of the South China Sea, which then dictated the size and composition of the desired fleet to be deployed.

In reality, while Singapore was certainly essential to an offensive posture aimed at the maximum end state and executed over several years, that did not make it a prerequisite for achieving adequate sea control west and south of the Malay Barrier. The Royal Navy would demonstrate that it could operate a substantial fleet from Ceylon with minimal heavy support facilities in the period 1942–44, just as it chose to move the Mediterranean Fleet from Malta to the minimally equipped, but more secure, Alexandria during the Abyssinian crisis of 1935/36 and again from 1939–43.

The loss of Singapore did not therefore imply the loss of sea power in the eastern Indian Ocean and an imminent threat to India and Australasia (if that is what Chatfield meant by 'losing' the Far East). It might make the sustained operation of a major Royal Navy fleet temporarily more difficult, but the potential resources and options that could be generated using the assets of India and Australasia would compensate. As Backhouse stated in 1939, the loss of Singapore would be 'serious', but it did 'not mean the loss of the Eastern Empire for all time'.[71] Meanwhile, Chatfield's argument that the Mediterranean was always recoverable so long as Britain held a strong position in the Middle East, serviced from the Indian Ocean, was a reasonable one to make in 1937, with Italy as the opponent here rather than Germany. Perhaps Chatfield still understated the scale of the military challenge in practice, and the strategic stakes would look much higher under the threat of German attack in 1941/42. His related argument that the Far East, by which he presumably meant Malaya, was not recoverable was less convincing. The military challenge involved in recovering Mediterranean interests and Malaya was similar.

The purpose of this strategy digression is not to argue that the chiefs of staff and Admiralty should now have begun contingency planning to dispense with Singapore. The Japanese threat to Southeast Asia was still remote. Britain could hold the barrier with a reduced fleet and, as Chatfield emphasised, the Royal Navy could expect to get stronger, not weaker, in the coming years. It is, rather, to demonstrate that the chiefs of staff and Admiralty were locking themselves into a rigid mindset that linked the survival of the core eastern empire[72] to the fate of Singapore. In reality, the one did not follow from the other. Critics of the Singapore strategy are right to highlight this rigidity of thinking, and to see it looming large over the eventual fall of Singapore. However, the same critics too often fail adequately to distinguish 'ends', 'ways' and 'means'. Presumed Royal Navy inability to send a fleet after 1938, loss of Singapore in 1942, and a belief that Britain was unable then to provide adequately for the security of India and Australasia, have become inextricably linked. Not only is this linkage misconceived, but the starting point and end point is also wrong. The Royal Navy always had the capacity to send a competitive fleet at least to the Indian Ocean, so long as it accepted opportunity costs elsewhere, usually in the Mediterranean. In early 1942 it did deploy such a fleet, and the loss of Singapore did not prevent this. The Royal Navy was also still capable in 1942 of exercising sufficient sea power to protect the core eastern empire in a much bleaker context than that envisaged pre-war.

There is a further issue regarding the investment in Singapore in the 1930s. Singapore has often been portrayed as a symbol without substance, but symbolism mattered. Chatfield demonstrated the value of symbolism in his 1934 letter to Fisher. Japanese ambition beyond China could best be countered by having 'a sufficient fleet recognised as being able to go out to Singapore and secure Britain's strategic position'.[73] This was the 'fleet in being' concept much favoured by Churchill later as prime minister. The fleet did not have to be in the Far East to deter Japan. Deterrence held, so long as Japan believed it was credible it could deploy. Visible investment in Singapore symbolised British commitment to Far East naval defence and gave Britain options. Hoare emphasised this at the Imperial Conference: 'By our action in building, developing and equipping the naval base at Singapore, we have advertised to the world in general, and Japan in particular, our intention to maintain imperial interests in the Pacific'.[74]

Singapore as a 'symbol of British resolve and capability' in the Far East also helped convince the United States that Britain remained committed to protecting its interests in the region and therefore to encouraging strategic co-operation.[75] Japanese uncertainty over the nature of that co-operation then enhanced deterrence, and was one reason that Japan made no move against Britain for more than two years after September 1939. If this argument is even partly accepted, it fully justified the money invested in the base. Japanese sources certainly confirm there was no serious discussion of 'southern expansion' in Japanese leadership circles until late summer 1940, following German victories in Europe, and no detailed planning for a potential attack on Malaya and Singapore until early summer 1941.[76]

Immediately following these 1937 Imperial Conference papers, the Joint Planning Committee produced an appreciation of the situation in the Mediterranean and Middle East in the event of an early unilateral war against Italy. This reflected Italy's new status as a possible enemy in the wake of the Abyssinian crisis, and the implications posed by a Mediterranean war for Britain's Far East strategy.[77] The paper complemented the earlier Far East appreciation, and exposed issues that would ultimately bring a significant shift in how the risks to the eastern empire were perceived. It also foreshadowed key aspects of overall British strategy in the coming war. The paper emphasised that Britain was immensely stronger than Italy, and through its control of both ends of the Mediterranean could cut Italy's access to its African empire and eliminate much of its trade. However, Italy held two powerful cards: its central position enabling it to threaten or cut Britain's primary sea and air routes to the Middle East and eastern empire; and its ability to threaten Egypt and the Suez Canal from Libya.

These Italian advantages led to three enduring conclusions for future British strategy. First, the confirmation that Malta was too vulnerable as a base for more than light Royal Navy forces, even though it had the only dock capable of taking a capital ship between Gibraltar and Singapore (when the latter was complete). The main fleet would have to base in Alexandria, which imposed time and distance challenges in controlling the central Mediterranean. Secondly, the naval effort required to move British merchant and military traffic through the Mediterranean with reasonable security in the face of a hostile Italy would be disproportionate. In war, therefore, the Mediterranean would be closed and all traffic diverted round the Cape. The economic loss from such diversion was manageable. Thirdly, the defence of Egypt was critical to the security of the Suez Canal, Alexandria, and Britain's wider position in the Middle East. Since Egypt could not be reinforced rapidly through the Mediterranean, sufficient forces must be 'pre-positioned' to meet any Italian attack.[78] The issue of Egypt now preoccupied Chatfield. In August he wrote to the Commander-in-Chief Mediterranean, Admiral Sir Dudley Pound, enclosing a copy of the Mediterranean and Middle East appreciation, and commented:

'If we have trouble with Italy, the Navy can win the war slowly, but the Army and Air Force can lose it in Egypt, rapidly, and therefore it is the defence of Egypt that will be our main preoccupation'.[79]

There was one striking omission in this draft. It noted that the closure of the Mediterranean would have no significant repercussions for oil supplies, since all empire requirements west of Suez could be met from the western hemisphere. It did not, however, highlight the continuing importance of Middle East oil supplies to the eastern empire. From late 1936 to late 1938 a series of detailed assessments were produced by the Oil Board (a strategic committee comprising representatives from key government departments and industry) into the oil supplies available to the empire in the event of war. The board considered the scenario of a European war (OB 162, 1936), the effect on supplies of a closed Mediterranean (OB 189 of 22 February 1937), supplies in a Far Eastern war only (OB 233 of 8 February 1938) and, finally, supplies in a simultaneous war in both Europe and the Far East (OB 290 of 23 December 1938) with Mediterranean either closed or open. The studies looked not only at available supplies, but also tanker availability, and embraced both military and civil requirements. The scale of research and quality of presentation was impressive.[80]

The issues exposed in the Mediterranean appreciation complicated the defence of the eastern empire from Japan in several ways. Deploying, concentrating and sustaining a fleet in the East would be more difficult. Throughout the interwar period, Royal Navy plans assumed the Mediterranean Fleet would deploy to Singapore in the event of a Far East crisis and that Commander-in-Chief Mediterranean would command the Far East fleet once it assembled.[81] This was the key reason for basing a large fleet in the Mediterranean. Closure of the Mediterranean through war with Italy would not prevent transfer of the Mediterranean Fleet through the Suez Canal, but reinforcements and supplies direct from the United Kingdom via the Cape route would take longer, as would any redeployment back to Europe to deal with Germany. Plymouth to Singapore via Suez at 8100 miles was just under a third shorter than the Cape route at 11,400 miles. For the Mediterranean Fleet based at Malta, the journey to Singapore reduced to about 6000 miles via Suez.[82]

Any losses suffered in a Mediterranean war would reduce forces available to counter Japan, although much naval action in the Mediterranean theatre might be discretionary. The prospect that the Royal Navy would suffer losses in a war with Italy, compromising its ability to deal with Japan, was an abiding Admiralty concern, not least for Chatfield, from the Abyssinian crisis onward. Chatfield admitted reluctance to see the Royal Navy drawn into war over Abyssinia. 'Our naval responsibilities were worldwide but we still had a one power standard.' 'If we lost, as we were bound to lose, some ships in a

Mediterranean war, we should be in a serious position as regards Imperial Security for many years. Ships cannot be built in a day.'[83]

A bigger problem was the resource cost imposed by the need to secure Egypt against potential Italian attack. The appreciation demonstrated that the line taken by Chatfield at the Imperial Conference, that the Mediterranean could always be temporarily evacuated and sealed off to allow concentration on the Far East, was over-simplified. A commitment to hold Egypt and the canal would be significant and would require trade-offs with Far East forces, especially regarding scarce air power. There was another important strategic circularity here similar to that at Singapore. If the primary argument for defending Egypt was to protect the canal, then with the Mediterranean closed, the main purpose of the canal was reduced from 'key artery of Empire' just to protecting Egypt.[84] How much did Egypt then really matter and what cost was justified to protect it? Captain Victor Danckwerts, as Director of Plans, put the matter succinctly in early 1939. If Singapore was lost, the eastern empire was at Japan's mercy. There was little purpose then in holding Egypt, where the principal reason for Britain's presence was to protect the canal. The only use of the latter was as a highway to an empire which Britain would be in the process of losing. In any case, the Royal Navy did not propose to use the canal as a highway in a war with Italy.[85]

British, and subsequently American, strategists would return to this issue at regular intervals through to the autumn of 1942. The most powerful exponent of the British interest in Egypt specifically and the Near East generally, at this time, was the Ambassador, Sir Miles Lampson (later Lord Killearn). Lampson directed British interests in Egypt continuously from 1934–46. During the winter of 1937/38 he conducted a determined and substantially successful campaign, often to the visible annoyance of the chiefs of staff, to get the defences of Egypt upgraded. In November he insisted that 'our state in Egypt and the Near East is as important as our interest in defending French frontiers and cannot be regarded as a secondary issue'.[86]

Strategic assessments by the chiefs of staff and other government departments during 1937/38 often refer to 'wider Middle East interests' or 'our wider position in the Middle East', without spelling out why this mattered. The final version of the Mediterranean appreciation in February 1938 made some effort to assess the worst case consequences following Italian control of the eastern Mediterranean and even the loss of Egypt on Palestine, Iraq and Saudi Arabia. It suggested most of these consequences were manageable. Although it did not say so, an obvious conclusion, therefore, was that any losses here were less important than those resulting from a determined Japanese attack in the Far East.[87]

There were ultimately two decisive arguments for holding the canal, though their expression remained distinctly opaque in late 1937, and they neither featured in the Mediterranean appreciation nor other policy papers at this time. First, to enable Britain to deploy and sustain forces that could guarantee the western boundary of the eastern empire and protect Middle East oil from attack from the west without the use of any Mediterranean transit. And, secondly, the ability to deploy and sustain a substantial Royal Navy fleet able to assert decisive control over the eastern Mediterranean, again independent of Mediterranean transit. There was perhaps one more factor, the ability to prevent Italian and German naval forces reaching the Indian Ocean.

The potential closure of the Mediterranean and the growing realisation that Egypt was a substantial and inescapable commitment was one of two problems that complicated Far East defence strategy at the end of 1937. The other was the deterioration in the Far East outlook caused by the outbreak of war between Japan and China in July. This had three consequences. It rendered any realistic prospect of a diplomatic understanding with Japan void. During the first half of 1937 there had been genuine hope that a revival of British naval strength, trade concessions, and a more enlightened Japanese attitude to China, could lead to agreement. This would then alleviate Britain's 'strategic nightmare' of conflict in three theatres.[88] The Sino-Japanese war now raised the possibility of an early clash with Japan over British interests in China, which might not be easily contained. It also meant Britain would be increasingly constrained in the Far East by the need to avoid alienating the United States, making the Japan problem more difficult to manage.

Against this background, the winter of 1937/38 is often viewed as a watershed in Britain's approach to imperial defence. It was apparently the point when the political and military leadership recognised that the triple threat, and the possibility of simultaneous war in three divergent theatres, was an insoluble strategic dilemma. Britain, therefore, embarked on a path of messy, and often shabby, strategic compromises, diplomatic and military. One of these was the effective shelving of any serious commitment to send a fleet to the East while maintaining to the Dominions that the commitments given at the Imperial Conference in June remained firm. The Anglo-American discussions over a joint show of force in the Far East at the turn of 1937, following the Japanese attacks on American and British vessels in the Yangtze, have been described as 'the moment of truth for the Main Fleet to Singapore strategy':

Preparations had been made, Anglo-American staff talks were in progress: all that remained was the political decision to despatch the fleet. In the event those critics of the main fleet notion who had always maintained that when it came to the point European considerations would prevent the despatch of the fleet were proved right.[89]

Actually, all that this affair demonstrated was that neither the Cabinet nor the Admiralty were prepared to despatch two-thirds of the active Royal Navy to protect British commercial interests in China, and perhaps risk a major war. It did not follow that no action would, or could, be taken to protect a British colony such as Hong Kong and, even less, did it suggest that the concept of Singapore as one of two keystones of empire defence, critical to the defence of India and Australasia, was now abandoned.

However, it is not difficult to demonstrate that chiefs of staff attitudes were indeed bleaker by the end of 1937. A report to the Committee of Imperial Defence that November concluded with a much quoted passage:

> Without overlooking the assistance we would hope to obtain from France, and possibly other allies, we cannot foresee the time when our defence forces will be strong enough to safeguard our territory, trade and vital interests against Germany, Italy and Japan simultaneously. We cannot, therefore, exaggerate the importance, from the point of view of Imperial Defence, of any political or international action that can be taken to reduce the number of our potential enemies and gain the support of potential allies.[90]

Such quotes still require context. The chiefs did not judge war with any of the 'triple alliance' group as imminent, nor did they assume war with one member would automatically translate into war with the other two, though they recognised an 'increasing probability'. Chiefs of staff assessments during 1938 were clear, for example, that Italy and Japan would seek to exploit any opportunities arising from British preoccupation in a war with Germany. But they rightly assessed that Italy would see much to lose, and therefore be cautious, while Japan was increasingly bogged down in China. Nor did they see Britain engaged in a hopeless armament race it was bound to lose. On the contrary, they were still confident that, given time, Britain would get relatively stronger and ultimately strong enough to deter aggression against the empire. Two earlier sentences from the same document as that quoted above read:

> Even today we could face without apprehension an emergency either in the Far East or in the Mediterranean, provided that we were free to make preparations in time of peace and to concentrate sufficient strength in one or other of these areas.
>
> [...]
>
> So far as Germany is concerned, as our preparations develop, our defence forces will provide a considerable deterrent to aggression.

At the beginning of 1938 Chatfield did not see the strategic problem posed by the triple threat as 'insoluble' (his term). He had faith in Britain's underlying economic resources compared to its enemies, once they were properly mobilised, although he did worry about the pace of rearmament and the need to buy time. Throughout 1938/39, the chiefs of staff were clear that Germany was better prepared for early war than Britain, but they also judged that Britain and France were superior in general economic strength to Germany and Italy. This would be decisive in a long war.[91] Reducing the number of enemies, at least temporarily, through diplomatic means should be viewed in this light. This aspiration was directed mainly at Italy, though Chatfield still harboured hopes that an understanding could be reached with Germany. However, he was coldly realistic about the limits of such accommodation and how long it would last.[92]

Many accounts of this period have not sufficiently emphasised that strategy involves managing risk and making choices. Britain had to find a credible way of defending its empire with the resources currently available and those in the pipeline. It could not do everything, but it could identify what mattered most at any given time and plan accordingly. The chiefs of staff put the 'balance of risk' argument well when arguing for reinforcing Egypt in February 1938. They identified the trade-offs between extra air and anti-aircraft assets in Egypt, where they could make a significant difference against the need to maximise air defence capability against Germany as quickly as possible.[93] The strategic planning trail at Committee of Imperial Defence and chiefs of staff level throughout the period 1935–39 consistently demonstrates a clear framework of overall imperial security priorities and good judgement of relative risk. Until December 1941 British Empire territorial losses were confined to the Channel Islands. Judged on that basis, given the forces ranged against her, British risk management was remarkably effective.

As regards the Far East, from autumn 1937 until early 1939 there was no significant change in the strategic principles and priorities laid down at the Imperial Conference. These echoed those established by the DRC, and, as Chapter 1 showed, Royal Navy prospects for achieving a credible two-hemisphere navy remained firm through this period. Chiefs of staff papers throughout 1938 demonstrate that neither the potential hostility of Italy nor the risk of the Mediterranean being closed caused any significant tilt towards giving higher priority to Mediterranean defence, let alone a reversal of the Far East first strategy, at this stage. The one important adjustment was the limited build-up of land and air forces in Egypt for the reasons described earlier. This can be viewed as the first real modification of the DRC strategy to concentrate defence effort on Germany and the Far East, foreshadowing a shift in imperial priorities in the spring of 1939. However, decision-makers at the time almost certainly saw this Egypt investment as only a slight deviation from established policy.[94]

Beyond that, the final version of the Mediterranean appreciation, approved by the chiefs of staff in February 1938, demonstrated willingness to accept remarkable risks in the Mediterranean theatre in the event of a simultaneous three-power war. When it was approved by the Committee of Imperial Defence on 25 March, the implications posed by closure of the Mediterranean provoked little discussion and certainly no push to alter existing strategic priorities. The prime minister indeed emphasised that preparations against Italy must still take third place.[95] Under the three-power war scenario, the main Mediterranean Fleet would still deploy to the East, leaving only a few submarines and light surface forces. The chiefs not only accepted that Italy would then control the eastern Mediterranean, but that even military supplies to Egypt through the Red Sea could not be guaranteed against Italian interdiction.[96] This willingness to accept risks in the Mediterranean is striking, given the massive superiority the Italians would have in the theatre in land and air power, quite apart from naval supremacy following withdrawal of the Royal Navy fleet. The Italian air advantage was put at 6:1 in numbers, and most of their aircraft were judged competitive, if not superior, to the Royal Air Force in quality. During the rest of the year, chiefs of staff assessments reiterated that British forces in Egypt could not count on reinforcements after war broke out, and must rely on forces and supply stocks already in place.

Acceptance that control of the Mediterranean, with the exception of Egypt, would be sacrificed if Japan intervened in a European war where Britain was fighting against both Germany and Italy was repeated in chiefs of staff assessments prepared before and after the Munich crisis, and in a major European appreciation completed in February 1939.[97] The August 1938 assessment, completed in the run-up to the Munich crisis, acknowledged that after despatch of a fleet to meet the intervention of Japan, Britain's Mediterranean possessions would be in a 'state of siege'. It also noted that France would lose 50 per cent of its oil if Italy blockaded the Iraq pipeline terminals at Haifa in Palestine and Tripoli in Lebanon. The later European appreciation recognised that Italy might be able to attempt seaborne landings in Egypt and Palestine and conduct a bombardment of Alexandria.

The consistent resistance of both Cabinet and chiefs of staff in this period to holding any formal staff discussions with the French about potential co-operation in the Mediterranean theatre confirms that no general change in Mediterranean strategy was contemplated during 1938. Admiralty resistance to naval co-operation, led by Chatfield and endorsed by the Committee of Imperial Defence, can be viewed as a serious policy error. It not only appeared perverse, given the scale of naval threat now facing Britain in three theatres, but a lost opportunity to exploit the potential vulnerability of Italy.[98] Chatfield even questioned whether it was to Britain's advantage to be allied to France in the event of an Anglo-Italian war.[99] His justification here was that any military advantages from formal collaboration with the French, which would inevitably be directed primarily at Germany, were outweighed by the 'grave risk' of precipitating the 'irreconcilable suspicion and hostility of Germany', when rearmament was still at an early stage. The related argument against collaboration in the Mediterranean theatre was that any perceived Anglo-French alliance there would inevitably encourage Germany to align formally with Italy.

Chatfield's case here was that Britain could deal comfortably with Italy in a single-handed war, even if France stood aside and denied use of its naval facilities, a scenario which was always possible. However, the probability of German intervention alongside Italy as the consequence of French support provided under an Anglo-French agreement meant Britain would then face a much tougher proposition, and possibly global, rather than theatre, war.[100] Despite these arguments, after strong French political representations, the Cabinet directed in April that limited military exchanges should nevertheless take place. The chiefs successfully insisted that these should be restricted to the level of military attachés. The subsequent naval discussions were confined to the scenario of war against Germany and comprised minor information-sharing, but no planning for joint dispositions or operations.[101]

Chatfield's continued resistance to full staff talks through 1938 did not mean he discounted the value of French support in the event of active conflict. He was clear that if a Royal Navy fleet had to be sent to the Far East, as seemed likely at the turn of 1937/38, French cover to help protect British trade and communications in both the Atlantic and Mediterranean would be essential 'to avoid our communications being cut behind our backs'. However, he believed that this cover could be negotiated while the Royal Navy fleet was preparing to deploy.[102] In short, Chatfield judged Britain could get the naval support it needed from France once conflict was underway or imminent, but engaging in a formal undertaking prior to conflict would narrow its strategic options to no advantage. This judgement can be questioned, but his position was understandable.

The conclusion of the Mediterranean appreciation that in any war with Italy, whether single-handed or part of a global conflict, the Mediterranean would be closed to through traffic both merchant and military, has attracted little attention. Yet, as the British military leadership quickly recognised, this had strategic implications that went beyond the defence of Egypt and deployment of the Far East fleet. By substantially increasing the transit time to all key territories in the East, it meant the eastern empire and British interests in the Middle East would be largely isolated from the United Kingdom homeland in wartime, and would need therefore to be more militarily self-sufficient. Admiral Sir Dudley Pound as Commander-in-Chief Mediterranean put this well to the Admiralty at the end of 1938:

- With present communications and long range aircraft, the Mediterranean has become a very small place.
- Italy will not fail to make full use of her advantageous geographical position and of her strength in long range aircraft.
- Movement of a single auxiliary from say Malta to Alexandria will become a major operation.
- The Central and Eastern Mediterranean, though seemingly one of the nearest of foreign stations, becomes, when using the Cape route, the most distant of all save China.

The war demonstrated that these were prescient points.[103]

A major review into the defence of India in May 1938 accordingly highlighted the need for a strategic reserve based east of the Mediterranean to provide adequate security for the eastern empire against threats from both Japan in the east, and Italy and Germany in the west. This review arguably triggered a process that would ultimately see India and Australasia providing most of the manpower to defend the eastern empire in the coming war, and also become significant producers of military material.[104] The closure of the Mediterranean also vastly raised the importance of the security of the Indian Ocean, not only for the protection of trade but also military traffic, vital war materials including oil, and the route to Egypt. By early 1939 this reassessment was influencing the role of the putative Eastern Fleet, which should have 'sufficient strength to protect the Dominions and India and give cover to our communications in the Indian Ocean'.[105] The true importance of the Singapore base, and therefore the defence of Malaya to Far East naval defence can certainly be debated, but the Indian Ocean was now becoming an inescapable naval commitment.

1939: A new balance between Far East and eastern Mediterranean

The European appreciation[106] approved by the chiefs of staff on 15 February 1939,[107] was the last formal strategic appreciation completed before the outbreak of war. As its name implied, it concentrated primarily on the risks and consequences of a conflict in Europe, where Britain and France were ranged against Germany and Italy. It assumed that, because of her preoccupation with China, early Japanese intervention was now unlikely, unless the western Allies were facing defeat, thus offering Japan easy pickings.[108] This assumption drew on Foreign Office guidance and accurately reflected Japanese attitudes.[109] The paper, therefore, allocated Royal Navy strength, including the entire capital ship force, between the Atlantic and Mediterranean on a ratio of two to one. The standard China and East Indies squadrons were left to watch Japan.[110] The strength of these squadrons was broadly the same as that during the 1937

Imperial Conference. If, against current expectation, Japan did intervene then the 1937 Imperial Conference priorities would stand. The despatch of a fleet to Singapore 'would be imperative'. Royal Navy forces would be withdrawn from the Mediterranean, with France left to restrain Italy from its bases in the west. The empire would then be faced with 'an immense aggregate of armed force which neither present nor projected defence was designed to meet', and the outcome of the war would depend on holding key positions until other potential allies, notably the United States, intervened.[111]

Although the European appreciation suggested that strategy for defending the eastern empire in a global war against all three Axis powers was essentially unchanged from 1937, it introduced two qualifications to prevailing policy that Far East naval defence took absolute priority over the Mediterranean. It displayed ambitions for early offensive naval action against Italy which, whatever the merits in a war confined to Europe, would make it more difficult to extricate forces for the Far East, should this prove necessary.[112] In addition, although a fleet would certainly be sent to the East if Japan intervened, 'its strength must depend on our resources and the state of the war in the European theatre'. These qualifications were sponsored by the new First Sea Lord, Admiral of the Fleet Sir Roger Backhouse, who had succeeded Chatfield in August 1938. He had strong support from the new First Lord, Lord Stanhope. Together, through the winter of 1938/39, they encouraged the British political and military leadership to consider a more flexible strategy for the naval defence of the eastern empire, although when the European appreciation was drafted, their new thinking was still evolving. The qualifications reflected a growing view that the Mediterranean theatre posed new risks and opportunities. But, just as much, they reflected perceptions that the immediate risk from Japan had reduced, and that a more realistic assessment of the naval forces needed for early war with Germany was required, in the face of continued delays in capital ship modernisation.

The possibility that strategic interests in the Mediterranean might make it desirable to delay and/or reduce the size of fleet sent to the Far East as a deliberate choice was raised for the first time when the Committee of Imperial Defence considered the European appreciation on 24 February. Stanhope took the lead in questioning withdrawal from the eastern Mediterranean, while Chatfield argued forcefully for continuing to give absolute primacy to the Far East. As the prime minister noted, Stanhope's choice would conflict with the guarantees given to the Dominions at the 1937 Imperial Conference, which had been 'categorical and unqualified', and he wondered whether Dominion leaders should now be advised that policy might need 'adjustment'. Chatfield, now Minister for Defence Co-ordination, proposed a Strategic Appreciations Committee be formed to consider this issue further.[113]

This 'adjustment' to the established Far East policy advocated by Stanhope has encouraged a belief that Backhouse was a strategic 'revisionist'.[114] The suggestion is that he regarded the deployment of a substantial proportion of the Royal Navy to the Far East as impractical and believed that, after securing home waters against Germany, the immediate priority should be to concentrate against Italy in the Mediterranean.[115] Any claim that Backhouse arrived at the Admiralty already disposed to a radical overhaul of Far East naval strategy is unconvincing. He provided formal reassurance on the despatch of a Far East fleet to Australia in November.[116] He endorsed the European appreciation which, despite his qualifications, reaffirmed Far East priority over the Mediterranean. During his brief tenure, he never formally questioned the concept of Singapore as 'keystone'. Just before falling ill in March 1939 with the brain tumour that would kill him,[117] he told Stanhope that he had 'always thought it necessary to send a fleet of a certain size to the East if Japan became threatening'.[118]

Backhouse did not, therefore, question the fundamentals of empire defence. However, he did bring new critical scrutiny to the Far East problem, and differed from Chatfield in several respects. He believed that a sharper distinction could be drawn between the vital core of the eastern empire, India and Australasia, and more discretionary interests in China; he thought the 'core' could be adequately protected in at least the first stages of a war with forces short of a full fleet; and he hoped this could release resources for a more active strategy in the Mediterranean.

Backhouse also recognised that the 1937 projections for a Far East fleet were over-optimistic and that the maximum available capital ship strength was unlikely to exceed five until 1940.[119] Three capital ships remained under major reconstruction in early 1939, *Renown*, *Valiant* and *Queen Elizabeth*, with the first now not expected to complete until September and not fully operational until the end of the year. These reconstructions were originally planned to complete by the summer, restoring maximum availability to fifteen ships.[120] In addition, *Hood* and *Revenge* were undergoing short refits until late summer 1939, though both could be mobilised at twenty-eight days' notice. The European appreciation allocated eight capital ships to the Atlantic following full mobilisation and three to the eastern Mediterranean. Backhouse now viewed six as the minimum safe force to contain Germany, leaving a theoretical maximum of five for the Far East, three withdrawn from the Mediterranean, and two from the Atlantic. German strength in 1939 was the same as that projected in 1937, when Chatfield thought four ships would be sufficient to contain it. Backhouse's figure was a more realistic assessment of what was required to deal with the German raider threat, whereas Chatfield had cut the home force to an absolute minimum, in order to generate credible numbers against Japan.

Backhouse argued that five ships would still be enough to protect communications in the Indian Ocean, although insufficient to take on the main IJN fleet, which ruled out operations north of Singapore, where he accepted Hong Kong might well be lost. Here he noted that British interests in China were essentially commercial. If the China trade was lost to Japan, it would be difficult to justify any strategic interest in Hong Kong. Singapore was an entirely different case. It should be held 'with all our might'.[121] However, he never specifically addressed the issue of whether a fleet significantly inferior to the IJN would be able to secure Singapore if the Japanese mounted an all-out attack. He judged such an attack most unlikely unless a war in Europe was going badly, but thought that it would be possible to keep communications open through the Indian Ocean and bolster Singapore with more troops and aircraft.[122] He also placed new emphasis on the US Navy as a restraining factor on Japan.

In essence, Backhouse was merely addressing more honestly and formally issues relating to strength and timing of reinforcement recognised as far back as 1937. These were that force redistribution to create a Far East fleet when war was already underway in Europe might take a considerable time, that rapid reinforcement of Singapore with land and air forces from India would therefore be essential, and might involve some risk, and that the 'period before relief' would probably be exceeded. Implicit in all this was the likelihood that there might well be an advance guard from the Mediterranean, including capital ships, before the full strength could deploy. The practical difference, therefore, between Backhouse's views on Far East reinforcement and existing Admiralty planning, or indeed the caveats Chatfield had already expressed in 1937, was limited.

Where Backhouse and Stanhope did break new ground was in arguing that if Japan intervened when war was already underway in Europe, then delaying reinforcement and reducing its strength could be a deliberate strategic choice, rather than a consequence of inherent delays in force redistribution. If the loss of everything north of Singapore was discounted, then it was possible to carry risk. They promoted this argument further during the first two meetings of the Strategic Appreciations Committee convened by Chatfield at the beginning of March. This committee was another subcommittee of the Committee of Imperial Defence and brought together the three chiefs of staff, the three service ministers, and a selection of other ministers with relevant expertise under Chatfield as Minister for Defence Co-ordination and chairman.[123] Stanhope did not accept the view that 'if we do not send a fleet immediately, we will lose Australasia and India'. Backhouse questioned key terms in the 1935 DRC formula: 'acting on the defensive' or 'serving as a deterrent'. They were open to interpretation. Interpretation also applied to the 1937 commitments. The commitment was to send a fleet 'but we did not specify when', or, he might have added, in what precise strength. In sum, Backhouse and Stanhope favoured a more flexible and graduated response to any Far East threat, rather than the automatic and early despatch of the maximum possible fleet.

If there was an element of choice over when to deploy forces to the East and in what strength, then the Royal Navy could maintain stronger forces in the eastern Mediterranean and for longer, perhaps for six months, even after Japanese intervention. Backhouse and Stanhope here pressed two points. It would enable the Royal Navy to deliver some hard blows against Italy that would not only reduce the naval threat she posed, but might even knock her out of the war. In addition, they emphasised a more political point, the role of the Mediterranean Fleet as guarantor to Greece and Turkey, and to Britain's wider position in the Middle East, where Stanhope thought 'things might go very wrong'.[124] These Admiralty views would be influential in driving growing awareness in wider British government circles that Britain had fundamental security interests in the eastern Mediterranean beyond control of Egypt and the canal.[125]

Chatfield felt this Mediterranean-orientated policy not only broke the 1937 undertakings to the Dominions but put the eastern empire at risk. Both claims were overstated. It was true that Britain had assured the Dominions that no risk in the Mediterranean would prevent the despatch of a fleet to the East. However, Chatfield had also emphasised that if a European war was already underway, the arrival of a fleet would be 'considerably delayed', and capable only of a 'defensive role'. A 'defensive role' surely suggested the need to distinguish between critical Far East interests and those that were discretionary, as Backhouse and Stanhope were now attempting to do. These two meetings do not show Chatfield at his best. He comes across as pedantic, legalistic and, at times, disingenuous.

The new thinking promoted by Backhouse and Stanhope drew on ideas developed by the retired Admiral Sir Reginald Drax,[126] brought in by Backhouse to provide independent advice on strategy. Pound and Cunningham, who was now Deputy Chief of Naval Staff, were probably also influential in pressing the case for the Mediterranean to have greater priority.[127] Indeed, the first official proposal for a Mediterranean offensive came from Pound, as Commander-in-Chief Mediterranean, in November 1938. He advocated simultaneous British and French land and air offensives mounted against Libya from Egypt and Tunisia respectively. The Royal Navy would have a conventional supporting role primarily directed at cutting Italian supply lines. He was told by London that British land and air forces in Egypt were quite inadequate for such a scheme.[128]

Drax was one of the Royal Navy's few intellectuals and widely recognised as a strategist.[129] He was also a controversial figure. In late 1937, in his final posting as Commander-in-Chief Plymouth, he had clashed with Chatfield when he savaged a naval staff paper, 'Appreciation of War with Germany (1939)', for lacking offensive spirit. In a stinging rebuke, Chatfield accused him of not understanding the overall strategic context Britain faced, with threats from Italy and Japan, as well as Germany. In future, Drax was to make proposals of a 'definite and tangible nature and not in the form of generalisations'.[130] By contrast, Drax was trusted by Pound and Churchill. Pound sought help from Drax in revising the Mediterranean Fleet Fighting Instructions. He also used him as an adviser throughout his tenure as First Sea Lord, often to develop arguments to counter Churchill's wilder schemes. With Churchill's approval, Drax was also appointed Commander-in-Chief The Nore from late 1939 until mid-1941.[131]

Drax produced two main ideas for Royal Navy deployment in a global war in 1939 against three enemies.[132] He argued first that Far East naval reinforcement should be reduced to a minimal 'flying squadron', comprising two *Queen Elizabeth*-class battleships, a carrier, and a flotilla of Tribal-class destroyers, which, added to the China and East Indies squadrons, would prevent Japan doing 'serious damage' in the first six months of a Far East war. Speed and mobility could compensate for reduced size, at least in the short term.[133] Deploying a 'flying squadron' would then allow the Royal Navy to concentrate a maximum force in the Mediterranean to 'crumple' Italy within his 'six month Far East window', while containing Germany. The 'flying squadron' has often been commended as an innovative alternative to the traditional Far East naval strategy by those who judge that by 1939 it was fast losing credibility. However, they invariably focus more on the supposed originality of Drax's thinking, than explaining how the 'flying squadron' would translate into practical strategy.[134] They also exaggerate his influence in tilting the Royal Navy towards a more Mediterranean-orientated policy.[135]

There are problems with both Drax ideas. He did not define what qualified as 'serious damage' in the Far East. If the goal was to secure the Indian Ocean against IJN incursion, guard Australasia, and perhaps allow judicious raids against isolated IJN targets, then his proposed force was sufficient. It was more doubtful whether it could guarantee the security of Singapore for a six-month period. Drax ducked this question, as have those who commend his originality. (He expressed reservations about Singapore as an operating base, judging that the Japanese could easily bypass it.[136]) Drax's force allocations, which assumed twelve capital ships available through 1939, were probably optimistic, even after mobilisation. If five were required in the Atlantic (one less than Backhouse stipulated was necessary), and two went to the 'flying squadron', that only left five for the Mediterranean. His Mediterranean 'reinforcement', therefore, only added the two *Nelson*s to the allocation already made in the European appreciation. The 'crumpling' of Italy accordingly rested on the deployment of five battleships here, rather than three. It also assumed that the Royal Navy battle-fleet could operate in the central Mediterranean and off the Italian coast in the face of Italian air power, whereas Pound was pretty sure it could not; that coastal bombardment could achieve important economic and political effect; that the Italian battle-fleet would accept battle with a superior Royal Navy force on Royal Navy terms; and that an Italian defeat (of, say, Taranto proportions) would cause Italy to sue for peace.[137]

There was also an inherent weakness in the composition of his 'flying squadron'. To be effective, this should have combined battlecruisers and carriers, units with similar speed, on the lines of the future Force H. The *Queen Elizabeth*s, at 24 knots, were slower than the Royal Navy carriers, but, more important, slower than all IJN capital ships. The four *Kongo* battlecruisers could do 30 knots after reconstruction, while the six battleships were all capable of 25 knots. They also decisively outranged the two unmodernised *Queen Elizabeth*s and the 'R' class. The Drax force, therefore, could neither fight a superior IJN force, nor guarantee to avoid it. To be fair, Backhouse (and perhaps Drax too) would have preferred to deploy the Royal Navy battlecruisers in the East, but they were needed at home to counter the fast German ships.

The views expressed by Backhouse at the Strategic Appreciations Committee reflected Drax's ideas and even his language. Backhouse speculated that two *Queen Elizabeth*s (the 'flying squadron') might be sufficient to control the Indian Ocean, and spoke of dealing with Italy by 'striking (her) a series of hard blows at the outset'.[138] He evidently found Drax's proposed force distribution helpful in working through how a flexible and discretionary Far East reinforcement policy might work in practice. He also welcomed Drax's offensive mindset, in contrast to the conservatism of Director of Plans. However, talk of a 'Backhouse/Drax School' goes too far.[139] Such a term implies the two had discussed and agreed a common view on future strategy. This had not happened by the time Backhouse departed. His views then were still evolving. His parting comments to Cunningham and Stanhope show that he saw the final Drax report as an important contribution, but not the definitive answer to Royal Navy force distribution.[140] For Backhouse, the 'flying squadron' was evidently one way in which flexible reinforcement might be applied. But, as Cunningham would shortly emphasise, the precise nature of reinforcement would depend on a variety of circumstances, and was also likely to be a staged process. As to a more activist approach against Italy, both Backhouse and Cunningham were more restrained than Drax about what was realistic.

Drax's ideas were therefore one of several catalysts encouraging the Royal Navy leadership during the first months of 1939 to adopt a more flexible approach to Far East reinforcement. The policy of flexible reinforcement which Backhouse was reaching for, and Cunningham would shortly endorse formally, was partly a necessity imposed by limited resources. It also provided a means of exercising deliberate strategic choice. Flexible reinforcement, using the actual term 'flying squadron', was incorporated in the revised Far East war plan issued in June.[141] The term then lapsed after the summer, but the option of deploying a fast mobile defensive force in the first phase of a Far East war survived. The naval staff adopted exactly this principle in their contingency plans from late 1940 to deploy Force H as immediate reinforcement to protect the Indian Ocean in the event of Japanese intervention. Churchill was applying similar thinking in pushing for what amounted to a Force H-plus in the Indian Ocean in the late summer of 1941.[142]

The Australians picked up on the discussions at the first Strategic Appreciations Committee meeting and sought formal clarification on naval reinforcement policy at prime ministerial level. This provoked an important response from Chamberlain to Dominion prime ministers on 20 March.[143] It remained the intention to despatch a fleet to the Far East if Japan intervened, but its size would depend on the state of any European war and losses sustained. Nevertheless, Britain intended to achieve three objectives: the prevention of major operations against Australasia or India; the protection of imperial communications; and preventing the fall of Singapore. Backhouse sent a similar message on naval channels. This admitted that the strength of the fleet that could be sent to the Far East was under review. However, Backhouse emphasised it would be sufficient to protect communications in the Indian Ocean and to deter any Japanese expedition against Australia. This aligned closely with Chamberlain's text.[144] Backhouse had earlier insisted that an expedition to Australia was currently beyond Japan's power due to distance and lack of a forward base from which to mount it.[145]

Chamberlain's message can be viewed as a skilful formula which reaffirmed the intention to defend the Dominions, while declining to commit to precise forces or timing. The elaborate plans of fifteen years were therefore abandoned for a vague promise.[146] This understates its significance. His first point was not new, but merely repeated Chatfield's caveat at the Imperial Conference. The Australians nevertheless did take it as a significant weakening of British commitment. The focus on the 'three objects' was a more important change. It implied Britain would now focus only on the inner core of the eastern empire and would not contest Japanese aggression north of Singapore. That could be seen as either weakening of commitment or realistic concentration on what really mattered. Although they reflected discussion at the Committee of Imperial Defence on 24 February, these messages from Chamberlain and Backhouse signalled a policy shift that went beyond the conclusions of that meeting and pre-empted the Strategic Appreciations Committee debate. They confirmed two things. First, Far East reinforcement would no longer be automatic, but based on a comparative risk assessment between Far East and Mediterranean interests. Secondly, Far East defence would now focus on an inner core, and interests north of Singapore were dispensable.

Meanwhile, in parallel with the Strategic Appreciations Committee deliberations and Chamberlain's initiative, the chiefs of staff, with Cabinet approval, finally began full staff talks with France in London on 29 March. This move towards formal military co-operation reflected the sharp deterioration in the international outlook since the autumn, recognition that there was now little prospect of limiting German ambitions, and the increasing likelihood that Italy would ally with Germany in a European war. Settling the terms of these talks was a protracted process. The chiefs had agreed in principle in November that a deeper level of exchange was required, and that talks should cover Italian intervention, and therefore potential co-operation in the Mediterranean and Middle East. Cabinet approval was not achieved until early February and the scope of the talks was then defined in early March.[147] The underlying assumption was that Britain and France would be allies in a general war against Germany and Italy, with the additional possibility of Japanese intervention. There would now be a full exchange on the Mediterranean and Middle East. Agreeing the talks had taken inordinate time, but the level of exchanges now contemplated went beyond those conducted prior to 1914.[148]

The British position at the staff talks followed the recommendations in the European appreciation. A sanitised version was shared with the French before the talks to brief them on the latest British thinking.[149] The appreciation defined how Britain expected an alliance with France to work in all potential war theatres. Britain had already decided, therefore, before engaging with the French, how it proposed to manage a war against the combination of Germany and Italy, what goals were realistic against the latter in the Mediterranean, and how it would balance Mediterranean and Far East interests in the event of Japanese intervention. It included a section 'Anglo-French action in the Mediterranean area', directed at securing joint interests in this theatre and ultimately defeating Italy. This set out force dispositions, allocated areas of responsibility, and identified both critical defensive priorities and opportunities for inflicting early damage on Italy. It expected France to allocate about half its naval strength to control the western Mediterranean and to support action against Italian communications in the central Mediterranean.

Britain was willing to listen and, indeed, defer to French views on operations against Germany on the 'western front', but the French exerted no significant influence over British plans for a naval war in the Mediterranean and Far East theatres.[150] Indeed, the chiefs of staff apparently entered the staff talks assuming that France would automatically fall in with British plans and dispositions for the Mediterranean and Middle East and further eastwards. The update produced by the chiefs of staff for the Committee of Imperial Defence at the end of May, conveying results from the first two sessions with the French, suggests they were correct.[151] Here, the specific naval agreements for both the Mediterranean and Atlantic theatres endorsed Admiralty aspirations set when the prime minister visited Paris the previous November.[152]

If Britain and France were at war with Germany alone, the Royal Navy anticipated easily dealing with the German naval threat, but still wanted the two French *Dunkerque* battlecruisers available in the Atlantic to help round up *Deutschland*-class raiders. Along with the three Royal Navy battlecruisers, the *Dunkerque*s were the only ships which combined sufficient heavy armament and speed (eight 13in guns and 29 knots) to catch and destroy a *Deutschland* in a single-ship engagement. Equally important, they were a match for all the Italian capital ships prior to the arrival of the *Littorio* class in 1940. France should also provide adequate escort forces to protect its coastal trade. If Italy was also hostile, the Royal Navy wanted one *Dunkerque* to stay in the Atlantic, but expected the French to deploy the bulk of their fleet in the western Mediterranean to counter the Italians, and not least the large Italian submarine force. If Japan intervened, the Royal Navy would despatch a fleet to the Far East, and in consequence might no longer be able to control the eastern Mediterranean. The Royal Navy then expected France to assume a larger responsibility for containing Italy in the Mediterranean, in return for Royal Navy protection of communications through the Indian Ocean to the Far East.

In presenting their proposals for the Mediterranean and Middle East, the British took little account of specific French needs in these theatres, notably the importance to them of oil from Iraq. (The French emphasised that this oil would need to be transported via the Suez Canal if the Mediterranean were closed to shipping, although it was later agreed that Iraq oil was not critical. French needs in wartime could be met from other sources.[153]) Nor did French thinking influence British plans in the Mediterranean over the five months between the onset of staff talks and the outbreak of war. The French certainly pressed in two areas: the need for stronger forces in Egypt; and the scope for a greater offensive effort against the Italians in Libya.[154] The desirability of reinforcing Egypt was already acknowledged in the European appreciation. The French merely encouraged the British to do what they already wanted to do anyway, once resources permitted. The desirability of French action against Libya from the west, in order to discourage any Italian move against Egypt, had also featured in the appreciation. Again, it is doubtful any French influence persuaded the British to give an offensive in Libya priority over naval bombardment of the Italian coast. Proposals for direct attacks on the Italian mainland had never got much traction, and certainly not from Pound. If the French were willing to execute a more powerful thrust against Libya from Tunisia, this would have British support, since it aligned with existing British strategy for the theatre, and the hope that Italy would prove fragile under pressure. However, Britain could not spare additional resources of its own for an offensive against Libya, and there were soon doubts about the real level of French commitment.

The British took little notice of French pressure to forego naval reinforcement of the Far East in the event of Japanese intervention, rather than risk losing control of the eastern Mediterranean. They insisted Singapore must be held. However, during the spring, they also formally adopted the much more flexible policy for both the scale and timing of Far East reinforcement suggested by Backhouse and Stanhope at the Strategic Appreciations Committee. The eastern Mediterranean would now not be 'lightly abandoned', and the distribution of naval forces between this theatre and the Far East would depend on the comparative level of risk. This new policy went some way to meeting French fears for the eastern Mediterranean but, as already noted, the British embraced it for their own reasons rather than deference to French wishes.

The formal outcome of the Strategic Appreciations Committee review of naval policy in the Far East is summarised in a much quoted passage in an Admiralty memorandum signed by Cunningham as DCNS on 4 April and approved by the Committee of Imperial Defence on 2 May:

> There are so many variable factors which cannot at present be assessed, that it is not possible to state definitely how soon after Japanese intervention a fleet could be dispatched to the Far East. Neither is it possible to enumerate precisely the size of the fleet we could afford to send.[155]

This conclusion is usually interpreted negatively. It surely implied that, with limited Royal Navy resources, Britain's strategic dilemma was now insoluble, and 'variable factors' was a convenient term to mask the reality that despatching a significant fleet to the East was now a remote prospect. However, the memorandum can be interpreted more positively. The 'variable factors' which appeared in many subsequent documents through the summer included:

- The number of capital ships (and other forces) available when Japan intervened. This number might reflect war losses if war was already underway in Europe as well as the ships coming out of rebuild from autumn 1939 onward.
- The overall strategic situation. Was Britain already at war, with Germany alone, or with Italy too, and with what result? Was there a prospect of achieving an early decisive blow against Germany or Italy?

- The strategy adopted by Japan. Ambitious and aggressive or confined to minor commerce raiding.
- The attitude of the United States and Russia as restraining factors on Japan.
- The adverse impact of Royal Navy withdrawal from the eastern Mediterranean on the attitude of Greece, Turkey and the Muslim world.

There were genuine unknowns here. It was certainly difficult to predict whether Japanese intervention would pose an immediate threat to critical interests or take effect only slowly with losses Britain could bear. It was equally difficult to judge in advance the political and strategic costs of withdrawing the Royal Navy from the eastern Mediterranean. Although this memorandum was released contemporaneously with the first round of the staff talks with France, it made no direct reference to either French naval support or French interests.

The memorandum was endorsed by the Strategic Appreciations Committee on 17 April. The committee stressed: 'offensive operations against Italy offered the best prospect of speedy results and should not be lightly broken off'; and the 'importance of affording moral and material support to our allies in the Near East, Turkey, Greece and Egypt'.[156] Given the perceived opportunities and risks in the Mediterranean, then keeping deployment options flexible until potential threats in the Far East took effect surely made sense, so long as the trade-offs were understood and did not cross over into self-deception. It is worth noting that Cunningham had not mentioned offensive operations in the Mediterranean in his original memorandum.

Cunningham's memorandum certainly confirmed that Britain could not meet all naval threats simultaneously. Its strength lay in arguing that Britain still had strategic choice. One choice, as Backhouse and Stanhope had stated at the first Strategic Appreciations Committee meeting, was deliberate delay in Far East reinforcement while Japanese intent became clear. However, the memorandum also had a major weakness not addressed at either the Strategic Appreciations Committee or the Committee of Imperial Defence. It established the choices Britain faced in allocating its finite naval resources, and the factors that should influence those choices. But it did not spell out the strategic objectives and risks against which those choices must be made. It gave good reasons why the scale and timing of Far East reinforcement could be kept flexible, but did not define the minimum force to secure Chamberlain's 20 March objectives against determined Japanese attack.

On 2 May the Committee of Imperial Defence endorsed the Strategic Appreciations Committee recommendations with little further debate. If a choice must be made between temporarily abandoning the eastern Mediterranean or the Far East, then this decision must be taken by the government of the day, taking all relevant factors into account. The prime minister recognised that, in balancing

Mediterranean and Far East interests, there was a scaling down of previous assurances to the Dominions, but his 20 March telegram had adequately addressed this. If Britain was defeated, then the fate of the Dominions was sealed. Britain would do all it could to protect them, but must concentrate on the 'main enemy'.[157] The committee did agree it was desirable to brief the Americans on the new policy. They were informed through a special Admiralty emissary, Commander T C Hampton, who had two meetings with the US Navy Chief of Naval Operations, Admiral William Leahy, at the beginning of June. This meeting and its consequences are discussed in Chapter 4.[158]

The prime minister was too sanguine about his 20 March assurances to the Dominions. His belief was genuine that Britain's ultimate commitment to their defence, if they were directly threatened, had not changed. However, the new flexibility over the timing and scale of reinforcement introduced on 2 May inevitably raised doubts in Dominion minds over whether the promises could and would be met in practice. Flexibility also had to translate into war plans the Dominions would find credible. The Admiralty quickly recognised this and managing Dominion expectations was a constant problem through the summer and beyond. Meanwhile, the Dominions received a less detailed, and perhaps less honest, account of evolving naval strategy than the Americans received via Hampton. This reinforced suspicion and anxiety in the short term, and then rankled for long afterwards.[159] Nevertheless, the Dominions should have recognised that there was no longer any guarantee of the automatic despatch of a full fleet, and that the purpose of reinforcement now was to secure communications in the Indian Ocean, and deter a major expedition against Dominion territories themselves.[160]

The outcome of the 2 May meeting has been presented as flawed and dishonest. It was flawed because it abandoned the policy of countering any hostile move by Japan with the immediate deployment of a competitive fleet without putting in place a credible alternative. The dishonesty lay in suggesting to the Dominions that nothing fundamental had changed. The government knew it could no longer promise a fleet would be sent out at any given time, but would not drop the Singapore strategy entirely and replace it with something else. What remained was the worst of both. The promise was not retracted, but the commitment to implement it at a fixed time was.[161]

There are two problems here. It implies a single, rigid, Singapore strategy, whereas the term embraced a range of options. Adopting a more flexible approach to Far East naval reinforcement in both timing and scale did not, in itself, invalidate a strategy to counter Japan based primarily on naval force. Nor was such flexibility new. Those who criticise the lack of a credible alternative also seem unclear whether the problem was failure to set appropriate imperial priorities in the face of a looming three-enemy war, or failure to implement credible plans to meet those priorities. Thus one critic accuses Britain of failing to adapt grand strategy and 'making the situation fit the plan' (whereas, in reality, strategy was significantly adjusted). He commends the Admiralty for adopting the Drax proposal for concentration against Italy (which it never did, at least in the way proposed by Drax). He then accuses the Admiralty of not following through and dropping the 'Singapore strategy' by adopting the 'flying squadron' (which, in some respects, it did do).[162] Another critic commends Backhouse and Drax for strategic innovation with their focus on the Mediterranean, but doubts the viability of the 'flying squadron', seeing it as 'not much improvement on the old Singapore Strategy'.[163]

This all begs the question of what could have been done differently. In the late spring of 1939 the real challenge for Britain with Far East reinforcement was to find a coherent solution which drew together the flexibility over force distribution proposed by Cunningham, and the more limited strategic objectives now set by Chamberlain. Ultimately, given the conflicting demands in Europe and the Mediterranean, there were two issues. Was it still possible in the worst scenario of all-out Japanese attack to generate sufficient forces to protect Singapore, which remained one of Chamberlain's objectives? Was Singapore really essential to the naval defence of the eastern empire, or could Chamberlain's 20 March inner core be adequately guaranteed with smaller forces operating from Ceylon and Australia?

By 1939, dispensing with Singapore as 'keystone' was difficult. If Backhouse and Cunningham had remained together at the Admiralty they might have attempted this. This was evident in their reaction when Danckwerts, as Director of Plans, repeated in trenchant terms at the end of March the standard Admiralty case for prioritising the Far East over the Mediterranean. If Singapore was lost, the eastern empire was at Japan's mercy. Cunningham thought this overstated and that 'denuding the Mediterranean might be disastrous'. Backhouse agreed. Japan would not attack southwards unless a European war was going badly for Britain. Three or four capital ships would suffice to protect core interests in the East. Japan would have to consider potential intervention by the United States, and Singapore defence could be enhanced with land and air assets. Losing Singapore would be serious, but the Far East position would be recoverable.[164]

The difficulty in explaining what an alternative Far East naval policy might have looked like in 1939 also reflects the muddled way in which the perceived strategic imperatives in the Mediterranean evolved across that year. Three arguments for giving greater naval priority to the Mediterranean must be distinguished here: the concept of the knockout blow against Italy, which was short-lived; the Balkans as buffer against the Axis and possibly as a base for an Anglo-French offensive; and the eastern Mediterranean as barrier to protect Middle East oil and the access routes to the eastern empire from the west.

On 2 May the Committee of Imperial Defence gained a much more optimistic impression of the prospects for early results against Italy than either the chiefs of staff or the Royal Navy leadership felt was achievable. It is not clear how this happened. The Joint Planning Committee had informed the chiefs five weeks earlier that an early knockout of Italy was not realistic. They stressed, in line with the response to Pound at the end of 1938, that no land or air forces were available for offensive operations and that the impact of naval power in isolation would be limited, possibly incurring more loss than benefit. Effort should therefore remain focused on the defence of Egypt.[165] It is true that Backhouse remained bullish about Italy up to his departure, telling Cunningham that: 'Seizing her colonies, bombarding oil storage and cutting her supply lines might bring results'.[166] Cunningham did not, however, reflect this in his 4 April memorandum for the Strategic Appreciations Committee. Later in the month, as Acting First Sea Lord, he emphasised that there were still no plans for offensive operations in the Mediterranean. Subsequent guidance to Mediterranean commanders-in-chief set modest aims. The primary goal in war with Italy was to make her position in Africa untenable. The Royal Navy would close the two ends of the Mediterranean, cut the routes to Libya and Ethiopia, and exert general pressure where possible, but there was no reference to action against the Italian mainland.[167] Pound confirmed this policy in early July soon after taking over as First Sea Lord.[168]

Surprisingly, it still took nearly three months for Chatfield to admit, with some embarrassment, that the early knockout was indeed not possible and that 'ministers might have been misled'.[169] Perhaps the best insight into this controversy is an exchange between Pound and Cunningham at the end of July. Pound wrote:

I do not know who gave the politicians the idea that it (knocking out Italy) could be done but it seems they expect it and are now undergoing the rather painful process of being undeceived. Italy can only be knocked out either by her armies being defeated or by being laid waste by air. We cannot do either of these things at the beginning of the war and it is left to the navy to do the knocking out. I can only imagine they thought the fleet would steam slowly along the Italian coast and blow it to bits which, if it were possible, would not knock Italy out.

Cunningham responded:

I think the phrase 'knocking Italy out of the war' was coined by the politicians themselves. They were never given to understand that Italy could be knocked out in a week or so. What they were told was that if Libya was completely cut off and the Italians kept fighting it was most likely that Libya followed by Abyssinia could be out of the war in about six months. Further, that the surrender of the army in Libya coupled with attacks on the Italian coast where material damage can be done would have a great moral effect and might well cause the Italians to lose heart and think they had had enough.[170]

Cunningham's interpretation was broadly consistent with the aspirations set out in the February European appreciation and subsequently shared with the French.

The saga of the 'knockout blow' did not show British strategy at its best, but in determining naval deployment, it did not ultimately matter. By late April the more convincing argument for a strong naval presence in the eastern Mediterranean was gaining traction, the fleet here as ultimate guarantor of Britain's commitment to Greece and Turkey, the security of Egypt and the Levant and, behind them all, the strategic interests of the Middle East. These wider interests were emphasised by Stanhope at the 2 May meeting, but took on sharper definition over the second half of 1939. By early December the chiefs of staff had identified three fundamental British strategic interests in the Middle East: the security of the canal on which control of the eastern Mediterranean depended in the face of a hostile Italy; the Anglo-Iranian oilfields; and the routes to northeast India. The defence of these needed strategic depth,[171] which required the support of Turkey and control of Iraq, Iran and Egypt. Turkey was 'the first line of defence for the Suez Canal from the north'. Nevertheless, they still emphasised that: 'Our interests in the Middle East, important as they are, are not as important as the security of France or Britain, or of Singapore.'[172]

All this justifies a more positive view of evolving British strategy for defence of the eastern empire across 1939. Given the range of risks Britain now faced, and the different ways they might take effect, a degree of muddle and ambiguity was perhaps excusable. However, the British strategy process was still generally good at identifying what mattered most, capable of correcting errors such as the 'knockout blow', and avoiding simplistic panaceas. By early summer Britain's political and military leadership had reached consensus on a new set of principles that would guide strategy for the defence of the eastern empire through the first half of the coming war. First, the core interests in the Far East were the protection of Australasia, India, Singapore and the communications between them, primarily in the Indian Ocean. Secondly, a serious Japanese threat to this core would take time to develop, giving Britain discretion over the size and timing of naval reinforcements. Immediate deployment of a full fleet was not an automatic prerequisite to defend this core.

Thirdly, there were now interests in the eastern Mediterranean that at least matched, and perhaps took precedence over, all Far East interests beyond the core. Fourthly, there would have to be a trade-off between eastern Mediterranean and Far East dictated by the relative level of risk and benefit at any given time. There were too many variables here to fix the level of Far East naval reinforcement in advance. Finally, France in the Mediterranean, and the United States in the Far East, could help reduce the risk inherent in the trade-offs between the two theatres.

In the face of a now probable three-enemy war, these five principles marked both an important change, but also a logical evolution in the desired strategic end state for defence of the eastern empire defined in 1937. The maximum achievable end point in a war with Japan had reduced to securing the core eastern territories and Indian Ocean, while on the western boundary the minimum desired goal now encompassed control of the eastern Mediterranean, rather than solely Egypt and the canal. Meanwhile, a new Far East war plan issued on 15 June was the Admiralty's initial, if somewhat flawed, attempt to define the 'ways' and 'means' to achieve these revised end points with the naval resources available in mid-1939.

These principles also featured in the final conclusions of the Anglo-French staff conversations, which recognised that British interests predominated in the Far East theatre. In a war against all three Axis powers, the European theatre must have overriding priority, since defeat here would automatically lead to the collapse of the Allied position in the East. It was also important to support the eastern Mediterranean powers and pursue early success against Italy. Initial strategy in the Far East must therefore be defensive. However, Singapore could not hold out indefinitely in the face of determined attack by Japan. Naval reinforcements must be sent at some stage, but it was impossible to decide in advance their precise scale and timing. The British and French governments must agree the appropriate distribution of Royal Navy forces between Mediterranean and Far East in accordance with the relative level of risk. Plans must address a range of options 'including two extremes': 'the practical abandonment of naval control temporarily in the Far East, or the Eastern Mediterranean'.[173] The staff talks had also clarified that if Britain did withdraw from the eastern Mediterranean, there was no prospect of French naval forces even partially filling the gap. Their effort would remain restricted to the western half of the sea, where the two *Dunkerques* would be withdrawn from the Atlantic to ensure adequate cover.[174]

There was one more contribution to this emerging consensus on flexible reinforcement. Churchill sent a 'Memorandum on Sea Power 1939' to Chamberlain, with a copy to Chatfield on 27 March. He argued that Germany would be too preoccupied with securing the Baltic to pose much naval threat to Britain in the first phase of a war. If Italy was hostile, Britain should therefore concentrate on mastering the Mediterranean, which the Royal Navy could do in 'two months'. The Italian armies in Africa would then be 'cut flowers in a vase', and easily wrapped up. Failure to take the initiative here would risk an Italian invasion of Egypt under German leadership, with disastrous consequences. Meanwhile, Britain must not be distracted by the threat from Japan. If she intervened, British interests in China, including Hong Kong, would be 'temporarily effaced', and it was pointless wasting effort to protect these. 'We must bear losses for the sake of the final result'. However, the likelihood of an attack on Singapore requiring a seaborne expedition across 3000 miles against a heavily armed fortress was remote. The Japanese were cautious people, would recognise the risks, and wait until matters were decided in Europe. Singapore could anyway easily hold out for six to twelve months while Italy was liquidated. No invasion of Australia was possible while Singapore stood, and anyway that concept was 'ludicrous'. It was reasonable to provide Australia with a 'guarantee' of protection, but 'in our own way' and 'in proper sequence'.

Chatfield told the prime minister that he agreed with this assessment, including concentration on Italy, although wrapping up the Mediterranean would take at least six months.[175] The paper is a fascinating preview of Churchill's personal strategic position in the coming war. His attitude here towards Japan would be little modified through 1940 and 1941. Substantial sections of this paper would be lifted wholesale for his formal guarantee to Australia as First Lord in November. It is possible Churchill's intervention helped tilt the Strategic Appreciations Committee and Committee of Imperial Defence in favour of an offensive against Italy, even though this idea did not last long. It was probably also influential in discouraging any inclination to risk war with Japan over China interests when the Tientsin crisis erupted in June.[176] Chatfield's new enthusiasm here for a Mediterranean offensive, while it reflected the emerging Strategic Appreciations Committee consensus, was at odds with the personal position he had taken at those meetings. His six-month assessment also clashed with the emerging Joint Planning Committee advice that such an offensive was completely unrealistic.

Meanwhile, the Admiralty moved rapidly to apply the new 2 May comparative risk policy in its war plans. Danckwerts as Director of Plans produced a revised version of Naval War Memorandum (Eastern), the Far East war plan, just three days later. This was based on the Strategic Appreciations Committee recommendations approved by the Committee of Imperial Defence, but specified the number of capital ships and other forces to be sent to the East under three different scenarios. If Japan intervened simultaneously with Germany and Italy and with the United States neutral, then four capital ships, along with a carrier and supporting forces, would be sent. If the United States was an ally, two capital ships would go, with similar supporting forces. Danckwerts judged here that with the United States involved, a direct attack on Singapore was unlikely. If Italy was neutral, or knocked out, then a maximum capital ship force of seven ships would deploy. He also reminded Cunningham that copies of the Far East war plan were held by the Dominions. If the amended version was approved, they would now receive details never previously shared with them, of Royal Navy force distribution in a triangular war.

Cunningham approved this draft on 16 May, along with an abbreviated version for Commander-in-Chief China, Vice Admiral Sir Percy Noble, to use in local discussions with the French. Here, in place of the three separate scenarios outlined above, reinforcement policy following Japanese intervention read as follows:

> Whilst it is not open to question that a capital ship force would have to be sent to the Far East, its composition cannot be forecast at present. In the most favourable situation at home and in the Mediterranean, a battleship fleet of seven or eight ships might be sent. In other circumstances it might only be possible to despatch a small force in the form of a 'flying squadron'.

The likely composition of this 'flying squadron' was virtually identical to that proposed by Drax two months earlier. It was the first appearance of the term 'flying squadron' in a formal planning document. It is not clear why Danckwerts had not used this language in his original draft. It may simply be that he wished to set out the reinforcement options in more detail.[177]

However, at some point after 16 May the 'Composition of the Fleet to be sent to the Far East' in the revised war plan was adjusted to the formulation sent to Commander-in-Chief China. This had important consequences. The original had established minimum reinforcement forces for specific scenarios. The underlying implication was that further forces up to the maximum seven or eight capital ships would be sent in the event of an all-out Japanese attack on Singapore, achieved through full withdrawal from the Mediterranean. Perhaps by introducing the specific term 'flying squadron', Danckwerts merely intended a convenient abbreviation for 'initial light reinforcement', a covering force pending a full fleet later, if needed. However, by missing out the word 'initial' and stating that 'it might only be possible to despatch a small force', his plan now implied there were circumstances in which reinforcement might never exceed a 'flying squadron'. His proposed plan therefore suggested a different concept of Far East defence without deployment of a full fleet, and without explaining the implications. Such language would certainly cause shock in the Dominions.

The revised war plan therefore reflected and exacerbated the crucial weakness in Cunningham's memorandum. It illustrated how the new flexible reinforcement policy might be applied in practice, but nowhere defined the objectives such reinforcement was to achieve. Thus the maximum force of 'seven or eight' capital ships was based on what might now be generated after leaving the essential minimum in the Atlantic and withdrawing from the Mediterranean. It did not identify Chamberlain's 20 March goals, and so offered no view on whether such a maximum force was adequate to meet them. Nor did it specify what the minimum 'flying squadron' might achieve. Nothing was said about operating north of Singapore.

Despite these shortcomings, the new war plan, including the 'flying squadron' reference, was approved by Rear Admiral Tom Phillips, who took over from Cunningham as DCNS on 25 May. It was then formally issued to commanders-in-chief and other operational commanders on 15 June.[178] It presumably had the endorsement of Pound, who took over as First Sea Lord on 7 June. The claim, often made, that Pound and Phillips rejected the concept of a 'flying squadron' when they arrived in the Admiralty, and immediately insisted that Japanese intervention must be countered on traditional lines with a full fleet is not correct. In mid-June they were content for the term 'flying squadron' to be used. They neither questioned the context in which the phrase was used, nor the implication that a 'flying squadron' might be the only force sent. If they were unhappy with the new plan and its failure to set strategic objectives for the force to meet, they could easily have asked Danckwerts, who remained Director of Plans, to postpone circulation to permit revisions.

Phillips did, however, quickly recognise Danckwerts' concern that the Dominions were not yet briefed on the new Far East reinforcement policy. He notified the chiefs of staff of the 'slight divergence' between the prime minister's 20 March message, which was the latest guidance on reinforcement given to the Dominions, and the subsequent position endorsed by the Committee of Imperial Defence on 2 May. The Dominions held copies of the Royal Navy's Far East war plan, and it was undesirable they should receive the new version before being informed at appropriate political level that policy had changed.[179] The prime minister had stated that 'it remained the intention to despatch a fleet to the Far East if Japan intervened', but its size would depend on the state of any European war and losses sustained.[180] By contrast, the Committee of Imperial Defence, reflecting Cunningham's memorandum, had agreed: 'There are so many variable factors which cannot at present be assessed that it is not possible to state definitively how soon after Japanese intervention a fleet could be despatched to the Far East. Neither is it possible to enumerate precisely the size of fleet we can afford to send'.[181]

Phillips was undoubtedly correct that, while the underlying British intent behind these statements might not be substantially different, the Dominions would interpret the Committee of Imperial Defence statement as a further weakening of commitment. This would be powerfully confirmed if and when they saw the reinforcement section with its 'flying squadron' reference in the new war plan. This issue was raised at the committee on 26 June. The consequences that flowed from that meeting, which included significant changes to Far East war planning and the withdrawal of both the new war plan and references to 'flying squadrons', are explored later.

The formal introduction of the new flexible reinforcement strategy by the Admiralty in its new war plan coincided with the episode known to history as the Tientsin crisis. The origins of this crisis lay in the growing Japanese impatience over the constraints posed on their operations and ambitions in China by the Western concessions. The presence of Chinese resistance groups within the concessions was perceived by the Japanese as especially provocative, and triggered specific threats against the British concession of Tientsin. A Japanese assault on what was effectively British territory had the potential to trigger a much wider British-Japanese confrontation and, in the worst case, war.[182] The crisis therefore put the new policy of 'flexible reinforcement', based on Cunningham's 'variable factors', to its first test.

It posed several questions and challenges. First, given the present threatening situation in Europe, was Britain still willing and able to use force, or at least the threat of force, to defend its interests in China? Initially, that meant using naval power to enforce economic sanctions against Japan. That might well provoke a trade war, which then risked escalating into Japanese action against British territories across the Far East, ultimately including an attack on Singapore. Or did Britain now stick to the reduced goals established by Chamberlain on 20 March, which meant China interests were ultimately dispensable? Next, how would the policy of flexible reinforcement apply if war, or at least military confrontation, broke out in the Far East before it did in Europe? The planning assumptions from the European appreciation onward had all assumed a scenario where Japan might intervene at some point after Britain was at war with Germany and Italy. What level of force could safely be deployed to deal with a reverse scenario? Finally, if Britain sent no forces to the Far East, backed down over Tientsin, and was seen to do so, what impact would this have on the Dominions?

The various chiefs of staff papers which defined the options available to the government to meet the Tientsin crisis are often used to demonstrate Britain's inability any longer to generate a competitive Far East fleet, and therefore the effective collapse of the Singapore strategy.[183] As with the earlier China crisis in the winter of 1937/38, they do no such thing. What the papers and the subsequent deliberations at the Committee of Imperial Defence convey is the deep reluctance of the chiefs and Admiralty to take risks with naval security in the Atlantic and Mediterranean in order to generate a maximum fleet to protect commercial interests in China, when the capital ship force was at its lowest. Scrutiny of the Tientsin papers has focused on the mathematical contortions the Admiralty was obliged to undertake by Chatfield to demonstrate that it might just be possible to produce seven capital ships for the Far East by early autumn, and whether such a force would be credible both in encouraging Japan to an acceptable settlement, and adequate if it came to war. It is rightly argued that, given current capital ship availability, the Royal Navy would have struggled to produce more than five or six ships before late autumn. It is also true that, in drafting these papers, judgements that rated IJN efficiency at 80 per cent of the Royal Navy were arbitrary and convenient rather than based on any hard intelligence.

This focus on the mathematics merely underlines the impossibility of the Royal Navy matching three different enemies in three different theatres in the circumstances of mid-1939, and rather misses the point. The difficulty was that generating an adequate fleet for a confrontation over China would require deployment well north of Singapore in waters advantageous to Japan. Government and chiefs of staff reluctance to contemplate this in the face of the current threats in Europe did not mean it was now impossible to meet Chamberlain's more bounded 20 March objectives. Here there are important insights in the Tientsin papers and in subsequent changes to Admiralty planning. They show the scale of Royal Navy force the Admiralty judged was required to meet different levels of Japanese attack in mid-1939, how far these forces could be generated, and the consequences for other theatres.

The papers indeed established a framework for addressing the naval risk posed by Japan in a three-enemy war that would remain extant until the end of 1941. They identified first the minimum level of reinforcement for the eastern theatre manageable without incurring significant additional risk in other theatres. This comprised two capital ships, one carrier, two cruisers and one destroyer flotilla.[184] This was the 'flying squadron' defined in the 16 May brief for Commander-in-Chief China, and implicit in the final version of the new Far East war plan. The papers also specified for the first time what this force could achieve. When added to the China Squadron, it might secure communications in the Indian Ocean against raids, and deter major operations against Australasia. It could not hold, or even remain in, Singapore if the Japanese moved south in strength. As already noted, this anticipated the small 'immediate response force' to secure the Indian Ocean, central to Britain's contingency planning against Japanese intervention from mid-1940 until late 1941.

The papers then established the maximum force deployable to the Far East from autumn 1939, following full mobilisation and withdrawal from the eastern Mediterranean. This was seven capital ships with appropriate supporting forces, sufficient to secure Singapore and shield Australasia and the Indian Ocean against a full-scale Japanese attack. However, the chiefs of staff stated categorically that it would not be strong enough to contest the area north of Singapore. Nor could it protect Hong Kong. By carrying significant risk in the Mediterranean, and some risk at home, the Royal Navy could therefore still generate sufficient forces to meet Chamberlain's limited 20 March goals in full. The chiefs and the Admiralty nevertheless insisted that these risks were only acceptable to protect critical empire interests. It made no sense to get into a war over China at this time. This concept of a 'maximum fleet', generated primarily from eastern Mediterranean resources, as an ultimate safeguard against a direct and immediate threat to the Dominions and Indian Ocean would also persist in contingency plans through 1940/41.

The Committee of Imperial Defence considered the use of naval force to back potential economic sanctions against Japan over Tientsin on 26 June. Chamberlain declared that sooner or later, if war broke out, Britain would have Germany, Italy and Japan ranged against her. The attitude of the United States was uncertain and France the only ally. He accepted the advice of the chiefs of staff that the maximum fleet which could be generated would be insufficient to operate safely north of Singapore. In consequence, Britain could not stop Japan freezing her out of China. He assumed his colleagues would agree there was no point in Britain initiating retaliatory action which risked a more general war. If Japan initiated such a war, that would be a different matter. He agreed to inform Australian and New Zealand representatives of this thinking, and did so on 28 June, when he also reaffirmed the assurances in his 20 March message. If a fleet deployed at this time to the East, the temptation for Germany and Italy to take advantage would be irresistible. Sending a less than adequate fleet would be pointless. Britain was understandably not going to risk war for its China trade.[185]

The Tientsin deliberations have further fed the belief that Pound as incoming First Sea Lord in early June, and Phillips[186]as his new DCNS,[187] rejected any concept of Far East reinforcement other than a full fleet. They therefore banned all reference to the term 'flying squadron' and the work of Drax.[188] In contrast to the flexible Far East reinforcement strategy initiated by Backhouse and formalised by Cunningham, Admiralty policy now reverted to the traditional view that a threat from Japan could only be countered by early deployment of a full fleet. This, in turn, implied that the Far East retained absolute priority over the Mediterranean. This belief largely rests on directions from Phillips relating to the new War Memorandum (European), the Royal Navy war plan for the European theatre. Following the Tientsin meetings, Danckwerts argued that plans to deal with Japanese intervention when war was already underway in Europe were better covered in War Memorandum (European) than War Memorandum (Eastern). Phillips as DCNS approved this change on 5 July but stipulated:

- The memorandum should emphasise the Royal Navy could not resource three fleets.
- Security of home waters had priority.
- A Far East Fleet must have sufficient strength to face Japan in line with chiefs of staff Tientsin recommendations.
- Providing a Far East Fleet would therefore require the British government to choose between Far East and eastern Mediterranean. The choice would depend on circumstances.
- References to 'flying squadron' should be deleted.[189]

Two distinct issues must be addressed. First, did Phillips, and Pound as his superior, privately doubt the wisdom of the new policy which balanced Far East and Mediterranean interests? Did they wish to revert to the more purist position adopted by Chatfield in the initial Strategic Appreciations Committee discussions? Alternatively, did they accept the need for choice 'depending on circumstances', but resist the idea of flexible reinforcement, fearing this would lead to divided forces and a belief that Far East defence could be achieved on the cheap? It is tempting to see links here with the debates over Far East reinforcement which would take place in the summer and autumn of 1941.

The first issue is easily answered. Phillips took over from Cunningham as DCNS at the end of May, and Pound arrived from the Mediterranean to take over as First Sea Lord on 7 June.[190] Phillips, therefore, acting on behalf of the Royal Navy, personally approved the chiefs of staff update to the European appreciation[191] and the report and recommendations arising from stage II of the French staff talks.[192] These papers reinforced the policy of comparative risk and flexibility over Far East naval reinforcement agreed at the 2 May Committee of Imperial Defence meeting, but put the consequences of that policy even more starkly. They confirmed that the timing and scale of Far East naval reinforcement depended on balancing the risks there against the position in Europe and the Mediterranean when Japan intervened. Britain's initial stance in the Far East would certainly be defensive, and 'at the outset allied naval forces in the Far East may not exceed their peacetime strength'. There is no evidence in the preparation of these papers, or in subsequent discussion, that Phillips disputed the need to balance Far East and Mediterranean interests. Neither he nor Pound argued the case for automatic Far East primacy either in their early months in office or indeed, in admittedly different circumstances, following the collapse of France the following year. The need to choose according to circumstances repeated in the instructions to Danckwerts on 5 July may be taken at face value.

The second issue is more complicated. Were Pound and Phillips opposed in principle to flexible reinforcement? Did they believe any fleet sent to the Far East must be 'adequate' to counter the full IJN fleet, and that there was no point in sending a lesser force? As discussed, they approved the new Far East war plan, which endorsed flexible reinforcement and specifically referred to the 'flying squadron' concept. They both valued Drax as a strategist. However, the preparation of the Tientsin papers under Phillips's guidance obliged the naval staff to tackle the issues which the Cunningham memorandum and subsequent war plan revisions had ignored. Specifically, what were the key objectives which Far East naval reinforcement had to meet, and could adequate forces be generated to meet these if it proved necessary?

Tientsin brought home to the naval staff, the chiefs of staff and the Committee of Imperial Defence the outer limits of the new comparative risk policy with the current naval forces available. The advice from Pound and Phillips was that only a small reinforcement force could be generated without compromising vital interests in home and eastern Mediterranean theatres. In effect, a Drax-style flying squadron, although they did not use this term in the Tientsin papers. Such a force could not credibly deter Japanese action in China. Nor could it guarantee Singapore against a subsequent Japanese attack. For this specific crisis, at this specific time, it had little value. Under pressure from Chatfield, they had then demonstrated that generating a fleet sufficient to break the maximum likely Japanese attack and secure Singapore was still possible within current Royal Navy strength, but only if the Mediterranean was abandoned and some risk carried at home. This 'maximum' Royal Navy fleet would be significantly smaller than the maximum IJN fleet in all categories of warship. It followed that its role must be strictly defensive. It could not operate north of Singapore, and could not credibly exercise influence over Japan in China, as Chamberlain and the Committee of Imperial Defence accepted.

The Tientsin papers therefore highlighted the issue ducked by Drax, by the Cunningham memorandum, and by the new war plan. Flying squadron reinforcement of the China and East Indies fleets could protect the Indian Ocean and Australia, and indeed Singapore, against limited IJN raids. It could not break a siege of Singapore supported by the full IJN fleet. The security of Singapore still 'ultimately' rested, as it always had, on the ability and will to deploy an 'adequate' fleet. 'Ultimately', there was no escaping the need to choose between Mediterranean and Far East, and accept the consequences. The key word here is 'ultimately'. The Japanese would not necessarily attack Singapore immediately, and if they did it was expected to hold out for a minimum of ninety days and later 180.[193] In practice, it might still be possible to defer a final choice between Mediterranean and Far East, and therefore the despatch of a fleet, for a considerable period. The new European war plan reaffirmed this, thereby confirming that Pound and Phillips still believed that immediate deployment of a maximum fleet should not be the automatic response to any Japanese intervention. There were also potential scenarios, such as a concerted attack on British trade by IJN surface raiders, where limited reinforcement, including capital ships, but well short of a fleet, made sense. Nevertheless, to meet the full objectives defined by Chamberlain on 20 March, now reaffirmed to the Dominions during Tientsin, the Royal Navy would have to produce a competitive fleet.

The problem of how to communicate to the Dominions the 'comparative risk policy' agreed on 2 May was unresolved when the Tientsin crisis broke. It was rendered more difficult by a telegram from Australian Prime Minister Robert Menzies which reached Chamberlain on 24 June, two days before the Committee of Imperial Defence were due discuss the issue. Menzies sought assurance that, in a war with Japan, 'the United Kingdom Government would send a fleet to Singapore within appropriate time capable of containing the Japanese Fleet to a degree sufficient to prevent a major act of aggression against Australia'. At the Committee of Imperial Defence meeting, Chamberlain agreed both to reiterate his 20 March assurances directly to Menzies and to underline them with the Dominion representatives in London, whom he duly saw on 28 June. This British position was further reinforced at a meeting chaired by the Dominions Secretary on 11 July. The Australian High Commissioner Stanley Bruce was evidently unconvinced by these assurances, but formally Britain had now confirmed from the highest political level its intent to despatch a 'fleet' if Japan intervened. This would be sufficient to protect Singapore, the Dominions and the Indian Ocean, albeit still with caveats over its precise size.[194]

Given these further assurances to the Dominions, it was obvious that the existing formula on force composition in the newly issued Far East war plan could not be passed to them unchanged. The suggestion that only a 'flying squadron' might be possible as reinforcement was not consistent with Chamberlain's renewed promise of a 'fleet' as ultimate guarantee. But, leaving aside the promise to the Dominions, a credible war plan for the eastern theatre must demonstrate that the Royal Navy could still generate a fleet strong enough to relieve and hold the vital Singapore base against maximum Japanese opposition. Danckwerts' proposal on 4 July that it would be more logical for the impact of Japanese intervention to be addressed in the European war plan rather than the Far East plan, now gave Phillips the opportunity to address these two issues. Hence the instructions issued to Danckwerts the following day.

The new Far East sections of the European war plan were issued on 4 August.[195] The revised Far East plan was then withdrawn after a lifespan of little over a month.[196] The existence of two plans within such a short period has been overlooked. Yet the differences are revealing. The new European plan now clarified the minimum forces to meet requirements in the home and Mediterranean theatres in the event of a European war. These were based around six and three capital ships respectively. Crucially, it now also defined the military objectives in the Far East, namely those set by Chamberlain, but also the ability to exert sufficient economic pressure on Japan to bring about her ultimate defeat. To achieve these objectives, a fleet deployed to the Far East must be strong enough to accept action against the Japanese fleet if it came south in full strength. In line with the earlier Tientsin papers, the minimum strength here was seven capital ships with appropriate supporting forces, including two carriers. The European plan recognised the desired strengths across three theatres could not all be met with current resources. Since the home theatre had absolute priority, providing the necessary forces for the Far East would require a trade-off between Far East and eastern Mediterranean risks, on the basis of the now familiar Cunningham factors.

The plan then defined how the required Far East fleet could be generated after allocating sufficient forces to deal with Germany as primary enemy. The allocations took account of the availability of the battlecruiser *Renown* due to complete rebuild in September and the battlecruiser *Hood* and battleship *Revenge* due out of short refit by the end of August. The minimum home fleet to deal with Germany would then comprise the three battlecruisers, *Hood*, *Renown* and *Repulse*, needed to cope with Germany's fast ships, three 'R'-class battleships and three carriers. Other forces would include two 8in cruisers, fourteen 6in cruisers, twenty-six destroyers and eighteen submarines. Set against German strength at this time, this was a substantial force. The required Far East fleet would involve full withdrawal from the eastern Mediterranean, although significant light forces would be allocated to secure the Red Sea and Persian Gulf from Italian attack.

The new plan also now emphasised that Japan could adopt an aggressive strategy, including an offensive against Singapore, at the outset of a war. In this case, a fleet should be sent 'as early as possible to prevent the loss of our only fleet base in the Far East'. The equivalent paragraph on 'Composition of the Fleet to be sent to the Far East', which had proved problematic in the Far East war plan read: 'if a force is sent to the Far East it must be capable of engaging the main Japanese Fleet under conditions favourable to ourselves.' The sample fleet for August 1939, including the existing China and Australia squadrons, comprised seven capital ships (two *Nelson*s, three *Queen*

*Elizabeth*s and two 'R'-class), two carriers, seven 8in cruisers, ten modern 6in cruisers, fifty-five destroyers and fifteen submarines.

Despite its firm commitment to providing an adequate fleet, the new plan retained the flexibility over the timing of reinforcement initiated by Cunningham. In line with Phillips's instructions, it duly omitted all reference to 'flying squadrons'. From the Dominion viewpoint, there was now nothing in the text to suggest that reinforcement would be less than an 'adequate' fleet. But nothing in the text prohibited a graduated response to reinforcement either. On 18 August, when the Tientsin crisis was dying down and deploying a fleet to the East was unlikely, Pound told Cunningham there remained an option of 'sending a weaker force of two battleships to the Far East', in which case Vice Admiral Sir Geoffrey Layton, Cunningham's deputy, would go with the battleships *Barham* and *Malaya*.[197] Assuming a carrier was included here, which seems probable, such a force would have replicated Drax's flying squadron. Flexible reinforcement therefore remained in place in practice, even if the European war plan no longer included it formally as an option. As already noted, there would be contingency plans for limited reinforcement with what was a flying squadron in all but name in the Indian Ocean throughout 1940/41.

The revised European war plan represented the final position on Far East naval reinforcement before the outbreak of war with Germany a month later. The strategic objectives for the Royal Navy in the Far East theatre were now those set by Chamberlain on 20 March, and repeated to the Dominions at the end of June. The timing and pace of Far East naval reinforcement to meet these objectives once Japan opened hostilities still depended on the comparative level of risk in that theatre compared to the eastern Mediterranean, in accordance with Cunningham's 'variable factors'. The 'maximum' fleet identified in the plan as potentially available for Far East deployment therefore represented the maximum 'means' available from late 1939, after making provision for the home theatre, to protect the two boundaries of the eastern empire.

The resources for this 'maximum' Far East fleet, including all capital units, would remain in the Atlantic and East Mediterranean, as in the European appreciation, for as long as possible. No reinforcements would be sent to the East unless Japan began serious raids on empire communications or moved in strength against Singapore. There was one exception. China Squadron forces on detachment in the Red Sea and Aden would return east immediately on the opening of hostilities with Japan. These comprised a division of destroyers and four submarines. Australian and New Zealand cruisers would also return east.[198] A Japanese raiding strategy would probably still be met with forces somewhat short of the full fleet, a form of 'flying squadron' in practice even if the actual term was now 'politically incorrect'. Despite the formula now adopted to reassure the Dominions, Britain would only send the full fleet if Singapore or the core eastern empire territories were directly and immediately threatened and not as a mere deterrent. She could reasonably hope that such a deployment would not prove necessary. The concept of a 'maximum fleet', generated primarily at the expense of the eastern Mediterranean, remained extant in 'worst case' contingency planning, even after the fall of France and through 1941, to meet an imminent and direct Japanese threat to Australia, although by then the fleet was more likely to base in Ceylon than Singapore.

If the worst case had materialised in late 1939, could the maximum fleet have met Britain's reduced strategic goals in the East? Director of Plans estimated that the maximum IJN fleet supporting an attack on Singapore in 1939 might be seven or eight capital ships, four carriers, eight 8in cruisers, and a proportionate number of ancillary forces. This was based on 75 per cent availability. This was a reasonable threat estimate given overall IJN strength at this time, the problems of supporting such a force at long distance, and the need to guard against American intervention. The Royal Navy 'maximum' fleet would be competitive in all categories except carriers, but would have some land-based air support too. It was smaller than the 1936 fleet but the goals now were more limited. Its role was strictly defensive. It would not operate north of Singapore. Deploying such a fleet would leave no safety margin at home against Germany in the event of war losses. It would open Britain to considerable political and strategic risk in the Mediterranean, although the chiefs of staff judged Egypt could be held.

In assessing Royal Navy competitiveness, there is inevitably a tendency to view Japanese potential in 1939 through the optic of what they achieved in late 1941. The Japanese had done no planning for an attack on Singapore, or a general war against Britain at this time. Indeed, the Japanese made no active preparations for an attack on Singapore or Malaya until August 1940, when studies began in the operations section of the army general staff. Even then, planning moved slowly and was not complete until October 1941. Intelligence was limited, and particularly poor on the northern coast of Singapore island and Johore. In 1940 the Japanese army still possessed no detailed map of the Singapore area.[199] When he visited Germany in 1940, General Tomoyuki Yamashita, future commander of the 25th Army and conqueror of Singapore, discussed an attack on Singapore with senior German officers. They all insisted that capture of the base would take up to eighteen months and require a minimum of five divisions.[200]

The IJN was a powerful opponent in 1939, but much less powerful than two years later. By contrast, the standing Royal Navy forces based permanently in the Far East were far stronger. The combined total for the China and Australia squadrons following the return of detached units in the Red Sea and

Persian Gulf comprised one aircraft carrier, four 8in cruisers, six modern 6in cruisers, nineteen destroyers, fifteen submarines, seven escort vessels and various light forces.[201] These forces alone, if well-handled, especially the submarines, could inflict significant damage on any force attacking Malaya.

Equally important, the Japanese at this time had no embarkation points from which to mount a seaborne attack, or airfields to support it within 2000 miles of Singapore.[202] It would be a formidable undertaking to provide the fuel to sustain an IJN force at this distance, requiring a substantial tanker fleet and a safe anchorage from which to refuel. In contrast, the Royal Navy had reliable facilities and large fuel reserves at Ceylon. To mount a credible attack on Singapore, the IJN required sustained air superiority, which depended on its carrier force. The IJN only had three fleet carriers available at the time of the Tientsin crisis, although a fourth (*Hiryu*) commissioned in July. With two light carriers added, a maximum effort by this IJN carrier force would have an initial numerical advantage over the combined British carrier and land-based air forces of at least two to one. However, the IJN carriers would have been vulnerable to attrition, not least from submarine attack. With air superiority eroded, the risk of British forces successfully interdicting IJN communications would be high. Troop transports would be especially vulnerable. IJN aircraft had no significant quality lead over British aircraft at this time. The British were well aware of the threat posed by carrier attack, and undertook a major exercise in early 1938 with the carrier *Eagle* posing as an IJN carrier supporting a landing force. *Eagle*'s mock attacks were successful, raising uncomfortable implications which the British attempted to address over the next year.[203]

Overall, if it came to a full confrontation with the IJN in late 1939, the total Royal Navy fleet generated after full reinforcement would be smaller than advisable. But, despite the present limitations of Singapore as a base, the challenge to the Royal Navy in supporting such a fleet with limited defensive objectives would be less than that confronting the Japanese.

The post-Tientsin reinforcement policy emerged under the direction of the new Admiralty team comprising Pound and Phillips. Together with Churchill, they become the three central figures influencing the naval defence of the eastern empire for the remainder of the period covered by this book. The previous chapter argued that Phillips made a more important contribution to Royal Navy capability and performance during his time as Director of Plans and DCNS/VCNS than generally acknowledged. This is a good moment therefore to consider Pound's tenure as First Sea Lord. As already stated, he took up the post on 7 June 1939. He fell ill from a malignant cerebral tumour at the end of August 1943 while visiting the United States and Canada for the Quebec summit conference, formally tendered his resignation to the Admiralty

Board on 20 September on return to the United Kingdom, and died just a month later on Trafalgar Day, 21 October.

Pound is generally portrayed as the *faute de mieux* First Sea Lord, appointed due to Backhouse's unexpected death, and because events, and perhaps poor succession planning by Chatfield, had removed all credible alternatives.[204] The implication is that he was promoted to a post where he performed adequately, but ultimately lacked the qualities to lead the Royal Navy to best effect during its ultimate challenge.[205] Four failings are commonly identified in Pound: that he lacked the strategic vision to conduct a global naval war; that he was a chronic 'centraliser' and 'back-seat driver' unable to delegate, a characteristic that Phillips supposedly reinforced rather than balanced; that he was unable to stand up to Churchill; and that his performance was compromised by poor health and fatigue.[206] Much attention has focused on the last two issues. In the case of health this is partly because key witnesses, and therefore historians, have been unable to agree whether poor health impaired Pound before his final year in post, both sides of the argument attracting powerful partisans. It is also because poor health and tiredness are viewed as an important influence on his performance under the other three headings.[207] Robin Brodhurst has produced the only full biography of Pound and has viewed all the research, as well as consulting modern medical opinion, and doubts health and fatigue were major factors before 1943.[208]

The degree to which Churchill overrode professional advice from Pound, or directly intervened in operational matters, thus circumventing Pound's authority, has also proved controversial, with Roskill, as official historian, especially critical both of Churchill's interference and Pound's reluctance or inability to confront him. It is not hard to find examples of Churchill intervening in the operational chain of command directly or indirectly. It is rather harder to find examples where such interventions either cut across Admiralty intent or produced outcomes the Admiralty did not want. Brodhurst also argues rightly that Pound was good at handling Churchill. He deliberately avoided the type of head-on collision, implicit in the 'standing up to Churchill' sought by Roskill, in favour of wearing the prime minister down with reasoned argument, which was invariably successful.[209] The case above all others which is quoted to illustrate Churchill riding roughshod over Pound's advice is the deployment of Force Z in late 1941. As this book will demonstrate, the reality of the positions taken in this debate is almost the opposite of the historical consensus.

The accusation that Pound was out of his depth in global strategy is often made, but rarely backed with convincing argument. Pound was perceptive in recognising that the Mediterranean would be closed in wartime and also in recognising the strategic importance of the eastern Mediterranean. His response to the fall of France and his focus on what was truly essential to British survival through 1940/41 was equally sound. So was his early grasp of the strategic importance of the Indian Ocean. It is not evident that any of those who might have replaced Pound during his tenure were better strategists, and that includes Cunningham. Nor is it apparent that he was less able as a strategist than any of his chiefs of staff colleagues, with the notable exception of Brooke.

Pound was certainly instinctively a 'centraliser', who favoured strong central direction both in the Mediterranean Fleet and in the Admiralty. However, the Royal Navy of 1939 devolved considerable responsibility to its operational commanders, and the claim that he persistently meddled in detail at the expense of the big picture or regularly interfered on the turf of commanders-in-chief looks overdone. There is little evidence to suggest Cunningham in the Mediterranean, or Admirals Noble and Horton during their tenure in Western Approaches Command, felt Admiralty interference was an issue. There are well-known examples relating to the Home Fleet, notably the *Bismarck* operation and the PQ17 convoy disaster, but these reflected special political or intelligence factors and were understandable, if not always excusable. As to the eastern theatre, this book will show that closer Admiralty direction might well have been beneficial in both the Force Z episode, and with Somerville at Ceylon the following April.

Pound's judgement of people has also been questioned. He undoubtedly made some bad appointments, of which sending Rear Admiral Sir Henry Harwood to take over from Cunningham as Commander-in-Chief Mediterranean in early 1942 was probably the worst. Other appointments proved inspired, notably Somerville at Force H and later to the Eastern Fleet, and Horton to Western Approaches. Whatever the carping over Phillips from more senior admirals, he proved an exceptionally able VCNS and an ideal complement to Pound in the first two years of war. Pound was not a natural delegator, but he did delegate enormously to Phillips.

It is ironic that the historical view of Pound has focused so much on his perceived weaknesses, when his tenure as First Sea Lord coincided with the period of the Royal Navy's greatest triumphs. He directed the Royal Navy through a period when Britain faced 'a combination of maritime enemies by whom she should, rationally speaking, have been defeated',[210] and brought it to the point where victory was in sight everywhere. Results should speak for themselves, and they suggest Pound was a lot more than just 'the pilot who weathered the storm'.[211] Possibly Pound's historical profile as a chief of staff has also suffered by comparison with chiefs of staff colleagues, either because they demonstrated a specific strength (Brooke as a strategist), or because they are judged primarily for what they did before or after their tenure as a chief (Dill in Washington, or Cunningham in the Mediterranean).

The policy of minimum and flexible reinforcement sufficient to guarantee security of the eastern empire core was reaffirmed by the War Cabinet and conveyed to the Dominions in November 1939 after the outbreak of war. Churchill, now First Lord, produced a paper to reassure visiting Dominion ministers that Britain could and would protect Australasia against any 'serious' Japanese attack. It repeated an unambiguous commitment that, if Britain were forced to choose between its Middle East interests and the defence of Australia, the latter would take precedence. While the paper aimed to provide the robust reassurance judged important in winning consent for the deployment of Dominion forces overseas, it was careful to distinguish between the scale of fleet needed to combat Japan in its home waters, and the now more limited requirement to deploy a force sufficient to deter attack on Singapore or Australia. It emphasised the difficulty Japan would have undertaking a long-range siege. It also included, with typical Churchillian rhetoric, the famous and emotive phrase that 'duty to kith and kin' would take precedence over the Mediterranean.[212]

Two points in the paper deserve emphasis, because they reflect Churchill's personal perspective on Far East naval reinforcement, which he would regularly underline over the next two years. The first was the concept of 'the fleet in being': 'The power of a predominant fleet is exercised simultaneously in all quarters of the world in which it has bases. This is irrespective of the position it occupies at any given moment provided that it is not permanently tied to that station.' Deterrence, in other words, rested as much on the *possibility* of deployment as its actuality. The second and related point was that ships 'could not be left idle' in wartime, waiting for an attack that might never come. As Churchill told Richard Casey, Australian Minister of Supply and leader of their delegation, and High Commissioner Stanley Bruce on 20 November, there would be no question of moving powerful forces to the East on the mere threat of Japanese attack. It was necessary to wait until such a threat took effect.[213] These points neatly underlined the policy reached over the summer – prepare to protect the 'core', but do not send reinforcements until we have to. Neither policy nor plans changed during the first months of 1940, until the collapse of France and the intervention of Italy sharply reduced Britain's options in the Far East.

The case for strategic flexibility
Britain's strategy for defending its eastern empire from Japanese attack through naval power in the late 1930s remained broadly credible. The concept of deploying a substantial fleet to the East to counter any attack on British territory and interests would have still looked plausible to Japan. The goals set by British decision-makers were generally limited, and within available

resources, given that until the very end of the decade a major conflict was unlikely and allowed considerable political discretion. The strategy was neither 'eviscerated'[214] nor reduced to 'a hollow gamble'[215] by the rise of the triple threat. It was not fatally compromised by the need to protect interests in the Mediterranean. Nor did the strategy fail to adapt to new circumstances. On the contrary, from late 1938 Britain's leadership moved towards a new consensus on balancing the needs of the eastern Mediterranean and Far East by focusing on a critical 'inner core' of eastern empire interests and making naval reinforcement plans more flexible. This flexibility was neither an empty gesture nor deception. It was backed by clear priorities and detailed force allocations. Those forces remained strong enough at this point to retain command of the Indian Ocean and severely disrupt a full-scale Japanese attack on Singapore, for which the Japanese had yet to do any planning.[216]

PART II

Existential War in the West

3

Securing Eastern Empire War Potential
after the Fall of France

This chapter and the next one describe the evolution of British strategy for defence of the eastern empire from the fall of France in June 1940 until the summer of 1941, when the German attack on Russia and the Japanese move into southern Indochina fundamentally changed the strategic picture. This chapter shows how from mid-1940 Britain tried to establish a limited defensive screen against Japanese intervention in the Far East while it concentrated on the existential threat to the United Kingdom homeland from Germany, and the prospect of a combined German and Italian assault on the western boundary of the eastern empire in the Mediterranean and Middle East. This policy laid the ground for future strategic failure in Malaya and Singapore. This was not simply because, with limited resources, Britain prioritised the defence of the Middle East.[1] It was, rather, because it insisted on holding a forward position in two theatres simultaneously, which in the Far East meant controlling a far larger area than anything contemplated pre-war. Chapter 4 examines how the relationship with the United States influenced British strategy in this period.

The present chapter explores why Britain adopted its forward position in the Middle East, which absorbed a steadily increasing share of military resources between autumn 1940 and the Japanese attack twelve months later. This included the major part of the Royal Navy's best carrier power and almost all the modern land-based air power that could be spared from the United Kingdom for deployment overseas. This severely limited the quantity and quality of resources available to counter Japanese aggression at the eastern end of the empire. Although the trade-off between these two boundaries of the eastern empire, in both of which naval and air power were decisive elements, has long been recognised, insufficient attention has been given to the issues judged most important by decision-makers at the time. By the spring of 1941 Britain's war leadership had identified three critical reasons for holding a forward position in the Middle East:

- The influence this position exerted on German access to the Iberian Peninsula and northwest Africa, with consequent implications for the security of the Atlantic lifeline;
- The denial of Iraq oil to the Axis;
- The security of the western boundary of the eastern empire and the Persian oil, without which it could neither survive economically nor generate its full war potential.

Investment in the Middle East also highlighted the importance of the Indian Ocean supply routes and their potential vulnerability to Japanese attack, and therefore a growing awareness of interdependence between these theatres by the summer of 1941.

The second part of the chapter explores the implications raised by the new chiefs of staff Far East appreciation of July 1940, which shaped defence policy in this theatre over the next eighteen months. Although the approach taken by this appreciation appeared defensive, with outwardly sensible recommendations focused on minimum reinforcements to hold Malaya and thus Singapore, the underlying strategy it embraced was regressive. Instead of building on the more flexible defensive thinking of 1939 that focused on the security of the Indian Ocean and inner core of the eastern empire, it reverted to a wider strategic goal of holding Japan north and east of the entire Malay Barrier, in order to secure Singapore. This resurrected the more ambitious 1937 strategy to control at least the southern sector of the South China Sea, which was beyond Britain's resources in 1940/41. Furthermore, it insisted the optimum way to achieve this wider goal was through the traditional deployment of a battle-fleet rather than a modern integrated 'all arms' approach. The problem identified with the 1937 Far East appreciation in Chapter 2 took effect. Deploying a fleet to Singapore was no longer just one way to achieve a strategic end: holding the base became the end itself. It was the failure adequately to distinguish between ways and ends, more than lack of means, that would bring disaster. The Admiralty, who continued to exert the dominant influence on Far East strategy, were primarily responsible for this.

The case for holding a forward position in the Middle East
The fall of France made it much harder for Britain to control the sea areas and communications essential both to protect the empire and successfully prosecute the war. The loss of French naval support was less serious than the size of the French navy suggested. The French navy had contributed little to operations against German surface forces in either the Atlantic or Norway, and brought little value to the defence of Atlantic convoys against the submarine threat.[2] The loss of French forces as a counterweight to Italy in the western

120

Mediterranean was more serious, but even this gap proved manageable. The prospect that Germany would acquire French capital ships, including those nearing completion, was a bigger risk, but the likelihood of this was minimised by mid-July.[3] Four modern French ships were of particular concern. One of the two battlecruisers, *Dunkerque* was immobilised for at least a year by the British action at Oran. The *Strasbourg* escaped to Toulon. Of two new battleships, the nearly complete *Richelieu* was disabled by Fleet Air Arm torpedo attack at Dakar on 8 July. *Jean Bart*, still some way off completion, was out of German reach at Casablanca. The attack on *Richelieu* was noteworthy for the first use of Mark XII aerial torpedoes with advanced duplex warheads employing a magnetic proximity fuse.[4]

The real damage to Britain's naval position lay in German access to bases on the French Atlantic coast, which vastly complicated Royal Navy defence of the critical Atlantic trade routes. There was also a change in the status of French territories overseas, to a position somewhere between unfriendly neutral and outright hostile. The primary benefit of the French bases was to the German U-boats. These could deploy far more quickly and safely from the west coast of France than from Germany, where they faced a long exposed transit to their patrol areas. With these Atlantic bases effective patrol time virtually doubled.[5] For the same reasons, French bases also helped with surface raider deployment both by warship and converted merchant vessel, and French airfields extended the opportunities for air attack on Atlantic and coastal shipping.

For the next two and a half years, Britain also faced a constant risk that Germany or the other Axis powers would exploit other French territory against her, whether on the Atlantic coast of Africa, in the Mediterranean, or the Far East. Japan indeed moved rapidly to take bases in northern Indochina, making an attack southwards a much more feasible proposition. The ostensible reason for this intervention, negotiated with the French colonial authorities over the period June–September, was to cut aid to China and provide a new launching point for military operations against her.[6] The possibility of wider southern expansion to achieve economic control over Southeast Asia and the Netherlands East Indies was also discussed for the first time, as the Japanese assessed the consequences of the German victories in Europe. However, there was no agreed strategy to achieve this yet, and the IJN was resistant to risking military confrontation with the Western powers.[7] Indeed, Vice Admiral Nobutake Kondo, Vice Chief of Naval Staff, told the Japanese emperor on 26 September that the IJN had no operations plan for a war with Britain.[8]

Countering these new risks in the Atlantic and Mediterranean tied up significant extra Royal Navy and Royal Air Force resources in a way never anticipated pre-war. It was much more difficult to release forces to counter Japanese intervention, even with the more flexible reinforcement policy which had emerged in 1939. It is often argued that it was the fall of France that finally rendered the Singapore strategy impossible.[9] However, that is true only if that strategy is defined within very narrow limits. Britain certainly lost Singapore in 1942, but it held India and the Dominions, and maintained adequate control over Indian Ocean communications. It also despatched a larger fleet to the Indian Ocean that year than it deployed in any other theatre during the Second World War.

Before exploring how Britain adjusted its naval strategy to meet these new circumstances, we should ask whether it is true that the loss of France and the consequences that would follow were never seriously considered by the Admiralty, and that no contingency plans were therefore contemplated. At the end of 1937, the chiefs of staff judged, almost certainly correctly, that Germany lacked adequate land forces 'to overrun France quickly'.[10] This remained the conclusion of their much more detailed appreciation completed in September the following year in the run-up to the Czechoslovakia crisis. This did acknowledge that German occupation of the Low Countries and northern France would make attacks on Britain easier. However, perhaps significantly, it added that even the total defeat of France, 'while it would enable Germany to attack Britain from a more advantageous position', 'would not necessarily be decisive'. The chiefs evidently saw the primary threat to Britain at this time as an all-out German air offensive. This would be 'the only way of achieving a rapid result' against Britain as Germany's most dangerous enemy before the superior economic strength of the Allies took effect.[11]

The ability of France to withstand a determined German attack on its northeast frontier was then reviewed extensively by the chiefs of staff at the beginning of 1939. The Joint Planning Committee advice, which the chiefs accepted, was that in most circumstances France could hold out for a considerable period, but it would be unsafe to assume she could do so indefinitely. This questioning of French capability reflected growing awareness in Paris and London that the Munich agreement had effectively dismantled Czechoslovakia's military power, and therefore significantly increased Germany's comparative military advantage over France.[12] This led the chiefs to question whether, contrary to current policy, it might be necessary to prepare a British field army for deployment to France in war. If France was defeated, not only would prosecution of a successful war against Germany be compromised, but Britain would have failed to achieve one of its key strategic goals, namely the defence of France. Here they specifically underlined the critical threat to the security of the United Kingdom homeland arising from German acquisition of French ports.[13]

This thinking was reflected in the European appreciation in February 1939 which stated: 'If France were forced to her knees, the further prosecution of the war would be compromised'; and, 'It is difficult to say how the security of the United Kingdom could be maintained if France were forced to capitulate'.[14] These judgements marked a distinct shift from the September 1938 appreciation. They accelerated the staff talks with the French, which in turn led to the wide range of collaborative measures agreed by end May, and referred to in Chapter 2, including the extensive framework of naval co-operation.[15] They also led to successive decisions over the coming months to deploy significant British air and land forces to France in the event of war to stiffen French defence.[16] The Admiralty also demonstrated that it was alert to the consequences of Spain becoming an active ally of the Axis powers. This would provide Germany and Italy with the use of an extensive stretch of Atlantic and Mediterranean coast in Spain and in North Africa, as well as further threatening France.[17]

The strategic position following the outbreak of war in September 1939 differed from that anticipated in the European appreciation in crucial respects. Italy remained neutral and it was soon clear that early Japanese intervention was also unlikely. These positives, however, were offset by the German-Soviet pact which enabled Germany to concentrate its forces in the West and reduced the effectiveness of the Allied blockade. British assessments through the winter of 1939/40 and up to the eve of the German offensive in the West nevertheless remained confident that with Germany the only enemy, superior Allied economic potential would prove decisive in the long term, and that France was still strong enough, with steadily increasing British forces deployed in support, to contain any early attack.[18] In the spring of 1940, Britain was also confident it had the upper hand at sea and, in particular, could deal with the U-boat threat.[19]

The chiefs of staff first contemplated the possibility of French collapse, following the German attack on 10 May, just nine days later on 19 May.[20] They instructed the Joint Planning Committee to produce an assessment of the implications, which was completed on 25 May.[21] Given the speed and stress under which this was produced, it was a remarkable document. It arguably provided a basic template for British strategy for the rest of the year and, in some respects, well beyond. It recognised that Britain's naval position would be made much more difficult by German access to French ports, potential loss of control in the western Mediterranean if Italy entered the war, and the even worse scenario of Spanish intervention, which would immediately threaten Gibraltar and provide the Axis with a longer coastline from which to challenge Britain. The assessment nevertheless judged that the Royal Navy was strong enough to counter any German threat in home waters, to protect the vital Atlantic supply line to Britain's west-coast ports, to control entry to the Straits of Gibraltar even in the worst scenario by seizing bases at Casablanca and in the Atlantic islands, and to maintain a fleet in the eastern Mediterranean to secure Egypt and contain Italy. It would not, however, be possible to send any significant forces to the Far East if Japan intervened. Here Britain would have to rely on the United States.

Three main questions arise from these British assessments. First, did the Admiralty and chiefs of staff recognise the risks to Britain's naval position that would follow a French defeat? The answer here is a qualified 'yes'. The qualifications were that until May 1940, the risk of a rapid collapse was judged very low and if it did occur, German naval resources were too limited to allow it to exploit its geographical gains in the short term. Air power was a different matter. Secondly, was the chiefs of staff judgement up to May 1940, from which the Admiralty inevitably took its lead, that France should be able to withstand a German land offensive for a considerable period, a reasonable one? The latest assessments of Germany's 1940 campaign in the West demonstrate that Germany had little material advantage, either quantitative or qualitative, over its Allied opponents. Nor did it consistently apply a revolutionary combined arms doctrine. Success reflected the brilliant application of more traditional aspects of the military art: overwhelming concentration of force at a vulnerable point, and surprise.[22] No reasonable assessment of the comparative military balance over the period 1938–40 could have anticipated the scale and pace of the subsequent victory. British judgements that France could hold at least for a considerable period were reasonable.

Finally, if Britain had been more sceptical of French ability to withstand a German attack from, say, early 1938, would it have altered its naval rearmament programme or its proposed war plans and dispositions? There are several points here. A more pessimistic judgement of French prospects would not have affected the Royal Navy alone. It is conceivable more funds might have been released for rearmament, but any addition might well have gone to the Royal Air Force and to preparing a larger British Expeditionary Force. In so far as the Royal Navy supported the need for a land force contribution from early 1939 to bolster French defence, it did so in the knowledge that investment in risk reduction here would potentially come at the expense of the future naval budget. It is tempting to say the Royal Navy might have allocated more resources earlier to anti-submarine vessels. This surely shows too much hindsight and ignores the opportunity cost of such diversion. The Royal Navy had to take account of all the threats it faced from three potential enemies, not just a somewhat higher possibility that Germany might conduct a large-scale Atlantic trade war, if and when it built the forces to exploit the bases it might capture. As argued earlier, the fact that the Royal Navy was able to cope with both the loss of France and entry of Italy into the war suggests that it got both its rearmament balance and its force distribution about right.

The most authoritative assessment of how the British leadership saw Britain's overall strategic position following the fall of France is the chiefs of staff Future Strategy paper of 4 September 1940.[23] At the level of grand strategy, this established a blueprint for how victory might still be achieved by wearing down Germany as the primary enemy through economic attrition, using naval blockade, bombing and subversion. Its genesis lay in earlier papers prepared by the Joint Planning Staff from mid-July onwards, notably for the visiting American delegation led by Rear Admiral Robert Ghormley at the end of August.[24] The vision conveyed in the Future Strategy paper was perhaps more an expression of faith than a realistic war plan. Britain was potentially strong enough to cope with a wider war embracing Italy and the Mediterranean, but only within a defensive framework. Anything more ambitious depended on United States support.[25] However, the paper is also important for its analysis of comparative force levels and its assessment of the immediate strategic vulnerabilities and potential opportunities confronting both Britain and the Axis. The basic concept of 'wearing down' Germany certainly influenced immediate British priorities and choices. The security of the United Kingdom homeland and the defence of the other interests and territory perceived as critical to the future war effort was, for the moment, the primary concern.

The authors of the paper believed that the Royal Navy could maintain adequate naval superiority over Germany and Italy until August 1942. No special significance attached to this date. The paper merely projected comparative force levels, using estimates of current strength and anticipated production, to 1942. There was no implication that the balance would fundamentally change at that point. The active hostility of France would be a significant additional commitment, but would still not dangerously weaken British control of essential sea areas. The projections for German and Italian naval strength, including German U-boat production, were broadly accurate, although they slightly overstated commissioning of German heavy surface units. The paper estimated seventy U-boats on 1 August, whereas the true figure was fifty-nine, and 157 (or 130 allowing for wastage) by 1 August 1941, when the true figure would be 153 on 1 July that year.[26] It correctly anticipated that only two new battleships, *Bismarck* and *Tirpitz*, would be available before 1942, but assumed incorrectly that there would also be two aircraft carriers and a fourth *Hipper*-class heavy cruiser by end 1941. None of these three were ever completed.

The paper was more confident that Britain could retain naval supremacy in the Atlantic and Mediterranean than when the implications of French defeat were first addressed at the end of May.[27] This probably reflected three factors: better understanding of German naval losses in Norway; the neutralisation of the French fleet; and the naval supremacy established in initial engagements with Italy. The first point was especially important. Not only was the remaining German surface force quite incapable of supporting an invasion operation, but only two heavy units would be available for Atlantic raider operations for the rest of 1940. In the Norwegian campaign the German navy lost three cruisers, including the brand new *Blücher*, one of its only two heavy cruisers, ten destroyers and six U-boats. In addition, the battlecruisers *Scharnhorst* and *Gneisenau* and pocket battleship *Lutzöw* were all badly damaged. The first two would not be operational again until the end of the year, and *Lutzöw* not until well into 1941. This left only the pocket battleship *Admiral Scheer* and heavy cruiser *Hipper* potentially available for Atlantic raider operations or, indeed, to support an invasion of the United Kingdom. The latest account of the Norwegian naval campaign argues that the German surface navy, small before the campaign, 'was crippled virtually beyond recovery'. This is an overstatement but underlines the scale of loss.[28]

Churchill was aware of German naval weakness by early August. On 11 August he told the prime ministers of Australia and New Zealand that 'the German Navy is weaker than it has ever been' and is reduced to 'only one pocket battleship, a couple of 8in *Hipper*s, two light cruisers, and perhaps a score of destroyers'. Apart from the addition of an extra *Hipper*, this assessment was essentially correct.[29] The scale of German loss in Norway equated to the best outcome from the six-month offensive against Germany postulated by Drax in early 1939. Meanwhile, the early successes over Italy included the hit by the battleship *Warspite* on the Italian battleship *Giulio Cesare* at Calabria on 9 July 1940, the sinking of the cruiser *Bartolomeo Colleoni* by the Australian cruiser *Sydney* on 18 July, and early attrition of Italian submarines, where twenty were sunk by the end of 1940, representing about 25 per cent of their operational force.[30]

In addition to these British successes, German U-boat strength had not increased at all in the first year of the war, while numbers actually deployable on the frontline had dropped by a third from thirty-nine to twenty-seven. Frontline availability would continue to fall to a low point of twenty-two in January 1941.[31] Even by January 1942, when overall U-boat strength at 249 was growing very fast, the actual number of sixty-five available for deployment in the North Atlantic had still not doubled from September 1939. (There were also then twenty-one available in the Mediterranean.)[32] Numbers operational at sea, when allowance is made for rest and maintenance, were much less, at between 50–70 per cent of frontline strength. Britain, meanwhile, increased its deployable Atlantic escort capability between September 1939 and January 1942 with around forty new destroyer escorts, some two hundred new corvettes and about forty old destroyers from the United States. Allowing for losses, escort strength more than tripled over this period with overall escort numbers rising from 100 to about 370.[33]

The Future Strategy paper assessed that the forces required for adequate superiority over Germany and Italy in the new strategic circumstances left no margin for the foreseeable future to deal with any Japanese intervention. The most force that could be deployed to the eastern theatre was a small 'hunting group', probably comprising a battlecruiser and carrier, to deter IJN raider action in the Indian Ocean. The paper nevertheless stressed the continuing importance of holding Singapore as a potential base for a fleet in being, and as a foothold, along with Malaya, for recovering any losses when stronger forces became available. Perhaps optimistically, it emphasised the intent of finishing the European war with a fleet sufficiently strong to secure and, if necessary, re-establish, Britain's position in the East against the strongest anticipated Japanese fleet. This concept of Singapore and Malaya as 'foothold for recovery' reflected Chatfield's line at the 1937 Imperial Conference.

Apart from a direct attack on the British homeland and a continuing assault on the Atlantic shipping routes, the paper saw two immediate areas of risk. First, an Axis drive southwest through Spain to seize Gibraltar, secure the western Mediterranean, and acquire bases on the West African coast. This would break the British blockade and support the Atlantic offensive. Secondly, an attack on Egypt to secure the eastern Mediterranean, force the withdrawal of the British fleet there and open up access to the Middle East and its oil, and to the Indian Ocean. The first risk followed directly from the fall of France and was certainly a real one. Throughout the autumn, the Germans did indeed try hard to draw Spain into the war, and their broader strategic aspirations were closely aligned to British fears. German goals here were summarised in Führer Directive No 18 of 12 November 1940 which defined plans for the capture of Gibraltar and subsequent acquisition of bases in the Atlantic islands and ideally northwest Africa.[34] According to Colonel General Franz Halder, chief of the German general staff, the idea of attacking Gibraltar was under discussion as early as 30 July. Other options identified for bringing pressure against Britain at this time were to support the Italians in an attack on Egypt; to attack Haifa; to attack the Suez Canal; and to encourage Russia to move on the Persian Gulf.[35]

However, the Spanish leadership, under General Franco, was unwilling to commit to Germany, unless she could guarantee benefits that would outweigh the economic damage from subsequent British blockade. Here Spanish aspirations in North Africa were in competition with French and Italian interests which Germany was reluctant to confront. Spain was sceptical British naval power would be easily dislodged from the Mediterranean. As the British had already calculated, the retention of a powerful fleet in the eastern Mediterranean, in addition to the newly established Force H at Gibraltar, encouraged Spanish caution.[36] Spain was well aware how dependent she was on British goodwill for oil and most of her food. Britain calibrated supplies with great skill, to ensure she had no chance to build up a cushion of stocks.[37] Substantial British bribes to the Spanish military leadership were also influential.[38]

The second risk identified by the Future Strategy paper was an elaboration, in the new circumstances, of the risk to the Middle East identified during the discussions in the Strategic Appreciations Committee in early 1939. The paper's analysis of the Middle East position is especially important because it identified the strategic goals here, and the strategic rationale underpinning those goals, which determined the huge British investment in this area over the next three years.

The importance that the Future Strategy paper, drafted at the end of August, placed on Britain holding Egypt and the eastern Mediterranean, with a strong fleet here as guarantor, built on an evaluation done two months earlier by the Joint Planning Committee.[39] In June the Planning Committee acknowledged there were strong arguments, already advanced by the naval staff, for withdrawing the bulk of the Eastern Mediterranean Fleet to meet the heightened risks in the Atlantic and to seal the western entrance of the Mediterranean, in the event of French collapse. The naval staff correctly highlighted the increased risks to Britain's Atlantic trade resulting from German access to French ports, and possibly Spanish bases too. However, they largely ignored the benefits Germany and Italy might gain from easy access to the Black Sea, and overstated the limitations of Alexandria as a base.[40] The Planning Committee, however, saw powerful political and strategic arguments which currently outweighed the naval case for withdrawal. Holding Egypt without the fleet might be difficult, Turkey might then tilt towards the Axis, and a wholesale collapse in Britain's position across the theatre could follow. The effectiveness of the British blockade would be seriously compromised. These arguments were developed and tightened at the beginning of July, and brought together in a telegram from the chiefs of staff to the Dominions and relevant overseas officials and commanders. This set out the rationale for holding the Middle East, and stressed the significance of Persian oil. It also expressed confidence that Britain could cope with Italy, so long as the Eastern Mediterranean Fleet remained in place.[41]

These factors again featured in the Future Strategy paper, but the arguments for holding the eastern Mediterranean were now tightened further. The most important new arguments related to oil. The paper rightly identified shortage of oil as a major Axis vulnerability. It assessed total German oil receipts (production and imports) for the year beginning 1 June 1940 at 7.6 million tons. True capacity was actually about 1 million tons greater, because synthetic production was by this time about 1.0 million tons higher than the British estimate of 3.3 million tons. British figures, including stocks available across occupied Europe, were otherwise accurate. If Germany could enjoy 'tranquil trade' from the Black Sea through the eastern Mediterranean to Italy and France, she could increase oil imports by 3 million tons per year or about 35 per cent of Germany's projected 1940 supply. This figure assumed about 1 million tons additional supply from Romania, above the 2 million tons from that source already provided by land and river routes, where the Germans would suffer disruption over the winter of 1940/41. The remaining 2 million tons would come from Russia. The obstacle to such tranquil trade was the Eastern Mediterranean Fleet, which also impeded Germany from reaching the Iraq oilfields through Turkey or Syria, while preserving their use for Britain.[42] Here the paper emphasised that while Germany would not be able to exploit Iraq oil in the short term, since Britain would destroy the infrastructure, she could deny it to Britain and ultimately threaten the Iranian fields and the refinery at Abadan.[43]

This British assessment of the Axis threat to the Middle East was entirely logical and the option of an attack here, both to weaken Britain's position and reap economic benefits by breaking the blockade, was regularly aired within the German leadership through the second half of 1940.[44] However, German aspirations were much less coherent than the British assumed. There were two reasons for this. Dislodging Britain from the Middle East would be a far more complex operation than an attack on Gibraltar through Spain, and would compete for resources with a 1941 attack on Russia, to which the German Führer Adolf Hitler was broadly committed from end July.[45] Also any major German intervention in North Africa or the eastern Mediterranean would cause tensions with Italy who saw this as her sphere.

For these reasons the German leadership never conducted a serious analysis of the strategic benefits, risks, and feasibility of a drive into the Middle East at this time. A partial exception here is the German naval staff, who produced detailed arguments in favour of a Mediterranean strategy, which were put to Hitler by Grossadmiral Raeder in September and again in November. However, Hitler evidently saw the Mediterranean as a distraction from the Russia campaign to which he was now committed, even though Raeder suggested that the Middle East could provide a base from which to seize the Caucasus oilfields, making an attack on Russia in the north unnecessary. Raeder ultimately lacked both the power base within the Nazi leadership, and the naval capability from which to make a convincing case. He also had to admit that some of his objectives, notably the seizure of Atlantic islands, including the Canaries and Azores, were impractical in the face of British sea power.[46]

Oddly, the possibility of gaining control of Middle East oil reserves for German use played little or no part in the Mediterranean debates that autumn. In particular, it appears there was no serious assessment of the prospects of acquiring and exploiting Iraqi oil.[47] This was partly due to the lull in major military activity following the fall of France through to the Balkan operations in the spring of 1941. This made the German oil position better than at any other time in the war. However, it also reflected the decision to attack Russia where a prime objective was indeed early seizure of the Caucasian oilfields. In November Reichsmarschall Hermann Göring told General Georg Thomas, chief of the war economy and armaments department, that Hitler believed Germany must get possession of the Caucasus oilfields, 'since without this large-scale aerial warfare against England and America is impossible'.[48] By early 1941, as serious planning for Barbarossa accelerated, Thomas confirmed that capturing the Caucasus fields was essential to preserve Wehrmacht operational capability. By May Wehrmacht operations staff were anticipating a monthly shortfall of 300,000 tons by September.[49] The Iraq oilfields did feature in army plans issued in the autumn of 1941 as an objective for late 1942 following successful capture of the Caucasus.[50]

Given this inability to articulate decisive benefits for a Mediterranean offensive, the subsequent German intervention in the theatre from early 1941 was essentially motivated by defensive factors. These were protecting the Romanian oilfields and facilities from potential attack, securing the Balkans as a southern flank prior to the attack on Russia in June, keeping Italy in the war, and occasional opportunism, such as the intervention in Iraq in May. The security of Romanian oil was certainly a significant factor behind the German intervention in Greece and the subsequent decision to take Crete, which Hitler feared could be used to mount air raids against the oilfields.[51] These defensive and opportunistic themes are illustrated in successive Führer Directives: No 18 of 12 November 1940 which focused primarily on Gibraltar, but mentioned limited support to the Italians against Egypt and the need to secure the Balkans; No 20 of 3 December 1940, which defined operations to secure the Balkans in more detail; No 30 of 23 May 1941, exploitation of the anti-British rising in Iraq; No 32 of 11 June 1941, which defined plans for a series of offensives to take control of the Mediterranean and Near East after the collapse of Russia. Only the last displayed real ambition with concerted drives on Gibraltar, the Suez Canal via Egypt, and into Palestine and Iraq/Iran from Bulgaria through Turkey. However, it represented a wildly optimistic vision for what might become possible in 1942 following victory in Russia, and comprised vague aspirations rather than any coherent strategy for undermining British imperial power.[52]

While the denial of oil and other economic resources to the Axis were alone viewed as compelling British arguments for holding the eastern Mediterranean, the Future Strategy paper also resurrected many of the arguments from early 1939 in favour of early action to drive Italy out of the war. The immediate opportunities, as identified then, were to sever access to her African empire and then eliminate it, tighten the blockade of her trade, and harry her fleet. Having identified the dual benefits, offensive and defensive, of holding a forward position in the eastern Mediterranean, the paper nevertheless identified a fall-back position if Axis forces proved too strong or demands elsewhere required the withdrawal of the fleet, including a Japanese threat to the eastern empire core. Here, a more extreme version of the Chatfield 1937 policy would take effect. Forces would be withdrawn from the Mediterranean, the canal would be blocked, and in the last resort Britain would retire to a line from East Africa to Iraq, holding the Persian Gulf, Aden and Kenya. While the paper did not spell out the circumstances in which the 'last resort' might take effect, it stated that, in the face of a direct and immediate threat to Australasia, Britain would abandon its position in the Middle East and Mediterranean to come to its aid.

As with the plans developed during 1939, the decision to hold and exploit a position in the eastern Mediterranean did not make it impossible to place a substantial fleet in the Far East, or at least in the Indian Ocean. Not only could the Eastern Mediterranean Fleet be withdrawn *in extremis* but, in theory, the Indian Ocean could be given greater priority at any time. However the decision meant forces available to meet potential Japanese intervention were still reduced in crucial ways. The build-up of adequate Royal Navy forces in the Mediterranean required reductions in the China Squadron, which by autumn 1940 was a pale shadow of its 1939 strength. By mid-1940 the carrier *Eagle*, all but one of the 8in heavy cruisers, most of the modern destroyers, and the fifteen submarines of the 4th Submarine Flotilla had been withdrawn. Almost all these forces went to the Mediterranean. Most of the submarines went to Malta, which proved an unwise deployment. These large boats of the 'O', 'P' and 'R' classes were ill-suited to the clear waters of the Mediterranean, where they were vulnerable to aerial spotting and many were quickly lost.[53] By late July the remaining forces east of Suez were reduced to one 8in cruiser, two modern 6in cruisers, four old 6in cruisers, six armed merchant cruisers, five old destroyers, and three anti-submarine escorts.[54] Sustained commitment to the Mediterranean would inevitably entail steady losses, limiting options for any future Far East naval reinforcement. Indeed, by the end of 1941 the Royal Navy had lost, in vessels either sunk or damaged, virtually all the frontline with which it started that year in the Mediterranean. But the most critical penalty paid in the Far East was in land-based air power where, through 1941, the Middle East absorbed almost all the modern air resources available for deployment from the United Kingdom to overseas theatres.

131

If the consequence of the commitment to the eastern Mediterranean was to leave the Far East increasingly exposed to Japan, then the obvious question is whether this commitment was justified. Were the risks and benefits valid, as perceived by Britain's leadership in autumn 1940, especially in regard to oil? Or was the Mediterranean actually a strategic dead end, offering no decisive advantage to either side? Investment would then have been discretionary, with the net result that Britain in particular expended huge resources for negligible gain.[55]

The charge that the Mediterranean was an irrelevant sideshow rests heavily on viewing the theatre and its prospects with hindsight of the German-Russian war that began in mid-1941. In mid-1940 British decision-makers clearly faced other possible futures. Assessments of British Mediterranean strategy devote little attention to the issue of Middle East oil supplies, although this is a central theme throughout British strategy papers in the period 1940–42. They largely ignore the southern supply route to Russia, which became an increasingly important factor in British and American minds from late 1941. They also show little awareness of the critical linkage between the Mediterranean and Atlantic campaigns, though this loomed large in German and American, as well as British, thinking. Finally, while there are legitimate arguments over the extent to which the offensive phase of the Mediterranean campaign from mid-1943 displaced effort that could have been better applied in northwest Europe, these considerations should not be confused with the rather different risk–benefit balance which applied in 1940–42.

British withdrawal or defeat in the Middle East would have given the Axis some valuable prizes, notably a sea route for Romanian oil, safe access to raw materials in Egypt and Turkey, and denial of Iraqi oil to Britain, even if Germany could not exploit this itself. In fact, while Iraqi oil was useful to Britain, it was not critical. For practical purposes, with the closure of the Mediterranean it could only be used to supply British forces and territories from the pipeline terminal at Haifa in the immediate eastern Mediterranean area. If Britain withdrew from the eastern Mediterranean, then clearly the oil could not be accessed, but nor would it be needed. In addition, the loss of Iraqi oil could easily be replaced from the Persian fields. These economic losses in the Middle East would not therefore have been critical to Britain, so long as the Iranian fields and Abadan were protected, and naval control was retained in the Red Sea and Persian Gulf. Falling back here would also have enabled valuable resources to be redeployed elsewhere.[56]

The immediate case against withdrawal lay in damage to British morale and her standing with the United States and key neutrals, also the compromise of the blockade, still a key element of British strategy, and belief that this was the only fighting theatre which could contribute to 'wearing down' Germany.[57] These factors certainly carried weight with the British leadership, as did the argument that effective defence of the Persian Gulf and Indian Ocean required strategic depth. However, a key point is whether this justification for forward defence is sufficient, or whether the strategic stakes in the Middle East were in fact rather higher. We need, therefore, to examine the factors that made the Mediterranean and Middle East a more decisive war theatre in the period 1940–42, and especially the issue of oil.[58] Middle East oil is hardly mentioned either in accounts specific to the Mediterranean and Middle East campaigns, or the prominent general histories of the Second World War.[59] Yet it is a dominant theme through chiefs of staff and Joint Planning Committee papers in 1940–42.

Britain had the brief prospect of a lasting strategic advantage early in this period through exploiting Operation Compass, the victory over the Italians in early 1941 led by Lieutenant General Sir Richard O'Connor. Originally conceived as a raiding operation, Compass achieved the capture of Cyrenaica and virtual destruction of the Italian army in North Africa comprising ten divisions; 130,000 prisoners were taken, along with 380 tanks and 845 guns, for less than 2000 British Empire casualties.[60] The subsequent seizure of all of Libya before the Germans could intervene was certainly a militarily feasible opportunity. Expelling the Axis from North Africa would have enabled Britain to control the central Mediterranean, and secure Malta. It might then have released significant air and ground forces for the Far East, rendering the painful strategic trade-offs later that year unnecessary. British sea and air power would have made an Axis reinvasion of North Africa virtually impossible. It would have vindicated the Future Strategy case for early action against Italy and, indeed, some of the pre-war 'knockout blow' thinking.

There is an argument that failure to seize this opportunity rendered Britain's Mediterranean strategy essentially negative. It felt obliged to deny the Axis assets, the use of the Suez Canal and access to the Indian Ocean, the oilfields of Iraq and Iran, which, while not intrinsically valuable to Britain, could in British eyes provide war-winning potential for the Axis. It can also be argued that British fears were exaggerated, since gaining the Suez Canal or Iraqi oilfields could not bring any decisive effect for Germany and Italy, at least in the short term. Britain could still control the exit from the Red Sea, while getting useful yields from the Iraq fields would take Germany at least a year and make only a modest contribution to her overall oil needs. The pre-war yield of the Iraq Kirkuk fields was about 4.5 million tons per annum. The oil was delivered to the Mediterranean coast by a pipeline which forked at the Syrian border, with a northerly arm going to the port of Tripoli in Lebanon and a southerly arm to Haifa in Palestine. In the face of any imminent threat to the Iraqi fields, Britain would have destroyed wells, pumping stations and sections of pipeline. Assessing how long it would take the Germans to restore a useful output is difficult, but achieving an output of 2 million tons via the Tripoli line, part of which was on Vichy territory and difficult for Britain to access, within twelve months seems reasonable. This estimate reflects the difficulty Germany had in recovering any yield from the Caucasus wells it captured in late 1942 in the Grozny area.[61] The pre-war output of the Iranian fields was around 11 million tons per annum and their productive potential was much higher. However, the geographical location of these fields and the Abadan refinery meant they could only be effectively exploited through the Indian Ocean. Germany and Italy had no prospect of secure access here unless Japan could seize control of this sea area on their behalf.

This negative case understates the strategic benefits for the Axis in the Middle East and their potential to damage the British and Allied cause in several ways. It is important to highlight the difficulties Germany faced in exploiting the Middle East oilfields but, if Iranian oil was beyond reach, gaining 2 million tons a year from Iraq in mid-1942, rising to perhaps 4 million tons from 1943, was credible. This additional supply must be set against a total available to Germany from all other sources of about 10 million tons per annum over the two years 1942/43. This not only had to feed Germany's own needs and war effort, but much of occupied Europe as well.[62] Iraq oil might therefore have added somewhere between 20 and 40 per cent to Germany's oil supply in that period. This would have made a substantial difference to her war potential, where shortage of oil imposed increasing limitations on mobility and fighting capability through 1941 as reserve stocks and supplies captured in France ran down. In May that year there were even serious proposals for a partial 'demotorisation' of the Wehrmacht, while in February the Italian navy was threatening to suspend all operations in the Mediterranean unless supplied with 250,000 tons of fuel.[63] German stocks of naval fuel were just 280,000 tons at that time, and would fall to half that figure by the end of 1942. Meanwhile, stocks of aviation fuel halved from 613,000 to 333,000 tons between 1940 and 1942.[64]

It follows that even 2 million tons of Iraq oil would have made a big difference to Germany's war effort. It might have provided decisive advantage in the critical turning points of the Russian campaign and certainly given Germany more options. It is striking that German successes in 1941/42 rested on consumption that was barely a third of that enjoyed by the British Empire, where total planned use across 1941 was 32.6 million tons. In addition, Britain had stocks (home and overseas) of some 9 million tons, equating to a whole year of German output, with 6 million tons belonging to the Admiralty alone.[65] Germany's fragile oil position underlines why control of the Balkans in order to secure the annual 2 million tons of oil from Romania was so important. Without this supply, its war effort would probably have collapsed.

While Britain dominated the eastern Mediterranean and held a substantial position in the Middle East and North Africa, she presented at least a potential threat to Germany's most important external source of oil, which Germany had to counter.[66]

Furthermore, if Germany had established a position in northern Iraq and Iran in 1941, this would have facilitated a drive north to seize the Caucasus oilfields the following year, a move that might have caused the collapse of the Soviet Union. The key factor preventing Germany realising these substantial strategic benefits in Iraq and Iran was the Eastern Mediterranean Fleet. It is therefore wrong to suggest that Axis control of the Suez Canal would bring little value, since the canal was essential to the Royal Navy's hold over the eastern Mediterranean. Without it, even if the fleet retired temporarily to Haifa following loss of Alexandria, it would be a fast-wasting asset.

If Germany controlled Iran, or even just the Iraqi port of Basra, it could also deny use of the Iranian oilfields and the Abadan refinery to Britain, even if it could not exploit these assets itself. By 1941 Britain's lack of shipping resources meant Abadan could only supply the Middle East and territories bordering the Indian Ocean. Supply from here to the United Kingdom was abandoned, while requirements in India, Malaya and Australasia could be met from the 5.7 million tons produced in the Netherlands East Indies and Burma fields. Abadan's output that year at 5.5 million tons was therefore its lowest in the war, although it still supplied about 18 per cent of total British Empire oil consumption this year, including about 50 per cent of that in the eastern empire. Its contribution would increase sharply from the beginning of 1942, both to replace the lost supplies from the Netherlands East Indies and Burma, and to meet the new demands of the eastern war, rising to 8.3 million tons over that year alone.[67] Nevertheless, even in 1941 it effectively underpinned the whole British Empire fighting effort in the Middle East theatre, for which most of the manpower came from eastern empire territories.[68]

The joint planning staff were also acutely aware during the first years of the war that Britain was responsible for maintaining oil supplies for the whole eastern hemisphere, apart from the Soviet Union and territories under Axis control.[69] They recognised that the Far East oil supplies were always vulnerable to Japan, and shortage of shipping meant this output could not easily be replaced from elsewhere. Abadan had spare capacity and was far closer than any alternative for feeding territories adjacent to the Indian Ocean. By the final year of the war, total eastern empire oil consumption would reach 17.8 million tons, with Abadan providing 12.5 million tons or some 70 per cent. Abadan output was then more than double that of 1941.[70] The loss of Abadan at any point in the war would therefore have had serious consequences for the overall British war effort, perhaps reducing it as much as 25 per cent by 1942, on the economies of the eastern empire and on the security of India. It certainly would have made the overall Allied task much harder, even after American intervention.[71]

Against this background, it is not easy to assess the specific influence of British naval power on Axis prospects in the Middle East and the possible consequences of the withdrawal of the Mediterranean Fleet in June 1940, as the naval staff originally favoured. The Axis would certainly have been able to dominate the northern half of the eastern Mediterranean and British inter-vention in Greece would have been impossible. However, that might then have allowed Britain the necessary resources to clear Italy from North Africa, providing a decisive win there. That, in turn, could have encouraged Britain to redeploy a fleet to the eastern Mediterranean to bolster Turkish neutrality and prevent any Axis seaborne initiative against Syria. If exploration of such counterfactuals rapidly becomes fruitless, it nevertheless underlines key points. There were significant strategic benefits for Germany in the Middle East, as Raeder at least recognised. However, realising those gains would have required the deployment of substantial forces, with implications, therefore, for the timing and conduct of the attack on Russia. Essentially, Germany would have needed to execute the all-out Mediterranean offensive from late 1940, which they subsequently outlined in Führer Directive 32 of June 1941, and as the British expected them to do. This would have meant delaying an attack on Russia until 1942. The logistic challenges of such a Mediterranean offensive were formidable but not insuperable.

Success did, however, require the neutralisation of the Eastern Medi-terranean Fleet. So long as it was in place or could be rapidly redeployed from the Indian Ocean, Axis options in the theatre were always constrained, at least until air power could be positioned to deal with it. Here, in so far as Germany contemplated a serious Mediterranean option at all at the turn of 1940/41, it is likely that British naval power had a discouraging effect rather greater than its real strength justified, given the damage the Royal Navy was to suffer at Crete. In that sense, the Eastern Mediterranean Fleet did indeed prove the ultimate guarantor of Britain's position in the Middle East, as recognised in the debates of early 1939.

The importance of British investment in the Mediterranean during 1941 is underlined in a strategic survey produced by the German supreme command (OKW) on 28 August 1941, which reviewed Germany's options following the anticipated defeat of Russia. It was approved by Hitler and issued to the three service chiefs, Field Marshal Walther von Brauchitsch, Göring and Raeder.[72] It assessed that Britain and the United States knew it was impossible to beat Germany on the continent. Their basic strategy, therefore, would be to increase Germany's supply problems, and use air power further to weaken the Axis position. They also knew invasion of the United Kingdom could be discounted at present. Britain's immediate objectives would therefore be to clear the Axis from North Africa, with direct American intervention in West Africa a possibility, use naval and air power to dominate the Mediterranean, tighten the blockade and collapse Italy. Britain would establish direct contact with Russia through Iran, to sustain her will to resist, and deny Germany access to Caucasus oil. She would also strive to keep Spain and Turkey neutral. Germany had to defeat Britain, but could only achieve this through direct invasion or siege warfare. The former would involve a massive reallocation of military resources not possible until late 1942. A successful siege meant sinking one million tons of shipping per month and also required a large shift in resources. However, effective operations in the Atlantic required bases in Spain and West Africa. Ideally, this would be achieved by drawing France, Spain, and hopefully Turkey, into a collaborative alliance with the Axis, but the political and military challenges in achieving this were formidable, and depended on defeat of Russia first. The collapse of Russia was therefore the primary goal, to which everything else must be subjected. Only then would it be possible to mobilise an all-out effort against Britain in the Atlantic and the Mediterranean. In the meantime, pressure should be applied to France to reduce the risk of British/American intervention in her African colonies. German operations in the eastern Mediterranean would be impracticable before the Caucasus was under German control.[73]

This OKW survey was in some respects an extension of Führer Directive 32, but it ranged far wider, and was remarkable for the degree to which it recognised the dangers in British strategy in the Mediterranean.[74] There is no sense here that Germany viewed the Mediterranean as an unimportant sideshow. On the contrary, it saw the Mediterranean as fundamentally linked to the prosecution of a successful Atlantic trade war, which was the preferred means of defeating Britain. This link has been little recognised.[75] It is also striking that within two months of the opening of the Russian campaign, the German leadership should have focused on the potential importance of the Iran supply route to keeping Russia in the war. As Chapter 8 will show, this may indeed have been critical to Russian survival in the second half of 1942. There is clear recognition in this survey that British mastery of North Africa would deny Germany the French and Spanish support without which defeat of Britain might well prove impossible. There is thus a neat parallel with Britain's assessment of its own position in the Mediterranean and Middle East theatre. Neither side can lose the war here but, without holding it, the war may be difficult to win. This perception is crucial.

The German survey further underlines how important the Middle East was to Britain's overall position, both to contain German power and to maintain the economic viability and war potential of the eastern empire. Britain could not know, when her initial calculations were made following the fall of France, that Germany would attack Russia the following year. As she continued to pour resources into the Middle East in mid-1941, she could not know whether Russia would survive, nor, of course, how and when the United States might enter the war. However, if a copy of the German survey had reached Churchill that autumn, it would surely have vindicated his conviction during the previous twelve months that Britain's position in the Middle East came second only to the defence of the United Kingdom. Loss of the Middle East would not immediately lead to defeat, but it would, at a minimum, threaten the survival of the eastern empire, and make the task of defeating Germany virtually impossible. This was an argument on which the chiefs of staff were initially more ambivalent.

Germany's survey would also have endorsed two other elements of British strategy in the fall of 1941. It would have confirmed the British case for a maximum effort to dislodge the Axis from North Africa by the spring of 1942, with the consequence that risk must be carried in the Far East. It would have validated Churchill's emerging view that if America entered the war, she should join Britain in an early attack on northwest Africa. In short, the survey was the best possible support for the strategy Churchill would successfully promote in his 'WW1' paper at the Arcadia Conference with the Americans after their entry into the war in late December. If WW1 amounted to one of the great state papers of the war, the German survey of 28 August deserves recognition as a worthy Axis counterpart, even if it was not, in the end, a strategy the Germans felt able to execute.[76]

A new Far East strategy and its weaknesses

The September 1940 Future Strategy paper did not address Far East defence in detail. However, its references to the continuing importance of Singapore, the contingency of deploying a task force to protect the Indian Ocean, and the 'last resort' commitment to Australasia, reflected a detailed Far East appreciation prepared for the chiefs of staff at the end of July and approved by the War Cabinet on 15 August.[77] This new appreciation was a comprehensive review of British military policy in the theatre, designed to address the drastic shift in priorities necessitated by the fall of France, and the risk that Japan would now exploit British preoccupation in Europe to move against British interests in the East. It established a new baseline for assessing defence needs in the theatre over the remaining sixteen months of uneasy peace. Most subsequent planning papers linked back to it, and its recommendations on force levels acquired the quality of almost holy writ.

The urgency in completing this appreciation, despite obvious pressures elsewhere, reflected growing indications of Japanese aggression towards British interests in China, and especially tension over the Burma Road. The joint planning staff addressed this problem on 24 June. They argued that 'the strategic importance of our position in the Far East remains as great as ever', that land and air reinforcements would have to compensate for inability to deploy a fleet and that these must come primarily from Australia and India.[78] The chiefs of staff assessed that the increasing Japanese hostility demonstrated Japan's overall aim of excluding western interests from the Far East and of acquiring control of the strategic economic resources of the area. To achieve this ambition, the chiefs judged that Japan must ultimately capture Singapore. Otherwise the existence of a Royal Navy fleet anywhere in the world would remain a threat. They also judged that, while an early attack on Malaya or Singapore was possible, Japan was more likely to pursue expansion step by step through Indochina and Thailand, avoiding direct confrontation with the British Empire or the United States until the position in Europe was clearer. This was a sensible assessment which correctly reflected Japanese thinking at this time.[79]

The appreciation explained that the two key assumptions underpinning the last major review of Far East defence in 1937,[80] summarised in Chapter 2, were no longer valid. These were that any threat to Far East interests would be seaborne; and that Britain could send to the Far East within three months a fleet sufficient to protect the Dominions, India, and Indian Ocean communications. The Japanese advance into southern China, the development of communications and airfields in Thailand, the vulnerability of Indochina following French collapse, and the increased range of modern aircraft had created an overland threat to Malaya, against which the arrival of a fleet could only partially guard.

The scale of Japanese attack anticipated in the appreciation, drawing on advice from the Joint Intelligence Committee, was an accurate assessment of what Britain would face sixteen months later. The forces available to Japan for 'new adventures', beyond existing commitments in the China war and watching Russia, comprised ten battleships, seven carriers and substantial supporting forces; six to ten divisions, along with the necessary shipping to project at long range; and up to 423 land-based aircraft and 281 carrier-borne aircraft. The assumption that Japan would probably attack through Thailand, accompanied by a seaborne assault on northern Malaya, supported by aircraft based in Thailand and Indochina, was correct.

Meanwhile, the collapse of France, the development of a direct threat to the United Kingdom, and the need to retain naval forces in European waters sufficient to match both the German and Italian fleets, all made it temporarily impossible to despatch an adequate fleet to the Far East should need arise. Without a fleet it was impossible to prevent damage to British interests, but the

139

appreciation argued the damage could still be contained, providing a foothold for recovery when resources allowed. It saw three ways of achieving this aim:

- buying time through concessions to Japan;
- compensating for the lack of a fleet by relying on air power and reinforcing the land defences of Malaya;
- building a common front against Japanese aggression with the Americans and Dutch, the latter as the colonial power holding the Netherlands East Indies.

Although the appreciation judged that the attitude and capability of the United States would be a constraining factor on Japan, it did not itself include any specific recommendations for improving co-operation with the Americans.[81]

A copy of the appreciation was sent to Far East commanders on board the merchant vessel SS *Automedon*. She was intercepted and sunk by the German raider *Atlantis* on 11 November 1940, northwest of Sumatra, and the secret documents she was carrying were captured.[82] The Germans shared the appreciation and other material with the Japanese naval staff. It is suggested this intelligence windfall was influential in persuading the Japanese to strike south against Malaya and the Netherlands East Indies.[83] The appreciation clearly provided a valuable insight into British thinking, and certainly confirmed that Britain would avoid military confrontation unless its own territories were attacked. However, the news that Britain would struggle to provide a fleet was hardly surprising. The air and land reinforcements antici-pated in the appreciation would have looked significant to the Japanese, and they could not know in December 1940 that much of this build-up would be deferred. Overall, set against the other factors the Japanese had to consider in contemplating a move into Southeast Asia – above all the American response, but also the evolving strategic picture through 1941 – it seems unlikely the *Automedon* capture had more than a marginal impact on Japanese decisions.

This August 1940 appreciation is generally portrayed as a reasonably honest assessment of Britain's predicament in the Far East. Inevitably, its bleak conclusions have often been interpreted as the final death of a naval strategy for defending the Far East empire, which by 1939 had lost credibility. Much attention has also focused on flaws in the new air-based strategy, not least the subsequent refusal of the prime minister to authorise the recommended resources.[84] However, although the appreciation acknowledged the changing strategic context for Far East defence, it insisted that defence here remained essentially a naval problem. The 'security of India, Malaya, and Australasia depends on our ability to control the sea communications leading to them' and the 'foundation of our strategy remains basing an adequate fleet in Singapore'. To oppose successfully the maximum fleet the Japanese might send south (ten battleships, seven carriers and supporting forces), the Admiralty now maintained that a fleet comprising nine capital ships (one less than Japan), together with a comparable strength of carriers, cruisers and destroyers, was required. This was a larger force than anticipated during the 1939 Tientsin crisis, and clearly impossible given current commitments in the Atlantic and Mediterranean. The desired capital ship force could only be achieved by withdrawing capital ships from the Mediterranean and Atlantic escort, and reducing the Home Fleet below an acceptable level. Even if this were done, which would give the Italians freedom to raid the Atlantic, there were insufficient cruisers and destroyers to make a Far East fleet viable.[85]

Despite the 'temporary impossibility' of sending an 'adequate' fleet, there would be some naval reinforcement. Once Japan intervened, a task force, broadly similar to Drax's 1939 flying squadron, although this term was not used, would be sent to Ceylon to cover the Indian Ocean, including the vital communications to the Middle East by the Cape route. This required speed, to avoid a superior IJN force, and might be drawn from the new Gibraltar force. This force, now known as Force H, comprised two capital ships and an aircraft carrier. By the autumn, the established contingency plan was to deploy Force H from Gibraltar in the event of war. For most of the period from then until December 1941, Force H comprised the modernised battlecruiser *Renown*, the modern fleet carrier *Ark Royal*, and the modern cruiser *Sheffield*. Force H would be replaced by two 'R'-class battleships or the two *Nelson*s once the first two *King George V*s became available to the Home Fleet in the spring of 1941. This Force H deployment would give 'a measure of security' if the IJN was 'un-enterprising'.[86]

When it considered the appreciation on 8 August, the War Cabinet also agreed to reassure the Dominions that the commitment to redeploy the Eastern Mediterranean Fleet to meet a direct and immediate threat to the Dominions stood.[87] This reassurance may have been decisive in persuading Australia to deploy troops to Malaya.[88] This promise, which Churchill would regularly reaffirm over the next two years, was politically expedient. Nevertheless, for Churchill, it not only reflected the emotional pull of 'kith and kin', but also ultimate priorities. The strategic decisions of early 1942, to put reinforcement of the Eastern Fleet above the needs of the Mediterranean, when the risks to both Indian Ocean and Mediterranean were at their height, show that *in extremis* the promise was indeed kept.[89] However, Churchill also always felt it was up to him and not the Australians to judge when the promise should take effect and with what level of force. This inevitably rankled in Australia.[90]

This assurance to the Dominions must be weighed against the reality of Royal Navy strength and distribution across the sixteen months from August 1940 to the outbreak of the Far East war in December 1941. During this period the Eastern Mediterranean Fleet always had at least three *Queen Elizabeth*-class battleships (with two modernised) and, until late May 1941, at least one modern fleet carrier. The movement of both Force H and the Eastern Mediterranean Fleet to the Indian Ocean would therefore generate a maximum force against Japan of four capital ships (with three modernised) and, for most of the period, two modern fleet carriers. This was broadly the level of force Backhouse had judged adequate to secure the Indian Ocean during the debates of early 1939. In the Atlantic, for the rest of 1940 the Home Fleet countered the reduced German threat with two fast battlecruisers, two *Nelson*s as heavy support and a fleet carrier. This left an expected five battleships (usually four 'R' class and one unmodernised *Queen Elizabeth*) and one fleet carrier available for Atlantic convoy escort against German surface raiders and as a general reserve. About half available Royal Navy strength in modern cruisers and fleet destroyers, over this period, was divided, in broadly equal numbers, between the Home and East Mediterranean fleets. The other half was deployed on trade protection, primarily in the Atlantic. The distribution of major units here was close to that in the European appreciation of early 1939. Maintaining this deployment between Atlantic and Mediterranean was tight, as war losses and damage took effect, but three new battleships, one rebuilt battleship, and four fleet carriers were commissioned during the period. This allowed sufficient resilience to cope with the evolving naval threat from Germany and Italy and, by mid-1941, a growing margin from which to find a defensive force for the Indian Ocean if and when it proved necessary.

Furthermore, despite the limits to British naval power set out in the new Far East appreciation, the established Far East war plans remained extant in the background. Indeed, as Chapter 4 shows, within six months they were being brushed off and updated, even if actual execution remained a remote contingency.[91]

At one level, therefore, the appreciation was a reiteration and a logical extension of Chamberlain's March 1939 commitment, rather than a fundamental break with the past.[92] Substantial naval forces would still be deployed to meet a critical threat to the eastern empire 'inner core'. The trade-offs between the eastern Mediterranean and the Far East, and the 'Cunningham factors' underpinning them, rehearsed at such length in 1939, still applied. However, the stakes in withdrawal from the Mediterranean were now rather higher. The concept of minimum and maximum reinforcement also continued. However, for a 'maximum' effort, now the Admiralty appeared again to want a fully competitive fleet. If the requirement was to prevent a Japanese expedition reaching Malaya in current circumstances, that was a reasonable aspiration (if out of reach in resource terms). It was not necessary for the more limited objective of holding the Indian Ocean and protecting

Australasia. Meanwhile, the idea that Singapore might need to depend on land and air power for an extended period was hardly new, as Chapter 2 has demonstrated. The 'period before relief' was now effectively open-ended, but even Chatfield had raised the possibility of it lasting up to a year in 1937.

This insistence in the appreciation that 'the foundation of our strategy' remains 'the basing of a fleet on Singapore' encouraged the belief that, while aspects of the Japanese threat had altered, the traditional 'ends, ways and means' to counter it remained valid. In reality, the Far East defence problem had altered fundamentally and required a complete rethink. Without this, Britain faced strategic failure. There were three challenges here.

First, the increasing likelihood that Japan could attack Malaya overland from Thailand, exploiting the improvements made to land communications in western Malaya in the late 1930s.[93] The appreciation acknowledged that a fleet could only 'partially' guard against this, but even that was optimistic.

Secondly, modern air power meant the Singapore base could potentially be rendered unusable, and naval operations gravely hampered, if the Japanese acquired airbases anywhere within 300 miles of Singapore. This figure reflects contemporary estimates of the German air threat to Alexandria from bases in eastern Libya and western Egypt.[94] These are an excellent guide to assessing the Japanese air threat, because the scale of attack anticipated against Alexandria, 200 long-range bombers, 200 dive-bombers, and 250 fighters, was very close to that projected for Singapore by the Joint Intelligence Committee at this time, and indeed deployed by the Japanese in December 1941. There was little practical difference between German and Japanese capability against this type of target. It was judged that for an enemy force of this size to achieve serious effect against the fleet in Alexandria, through sustained daylight bombing against a fighter defence of three squadrons, it would be necessary to reduce the attack range to 300 miles or less, both to generate adequate sorties and allow fighter escort. Below 300 miles, the threat might be too great to allow the fleet to remain. The implication was, therefore, that Britain must now defend all of Malaya.

The third challenge was protecting the Netherlands East Indies, which offered an attacker both airbases and multiple launching points for a land attack on Malaya. The security of Singapore thus depended on at least the adjacent areas of this territory, notably Sumatra, remaining in friendly hands. However, the Netherlands East Indies, easily accessible and poorly defended, were now highly vulnerable to a Japanese attack at their chosen place and moment, which a Royal Navy fleet would have difficulty contesting. The traditional scenario as put by Churchill to the Australians in November 1939 no longer applied, where a Royal Navy fleet arrived to sever the communications of a Japanese expeditionary force projected at long range to besiege Singapore Island itself.[95] Nor was it sufficient to deploy air power, which could temporarily substitute for a fleet in this standard scenario. In practice, the effective defence of Singapore now required Britain or its allies to hold the land, sea and air space within a radius of 300 miles of Singapore, and to be able to contest a significant area beyond that.

The appreciation implicitly recognised this by stating that, in the event of war, Malaya, Burma and the Netherlands East Indies must all now be defended to protect Britain's position in the East. Malaya must be held to deny Japan airbases for close attack on Singapore, but also because the food supplies necessary for Singapore to withstand a long siege were in the north. Burma was important to the defence of Singapore because it was a crucial staging point for air reinforcements. Japanese bases in the Netherlands East Indies would 'directly threaten our vital interests', endangering sea and air communications and Singapore. While the appreciation did not distinguish between different parts of the Netherlands East Indies, the most vital territory for the defence of Singapore was clearly Sumatra and, to a lesser extent, Java. Over the next year this ambitious aspiration for theatre defence would translate into a more defined military objective of holding a defensive line from Lashio in eastern Burma, significant because it was the starting point of the Burma Road into China, and then a crescent just north of the Malay Barrier to Tonga, east of Fiji.[96]

This was a huge additional commitment beyond Chamberlain's March 1939 core. A realistic assessment of the resources required to protect Malaya alone against the anticipated scale of Japanese attack would surely suggest figures analogous to those currently being projected to hold Egypt. And even if Britain provided adequate forces to secure Malaya, it must rely on the Dutch to protect the Netherlands East Indies and deny the Japanese the bases that could compromise the defence of Singapore and provide access to the Indian Ocean and Australasia. The chiefs of staff recognised Britain could do little to support the Dutch, but the Dutch were unlikely to hold off a Japanese attack themselves.[97] This was a conundrum much discussed, but never adequately addressed in the new defence plans. It made sense to develop joint defence measures with the Dutch, and some progress was made through 1941. Britain could never solve the harsh reality that the limited defences of the Netherlands East Indies left Singapore fatally exposed to attack from multiple adjacent locations. Even if reinforced defences of Malaya were strong enough to halt an initial Japanese attack, by occupying key points of the Netherlands East Indies, the Japanese could impose a sea and air blockade and even the strongest Royal Air Force presence would then become a wasting asset.[98] The Joint Planning Committee recognised most of the challenges in defending this wider space in February 1941, when it addressed the consequences of an imminent Japanese attack southward suggested by intelligence and diplomatic reports. This is known as the 'February crisis'. They correctly anticipated how Japan would exploit its access in southern Indochina, Thailand, including the Kra Isthmus, and the Netherlands East Indies the following December, and predicted that Singapore could be bombed from bases in southern Indochina.[99]

In insisting that the Far East defence problem remained essentially naval, the naval staff also demonstrated a surprising rigidity of thinking in the Far East appreciation and subsequent papers. The rigidity lay in believing that if only an 'adequate' battle-fleet could be based at Singapore, this alone could still deter and counter a damaging attack by Japan.[100] But, from August 1940 through to the outbreak of the Far East war, neither the naval staff nor the Royal Navy leadership in theatre addressed the practicalities of contesting the South China Sea with a battle-fleet, despite emerging war experience in the Mediterranean and elsewhere. Any Japanese expeditionary force bound for northern Malaya would now have to be engaged at a considerable distance from Singapore, either off the Indochina coast, or in the Gulf of Siam, or well to the east if heading to targets in the Netherlands East Indies. Here a Royal Navy or US Navy force would now not only face an IJN battle-fleet and substantial carrier fleet, but also land-based air power in Indochina, and possibly in Thailand. Such a force would therefore be at high risk unless it operated under its own defensive air umbrella. However, from the Far East appreciation onward, there is little sign that the naval staff saw 'adequate' air cover as an essential prerequisite for successful operations north or east of Singapore by their 'adequate' fleet. In August 1940 the Royal Navy had yet to experience the full force of the Luftwaffe in the Mediterranean, but already Norway, Dunkirk, and even the Italians at Calabria in July,[101] had demonstrated how vulnerable ships were to air attack when in range of land bases. The rapid German seizure of airbases in Norway and the subsequent operations against the Home Fleet were also an obvious example of what Japan might achieve in southern Indochina.

This continued insistence that Far East defence rested on naval power, the whole panoply of pre-war strategy and planning that underpinned this perception and the persistence of a mindset, at least in this theatre, that 'fleet' and 'battle-fleet' were synonymous, discouraged the fundamental reassessment of the defence problem that was needed. It should have been evident to the chiefs of staff, the wider military leadership, and even the Admiralty that, assuming a battle-fleet could be established at Singapore, this fleet could not alone secure the base, any more than a battle-fleet on its own could protect Alexandria from land and air attack launched from Libya. Nor could it guarantee protection of the much extended critical defence space defined in the Far East appreciation. It could not, therefore, be the 'foundation of our strategy'. If the desired strategic 'end-point' really was to hold Malaya, Burma and the Netherlands East Indies, a mix of naval, air and land components was required, comparable to those the appreciation expected Japan to deploy. If Britain and her allies could not find the necessary resources, then the end-point should be adjusted. In the event, Britain persisted with a strategic end for which ways and means were quite inadequate.

This failure had three important consequences for the Royal Navy's position in the Far East when the Japanese attacked in December 1941. First, it meant that the recommendations for enhanced land and air defence were viewed more as temporary stopgap or holding operation than essential complement, let alone permanent substitute, for the traditional fleet. This perception encouraged London planners and the chiefs of staff both to limit the scale of land and air forces allocated to the Far East, and to accept delay in their build-up. Secondly, it encouraged Britain's war leadership, but especially the Admiralty, to see the US Navy as the primary answer to Far East defence. If the Royal Navy could not provide a 'main fleet to Singapore', then the United States should be persuaded to substitute. This would further enable Britain to keep its land and air investment in the Far East to a minimum. A traditional 1937-style British 'main fleet to Singapore' framework showed little regard for either American needs, or the new strategic context following the Japanese advance into northern Indochina.

Finally, the chiefs of staff and, even more, the prime minister failed to see the negative linkage between a minimalist approach to air reinforcement of Malaya and the prospects of achieving the desired US Navy deployment. From September 1940 onward, the chiefs and prime minister used the hope of American intervention as a justification for going slow on air reinforcement. Not surprisingly, the United States saw this as, at best, a lack of seriousness, and at worst a plot to trap them in a British war.[102] Ironically, going slow on air reinforcement also meant that when the United States did make a serious commitment to the theatre in the final months of 1941, but through air rather than naval power, the British air contribution remained too weak and ineffective for the combined Allied air strength to persuade Japan to pull back.

The unrealistic expectations of American support meant Royal Air Force strength in Malaya in December 1941 was weaker than it might otherwise have been. This had serious implications for the Royal Navy. It rendered the Admiralty plans for a new Eastern Fleet, which emerged in the autumn of 1941, deeply flawed, and meant there was scant prospect of adequate air cover for Force Z. The truth was that by late 1940, air power and naval power were interdependent and complementary. It was an illusion to think one could substitute for the other. As Chapter 4 shows, Britain's unwillingness either to make a serious contribution to defence of the Malay Barrier, or bring flexibility to how it could best be achieved, compromised efforts to achieve a practical joint American-British-Dutch defence plan. As a result, when it did become possible to provide significant Royal Navy reinforcements for the Far East in autumn 1941, Admiralty planners defaulted to a variant of their Far East war plan that might have made some sense against a 1937-type IJN threat, but was quite inappropriate for the current circumstances.

The Far East appreciation stated that until a fleet again became available, defence of Britain's interests must depend primarily on air power. The failure to implement the appreciation's recommended air strengths is viewed as both a prime cause of overall British defeat and a contribution to the loss of Force Z.[103] The 180 frontline aircraft (with many obsolete) on 7 December 1941[104] are compared to the 336 modern aircraft originally promised in the appreciation. This headline deficit is misleading. A substantial part of the 336 planned comprised reconnaissance aircraft, and it included an allocation to cover the Indian Ocean and Borneo, as well as Malaya. The recommended fighter and bomber strength for Malaya was sixty-four and ninety-six respectively (the latter including thirty-two torpedo bombers). This proposed fighter/bomber force was supposed to counter a Japanese combined fighter/bomber scale of attack on Malaya of about six hundred,[105] a Japanese advantage of nearly 4:1, as well as interdict any invasion fleet at sea and, hopefully, significantly degrade a Japanese landing.[106] These odds were daunting, even assuming the Royal Air Force enjoyed a quality edge in aircraft,[107] organisation, training and experience.[108] In the event, the British fighter/bomber total when the Japanese attacked in December 1941 was not far below the recommended 160 and, in the case of fighters, there were substantial reserves.[109] The subsequent disastrous Royal Air Force performance partly reflected poor deployment and training, limited operational experience, and an element of obsolete aircraft within the total. It also suggested that the problem was not only the slow pace of reinforcement during 1941, but that the original target strength was completely inadequate.

In reaching their recommended Far East strength, the starting point for the Joint Planning Committee was the anticipated scale of Japanese attack and an assumed Royal Air Force quality advantage. They also took account of the 346 aircraft the Dutch were expected to have in the Netherlands East Indies by late 1941. A further factor was what could reasonably be allocated from overall British production. Here the chiefs of staff Future Strategy paper is a valuable guide to the overall air production and deployment priorities in August 1940. Its proposed strength for Malaya represented 10 per cent of projected 1942 overseas fighter strength and 16 per cent of 1942 overseas bomber strength. The planning staff no doubt judged this an achievable target and a reasonable maximum for a theatre where hostilities were not yet underway. The projected 1942 strengths assumed 160 fighters and eighty light bombers obtained from Britain's overseas aircraft orders, many of which would indeed go to Malaya. However, these Future Strategy projections seriously underestimated wastage in protracted combat, of which there was only limited experience in mid-1940.[110]

The Far East appreciation was therefore an odd mixture. It demonstrated good understanding of potential Japanese objectives,[111] and how Japan might achieve them. It also showed reasonable awareness of the changed strategic environment and its implications. There was inexorable logic behind its conclusion that Japan's growing ability to deploy land and air power much closer to Singapore meant that defence now required more strategic depth. However, the underlying strategy was regressive rather than progressive. Instead of adopting the more flexible defensive thinking of 1939, focused on the security of the Indian Ocean and inner core of the eastern empire, it effectively committed Britain to controlling a vast area north and east of the Malay Barrier, which it argued was still best achieved through deployment of a traditional battle-fleet. Underlying the appreciation was a circular argument. Singapore had been created to project a battle-fleet to coerce Japan but it now required a battle-fleet to protect the base itself so that it could maintain a battle-fleet. In reality, as events would show, the eastern empire did depend on the security of the Indian Ocean, but this did not require Singapore, and nor was a battle-fleet the sole arbiter of maritime control, as Mediterranean experience was demonstrating. Deploying a fleet to Singapore was still a reasonable way to secure the strategic end of protecting the inner core of the empire in the context of the late 1930s, but protecting the base had now become the end itself.

The argument that Britain's Far East strategy failed in 1941 because it could no longer deploy a fleet and refused to address the consequences is wrong. Britain could, if needed, still find a fleet sufficient to meet the limited 1939 objective of securing the Indian Ocean, even in the dire situation of late 1940. It would certainly demonstrate it could do so in early 1942. The Royal Navy failure in late 1941 was not inability to provide an adequate fleet, but not recognising the limitations of a fleet in the new strategic circumstances and insistence, nevertheless, on deploying an inappropriate force against unrealistic strategic goals.

Two questions now arise. The first is why, during the debates around the Far East appreciation, and later, as it became clear that reinforcements for Malaya would remain well below agreed requirements, the role of Singapore as 'keystone' of eastern empire defence was never challenged by the chiefs of staff. The Americans did not believe Singapore could be defended with the resources the British were prepared to commit.[112] American planners also saw the base as expendable believing (correctly, as it turned out) that British imperial communications could be adequately secured without it.[113] Certainly, it was the only base in the eastern hemisphere with all the facilities required for long-term support of a fleet, and it had the only dock east of Durban capable of taking capital ships or carriers.[114] However, Malta represented in almost all respects an equivalent strategic asset, which the Royal Navy had judged too vulnerable to use as a fleet base in wartime, and possibly also indefensible. There were alternative potential bases that could support naval cover for Australasia and the Indian Ocean, notably Colombo and Trincomalee in Ceylon, and Darwin or Perth in Australia. Again, the Mediterranean offered a precedent. If Alexandria was an effective operational base for the eastern Mediterranean, then Ceylon could surely fulfil the same role for the Indian Ocean. The level of military investment in Egypt and the eastern Mediterranean already underway in the autumn of 1940 also demonstrated the potential commitment required to keep Singapore viable.

There are perhaps several reasons the Mediterranean parallels did not trigger a rethink, at least at this time. There was the long history behind the 'main fleet to Singapore' idea, and the vast amount of political, military, economic and emotional capital Singapore therefore represented.[115] The Far East appreciation showed that the idea of naval power as the 'foundation' of Far East defence and its dependence on Singapore persisted, and was inextricably linked in a way not entirely logical. The British representative at the ABC-1 Anglo-American staff talks in early 1941, Rear Admiral Roger Bellairs, emphasised this point when he told the Americans that the importance of Singapore went beyond the strictly military:

> The maintenance of a fleet base at Singapore is a cardinal point in British strategy. The conception is based not only on purely strategic but political, economic, and sentimental considerations, which even if not vital on a strictly academic view, are of such fundamental importance to the Empire that they must be taken into account. We are a maritime power, various Dominions and Colonies held together by trade routes across oceans. The home population is dependent on imported food and overseas trade. The security and population of India is our trust and responsibility. Defence of all their interests is vital to our war effort and depends on the capacity to hold Singapore and in the last resort to base a battle-fleet there.[116]

Governments find it difficult to overturn long-established policy, and to admit that the investment in the base and its defences of perhaps £10 million since 1935 was effectively wasted would be even harder.[117] Personalities were important too. Pound and Phillips, now driving the Admiralty, had largely created the Singapore strategy.[118] As discussed in Chapter 2, symbolism played a role not least in underpinning the 'fleet in being' concept.[119] The Far East appreciation also embedded the idea that, so long as Singapore held out, Britain had a foothold from which it could eventually recover its position in the Far East, a variant of Chatfield's argument in 1937.[120] Finally, in August 1940 there were still compelling arguments of 'time and distance'. Even with their new base at Hainan, the Japanese were still over 1000 miles from northern Malaya. They were not yet in southern Indochina and an air threat from there would take time to develop. Britain, therefore, had time in which to improve its defences and, above all, fashion a deterrent alliance with the Americans and the Dutch to make holding Singapore and the Malay Barrier a more credible proposition.

The second question is whether, if Singapore had to be held, it could be done with a smaller security perimeter around it. More effective and economical options for providing adequate defensive depth in Malaya have been suggested over the years rather than the plans actually implemented in 1941.[121] It was clearly not necessary to hold all of the Netherlands East Indies to cover Singapore. Holding Sumatra and its offshore islands might be sufficient. Given the very limited British forces available, deploying bomber squadrons to Borneo, as the Far East appreciation suggested, made little sense. An agreement to support the Dutch in holding Sumatra might have enabled preparatory investment in air and sea reinforcement routes, and permitted joint concentration on a more limited, but more effective, defence perimeter. Major General Ian Playfair, chief of staff to the American-British-Dutch-Australian (ABDA) joint Far East Command formed after the Japanese attack, argued that Malaya fell when France fell. It was impossible to build up its defences to meet the changed scale of Japanese attack resulting from their access to airfields in Indochina. Had it been politically possible, the right tactical answer to the threat from Indochina was to incorporate Malaya and Sumatra into a fully integrated defensive zone under a single command. This zone could then exploit 'defence in depth', basing aircraft in Sumatra out of Japanese reach, and then deploying them temporarily to forward airbases in Malaya. He emphasised the importance of submarines, mining and light naval forces in securing this zone. Playfair's views deserve attention, not just because of his ABDA role, but because he was Director of Military Plans and the army representative on the Joint Planning Committee through much of 1940/41.[122] However, as discussed in the next chapter, Dutch political support for such a joint scheme would have been unlikely until well into 1941.

While the Far East appreciation had critical weaknesses if assessed as a long-term strategy, it should not be judged too harshly. Given the overall problems facing Britain in August 1940, the uncertainties over whether and how Japan might intervene in the war, and the reasonable possibility of significant

American support in the Far East, its immediate recommendations were sensible enough. Provision of the proposed reinforcements did not irrevocably commit Britain to a particular defence strategy. They were needed in the theatre under any likely scenario. They could provide a necessary core on which to construct a more credible Allied defence of the Malay Barrier and to reinforce this when war broke out. But if the concept of holding Singapore were ever abandoned, they were equally necessary to support defence of the Indian Ocean.

In the event, the Far East appreciation proposals for reinforcement met immediate resistance from the prime minister. In a minute to Ismay on 10 September, and subsequent comments to the chiefs of staff, Churchill challenged much of the appreciation's case.[123] Using arguments almost identical to those he used in November 1939, he insisted the threat to Singapore over long, exposed lines of communication from Japan was overstated, and that its prime defence remained a fleet whose protection applied whether on the spot or at a distance. The recently reinforced Mediterranean fleet could easily be redeployed east if required. He still saw Singapore as a 'fortress' which could hold out until relieved, ignoring the hard geographical realities imposed by the Netherlands East Indies problem. He rejected the idea of trying to hold all of Malaya, 'a country as large as England', with current resources, and dismissed the Japanese air threat to Singapore itself. The chiefs tried to educate the prime minister ten days later, but their arguments were not compelling, and had little effect.[124] Churchill accepted it was not feasible to send a fleet for the present, but the Japanese 'would never be certain what we might do'. The concept of deterrence remained valid. The presence of a substantial US Navy fleet on their flank would encourage the Japanese to be cautious. Meanwhile, the Middle East must have priority for overseas resources. Churchill's assessment was accurate as regards the attitude of the IJN at this time. The Japanese army was more inclined to take risks in pursuing an expansionist policy to the south, but there was still a broad consensus that war with the United States would be unwise.[125]

The chiefs of staff were correct in emphasising that Singapore would only be viable as a base if the Japanese were kept at a distance. The prime minister was right to question whether it was credible to find forces to hold Malaya, given the demands of the Middle East. The chiefs failed to confront the prime minister with the Netherlands East Indies problem, and they did not explain the new limitations on what a fleet alone could achieve. Nor did they argue that operation of a fleet depended on establishing adequate air support in the theatre. The distance of the nearest Japanese bases gave the discussions a hypothetical quality, but the chiefs had acquiesced in arguments raised by the prime minister which they should have challenged, and had begun a pattern of deferring awkward problems.

Meanwhile, the prime minister's attitude would remain remarkably consistent for the next fifteen months. Entrenched scepticism that the Japanese would mount a long-range attack against Singapore, and an erroneous belief that Singapore was a Verdun-type fortress, played a part here. More important was his view that, with the notable exception of Australasia and India, nothing in the Far East matched the importance of the Middle East, and that the United States would act as a brake on Japanese ambition. These factors made him willing to carry risk in the Far East, but successive personal interventions across 1941 also demonstrate that he never accepted the concept of Singapore as a 'keystone' of empire defence ranking alongside the United Kingdom. The view that if he had better understood the vulnerability of Singapore, he would have sanctioned more resources is wrong. He would always have accepted the loss of Singapore rather than compromise on support for the Middle East or Russia.[126]

The proposed reinforcements were revisited four months later when the joint planning staff reviewed the recommendations of Far East commanders. Their assessment, which took the Far East appreciation as a baseline, comprised a 'tactical appreciation', and the conclusions of a defence conference held at Singapore in October.[127] These reviews were comprehensive and, with the benefit of hindsight, impressive. The assessments of Japanese intent, likely operational execution and scale of forces were both prescient and realistic. Neither the estimates for Japanese frontline air strength nor the intelligence available had changed much between the August appreciation and the November commanders' assessment, but the commanders' dispositions were more realistic. Inevitably, given the gap already evident in the appreciation between potential Japanese strength and resources currently allocated to defence of Malaya, the commanders argued for significant additions to the reinforcements proposed in August if the military objectives of the chiefs of staff were to be met. The most obvious increase was to raise air strength to a total of 580 frontline aircraft, including 144 fighters (up more than 100 per cent)[128] and a strike force of 192 (up 100 per cent[129]) actually based in Malaya. At the time this assessment was prepared, the only modern aircraft in Malaya were a combined total of forty-eight Blenheim I and Hudson bombers with just thirteen in reserve. There were still no fighters.[130]

The commanders' recommended force levels assumed the Japanese had acquired bases in Indochina and southern Thailand (as indeed they would do between July and November 1941), but had not established themselves in the Netherlands East Indies and would not do so during an attack on Malaya. They questioned whether the Netherlands East Indies assumption was valid. If it proved incorrect (as proved the case in December 1941[131]), the scale of air attack on Malaya would significantly increase, landings would become possible on the west coast, and Singapore risked blockade. To deal with this, their proposed scale of forces would need to increase further. These assumptions largely explain the force additions to those in the August appreciation. They also reflected the commanders' recognition that providing replacement aircraft from the United Kingdom or Middle East in the face of a Japanese attack might prove difficult, and initial numbers and reserves must reflect this.[132] Here, it is not clear how far they considered the vulnerability of the air route from Burma to rapid Japanese interdiction.

The chiefs of staff broadly accepted the joint planning staff view that the commanders had 'overstressed' the inadequacies of the proposed August reinforcement programmes, and that the original force levels should stand, apart from small enhancements to land forces.[133] The planning staff rejected any increase in air strength beyond the August target of 336. They noted the Japanese had never fought a first-class power and doubted they were more effective than the Italians. This is one of the first occasions the analogue of the Italians was used as a measure of Japanese effectiveness in strategic papers. In so far as this related to air fighting capability, and certainly capability at sea, it was misleading. Cunningham, as Commander-in-Chief Mediterranean, described Italian high-level bombing of the Mediterranean Fleet at Calabria in 1940 as 'most frightening' and was 'seriously alarmed' for his older ships.[134] The planning staff must have known this, but insisted recent British performance in North Africa and the Battle of Britain showed that superior numbers could be countered by mobility and power of concentration. Much of the planning staff treatment here was superficial or erroneous, and the careful arguments of the local commanders were countered with flat assertion.

Nor did the planning staff view reflect poor intelligence, which at Joint Intelligence Committee level remained an accurate guide. The Joint Intelligence Committee provided an update on the threat to Malaya which was available to the chiefs of staff when they considered the planning staff review. The committee confirmed that Japan could deploy ten divisions at short notice, though shipping might only be available for four. These would be supported by 336–432 land-based aircraft from southern Thailand and a further 290 carrier-based. Naval forces could include the entire IJN battle-fleet of ten capital ships and seven carriers.[135] When the Director of Military Intelligence (DMI) reviewed this assessment in the wake of the Japanese attack exactly a year later, he noted that the predicted naval and army scale of attack 'was excessive', while the air scale was 'remarkably accurate'.[136]

There is no evidence the prime minister exerted influence before the chiefs endorsed the planning staff recommendation, but both knew how reluctant the prime minister had been to sanction investment in the Far East the previous September. The prime minister had not changed his view. When he saw the chiefs of staff papers on the commanders' assessment he reiterated his opposition to any significant 'diversion' of forces to the Far East. The planners felt obliged to confirm that not only was 336 a ceiling, but it was a target to be reached only by the end of 1941, if then.[137]

Reviewing the case made by the local commanders, and the intelligence available, it is hard to see how the planning staff felt their original scale of defence could cope. However, the planners and chiefs of staff could argue that the threat had not fundamentally changed, and that commanders always ask for more resources than they need. The known poor relationship between the army and air commanders in Singapore also made it easier to criticise their recommendations.[138] More important was the fact that the Japanese were not yet in southern Indochina, let alone Thailand, suggesting there was time to build up reinforcements. Nevertheless, the planners had also recently suggested to the vice chiefs that the minimum guaranteed warning time of an attack on Singapore (then five days) should be reduced. This reflected the inability of the Secret Intelligence Service (SIS) to provide any 'war warning', and the possibility the Japanese might now mount an invasion from Camranh Bay, just three days' steaming from northern Malaya. Warning would then be completely dependent on air reconnaissance.[139]

The planners could also argue that, despite the relentless resource pressures Britain faced at this time, the reinforcements earmarked for Malaya over the next six months were not only significant compared to the present baseline, but comparable to what was currently reaching the Middle East where there was an active war underway: 170 Brewster Buffalo fighters were on order from the United States, to be delivered between January and July, with three squadrons to form by mid-year and the possibility of a further two by end 1941. Twenty-four American Glenn Martin Baltimore bombers were expected by July, with eight per month thereafter. The first of two Beaufort torpedo squadrons, drawing on aircraft built in Australia, was to form by June, with fifty aircraft available by the end of the year.[140] The Baltimores and Beauforts were state-of-the-art strike aircraft. By contrast, it is customary to dismiss the Buffalo as obsolescent and useless. It was certainly no Spitfire, but with the right servicing support and good pilots it was capable of performance close to a Hurricane, and was therefore an adequate counter to current Japanese bombers.[141]

To ease the shipping burden, the American aircraft were to be shipped direct from the United States. Had these deliveries from the United States and Australia proceeded to schedule, there would have been seven strike squadrons of modern aircraft in Malaya by December, together with substantial reserves, although not all would have been fully operational. With 112 frontline aircraft, this total would have been very close to the Far East appreciation target strike force of 128 including the Borneo element. Meanwhile, at the beginning of 1941 there were still only three Hurricane squadrons in the Middle East and only eighty-seven aircraft had arrived there since the beginning of September, although the bomber position here was better with a first-line strength of fifteen squadrons.[142] Attrition over the next four months, including the losses in Greece, would mean force levels had not improved here by the end of April.[143]

In the event, there were severe production delays in both the United States and Australia which badly disrupted the reinforcement schedule for Malaya. The Baltimores never arrived and had to be covered by less capable Hudsons, whose primary role was reconnaissance. Only six Beauforts were delivered by December, and none were operational. The five planned Buffalo squadrons were in place by then, but only two were properly worked up.[144] Making due allowance for these delays, which were not easily foreseeable in January, the decision to retain the 336 target would be more defensible if there had been a definite date for completion of the programme. The Far East appreciation had originally set a target date of 'end 1941'. This date had now been made conditional on available resources and commitments elsewhere. Above all, there should have been more awareness that what was required was investment in overall capability: experienced pilots and maintenance personnel, radar and command and control, as well as up-to-date aircraft. The Royal Air Force could have defeated a substantially larger Japanese air force with a system which linked these capability elements together, as in the United Kingdom.[145]

At the beginning of 1941, therefore, Britain had accurately assessed the risks posed by Japan. It had devised a holding strategy to limit those risks and protect its vital interests, pending an improvement in its overall strategic position and the benefits of growing war production. The strategy relied on holding Singapore to give credence to the deterrent value of a fleet in being, using enhanced air power to keep the Japanese at an acceptable distance from Singapore and drawing the United States into an alliance, along with the Dutch, all to dissuade Japan from southern adventures. But there were three fundamental flaws in this strategy. First, if the United States was unwilling or unable to provide a credible military deterrent against Japan, the resources Britain was notionally willing to provide by end 1941, even in concert with the Dutch, were quite inadequate to meet the desired goal of holding the Netherlands East Indies and Malaya, or even a lesser goal of Malaya, Sumatra and Java. Secondly, Britain's increasing commitment to the Mediterranean and Middle East, designed to meet the opportunities and risks posed by that theatre, would further reduce resources for the Far East. Thirdly, the prime minister did not believe in important elements of the strategy. This was also likely to compromise the build-up of adequate air power, leaving Malaya wide open to attack in the north, and making any naval operation north of Singapore a high-risk enterprise. In the new circumstances, a fleet unable to operate north of Singapore could not guarantee its protection.

There was a further problem. Japan's primary goal in Southeast Asia at this time was to ensure strategic resources, above all oil. It still hoped to achieve this peacefully and avoid military confrontation with either the United States or Britain. Through 1940 neither the Japanese army nor the IJN were prepared for a war with either power. The situation in China was unsatisfactory, and Russia was an anxiety. Without stability in the north, invasion in the south was risky.[146] By the spring of 1941, the IJN general staff had still only completed a rough study of potential war strategy against the United States or Britain on a total war scale. The only planning against Britain had focused on Hong Kong. There was still no expectation of all-out war against either the United States or Britain in the near future.[147] So the British were correct in seeing the attitude of the United States and Russia, and the military position in China, as factors that imposed a brake on Japanese ambition.

However, Japan also viewed military co-operation between Britain and the United States as a direct threat to her national security, especially if it threatened her oil. Until spring 1941 there were differing views on the likelihood of such co-operation. There was even a view in the army general staff that an attack on the Netherlands East Indies to secure its oil would not provoke British intervention. However, the army and the IJN were agreed that Japan must go to war if the United States cut its oil supply or the US Navy fleet came to Singapore.[148] The more, therefore, that Britain drew the United States into her Far East defence arrangements, the greater the risk of provoking the very attack she feared. This was especially true of the IJN's position in the Japanese internal debates during the winter of 1940/41.[149]

British lobbying to encourage forward deployment of the US Navy Pacific Fleet, preferably at Singapore, but otherwise at Manila, and American rejection of such deployment at the ABC-1 staff talks which ended in March 1941, is described in the next chapter. There is a general consensus that without American willingness to make a clear-cut commitment to contain Japan, Britain's Far East dilemma was not soluble without diverting substantial resources from the Middle East. This applied especially to air power, but also specialist land equipment, notably tanks and artillery.[150] However, American intransigence over forward basing did not end the prospect of constructing a naval deterrent. US Navy intervention in the Atlantic could release sufficient Royal Navy forces to resurrect an eastern fleet, and the US Navy Pacific Fleet could still exert influence on Japan from Pearl Harbor. Throughout 1941, therefore, the desirability of enhancing Far East air and land reinforcements to Far East appreciation standard continued to be qualified by the possibility of reverting to the traditional naval strategy, or at least creating a sufficient British/American naval deterrent to discourage a Japanese move south. Later in the year, the United States would fundamentally alter its position on forward basing, with the commitment to establish a large strategic air force as a regional deterrent in the Philippines. This further encouraged Britain to think it could maintain a minimum reinforcement policy.

The strategic trade-off between Middle East and Far East in 1941

There were two constraints on the supply of military equipment and skilled personnel from the United Kingdom to overseas theatres, which limited the scale and pace of land and air reinforcements for the Far East. These were the need to maintain strength in the United Kingdom homeland against the perceived continuing risk of invasion,[151] and the limitations of shipping which, with occasional exceptions, had to take the Cape route. Successive chiefs of staff assessments through early 1941 show that the threat of United Kingdom invasion was still taken seriously, that force levels here, including air, were judged barely acceptable to counter this risk, and that any supplies sent overseas could not be retrieved in time to meet an attack. This explains why Fighter Command continued to expand through 1941 (seventy-five daytime squadrons in January and ninety-nine by September, compared with fifty-eight in July 1940), and how this limited the transfer of the most advanced aircraft overseas. With the benefit of hindsight, a case can be made that Britain over-insured with forces in the United Kingdom in 1941/42, at the expense of overseas theatres. That is not how it appeared at the time. Even if Britain had been willing to release more forces overseas, the necessary shipping space did not exist.

Given these two constraints, more reinforcement of the Far East, especially in aircraft, could only be achieved at the expense of the Mediterranean/Middle East theatre. The first part of this chapter explained why the loss of the Middle East would threaten the survival of the eastern empire, and perhaps make the defeat of Germany impossible. That was bound to make any diversion from this theatre through 1941 unpalatable. However, the fact that Britain began significant diversions immediately the Japanese attacked in December, and generated substantial resources for the Indian Ocean theatre in the first half of 1942, without apparently damaging its Middle East position, suggests it could have made different choices earlier.[152] Earlier diversion, especially if co-ordinated with American reinforcement in the Far East, might have persuaded Japan to hold back. It might also have reduced the early British losses to Japan. It would certainly have made the strategic position in the Indian Ocean in the spring of 1942 much less dangerous than it became. The remainder of this chapter considers how real the choices really were, how far alternative trade-offs between the two ends of the eastern empire were discussed, and what impact such alternatives would have had if implemented.[153]

It is important to emphasise how vulnerable the British position in the Middle East seemed at the end of April 1941, following German intervention in the

Balkans and North Africa. It was underlined in the Joint Planning Committee assessment prepared for Australian Prime Minister Robert Menzies on 28 April, which reviewed the immediate threats to the Mediterranean and Middle East, and the implications Axis moves here might have on Japan's actions in the Far East.[154] The assessment described a potential two-pronged offensive in the eastern Mediterranean directed at Iraq via Turkey in the north, and against the Suez Canal and Alexandria in the south. It emphasised the current superiority of German air power here and the threat it posed to British naval bases and operations. The planners judged Germany's ultimate goal was to destroy Britain's position in the region and capture Middle East oil supplies. They also anticipated a simultaneous operation through Spain to seize Gibraltar. Essentially, they argued the Germans would now attempt to execute the very strategy that they would shortly embrace in Führer Directive 32 and the August German staff appreciation highlighted earlier as their ambition for 1942.

To meet the most immediate threat – to Egypt – there were only four British Army divisions facing six Italian and up to four German. There were only three Royal Air Force fighter squadrons in Egypt, and seven bomber squadrons, though it was hoped to increase these to six and ten by the end of May. The planners assessed it was still possible to hold Egypt and the Levant, but reserves were limited and British reinforcement lines round the Cape were far longer than those of the Axis. The worst-case scenario was therefore a retreat to Sudan and the Persian Gulf, blocking the canal, destroying the oilfields and denying the Axis access to the Indian Ocean. If Japan intervened in current circumstances, the only certain reinforcement was the Indian Ocean task force. Additional naval reinforcements would depend on circumstances, and here the planners listed a variant of the 1939 Cunningham factors.[155]

The suggestion of strategic retreat provoked a sharp intervention from the prime minister in the form of a 'Directive' to the chiefs of staff.[156] This stated categorically that Japan was unlikely to enter the war unless there was a successful invasion of the United Kingdom. Fear of American intervention was a powerful restraint, and Japan would recognise that even defeat for Britain in the Middle East would not help her much, since British forces there could be transferred to the Far East theatre. Loss of the Middle East would, however, be a disaster 'of the first magnitude' for Britain, second only to 'invasion and final conquest'. Every effort was therefore to be made to hold the forward line, and there was no question of strategic withdrawal. No reinforcements were to go to the Far East beyond the modest upgrade in progress.

This 'political' guidance was eminently clear, but the chiefs felt it overstated the importance of Egypt. They initially argued that Britain could survive the loss of the Middle East and continue the war, so long as the United Kingdom homeland, Malaya, the Cape and essential sea routes remained secure. It is striking that they referred here to 'Malaya', not 'Singapore'. This reflected their belief that holding Malaya was now necessary to protect Singapore, but also underlined the point that defending Singapore and Malaya had become an end in itself, rather than a means to an end. Ismay recognised that if this assessment reached the prime minister, it would trigger an 'explosion', given his antipathy to holding all Malaya.[157] He persuaded the chiefs to temper their view and avoid any direct challenge to the prime minister's order of priority. Their revised advice was: 'Life would continue after the loss of the Middle East so long as we do not lose the UK or the Battle of the Atlantic'. Reference to Malaya as a prerequisite of survival was dropped.[158] The Chief of the Imperial General Staff, General Sir John Dill, separately reminded the prime minister that Malaya formally still ranked second in Britain's strategic priorities.[159] The prime minister responded that the United States remained a decisive deterrent to Japan, that an attack on Singapore was unlikely, and less dangerous than a Japanese attack on shipping, that its defence required 'only a fraction of the forces' needed in Egypt, and that he could not agree even the loss of Singapore outweighed the loss of Egypt.[160]

The prime minister's directive, read as a set piece, was stronger on exhortation than logic. However, he set out the underlying rationale for his commitment to the Middle East in a parallel letter to President Roosevelt, who had also suggested strategic withdrawal.[161] Here, Churchill stressed the influence that holding a forward Middle East position had on Spain, Vichy, Turkey and Japan. Loss of the Middle East would trigger a cascade of wider losses, which would threaten the security of Atlantic and Pacific communications, and make a war in which the United States and the British Empire were ranged against the Axis a 'hard, long and bleak proposition'. Speaking privately afterwards, he noted that the issue was not 'whether we shall win or lose', but whether the war is 'long or short'. 'With Hitler in control of Ukrainian wheat and Iraq oil', British staunchness would not 'shorten the ordeal'.[162] Churchill's picture here of the stakes in the Mediterranean and Middle East, and not least the Atlantic connection, shows an uncanny similarity to the view the German general staff would take in August, and reveals a depth of strategic insight apparently beyond the present chiefs of staff.

Given the stakes as Churchill saw them, the Joint Planning Committee assessment underlined how limited the immediate air strength in Egypt was to deal with the most pressing Axis threat. Not only was the anticipated British strength by end May a bare minimum defensive force but, as the prime minister was well aware, it compared favourably with aircraft already in Malaya, and anticipated in the next few months from American sources. Aircraft supply for Malaya had been discussed at the Defence Committee meeting of 9 April, just three weeks previously. It had then been agreed that supply direct from the

United States was the best means of meeting Malaya's needs, and it did not make sense to add Hurricanes from the United Kingdom. The prime minister could reasonably expect at this time that Malaya would have sufficient Buffaloes for five fighter squadrons, and sufficient Baltimores and Beauforts for four new bomber squadrons, by late summer.[163] His refusal to countenance any diversion to Malaya is therefore understandable. And given the imminent risks to Crete, and in Syria and Iraq, it is equally understandable that he pressed for maximum additional air reinforcement to the Middle East.

On 15 May the Chief of Air Staff, Air Chief Marshal Sir Charles Portal, responded therefore with plans for an approximate doubling of frontline strength in the Middle East/Mediterranean theatre by mid-July, although this was still only 80 per cent of the anticipated German fighting strength in the Mediterranean. Frontline strength would rise to 40.5 squadrons and 692 aircraft. Portal's total included seventeen squadrons of Hurricane fighters and seven of the American equivalent P40 Tomahawks; 862 aircraft were to be shipped between 1 May and 15 July, with 300 aircraft per month thereafter to meet wastage.[164] This strength was broadly achieved on schedule, but by early July, the need to improve defences in the Levant, Iraq and Iran had raised the target by a further 50 per cent to 62.5 squadrons. Ismay informed the prime minister at the beginning of July that fighter deliveries to the Middle East were exceeding those planned, with 402 delivered in May/June against a target of 341. This was just under half the combined monthly production for Hurricane II, Spitfire II and Spitfire V of 420 in those two months. Meeting the bomber target, meanwhile, involved significant penalties to Bomber Command.[165] Overall, there would be forty-eight squadrons in the Middle East by late August, including twenty-three fighter and seventeen bomber squadrons. By that time, the long-term target strength had risen dramatically to a total of ninety squadrons planned in the theatre by spring 1942.[166] These figures demonstrate that the need to match the German threat in an active war theatre meant diversion to the Far East was not feasible before mid-July, nor did the direct deliveries to the Far East planned from the United States appear to make it necessary. After July, there was, in theory, sufficient strength to make diversion possible. This coincided with the Japanese move into southern Indochina, and awareness of growing delays to deliveries from the United States and Australia. However, there were also now new arguments against diversion.

It is clear from the various papers circulating at the beginning of May that the chiefs of staff believed the defence of Malaya was ultimately more important than Britain's position in the Middle East.[167] It is equally clear from the prime minister's exchanges with Dill that he did not agree with this order of priority. Nor did Ismay, who stated after the war:

If you will read the minute Dill sent to Winston in May 1941, you will see what I regard as the most extraordinary document that has ever seen the light of day. Put yourself in the PM's place and ask yourself whether you would have much confidence in the strategic advice of a man who put his signature to that document.

Ismay believed this exchange was decisive in convincing Churchill that Dill had to be replaced as Chief of the Imperial General Staff.[168]

The chiefs' belief that Malaya should rank above the Middle East was nevertheless further underlined during the preparation of two major strategic assessments in May and June. These were a Mediterranean and Middle East appreciation[169] and a wider review of Future Strategy.[170] These explain how the chiefs viewed the comparative claims of the Middle and Far East during the second quarter of 1941, before the German attack on Russia and Japan's move into southern Indochina substantially altered the strategic picture. The first draft of the Middle East appreciation not only insisted that the security of Singapore[171] ranked immediately after the United Kingdom homeland, reflecting Dill's earlier arguments to the prime minister, but went further, claiming that 'the loss of Singapore would vitally affect Britain's ability to continue the war', whereas the loss of the Middle East, while a disaster of the first magnitude, was not vital in the same way. It justified this priority for the Far East by emphasising that the loss of Singapore would cut sea communications with Australasia, threaten control of the wider Indian Ocean, put the stability of India at risk, and impose economic losses for both Britain and the United States in oil, tin and rubber.

The draft also drew on a recent Joint Intelligence Committee assessment[172] to argue that although war had not yet broken out in the Far East, Japan's ambitions were clear and Britain's difficulties in the Middle East could encourage an early strike. The actual scale of attack the Japanese could bring to bear reflected earlier assessments, but was more detailed. The assessment confirmed that eight divisions could be made available at short notice, with adequate ship lift for six at one time, and the Japanese had considerable experience of combined operations. The air threat had risen slightly to a maximum of 450 land-based aircraft and 340 carrier-borne, although the limitations to airfields in Indochina and Thailand would reduce the scale of air attack that could be generated at one time. Air capability was still assessed to be similar to the Italians. Given this threat, land and air forces in Malaya remained far below the minimum necessary for security, and three months were required to ship supplies to Singapore. Resources needed for the Far East were exactly those needed in the Middle East, but quantities required for the Far East were small, and could make all the difference to securing a vital British interest. Equivalent resources in Egypt would have limited impact. As the Joint Planning Committee subsequently stated: 'We should not spoil the ship for a h'ap'orth of tar'.[173]

This emphasis on the Far East was substantially softened in the much abbreviated final version of the Middle East appreciation. Here, Singapore 'remained a vital interest' since it was required to secure sea communications in the Indian Ocean, but a Japanese attack was unlikely and the United States posed a powerful deterrent. 'Menace remained' and some reinforcement was required, but no target was set for this. The appreciation in its final form, sent as a telegram, under the prime minister's signature, opened by stating that invasion of the United Kingdom 'probably remains Germany's 1941 objective' and that, apart from the battle of the Atlantic, the enemy main effort was now directed to the capture of Egypt. The word 'probably' may have indicated the growing signs of an early attack on Russia from Ultra intercepts.[174] The appreciation concluded that it was not possible to be strong everywhere, and risks must be accepted, including in the Far East. This was a radically different view of how the Far East featured in Britain's war from the first draft. The language clearly reflected input from the prime minister.[175] As we will see in the next chapter, Churchill's scepticism over attempts to portray Singapore as a 'keystone' had already been evident during the ABC-1 staff talks with the Americans in February. Here he had castigated the Admiralty negotiating team for using 'extreme arguments', such as Singapore having priority in empire considerations, and told the First Lord and First Sea Lord that, if Singapore were captured, a fleet could be based in Australia to protect it from invasion.[176]

It is extraordinary, therefore, that the Far East section of the Future Strategy paper issued three weeks later on 24 June reverted back to the Middle East appreciation first draft, insisting: 'Singapore is vital to us', 'by its loss we should lose control of sea communications with Australia and New Zealand', and 'it is of the utmost importance to take, as soon as possible, the necessary measures for its defence'.[177] These two expressions of Far East policy were miles apart, and there should surely have been effort to reconcile them.[178] The primary responsibility here lay with the chiefs of staff. The prime minister had given clear political direction on Britain's strategic priorities. If the chiefs did not agree, as they evidently did not, it was up to them, through the Joint Planning Committee, to test the arguments and present an alternative case.

Here the various papers from late April through to late June had raised important questions. First, what was the basis for the chiefs' argument that the defence of Malaya ranked second only to the United Kingdom? That was certainly the position at the 1937 Imperial Conference but that priority had been heavily qualified in 1939. There was no mention of second priority for Malaya in the 1939 European appreciation, nor in the 1940 Far East appreciation, nor in the 1940 Future Strategy paper. In the first major strategic briefing given to the Americans, when a team led by Rear Admiral R Ghormley visited London in August 1940, the chiefs stated that the United Kingdom and Egypt were the 'vital theatres', and gave no indication that the Far East was viewed as second priority.[179] It was pointless to resurrect a pre-war priority in the utterly changed circumstances of 1941. Major General Sir John Kennedy, Director of Military Operations, later claimed from the perspective of December 1941: 'The British Chiefs of Staff, since before the war, had always accorded to the defence of Singapore a higher priority even than the defence of the Middle East; but this had been lost sight of by the British Government during the last year and a half'. This was disingenuous. The chiefs had not formally reaffirmed the priority at any point between spring 1939 and spring 1941, and they certainly had no political endorsement for it.[180] Dill had referred the prime minister to his oft repeated guarantee to the Dominions but, as Dill well knew, that guarantee applied only to a 'direct and immediate threat' to the Dominions themselves, and did not automatically imply overriding priority for Malaya.

Secondly, were the arguments put forward by the Joint Planning Committee, and apparently endorsed by the chiefs, in support of second priority for Malaya valid? Was it really true that 'the loss of Singapore will vitally affect our ability to win the war'? Was it right that the loss of Singapore would cut communication with Australasia?

Thirdly, even if Malaya was to have second priority, what did this mean in practice? What were the defence goals? The chiefs had insisted in the Far East appreciation that all Malaya must be defended to protect Singapore. The prime minister disagreed and the conflict here also ought to be reconciled. The chiefs knew Singapore and Malaya depended on the security of the Netherlands East Indies, but the implications here had never been tackled. The prime minister had told Dill the defence of Singapore required just a 'fraction' of the resources required in the Middle East, and Dill had acquiesced.[181] Logic surely suggested that the whole Malay Barrier could not possibly be defended against the Japanese scale of attack, recently confirmed by the Joint Intelligence Committee, with a 'fraction' of Britain's current Middle East forces. Was Dill merely suggesting the rather arbitrary Far East appreciation reinforcements would be enough?

In assessing the risks in the Far East during 1941, the performance of the Joint Intelligence Committee was broadly excellent. Throughout the year, it achieved a strikingly accurate forecast of Japanese intentions and strategy in Southeast Asia, and the landward attack on Malaya ranks as one of the most widely predicted operations of the Second World War. Headline estimates of Japanese capabilities and scales of attack were also generally accurate. These intelligence assessments were especially impressive, given the complex nature of Japanese decision-taking, and the fact that final decisions on southern operations were only made in the autumn.[182] In judging Japanese intent, the one striking failure was not anticipating that Japan would attack Britain and the United States simultaneously.[183]

At the end of June 1941, the fundamental questions bearing on Britain's priorities in the East were still unresolved. The chiefs of staff supported Middle East reinforcement, but only on condition it posed no risk to the United Kingdom homeland or Malaya. They remained committed to early completion of the Far East appreciation reinforcement package, and it appeared there would be sufficient surplus from the Middle East air build-up by August to cover a looming shortfall in Far East re-equipment owing to delay in American deliveries.

However, over the next six weeks there was a remarkable shift towards the prime minister's position that the Middle East should have overriding priority. The key influence here was the German attack on Russia on 22 June. This created the new risk, in the event of early Russian collapse, of a German drive into the Middle East, either through Turkey or from the north through the Caucasus.[184] But it also offered a window of opportunity to drive the Axis from North Africa before Germany could redeploy forces from Russia.[185] The new northern risk to Britain's position, along with the proposed offensive, which would proceed as Operation Crusader in November, meant the effort to build maximum possible strength in the Middle East, especially in armour and air power, received further momentum. Until October the Middle East commanders tended to overestimate German air strength in North Africa and also feared, with some justification, that additional air forces could be transferred from Russia if fighting died down there during the winter. These factors, and the desire to achieve air superiority for a Libyan offensive, maintained the pressure to maximise air reinforcement to the Middle East and avoid diversion.[186]

By 20 July the Joint Planning Committee, contemplating an imminent Japanese move into southern Indochina, and in a complete reversal of their position a month previously, now argued against diverting additional air resources from the Middle East to Malaya, although they advocated some small enhancements to land forces.[187] There was an obvious irony here. The planners were highlighting the same Indian Ocean risks as they had in May with their 'h'ap'orth of tar' argument for Malaya reinforcement, but now from Germany rather than Japan, and using the risks to bolster the Middle East at the expense of the Far East. This reflected the prime minister's attitude. On 16 July he reiterated to the chiefs of staff his conviction that Japan would not attack Britain in present circumstances but, if she did, the United States would intervene. He accepted the likelihood of an imminent Japanese move into southern Indochina merited further precautions, but only without risk to other theatres.[188]

The seeming relentless priority now being given to the Middle East was criticised by the Americans, who were a key contributor of equipment. They felt the investment was disproportionate to either benefit or risk.[189] Roosevelt's special adviser Harry Hopkins privately revealed that the United States military viewed the British position in the Middle East as 'quite hopeless', and further reinforcement would be akin to 'throwing snowballs into hell'.[190]

This growing criticism caused the chiefs of staff to commission the Joint Planning Committee to produce one of the most important papers of the war.[191] It brought together in a comprehensive form, for the first time since the start of the war, all the various arguments used to justify Britain's investment in the Middle East to date. It identified two critical interests Britain had to defend: access to the Indian Ocean, control of which came close second to the Atlantic in generating the maximum empire war effort; and Iranian oil and the Abadan refinery, which were essential to sustain eastern empire lifelines and production.[192] Their security required defence in depth. Withdrawal to East Africa and the Gulf would not only mean huge economic and material loss, but would tilt Spain and Turkey into the Axis camp, with serious consequences for the Atlantic battle in the case of the former. The paper also defined 'offensive' opportunities: tightening the blockade; knocking out Italy; wearing down German air strength; and joining up with Russia through Iran and the Caucasus.

The one surprise was the emphasis on preventing German and Italian access to the Indian Ocean, as opposed to the strategic space centred on Iraq and Iran. As noted in Chapter 2, the Suez Canal was vital to sustaining the Mediterranean Fleet and, therefore, Britain's whole position in the Middle East. But if the British had been forced out of Egypt, they would have blocked the canal and it would have taken the Axis months, perhaps even a year, to clear it. Even then, under the most optimistic scenario this would only have provided access to the Red Sea, which Britain could easily dominate at its southern end. Although Germany and Italy did discuss joint operations in the Indian Ocean at the Friedrichshafen naval summit in June 1939, neither apparently contemplated serious fleet operations or incursions by heavy units, as opposed to raiding operations by light forces and submarines from Italian bases in East Africa.[193] By mid-1941 all these Italian bases had been lost.

The 'offensive' opportunities identified in the paper deserve further comment. The contribution of the Mediterranean theatre to 'wearing down' Germany, certainly at this stage of the war invariably receives little credence. The tiny German land forces actively engaged in North Africa are inevitably compared with the huge German army commitment in Russia. However, the contribution the Mediterranean theatre made towards engaging and wearing down German air power in 1941/42 was considerable. When the chiefs of staff discussed the paper on 24 July, Portal suggested it would be possible to engage up to 30 per cent of Germany's air strength in the Mediterranean and Middle East theatre.[194] This aspiration proved over-ambitious, but it appears that Germany had about 16.5 per cent of its frontline air strength in the Mediterranean and North Africa by late autumn 1941, rising to an average of at least 20 per cent from spring 1942 through to summer 1943.[195] More significantly, by end December 1941 Germany was deploying more frontline aircraft against Britain in the western and Mediterranean theatres combined (1650 aircraft) than it was on the whole eastern front against Russia (1563 aircraft). In particular, the number of German fighters deployed in the two western theatres was almost double that in the East. The British air effort in the second half of 1941 was therefore crucial in limiting the number of aircraft the Germans could deploy in Russia. This, together with the British lend-lease contribution at this time, probably played a significant part in enabling Russia to survive the German assault on Moscow.[196] As Chapter 8 will demonstrate, the supply route to Russia through Iran would prove equally important in maintaining the Russian war effort through the winter of 1942/43.

Overall, this paper therefore provided a compelling rationale. It brought new strategic coherence to the vision the prime minister had been expressing for months, not least in his May exchange with Roosevelt. It also brought much needed coherence and intellectual weight to chiefs of staff understanding. When the response to the Hopkins criticisms was initially discussed by the chiefs on 22 July, the arguments aired in favour of the Middle East strategy were somewhat banal.[197] It set the strategic goals Britain would pursue in the Middle East and Mediterranean theatres through to 1943. The immediate resources required to achieve this comprehensive new strategic vision were set out in a parallel paper circulated a week later.[198]

The importance of holding the Middle East was further underlined by the chiefs of staff in a general strategy paper prepared for the Placentia Bay summit conference with the Americans in early August. Here, the chiefs now agreed the Middle East must have first call on overseas resources. They emphasised the need for strategic depth to deny access to the Indian Ocean and protect Persian oil. 'Loss of our position in the Middle East would have disastrous effects'. Singapore, meanwhile, was essential to maintaining sea communications with India and Australasia, but its defence needs would now have to be balanced against requirements in other theatres.[199]

The need set out in these papers to generate the maximum empire war effort and the specific contribution of the eastern empire to that war effort requires more explanation. By December 1941, total British Empire land forces in the combined Middle East and Far East theatres comprised the equivalent of sixteen divisions, with the Indian Army providing six, Australia four, New Zealand one, and South Africa two. These thirteen non-United Kingdom divisions represented about 23 per cent of total British Empire fighting manpower available for ground force deployment at this time, although India and Australia had additional land forces for domestic defence and security. The Indian Army was now expanding fast, reaching 900,000 personnel by the end of 1941, rising to over 1.5 million by the end of 1942.[200] The percentage ground force contribution from these four empire territories actually deployed to fighting fronts remained broadly constant for the rest of the war as empire forces steadily expanded. The percentage manpower contribution of the same four territories to British Empire air and naval strength was much less, although often of high quality. Many air personnel were incorporated directly within British units. The percentage contribution of fighting manpower from these four territories is also reflected in their casualty rate, which was about 19 per cent of all British Empire casualties over the whole war.

As the war progressed, the core eastern empire territories were also increasingly able to equip and support the land forces they generated from their own productive resources, with the important exception of heavy weapons. Production of major weapons, ie aircraft, tanks and ships, within eastern empire territories was negligible before 1942 and remained limited after that, reaching at most 5 per cent of overall empire effort over the whole war, with shipping the most important component.[201] Beyond this direct fighting contribution, the eastern empire made a wider and critical contribution of raw materials and food. By the end of 1942, India's financial contribution to the support of the combined Middle East and Far East theatres equalled that of Britain.[202] As this chapter has already demonstrated, oil from Persia and Iraq serviced the entire British Empire war effort east of Malta and the Cape. These various eastern empire contributions to the total British war effort explain the advice to the War Cabinet in mid-1942 that the loss of Abadan might reduce that effort by 25 per cent.[203] This 25 per cent figure certainly appears a reasonable estimate for the eastern empire war effort, although what proportion of this would have been eliminated in practice by the loss of Abadan is impossible to calculate.

It can still be argued that the eastern empire brought Britain no net military benefit, and could only contribute to defending its own territories. Despite the empire contributions, Britain also incurred substantial net costs in defending the East. In particular, the war transformed India's financial relationship with Britain from debtor to substantial creditor. By the end of 1945, India's claim on Britain would reach the extraordinary total of £1321 million.[204] The main counter-argument here is the overall strategic case for holding the Middle East, set out in this chapter. The eastern empire, together with South Africa, provided about two-thirds of the fighting manpower for the Crusader offensive in November 1941. It would have been impossible to hold a forward position in the Middle East during the period covered by this book without eastern empire manpower. One other point deserves note. If Australia and New Zealand had spent the same proportion of national income on defence in fiscal year 1937 as Britain, they would have contributed £37 million extra to empire defence resources. This was significant when set against a budget for the Royal Navy that year of £102 million. Indeed, over a period of years, the Dominions could have paid for most of the Far East fleet they began to fear would not appear.[205]

The chiefs of staff endorsement of the Middle East as Britain's main overseas priority, and the new stress placed on protecting the Indian Ocean and Persian oil if Britain was to maximise its war effort, ought logically to have spurred the chiefs to commission a parallel review from the Joint Planning Committee into 'the strategic necessity of holding our present Far East position'.[206] The Japanese move into southern Indochina at the end of July further emphasised the need for this. Such a review would surely have identified that the defensive goals established in the 1940 Far East appreciation were not achievable with available resources, and that the deterrent effect of the United States was currently insufficient to fill the gap. It would therefore have exposed just how much risk Britain was now carrying in this theatre. A chiefs of staff update on Far East defence produced for the War Cabinet at the end of July fell far short of the searching reappraisal required. It merely confirmed the existing strategic aspiration, to hold, in collaboration with the Dutch, a defensive 'crescent' from Lashio in Burma to Tonga in the South Pacific, with Singapore as the keystone. It summarised the forces currently available to hold this line.[207] The chiefs emphasised that, in accord with the Far East appreciation, defence would continue to depend initially on the flexible deployment of air power. They acknowledged air strength for Malaya was still barely 50 per cent of that recommended in the appreciation, with little prospect of improvement before the end of the year.

Within six weeks, the chiefs of staff formally confirmed there would be no further air reinforcements for the Far East until 1942.[208] This reflected the continuing demands of the Middle East, but also the new requirement to provide urgent aid to Russia.[209] British planners estimated that as a result of diversion to Russia, over the nine months October 1941 to June 1942, the Royal Air Force would lose 1800 fighters from United Kingdom production and 1800 assorted aircraft from American production. United Kingdom fighter squadrons would therefore need to be capped, and upgrades to the Middle and Far East put on hold. The diversion of 200 Hurricane Mk IIs to Russia during the autumn has drawn specific criticism, on the grounds that they could have been better employed in the Far East.[210] There are two points here. First, the allocation to Russia was a political choice easier to criticise with hindsight than in the autumn of 1941, when any contribution that might keep Russia fighting seemed critical. Secondly, the real limiting factor for Hurricanes in autumn 1941 was shipping space and the capacity of the trans-Africa Takoradi air reinforcement route. Whatever went to the Far East on these routes reduced what went to the Middle East.

If there was to be no early air reinforcement, then American intervention in the war became the critical factor in Far East defence. The July update paper hoped that, at best, this would deter the Japanese. Failing that, it would enable the despatch of a Royal Navy fleet (by releasing resources in the Atlantic), provide an advance base in the Philippines, and discourage the Japanese moving all their forces south. This may be the first reference to the prospect of a Royal Navy fleet based in the Philippines, which would take on increasing significance in the coming months. The inclusion of this reference in a Joint Planning Committee paper must have been sponsored by Director of Plans on behalf of the naval staff. It reveals, therefore, how easily the Admiralty defaulted to its longstanding Far East war plans. Release of Royal Navy forces for an eastern fleet through US Navy substitution in the Atlantic is described in the next chapter.

The July update on the Far East lacked credibility. It did not address the likely scale of Japanese attack and therefore the complete inadequacy of available forces to hold the proposed defensive line. The chiefs of staff did ask the Joint Planning Committee to clarify what early reinforcements were possible, but were unwilling to sanction diversions from the Middle East. The planners merely set out existing force levels for each service, identified reinforcements that could be provided in thirty days, and additional forces 'later'. The identified Royal Navy reinforcements broadly coincided with the forces Pound would propose to the prime minister for Indian Ocean reinforcement in their exchange of minutes two weeks later (discussed in Chapter 6).[211] The chiefs no doubt deferred to the prime minister's political judgement that Japan would not attack and that if she did, the United States would intervene, but they had a responsibility to spell out the risk being carried and its full consequences. Kennedy claims that he and Dill discussed the Far East situation on several occasions immediately following the Japanese attack on 7 December. They felt there was little hope for Singapore, as naval and air forces were lacking and the army units were short of tanks and other specialist weapons. They agreed, however, that reinforcements had not been feasible, given the needs of other theatres. This, however, begs the question as to why defence goals in the Far East were not made more realistic, and why they had both been arguing in May that Malaya was essential to empire defence.[212]

The chiefs of staff therefore did not satisfactorily address the time lag before Royal Navy or other reinforcements could reach the theatre in the event of war, the dependence of any new Royal Navy deployment on air power, or the current limits on American fighting effectiveness, all issues within their remit. Nor did they insist on a clear programme for filling the obvious force deficiencies, which had now been reaffirmed, within a reasonable timescale. A more honest appraisal drafted in early August, given the decision to prioritise the Middle East, would have endorsed the American view that Singapore was not defensible with existing resources. (Ironically, that is not quite how the Japanese saw matters at this time. At the end of September, as they finalised preparations for the Malaya operation, they still anticipated that owing to the air and naval strength of the Allies at Singapore, progress along the Malayan peninsula would be extremely slow.[213]) Faced with this appraisal, the War Cabinet would then have had a choice. Either to set a more limited goal of an 'outer ring' defence, aimed at protecting Australasia and critical Indian Ocean communications from Ceylon,[214] acknowledging that the role of the forces in Malaya and Singapore was now essentially to buy time. Or to accept more forces must be diverted from the Middle East, transferring risk there and potentially compromising the Crusader offensive. It is possible to see how such an alternative, more limited goal would have looked, because the joint planning staff had to address precisely this challenge six months later in February 1942.

This failure adequately to address the risk posed by the Japanese move into southern Indochina was a key turning point. Given the time lag in moving forces to the East, it was the last moment when Britain had the option of injecting sufficient air forces to buy enough time, when Japan struck in December, to enable more substantial reinforcements to arrive. It is important to be clear, therefore, what level of diversion from the Middle East at this time was logistically achievable, and what the consequences in the two theatres would have been. A minimum diversion would have reallocated four bomber squadrons to Malaya to replace the delayed Baltimores and Beauforts due from the United States and Australia. A maximum diversion might perhaps have added four squadrons of modern fighters. (It is worth noting that on 3 September, Pound advocated sending two of the twenty fighter squadrons earmarked for the Middle East to Malaya instead, a move categorically rejected by the prime minister.[215]) Following the Japanese attack in December, the joint planning staff recommended the transfer of a slightly larger air group to Malaya and Burma than the 'maximum' diversion suggested here. It comprised six light bomber and seven fighter squadrons, which it judged would not unduly compromise Middle East security. Admittedly, by this time, the Crusader battle was largely over, so the immediate risks in diversion were reduced.[216]

Moving the maximum force, along with 100 per cent reserves, spares and support, in time to be operationally capable by December would have been just possible. In the five months March to August 1942, 1000 aircraft (of broadly similar type to those projected here) were shipped, mainly via the Middle East, to India to achieve an effective strength of 500. The suggested maximum reinforcement for Malaya would involve moving just over 250 aircraft, including 100 per cent reserves, in three months. For the strike squadrons, most of the support structure was already in place.[217] The consequence in the Middle East would have been a reduction in Royal Air Force strike capability for the Crusader battle in November of about 20 per cent. Given how closely fought Crusader was, this might therefore have tipped a narrow victory into defeat. Assessing the impact of even the maximum force in Malaya is more difficult. It would have virtually doubled Royal Air Force fighting power, might well have saved Force Z, at least initially, and probably delayed and complicated the Japanese advance.[218] It is also hard to gauge whether such reinforcements would have had any deterrent effect on the Japanese. Taken in isolation, it seems unlikely, although the Japanese did fear the cumulative impact of western reinforcements through the winter. They had also overestimated Royal Air Force numbers in Malaya by nearly 100 per cent and Dutch air strength by 50 per cent without being dissuaded.[219]

Thereafter, the continuing survival of Singapore would have rested on which side could reinforce most quickly. Here the Japanese held the advantage, as well as the opportunity to increase their initial scale of attack. One way to look at this is to calculate the maximum force the Japanese could devote to Malaya if they reinforced their initial attack with air and ground forces moved from the Philippines after the initial campaign there (about three weeks in), and made some adjustment to their attack plans for the Netherlands East Indies. The Japanese Malaya attack force could then be raised to as much as 1200 (as opposed to 600) aircraft and ten (compared to four) divisions. To combat this, Britain might need 1000 aircraft and eight divisions, force levels never realistic with even a minimal holding operation in the Middle East through 1941. They were only partly achievable if Crusader and aid to Russia had both been abandoned. Such figures can only be hypothetical, but the basic point that Japan had enough capacity to counter a significant British diversion from the Middle East prior to their attack seems valid.[220] That said, the sheer ambition of the Japanese goals in the first months of the war meant their forces were stretched under any scenario, with little margin to meet unexpected setbacks. The British defeat at Singapore Island came just as Japanese supply lines were failing. If the British had held the Japanese at bay a little longer, the overall Japanese timetable would have been badly disrupted, with unpredictable consequences.[221]

The reinforcement argument is, anyway, academic. Given the priority placed on Crusader and the comparatively small air advantage Britain was perceived to enjoy in North Africa, there was no prospect the prime minister or chiefs of staff would have countenanced a diversion during the August and September window when it could make a difference. The need for maximum air power to support the Crusader offensive was emphasised when Middle East commanders met the Defence Committee on 1 August and a start date was set for 1 November (subsequently delayed to 18 November).[222] The margin of air advantage enjoyed by the Royal Air Force for Crusader continued to be argued between Middle East Command and London during October.[223]

The Admiralty appears to have been oddly passive in the debate over strategic trade-offs between the Middle East and Malaya in the spring and summer of 1941. Given that they were the historic architects of a Far East naval strategy, in which both the present First Sea Lord and VCNS had played a personal role, and which remained Britain's preferred option, there is little sign of naval staff pressure to make the defence of Singapore more credible. As the next chapter shows, the Admiralty knew by February that there was no chance of a US Navy fleet basing at Singapore, and only limited deployment forward of Hawaii. Unless the United States entered the war and replaced Royal Navy forces in the western Atlantic, there was also no prospect of the Royal Navy deploying more than a small Indian Ocean task force. The Admiralty assumed, therefore, that in the event of war, Japan was likely to achieve a foothold in Malaya, and while Singapore might not fall, the naval base might be unusable.[224] The assumption was that the Japanese could conduct air attacks from Thailand and northern Malaya, and also prevent sea access if they seized Sumatra and Java.

From February through August, both Pound and Phillips judged that the main threat to Britain in a war with Japan fought without American support was not the loss of Far East possessions, but attack on the vital communications in the Indian Ocean, including those that sustained the Middle East. [225] Phillips reiterated this point in trenchant terms at the beginning of August. Here he emphasised that the Admiralty had revised their view of what was vital. Trade in the Indian Ocean and Pacific was vital, while defence of the Kra Isthmus was not. The Admiralty had insufficient resources to deal with Japanese raiders and expected minimal help from the United States, who were mainly focused on the Atlantic. The longstanding promise to the Dominions to withdraw the Eastern Mediterranean Fleet to protect them predated the scale of Britain's commitment to the Middle East.[226]

This was a reasonable view of priorities in the circumstances and, indeed, a logical evolution of the Chamberlain principles of March 1939. However, the

172

Admiralty can still be criticised on three grounds. First, if they really did judge that Singapore was now effectively dispensable to the naval priorities that most mattered, then they should have taken a lead in calling for a major rethink on Far East strategy and resources. Secondly, as part of such a rethink, they should have emphasised that the concept of retaining Singapore as a naval base, or 'as a foothold for recovery', now only made sense if sufficient air power could be provided to protect the base and cover fleet operations. By mid-1941 Mediterranean experience demonstrated that one was not possible without the other. Cunningham made this point particularly well to the Admiralty in April.

> The key to the situation here and the one which will decide the issue of our success or otherwise in holding the Mediterranean lies in air power. We can probably manage on land and on sea with forces reasonably inferior to the enemy but we cannot do so if also inferior in the air. I consider that no half measures will do. If HMG want to hold the Mediterranean, adequate air forces must be sent.[227]

Finally, they should have done much more in this period to prepare Ceylon as an alternative operating base, drawing on the experience of Alexandria. As Chapter 6 will demonstrate, in August the Admiralty was poised between a judicious defensive strategy focused on the Indian Ocean, and a tendency to default to the traditional framework of Far East war plans.

The fatal illusion: forward defence in two theatres
This chapter draws four main conclusions. First, Britain's continuing commitment to the eastern Mediterranean and Middle East following the fall of France was influenced by two critical factors. These were the need to secure the western boundary of the eastern empire and protect access to the Indian Ocean and Iranian oil, to enable Britain to generate the full war potential of that empire, deny vital resources to the Axis, and later establish direct contact with Russia; and the influence that Britain's position in Egypt exerted on attitudes in Spain, Vichy and Turkey, and the prospect of Germany extending its control of the Atlantic coast. These two factors dictated the need to hold a forward position in the Middle East. The military resources generated by the eastern empire made it possible.

Secondly, Britain's leadership failed adequately to recognise how fundamentally the defence problem at the other end of the empire in the Far East had changed. Britain could no longer protect and use Singapore as a base without denying Japan access to a substantial area around it. Britain could only generate the air and land forces to achieve this by diverting them from the Middle East. Sufficient diversion was never possible in 1941 without putting the eastern empire and the oil to sustain it at serious risk from Axis attack in the west, and undermining Britain's wider ability to prosecute the war. Britain could pursue a forward defence policy in one theatre, but not both.

Thirdly, Britain's war leadership allowed the protection of Singapore to become an end in itself, rather than seeing it as just one means to secure the critical core of the eastern empire, rightly identified in 1939. The chiefs of staff were primarily responsible for failing to conduct a searching reappraisal of Far East strategy in mid-1941 as they had in the Middle East.

Finally, the Admiralty remained too attached to a narrow interpretation of pre-war strategy that was inappropriate to the opportunities and capabilities now available to the Japanese, and failed to draw obvious lessons from the Mediterranean war.

4

The American Relationship, ABC-1 and the Resurrection of an Eastern Fleet

This chapter describes the evolution of the naval relationship with the United States from the first formal exchanges on naval co-operation in the Far East in early 1938 to the first American-British summit at Placentia Bay in August 1941. This initiated active US Navy escort operations in the Atlantic, thereby releasing Royal Navy forces for deployment in the East. The chapter concentrates primarily on the period following the fall of France and how American attitudes influenced British naval strategy for protecting the eastern empire over the next twelve months. The collapse of France, and the American perception that without substantial assistance British defeat might quickly follow, led the United States to prioritise the Atlantic over the Pacific. This decision was enshrined in their Plan Dog memorandum of November 1940 and confirmed in the first formal American-British staff talks in early 1941, known as ABC-1. Plan Dog, however, effectively eliminated the British hope that the United States would take responsibility for guarding their naval flank in the Far East. It obliged the Royal Navy leadership to adopt a compromise American proposal, whereby the United States would relieve sufficient Royal Navy forces in the Atlantic to enable the Royal Navy to create an eastern fleet to secure the eastern empire against Japanese intervention in the war. Unfortunately, it still proved difficult to translate the ABC-1 strategic principles into practical plans for co-operation in the Far East, and failure here would ultimately encourage the Admiralty to embrace an unwise forward deployment strategy with inadequate forces in the autumn of 1941.

A gradual meeting of minds
During the 1930s the Anglo-American naval relationship progressed steadily from one marked by rivalry and suspicion[1] towards cautious friendship, based on growing awareness of common interests, especially in dealing with the naval threat posed by Japan in the Far East.[2] This trend was evident in the exchanges

between the two countries around the two London naval conferences in 1930 and 1936. These largely restored the trust and understanding that had been partly lost in the decade after the First World War.[3] However, it was the visit of Captain Royal Ingersoll, the US Navy Director of Plans, to London in January 1938 which marked a step change. The visit established agreement for the Far East theatre on 'strategic co-operation, respective spheres of action, reciprocal use of facilities, and common codes'. Mutual war plans were also shared.[4] Nevertheless, the real impact of this visit, and subsequent exchanges over the next eighteen months, notably the visit by Commander Hampton to Washington in June 1939,[5] was inevitably limited without agreement by the British and American governments on specific joint objectives to restrain Japan and the use of joint naval power to achieve them. There were too many political constraints and doubts on both sides to make this feasible. By September 1939, therefore, the relationship was friendly and consultative, but remained well short of any formal commitment.[6] However, these naval exchanges in 1938/39 were still significant in fostering a wider network of Anglo-American relationships focused on international security, especially in the Far East. The two countries began to recognise that they shared parallel goals, similar strategic evaluations, and common approaches. In that sense, the naval exchanges were the first tentative steps in creating the 'Grand Alliance' initiated at Placentia Bay in 1941.[7]

The Ingersoll and Hampton meetings[8] had enduring influence on the subsequent development of the Anglo-American naval relationship in 1940/41 in several respects.[9] The first is the concept of 'spheres of interest' and division of labour. Ingersoll and his Royal Navy opposite number, still Captain Tom Phillips, agreed that in containing Japan, the Royal Navy would assume responsibility for the Indian Ocean, Australasia and the South China Sea as far as the Philippines. The US Navy, meanwhile, would cover the western and northern Pacific, including Fiji and Samoa, again up to the Philippines. This division was geared primarily to the enforcement of economic sanctions and the conduct of a trade war against Japan. In 1938 it had logic and offered the Royal Navy significant benefit, the possibility of securing the area as far as Hong Kong with a rather smaller force than if operating unilaterally. But it also established a division that the Americans would continue to promote through 1941, when Britain had scant prospect of resourcing her defined sphere. It is also worth noting that at the Hampton meeting, Leahy went rather further than the Ingersoll spheres of interest which focused on the Far East. He suggested that if the United States joined Britain and France in a war against the three Axis powers, the US Navy Fleet should control the Pacific while the 'Allied Fleets' (ie Britain and France) covered European waters, the Mediterranean and the Atlantic. The Indian Ocean was not mentioned. Since

Pound and Phillips were the recipients for Hampton's report in 1939, it was then natural they would promote a similar division in mid-1940.[10]

Secondly, the British took some encouragement from both the Ingersoll and Hampton meetings, especially the latter, that in the event of aggressive moves by Japan against the western powers, the Americans would be willing to base significant forces at Singapore, reducing the scale of British force required. Leahy volunteered his 'personal view' to Hampton that in a joint war against the Axis, the US Navy Fleet should move to Singapore in sufficient force to engage the Japanese fleet on passage and therefore also on arrival. He was opposed to sending a weaker force, but stressed the importance of a British contribution, including capital ships, to underline that this was a joint force.[11] Given such encouragement, the British would pursue this idea determinedly in late 1940.

Thirdly, the Ingersoll meeting encouraged the Admiralty to look favourably on the Philippines as a forward operating base that would get over many of the problems inherent in Hong Kong.[12] This too would influence Admiralty thinking both in late 1940 and again in the final run-up to war in late 1941.

Finally, the Ingersoll meeting established a principle of sharing sensitive information that would extend into limited technical exchanges in 1938/39, and then much more substantial intelligence-sharing after the outbreak of war. The Admiralty Board first authorised a framework under which technical information would be shared with the US Navy in May 1938, when it agreed the Americans would be treated 'exceptionally'.[13] In the second half of 1940 the Royal Navy answered no less than 395 information requests from the US Navy through the Bailey Committee, whose status is explained shortly.[14] This level of sharing clearly reflected the impact of war, but also showed how the Ingersoll meeting had broken a barrier in establishing trust and confidence.

The Atlantic comes first

As discussed at the beginning of the last chapter, the collapse of France made it much more difficult for Britain to retain control of all the sea areas she judged vital to her survival and to her ability to prosecute the war. During the month of June, she faced not only German control of the French Atlantic coast and the entry of Italy into the war, but the prospect of Japanese and Spanish intervention too. The bleak outlook inevitably fostered hopes of American intervention on Britain's side and, at a minimum, help in securing the Atlantic. Pound as First Sea Lord accordingly set up a committee under the retired Admiral Sir Sidney Bailey to determine what naval assistance Britain should seek from the United States and how this should best be co-ordinated. It met for the first time on 20 June. The key members of the Bailey Committee, as it was named in contemporary papers, apart from Bailey himself, were Rear

Admiral W S Chalmers and Captain L Curzon-Howe. The latter was the recently returned naval attaché in Washington and had attended the Hampton talks in that role in June 1939.[15]

The Bailey Committee focused on three distinct issues: it provided advice on where American operational assistance was most needed; it advised on how an operational partnership could best be managed, drawing on experience in the First World War; and it conducted an audit of Royal Navy capability and war experience to date, to provide a pool of knowledge that could be shared with the US Navy to support a future operational relationship.[16] Its initial recommendations on operational assistance, completed on 9 July,[17] started with the Royal Navy's global priorities. For the immediate future, these were to secure home waters, the Atlantic supply route and the Mediterranean. While the naval staff certainly wanted the United States to protect British interests in the Far East, this was not a primary interest at this stage. Indeed, under its initial terms of reference, the Bailey Committee was not even asked to consider Japan as a possible belligerent.[18] The staff hoped a strong American presence in the western Pacific would restrain Japan, but expected the United States to do only what it would do anyway to meet its own interests in the area. If the United States kept the theatre peaceful, then it could provide much-needed support in the more important Atlantic theatre. There was also an obvious difference between the American role in the Pacific and the Atlantic. Deterrence in the former could apply in peacetime. Support in the Atlantic depended on American entry into the war.[19]

These naval priorities identified by Bailey foreshadowed the main risks and opportunities defined in the Future Strategy paper at the end of August. They were also confirmed in a briefing by the First Sea Lord for the prime minister on 2 August. This covered the redistribution of the Royal Navy in the event of war with Japan, with the United States neutral. It emphasised that security of home waters came first. If Britain was to hold the Middle East, a fleet was required in the eastern Mediterranean and a force was required at Gibraltar to prevent any Italian breakout into the Atlantic. The final requirement was defence of trade in the Indian Ocean, although this was less important than the Atlantic. For the last, it identified for the first time an Indian Ocean defence force comprising the battlecruiser *Renown*, the carrier *Ark Royal*, two 8in cruisers, some modern 6in cruisers, if available, and six destroyers. It also assumed all Australian and New Zealand forces would return to home waters. Significantly, Pound saw Trincomalee as a better base from which to protect Indian Ocean trade than Singapore.[20]

The low priority placed on the Far East in Bailey's initial work explains why the August Far East appreciation did not include specific recommendations for developing American co-operation. However, low priority for the Far East did not mean Britain had no views on how co-operation there with the Americans might evolve. As early as 25 May, when the chiefs of staff assessed Britain's prospects if France fell, they concluded that Britain should rely primarily on the United States to 'safeguard our interests in the Far East'.[21] Given the argument that would erupt over the ranking of Singapore in empire priorities the following spring, it is noteworthy that at this time Britain's position in the eastern Mediterranean took precedence over Singapore. By the end of June, the Joint Planning Committee had gone further and established the aspiration that 'it would be convenient for the United States to assume operational control over the whole Pacific Ocean, including the entire British China Station'.[22]

Furthermore, Bailey's first report to the First Sea Lord not only anticipated that the United States 'will continue to maintain a strong fleet to safeguard our joint interests in the Pacific and Far East at least until Japan makes her attitude clear',[23] but assumed that if a capital ship force was required at Singapore, the Americans might be willing to provide this. This expectation that the United States might be willing to base a capital ship force at Singapore reflected the British view that Singapore was the only logical option in the Far East theatre, given the lack of significant facilities in the Philippines. It also inevitably reflected the comments made by Admiral Leahy to Commander Hampton in June 1939. More recently, on 16 April the US naval attaché, Captain Alan Kirk, had asked Phillips as Deputy Chief of Naval Staff whether the US Navy would be able to use Singapore in the event of a Japanese attack on the Netherlands East Indies.[24] Churchill, who was, no doubt, aware of the Hampton background from his time as First Lord, and certainly aware of Kirk's inquiry, had also raised the possibility of the United States using Singapore in his first letter as prime minister to President Roosevelt on 15 May.[25] Roosevelt pointedly did not offer any encouragement on the Singapore suggestion in his reply three days later. However, he did decide in concert with Admiral Harold Stark, the new Chief of Naval Operations, that the US Navy Pacific Fleet should remain at Pearl Harbor after manoeuvres held there in May, rather than returning to its normal base at San Diego.

British ideas for an American contribution to Far East naval defence had not moved beyond the aspirational when the chiefs of staff briefed the American fact-finding mission led by Rear Admiral Robert Ghormley at the end of August. Ghormley, as US Navy Director of Plans, had accompanied Leahy to his meeting with Hampton in June 1939 and he became Assistant Chief of Naval Operations later that year. By background, therefore, he was well placed to address Far East co-operation. The chiefs drew on the newly completed Future Strategy paper for their briefing, along with the Far East appreciation for the Far East element.[26] However, they neither emphasised the Far East as a current priority, ranking it behind the United Kingdom homeland, the Middle East, and even West Africa, nor sought specific assistance in the theatre. Once again, there was no suggestion at this meeting that the defence of Singapore ranked second in empire priorities, as Dill would argue the following spring. Reflecting the Bailey line, the chiefs merely made the general observation that given Britain's present inability to provide a fleet for the Far East, 'the immense value of active US Navy co-operation' was obvious. The support of a US Navy battle-fleet would be 'transformational'.

Ghormley did press Pound on British reaction to a hypothetical US Navy transfer of part of their Pacific Fleet to the Atlantic. Would Britain then reinforce Singapore or give priority to the Mediterranean? Pound responded that it would be 'strategically unsound' to send a force of insufficient strength to meet the Japanese fleet, unless it could be sure of getting there first. In present circumstances, with inadequate forces under any likely scenario, it was better to concentrate on controlling the Indian Ocean, rather than try to reach Singapore with insufficient forces. Pound clarified that a 'sufficient' Royal Navy fleet now meant a strength one battleship less than the IJN total: ie nine ships, along with appropriate supporting forces. That implied 'six or seven destroyer flotillas', which could not possibly be provided at present. Pound's response, whatever its merits, was a revealing insight into his thinking on Far East reinforcement, which would remain consistent up to September 1941.

Following the discussion with the chiefs of staff, Pound gave Ghormley a version of the full Bailey report. This provided a basis for a series of meetings between the Bailey Committee and Ghormley through September and October. Only the first of these, on 17 and 18 September, addressed strategic issues and operational assistance in any detail. The other meetings were mainly technical briefings. On 17 September Bailey again stressed the value of American naval support in the Far East, and stated that moving the US Navy Pacific Fleet to Singapore, Australia or the Philippines 'might keep Japan quiet'. Ghormley made no response, other than to stress the difficulty in maintaining and protecting lines of communication when the fleet deployed forward, given the bases available to the Japanese in the western Pacific. Bailey neither pressed the issue of Far East support in general, nor the use of Singapore in particular. He laid at least equal emphasis on the value of American support in the Atlantic. Ghormley was left clear that American cover in the East was an important British aspiration, but there were no specific proposals at this stage.[27]

There were two catalysts that encouraged Britain to translate its general aspiration for American naval cover in the Far East into a more specific commitment. The first was the need for a credible policy towards the Netherlands East Indies in the event of Japanese attack there. As the Joint Planning Committee stated on 2 October, war with Japan would seriously prejudice success against Germany. However, Japanese occupation of the

Netherlands East Indies would soon neutralise the Singapore base and render it unusable. Britain could not, therefore, allow undisputed occupation, but any support for the Dutch would be ineffective without prior staff discussions. The chiefs of staff concluded that these should proceed, but without any binding British commitment to intervene. Inviting American participation would clarify their attitude towards defence of the Netherlands East Indies, and hopefully minimise British liability.[28] The second catalyst was the signing of the Tripartite Pact by the three Axis powers on 27 September. This raised the potential risk of Japanese intervention and resulted in a specific proposal from the American Secretary of State, Cordell Hull, for private staff discussions to explore common defence possibilities.[29] The War Cabinet tasked the chiefs of staff to develop proposals for such talks, but it was soon apparent from the British ambassador in Washington that Hull had overreached. There was no prospect of full staff talks until after the American presidential election in November.

The chiefs of staff therefore agreed that more informal exploratory talks on the Far East should be held with Ghormley in London, and the United States would also be invited to send a representative to attend the staff talks with the Dutch at Singapore.[30] In preparing draft instructions for the British delegation meeting Ghormley, the Joint Planning Committee confirmed that, during earlier discussions with Ghormley, the Far East problem had only been addressed within a wider global context, and not as a specific issue. The British objective now should be to establish the employment of American, British and Dutch forces in the Far East theatre if all three were involved in a joint war with the three Axis powers. The planners argued that American intervention would prevent a Japanese attack on Australasia and the presence of a US Navy battle-fleet in the theatre would much reduce the risk of seaborne attack on Malaya, although the possibility of land or air attack would remain. The United States should be invited to take 'our Naval Far Eastern War Memorandum' as the basis for discussion, with the US Navy Pacific Fleet substituting for the Royal Navy Eastern Fleet. The key question, therefore, was how far the United States could make up the British naval deficit and from what base(s). Singapore, Hong Kong, Manila, Guam and Honolulu were all listed as possibilities.

The Planning Committee emphasised that the British war plan would need modification, because the Far East 'defence problem' now embraced the Netherlands East Indies and Philippines, as well as specific British interests. Manila would be a good advanced base, while Hong Kong would probably be unusable. In line with long-established Admiralty strategy, the committee still saw 'economic pressure' as the primary means of bringing Japan to heel. Given that the United States was likely to provide the bulk of forces, the committee recommended that all British naval forces in the China Fleet area should come under American command, with the Indian Ocean remaining a British responsibility. American ability to provide shore-based bombers and fighters for Malaya and the Netherlands East Indies should also be investigated.[31] These draft instructions were approved by the chiefs of staff the following day, 16 October, and a summary despatched to Commander-in-Chief China to use as the basis for staff talks with the Dutch at Singapore.[32]

The Joint Planning Committee did not spell out which 'Far Eastern War Memorandum' they were referring to in these draft instructions produced on 15 October. However, a précis of Naval War Memorandum Eastern was now produced and circulated on 20 October, under the signature of Colonel E I C Jacob as secretary to the United Kingdom delegation established for the deferred staff talks, but now focused on the Ghormley meeting. Its introduction confirmed that this was the 1937 version of the War Memorandum, 'drawn up to give effect to the 1937 Far East appreciation'. It recognised that this plan was based on 'the situation then existing', and in many respects was not applicable to the present situation.[33] At the chiefs of staff 23 October meeting, Phillips as VCNS insisted that the latest August 1940 Far East appreciation was inappropriate for the proposed discussions with the United States (and potentially the Dutch too). It assumed no fleet was available in the Far East, since Britain could not send one. If the objective was now to persuade the United States to provide the necessary fleet instead, then the strategy for dealing with Japan outlined in the earlier 1937 Far East appreciation was a better basis on which to open talks. This would also avoid tasking the planners with producing a fresh appreciation.[34]

The Americans were unhappy even with more limited exploratory talks, and insisted that discussion with Ghormley on the Far East was confined to a bilateral exchange of information.[35] Ghormley accordingly produced a list of written questions: the composition of current British and Dutch forces; planned reinforcements, strategic disposition and command arrangements; what exactly was required from the United States, and what level of American forces could be supported. He also issued a warning. The United States wanted to help keep the Japanese out of Malaya and the Netherlands East Indies. However, before contemplating any military assistance, they would need evidence that the British and Dutch were making a maximum commitment themselves to defending their territories. The British immediately responded to Ghormley with information on force levels, based on those in the August Far East appreciation.[36]

The British answer to Ghormley's key question – what exactly was required from the United States in the Far East – was then identified in an internal appreciation produced for the chiefs of staff by Rear Admiral Roger Bellairs, who had been nominated to lead the British delegation to the deferred staff talks. He would subsequently represent Britain at the ABC-1 talks in January.[37] This was a significant evolution of the Joint Planning Committee mid-October draft instructions described above, and effectively replaced them. It re-emphasised the traditional view that Far East defence was essentially a naval problem and, following Phillips's guidance, drew on the principles, and even language, of the 1937 Far East appreciation and its associated war plan. The British proposal now was that the United States should counter any Japanese southward move directed at Malaya and/or the Netherlands East Indies by basing a substantial fleet at Singapore. This fleet, with a suggested minimum strength of eight capital ships and three carriers, should be strong enough to engage any IJN fleet, to disrupt Japanese communications, thus rendering any expedition against Allied territory impossible, and to prevent Japanese interference with Allied trade.

It is not clear how the strength of the desired US Navy fleet in Bellairs's paper was calculated. It did not directly equate either to the Royal Navy strength defined in the 1937 appreciation, which recommended ten capital ships, or the maximum fleet of seven ships proposed in War Memorandum (European) in August 1939. Nor did it meet the Admiralty view expressed during the Tientsin discussions that the minimum acceptable strength for a competitive fleet was really one ship less than the maximum IJN strength, which would mean nine ships. It was apparently a compromise between all these estimates. As explained in Chapter 2, the post-Tientsin fleet of August 1939 also had the limited defensive goals of protecting Singapore and covering the Dominions. It was not judged strong enough to operate north of Singapore. The goals now defined for the proposed US Navy fleet were more ambitious, so logically required a larger fleet. But Bellairs was also clear that the diversion from the more important European theatre should be the minimum necessary to achieve these goals. Bellairs's figure of three carriers did not link to any previous British formula or plan. In 1937 the Royal Navy hoped to deploy four carriers in a Far Eastern war, while in 1939 the maximum it thought feasible was two. The figure three perhaps merely represented the minimum carrier strength the IJN were expected to deploy,[38] or the current US Navy carrier strength the Admiralty believed was available in Pearl Harbor.[39]

Bellairs argued that Singapore was geographically a better base than Hawaii for the proposed US Navy fleet, but emphasised the importance of Manila as an advanced operating base if the fleet was to interrupt Japanese com-munications through the South China Sea and cover Allied territories. He expected Japan to neutralise the Philippines before moving south. Finally, Bellairs proposed that the Royal Navy establish a task force in Ceylon, and the US Navy, one at Hawaii, to secure communications and protect trade in rear areas. The former was the battlecruiser and carrier combination identified in the August Far East appreciation. If no Japanese attack on trade developed in the Indian Ocean, this force could move to Singapore and support operations in the South China Sea.

These Bellairs proposals of 8 November require context. The Bailey report, the engagement with Ghormley, the need to respond to the on–off staff talks – which had spurred Bellairs's work – and, not least, the progress of the war since the fall of France, had all helped Britain to reassess its naval priorities. Britain had to decide where its resources should best be concentrated, and to clarify what it wanted from the United States. By early November it had a coherent view of the global naval strategy it wanted to pursue, and where it wanted American help. The Royal Navy leadership was clear that Europe was the decisive war theatre, and Germany the main opponent to be beaten. If Japan intervened, strategy should be defensive and focus only on holding Singapore and the Netherlands East Indies, and denying access to the Indian Ocean. This is evident in Pound's redraft of a brief prepared for the American president at the end of October.

> The outcome of the war would depend on the defeat of the Axis powers in Europe. When this is achieved the Japanese problem will be simple and even if we had made no progress in defeating that country in the meantime it is most probable she would give in after the Axis powers in Europe had been defeated. The defeat of Japan on the other hand by our combined forces would do little if anything to hasten the defeat of the Axis in Europe.[40]

The naval staff judged that Royal Navy forces were insufficient to meet current commitments in the Atlantic and Mediterranean and on the wider trade routes.[41] Royal Navy forces to meet a threat from Japan could only be provided at the expense of Europe and the risk of further compromising success in that theatre. Nevertheless, the staff insisted that 'failing other sources' (ie the United States), the necessary forces would somehow be found to protect the Far East, especially Australia, if necessary by withdrawal from the Mediterranean.[42] It was desirable therefore that American-British co-operation should focus first on the containment of Japan and the minimum US Navy forces required for this. Once Far East defence needs were met, the balance of US Navy forces could be deployed to assist the Royal Navy in the Atlantic.[43] This was the argument the British began putting to the American political and naval leadership, primarily through two meetings with Ghormley in the second half of November, but also through Lord Lothian, the British ambassador. The latter returned to Washington after a visit to London, where he was briefed by Pound at the same time as the Ghormley meetings took place. These briefing operations drew on the Bellairs paper to make the more specific case for basing a US Navy fleet at Singapore.

In London the arguments, including the case for a US Navy fleet at Singapore, were first put to Ghormley by Pound on 19 November.[44] Bailey and Bellairs then followed up with a more detailed presentation, drawing on the Bellairs paper, now approved by the chiefs of staff, on 22 November.[45] Bailey's agenda for this meeting, drawn up the previous day, was revealing:

- Seek a decision in Europe;
- Remain on the strategic defensive in the Pacific;
- Singapore the key position;
- Minimum force at Singapore to contain Japanese naval activities;
- Possible scale of attack on United States west coast and countermeasures;
- Our estimated requirements and available forces;
- United States forces that can be made available.

The British thinking encapsulated in the Bellairs paper has been criticised, and even savaged, as both unrealistic, and showing arrogant disregard for American interests.

The British, strong in procedures and preparation, were weak in understanding American sensitivities and prejudices. To suppose that America would agree to send its fleet to a colonial outpost or meekly submit to the principle that initiatives for American involvement would emanate from London was to engage in day dreams bordering on the hallucinogenic.[46]

From Washington's perspective, Britain's view seemed 'incredibly selfish and parochial'. American policymakers were not confident of Britain's survival. In these circumstances, to leave the US Navy Fleet at Hawaii, rather than withdraw it to the United States, seemed controversial, while to move it 6000 miles further away to Singapore looked 'treasonably irresponsible'. Sending a detachment to the Asiatic Fleet was almost as dangerous. Keeping it at Hawaii was therefore 'a tolerable compromise'.[47] The British attitude 'ignored not only the totally changed strategic situation in the area but also the unlikelihood of the Americans being willing to substitute their fleet for that of Britain in a British plan conceived originally to defend British imperial interests'.[48] Some of these criticisms are justified, but they also merge the misreading of American thinking, the substantive issues, and weaknesses in how they were then presented, in a way that confuses rather than illuminates.

The Bellairs paper had some logic and credibility if it is judged solely as a strategy to defend Allied[49] interests in the 'Far Eastern' theatre (comprising Malaya, the Netherlands East Indies, the Philippines and China), as opposed to wider American security needs across the Pacific. The fact that American 'means' were to be applied to give effect to a long-standing British strategy for countering Japan did not imply the strategy was inappropriate for important

American priorities in the Pacific theatre. Deployment of a US Navy fleet to Singapore certainly solved a specific British problem. But the British could reasonably argue that this was the best way to achieve a common desired strategic end. This was sufficient control of the South China Sea to secure essential joint, not just British, territories and interests, and apply enough economic pressure to discourage a Japanese advance. Singapore was not promoted over Manila for selfish strategic or geographic reasons, but on the practical basis that Manila lacked facilities, as the Americans acknowledged. The British could also argue that their proposals were a reasonable evolution of the ideas aired in 1938/39 in the discussions with Ingersoll and Hampton.

Although the British did not know it, their proposals aligned closely with a US Navy plan, developed in autumn 1939, to deploy their Pacific Fleet to Singapore and then drive northwards to secure the Malay Barrier and the Philippines. This plan was known as Rainbow 2. It was designed to address the type of strategic scenario that now prevailed.[50] Furthermore, a reduced version of Rainbow 2, known as 'Asiatic reinforcement', was still being actively developed until early January 1941. That month Commander John McCrea visited the Commander-in-Chief Asiatic Fleet, Admiral Thomas Hart, bringing a copy of this variant, the Rainbow 3 war plan and a message from Admiral Stark, as Chief of Naval Operations. 'Tell Admiral Hart that, consistent with a strong policy, there will be no backing down (with Japan). The President, Secretary of State, Welles (Under Secretary of State), and Navy Secretary Frank Knox, do not desire war with Orange (Japan). However, there will be no weakening or appeasing.' McCrea briefed that Rainbow 3 envisaged reinforcing the Asiatic Fleet with a carrier, cruiser division and destroyer squadron, tripling Hart's force. Stark also anticipated that Hart's force would co-operate with the British and Dutch in the defence of the Malay Barrier. Two days after McCrea's departure on 20 January, and just a week before the American-British ABC-1 staff talks commenced, Hart was informed that Rainbow 3 was to be superseded. There would be no Asiatic reinforcement. The ships would go to the Atlantic instead.[51]

Despite these qualifications, the Bellairs paper had four major weaknesses which became increasingly evident under American scrutiny. The first problem was the force distribution it proposed between Pacific and Atlantic theatres. The British claimed to want a defensive strategy in the Far East, deploying, in Pound's words, 'the minimum forces necessary to hold the Japanese', so that maximum forces could be concentrated in the European and Atlantic theatres, 'to hasten defeat of Axis powers that alone can end the war'.[52] However, as Ghormley pointed out, the distribution of US Navy capital units, proposed by Britain, between Singapore, Manila and Pearl Harbor would leave little surplus of major US Navy units available for the Atlantic. The British consistently argued that the minimum US Navy fleet required in Singapore was nine capital ships (one less than the overall IJN strength in 1940) and three carriers. They also proposed a further carrier in Hawaii, therefore absorbing all but one of the US Navy's 1940 carriers. These figures underestimated the problems in supporting and maintaining a US Navy fleet at a huge distance from its normal bases, or the political difficulty of selling a policy which had no US Navy capital ships deployed outside the South China Sea. If the US Navy did deploy nine capital ships to Singapore, it was inconceivable the remaining three ships presently in the Pacific Fleet would be released to the Atlantic.[53]

Yet the British did also want a substantial US Navy contribution in the Atlantic. The scale of American commitment desired here was apparent when the British Ambassador, Lord Lothian, met the naval staff (comprising VCNS, Bailey, Bellairs, and Director of Plans) on 9 November. They suggested that to meet Atlantic requirements, the US Navy would need to withdraw two battleships, two carriers, and seven modern cruisers from the Pacific. This transfer was not consistent with the requirements set out in the Bellairs paper approved by the chiefs of staff only the previous day.[54] The British figures did not add up. The size of the US Navy fleet they proposed for Singapore seemed larger than required for a limited defensive strategy against Japan, and they overstated overall American strength. While British figures credited the US Navy with fifteen capital ships, one of these, *Arkansas* armed with 12in guns, was effectively a training ship, while six others were of limited military value, comparable to the Royal Navy 'R' class.

The second problem, identified by Bellairs himself, was the inadequate state of the Singapore and Malaya defences. It would be difficult to induce the Americans to send a fleet to Singapore if they lacked confidence the base would still be there when they arrived. The Americans were well informed on the state of Singapore and Malaya defences through their observer at the Anglo-Dutch staff talks. They had justifiable doubts that Singapore yet had the facilities capable of supporting a substantial fleet. Insistence by the chiefs of staff that Bellairs's concerns were exaggerated, and Singapore could withstand a long siege, was unconvincing.[55] Worse, the failure to acknowledge the present weakness of defending forces, and failure to demonstrate commitment to providing substantial reinforcements, disregarded Ghormley's warning that the British and Dutch must make a serious contribution to Far East defence.

This warning was repeated by Stanley Hornbeck, the special adviser to the US Secretary of State Cordell Hull, in two conversations with the Washington embassy in late November. Hornbeck was well known to the British as the American government's foremost expert on Far Eastern affairs, having headed the Far Eastern division in the State Department from 1928–37. He was broadly sympathetic to British needs in the Far Eastern theatre and understood the importance they placed on Singapore. He stressed that not only must the United States see that Britain was making a serious effort to upgrade Far East defences, but that no American naval officer he had spoken to favoured sending US Navy ships to Singapore.[56]

The third problem was the lack of air power in the theatre. The proposed US Navy fleet would have its own air component, but it would still be significantly outmatched by the air forces the Japanese could bring to bear. The Bellairs paper did not address the limitations this would impose on naval operations in the South China Sea, as already discussed in Chapter 3. Pound apparently believed it was not necessary for the proposed fleet to operate at any distance from Singapore, but that hardly squared with the need to counter a Japanese expeditionary force to northern Malaya, or the aspiration to cover the Philippines.[57]

Finally, the British argument that a US Navy fleet based at Singapore could provide adequate deterrence against an IJN attack on Hawaii or raids on the United States west coast was dubious. The naval staff argued that any raid would be executed by cruisers and carriers, and would be constrained by logistics and the threat of American land-based air power. They conceded that interception of a raiding force would be easier if the US Navy Pacific Fleet was based at Hawaii, but the area of sea to be swept was still very large. If, by contrast, the US Navy Fleet operated with 'energy and initiative' from Singapore and Manila, it might pose sufficient threat to deter Japan from releasing a raiding force in the first place.[58]

It was probably true that the material damage the Japanese could inflict here was limited. However, they could, as Lord Lothian, pointed out when he met Pound on 8 November, interrupt the communications across the Pacific on which the support of the US Navy fleet depended. The US Navy had identified Japanese interdiction of communications as a major problem with Rainbow 2. They had anticipated that reinforcements and supplies for a Rainbow 2 fleet deployed at Singapore would need to be routed via the South Atlantic and Indian Ocean with Royal Navy assistance.[59] Lothian was also inevitably much more aware of the political impact of any Japanese raids on the United States Pacific coast than the Admiralty appeared to be.[60] He accordingly asked for more detailed advice on the Japanese scale of attack that might be generated against the United States west coast. Director of Plans' subsequent arguments here were still not convincing and certainly did not address the threat to Pacific communications.[61]

The completion of Bellairs's paper, and the wider conclusions reached by the Royal Navy leadership on how the United States could best support Britain's global naval strategy, coincided almost exactly with a fundamental review of American strategy by Admiral Stark. Stark's review is known to history as the

Plan Dog memorandum. It received this label because Stark set out four strategic options for the United States labelled A to D and recommended that the last, option D for 'dog', should be pursued. This was an 'Atlantic first' strategy.[62] Plan Dog was much more than a review of naval strategy. It was, in effect, a national security review, which outlined not only the overall strategic risks and choices the United States faced in October 1940, but anticipated the strategy the United States would adopt over the next five years.

Stark's core conclusion mirrored that of the British, that Europe was the decisive war theatre and that victory here was essential to America's future. If Britain lost, then in a much-quoted phrase, America might not 'lose everywhere', but was in danger of not 'winning anywhere'. Stark did not think Britain could win in Europe without substantial American support, which would limit what the United States could do in the Pacific. In essence, the United States must pursue an 'Atlantic first' policy, try to avoid war with Japan, but, if conflict did arise, ensure operations in the Pacific did not compromise the primary effort in the Atlantic. The memorandum is also striking for its emphasis on the Mediterranean. It judged that the defence of Egypt and then Gibraltar should be Britain's current priorities after the United Kingdom homeland, as indeed they were, and should take preference over the Far East. Stark forwarded the final version of his memorandum to the Secretary for the Navy, Frank Knox, on 12 November 1940.[63]

While Stark's paper was immensely important in pushing the United States towards a coherent national security strategy, in advocating a defensive strategy in the Pacific it confirmed a shift in policy that was already well underway. The fall of France and the prospect that Britain might also suffer rapid defeat had inevitably focused American attention on defence of the western hemisphere since the early summer.[64] In addition, the financial stringency imposed on defence budgets in the aftermath of the Depression meant that by 1939 the United States lacked the capability to conduct a full offensive war against Japan in the Pacific, let alone a war against multiple opponents in two hemispheres. By 1940 a substantial naval rearmament programme was gathering pace, but the results would not begin to appear until well into 1942. Meanwhile, there had been a steady reduction in the scope of American war plans for the Pacific towards the concept of a limited war fought with limited means to secure modest objectives.[65] Financial constraints apart, these more limited goals reflected the distaste felt by Congress and the American public for offensive war, and recognition that American interests in the Far East were less valuable than those of Britain and other colonial powers. British ambitions for a major US Navy fleet at Singapore showed insufficient awareness of these limitations on American intent and capability as well as American warnings, repeated by Ghormley, that American support in the Far

East could only be contemplated if the British and Dutch were seen to be helping themselves.

The British were first alerted to the existence of Plan Dog on 31 October by the Bailey Committee representative in Washington, Captain Arthur Clarke.[66] He was shown a first draft by the Head of US Navy War Plans, Captain Richmond (Kelly) Turner. Clarke had already been shown the complete Rainbow 3 plan, the current US war plan for the Pacific, a week earlier on 23 October. As explained earlier, Rainbow 3, which replaced Rainbow 2, provided significant reinforcement to the Asiatic Fleet. It also envisaged a limited offensive in the central Pacific.[67] Clarke now reported Stark's assessment that a full offensive war against Japan would absorb all American naval and industrial resources, leaving the US Navy unable to provide the minimum assistance in the Atlantic and Europe necessary to avoid a British defeat. If Japan forced war upon the United States, it would therefore adopt a defensive posture. This appeared to imply maintaining a reasonable fleet in the central Pacific and some small reinforcement to co-operate with British and Dutch forces in the Far East. But ultimately the United States was prepared to accept the loss of the Philippines, the Netherlands East Indies and Singapore.[68]

Given the authority of Clarke's insight, it appears odd that neither the Royal Navy leadership nor the chiefs of staff now questioned whether the emerging Bellairs strategy, which was not approved until 8 November, was still feasible. There were two reasons for the lack of an immediate rethink. In the first place, the naval staff saw pleasing agreement on the basic principle that there should be a defensive strategy in the Pacific while the main effort focused on the vital European theatre. The difference, therefore, was over the implementation of a defensive strategy, and here they hoped the United States could yet be convinced of the key role of Singapore. The purpose in basing a fleet there was not initially to take the offensive, but to contain Japan. In what proved a prophetic insight, the Director of Plans, Captain Charles Daniel, added that, if the United States could not be persuaded, 'we might, under certain circumstances, have to send a powerful squadron ourselves to Singapore to the detriment of our offensive in Europe'. An 'uneconomical procession' of British and American forces to the eastward would then be set in motion.[69]

The second reason was that Pound received a letter from Ghormley on 13 November, seeking a meeting to discuss an assumption being made in the Navy Department that Britain 'can and will' prevent any aggression against the western Atlantic and western hemisphere by the Axis powers.[70] This conflicted with Clarke's report, and suggested American policy was still under development and thus susceptible to influence. As Daniel put it, if Clarke's reading was right, the United States was adopting a more defensive posture in the Pacific and more help in the Atlantic, 'than we want'.[71]

On 21 November Clarke reported that Stark's paper, with a firm recommendation for option D, and the support of the United States Army, had been sent to the president. Clarke confirmed that, although the final paper had more detail, the core arguments were the same. He also added several crucial points. The status given to the paper suggested option D was now likely to become official policy. He gave details of the other three policy options (A–C) which underlined the significance of the 'Atlantic first' recommendation at D. Clarke also emphasised that substantial American intervention in the Atlantic was not only judged essential to secure victory, but now also to avoid British defeat.[72] It is not clear whether Bailey and Bellairs saw this telegram before they met Ghormley the following day, and it is unlikely it would have caused them to alter their planned briefing of Bellairs's 8 November paper. Ghormley was also unsighted on evolving American policy. Turner told Clarke he had not been briefed on Stark's Plan Dog paper and the British were not to display knowledge of this.[73]

Despite this apparent commitment to Plan Dog, the British continued to get conflicting signals. On 30 November Turner informed Clarke that he was preparing contingency plans based on option C of Stark's paper rather than D. Option C, summarised by Clarke ten days earlier, read: 'Abandonment of full offensive against Japan and adoption of a policy of rendering maximum aid to Britain in European and Far Eastern areas. This might prevent Japan achieving large successes in Malaysian area but would not permit despatch of sufficient weight to European area to ensure Germany's defeat'.[74] This option involved strengthening the Asiatic Fleet to ensure the Malaya area could be held, while maintaining the main body of the US Navy Fleet at Hawaii. Clarke subsequently clarified that this 'Asiatic reinforcement' would comprise one carrier, five heavy cruisers, one light cruiser, twenty-two destroyers, seventeen submarines and thirty-six flying boats.[75] The corollary was that there would only be limited Atlantic reinforcement (although from the British viewpoint it would still be significant) and this would be made up of three battleships, two carriers, five heavy cruisers, four light cruisers, twenty-nine destroyers, and fifty-six submarines.[76] Turner suggested that, while the US Navy remained committed to D as the best option, they thought they might yet be overruled.[77] Turner was not yet aware of the British proposals for US Navy deployment to Singapore put to Ghormley on 19 and 22 November. Incredibly, Ghormley's report covering these discussions did not reach the Navy Department until 5 December.[78]

The beginning of December now brought two crucial, and linked, developments. The first was the American decision to proceed with staff talks in Washington, in which a joint naval strategy would be a dominant theme. The British learnt from Lord Lothian on 29 November that the president had authorised the talks.[79] However, Ghormley was not informed until 2 December, when the Navy Department instructed him to prepare to return to Washington to participate. The second development was a firm American message, delivered in both Washington and London, that the British proposal to base a major US Navy fleet at Singapore was unacceptable. Turner spoke to Clarke with typical bluntness. The British proposal reflected selfish interests and took no account of American needs. It was 'equivalent to America proposing to despatch the British Mediterranean Fleet to Singapore to safeguard the Philippines'. Staff talks would be pointless if the British persisted. Turner did, however, confirm that the significant Asiatic Fleet reinforcement of 30 November remained extant.[80] Ghormley reinforced this American position with Bailey. Deploying the US Navy Fleet to Singapore would be widely perceived as 'pulling British chestnuts out of the fire'. He personally recognised the vital importance of Singapore to the British Empire and therefore, indirectly, to the United States. However, this was not grasped by American public opinion, nor indeed the Navy Department.[81]

Churchill naturally observed these exchanges closely. He responded enthusiastically to the initial reports on Plan D, seeing it as 'strategically sound' and 'highly adapted to our interests'. Britain should strengthen Stark's argument and do nothing inconsistent with it. Importantly, he saw little difference in deterrence effect between a US Navy fleet based at Singapore or Honolulu.[82] He therefore instructed the Admiralty not to contest Stark's strong opposition to Singapore basing.[83] Pound accordingly sent temporising replies to both Stark and Ghormley, stressing that the British delegation to the coming staff talks would approach matters with an open mind.[84] Churchill was undoubtedly focused here on the big prize, consolidating American support for Britain where it most mattered, and ideally bringing her into the war. It is more debatable whether he fully understood that in committing to an 'Atlantic first' policy, the United States would no longer have a superior fleet on Japan's flank, and that Far East requirements would have to assume higher priority for Britain if they were to take lower priority for the United States.[85]

Meanwhile, there was a significant meeting at the Admiralty on 10 December.[86] With the exception of Pound, this brought together all the key members of the naval staff dealing with Far East policy and the potential US Navy role. Those present were VCNS (Phillips), ACNS (F) (Rear Admiral Sir Henry Harwood), Director of Plans (Captain Charles Daniel), Bailey, Bellairs, and Rear Admiral Victor Danckwerts. The latter was the previous Director of Plans and about to head the British naval delegation in Washington. The meeting is important for three reasons: it encapsulated naval staff thinking on the Far East at this time; it established Britain's opening naval position for the forthcoming staff talks; it also outlined a better naval outcome for the eastern theatre at the forthcoming talks than would be achieved.

The meeting agreed that Singapore remained the best option to base a fleet to deter a Japanese move south, but recognised it would be hard to get the US Navy to accept this. A key issue, therefore, was whether a fleet based at Honolulu could meet British needs. Threatening the Japanese homeland, including Tokyo and other cities, with attack by carrier-based aircraft might achieve the desired deterrence, but it was not clear whether the US Navy would countenance this, or whether it was logistically possible over a range of 3350 miles. It is intriguing that the British raised this idea. The group no doubt had in mind the successful Fleet Air Arm attack at Taranto, exactly a month earlier, as an example of how even a single carrier could achieve strategic impact. However, the reference to 'Tokyo and other cities' suggests they had civilian, rather than military, targets in view. They clearly wanted to achieve the maximum political effect to persuade the Japanese leadership that deploying the bulk of its naval forces southward was too risky. This appears to be the first time that the Royal Navy contemplated using naval aircraft against civilian targets, although it was a logical evolution of what the Royal Air Force was doing against Germany, and the plans to bombard Italian coastal targets with battleship gunfire. The idea anticipated the American raid on Tokyo in April 1942 using two-engine land bombers flown from US Navy carriers. This operation, led by Lieutenant Colonel James Doolittle, did achieve a marked political effect although it did negligible damage and was immensely complex to mount.

If the US Navy would not contemplate carrier strikes, then Britain would argue that a limited offensive role from Honolulu would be insufficient, and hopefully convince the US Navy of the need for more forward basing. If carrier attack was feasible, Britain should accept Honolulu as the primary US Navy base, but push for strengthening the Asiatic Fleet with two capital ships and the maximum possible air and submarine force at Manila. The Royal Navy would probably also bolster Far East defences by early deployment of Force H to the Indian Ocean.[87]

Accounts of American-British naval negotiations at the end of 1940 usually move directly from the American decision to open staff talks, and their parallel message that deployment to Singapore was unacceptable, to the opening of the ABC-1 talks on 29 January 1941. They imply that the British delegation effectively ignored Churchill's direction to defer to American views on Singapore by resuming their lobbying almost as soon as the conference opened. One account describes 'an unresolved difference' between the chiefs of staff and prime minister over Far East policy. 'For a time the British delegation at the conference seemed more intent on forwarding the strategy of the Chiefs of Staff and in the process almost broke up the Washington meetings.'[88] Such accounts exclude the instructions for the United Kingdom delegation issued on 19 December, following approval by the Defence Committee two days earlier.[89] These instructions reveal important shifts in British naval policy towards the Americans from the position taken with Ghormley in late November.

The 'General Instructions' stated that in a war against all three Axis powers, it was British policy to give priority to the European theatre and defeat Germany and Italy first. However, the security of the Far Eastern position, including Australia and New Zealand, was also essential to British strategy and the retention of Singapore as key to defence of those interests must be assured. The separate 'Instructions for the Naval Delegates' confirmed the British view that an 'adequate force' should be provided in the Pacific while meeting requirements in Europe. It recognised, however, that the location of a potential eastern fleet was 'unsettled'. The British view remained that Singapore was the right strategic option, but it seemed the United States might not accept this. They apparently favoured an eastern fleet at Hawaii, with a 'limited offensive role'. The naval delegates were accordingly instructed to explore how adequate deterrence could be achieved from Hawaii, using precisely the arguments identified at the 10 December Admiralty meeting described above. This was consistent with Churchill's directive at the Defence Committee that the British delegates could explore American thinking but must ultimately defer to their position on all matters concerning the Pacific. Britain should not be asking the United States 'to come and protect' Singapore but, rather, offering its facilities for their use.[90] Pound stated that the chiefs of staff fully agreed with the prime minister's view.

The instructions then defined how the British wanted American naval forces distributed between the European and Pacific theatres. Here they underlined the sheer scale of commitment the British now required from the US Navy in the Atlantic and western Mediterranean. These were already evident in the figures proposed by Bailey to Ghormley on 22 November. However, the new figures prepared for the staff talks contained important changes. The British now wanted the US Navy to take over responsibility for the Gibraltar Force controlling the Straits and western Mediterranean, as well as providing the Atlantic support identified by Bailey. The US Navy would, therefore, effectively take over the Mediterranean sphere assigned to the French in the 1939 Anglo-French staff talks, as discussed in Chapter 2. Overall, the British now required four US Navy carriers for the European theatres, leaving just two available to cover the Pacific and Far East.[91] The British were therefore proposing a much larger naval commitment to the European theatres than the US Navy had yet contemplated, with inevitable consequences for defensive cover in the East, leaving aside the argument over Singapore basing.

The total British proposals for US Navy forces in the combined Atlantic and western Mediterranean theatres were now five battleships, four carriers, eighteen cruisers, seventy-two destroyers, forty submarines, and significant light anti-submarine forces in addition. By comparison, the Pacific Fleet would have ten battleships, two carriers, seventeen cruisers, ninety-three destroyers, and eighty submarines. Under these proposals, the Pacific Fleet would still have twice as many battleships as the new Atlantic Fleet, but it would have fewer carriers and would also have its light forces much reduced. It would therefore retain battleship equality with the IJN, but would be far weaker in the crucial categories of carriers and cruisers.

This British emphasis on Atlantic reinforcement has been underestimated in established accounts of the American-British naval relationship in both the run-up to the ABC-1 talks and the conference itself. These accounts have focused primarily on the arguments over Far East strategy. They have also stressed that it was American concern over Atlantic security which effectively ruled out basing any substantial US Navy force forward of Hawaii. These American fears were real, but the British did much to encourage those fears in the last two months of 1940, when American policy was still evolving.

There were three problems with this British negotiating position for ABC-1. In the first place, the total Allied force, primarily American, recommended for the Pacific theatre was much weaker than the potential IJN opposition in the crucial categories of carriers, cruisers, modern destroyers and submarines. The combined US Pacific and Asiatic Fleets on 1 December 1941 would have a strength which was quite close to British proposals: nine battleships, three carriers, twenty-four cruisers, eighty destroyers and fifty-five submarines. By comparison, IJN strength at that time was ten battleships, ten carriers, thirty-five cruisers, 111 destroyers and sixty-four submarines.[92] Even if the bulk of this US Navy force was concentrated at Singapore, as the British wanted, and tasked with a defensive holding operation confined to the Malay Barrier, the disparity in air power would now place it at a decisive disadvantage. If, on the other hand, it was based primarily at Hawaii, as the US Navy insisted, a force of two carriers would be far too weak to conduct more than a symbolic and high-risk operation against the Japanese homeland. In short, the British aspiration for American deterrence cover could not be met with the forces the British were recommending. There was a fundamental inconsistency between what they wanted the United States to do in the East to constrain Japan, and what they claimed they needed for the European theatres. A charitable explanation for this is that the British overestimated American naval power. A fairer, if harsher judgement, is that Royal Navy planning here displayed a tendency to indulge in wish lists that showed insufficient regard for strategic, operational, and not least logistic, realities.

The second problem was that in pressing for such substantial support in European theatres, the British confirmed American fears that they were facing potential defeat here, thus encouraging the United States to over-insure. Under the Rainbow 5 war plan that implemented Plan Dog, by July 1941 the US Navy had exceeded the British December target strengths for the Atlantic in all categories of warship except carriers (three in the Atlantic rather than four) and cruisers (thirteen rather than eighteen). Forces in the Pacific (Pacific and Asiatic Fleets combined) dropped significantly from the British targets (destroyers down to fifty-eight by July, compared to ninety-three, and submarines down to fifty from eighty).[93]

The British emphasis on Atlantic support, potentially at the expense of the Far East, requires more explanation. The September Future Strategy paper had expressed confidence that Britain could retain control of all vital sea areas in the European theatre, and there was no mention then of any critical dependence on US Navy resources. A strategic survey prepared for the forthcoming staff talks in mid-December shows why the September confidence was now being qualified.[94] It repeated that Britain faced three existential threats: invasion; crippling air attack; and seaborne attack on trade. The danger of the first two had receded, but Germany was now making an intense effort to defeat Britain at sea, using a combination of submarine, surface raider, minelaying and air attack, and exploiting the strategic advantage of the long continental seaboard. Here the survey noted the additional threat posed by a German move into Spain and against Gibraltar. In the five weeks to 3 November, shipping losses were 420,300 tons, a level comparable to the worst period of the last war. If losses continued at this rate, they could be fatal. Britain's maximum merchant shipbuilding capacity was 1.5 million tons per year, but it would require 3 million tons above that to make good losses. This was apparently the US Navy view as well. Admiral Stark stated in December that British ship losses had now reached 4.6 million tons per year. He forecast that at this rate Britain would not last another six months.[95] The survey concluded that holding out against Germany, for the moment, depended on maintaining seaborne supplies. To ensure this, Britain required all the help the United States could offer, especially in light escort forces, flying boats and merchant shipping resources.

This December survey was clearly drafted to make the case for American naval support, but it was a genuine assessment of how Britain viewed the naval risks in the Atlantic at this time.[96] Overall merchant ship losses in the second half of 1940 were 1.85 million tons for vessels over 1600 gross registered tons, of which at least 1.50 million tons were lost to U-boats. Monthly shipping losses from submarine attack were now three times the average monthly level over the first nine months of the war. The loss to U-boats was especially severe in October at 363,267 tons, a figure which would not be exceeded until February 1942.[97] This October figure was a warning of what the Germans might achieve with steadily growing U-boat output, the potential acquisition of bases in Spain and West Africa, and the diversion of Royal Navy destroyers to meet a new United Kingdom invasion risk in the spring.

The threat posed by German surface warship raiders was also now greater than at any point during the rest of the war. With repairs after the Norwegian campaign complete, and two new battleships and a heavy cruiser nearing completion, the British faced a potential force of eight major warships available for Atlantic raiding duty, compared with just two in September. Germany now had scope for several simultaneous operations and the large raiders could only be dealt with by capital units. The pocket battleship *Admiral Scheer* commenced a five-month sortie in October, during which she ranged as far as the Indian Ocean. The heavy cruiser *Hipper* made sorties in December and February. The battlecruisers *Scharnhorst* and *Gneisenau*, which returned to operations in mid-December, made a successful two-month Atlantic sortie in January 1941, destroying more than 100,000 tons of shipping, arguably the only raider operation which had strategic effect.[98] The battleship *Bismarck* and heavy cruiser *Prinz Eugen* would become operational in May 1941, and the battleship *Tirpitz* a little later.

Although the British could not know this in December, their raider counter-measures would prove sufficiently effective in the first half of 1941, not only to prevent their worst-case raider scenarios, but to ensure the overall raider results were distinctly modest. The eight German warship raiders (one battle-ship, two battlecruisers, three pocket battleships and two heavy cruisers) deployed in the first twenty-eight months of the war sank just fifty-nine ships, and a total of 297,909 tons, for the loss of *Bismarck* and *Graf Spee*.[99] By the end of 1941, the remaining force was corralled in French ports or Norwegian waters, and the prospects for Atlantic breakout were slim. Raiding operations by major surface warship were essentially over.[100] From 1940 the Germans also used armed merchant raiders with rather better results, a total of seven deployed during 1940/41 sinking ninety-eight ships, and a total of 593,171 tons, against three raiders destroyed by the Royal Navy.[101]

The important shipping figure for the British was the net loss after gains from new build and acquisition were taken into account.[102] This was not yet critical in December 1940, since the net loss for vessels over 1600 gross registered tons (which were clearly those responsible for ocean transport) in the second half of 1940 was just 664,000 tons. However, the British could see it was rising rapidly, and they were aware that many of the shipping gains in the second half of 1940 were one-off acquisitions and seizures that could not be repeated.[103] In the first half of 1941 net loss would rise to 1,212,000 tons, a rate that could not be sustained indefinitely.[104] Remarkably, the second half of 1941 would bring a net gain of 229,000 tons, reducing the net loss overall for

1941 to 983,000 tons. This reflected not only the impact of Ultra intelligence, evasive convoy routing, and increased British escort strength, but also the impact of American naval escort in the western Atlantic.

This positive shift lay in the future and from the present British perspective, active American naval support in the Atlantic to ensure supplies, along with long-term shipping output, looked essential to survival. Nevertheless, in making their case, both internally and to the Americans, the British did not adequately distinguish between the essential and 'nice to have'. Convoy escorts, flying boats, and shipbuilding resources were 'essential', as the 13 December Joint Planning Committee survey stated. Three carriers and six cruisers to form 'raider hunting groups' were 'nice to have' in the Atlantic, but would also make a substantial and much-needed difference to Pacific strength. The same applied to battleships beyond those required to replace the Halifax escort force. It is possible that by early January Pound had recognised that Britain had overstated its needs in the Atlantic, and that this would pose problems for the Far East. He told Ghormley that three US Navy battleships, along with modest supporting forces, and the current US Navy escort forces, would be sufficient to prevent any aggressive Axis moves against the western hemisphere and assist convoy work. Carriers were not mentioned. There was a huge difference between Pound's line here and the ABC-1 instructions approved three weeks earlier. Ghormley nevertheless reported to Stark that it would be 'dangerous' to count on Britain holding the Atlantic without considerable American assistance.[105] Despite Pound's second thoughts, the overall result was that, with British encouragement, the US Navy had more forces, especially major units, in the Atlantic in 1941 than were justified by the underlying strategic realities. This not only reduced deterrence cover against Japan, but ensured overall Allied dispositions in the East would be less effective than they might otherwise have been.

The impact of Atlantic lobbying on the Americans is evident in Table 6 below.

Table 6 United States Naval Forces in the Atlantic 1940/41

	Royal Navy Deficit Director of Plans 9/11/40	Bailey 22/11/40	British ABC-1 19/12/40	Rainbow 3 7/12/40	Rainbow 5 31/7/41
Capital ships	4	5	5	3	6
Aircraft carriers	5	2	4	2	3
Cruisers	18	20	18	9	13
Destroyers	82	77	72	45	81
Submarines	N/A	60	40	56	63

Notes:
(i)   Column 1 is extracted from Director of Plans' note for VCNS dated 9 November 1940, 'Commitment of our Naval Forces', ADM 199/1159, TNA. This defined overall force requirements for various theatres along with ships actually available on 11 November 1940. It therefore identified the deficit the Royal Navy perceived at this time in the Atlantic and western Mediterranean which they hoped the US Navy would fill. Director of Plans specifically stated – 'From the appendix it will be seen that our present numbers are totally inadequate for the task and it is for these reasons that the proposed dispositions of the American Fleet have been put forward'. The deficit figures closely match the figures for support desired from the US Navy in the Atlantic subsequently provided by Admiral Bailey to Rear Admiral Ghormley on 22 November (Column 2).
(ii)   Column 2 is extracted from the American naval dispositions proposed for the Atlantic provided by Bailey to Ghormley on 22 November. The figures are included in Bailey's record of the 22 November meeting, in ADM 199/1159, at Appendix II.
(iii) Column 3 is extracted from the British proposals for US Navy forces in the Atlantic and western Mediterranean included in the Instructions for Naval Delegates in COS (40) 1052 of 19 December 1940, 'British – United States Technical Conversations', CAB 80/24, TNA.
(iv)   Column 4 is taken from US Navy War Plan WPL-44. The figures here accord closely with those provided by Captain Turner to Captain Clarke on 7 December 1940 and recorded in Washington tel 2952 of 6 December 1940, ADM 199/1232, TNA.
(v)   Column 5 is derived from US Navy War Plan WPL-46.

The final problem with the British negotiating position was the failure to recognise and exploit a missed opportunity. The British knew from Turner that the US Navy was contemplating substantial reinforcement of the Asiatic Fleet. Although the Americans had not said so, they could assume this would base at Singapore, or at least agree to fall back there if Manila became untenable. The British could have immediately encouraged Asiatic Fleet reinforcement in two ways: by suggesting early deployment of Force H to Singapore to support the Asiatic Fleet task force, instead of keeping it in the Indian Ocean; and by proposing a joint approach to building up air strength, along with the Dutch, in the Far East theatre. This might have achieved the basis of a modern joint task force which, with a modest upgrading of land-based air power, had sufficient strength and capability credibly to contest the southern part of the South China Sea in late 1941. The British could then have acquiesced in the main US Navy Fleet remaining at Hawaii, while pressing the US Navy to keep at least three carriers there rather than two.

There is no guarantee such a policy would have succeeded, given the growing US Navy commitment to the Atlantic, their reservations over dividing their forces, and doubts about the survivability of Singapore as a base. However, it would have demonstrated British flexibility and willingness to work within the grain of American thinking. It would have encouraged the Americans to be more collaborative through 1941, even if there was no immediate agreement. It would also have required the Royal Navy leadership to develop a defence concept for the Malay Barrier using something closer to the Drax 'flying squadron', rather than Pound's 'adequate battle-fleet'. Although this was, arguably, exactly the concept Cunningham and Somerville were applying with success in the Mediterranean, Pound showed no appetite to translate new thinking to the East. At his meeting with Ghormley on 7 January, he reiterated that his preferred option for Far East defence was a substantial US Navy fleet at Singapore. He seems to have made no effort to explore how deterrence could be achieved from Hawaii as set out in the ABC-1 instructions.[106]

Table 7 below illustrates the scope for alternative patterns of US Navy and Royal Navy distribution in the Pacific and Far Eastern theatres from December 1940 to July 1941.

Table 7 United States and Royal Navy Forces in the Pacific and Asiatic Theatres 1940/41

	US Navy				Royal Navy	
	Pacific Fleet		Asiatic Fleet		China Fleet	Force H
	Dec 1940	July 1941	Dec 1940	July 1941	July 1941	
	Rainbow 3	Rainbow 5	Rainbow 3	Rainbow 5		
Capital ships	12	9	0	0	0	1
Aircraft carriers	2	3	1	0	0	1
Cruisers	13	16	6	2	13	1
Destroyers	71	45	22	13	5	5
Submarines	38	33	17	17	0	0

Notes:
(i)   Column 1 derives from US Navy War Plan WPL-44. It shows the strength of the Pacific Fleet after the proposed despatch of Asiatic reinforcement (Column 3).
(ii) Column 2 from US Navy War Plan WPL-46. It shows the strength of the Pacific Fleet after transfers to the Atlantic and cancellation of Asiatic reinforcement.
(iii) Column 3 from Captain Turner's figures for Asiatic reinforcement provided to Captain Clarke on 6 December 1940 and recorded in Washington tel 2952 of 6 December, ADM 199/1232, TNA.
(iv) Column 4 from US Navy War Plan WPL-46.
(v)   Column 5 figures represent an average for the second half of 1941 taken from the table attached to Director of Plans minute dated 27 September 1941, ADM 116/4877, TNA. Only four of these cruisers were modern with the balance old vessels of the 'C' and 'D' classes.
(vi) Column 6 from Director of Plans minute dated 23 February 1941 which formally designated Force H as the 'Immediate Reinforcement' for the Indian Ocean in the event of Japanese intervention and confirmed its current strength. ADM 116/4877, TNA.

If the July strength of the Pacific Fleet (Column 2) is taken as a minimum, then the reinforced Rainbow 3 Asiatic Fleet as proposed by Turner to Clarke on 7 December (Column 3) would be met by holding back one carrier, four cruisers and nine destroyers from the transfers to the Atlantic in the first half of 1941.[107] (Following Pearl Harbor, the US Navy immediately transferred Task Force 17, comprising the fleet carrier *Yorktown*, two light cruisers, and four modern destroyers, from the Atlantic to the Pacific. The newly commissioned *Hornet* followed in January, leaving just the light carriers *Wasp* and *Ranger* in the Atlantic.[108]) This would still leave an Atlantic Fleet substantially larger than the Rainbow 3 fleet contemplated in December (Column 4 of Table 6) in capital ships, destroyers and submarines. This reinforced Atlantic Fleet would also remain strong enough to replace the Gibraltar Force on American entry into the war, thus relieving Force H for deployment to the Far East. The combination of Force H with a reinforced Asiatic Fleet and the existing China Fleet and Dutch forces would have yielded an overall Allied force of one modernised battlecruiser, two carriers, twenty-three cruisers,[109] forty destroyers and thirty submarines. This did not include significant Australia and New Zealand forces, comprising about five modern cruisers and five modern destroyers. This Allied force would have been broadly comparable in strength and capability to the IJN southern task force which executed the invasion of Malaya and the Philippines in December 1941. This comprised two battlecruisers, two small carriers, fourteen cruisers, fifty-four destroyers and eighteen submarines.[110]

The Royal Navy could not have provided Force H immediately in early 1941. What was needed was a clear joint strategy for holding Japan north of the Malay barrier, enabling local commanders to develop operational plans with confidence. In the event, Asiatic Fleet reinforcement died in mid-January as 'Atlantic first' took hold and Plan Dog translated into the Rainbow 5 war plan. To mark this, the US Atlantic Fleet was formally established under Admiral Ernest King on 1 February 1941. Prior to that there was a single US Navy Fleet based in the Pacific, with detached squadrons only in the Atlantic.[111] By promoting a major Atlantic transfer, the British therefore encouraged a process which meant they got the worst of all worlds before the ABC-1 talks even started. They lost the opportunity for meaningful co-operation with the United States in the Far East theatre, which would now be the subject of endless and unproductive wrangling through 1941. They ended up with a Pacific Fleet incapable of exercising credible deterrence. They got the promise of help in the Atlantic which was more than they needed, and much of which could not take effect anyway until the United States entered the war.

The ABC-1 staff talks and their impact on Far East naval strategy

The ABC-1 staff talks which began on 29 January 1941 lasted two months. The main accounts of these talks have important, and often surprising, gaps and misunderstandings.[112] There has been too much emphasis on the differences over Far East strategy and too little on the remarkable agreement on overall strategic priorities, as well as the important pre-hostilities co-operation initiated in the Atlantic theatre. In exploring the Far East arguments, most accounts give a partial and distorted view of what British goals actually were, and exaggerate the significance of apparent differences between the prime minister and the chiefs of staff and naval staff.[113] They also overstate the possibility that the talks might have broken down over the Far East.[114] None of the main accounts adequately explains how the concept of a Royal Navy eastern fleet came to be resurrected and endorsed by the Admiralty just three weeks into the talks, with major consequences for British naval reinforcement later in the year. They also omit important insights into how the Admiralty weighed the comparative importance of the Far East and Middle East at this time.

We have already seen the British objectives for ABC-1. The comparable American objectives prior to war were to ensure the security of the western hemisphere against intervention by hostile powers; to provide material and diplomatic assistance to the United Kingdom; to oppose by diplomatic means Japanese incursion into new territory. If the United States entered the war, its overall goal was the defeat of Germany and her allies, and its primary military effort would be made in the Atlantic and Mediterranean. It would prefer to keep Japan out of the war, but if Japan intervened, Pacific and Far East operations would aim to minimise distraction from the primary theatres.[115] There was much common ground with British policy in these initial overarching goals, and the arguments that would later erupt over the Far East were, therefore, not so much about end points, but rather the ways and means of achieving them.

Given the comparative start points, the striking feature of the final ABC-1 agreement from a British perspective is not just the clear commitment to dealing with the 'ultimate enemy' first, and the extent to which British proposals for American support in the Atlantic and western Mediterranean were agreed, but also how far it supported existing British views on overall grand strategy.[116] Thus ABC-1 endorsed the principles of blockade, a maximum air offensive against Germany and the early elimination of Italy. Critically, from the British viewpoint it also confirmed the need to maintain the British and Allied position in the Mediterranean, and to prevent any extension of Axis control in North Africa. Britain certainly failed to get its preferred outcome in the Far East, or even adequate assurances. Nevertheless, the United

States agreed that resources must be provided to guard against Japanese intervention and promised that in the event of war, the US Navy Pacific Fleet would operate offensively to weaken Japanese economic power and divert Japanese forces from Malaya. It also undertook to augment forces in the Atlantic and Mediterranean to allow the Royal Navy to release forces for the Far East. A United States Army memorandum neatly summarised the American naval commitment agreed under ABC-1 as follows: 'Initial US naval operations will be to maintain a strategic reserve in the Pacific in order to influence Japan against further aggression; and to relieve Britain of responsibility for shipping in the western Atlantic including the North Atlantic route to the British Isles'.[117]

The limits to American support in the Pacific and Far East theatres, and the prospect that Britain would have to deploy substantial naval forces of its own if it wished to secure Singapore, were clear within a week of the talks starting. In line with their instructions, but contrary to most subsequent accounts, the British team did not reopen the issue of US Navy basing at Singapore. They did try hard to explain why the security of Singapore mattered to their overall war effort, and the serious threats to Australasia, the Indian Ocean and, ultimately, the Middle East supply route, that they judged would follow its loss.[118] They also addressed the relative importance of the Middle East and Far East. There were powerful arguments why neither could be abandoned but 'on a long term view, the Far East is to the British Commonwealth of greater importance than the Middle East'.[119] In seeking American help, they focused on two points: how the US Navy Pacific Fleet would exert effective deterrence on Japan; and the desirability of the US Navy reinforcing its Asiatic Fleet, although without the parallel Royal Navy contribution suggested earlier.

The Americans insisted they would maintain sufficient forces in the Pacific to exert pressure on Japan, but that these must be concentrated at Hawaii. There would be no further detachments to the Far East theatre. They also questioned the ultimate importance of Singapore, dismissing the prospect of any significant Japanese threat to Australia or the Indian Ocean. The British delegation found American assurances that they could contain Japan from Hawaii inadequate, and judged that the Americans saw Malaya and the Netherlands East Indies as expendable. True to their instructions, the British pressed the Americans on the possibility of carrier attacks against the Japanese homeland at the third ABC-1 meeting on 3 February. The Americans brushed this option aside. Even with four carriers, such attacks would be too difficult, and the weight they could deliver 'ineffective'.[120] The Americans did not think Singapore was defensible with existing or planned forces, and felt any US Navy reinforcements, such as the carrier task group the British sought for the Asiatic Fleet, would be left exposed and vulnerable. Bellairs informed Pound on 4 February, after the third ABC meeting, that it was clear there was no prospect of inducing the Americans to move the Pacific Fleet to Singapore. Pressing them on this 'would do no good – indeed the reverse'. He would, however, continue to push them on exercising pressure from Hawaii and Asiatic reinforcement.[121]

The possibility that the British might provide their own reinforcement to the Far East if the Americans took over obligations in the Atlantic was first raised by Ghormley and the US military attaché, Brigadier Raymond Lee, before the talks started. The initial British response was revealing, in view of developments later in the year. It acknowledged that such assistance would release older battleships from escort duty, but their 'armour, endurance, and AA armament' were insufficient for duty either in the eastern Mediterranean or engaging the Japanese fleet unless supported by 'heavier types'. The 'older battleships' referred to were, of course, the 'R' class. Their limitations, fully acknowledged up to now by the Admiralty, have been noted in earlier chapters. Over the next six months, the Admiralty would move steadily towards the view that they might, after all, be capable of assuming a central role in a new eastern fleet.[122]

Turner pursued this option at the third ABC meeting on 3 February. One reason for ruling out Asiatic reinforcement was that American lines of communication to the Far East theatre were 'extremely hazardous', whereas British lines through the Indian Ocean were secure. He therefore proposed that the US Navy should further reinforce the Atlantic, thus releasing British naval forces for the East. It is arguable that the British had at least helped to bring this undesirable option on themselves. By emphasising the importance of Singapore to their war effort, they had provoked the response: 'Well, if it is so important, defend it yourself.' By proposing that the US Navy should take over the Gibraltar Force, as well as northwest Atlantic escort, an option the US Navy proved willing to accept, they had rendered the creation of an eastern fleet at least possible.

By 11 February Bellairs clearly felt the prospects were bleak of meeting his original instructions, the assurance of credible cover from the main US Navy Fleet at Hawaii, along with reinforcement of the Asiatic Fleet. The previous day the Americans had requested a British paper covering Japanese options for attacking Malaya; consequences arising from the loss of Singapore, assuming the US Navy Pacific Fleet remained active in the Pacific theatre; and whether Britain would send a fleet to the East if the United States provided compensating forces in the Atlantic.[123] He intended to have a last go at explaining the risks facing Britain in the Far East, in the hope this might yet unlock meaningful Asiatic reinforcement, but stressed that US Navy capital ships in Singapore must be ruled out. If the Americans would not budge on Asiatic reinforcement, he wanted to know whether the chiefs of staff would contemplate, as an alternative, the creation of a Royal Navy capital ship force following US Navy Atlantic reinforcement.[124]

204

Bellairs's message provoked the first of two important interventions by the prime minister, in which he famously accused Bellairs of making 'heavy weather'. The prime minister was relaxed about the US Navy basing at Hawaii, and disinterested in Asiatic reinforcement, arguing that if Japan intervened, events would draw the Americans forward. Significantly, he also saw no need for the US Navy to maximise their effort in the Atlantic and Mediterranean. The simple principle was that the US Navy should deal with Japan and limit assistance in the Atlantic to convoy escort. He dismissed the idea of a Royal Navy capital ship force as 'quite foolish'.[125] The prime minister might have been intuitively right here about what was really needed in the Atlantic, but it was not what the Admiralty had sought, and he had approved, in December. It also certainly fell far below what the Americans thought was now needed. The prime minister, therefore, not only chose to ignore the fact that Bellairs had been faithfully executing the instructions received from the Defence Committee, but he failed to understand the strength of American commitment to the Atlantic. Not for the last time, he also minimised the risks in the Far East.

Pound immediately challenged the prime minister's line on Royal Navy capital ship reinforcement and Pound's view prevailed in the reply to Bellairs.[126] He told the prime minister that to fight the three Axis powers, Britain and the United States required a battle-fleet in three theatres (home waters, Mediterranean and Far East). The ideal was a single fleet in each. The economical way to control the Pacific was a single battle-fleet at Singapore, strong enough to fight the Japanese fleet. A single fleet at Hawaii was not sufficient to deter Japan from moving south. Pound was obviously arguing here for power of concentration and economy of effort. However, he was also being over-simplistic. Theory was one thing and the practical reality of dealing with multiple threats across wide areas quite another. The Royal Navy effectively had two battle-fleets in the Mediterranean, and wanted the US Navy to provide a second one in the Atlantic. Pound continued that the Admiralty had not previously proposed sending capital ships to Singapore while the Americans maintained their fleet at Hawaii, because they hoped to convince the Americans to base in Singapore. If the Americans ruled this out, as now seemed certain, but sent six capital ships to the Atlantic and Mediterranean, Britain must decide whether to use the ships they replaced to create a capital ship force for the Far East. Pound judged that, if US Navy ships could take responsibility for Atlantic escort and Force H, it would be possible to create an eastern fleet comprising *Rodney*, *Nelson*, three 'R' class and *Renown*.

Within two days, on Pound's instructions, Captain Charles Daniel, Director of Plans, had completed detailed proposals for this new eastern fleet. He confirmed that if the US Navy would not be shifted from concentration at Hawaii, this would leave insufficient protection for the Dominions and essential communications in the Indian Ocean. The Royal Navy must, therefore, take on this task, for which capital ship cover was essential. So long as the Americans provided the Atlantic reinforcements they were now promising, it would be possible to create an eastern fleet based around six capital ships and one carrier. His proposed fleet would comprise the battleships, *Rodney* and *Nelson*, released from the Home Fleet by the commissioning of the new *King George V* and *Prince of Wales*, the modernised battlecruiser *Renown* and carrier *Ark Royal*, released by the Americans taking over the Gibraltar Force (Force H), and three 'R'-class battleships relieved by the Americans from the Halifax escort force. These heavy ships would be accompanied by ten cruisers and thirty-two destroyers. At this point, *Rodney* and *Nelson* were still the most heavily armed battleships in the world, and broadly comparable to the best IJN battleships, *Nagato* and *Mutsu*.

Daniel's dispositions assumed a total US Navy commitment to the Atlantic, as recently notified by Bellairs, of six battleships, three carriers, sixteen cruisers, and eighty-two destroyers. This Atlantic reinforcement compared with the Admiralty proposals in mid-December of five battleships, four carriers, eighteen cruisers and seventy-two destroyers.[127] Daniel noted that his new Eastern Fleet would be weaker than any fleet previously considered, but it would suffice to hold Malaya, given the American presence on Japan's flank. The proposed fleet was smaller than the 'maximum fleet' available for the Far East defined in Naval War Memorandum (European) in August 1939 by one battleship, one carrier, seven cruisers and twenty-three destroyers. The composition and therefore the quality of the capital ship force were similar to 1939, and no doubt Daniel used those dispositions as his start point. However, only *Renown* and *Ark Royal* from Force H, and to a lesser extent the two *Nelson*s, were equipped for the modern war environment of 1941. The proposed fleet was hardly competitive, therefore, with the forces the IJN were expected to have by the end of the year.[128]

These exchanges demonstrate unequivocally that by 15 February, two weeks into the ABC-1 talks, the prime minister, chiefs of staff and naval staff in London, and the United Kingdom delegation in Washington, all agreed that the US Navy Pacific Fleet would not shift from Hawaii, and any prospect of a major US Navy fleet basing at Singapore was a non-starter.[129] The prime minister judged the risk of Japanese intervention remained low, regarded a fleet at Hawaii as sufficient deterrent, and saw further probing into potential US Navy plans and dispositions in wartime as an unnecessary distraction from the core goal of cementing a grand strategic alliance. By contrast, the naval staff felt a US Navy fleet at Hawaii would provide inadequate cover for Singapore, the Dominions and Indian Ocean, and were prepared to cover the gap with Royal Navy resources. They agreed with Bellairs that a stronger

Asiatic Fleet and commitment to offensive operations by the Pacific Fleet would make Royal Navy cover more effective.

There were therefore still differences between the prime minister and naval staff, but they were not over Singapore basing.[130] The traditional interpretation of the prime minister's second intervention on 16 February, as a directive to the Admiralty to tell Bellairs to shut up about Singapore basing, is also wrong.[131] The prime minister here savaged Bellairs's latest report as a long-winded and pointless reiteration of ground already covered, and for reopening a basing argument already decided. Bellairs was certainly verbose, and provided a rather poor summary of his paper passed to the Americans to meet their request of 10 February. But on the substantive points, the prime minister's strictures were unfair. Reduced to essentials, Bellairs's paper defined the strategic importance of Singapore in standard British terms. It then argued that if it was not possible to place a capital ship force (either British or American) at Singapore, the US Navy Asiatic Fleet should be sufficiently reinforced to threaten Japanese communications in the South China Sea, thus rendering operations against Singapore more difficult. Responding to the prime minister, Pound agreed that Bellairs had argued 'that the US Fleet should be at Singapore rather than Hawaii'. (This was rather unjust to Bellairs. He had judged Singapore to be the only fully satisfactory strategic solution, while also recognising it was not possible.) However, Pound rightly disputed the prime minister's claim that Bellairs had advocated splitting the Pacific Fleet between Singapore and Hawaii.[132]

The prime minister's new intervention certainly underlined both his personal attitude to the negotiations with the Americans, and his prejudices over Far East defence. But it had minimal practical effect on the British policy already shaped by Pound and the naval staff between 12 and 15 February. This policy was effectively a role reversal. The US Navy would substitute for Royal Navy forces in the Atlantic, so they in turn could fill the gap the US Navy refused to take on in the Far East theatre. It was a compromise, and a poor substitute for the original British aspiration to persuade the US Navy to take over both Pacific and Far East naval defence. But whatever its shortcomings, it was a clear way forward, confirmed in new instructions from the chiefs of staff to Bellairs on 19 February.

These instructions incorporated conciliatory language, suggested by the prime minister, to soothe the Americans, and emphasised British acceptance of American naval dispositions in the Pacific theatre, which all key parties in London agreed were now immutable.[133] However, they also confirmed that Britain would now send a substantial fleet to the Far East, including six capital ships, as soon as the US Navy relieved Royal Navy forces in the Atlantic.[134] The chiefs of staff recognised that the Atlantic changeover would take time to implement. During the interim before Royal Navy forces arrived, the defence of the Malay Barrier would therefore depend heavily on American willingness to threaten Japanese communications. Furthermore, the Royal Navy fleet would be insufficient to take on the whole IJN fleet, so American pressure would be essential to prevent Japan sending a maximum force south. The chiefs still hoped the Americans would see merit in reinforcing the Asiatic Fleet but, significantly, they would prefer reinforcement here to come at the expense of the Pacific Fleet, not the Atlantic.[135]

These British queries over the time involved in Atlantic release and the effectiveness of American pressure from Hawaii could be interpreted as caveats, and they were subsequently discussed at length, notably on 26 February. However, in practice, the British had little option but to accept American assurances. The Far East deal implicit in these instructions was therefore the one incorporated in the final ABC-1 agreement. The relevant section is worth quoting:

> If Japan does enter the war, the Military Strategy in the Far East will be defensive. The US does not intend to add to its present military strength in the Far East but will employ the Pacific Fleet offensively in the manner best calculated to weaken Japanese economic power and to support defence of the Malay Barrier by diverting Japanese strength away from Malaya. The US intends to augment its forces in the Atlantic and Mediterranean to enable the British Commonwealth to release forces for the Far East.[136]

Despite some robust initial exchanges over Far East strategy, it was never likely the talks would break down on this issue. One account describes an 'extraordinary crisis over Far Eastern strategy that flared so dramatically in late February' and 'actually threatened the continuance of the conference and presumably of Anglo-American co-operation'. Britain, unable to protect an area it judged vital, was pushing America to a point where it risked the larger prize of American involvement in the war. The British discovered, therefore, the 'outer limits of coercion'.[137] This interpretation does not reflect the underlying objectives of the two parties and the record of the discussions. Above all, it overlooks the fact that effective agreement on the Far East had been achieved by 15 February. There could not therefore be a major 'crisis' over the substance of Far East strategy later in the month.

There was, it is true, a related row, which might have escalated if the British had not moved quickly to defuse it. Lord Halifax, the British ambassador, unwisely, and without Bellairs's knowledge, showed a copy of Bellairs's 11 February paper to the American Secretary of State, Cordell Hull. The American delegation saw this as 'political lobbying' against the agreed terms of the staff talks, threatening suspension until they received an explanation. Bellairs quickly provided assurances that this was a mistake which would not be repeated, and this was accepted. This row, however awkward for a few days, was about protocol rather than substance. The underlying reality was that both sides had too much political capital invested in the success of these talks to countenance failure. There was consensus on Atlantic primacy, and the British delegation arrived under clear instructions to defer to the Americans on the Pacific. The British would ultimately have accepted Hawaii basing on whatever terms the United States offered, and no Asiatic reinforcement. The US Navy offer to release Royal Navy forces from the Atlantic for the Far East was therefore a bonus, and the ready British acceptance made the outcome more collaborative and comprehensive than it would otherwise have been. It is important to stress that the president and State Department, including Secretary of State Cordell Hull, were almost certainly more understanding and supportive of the British position in the Far East than were the American military. They recognised the damage to British Empire cohesion and war fighting potential that might follow Far East losses. They also recognised that Malaya tin and rubber were vital to the American economy, and especially potential war production as well. Awareness of their views undoubtedly ensured the United States delegation remained constructive and disposed to find a way forward.[138]

The British decision to create an eastern fleet, subject to US Navy Atlantic reinforcement, has received little emphasis in accounts of the ABC-1 negotiations, and the subsequent implementation of the decision has been virtually ignored. Yet it is fundamental to understanding Far East naval policy and the evolution of Far East naval reinforcement over the rest of 1941 and, indeed, the first months of 1942. It is impossible to make sense of the well-known debates between the prime minister and Admiralty in August and October, which led to the despatch of Force Z, without understanding how the ABC-1 decision evolved. For the Admiralty moved swiftly to translate the 19 February instructions to Bellairs into a formal policy for Far East naval reinforcement.[139] Within a week, an initial outline of this policy had been agreed and communicated to Commander-in-Chief China. This signal included the succinct sentence: 'We have been asked if in the light of the above (US) dispositions we should be prepared to send a capital ship force to the Far East and have replied "Yes"'.[140]

The new policy stated that if the United States and Japan entered the war together, immediate reinforcements would still be sent to the Indian Ocean, comprising Force H and the Dominion naval forces in the Mediterranean. Force H still comprised the modernised battlecruiser *Renown*, the carrier *Ark Royal*, the modern heavy cruiser *Sheffield*, and five destroyers. The Dominion forces were made up of the modern Australian cruiser *Perth* and five Australian destroyers. Two submarines from the Home or Mediterranean Fleets would be added. Daniel as Director of Plans emphasised these forces were primarily to protect vital communications in the Indian Ocean, not to 'dispute Japanese control of the South China Sea'. He expected Indian Ocean routes to suffer heavy attack from surface raiders at the start of a war with Japan. This raider threat evidently referred primarily to raids by IJN heavy cruisers, but clearly incursions by IJN battlecruisers and carrier groups were possible too. The prime minister and First Sea Lord would see cruiser raiders as the main risk from the IJN through most of 1941.[141] This proposed Royal Navy Indian Ocean immediate reinforcement, along with Dominion cruisers already in the East, was a reasonable minimum response to this cruiser threat. It would have struggled to cope with one or more IJN hunting groups with capital units, let alone a major force of the type that would attack Ceylon in April 1942. This is relevant to the debate around *Prince of Wales* later in the year. As Daniel acknowledged, such a force could also do little to protect Malaya or the wider Malay Barrier.

Once the US Navy was fully mobilised and able to take on agreed responsibilities from the Royal Navy in the Atlantic and western Mediterranean, which might take some months, the main body of the new Royal Navy Eastern Fleet would concentrate and move to the Indian Ocean to join the 'immediate reinforcement', and then ideally move on to Singapore. The composition, mobilisation and deployment of this new fleet were reviewed again in early March,[142] in early April[143] and in May[144] with minimal change. Indeed, the plans first defined in mid-February would remain extant through the summer and autumn, and were still evident in a Joint Planning Committee paper issued the day before Japan attacked on 8 December.[145] As Chapter 6 will show, the deployment of Force Z in October is better seen as an evolution of these plans, rather than a fundamental departure.[146]

A more detailed exposition of the new Far East naval strategy was sent to Far East naval commanders in early April after the end of ABC-1.[147] It explained the respective British and American roles now agreed, and broke the proposed Royal Navy Far East naval reinforcement into two formal phases. Phase 1 covered the period before the arrival of the Eastern Fleet, with reinforcements comprising the 'immediate reinforcements' of Force H and Dominion forces. Phase 2 comprised the main Eastern Fleet, composed of five capital ships, ten cruisers and twenty-seven destroyers, which would concentrate at Freetown following relief by US Navy forces in the Atlantic. The plans anticipated that it would take eighty days from United States entry into the war to get the full phase 2 fleet to Singapore. If Singapore had fallen, which was considered unlikely, the fleet might use Port T at Addu Atoll in the Maldives as its main base. This is one of the first references to Port T, which will feature extensively in Chapter 8.

The naval staff also considered how Far East reinforcement should be modified if the United States entered the war against Germany and Italy, but Japan remained neutral.[148] Here they sought a balance between having sufficient forces close to the Far East theatre to be a credible deterrent to Japan, and to conduct initial defence if she attacked, without distracting from the primary goal of defeating Germany and Italy. The provisional conclusion was that the phase 1 force would be sent to the Indian Ocean, three 'R'-class battleships would be deployed on convoy escort in the Indian Ocean, and that, ideally, two other Royal Navy carrier task forces (centred on *Eagle* and *Hermes*) should be established in the Indian Ocean and South Atlantic area. It was also agreed that the two *Nelson*s were not suitable for raider hunting in the Indian Ocean, owing to their lack of speed. These proposals again provide important context for the arguments between the prime minister and naval staff which would take place in August.

ABC-1 is invariably portrayed as a setback for British Far East strategy. It is argued that the American naval assistance promised in this theatre fell far short of what Britain needed to defend an area she considered vital.[149] It is argued further that Britain had now ceded her independence in Far East strategy to the United States. 'The Admiralty had made every conceivable attempt to bring the USN into the fold, to set the agenda and to establish dominion over how the war would be fought and where, and had failed.' Far East strategy now depended 'less on demands from the Dominions' than 'sanctification' by the United States.[150] ABC-1 is thus presented as the beginning of a wider power shift, with Britain obliged to defer to American wishes and accept ultimate American naval dominance.[151] The British have also been accused of behaving 'self destructively' at ABC-1. They obtained an American pledge to beat Germany first, yet 'contrary to that intent they sought to gamble America's strongest military asset on a mission of extreme peril', pushing the Americans to move the bulk of their Pacific fleet forward to command the approaches to Malaya and the Netherlands East Indies, thereby exposing it to superior Japanese forces. The Americans would be protecting assets in which they had little direct national interest, while leaving Hawaii and California open to attack and making it more difficult to reinforce the Atlantic quickly in the event of British collapse. The British argument that their global war effort depended on the resources of Australasia and India, which in turn depended on the security of Singapore, is here judged specious. The fall of Singapore a year later did not collapse the empire war effort. By contrast, the loss of the Pacific Fleet off Singapore might well have caused the United States to turn its back on Europe to focus on Japan, with incalculable consequences.[152]

There are powerful counter arguments to these 'setback' interpretations of ABC-1.[153] First, ABC-1 both consolidated and promised broad American endorsement of Britain's overall 'grand strategy' for defeating Germany and Italy. The Far East outcome must be set in this wider context.

Both sides found ABC-1 invaluable. There was a fundamental agreement that Germany was the primary threat to the security of both countries, that the defeat of Germany and Italy was the priority, that the Atlantic lifeline between Britain and the USA must be secured and that a purely defensive deterrent policy should be maintained against Japan. Here was the core of Anglo-American co-operation – a commitment to mutual control of the Atlantic as the key to both countries' survival.[154]

The American endorsement obviously reflected American self-interest, but the scale of commitment to the Atlantic and the distinct commitment to the Mediterranean arguably went further than strict self-interest required.

The report by the United Kingdom delegation to the chiefs of staff concluded:

... there has never been any divergence of opinion in regard to the paramount aim of defeating Germany and the concentration of US forces in the Atlantic area for this purpose. Their view agrees with ours that the gravest danger to the Allied cause is the Axis threat against the sea communications of the British Isles, and that every help the US can give for protecting these communications should receive the maximum priority.[155]

It is vital to appreciate here that at the mid-point of the year, from the British perspective, the situation in the Atlantic remained as bleak as that painted in the December Strategic Survey, and the threat it posed to Britain's survival here came second only to invasion. In mid-June the Joint Planning Committee assessed that the rate of shipping loss was still an unsustainable 4.5 million tons per year, and the only prospect of improving the situation remained decisive US Navy intervention in the Atlantic.[156] It follows that for Britain's war leadership, any differences between Britain and the United States over support in the Far East (which, perhaps significantly, were not mentioned in this Joint Planning Committee paper) were far outweighed by what the US Navy could offer in the Atlantic.

Secondly, ABC-1 established the framework under which the United States would assume full responsibility for the security of Iceland, and for protecting convoys in the western Atlantic from September, three months before the United States entered the war. The immediate impact on Atlantic losses of this American intervention is hard to assess, but it possibly saved 500,000 tons of shipping in 1941 alone. Shipping losses from U-boats fell by about 50 per cent in the second half of 1941 compared to the first half (750,532 tons down from 1,548,182 tons). If the losses of the first half had been repeated in the second half, and a further adjustment is made for an average 60 per cent increase in frontline U-boat strength in the Atlantic, total losses for the year should have been around 4.0 million tons, whereas in reality they were 2.3 million tons, representing an apparent net benefit of 1.7 million tons.[157] Three factors contributed to this benefit: the breaking of U-boat Enigma from the end of June and the use of this Ultra intelligence in diverting convoys; the strengthening of Royal Navy convoy escorts as more vessels came available from new build; and the introduction of US Navy escorts in the western Atlantic. The last factor was a double win, because it not only meant convoys were relatively secure while under US Navy escort, but Royal Navy forces were released to increase escort support elsewhere.

It is impossible to produce definitive figures for the relative importance of these factors, though Ultra is usually awarded the greatest role, with a saving of perhaps 1.5 million tons frequently put down to this factor alone.[158] That seems significantly to underplay the other factors. If 1.7 million tons is taken as a reasonable figure for total shipping saved (there are clear limits to this sort of statistical exercise with so many variables), a contribution of 500,000 tons from US Navy escort seems feasible. The fall in losses in the second half of 1941 meant the overall losses from U-boats in 1941 at 2,298,714 tons were actually lower than for 1940, when they were 2,462,867 tons.[159] Shipping losses from all causes in all theatres were nevertheless still up by 10 per cent at 4,328,558 tons, compared to 3,991,641 tons in 1940.[160] The US Navy intervention in the western Atlantic also enabled the Royal Navy to begin Far East naval reinforcement well in advance of the Japanese attack in December, even if the reinforcement was mishandled, as discussed later.

Thirdly, there is a tendency to underestimate the degree of American support agreed at ABC-1 for Britain's position in the Far East. The role of the US Navy Pacific Fleet moved from theoretical deterrent, prior to the agreement, to active participation in a common strategy to contain Japan, and a promise to deploy offensively to draw Japan away from Malaya. The commitment to replace and thereby release Royal Navy forces in the Atlantic and western Mediterranean, especially Force H, was viewed by Britain as an uneconomic use of available Allied forces, but was a substantial American concession to meet a British interest which the United States felt was, at best, overstated. It was 'uneconomic' because, as the British pointed out on 26 February, the Allies ended up with a plan to deploy fifteen capital ships (six Royal Navy at Singapore and nine US Navy at Pearl Harbor) to check a force of ten IJN capital ships. It was a 'concession' because the US Navy was agreeing to substitute for Royal Navy ships rather than reinforce them. As a result, there would be no net increase in capital ship forces in the primary war theatre. The British certainly regarded the creation of their own Eastern Fleet through

Atlantic substitution as second-best to a US Navy fleet at Singapore, or even Asiatic reinforcement.[161] However, the war leadership as a whole, and certainly the Admiralty, appear to have embraced the ABC-1 solution as an acceptable alternative, even if it was inefficient. There is no sign that 'Atlantic substitution' was questioned, let alone criticised, when the chiefs of staff and Defence Committee successively reviewed and approved ABC-1.[162]

Finally, the accusation of self-destructive behaviour is a gross mis-representation of the British stance. The British regarded basing a US Navy fleet at Singapore as the most effective way to contain Japan, but they never insisted this was the only option. They never pressed the Americans to adopt it, and they had abandoned this option before ABC-1 opened. It is correct that, as matters turned out, the loss of Singapore had limited strategic impact on the war, therefore apparently vindicating that judgement of the American chiefs of staff. But that does not necessarily mean British fears of the wider risks posed to the Allies by Japanese conquest of Southeast Asia were unreasonable, even if they overstated the specific importance of Singapore, and were naive about the political and military constraints on American deployment. The risks were real. A determined Japanese effort might have taken Ceylon in the spring of 1942, destroyed the Eastern Fleet, cut Indian Ocean communications, and made Britain's position in the Middle East untenable.[163] That might not have knocked Britain out of the war, but the consequences would have been as great as the hypothetical loss of a Pacific fleet at Singapore, and might then reasonably be ascribed in part to American failure to commit more forces to Far East defence at ABC-1.

Critics of ABC-1 do not adequately address whether a better outcome to ABC-1 was possible, and what this might have looked like. As suggested earlier, it is just possible that the Americans would have maintained their commitment to Asiatic reinforcement if Britain had entered the negotiations with a more credible commitment to providing adequate forces to defend the Malay Barrier. This would not only have required deployment of Force H to Singapore as a 'matching force', but also a wider scale of force commitment on the lines of the Far East commanders' assessment at the end of 1940, but with additional light naval forces and, ideally, a few submarines. The last would be important to match the substantial American and Dutch submarine forces, and give the Royal Navy some influence over their deployment. Such a British commitment would have raised all the difficult trade-offs with the Middle East discussed in Chapter 3 and, given the stance of the prime minister, was never likely. Nor would the United States have easily compromised on their growing determination to provide the maximum possible force in the Atlantic. The problems associated with different national priorities and prejudices, and the inevitable misunderstandings and mistrust were formidable.

A second question which is ignored in assessments of ABC-1 is why Britain was so quick to resurrect the concept of a Royal Navy Eastern Fleet once it was clear the Americans would not shift from a defensive strategy based on Hawaii. The American refusal either to reinforce the Asiatic Fleet, or commit to offensive carrier operations against the Japanese homeland, let alone accept primary responsibility for defence north of the Malay Barrier, was a major disappointment, but did not fundamentally change the position established in the 1940 Far East appreciation. The chiefs of staff had never said then that direct American support was essential to a 'holding strategy' based on air and land power (although Chapter 3 has argued that in reality defence of the Netherlands East Indies did require this). If Far East defence without a fleet based in the theatre was judged viable in August 1940, then nothing obvious had changed to make it less so six months later. The British had certainly taken some comfort from the existence of an American fleet on Japan's flank when reviewing the Far East appreciation, but that comfort factor still applied. Failure to achieve the maximum aspirations from the Americans in the November Bellairs paper, or the lesser goals in the December ABC-1 instructions, merely took Britain back to the status quo ante. It did not automatically imply the need to create a Royal Navy Eastern Fleet. Britain still had choices. These included faster and stronger air reinforcement, or accepting Singapore was not defensible in all circumstances, as Churchill at least seemed willing to accept, and developing an 'outer ring' defence to protect Chamberlain's eastern empire inner core, as discussed previously.[164]

Even if Britain wished to take advantage of the US Navy transfer to the Atlantic to reinforce its Far East forces, then that did not necessarily imply a substantial battle-fleet capable of contesting the South China Sea in traditional terms. Britain could merely have deployed the Force H 'immediate reinforcement' further forward at Singapore, in substitution for the 'Asiatic reinforcement' carrier task force she sought from the Americans. There is indeed a puzzle here. Had the US Navy agreed to provide the Asiatic reinforcement carrier task force which was the core provision sought by Bellairs in his 11 February paper, then there would presumably have been no American offer of 'Atlantic substitution', and no Royal Navy planning to create a major new Eastern Fleet. The conclusion, therefore, is that the Admiralty believed Asiatic reinforcement along with the Pacific Fleet at Hawaii provided adequate Far East assurance. It follows that Force H at Singapore in substitution for Asiatic reinforcement would provide the same assurance. The Admiralty might still have required an additional carrier task force in the Indian Ocean to meet the putative IJN raider threat, but that was achievable without deploying a battle-fleet. The irony is that both Asiatic reinforcement and a putative Force H substitute equated to the Drax 'flying squadron' concept of 1939 and to Force Z plus carrier later in 1941.

There is no definitive answer here. The mid-February papers justifying the decision to create an eastern fleet show that the naval staff did not believe a US Navy fleet at Hawaii, along with the planned Royal Navy 'immediate reinforcements', could provide adequate cover for the Dominions or the Indian Ocean. They also evidently judged that the strategic penalties in the 'last resort' option of withdrawing the Mediterranean Fleet were greater now than six months earlier. They certainly judged the potential damage resulting from IJN attacks on Indian Ocean communications, including the vital Middle East traffic, to be much higher.[165] A further possibility, clearly in Pound's mind at this time, was that Japan might intervene in the war while the United States continued to stand aside, at least in the Far East.[166] He told the prime minister that in a war with Japan fought without American support, the main threat was not the loss of Far East possessions, but attack on vital communications in the Indian Ocean, including those that sustained operations in the Middle East. The only means of countering this threat at present (in 1941) was to withdraw naval forces from the Mediterranean, undermining all the successes so far achieved in that theatre, and giving Germany access to oil and other vital supplies. Japan's intervention would then have offset all the aid so far provided by the United States to Britain.[167]

Had Pound been aware of the American response to Bellairs's paper circulated three days later, he would have been even more concerned. This stressed that there was indeed no guarantee the United States would go to war with Japan if she attacked southern Indochina, Thailand, or even Malaya, while avoiding direct attack on American territory or interests. The United States could not assume direct responsibility for the defence of substantial parts of the British Empire. So far as possible, territorial interest should dictate how American and British forces were deployed.[168]

It is also essential to understand that committing to an eastern fleet in February 1941 was hypothetical. It clearly depended on American intervention in the Atlantic war, but the scope and timing of this intervention remained uncertain.[169] It depended on Japanese actions too. The American offer of 'substitution' gave Britain another option for Far East naval reinforcement beyond 'last resort' withdrawal from the eastern Mediterranean. Whether and in what form Britain finally exercised the option could, as with the Cunningham doctrine of April 1939, 'depend on circumstances at the time'. It must have appeared to the Admiralty, therefore, that given American intransigence on forward deployment and basing, Britain lost nothing in accepting the alternative American offer, which both widened her options and confirmed 'distant' American deterrent cover in the Pacific.

A related issue is what role the naval staff expected the hypothetical new eastern fleet to play in containing a Japanese southward attack. Here too a definitive answer is hard to pin down. Because of the inevitable uncertainties over how quickly substitution could take effect and because the proposed eastern fleet would be smaller than any previously contemplated by the Royal Navy, initial planning had a defensive cast. The April guidance to Far East commanders said it was difficult to prejudge the situation facing the phase 2 fleet on arrival in the Indian Ocean. It was unlikely Singapore would have fallen, but Japanese occupation of Sumatra and Java might make it unusable. Immediate priorities would then be to secure the Indian Ocean and safeguard vital communications. The fleet would operate initially from Trincomalee, or from the refuelling base and anchorage at Addu Atoll in the Maldives known as Port T. The thrust of the guidance was cautious and suggested that even if Singapore was available, any operations north or east of the base would be limited.[170] (Port T was one of four discreet anchorages identified to support movement of a fleet to the Far East when planning for this began in the early 1920s.[171] It featured subsequently in all Admiralty Far East war plans. However, there were no permanent facilities there until surveys to establish rudimentary refuelling and anchorage arrangements began in late 1940.[172])

The Admiralty doubts about the availability of Singapore were questioned by Far East commanders. Perhaps surprisingly, given their earlier pressure for more reinforcements, they argued that there were sufficient Allied submarine and air forces available to dispute control of the South China Sea, even in phase 1.[173] The reference to submarine forces here reflected the significant Dutch and US Navy strength in this arm. The Dutch had fifteen boats at this time, of which eleven were relatively modern. The US Navy force, within the Asiatic Fleet, built up through 1941 to a total of twenty-nine, with twenty-three of these modern. On paper, therefore, this was a substantial combined force. It should have presented a major threat to IJN operations, and certainly to vulnerable troop convoys. The judgement here, presumably originating from Commander-in-Chief China, Vice Admiral Sir Geoffrey Layton, himself a submariner, was therefore reasonable. In practice, when the Japanese attacked, the Dutch did perform well, but the American force was a major dis-appointment and achieved little. This reflected poor training pre-war, torpedo defects and lack of logistic support.[174]

While the Admiralty may have hoped that Atlantic substitution, at a minimum, extended their defensive options in the Far East, it was soon clear that the terms of the ABC-1 Far East settlement were less flexible than perhaps the British anticipated. Danckwerts, as Head of British Admiralty Delegation Washington, warned VCNS (Phillips) at the end of June that the Americans were inclined to be litigious over ABC-1. They regarded the contents as a 'definite commitment'. Even though most elements could not take effect until the United States actually entered the war, they viewed it as more 'sacrosanct' than justified by a constantly evolving global situation.[175] At the Riviera Summit at Placentia Bay in August, Turner noted that some aspects of the Future Strategy paper presented by the British were at variance with ABC-1. 'He regarded ABC-1 as still sound, and he considered that it had been drawn up as a guide to action, not only after the United States came into the war, but as a guide to British action before that.'[176]

The first problem was that Britain had assumed primary naval responsibility for the new Far East theatre defined in ABC-1. This was distinct from the Pacific and Australia and New Zealand areas also defined in the final report. The Far East area was bounded by latitude 30° N, longitude 140° E and the southern boundary of the Malay Barrier crescent. It therefore incorporated Formosa, the Philippines, the Netherlands East Indies, Indochina, Thailand and Malaya, and wide sea areas around them, including all of the South China Sea. It was an area of joint responsibility between Britain and the United States but, importantly, Commander-in-Chief China had 'strategic direction' over all naval forces in the area, except those directly committed to defence of the Philippines. In that sense, therefore, Britain had 'primary naval responsibility', although there was ample scope for ambiguity.[177] At the time of signing, Britain may not have fully understood how the United States would interpret this responsibility. However, it was soon evident that if Britain wanted American support in holding the Malay Barrier, this came at a price. Britain had to demonstrate a serious naval commitment to barrier defence and not just to holding the Indian Ocean. Britain, therefore, found it had rather less freedom over Far East naval reinforcement than it originally hoped.

The American chiefs of staff emphasised this to their British counterparts in early August when they rejected the report of the American-Dutch-British (ADB-1) Conference convened in Singapore in April to produce a joint operating plan for the Far East theatre based on the ABC-1 principles. Recognising that the strategy of the 'Associated Powers' in the Far East was defensive, this report defined two main objectives: the security of sea communications and security of Singapore. A 'subsidiary' objective was to operate air and submarine forces from the Philippines for as long as possible to threaten Japanese communications. The report purported to address the situation both before (phase 1) and after (phase 2) the arrival of a Royal Navy Eastern Fleet, but in practice concentrated on the former. During phase 1 it did indeed expect the Americans and the Dutch to take on all operations north of the barrier, while the Royal Navy focused on protection of Indian Ocean communications. It is not surprising that the Americans reacted negatively. Essentially, they were invited to bear the whole burden of protecting Singapore, whose ultimate importance they disputed, during phase 1.[178]

The Americans accordingly criticised ADB-1 for failure to appreciate 'the great strategic importance of holding the Netherland East Indies and particularly Sumatra and Java', adding 'it will be impossible to hold Singapore if the Dutch islands are captured by Japan'. They noted that during ABC-1 meetings the British had repeatedly stated that defence of the Malay Barrier was 'vital to the continued security of UK itself'. However, of forty-eight Royal Navy warships identified as immediately available on the outbreak of a Far East war, only three were allocated to defence of the barrier and none north of it. The Royal Navy proposed to devote almost all its forces to escort and patrol work, often far away from the position the British had insisted was vital. They accepted that the Royal Navy planned to constitute a 'strong Eastern Fleet' from forces released by the arrival of the US Navy in the Atlantic, which could make a significant contribution to barrier defence. However, the Americans viewed the arrival of this fleet as 'problematic'. In consequence, unless the Royal Navy planned a contribution to barrier defence in the first phase of a war, the United States would not allow the Asiatic Fleet to operate under Royal Navy strategic direction as ABC-1 had envisaged.[179]

This disagreement is important on several counts. It demonstrated first that the Americans recognised what Britain remained reluctant to admit formally, that Singapore was untenable without ensuring the security of Sumatra and Java. Through most of 1941 the Admiralty doggedly resisted providing any formal guarantee to the Dutch on defence of the Netherlands East Indies, despite regular pressure to do so from the Foreign Office. Churchill deferred to the Admiralty view. As one historian has aptly stated, the Admiralty showed 'a curious failure to distinguish between liabilities and obligations'. The defence of the Netherland East Indies was always a British liability in the sense that she could not afford, in the last analysis, to fail to support the Dutch. 'The assumption of a formal obligation would in no sense have increased this liability; indeed it might even have lessened it by improving defence co-ordination and thereby making an attack on the islands less attractive to the Japanese.'[180] While this assessment of the British attitude is broadly fair, two important qualifications are required. First, until early 1941, the Dutch governor general in the Netherlands East Indies held to a policy of 'aloofness' in dealings with Britain in the Far East, reflecting the Dutch tradition of neutrality. This did not improve the prospects of a formal British guarantee. Secondly, despite the political constraints on both sides, there were still sufficient confidential military exchanges from the late 1930s to enable joint Anglo-Dutch naval and air plans for defending the Malay Archipelago to progress rapidly after the spring of 1941, although it was a task far beyond their power.[181] Formal political co-operation with the Netherlands East Indies earlier might have pushed Britain to confront the true discrepancy between commitments and resources in the Far East theatre. But without a willingness to inject far greater resources, the practical difference to barrier defence would have been marginal.

Meanwhile, the United States had underlined that it was not prepared to take on the entire burden of helping the Dutch defend the Netherlands East Indies. If Britain attached such importance to security of the Malay Barrier, it must contribute. The United States Army War Plans Division was particularly wary of the apparent British intent to leave the naval fighting to the Americans and Dutch, pending the arrival of their Far East reinforcements. They recognised Royal Navy resources were limited, but argued the British could provide a reasonable force for the Malay Barrier if they did not scatter assets throughout the Indian Ocean.[182]

American objections to the British dispositions in ADB-1 were further emphasised during the Riviera Conference. 'Turner remarked that the initial British dispositions contained in the (ADB) Report showed practically all the British naval forces as being employed on British trade routes instead of operating along the northern line of the Netherlands East Indies. He considered this disposition unsound.'[183] American attitudes, therefore, began to sway both the shape of Britain's naval forces in the East, and their employment. Ultimately, the Royal Navy began to realise that only when it had a substantial force at Singapore would it exert any influence on the US Navy dispositions which it judged so vital to Far East defence. With the increasing risks of Japanese attack, and the consequent growing need to bind the Americans into Far East defence, the Admiralty was tempted to deploy inadequate Royal Navy forces further forward than was sensible in the circumstances.

A second problem was how the US Navy transfers from the Pacific to the Atlantic, executed in accordance with Rainbow 5 and the ABC-1 principles, translated into the practical intent and capability of the residual Pacific Fleet. The transfers began rapidly and their scale aroused concern in the Admiralty and other parts of the British war leadership, since the deterrent effect of the Pacific Fleet remained critical if the new strategy based on a small Eastern Fleet was to be credible. Inevitably, Churchill was a notable exception here. He was happy to see virtually any scale of transfer to the Atlantic if it promoted early American intervention, and was furious with Danckwerts in Washington for suggesting there would be British reservations. At the end of April, the Americans raised the prospect of a much more substantial transfer than anything previously contemplated under ABC-1. Turner told Danckwerts that the Pacific Fleet might be reduced to just three to four battleships, eight cruisers (only four modern), and thirty to forty destroyers.[184] The Defence Committee saw a tricky balance here. A reduction in the Pacific Fleet might encourage Japan to strike, while on the other hand, reinforcement of the Atlantic could suggest to Japan that early American entry into the war was more likely. It was also likely to have a positive effect on important neutrals such as Spain.[185] This caused the Admiralty to focus on the minimum acceptable Pacific Fleet, which it judged to be seven battleships and three carriers, and was indeed its final strength when the Japanese attacked.[186] There were differing views over transfers in the United States as well. In general, the War and Navy Departments, including their political leaders, Henry Stimson and Frank Knox, favoured a maximum transfer to the Atlantic, while both the president and the State Department, especially Cordell Hull, remained more anxious about encouraging Japan.[187]

By late May the Pacific Fleet had not only transferred a significant pro-portion of capital units, but also substantial support forces, and almost all its amphibious capability. Its freedom of movement westward was also severely circumscribed by Washington, in case further transfers to the Atlantic were needed.[188] Its ability, therefore, to conduct offensive operations that Japan would consider a major threat, with a realistic hope of diverting a significant part of the IJN away from the Malay Barrier, let alone inflicting serious damage, was limited in the short term. Despite these limitations, and the ambiguity from Washington, the Pacific Fleet remained formally committed to an offensive strategy through to the outbreak of war. It was, however, heavily outnumbered in critical areas such as carriers, and many aspects of its planning look badly flawed when viewed against subsequent war experience.[189]

Following a visit to Pearl Harbor together with Captain Clarke in early April, Danckwerts warned Pound to limit his expectations of what the Pacific Fleet could and would do.[190] It is not clear how much significance London attached to Danckwerts' report, but it should have raised hard questions about the validity of a British Far East strategy that still placed heavy reliance on the deterrent value of the Pacific Fleet and continued to use this as an excuse to go slow on Malaya air reinforcement. Pound's attitude is particularly hard to understand here. In the period leading up to ABC-1 and throughout the conference itself, a key British concern, never adequately satisfied, had been the effectiveness of US Navy deterrence conducted from Hawaii. As noted earlier, the Americans had dismissed the possibility of carrier attacks on Japan. Now Pound had received warning from Danckwerts that the Pacific Fleet was ill prepared for even the more limited offensive role agreed at ABC-1. Yet at the War Cabinet meeting on 8 May, which reviewed the British response to the proposed transfers from the Pacific Fleet to the Atlantic, the First Sea Lord 'thought the US Fleet left at Hawaii would be as capable of raiding the Japanese coast as the whole fleet now concentrated there'.[191]

Pound's professional advice, therefore, was that a significant transfer, some 25 per cent of Pacific Fleet strength, with more under consideration, would make no difference. Clearly, this could not literally be true for the position in the Pacific, whatever the advantages in the Atlantic, and it took scant account of Danckwerts' warning. Phillips, as VCNS, who had been so anxious to explore carrier raids on Japan in December, apparently now shared Pound's view. In March he had stated that unless Japan showed signs of definite intervention, a large Pacific Fleet based at Hawaii, 'making faces at Japan', 'was a waste'.[192] At the end of May he endorsed the view of ACNS (F) (Harwood) that US Navy transfers to the Atlantic would facilitate earlier release of Royal Navy capital ships for an eastern fleet.[193] The steady reduction in the US Navy Pacific Fleet also inevitably provoked nervousness in Australia and New Zealand, and pleas for Royal Navy reinforcements in compensation. Britain insisted this would only be possible when the United States became a belligerent, or at least took on operational responsibilities short of formal war.[194] Meanwhile, the policy of reinforcement from the eastern Mediterranean only as 'last resort' stood.[195]

The perils of compromise

The increasing American inclination to prioritise Atlantic security over the Pacific, following the fall of France, was strongly encouraged by Britain, who sought to channel American effort against Germany as primary enemy. By the end of 1940 Britain was seeking a scale of American naval contribution, not only in the Atlantic but also the western Mediterranean, which has been under-recognised. The resulting 'Atlantic first' commitment agreed at the ABC-1 staff talks was all that Britain hoped, helped to guarantee Britain's survival, and largely endorsed Britain's blueprint for defeating Germany. However, Britain overestimated American will and ability to cover two divergent theatres, and did not adequately recognise that the American help it sought in the Atlantic was not consistent with the scale and nature of American naval cover it wanted against Japan in the Far East. The Far East compromise of 'Atlantic substitution' agreed at ABC-1, although it was a second-best alternative, appeared to offer Britain additional options for securing its specific interests in the Far East, while retaining reasonable American deterrence cover as well. In reality, it promised forces that were too widely dispersed and too ill-suited to cope with the risk posed by Japan with any confidence.

PART III

July 1941: The Road to Disaster in the East

5

Royal Navy Readiness for a War with Japan in Mid-1941: Intelligence and Capability

The previous two chapters have explained why the defence of the Indian Ocean became an increasingly important factor in British strategic calculations during the first half of 1941. They also showed how American determination to prioritise the Atlantic over the Pacific obliged the Royal Navy to resurrect the concept of an eastern fleet to ensure adequate security against Japanese intervention in the war. The next chapter argues that for a number of reasons, the mid-point of the year marked a watershed for both Britain and the United States in their perception of the risk from Japan, and the start of a series of moves on both sides that led inexorably to confrontation at the end of the year. This chapter examines the Royal Navy's intelligence picture of the naval risk posed by Japan in mid-1941, as the prospects of her intervention increased, and as it became both possible and necessary to contemplate deploying significant naval reinforcements to the East. It also looks at the overall resources and capabilities available to the Royal Navy at this time to secure Britain's vital interests across the wider eastern empire and to provide any necessary reinforcements.

The Royal Navy picture of the IJN in 1941

For most of the interwar period, the Royal Navy viewed the IJN as both its most likely opponent in a future war, and the only naval power that posed a significant threat. In terms of size, the IJN ranked third after the Royal Navy and US Navy, its fleet spanned the full range of naval capability, it had established a fine tradition,[1] and was recognised as an innovator.[2] It was by any measure a powerful force, and therefore a key standard against which the Royal Navy judged its strength and capability. The strength of the IJN, current and projected, was not only a key determinant of the Royal Navy rearmament programme from 1935 onward, but had also shaped Royal Navy programmes in the 1920s and early 1930s, especially for cruisers and submarines.[3] The specifications of the County-class cruisers laid down from 1924 were largely dictated by IJN cruiser plans following the 1922 Washington Naval Treaty. The *Southampton* class laid down from 1934 were strongly influenced by the *Mogami* class. The 'O'-, 'P'- and 'R'-class submarines, laid down between 1924–29, were specifically designed to hold off an IJN fleet in the South China Sea, pending the arrival of the main Royal Navy fleet. Until 1940, defence of the Far East was seen as pre-eminently a naval problem, and the Admiralty dominated Far East defence policy and planning. Before 1937, this policy and planning had a theoretical quality, but Japan's invasion of China increased the risk of confrontation, and the prospect of an attack on British possessions. The 1937 imperial review and Far East appreciation represented a watershed in judging those risks. For all these reasons, the Royal Navy studied the IJN closely, drawing on both overt and secret intelligence sources.

The Royal Navy's intelligence picture of the IJN has received contrasting reviews. One influential interpretation is that poor intelligence and wishful thinking allowed the Royal Navy to create an image of the IJN that made it less threatening, and hence easier to manage. As the Royal Navy increasingly struggled in the late 1930s to provide a fleet to match the IJN, so it sought convenient evidence that Japan could neither sustain nor make effective use of a superior fleet. This led it to set IJN efficiency at 80 per cent of the Royal Navy, to underrate Japanese technical and industrial capacity and to believe that the IJN would be a cautious opponent. These factors encouraged a disastrous reliance on inadequate forces, culminating in the Force Z deployment at the outset of war.[4] This interpretation focuses too much on what was not known, rather than emphasising what was known and then concentrating on key gaps. It also fails adequately to distinguish between what was knowable and what was not knowable. It was not possible to predict the timing of a Japanese attack on Malaya with any certainty before autumn 1941, because no firm plan existed before then. Nor could the Royal Navy have predicted prior to 1941 that the IJN would group all its fleet carriers in a single task force to deliver strategic effect, because the IJN did not adopt this concept until early that year. Finally, it does not place intelligence within the wider context of political and military risk management. Perceived intelligence weakness must be weighed against the fact that British assessments of the forces the Japanese would deploy against Malaya were consistently good.

An alternative view of British intelligence performance in the run-up to war concedes that the Royal Navy's assessment of the IJN was mediocre, but argues the failings were compensated by system and circumstances. Royal Navy strategy, based on 'bean-counting' of warships and a rejection of best-case planning, was not distorted by any underestimation of Japanese quality, nor was the latter responsible for the loss of Force Z.[5] The Royal Navy may have failed sufficiently to recognise IJN technical achievements and innovation in tactical thought, especially in the use of naval air power, through the late 1930s. However, this was not in itself responsible for Britain's inadequate dispositions in the Far East in December 1941, which were more the result of circumstances and the demands of grand strategy. Royal Navy intelligence failings would not, therefore, have been significant, had Britain been able to despatch sufficient naval and air forces to the East to implement a defensive strategy. Proponents of this view have also, rightly, stressed that in planning for war with Japan, the Admiralty always wanted its naval forces to be larger than they were, always preferred numerical superiority over the IJN, and calculated the balance of forces on the basis that one Japanese warship equalled one British warship of equivalent size.[6]

In terms of unit numbers of IJN warships, Royal Navy 'bean-counting', or basic assessment of IJN order of battle, in mid-1941 was fairly accurate, though not perfect. An assessment prepared by the Naval Intelligence Division (NID) section responsible for Japan, NID 4, for the prime minister in late August 1941 gave an authoritative statement of overall IJN strength.[7] This got most numbers correct.[8] It overstated the number of operational destroyers (126 compared with an actual strength of 112) and submarines (eighty compared to sixty-five), but these errors were not significant and may be explained by the inclusion of units in reserve.[9] However, the assessment also contained important mistakes in displacement and armament, which represented a more serious underestimate of actual IJN fighting capability, especially air power. It correctly identified eight aircraft carriers, but underestimated the displacement of the fleet carriers *Hiryu* and *Soryu* and the light carrier *Ryujo* by about 40 per cent.[10] Overall aircraft capacity of the eight carriers was put at 362 aircraft, compared with an official IJN figure for embarked strength at this time of 473, an underestimate of about a quarter.[11] Six cruisers, the four *Mogami* class and two *Tone* class, were mistakenly listed with 6in guns, whereas in reality they were all by this time armed with 8in.[12] (The four *Mogami* class were initially fitted with fifteen 6in guns, since Japan had reached its London Naval Treaty limit on 8in cruisers, but they were designed to be upgraded, and this was done secretly in the late 1930s. Both the Royal Navy and US Navy missed this. The *Tone* class were built as 8in cruisers from the start, but NID 4 assumed they would repeat the 6in pattern of the *Mogami*s. NID 4 did not correct this error, shared by the Americans, until after the Battle of Midway when photographs of *Mikuma* and *Mogami* showed their main armament was ten 8in guns. NID 4 then concluded, rightly, that they had always been designed for upgrading to 8in, and assumed the two *Tone*s would now be similarly armed.[13] Finally, the assessment included a 'heavy armoured cruiser' of 14,000 tons, armed with six 12in guns, on trials which did not exist.

Estimates for the overall strength of the IJNAF produced during 1941 were also broadly accurate. In May that year the Joint Intelligence Committee assessed first-line IJNAF strength at 1496 aircraft, including 330 ship-borne. The figure for ship-borne air strength of 330 aligned closely with the subsequent NID 4 estimate for the prime minister in August. Given that the total included seaplanes and catapult reconnaissance aircraft, it underestimated carrier-borne strength, even allowing for the fact that there were only six carriers in commission at this time. (The large fleet carriers, *Shokaku* and *Zuikaku*, were still in build.) Meanwhile, the Joint Intelligence Committee assessed Imperial Japanese Army Air Force (IJAAF) strength at 886, giving a total Japanese frontline strength of 2384.[14] NID subsequently circulated a figure of 1600 for IJNAF first-line strength in August[15] and a later Air Ministry Weekly Intelligence Survey in December 1941 quoted a total IJNAF strength of 1561 with 547 ship-borne.[16] The latter report set IJAAF strength at 1108, giving an overall Japanese frontline in December of 2669. By then there were ten IJN carriers in commission, so deployed carrier air strength had grown accordingly from the May estimates.

These estimates during 1941 compare with an official Japanese figure for frontline IJNAF strength on the outbreak of war of 831 shore-based and 646 ship-borne aircraft, a total of 1477.[17] British estimates for ship-borne aircraft were fairly accurate for seaplanes and floatplanes, but underestimated the carrier total by about 25 per cent (338 in December,[18] as opposed to a real total of 473). The estimates for IJNAF land-based bomber strength were also in the right order, but there was otherwise no detailed breakdown of either land-based or ship-borne strength into either category, ie fighters, torpedo bombers, heavy bombers, etc, or specific aircraft type such as A6M Zero, B5N2 torpedo bomber, or Type 1 bomber, etc. Alongside the above estimates of frontline strength, evidence from early 1942 suggests that British intelligence departments had a surprisingly accurate view on the size of the aircraft reserve held by the Japanese at the start of the war. Drawing on Joint Intelligence Committee advice, Ismay informed the prime minister in early March that the immediate reserve at the start of hostilities for the two Japanese air forces was 650 aircraft.[19] Japanese figures show that the actual total for the IJNAF operational reserve was 309.[20] It is unlikely the IJAAF reserve was larger, so a combined estimate of 650 was about right.

The Joint Intelligence Committee report of May 1941 did not expect Japanese air strength to grow significantly over the next two years, judging that production only balanced wastage and re-equipment. Wastage calculations here, of course, took account of ongoing operational losses in China. For the

IJNAF, at least to end March 1942, this assessment was essentially correct. In the summer of 1941, production of naval aircraft of all types was only 162 aircraft per month and was only 179 per month over the first four months of war. Production was especially slow for the more modern combat aircraft, and this was compounded by the paucity of reserves noted above, which represented barely 25 per cent or less of frontline strength. There were only 415 Zero fighters available to the frontline at the outbreak of war and, as will be demonstrated later, carrier attack aircraft availability was depleting fast well before the Battle of Midway in June 1942.[21] Overall, these estimates for immediate pre-war Japanese air strength, frontline, reserves and production capacity were significantly better than the comparable estimates for pre-war German air strength, and far superior to the estimates of German air strength and production during 1940 and the first half of 1941. In 1939 German air force frontline strength was overestimated by 18.5 per cent, while 1940 German aircraft production was overestimated by a minimum of 23 per cent, and at one point by about 75 per cent.[22]

British military leaders have attracted harsh criticism for their lack of knowledge of Japanese aircraft performance. Although surviving records here are patchy, accurate performance tables for all Japanese aircraft in use at the outbreak of war had been circulated across the British intelligence community by mid-1941.[23] The exceptional range of many Japanese naval aircraft, including the new Zero fighter, was identified in these tables.[24] British intelligence also had a reasonably accurate picture of IJNAF aircraft armament. The main types of bomb carried were known, as were details of the Type 91 aerial torpedo.[25] The capability of the Type 91 has often been exaggerated, compared to the standard Royal Navy 18in Mark XII and XIV Fleet Air Arm torpedoes. In fact, specifications, performance and reliability were close. The Type 91 could, in theory, be dropped from up to 500m (1640ft) altitude, but authoritative Japanese sources state that despite the optimistic claims of the ordnance department, only 10 per cent would function correctly at 200m (660ft) and 50 per cent at 100m. In an operational context, the preferred standard drop was from a range of 400–600m (1300–2000ft) at 160–170 knots at a height of 30–50m (100–164ft). This was little different from the operational performance envelope of the Fleet Air Arm Albacore, although the latter was somewhat slower.[26] This intelligence on aircraft and armament had been absorbed within Far East air headquarters by early autumn 1941 at the latest.[27]

As regards Japanese air deployment, an August NID report identified eight Japanese airfields in Indochina, along with details of the upgrades underway at Saigon and Bien Hoa, which would both be used by IJNAAF aircraft that December. Significantly, this report also included a chart showing the operational radius for heavy bombers deploying from Saigon and Soctrang, demonstrating that Singapore and the Malacca Strait would be in range of aircraft with a normal bomb load.[28] A subsequent report provided details of the Type 96 IJNAF heavy bomber, correctly estimating it could carry 2200lbs (1000kg) to 950 miles. This report admittedly doubted Japan could afford to deploy more than 150 land-based aircraft for potential operations against Malaya and the Netherlands East Indies at this time, but this figure would be revised sharply upwards over the next three months.[29] In judging operational effectiveness, Far East air headquarters drew a distinction between the IJNAF, whose quality was rated high, and the IJAAF, who were rated mediocre.[30] This assessment would have been shared with the Far East Combined Bureau (FECB), whose role is described shortly, and the China Fleet.

The Royal Navy's primary measure of its strength against the IJN was the number and quality of capital ships. Here it was certainly not complacent. In March 1940 Churchill, then First Lord, sent a paper comparing Royal Navy and IJN capital ships to the War Cabinet. It pressed the case to resume building capital ships, suspended at the start of the war, in order to ensure adequate capability against Japan from 1942 onward. However, the paper is important for what it says about the existing balance. It stated that the IJN battle-fleet, which had been completely modernised, had a speed at least equivalent to the *Queen Elizabeth* class and considerably greater than the 'R' class. Japanese battleships also outranged the unmodernised Royal Navy ships. The paper stated correctly that all ten IJN capital ships had received modern, more efficient boilers and engines, new main armament guns of increased elevation, probably to 40 degrees, additional armour, including horizontal protection, and new anti-aircraft armament. It would be unsatisfactory to send any Royal Navy ships to the East unless they matched IJN ships for both speed and range. Only seven of the existing fleet did so. These seven comprised the four Royal Navy reconstructions undertaken between 1934 and 1940, namely the three battleships, *Warspite*, *Valiant* and *Queen Elizabeth*, and the battlecruiser *Renown*, along with the two *Nelson*s and *Hood*. The four modernisations took broadly the same form as the IJN applied to all ten ships, although there were also two partial modernisations. The paper noted that although the new *King George V* class would broadly match anticipated new IJN ships in numbers, they would be out-gunned. In addition, Japan was believed to have four 12in gunned battlecruisers in build.[31]

The September 1940 Future Strategy paper confirmed this assessment. It stated that Japan's modernised ships were 'superior to our own', and that the new battlecruisers could only be countered by a *King George V* or *Hood* or *Renown*.[32] NID 4 reminded Churchill of the IJN capital ship modernisation programme in August 1941, as he was beginning the debate with Pound over Far East naval reinforcement.[33] In March 1942 the naval staff stated that there was no recent information on IJN gunnery and RDF (radar), but there was no reason why the IJN should not be 'considerably superior in Long Range Direct Fire and Medium Range Blind Fire'.[34] The IJN had, in fact, put much effort into long-range gunnery with significant results in trials, but this was based on traditional techniques of visual ranging.[35] They never produced effective fire-control radar, which the Royal Navy had in most capital ships by this time. Royal Navy anxiety over IJN capital ship superiority persisted through most of the war. As late as 1944, a paper by the Director of Naval Intelligence (DNI) stated that the four older IJN battleships of the *Fuso* and *Ise* classes were superior to the modernised *Queen Elizabeth*s while the *Kongo*-class battle-cruisers were superior to the modernised *Renown*, although it recognised Royal Navy radar could, in practice, make a decisive difference.[36] This assessment was undoubtedly unfair to both the modernised *Queen Elizabeth*s and *Renown*, but it reflected an enduring Admiralty view. As regards gunnery performance, it is unlikely there was much difference between the two navies in long-range fire under good daytime conditions, but radar gave the Royal Navy a major advantage at night, or in bad weather.

An effective assessment of the Japanese naval risk to British interests could not rest solely on bean-counting. It required knowledge of IJN organisation, the location and movements of its key forces, their fighting effectiveness and, above all, timely warning of hostile intent. Here, despite limited resources, the intelligence capability available to NID by mid-1941 was good enough to enable the Admiralty and local Royal Navy commanders to reach reasonable conclusions on the scale, quality and timing of an attack. To provide the Far East intelligence picture, NID relied primarily on the Far East Combined Bureau, a joint intelligence organisation set up in 1936, combining personnel from all three services to support Far East commanders. The FECB was a visionary concept for its day, and represented what in modern parlance would be described as an all-source 'fusion centre'. Its primary roles were to give early warning of Japanese attack, build an accurate Japanese order of battle, naval, land and air, and provide operational intelligence once war had broken out. It also provided some set-piece assessments of Japanese capability, and occasional strategic overviews.[37] Although the FECB was a tri-service organisation, because of the Royal Navy's traditional pre-eminence in Far East intelligence, it was accountable to and administered by Commander-in-Chief China, not Commander-in-Chief Far East, and commanded by a Royal Navy captain. In the second half of 1941 this was Captain Kenneth Harkness. He was a gunnery officer, not an intelligence specialist, but capable, with a strong operational record and a good administrator. FECB, therefore, had a distinct naval bias. It devoted more effort to naval requirements and was more effective here than it was for the other two services.

Importantly, FECB collaborated closely with NID with inevitable advantages here for intelligence distribution and exploitation. Patrick Beesly, who worked for NID in the war, described FECB as a 'well thought out and comprehensive organisation, the first example of an inter-service effort in the intelligence field, and for NID its most important outstation'.[38] When it moved to Singapore from Hong Kong in 1939, FECB acquired its own Naval Operational Intelligence Centre (NOIC), modelled on that at the Admiralty, the Pacific Naval Intelligence Organisation, which provided a plot of all Axis naval activity from East Africa to the west coast of the Americas.[39] In his 1939 command review, Commander-in-Chief China, Vice Admiral Sir Percy Noble, stated that FECB had ensured he knew with complete confidence the whereabouts of all elements of the Japanese combined fleet on the outbreak of the European war. It also located the German pocket battleship *Graf Spee* during her brief foray into the Indian Ocean through long-range direction-finding (D/F) fixes.[40] In covering the IJN, FECB drew together intelligence from signals intelligence (SIGINT), human agents,[41] aerial reconnaissance, submarine surveillance, diplomatic reporting and open sources.

SIGINT contributed most value to the FECB intelligence picture and especially on the IJN. This term embraces different techniques: radio intercept; D/F; traffic analysis to extract operational value from the timing and pattern of radio transmissions; and the actual decryption of Japanese traffic, both military and diplomatic. FECB SIGINT collection and processing involved close collaboration with the Government Code and Cypher School (GC&CS), Britain's central SIGINT organisation administered by the Secret Intelligence Service (SIS). GC&CS seconded staff to FECB.

During 1941 the dominant input to tracking IJN strength, organisation, locations and movements was traffic analysis. Essentially, this involved monitoring the patterns of IJN radio transmissions by volume and type, and linking these with unit call signs, and even individual operators. Its effectiveness depended on the painstaking construction of IJN organisation and identities over time, and ability then to spot changes. FECB developed an advanced technique of radio fingerprinting which enabled it to build up a dictionary of individual IJN operators and follow their appearance on air.[42] D/F made a useful contribution in support, although there are differing views on its accuracy.[43] Lieutenant Commander S W Francis, who served in the FECB in 1941, later described how FECB could track both Japanese warships and naval air squadrons with considerable precision through traffic analysis and D/F fixing.[44] This enabled FECB to monitor the Japanese air build up in Indochina in late 1941, and potentially therefore to give an accurate assessment of the air threat to Force Z. It also enabled FECB to follow the formation and movements of the IJN southern task force earmarked for the invasion of Malaya. US Navy Intelligence was equally effective at traffic analysis, and from

February 1941 there was close co-operation between FECB and the US Station Cast at Corregidor in the Philippines.[45]

The story of the breaking of Japanese cyphers is inevitably complex. For much of the interwar period, GC&CS could read the bulk of Japanese diplomatic and naval traffic.[46] New high grade cypher systems introduced in 1938/39 then denied Britain access to the most important military and civilian messages until early 1941. The most significant changes were the introduction of a new diplomatic cypher, designated 'Purple' by the United States, and a new naval general cypher which became known as JN 25.[47] Britain then benefited from a remarkable American success in breaking the Purple cypher from September 1940 onward.[48] The Americans shared this success with GC&CS in February 1941, when a combined US Army and Navy team, known as the Sinkov–Rosen mission after their respective leaders, visited GC&CS at its Bletchley headquarters. They provided a decryption machine to enable the British to read intercepted Purple traffic directly. In return, GC&CS provided details of the German Enigma system.[49] By spring 1941 the Americans were reading between fifty and seventy-five Japanese diplomatic messages per day.[50] British independent output was somewhat less, largely due to more limited access to Japanese high-grade traffic, including some Washington embassy material.

Purple gave the American and British governments valuable insights into Japanese and German leadership thinking and intentions throughout 1941. The German access derived primarily from the reports to Tokyo from the Japanese ambassador in Berlin, Lieutenant General Hiroshi Oshima, who had excellent high level contacts.[51] The intelligence product from Purple intercepts was called 'Magic' by the Americans, and the decryption machines likewise 'Magic machines'.[52] Magic intercepts made an important contribution to Joint Intelligence Committee assessments in 1941. Their scope is also demonstrated in the titles of intercepts sent on a daily basis to the prime minister, especially in the second half of the year.[53] The post-war GCHQ summary of the SIGINT material available to the British and United States governments which provided war warning indicators in late 1941, including material relevant to Pearl Harbor, found that there was full sharing of Purple material in 1941. There was no evidence that the United States deliberately held messages back. The only omission from the British record were some of the final 'deadline' messages from the last stage of United States-Japanese negotiations in the first week of December.[54] One of the Purple machines provided by the Americans was despatched later in the year to FECB.[55] Although it apparently arrived in Singapore, it never reached FECB, and was lost in the chaos of the city's fall. Fortunately, it was not found by the Japanese, which would have disclosed the Purple operation, with disastrous consequences.[56]

In parallel with the Purple exchanges, DNI and GC&CS agreed to collaborate with the Americans on Japanese naval codes, especially JN 25 which was introduced in mid-1939. The first variant, which would become known as JN 25A was in force for eighteen months until December 1940, when JN 25B was introduced.[57] This exchange, which also began in February 1941, was initially conducted between FECB and the US Navy Station Cast at Corregidor in the Philippines, which were both then leading on JN 25.[58] Both parties brought valuable contributions to the table here, though the British initially contributed most. FECB supplied Corregidor with 'the latest JN 25 book, indicators and subtractor tables, on all of which the US Navy had no information'. The Americans provided a Japanese merchant ship code, an IJN personnel code and call sign data.[59] Co-operation between FECB and Station Cast then remained extremely close for the rest of 1941, with complete sharing of all intercepts and decryption results facilitated by an encrypted radio link.[60] Cast significantly extended FECB access to IJN traffic because they were far better placed geographically to monitor activity around the Japanese home islands. FECB also established a much more limited exchange with the Dutch SIGINT unit Kamer 14 based at Bandung in Java.[61]

The foundation work done on JN 25 by GC&CS and FECB from 1939–41 was critical in enabling both the British and Americans eventually to read this cypher at a level which could deliver operational intelligence.[62] It included input from Alan Turing, the mathematical genius recruited into GC&CS in 1938. Although GC&CS achieved some readability of JN 25 as early as September 1939, when it transferred responsibility to FECB, neither the British nor American teams obtained much operational value until December 1941 after the outbreak of war.[63] The two years 1940 and 1941 were required to understand the structure of the JN 25 system sufficiently to break complete signals and to overcome the problems caused by the Japanese shift to the new JN 25B variant in December 1940.[64] The fact that FECB personnel involved in decryption, but especially of JN 25, grew from five to forty between early 1940 and mid-1941 demonstrates the scale of effort and its importance.[65] Although the JN 25 work yielded little direct operational intelligence pre-war, it provided far better understanding of IJN communications practice, which was then used to improve traffic analysis.

The SIGINT intercept work described here was supplemented by intelligence from lower grade Japanese diplomatic cyphers, such as the Red system that preceded Purple and could be read by both Britain and the United States, other low-grade cyphers used by the Japanese consular network, and plain language intercept. In early 1941 GC&CS was reading nineteen lower grade Japanese cyphers and the United States Army Signal Intelligence Service was reading fifteen of these.[66] Purple was only used by the thirteen Japanese diplomatic missions Tokyo judged most important. The rest continued to use Red. Little of this wider civilian output directly illuminated IJN capabilities and operations, but it did provide further context for judging Japanese intentions. Neither Britain nor the United States achieved significant decryption of Japanese army cyphers during 1941.[67]

Intelligence gleaned from these SIGINT intercepts had obvious limitations. Even the highest quality Purple intercepts only offered occasional and partial indications into Japan's (or Germany's) ultimate political and strategic intentions. Without consistent and comprehensive access to JN 25 or equivalent IJA systems, it could provide no insight into high-level naval or military planning. The SIGINT that was available also told the Royal Navy little about the quality of the IJN, its specific weapons systems, its fighting effectiveness, let alone the detailed strategy and tactics it would apply in a war with Britain and its allies. Nor could it tell the Royal Navy much about the IJN's building programme. Human sources could potentially contribute to all these areas, but the highly secretive and well-protected Japanese system proved difficult to penetrate, either by SIS or the military attachés in Tokyo.[68] The poverty of SIS reporting on the IJN building programme is illustrated by an April 1939 report which summarised building underway at Yokosuka, Maizuru, Kure and Kobe. It was wrong in virtually every detail, confusing battleships and carriers under construction, and identifying three fictitious battlecruisers. The covering comment admitted that collection in Japan was very difficult, and that SIS was largely dependent on visiting Chinese agents.[69] Despite the difficulties they faced, the military attachés nevertheless still produced some useful insights. For example, the Tokyo naval attaché reported in mid-October that all units of the IJN had mobilised and moved to a war footing.[70] American exploitation of human sources was no more successful.[71]

One other source of intelligence on the IJN was available to NID, although by mid-1941 it was historic rather than current. This was submarine surveillance. The submarine *Regulus* conducted an intelligence-gathering patrol in Japanese waters in October 1939. This focused on the mouth of the Bungo Channel, the strait separating the islands of Kyushu and Shikoku, which gives access to the Inland Sea. It involved significant contact with the IJN combined fleet, producing valuable photographic intelligence of major IJN units. Some of these photographs were subsequently discovered by the Japanese in Singapore after its fall in February 1942.[72] *Regulus* left Hong Kong on 2 October and was operating close inshore at the mouth of the Bungo Channel for about a week, before returning to Hong Kong on 21 October. She sighted the carrier *Ryujo* on 8 October, dived to avoid another carrier the following day, and manoeuvred 'to close the Jap fleet' on 11 October.[73] *Regulus* covertly observed an IJN fleet exercise, including 'a brand new Japanese aircraft carrier', almost certainly *Hiryu*.[74] Simultaneously, the submarine *Perseus* patrolled the Kii Strait south of Osaka Bay 150 miles to the east. She did not encounter any IJN vessels, and was tasked primarily against suspect German merchant traffic.[75]

Such intelligence patrols were clearly frequent in the late 1930s and continued until all Royal Navy submarines were withdrawn from the Far East in mid-1940. *Regulus* herself was sunk in the Mediterranean in December 1940. The Japanese later discovered that *Regulus* had entered Shibushi Bay and Osaka Bay via the Kitan strait, all producing photographic intelligence, although it is not clear that all these incursions occurred in the October 1939 patrol.[76] What is clear is that the fifteen submarines of the 4th Flotilla were highly efficient and effective, and would have been a major threat to any IJN seaborne invasion forces. Significantly, Japanese anti-submarine measures were viewed as 'feeble'.[77] Had Royal Navy submarines remained in the Far East after mid-1940, they would certainly have corrected some of the intelligence errors regarding new IJN warships. The substantial US Navy submarine force within the Asiatic Fleet could also have contributed here, but it seems they were never used in this way, and they appear to have lacked the necessary aggression and risk-taking.[78]

In the absence of consistent high-level intelligence from human sources, or a substantial breakthrough into JN 25, British assessments of how their broadly accurate picture of overall Japanese order of battle would translate into an actual attack on the territory or interests of Britain or its Allies was based on two things: political and military judgement of risk, and warning indicators of imminent hostile intent. Risk judgement would take into account diplomatic insights from the Tokyo embassy, the current disposition of Japanese forces, geographic and logistic possibility and, not least, the existing Japanese military commitments in China. The more specific warning indicators were listed by FECB in December 1940.[79] The most important were troop and transport concentrations, unusual naval movements, and concentration of shore-based aircraft. Others included diplomatic exchanges, evacuation of Japanese nationals, reduction in commercial activity and reduction in commercial shipping. Virtually all the indicators identified by FECB proved their worth in the immediate run-up to war in late 1941.

From the August 1940 Far East appreciation, through to mid-1941, the core elements of the intelligence judgement here, reflected in both London and Singapore, were constant. They were that Japan could easily make available a southern expeditionary force of six to ten divisions, and that it had sufficient shipping to lift this from Formosa or Hainan. It could cover this force with most of the IJN's major units and could also deploy a substantial land-based air force of 350–450 aircraft. The judgement also reckoned Japan faced three major constraints in contemplating an attack on Malaya or the Netherlands East Indies: the challenge of distance, a minimum of 1150 miles from its embarkation points to the nearest targets; the possibility of American intervention against its long communication lines; and, above all, the need to acquire advanced airbases to achieve acceptable air cover for an invasion force. An attack relying solely on carrier air cover was clearly possible, but inherently risky. As FECB noted, it would also involve extensive naval activity, which was highly likely to be spotted.[80] A key assumption, therefore, which quite reasonably underpinned British calculations until the Japanese move into southern Indochina at the end of July 1941, was that the need to ensure air cover would lead Japan to a strategy of incremental advance and thereby provide warning.

These judgements are evident in the comprehensive Joint Intelligence Committee update published on 1 May 1941[81] and the deliberations in Singapore around an FECB threat assessment a month earlier on 4 April.[82] FECB stated that the nearest Japanese launch point to Kota Bharu was Hainan. Unless they established prior bases in southern Indochina or Thailand, air cover for an attack on Malaya would have to be ship-borne, and the maximum available force would be six carriers and three seaplane carriers capable of delivering seventy-five fighters, 206 strike aircraft and sixty assorted floatplanes. However, if Japan could obtain bases in southern Thailand, it estimated it could deploy a shore-based air force of 200 fighters, 200 light bombers, 150 heavy bombers and 100 reconnaissance aircraft. This estimate proved accurate. The total combined IJAAF and IJNAF strength deployed against Malaya in December was 564 aircraft. The IJAAF 3rd Air Group deployed 447 aircraft comprising 168 fighters, 108 light bombers, ninety-nine heavy bombers, and seventy-two reconnaissance aircraft. The reinforced IJNAF 22nd Air Fleet had thirty-six fighters, ninety-nine heavy bombers and nine reconnaissance aircraft. The breakdown by type was therefore almost exactly as FECB had anticipated six months earlier.[83] In commenting on this FECB assessment, general headquarters Far East air staff accepted these figures were credible, and discounted the ability of a carrier force alone to generate sufficient offensive strength. They judged, therefore, that Japanese plans must allow for the occupation of southern Indochina and Thailand, as well as holding back a considerable naval bomber force to guard against American intervention.

Following Japan's subsequent move into southern Indochina, Group Captain Lawrence Darvall, the senior air staff officer now also acting as chief of staff to the Commander-in-Chief Far East, Air Chief Marshal Sir Robert Brooke-Popham, stated in mid-August:

The great difficulty in attacking Malaya has been to provide shore-based air cover. Now the Japanese have the means of providing it from Indo-China, it is hard to believe they will not take advantage.[84] An ominous move will therefore be the preparation of southern Indo-China air bases for full operation including stocking with fuel and bombs etc. Aircraft can be flown in but ground support takes time. Once established, such forces could support a seaborne invasion sailing from Hainan or Formosa and not touching Indo-China.

This was indeed the approach adopted by Japan in December. The main Malaya attack force deployed from Hainan.[85] Darvall concluded:

The air position is a vital sine qua non for Japan. Preparation and stocking of Indo-China airbases is a critical intelligence indicator. The arrival of the Type Zero naval fighter[86] will be a definite indicator that Malaya is the target.[87]

In early September Darvall added that FECB now assessed that the current capacity of airbases potentially available to Japan within 500 miles of northern Malaya was 250 aircraft. However, he judged that Japan lacked the air resources to undertake more than one major campaign at a time; nor could it afford to pre-position fuel, bombs and support personnel in different theatres to allow rapid transfer of aircraft. Japan would have to choose, and this would provide the necessary warning indicators.[88] Brooke-Popham certainly absorbed these changing implications for the air threat following the end July move into southern Indochina, because he sent an updated assessment to the chiefs of staff on 16 September as a basis for calculating Royal Air Force reinforcements. However, he reiterated Darvall's point that the current airfield limitations in Indochina might restrict Japanese deployment to 250 aircraft at short notice.[89]

Overall, by early autumn both London and Singapore had got the likely scale of a southern attack about right, at least in terms of raw numbers and the way they would be applied.[90] Darvall was also right in emphasising the status of the Indochina airbases as the key warning indicator that an attack on Malaya was imminent, although significant changes in shipping and troop deployments were clearly also valuable pointers.

In addition to SIGINT, there were three important sources that could provide these warning indicators. These were the British consul in Saigon, William Meiklereid, who (unusually for Vichy-administered territory) had been allowed by the French to remain in place;[91] continuing SIS exploitation of its former liaison relationships with French intelligence officials in Indochina;[92] and the wider independent SIS agent networks in the region. All three would indeed provide crucial insights on the Japanese air and troop build-up in southern Indochina during November.[93] Brook-Popham was scathing about SIS performance at the beginning of 1941, soon after his arrival in Malaya.[94] Some of his criticism in regard to organisation, low-calibre personnel and failure to deliver quality strategic insights on Japanese intentions and capability was amply justified. However, in delivering tactical intelligence through the autumn SIS did better. It was not only able to track the build-up of Japanese forces for their southern operations in detail, but also provided accurate and timely warning of their specific targets in Malaya. In particular, the French liaison source Sectude provided 'ample warning of the attack on Siam and Malaya', including the 'correct date and actual places for landings as well as the strength and movements of the enemy invasion fleet'.[95]

While the warning indicators proved effective, estimating the fighting quality of a Japanese expeditionary force was more difficult. Neither FECB nor Darvall appear to have offered a direct view here. Darvall did, however, propose a figure of 120 (sixty bombers and sixty escorting fighters) for the likely Japanese daily sortie rate generated from 600 aircraft, which he judged 'not particularly serious'. This estimated sortie rate, which he implied drew on Battle of Britain experience, was not unreasonable if regarded as an average. The highest weekly sortie rates generated by the Luftwaffe for both bombers and fighters during the Battle of Britain were about three times their serviceable strength, but often well below this.[96] FECB's estimate of 550 Japanese bombers and fighters, at 75 per cent serviceability, would translate into a serviceable strength of 412. Applying the maximum Luftwaffe ratio, this would therefore generate an average weekly sortie rate of 1237 and therefore an average daily rate of 178. This was 50 per cent more than Darvall's figure, but the Luftwaffe only rarely achieved the full ratio of three times strength, and 120 was not far out as an average equivalent.

There are, however, obvious problems with such statistical comparisons. Sortie rates varied hugely on a daily basis, depending on weather and operational factors. Any capable airforce could generate much higher ratios for a limited period. Above all, the ratio of defending fighters to attackers in the Battle of Britain was about 1:3, whereas in Malaya in December it would be about 1:7. Malaya also lacked an equivalent radar-supported fighter-direction system, and the experience and skill level of Royal Air Force pilots based there was low compared to their United Kingdom counterparts, and certainly to the Japanese.[97] Overall, Darvall's assessment that the Japanese sortie rate was manageable was complacent, given the limitations of Royal Air Force fighter defence in both numbers and quality.[98]

Lack of quality intelligence from human sources meant assessments of future naval build depended on published Japanese budgets, which were, inevitably, often unreliable, on calculations of industrial capacity and availability of building slips, information acquired by the naval attachés, and occasional visual sightings by visiting British merchant vessels. Inevitably, the Royal Navy was also tempted to assume that IJN building plans would mirror those in European navies. There were two important things the Royal Navy got wrong on future IJN build.

First, it failed to identify the super-battleship programme. In late 1937 the Royal Navy assessed that Japan was commencing two new capital ships, almost certainly armed with 16in guns, and probably displacing 42,000–43,000 tons. SIS reported around this time that the new ships were to be armed with twelve 16in guns and displace 46,000 tons. However, DNI stated that subsequent information from secret sources (almost certainly again SIS) had suggested 'the definite possibility' of the ships having 18in guns, which 'could not be ignored'. These two ships of the Japanese 1937 building programme were *Yamato* and *Musashi*, of 72,000 tons and carrying nine 18.2in guns. The SIS reporting was thus some way out. But it helped convince the naval staff that the IJN ships were significantly superior to the *King George V*s then under construction, and that a response, the *Lion* class, was needed.[99] By 1940 the Royal Navy assessed the IJN would commission four new capital ships by 1942, the two 1937 programme at 40,000 tons (assessed displacement down somewhat since 1937) and two others of 35,000 tons, all now believed to be armed with up to nine 16in guns.[100] In reality, the IJN only planned a total of four *Yamato*s of which they completed just two, one in December 1941 and one in mid-1942.

Secondly, the Royal Navy believed in an entirely fictitious IJN battlecruiser programme. Until at least the end of 1941, the Royal Navy thought the IJN was building four battlecruisers, of around 20,000 tons armed with 12in guns, and even assumed the first of these, called *Ibuki*, had commissioned early that year. The genesis of this belief probably lay in an SIS report dating from late 1937 which stated that Japan was secretly building 'three cruisers with 12in guns'.[101] While this SIS report was clearly wrong, there was some underlying substance in that the IJN genuinely contemplated such ships in 1934, and may have deliberately propagated the idea as a deception for some while afterwards.[102] Mirroring may also have played a part in subsequent naval staff thinking. Since both the French and Germans had built such ships, the Royal Navy was inevitably susceptible to a belief the IJN would follow suit. SIS was then no doubt pressed to find further evidence. The enthusiasm with which at least some SIS agents reported the existence of 'battlecruisers' or 'pocket battleships', with specifications very similar to those of Germany, smacks of agents reporting what their case officers had told them to look for, and therefore presumably wanted to hear.[103]

Several important qualifications apply to these failings. Criticism of Royal Navy assessments of IJN building plans has mainly focused on NID studies in the period 1938–40.[104] However, a later FECB report on the IJN construction programme dated August 1941, although it still contained important errors, demonstrated that estimates of IJN build available to the Royal Navy were now closer to reality for all categories of warship.[105] This report correctly identified one battleship fitting out (*Yamato*, which would be commissioned in December 1941), and one building at Yokusuka (*Shinano*, the third *Yamato* class, which would be converted into an aircraft carrier). It mis-identified *Musashi*, the second *Yamato* class, fitting out at Nagasaki, and *111*, the fourth *Yamato* on the slip at Kure (never completed), as 'pocket battleships'. It correctly identified three aircraft carriers fitting out, which were *Shokaku* (commissioned August 1941), *Zuikaku* (commissioned September 1941) and *Taiyo* (also September). Total cruisers under construction were estimated at seven, as opposed to the reality of four. The figure of seventeen destroyers compared to an official Japanese figure of twelve, although the FECB figure may have included small escort vessels.[106]

In 1940, therefore, the Royal Navy thought the IJN would have four new battleships of 35,000–40,000 tons by 1942 and up to four additional 12in-gun battlecruisers. It also assumed the IJN could build at a rate of three capital ships every two years. Its own forward building plans reflected this.[107] In reality, the IJN completed two *Yamato*s by 1942, and lacked the industrial capacity to continue the programme beyond this. FECB had certainly not recognised the size and capability of the *Yamato*s, and it evidently never acquired definitive intelligence on precise IJN building plans. However, by focusing on industrial capacity and the status of key building slips, as of August 1941 it still had the number of new capital units, both capital ships and carriers, likely to be available by end 1942 about right. It also had realistic estimates for delivery of smaller units.

Unfortunately, although this FECB assessment was definitely shared with DNI, it was either not accepted in NID, or else was soon forgotten. By March the following year, NID estimates for IJN construction were not only badly off track again but bordered on the ridiculous. An NID note forwarded to the prime minister by the First Lord, A V Alexander, stated that one new battleship of 40,000 tons was in service, a second was imminent, and a further three were under construction. In addition, six battlecruisers of between 14,000–20,000 tons, with two nearing completion, and two carriers were also under construction. The prime minister had already queried whether Japan had the industrial capacity to support such a programme after seeing initial figures ten days earlier in a paper from the First Sea Lord.[108] It is unlikely he was convinced by Alexander's follow-up, which quoted distinctly doubtful sourcing.[109]

Ultimately, these NID errors over IJN capital ship plans did not much matter. The key point is that the Royal Navy made worst-case assumptions about the planned rate of IJN build for capital units and the timing of their appearance. Common sense balance was then applied by the political leadership, in several important instances by Churchill. The Royal Navy then got its own rearmament programme for capital units about right, as we saw in Chapter 1. Finally, it is worth noting that NID errors over the size, armament and build status of potential enemy combatants were not confined to the IJN. NID underestimated the displacement of the German *Scharnhorst* and *Bismarck* classes by around 20 per cent too.[110]

The Royal Navy picture assessed

By late summer 1941, NID and the naval staff had a broadly accurate picture of headline IJN strength in both ships and aircraft. They had also correctly gauged the scale of attack Japan could deploy against British interests. A tendency to play down IJNAF effectiveness, based on perceived poor performance in China, was balanced by an inclination to overstate the IJN quality advantage in capital ships. Estimates for IJN new construction and aircraft production had errors, but the latest FECB assessment demonstrated that with careful analysis of available information, the intelligence community was getting closer to reality here. They also had a good picture of IJN organisation and, through FECB, drawing primarily on SIGINT but also SIS sources, were able to track the movement of naval and air units in close to real time.

At the end of September NID stated that Japan was putting its fleet in a state of readiness.[111] In early October it noted the IJN had completed its annual reorganisation two months ahead of time.[112] By the end of the month it concluded that the IJN was on a 'war footing'.[113] Tracking of Japanese merchant shipping by the Ministry of Economic Warfare (MEW) was also accurate, and provided an additional pointer to likely hostilities.[114] In early October NID, drawing on MEW data, recorded that the number of Japanese merchant vessels at sea, which averaged 162 per month during the first half of the year, had declined to just forty since early August.[115] By the middle of the month MEW was reporting that normal traffic had virtually ceased, and by the end of October it had noted possible evacuee ships. NID subsequently stated that the Japanese government had taken control of all shipping on 8 October. The US Navy had similar intelligence on the withdrawal of Japanese merchant shipping, and in early November stated that merchant vessels were being inducted into the IJN 'in alarming numbers'.[116] Meanwhile, decryption of Purple diplomatic traffic and that from lower grade systems provided important insights into Japanese thinking and intentions at the strategic level.[117]

War warning

If British intelligence capability against Japan had strengths in early autumn 1941, there are still questions regarding its contribution over the following months. First, was the capability good enough to give precise and timely warning of an actual attack on Britain, as opposed to merely illuminating the potential to attack? Secondly, were there critical gaps in the British intelligence picture that would compromise Royal Navy dispositions and plans to meet an attack? On the first point, there is an argument that FECB, whose primary responsibility was war warning, failed to read Japanese intentions correctly in November and early December 1941, was late in spotting the significance of their southern deployment, and ultimately judged it was directed at Thailand rather than Malaya. Britain therefore 'received the worst of both worlds from FECB'. 'It rejected the FECB's assessments of Japanese capabilities, which were accurate enough to enable effective preparation, while accepting views on intentions that were wrong, and shaped by enemy deception.' FECB views here exerted significant influence in both London and Washington.[118]

This interpretation overstates FECB's role and influence. FECB was a critical SIGINT outpost, it was an important clearing house for intelligence collected from all sources within the region, and it had important specialist expertise on the Japanese military. Providing intelligence and local advice on war warning was certainly a primary task, but that did not make it uniquely responsible for war warning. A final judgement on Japanese intentions could only be reached in London. That was partly because London had unique intelligence, notably Magic, which was only shared with FECB on an occasional and sanitised basis, but also because only London had the full diplomatic context (including insights drawn from wider SIGINT intercepts) and, importantly, access to American thinking and assessments.

Ultimately, too, war warning was a matter of political and military judgement by Britain's war leadership. The intelligence community, of which FECB was a part, could offer specific insights drawn from SIGINT and human sources and suggest, up to the level of the Joint Intelligence Committee, what they meant. However, intelligence assessments could never be more than a guide, and the war leadership had to decide what weight to give them alongside other inputs such as reports from the Tokyo embassy or from the wide range of sources in the United States government. To take an obvious example, the prime minister, the War Cabinet and chiefs of staff would have placed as much weight on the assessment of Japanese intentions sent by the ambassador in Tokyo, Sir Robert Craigie, on 22 October following the fall of the Prince Konoye government, as any single Joint Intelligence Committee assessment, let alone a view from FECB.[119] Craigie showed remarkable foresight in pressing the argument for an early Japanese move south in the face of a prevailing consensus that they were still looking towards Russia. The War Office certainly backed his interpretation.[120] Diplomatic reports could also provide excellent military intelligence. A good example is the report on 13 November to the Foreign Office from William Meiklereid, the consul in Saigon, which summarised recent Japanese military movements in Indochina. This was crucial in convincing the War Office that the likely Japanese objective was Thailand, not the Burma Road.[121]

To criticise FECB for poor political intelligence is to fail to understand that this was beyond their power, and that senior local customers such as Brooke-Popham, who was critical of FECB failings here, should have recognised this. Without high-grade political sources, either human or SIGINT, middle-ranking military officers based in Singapore just did not have the relevant skills, experience or background to assess Japanese political or strategic intentions. Even if the sources had existed, and constitutionally they had come under FECB control (which in the case of any high-grade human sources acquired by SIS was most unlikely), none of the senior FECB staff serving in late 1941 were equipped to exploit, understand and present political intelligence in an effective manner.[122] Quality intelligence insights on high-level Japanese intentions could only have come from an SIS source with direct access to the Japanese leadership, which was never available, or from timely and revealing Magic intercepts, which were occasionally available in London, but rarely definitive and rarely shared with FECB.

It is also important not to be too selective in assessing the military indicators available to FECB, and their role in illuminating Japanese intentions.[123] With the exception of Purple, all the main sources of warning intelligence and their output were available to FECB. Partly as a result of Brooke-Popham's representations, but also the new SIGINT collaboration with the Americans, there were significant improvements in intelligence organisation by mid-1941.[124] Monitoring during November and early December of the Japanese air force build-up in southern Indochina, and (with American help) the formation of a southern naval task force, was impressive. However, the major jump in Japanese air force strength in Indochina only occurred in the final week before their attack. On 28 November Brooke-Popham, drawing on FECB, assessed there were 245 aircraft in Indochina. Japanese sources suggest this was almost exactly right.[125] By 6 December the FECB estimate had risen to 500, again about right.[126]

The combination of SIGINT and military indicators from FECB, plus some important collateral reporting from SIS, along with American warnings, meant Britain's war leadership were clear by end November that the Japanese were headed south, and that the sheer scale of forces allocated made hostilities likely and imminent. What was not foreseeable with existing British sources was the attack on Pearl Harbor, and all the consequences that flowed from that. Nor was it possible, without a source in the Japanese leadership, to be sure if an attack on Malaya itself was imminent, or whether the Japanese would briefly consolidate in Thailand first, or attack the Netherlands East Indies. Britain also failed to anticipate a simultaneous attack on the Philippines. War warning intelligence was, therefore, far from perfect through the autumn of 1941. However, as shown later, it was quite good enough to enable the Admiralty to avoid an exposed position in the Far East.[127]

Intelligence gaps and underestimation

A second issue is the existence of critical gaps in the Royal Navy's picture of IJN capability and the implications these had for its deployment.[128] The Royal Navy underestimated the size of the IJN's carrier-borne air force. It had no inkling that during 1941 the IJN would develop the concept of a multi-carrier strike force, organised and able to project power at a considerable distance, and implement the training and support to give this practical effect. It did not recognise how the IJN was training and deploying its land-based air strike forces alongside its fleet to create a single integrated offensive system, with each component able to substitute for the other. The Royal Navy was also unaware of IJN innovations in weaponry, especially long-range torpedoes. Finally, the Royal Navy did not realise how tactically innovative the IJN would be, not least in night-fighting, although this was also a Royal Navy strength. (In early 1942 the view took hold that the IJN did not like night-fighting and that this was something the Royal Navy should exploit. This belief seems to have originated with Layton, when Commander-in-Chief Eastern Fleet, although it also reflected pre-war impressions.[129] IJN successes in a series of night encounters with the US Navy in the second half of 1942, notably Savo Island and Tassafaronga, demonstrated that this view was rubbish. Nevertheless, the IJN did not always respond well when caught by surprise at night, as demonstrated by their performance at Balikpapan, Borneo, on 20 January and Bantam Bay, Java, on 28 February 1942. Their performance at Bantam Bay when their invasion force was surprised by the Australian cruiser *Perth* and the US Navy cruiser *Houston* was especially chaotic, even though they enjoyed huge superiority.)[130]

Underestimation of IJN air power was the most critical Royal Navy failing. It is important to understand why this occurred. As already discussed, NID, the naval staff, FECB and Far East commanders possessed most of the intelligence to create a reasonably accurate picture of IJN air capability. They knew the number of aircraft carriers and the specification of the aircraft they carried. They knew the strength and organisation of the land-based IJNAF, had accurate performance data for its aircraft, and in the second half of 1941 would accurately track its deployment in Indochina. They also knew the IJN had invested heavily in its air arm since the mid-1930s. The chiefs of staff 1937 Far East appreciation provided a broadly accurate assessment of IJNAF strength at that time. Significantly, it assessed there was little difference between IJNAF and Royal Air Force or Fleet Air Arm aircraft performance.[131] An exchange between DNI and the Director of the Naval Air Division (DNAD) in February 1940 estimated the IJN might still be spending 50 per cent more on its air arm than the Royal Navy. This estimate took account of expenditure on Royal Air Force Coastal Command.[132] The estimate put the strength of the IJN carrier air arm at 450 aircraft, although DNAD questioned (wrongly) whether these were all as modern as their Royal Navy equivalents. The equivalent Royal Navy frontline strength at this point was 264.[133]

Despite this awareness of IJN air investment, there is a puzzling absence of comment on IJN air capability, especially carrier capability, in British assessments of the balance of naval forces in the Far East through 1940/41. This absence of comment contrasts with the 1937 Far East appreciation. Although this had few references to carriers compared to capital ships, it did at least consider the carrier balance, and how four IJN carriers might be deployed in a hypothetical 1939 war. As already emphasised, the primary Royal Navy gauge for measuring relative strength was always the battleship. The importance the Royal Navy attached to IJN battleship modernisation is evident, but it apparently gleaned less detail on IJN carrier modernisation, and there are few references to it.[134] Nor did the Royal Navy consider how the arrival of four brand new IJN fleet carriers between 1937 and 1941 might change IJN attitudes to naval warfare. In forming its plans for a new eastern fleet in the second half of 1941, the Royal Navy sought equality with the maximum likely battleship force the IJN might deploy in the South China Sea, but assessed a single carrier was desirable rather than essential.

There are no contemporary assessments or views from senior Royal Navy officers which satisfactorily explain this disregard for IJN air power as a critical factor in the Far East naval balance when the Admiralty contemplated naval reinforcement during the second half of 1941. The omission is striking, given the important role that air power, including Royal Navy carrier operations, had played in both Atlantic and Mediterranean theatres by mid-1941. Indeed, throughout this year Cunningham bombarded the Admiralty (and on occasion the prime minister) with signals emphasising the crucial importance of adequate air cover (both carrier and land-based) if his fleet was to operate successfully. He underlined the impossibility of contesting the central Mediterranean without such cover. In November he insisted that operations in the central Mediterranean required a carrier 'stuffed with fighters'. Two carriers were 'better and safer than one', but one was 'essential'.[135]

Cunningham's views are important because, as explored in Chapter 7, there were striking analogies between the Mediterranean and South China Sea which the naval staff should have recognised. Explanations for not seeing these analogies are hard to find. One obvious factor is that none of the Royal Navy's European opponents operated carriers, so the Royal Navy had not needed to consider the implications of an air threat beyond the range of land-based aircraft during the war to date. A second factor was that, until the Japanese moved into southern Indochina, the sheer distance of the Japanese airbases meant the land-based air threat was more theoretical than real and immediate. This distance factor may then have linked in some Admiralty minds with an expectation that Royal Navy forces operating in the South China Sea would be able to call on British or American land-based air support. By mid-1941, experience in the Mediterranean should have suggested that with the known balance of forces on each side, little comfort could be taken from this.

A final factor is that the sheer geographical spread of Royal Navy commitments, together with war losses and damage, meant that before 1942 it rarely had more than one carrier available in any theatre of operations, and sometimes none. For example, there was no carrier in the eastern Mediterranean throughout the second half of 1941. As a result, with rare exceptions such as the attack on the Italian naval base at Taranto in November 1940, which achieved a strategic effect comparable to Pearl Harbor, the Royal Navy was obliged to deploy its carriers in a supportive role. This was either for local air defence or as a facilitator of fleet action through reconnaissance or attrition, rather than as a decisive weapon in its own right. This could explain why some of the naval staff saw a carrier for the Eastern Fleet as merely desirable rather than essential.

Nevertheless, by the end of 1941 there were also views within the Admiralty on the impact of air power at sea quite as revolutionary as any within the IJN or US Navy. In December the Fifth Sea Lord, Rear Admiral A L St G Lyster, told the Admiralty Board that the dominating factor in naval warfare was no longer the big gun, but the air striking force, whether shore-based or carrier-borne. Lyster saw no reason why a fleet of carriers only escorted by cruisers and destroyers should not be able to deal effectively with what was usually termed a 'well-balanced' fleet. This proposal to dispense with battle-fleets was far-sighted but radical at this time. Few senior officers in any navy would yet have gone this far. Lyster therefore argued for heavy investment in air power – 'particularly if we hope to compete with the Japanese Fleet in the Indian Ocean on anything like equal terms'. He added: 'If we do not provide our fleet with ample aircraft for both offence and defence, we are liable to get a caning'. Lyster was writing in the wake of Pearl Harbor and the loss of Force Z, but his views must have been moving in this direction through 1941 (he became Fifth

Sea Lord in April), and it is surprising that there is not more sign of his influence on Far East planning during the autumn. [136]

Royal Navy expectations of how the IJN would use carriers were inevitably likely to mirror its own thinking and current war experience. It would expect the IJN to divide its carrier fleet not just between Pacific and Southeast Asia theatres, but also to support independent hunting groups rather than bring them together as a single force. Until early 1941 this was actually a reasonable assumption.[137] It was only in January that year that the IJN decided to bring its carriers together as a single concentrated force in the 1st Air Fleet which came into being formally on 1 April. The creation of this force marked a revolutionary leap from predominantly single carrier operations to co-ordinated multi-carrier operations. Prior to that date, IJN carriers had often operated in pairs, but never as a foursome, let alone as six. Indeed, six fleet carriers only became possible with the commissioning of *Shokaku* and *Zuikaku* in the second half of the year. The revolution lay in moving from the role of carrier as a tactical weapon supporting the battle-fleet to a carrier task force that could use its combined air strike power to project strategic effect at long distance. The application of this revolution at Pearl Harbor was impressive for two reasons. First, the sheer number of aircraft dedicated to the attack, 183 first wave and 171 second wave, compared to anything that had gone before. And secondly, the solving of all the logistic and operating challenges to put them over the target.[138]

The leap was made possible by three elements coming together: motive, the need to incapacitate the US Navy Pacific Fleet, and availability and opportunity. In 1941 the IJN had the carriers, new aircraft and highly trained crews to consider operating in a new way, and the authority to make it happen, vested in the special status held by Admiral Isoruku Yamamoto as Commander-in-Chief Combined Fleet. The IJN translated this concept into a practical strategic weapon within barely six months, successfully solving numerous problems from a standing start, although in doing so they also stretched their resources very thin. While the IJN had a core of very experienced aircrew, the delivery of aircrew struggled to keep up with the demand created by an increase in carrier aircraft capacity of about one-third in the second half of 1941. The combat readiness of the 5th Carrier Division, comprising the new carriers *Shokaku* and *Zuikaku*, consequently suffered badly.[139] The characteristics so often emphasised as classic examples of early war IJN carrier doctrine were in reality, therefore, only a few months old, at most. IJN carrier doctrine had evolved very quickly – indeed, virtually mutating overnight.[140]

The IJN could do all of this in remote locations beyond the reach of Royal Navy or US Navy intelligence, and without the distraction of fighting a war.

These IJN doctrine innovations occurred alongside, and were facilitated by, a comprehensive aircraft re-equipment programme across the year 1941. This again was at best only partly visible to the western powers. The A6M Zero fighter and the latest marks of the Type 97 torpedo bomber and Type 99 dive-bomber were all introduced in the twelve months leading up to the outbreak of war. (The Royal Navy and Royal Air Force had details of the Zero by mid-1941, but it is not clear they realised it was designed primarily for carrier deployment.) It was virtually impossible for the US Navy or Royal Navy to spot this revolutionary change and appreciate its implications. To do so would have required not just extraordinary and timely insider intelligence access, but an equivalent military vision of what was possible, driven by similar strategic need.[141] Both the US Navy, and certainly the Royal Navy, faced different challenges, and neither had the luxury of concentrating its carrier power in a single theatre. It would be late 1943 before the US Navy could generate equivalent carrier power to the IJN 1st Air Fleet carriers, the 'Kido Butai', of late 1941.

Just as the Royal Navy failed to recognise the evolution of the IJN carrier fleet into a single concentrated force, so, together with the Royal Air Force, it failed fully to understand developments within the land-based components of the IJNAF. FECB, as already shown, was able to track IJNAF deployments in Indochina effectively in the autumn of 1941. However, it did not appreciate that the IJN had created a land-based equivalent to the carrier based 1st Air Fleet in the 11th Air Fleet, operating as a fully integrated component of the combined fleet under Yamamoto.[142] This was a concept that not only did not apply to the Royal Navy, where land-based maritime strike was a Royal Air Force Coastal Command responsibility, but had no parallel elsewhere in Europe or the United States. To be fair, Cunningham recognised the need for, and did his best to promote, exactly this concept in the eastern Mediterranean following the fall of Crete and the loss of all his carriers. However, inter-service politics made execution difficult, and it would be well into 1942 before something approaching this concept was put into effect, albeit on a much smaller scale to the 11th Air Fleet.[143] As a result, while intelligence got both IJN aircraft numbers and performance characteristics about right, drawing heavily here on traffic analysis, it failed to recognise that behind these numbers was a highly tuned weapon system dedicated to maritime strike.

Many of the senior Royal Navy officers most responsible for meeting the threat from the IJN cited underestimation of IJN power and effectiveness to explain the disasters that befell the Royal Navy in late 1941 and early 1942. Underestimation was inevitably linked with poor intelligence, an excuse that arguably became more popular with the passage of time. Pound stated, 'We all underrated the efficiency of the Japanese air forces and certainly did not realise the long ranges at which they could work'.[144] Vice Admiral Sir Henry Moore, who succeeded Phillips as VCNS, went further: 'We grossly underestimated the power and efficiency of the Japanese naval surface and air forces'. He added, 'this may have been due both to lack of intelligence and to faulty assessment of what we had'.[145] Godfrey as DNI, in his post-war unpublished memoirs, said, 'Japan, behind an impenetrable security wall, had built up a fighting machine about whose composition and intentions we knew very little. Both we and the Americans erred and there is hardly anyone entitled to say – "I told you so"'.[146]

The question is whether these claims hold up, or whether there is a strong element of *post facto* justification. In protecting reputations, blaming underestimation and, especially, poor intelligence was easier than accepting that defeat reflected poor strategic or operational decisions, or failure to provide the resources which intelligence suggested were necessary. It is striking that Layton, the Far East Naval Commander-in-Chief both before and after Phillips, when writing his contemporary account did not mention intelligence weakness or underestimation, and placed the blame entirely on inadequate forces, a failure to provide the strength 'we knew to be necessary'.[147] Layton's view was shared by Major General Ian Playfair, who as noted previously became chief of staff to the American-British-Dutch-Australian (ABDA) joint Far East Command formed in January 1942. In 1943 he identified 'fundamental defects' which had caused the loss of Malaya and then subsidiary 'contributory causes'. 'Not enough forces' came right at the top of his list. He too did not mention either poor intelligence or underestimation of the enemy as factors.[148]

Possible explanations for specific underestimation of the IJNAF have already been discussed. It is harder to support the claims of Moore and Godfrey that there was a wider failure, given the reality of the naval intelligence performance set out earlier in this chapter, and the generally excellent record of the Joint Intelligence Committee, of which Godfrey was a key member.[149] Nevertheless, Royal Navy assessments of the risk posed by the IJN clearly depended not just on knowledge of its headline strength, but also perceptions of its overall fighting quality and efficiency, the strategy and tactics it would deploy, and its ability to sustain operations over time. The thesis that the Royal Navy created a false image of the IJN which understated its effectiveness and, therefore, of the resources needed to counter it, is relevant here.

In judging how well the Royal Navy assessed its IJN opponent, some perspective on IJN strengths and weaknesses is required. The IJN's evolution of its air strike capability in 1940/41 was highly innovative, but it was based on the local concentration of a superbly trained force, rather than overall resource superiority, or any fundamental technical advance in military capability. The IJN, and especially the IJNAF, has been aptly described as 'so highly tempered it was brittle'.[150] Much of its equipment was superb by the standards of 1941 and the competition it immediately faced in the Far East theatre. But Japan lacked the industrial, technical, and logistic resources, and arguably the leadership and management insight, either to replace losses or to maintain a competitive edge against the western powers. The IJN also had major weaknesses in lack of radar, modern aircraft communications, poor anti-aircraft defence, indifferent damage control, and woeful anti-submarine capability, where it was years behind the Royal Navy. Aircraft communications were a particular weakness. IJN aircraft lacked even a basic VHF voice system until well into 1943 and the high-frequency Morse system, which was only fitted to strike aircraft and not fighters, was bulky and unreliable.[151] This lack of modern communications imposed severe limitations on the conduct of strike, reconnaissance and, above all, air defence operations.

Most important of all, Japan lacked the merchant shipping resources necessary to sustain its economy during a war with the western powers and to reap the benefit of its conquests, especially in regard to oil. Furthermore, the IJN had neither thought about trade protection, nor devoted any effort to procuring the relevant capabilities, drawing on Royal Navy lessons in the Atlantic. When it began the war, the IJN had just four dedicated anti-sub-marine escorts, and had no underwater detection equipment available at sea until August 1942.[152] At that time, the Royal Navy was deploying 2100 sonar-equipped ships.[153] IJN doctrine was narrowly focused on the concept of a decisive battle with the enemy fleet. Here it was 'ingenious, imaginative and beautifully crafted'. But it neglected the wider aspects of maritime power on which Japan depended, and underestimated the limitations of Japan's economic and industrial capacity which threatened rapid obsolescence.[154]

Some qualifications are nevertheless required. Japan commissioned more carriers than either Britain or the United States in 1942, almost compensating for its heavy losses that year, and it out-built Britain in this category over the three fiscal years 1942–45. It also tripled aircraft production across these years and introduced some competitive new designs. In some respects its wartime aircraft industry outperformed that of the Soviet Union. During the war years from 1942 to 1945, Japan also produced 3,392,814 tons of merchant shipping, including 986,159 tons of oil tankers. This was very close to British output over this period, despite the huge disruption from bombing Japan suffered from mid-1944. Without bombing, Japan might have out-produced Britain in merchant shipping.[155]

When due account is taken of all these factors, the evidence that the Royal Navy formally and consistently marked the IJN down on fighting efficiency is sparse. Three items are invariably highlighted: a 1935 report by the Tokyo naval attaché, Captain J P G Vivian;[156] the 1939 Tientsin papers, described in Chapter 2, which rated the fighting efficiency of the IJN at 80 per cent of the Royal Navy;[157] and the joint planning staff and Joint Intelligence Committee assessments during 1941 that Japanese air forces should be rated on a par with the Italians.[158] These items must be placed in context. The Vivian report attempted to identify traits in Japanese national characteristics and culture which might limit its efficiency. It undoubtedly attracted high-level interest in the naval staff when it appeared, but it has probably received more weight than it merits, simply because it has survived in the files, whereas alternative views have not. There is no evidence it had lasting impact, or ever represented a consensus. The 1937 Far East appreciation, two years later, assumed that, for planning purposes, the IJN had equal capability to the Royal Navy. Indeed, it specifically proposed the Royal Navy should aim for a capital ship advantage of twelve to nine.

The 1939 80 per cent rating appears to have persisted as a rough gauge of IJN quality over the next two years, but there is no sign this had any practical effect, either. It is also important to underline that the original reference was to maintenance, not to skill and commitment in battle. The IJN discovered serious design flaws in several classes of ships in the mid-1930s, notably the *Mogami*-and *Takao*-class cruisers and *Fubuki*-class destroyers. Correcting these involved major remedial work, with ships out of commission for long periods. It is likely the Royal Navy was aware of this and it may have contributed, therefore, to an 80 per cent availability factor.[159]

Admiral Sir William Davis, a captain serving as Deputy Director Naval Operations (Foreign) in 1941, later said:

Many of us (on the Naval Staff) would not agree with the estimate that the Japanese were only 80 per cent efficient compared with ourselves. We thought they were tactically rather rigid and also behind us in anti-submarine tactics. But frankly we knew nothing else (about their efficiency) and many of us thought it best to over-estimate rather than underestimate.[160]

That view rings true, and fits with the cautious approach the Royal Navy took on comparative battleship performance, as well as the experience gained in submarine surveillance operations. There was also some justification for questioning IJN fighting efficiency in terms of their inability to provide the logistic and personnel support necessary for a sustained war, and the Royal Navy may have acquired at least anecdotal evidence of this.[161] In that specific sense, the concept of an efficiency correction was defensible.

Ranking the Japanese air forces with the Italians was potentially more serious, if it implied they were an inferior opponent. As discussed in Chapter 3, it was one excuse for the chiefs of staff limiting Far East air reinforcement in terms of both numbers and quality, although it is harder to argue it was a decisive factor, given the pressures to prioritise the Middle East. It is not clear from the joint planning staff and Joint Intelligence Committee papers where the analogy with the Italians originated. It seems likely it was a Royal Air Force, more than a Royal Navy, judgement and, if so, it is difficult to judge how much it influenced Royal Navy attitudes. It may at the least have encouraged the Royal Navy to be more relaxed than was justified about the air threat to operations in the South China Sea in late 1941, and to pose fewer questions about IJN carrier power. While these comparisons with the Italian air force are viewed as pejorative (and this was undoubtedly intended by the joint planning staff), the Royal Navy, certainly Cunningham and Somerville, had learned to treat the Italian air force with respect in the central Mediterranean.

By late 1941 the Italians had achieved significant successes. For example, they had torpedoed four heavy cruisers, with varying degrees of damage, in four separate incidents between September 1940 and July 1941.[162] They had regularly attacked the fleet in Alexandria and conducted very disruptive mining operations in the Suez Canal. Finally, they had torpedoed and severely damaged the battleship *Nelson* during Operation Halberd, a convoy to resupply Malta run from Gibraltar in late September 1941, just two months before the Force Z operation. Ironically, *Prince of Wales* was part of the battleship escort, shooting down two Italian torpedo bombers.[163] In his memoirs, Cunningham was unequivocal about the high quality of Italian air performance at sea during the first part of the war. He stated that they appeared to have some squadrons 'specially trained for anti-ship work'; their reconnaissance was 'highly efficient' and 'seldom failed to find and report our ships'; 'bombers then invariably arrived in an hour or two'; 'Italian high level bombing was the best I have ever seen, far better than the German'.[164] This experience with Italian air performance at sea would surely have tempered any Royal Navy inclination to be complacent about IJNAF aircraft in Indochina if it had been recognised they were armed with torpedoes, and available intelligence on their range had been properly absorbed.[165]

Overall, the Royal Navy's picture of IJN capability, while it missed the impact of the 'revolution' in its approach to air power in 1941, was otherwise balanced and realistic. None of the key documents from 1937 onward show significant inclination to dismiss IJN fighting power, or to contemplate a major engagement except on 'favourable terms'. One final issue deserves mention. Churchill told the First Lord, A V Alexander, in September 1940 that 'The NID are very much inclined to exaggerate Japanese strength and efficiency'. This quote has been much repeated over the years and become part of the case against Churchill in assigning responsibility for the loss of Force Z. There are two points to make here. First, the quote is not consistent with the suggestion that the Royal Navy itself consistently underestimated the IJN.[166] Secondly, it is almost certain Churchill was recalling arguments over comparative battleship strengths when he was First Lord earlier in the year. He was frustrated that he was being asked to justify investment in additional Royal Navy build on the basis of what he felt was little more than speculation about IJN strength.[167] Not for the first time, he was subjecting his briefers to rigorous sceptical questioning.[168]

Chapters 6 and 7 explore how far the Royal Navy applied the intelligence picture of the IJN described in this chapter to shaping and executing a strategy for dealing with the naval risk posed by Japan, from mid-1941 through to the outbreak of the Far East war. The remainder of the chapter now looks at the resources available to the Royal Navy to defend the eastern theatre after mid-1940, and the Royal Navy policies and doctrine that influenced how those resources were used.

Royal Navy resources for an eastern war in 1941

Chapter 1 showed that Britain implemented a modified New Standard naval building programme over the three fiscal years 1937–39, designed to ensure adequate parity with the combined fleets of Germany and Japan by 1942. The outbreak of the European war in September 1939 triggered substantial changes to this programme. The plethora of new wartime shipping requirements, both new build and repair, and affecting both warship and merchant shipping needs, brought an immediate slowdown to previous plans. In May 1940, in order to meet the requirement for additional Atlantic escorts, merchant ships, and urgent army needs, pre-war orders were suspended for six capital ships, one aircraft carrier, eight cruisers and ten destroyers. In practice, most of the labour effort released here was diverted to the fleet destroyer and destroyer escort programmes, raising their manpower allocation by about 55 per cent.[169] Not only were those vessels already under construction, including those temporarily suspended, all completed within the next two years, a further eighteen fleet destroyers and forty-two Hunt class were progressively laid down after 1 June 1940 and commissioned before the end of 1942.[170] This enhanced destroyer output released older vessels for Atlantic escort, and was critical to supporting a new Eastern Fleet in 1942.

The suspended capital ships were *Howe*, the final *King George V*, the four *Lion* class and *Vanguard*. *Howe* was resumed in 1941 and completed in August 1942. *Vanguard* was laid down in October 1941, but not completed until 1946. The *Lions* were later cancelled and broken up on their slips. The aircraft carrier was *Indefatigable*, the last of the six *Illustrious* class. She was resumed in 1942 and completed in May 1944. Her sister *Implacable* was also much delayed, and completed even later in August that year. In September

1939 the naval staff had expected *Implacable* and *Indefatigable* to be commissioned in October 1941 and June 1942 respectively. Their availability in 1942 would have made a significant contribution to the Royal Navy's global commitments, and made the Royal Navy the strongest carrier power until late 1943.[171] The 1940 building programme agreed over the previous winter was also savagely pruned back.[172] The impact of these suspensions and cuts, alongside war losses, on Royal Navy strength in 1941 and 1942 is illustrated in Table 8.

Table 8 British Empire target naval strength

	August 1940	August 1941		January 1942		Deficit
Capital ships	13	16	(15)	18	(13)	5
Fleet aircraft carriers	4	7	(6)	7	(6)	1
Light aircraft carriers	2	2	(2)	2	(2)	0
Cruisers	57	71	(58)	75	(58)	17
Destroyers	173	224	(215)	252	(232)	20
Submarines	47	61	(52)	72	(57)	15

Source: Future Strategy paper, September 1940, and H T Lenton.
Target strengths reflect planned production following May 1940 suspension and cuts, but do not allow for war losses. Actual strengths achieved, which take account of real building rate, overseas purchases and war losses are given in brackets.[173] The figure of thirteen capital ships for August 1940 excludes *Queen Elizabeth*, undergoing modernisation until early 1941.

The message from these figures for Royal Navy resources available to counter the naval risk from Japan is stark. As a result of the demands of the European war, nominal Royal Navy strength in fleet units hardly changed from the time the Far East appreciation was issued in August 1940 and the outbreak of the Far East war in December 1941. In reality, the deficit against target strength was greater than displayed in the table, because the figures omit units under repair. Two fleet carriers and one battleship were out of action for between six and twelve months in August 1941 following war damage, and a further three capital ships were out of action for between six and eighteen months in January 1942. The number of modern or modernised capital ships able to engage Axis units on equal terms never exceeded eight in this period, and was often less.

The table also fails to bring out an acute shortage of modern fleet destroyers, since the destroyer figures in the table combine the categories of fleet destroyers and destroyer escorts. The Royal Navy entered the European war in 1939 with 103 modern fleet destroyers. By August 1940 war losses had reduced this figure to eighty-seven. There was a further net fall to eighty-three in August 1941, with a small increase to eighty-five by January 1942. However, during the second half of 1941, a further thirty destroyers were, on average, unavailable owing to damage or refit, so effective strength was rarely above fifty-five.[174] This was a quite inadequate number to meet fleet needs in three separate theatres and would be an important constraining factor in building up an eastern fleet in 1941/42. The shortage was exacerbated by the fleet destroyer suspensions ordered in May 1940, which inevitably extended the period where losses outweighed gains from build. The balance in the destroyer total in the table comprised destroyer escorts which fell into three categories: older vessels completed before 1920 to First World War design; around thirty-five old American destroyers acquired in the destroyer for bases deal in August 1940; and the new Hunt class which began commissioning in mid-1940 and reached a figure of forty-three by January 1942. The United States actually provided fifty destroyers, but around fifteen were transferred to the Royal Canadian Navy and allies such as the Royal Netherlands Navy. These American vessels took around six months on average to refit for Royal Navy use and were then of only limited value – barely satisfactory as Atlantic convoy escorts. The Hunt class were originally designed for Atlantic escort, but their sea-keeping was a disappointment, and they were generally deployed in coastal escort and in the Mediterranean, where they often operated as fleet destroyers with reasonable success.

On the positive side of the balance, the Royal Navy inflicted proportionately greater damage on Germany and Italy in the period up to December 1941. While nominal Royal Navy frontline strength grew over this period,[175] German and Italian strength in surface forces declined by about 40 per cent in each case. By end 1941, the Germans had lost one battleship, one pocket battleship, one heavy cruiser, two light cruisers and twelve fleet destroyers.[176] They had also lost fifty-three U-boats to end August 1941, almost the total strength at the start of the war.[177] The Italians had lost one battleship, three heavy cruisers, three light cruisers, twenty-four fleet destroyers and twenty escort destroyers. Italian submarine losses were also very heavy in this period, at thirty-eight against a total build of eighty-five between 1930 and 1942.[178]

Even more important, by diverting building resources away from fleet units from late 1939 onward to meet the requirements of the Battle of the Atlantic with the U-boats, and judicious management of merchant ship resources, Britain substantially compensated, through a mix of new build, requisition and capture, for the 9.1 million tons of merchant shipping lost during the twenty-eight months to the end of 1941.[179] Indeed, British-controlled shipping, comprising vessels over 1600 gross registered tons, actually rose from 17,784,000 tons at the outbreak of war in September 1939 to 20,693,000 tons at 31 December 1941.[180] This even included a net gain in the crucial category of oil tankers of some 1.2 million tons.[181] The Royal Navy commissioned about two hundred Atlantic escort vessels, primarily Flower-class corvettes, in addition to the destroyer escorts referred to above, across the two years 1940 and 1941, with about a third of these built in Canada.[182] This provided a critical margin over U-boat build in this period. Britain may not have been winning the Battle of the Atlantic at the end of 1941, but it was in no immediate danger of losing. This was a far better outcome than anticipated by the chiefs of staff in the Future Strategy paper of September 1940[183] and their Strategic Survey[184] prepared for the ABC-1 staff talks three months later. It demonstrated that Britain had got its immediate naval priorities right. The IJN would fail to do so. Finally, it is important to note that the Royal Navy would see a steady improvement in its overall destroyer situation in 1942. It would commission thirty-four fleet destroyers that year, more than double the numbers in 1941, and thirty-eight escort destroyers. Twenty-five fleet destroyers and eight destroyer escorts would be lost, but this still left a significant net gain in strength.

This resource picture explains why, as the Admiralty reviewed options for Far East reinforcement immediately following ABC-1, the only readily available force was Force H. This could be redeployed in emergency from Gibraltar, with the added prospect of the four 'R'-class battleships, if and when the Americans released them from Atlantic convoy escort. Five months later, by end August, the outlook was better. Admiralty planners could anticipate a small increase in capital ship availability by the end of the year as three *King George V* class came available, and three *Illustrious*-class carriers arrived from new build and repair. So long as there were no further losses, this would allow a defensive force of modern units to be established in the Indian Ocean by spring 1942, even without full US Navy 'Atlantic substitution' and relief of Force H. This resource situation underpinned the dispositions which the First Sea Lord presented to the prime minister in their correspondence in the last week of August, and which is examined in the next chapter.[185]

Royal Navy air capability in 1941

The Royal Navy required a strategy for dealing with Japan that took realistic account of its available resources in 1941. However, it also needed to apply the right capabilities and fighting tactics. Here, understanding the new potential of air power at sea and applying the lessons of the war to date was particularly important. Chapter 1 explained how the Fleet Air Arm entered the European war with obsolescent aircraft, and also faced low priority for development and production. Once the war got underway, a combination of prioritisation by the Ministry of Aircraft Production on key Royal Air Force types,[186] procurement mismanagement and shifting operational requirements caused development of the new generation fighter and strike aircraft ordered in 1939 and 1940 to move painfully slowly.

THE ROYAL NAVY IN EASTERN WATERS

Of the three aircraft taken forward, none ultimately reached service until 1943. Only one then proved operationally adequate, albeit not in its intended role. They were the Fairey Barracuda torpedo bomber, the advanced next-generation torpedo strike reconnaissance (TSR) aircraft to replace the Albacore and Swordfish; the Fairey Firefly specification N 8/39 two-seater escort fighter to replace the Fulmar; and the Blackburn Firebrand high-performance single-seat fighter. The failure of the Barracuda was partly owing to the cancellation of the advanced Exe engine by the Ministry of Aircraft Production in 1940 to concentrate on other engine priorities. This was a decision beyond the Royal Navy's control, but it led to substantial and unsatisfactory redesign. The development of the Firefly was inhibited by changing perceptions of fighter requirements and the best means of meeting these. It eventually proved a useful aircraft, but as a fighter-bomber and night-fighter rather than mainstream day-fighter, where it could not compete with contemporary US Navy fighters. It was not fully operational until 1944. The Firebrand was a high-performance single-seat fighter able to take on land-based aircraft, but was fatally compromised by hasty design and too many conflicting requirements.[187]

The Norwegian campaign persuaded the Fleet Air Arm that its most critical need was a dedicated naval fighter with sufficient performance to counter the latest land-based strike aircraft and their escorting fighters. Experiments here with radar-assisted fighter direction emphasised the desirability of an agile aircraft able to gain height and distance quickly for interception. The first Royal Navy radar-controlled interception at sea occurred on 23 April 1940, using the converted anti-aircraft cruiser Curlew as a radar picket. The Norway experience also demonstrated the potential for integrating new technology: radar, lightweight VHF communications (which were far ahead of the US Navy) and radio homing. Essentially, the Fleet Air Arm was now reaching for a 'Battle of Britain' fighter defence concept, based on new perceptions of the threat and available technology. Two factors, therefore, came together here to drive a fundamental shift in fighter philosophy: the threat from high-speed aircraft and the technical means to counter this threat with carrier-based fighters, using the emerging Royal Air Force fighter direction techniques.

The result was the specification of the new Firebrand single-seat fighter in July 1940,[188] and the decision to meet the gap before the Firebrand's arrival by ordering the Grumman F4F Wildcat from the United States, which the Royal Navy named the Martlet. This followed an extensive debate over how to reconcile the traditional requirement for a long-range escort fighter to support carrier strike forces, which in the Fleet Air Arm view required a dedicated navigator as well as pilot, and the new need to defend the fleet against high-performance attackers, where equivalent fighter performance was needed, implying single seat and acceptance of shorter range. The Admiralty continued to worry about the difficulties a single-seat fighter might face with navigation until well into 1941. The initial conclusion was that two aircraft were needed.[189] By September 1941 it was already clear the Firebrand was well behind schedule and could not be operational before mid-1943.[190]

Meanwhile, deploying the interim Martlet from Royal Navy carriers posed a problem. Without folding wings, none of the lifts in *Ark Royal* or the first three *Illustrious* class were large enough to accommodate them. The solution was to ask Grumman to produce a folding wing variant and eventually to adopt the US Navy practice of deck parking. Because of these limitations, the first Wildcats delivered were used in a land-based role for the defence of Scapa Flow. Designing and producing a folding wing took much longer than hoped, and the Admiralty briefly considered undertaking the work in the United Kingdom. In early 1941 it expected the folding wing variant to begin arriving in the middle of the year, but this proved wildly optimistic.[191] Nevertheless, at the end of 1941, the Royal Navy still assessed the Wildcat the best naval fighter in the world.[192] Trials had by now shown that it was more manoeuvrable than a Hurricane I, was faster at all heights up to 15,000ft, and climbed better too.[193] The Royal Navy ordered 100 aircraft in July 1940, 150 more in December 1940 and 200 in October 1941.[194] It appears a further eighty-one were taken over from French orders in mid-1940.[195] Grumman had originally promised delivery of twenty aircraft per month from late 1940, sufficient to equip the Fleet Air Arm frontline fighter force by the following autumn. This would have given Royal Navy carriers broadly the same fighter capability as the US Navy in confronting the IJN in late 1941 and in 1942. The US Navy had initially selected the Brewster Buffalo as its preferred naval fighter, but switched to the Wildcat in mid-1941, partly on the basis of British experience. The Wildcat then remained its primary naval fighter throughout 1942. The Buffalo, as we have seen, became the mainstay of British fighter defence in Malaya.

However, by the end of 1941 Grumman had delivered less than half the numbers contracted and paid for and, crucially, none had the folding wings, essential to the Royal Navy, which Grumman had also promised.[196] Churchill, who monitored the Fleet Air Arm fighter problem throughout 1941, described this as 'a melancholy story'.[197] In September that year, in typical fashion, he cut to the heart of the issue. 'All this year it has been apparent that the power to launch the highest class fighters from aircraft carriers may re-open to the Fleet great strategic doors which have been closed against them.' He instructed that – 'the aircraft carrier should have priority in the quality and character of suitable (aircraft) types'.[198] The latter was, of course, easy to say, but much harder to deliver. The US Navy, by then also acquiring Wildcats, blamed the delays on acute shortages of materials across the US aircraft industry, owing to concentration on the four-engine bomber programme.[199]

The end of 1941, therefore, found the Fleet Air Arm badly let down by American industry and desperately trying to plug its fighter gap through stopgap adaptations of the Hurricane and Spitfire, neither of which were really suitable for carrier operation. Once it became clear that Wildcat deliveries would be delayed, 270 Hurricanes were released to the Fleet Air Arm between February and May 1941.[200] Inevitably, some of these Royal Air Force releases were of poor quality.[201] Alexander again summarised the status of Fleet Air Arm procurement for the prime minister in early December. He explained why the Hurricane and Spitfire, although necessary as stopgaps, were inherently unsuitable for carrier operation. It remained essential to maximise Wildcat supplies until new British naval fighters were available, but supplies could only be assured by asking the United States to prioritise naval fighter over heavy bomber production.[202] Despite Alexander's insistence that the Spitfire was unsuitable, it appears that the possibility of converting Spitfires for carrier use, including the provision of folding wings, was considered as early as February 1940, but was ruled out at this time because of the impact on Fighter Command requirements. The idea was then resurrected in September 1941, technical issues were resolved by January 1942, and an initial order placed for 250 aircraft, by now designated the Seafire.[203] The modification of the Spitfire for naval use inevitably still took time, and the first twenty-eight aircraft were not delivered until July 1942. At that point, deliveries were expected to run at twenty-five per month and by late August the initial order for 250 was expanded to 452 for the end of 1943. This reflected the view by then that the Firebrand would have to be abandoned.[204]

Given the delay to the Barracuda, the Fleet Air Arm also considered the merits of purchasing strike aircraft from the United States. The current US Navy torpedo bomber, the Douglas Devastator, offered no significant performance advantage over the Swordfish or its Albacore successor, which began coming into service in 1940. The US Navy did have an excellent dive-bomber in the Douglas Dauntless SBD2, but the Royal Navy had long chosen to prioritise torpedo attack over dive-bombing, and its carriers had insufficient capacity to carry reasonable numbers of both types. There is a compelling argument here that the US Navy ended up prioritising the dive-bomber because its aerial torpedoes did not work satisfactorily. By contrast, the Royal Navy had excellent torpedoes.[205] The Fleet Air Arm was, however, impressed with the forthcoming Grumman TBF Avenger, which would prove the outstanding naval strike aircraft of the war. Two hundred were ordered in late 1941 under lend-lease, but did not reach the Royal Navy until 1943.

This background meant that until well into 1942, the Fleet Air Arm was largely dependent on obsolete biplane strike aircraft dating from the mid-1930s and a more modern fighter of interim design, the Fulmar, introduced in 1940.

Indomitable, completed in autumn 1941 with larger lifts and extra hangar space, was equipped with Hurricanes from the start, while modifications to *Illustrious* and *Formidable* in the United States in late 1941 enabled them to deploy Wildcats when they rejoined the fleet at the end of the year. While they were not competitive with the latest IJN and US Navy carrier aircraft, the limitations of the standard British Fleet Air Arm types can be overstated. The Fulmar, as primary fighter from 1940, could not match a Zero for speed or manoeuvrability, but it was still quite fast enough to catch the most modern loaded strike aircraft, and had other advantages both as an interceptor and reconnaissance aircraft. It was more robust than a Zero, could dive at 400mph (faster than almost all contemporaries and a speed which would cause a Zero to break up), had a four-hour endurance, and was an excellent gun platform with large ammunition capacity (which was a Zero weakness[206]), all of which, when allied to radar control, made it a useful defensive fighter.[207]

The Swordfish and Albacore torpedo bombers had reasonable range, a good communications fit, were married to an excellent torpedo, and their biplane manoeuvrability was an advantage in marginal flying weather. The Fleet Air Arm torpedo here was the 18in Mark XII introduced in 1940. Contrary to the impression often given that the Royal Navy was backward in aerial torpedo capability, the Mark XII could be dropped at up to 200ft (61m) and 150 knots, making it easily comparable to the IJN Type 91. It also had two speed options, an excellent warhead and the option of an advanced detonating pistol, the duplex magnetic proximity fuse.[208] In addition, it had gyro-angling so the attacking aircraft could offset, rather than flying direct at the target.

The Fleet Air Arm's Swordfish and Albacore torpedo bombers could not match their IJN counterparts for speed and range, but compensated through their ability to operate at night or in bad weather, and they had high reliability. It is doubtful either IJN or US Navy aircraft could have taken off in the conditions prevailing in *Ark Royal* on 26 May for the crucial attack on the *Bismarck*.[209] In addition, from early 1941 significant numbers were fitted with ASV air surface search radar, giving them a night and bad weather search and attack capability which neither the IJN nor US Navy could match. The first airborne radar sets, known as ASV 1, were deployed in Fleet Air Arm aircraft in late 1939, but were fragile and unreliable. The much improved ASV 2, with an effective range of about 15 miles to detect a medium-sized warship, began to be deployed in early 1941. The 825 Squadron embarked in the new carrier *Victorious* were entirely ASV 2-equipped, and this facilitated their night attack on *Bismarck* on 24 May. Some aircraft in *Ark Royal* were also equipped, enabling them to operate against *Bismarck* in the atrocious weather prevailing two days later.[210] Judged, therefore, as an overall weapon system, the Fleet Air Arm torpedo bombers were effective and competitive.

By the autumn of 1941, despite the limitations of its aircraft both in numbers and quality, the Royal Navy carrier fleet had achieved notable operational successes across different theatres and under different commanders, amply demonstrating that the Royal Navy was definitely not tied to a conservative battleship mentality. One measure here is that the Royal Navy had sunk or disabled five modern or modernised capital ships through aerial torpedo attack by end May 1941. At Taranto in November 1940, just eleven Fleet Air Arm Swordfish sank or disabled three modern or modernised Italian battleships, while eighty-nine IJN B5N2s were required to sink or disable five older US Navy battleships in the first-wave attack at Pearl Harbor. While the IJN is invariably credited with sinking the first capital units at sea (*Prince of Wales* and *Repulse*), the Fleet Air Arm had previously disabled a modern German battleship at sea (*Bismarck*) and come close to disabling another, the modern Italian battleship *Vittorio Veneto*, at Matapan.[211] They had also severely disabled the new French battleship *Richelieu* at Dakar on 8 July 1940.

The Royal Navy had also completed more modern carriers than either the IJN or US Navy, even if, for all the reasons discussed, it badly lagged both in the number and quality of frontline aircraft, together with trained and experienced crews. By autumn 1941 the Royal Navy had completed five large modern fleet carriers, against four by the IJN, and three by the US Navy. The IJN and the US Navy had also each completed a single light carrier earlier in the 1930s. Despite all its procurement problems and heavy wartime attrition, frontline air strength had almost doubled in size after two years of war, and it would continue grow steadily into 1942. Relevant figures here are as follows:[212]

Date	Sept 1939	Sept 1941	April 1942
Strike aircraft	140	198	196
Fighters	36	129	274
Total	176	327	470

Aircraft reserves by autumn 1941 were also substantial compared to those of the IJNAF. At the end of September 1941, alongside the frontline strength recorded above, there were 141 strike aircraft and seventy-two fighters allocated to training, a further 540 and 335 respectively in general reserve and fifty-seven and fifty-five in transit.[213]

The Royal Navy nevertheless had to divide its carrier fleet across four theatres, Atlantic, the two ends of the Mediterranean, and the Indian Ocean, and the initiation of the Russian convoys from late 1941 effectively added a fifth theatre, the Arctic. This made it impossible further to explore and train for the multi-carrier operations and mass strike tactics which the Royal Navy had investigated in the 1930s, and which the IJN developed so assiduously during 1941.[214] In theory, this left it poorly placed to handle a mass carrier engagement of the Coral Sea or Midway type, which the IJN and US Navy would experience in mid-1942. However, by mid-1941 the Royal Navy had made innovations which partly compensated for lack of numbers and quality of aircraft. Both the US Navy and IJN had embraced an operational philosophy based on the single massive strike, which made it difficult to manage the more flexible flying cycle required to handle the competing tasks and demands of a multi-threat environment.[215] The Royal Navy, by contrast, emphasised operational flexibility with rapid switches of aircraft tasking.[216] The evolution of this sophisticated multi-role flying cycle is well illustrated in some of the reports on Force H operations by Vice Admiral Somerville as early as autumn 1940. These show the execution of techniques and tactics, including radar pickets, which would still be in use in the 1960s, and were quite beyond US Navy and IJN capability at that time.[217]

The latest Royal Navy carriers had the most advanced radar of the day.[218] Aircraft communications systems and direction-finding homing were steadily improved. The Royal Navy continued developing and refining the techniques for long-range enemy raid detection and fighter direction that were first tried in Norway and employed during subsequent operations in the Mediterranean. Impartial testament to the quality of Fleet Air Arm operations at this time came from an American observer, Commander E G Taylor (US Navy), who served in the Fleet Air Arm in 1940 as a Royal Navy sub lieutenant. He informed the US Navy that the Fleet Air Arm in the spring of 1940 was in a desperate condition as regards pilots, aircraft numbers and quality, but did an excellent job with what it had through skill, innovation and new technology. Taylor described Fleet Air Arm fighter control techniques as very effective and far in advance of the US Navy which, in his view, was still not tackling the issue seriously at the end of 1941. Taylor subsequently played a part in Royal Navy procurement of the Wildcat, drawing on his war experience.[219] The US Navy was later impressed with, and subsequently largely adopted, Royal Navy air defence tactics demonstrated by the Royal Navy carrier *Victorious* when on loan to the US Navy Pacific Fleet in mid-1943.[220]

By mid-1941 the Royal Navy also had the basis of the action information organisation (AIO) that would revolutionise the way naval commanders used available information to drive operations. It would be followed with only minor incremental changes in the Royal Navy and US Navy through to the 1960s. The IJN had no radar at all before late 1942, totally inadequate airborne communications, and no real concept of fighter direction. IJN combat air patrols essentially ran themselves. This meant that IJN air defence was inefficient and susceptible to surprise.[221]

As described in Chapter 1, the Royal Navy had been experimenting with night flying operations, including night torpedo attack, since the early 1930s.

The scope for night attack pre-war was, however, limited because of the difficulty of conducting night searches before the advent of radar. It depended on night shadowing of an enemy already located at dusk, at which the Fleet Air Arm practised and became adept. However, during 1941, about half of the Royal Navy's strike aircraft were fitted with ASV, providing a genuine night search capability for the first time. This enabled the Royal Navy carriers to undertake attacks at night or in bad weather, conditions impossible for the IJN or US Navy.[222] Examples of night/bad weather operations were the attack on Taranto in November 1940, a night attack at a range of around 180 miles from *Illustrious*, and the previously mentioned bad weather attacks on *Bismarck* from *Victorious* and *Ark Royal* on 24 May and in the afternoon and evening of 26 May 1941. ASV was arguably crucial to the success of the Bismarck attacks, as emphasised by the commanding officer of 825 Squadron in *Victorious*. 'ASV proved to be of assistance beyond all measure. While remaining hidden from the enemy by cloud, my observer was able to give me a clear picture of own and enemy forces up to the very last moment of breaking cloud for attack'.[223]

By mid-1941 the Royal Navy had, therefore, acquired a much wider base of wartime experience in carrier operations than is often suggested. Some of this reflected the application and elaboration of pre-war thinking. The 'find, fix and strike' role on behalf of the battle-fleet evident at Matapan and the *Bismarck* operations fall into this category, and even the Taranto operation drew heavily on pre-war plans. The Royal Navy had formed a special committee to look at air attack on enemy bases in 1929, and investigated the merits of specialised weapons for this. Mediterranean Fleet orders in 1936 included instructions for shallow-water torpedo settings for an attack on Taranto.[224] However, in air defence the Royal Navy was breaking new ground with capabilities, not only radar but also VHF communications and 'identification friend or foe' (IFF), which were not available before the war. It was also becoming adept at exploiting the full range of carrier capabilities: search, strike against land and sea targets, air defence, and anti-submarine, which all featured in complex multi-threat scenarios such as Mediterranean convoy operations.

All of this had demanded much tactical innovation and a new approach to force composition. It was the Royal Navy which consolidated the concept of the fast multi-role carrier task force in this period, of which Force H was the supreme example. This model would not be embraced by the US Navy until much later, because until its new build battleships (*North Carolina* and *Indiana* classes) became available for the Pacific in late 1942, it had no capital ships fast enough to operate with its carriers, and it also lacked the oil tankers to support them until well into 1943. By contrast, the Royal Navy not only had its battlecruisers, but also widely used the modernised *Queen Elizabeth* class, significantly faster than their US Navy equivalents, alongside its carriers in both the Mediterranean and Indian Ocean. This not only ensured support against surprise surface attack, but also provided substantial anti-aircraft firepower. Finally, as proof that it could conduct the most advanced multi-carrier operations, the Royal Navy undertook a four-carrier operation against the most challenging opposition, air, surface and submarine, in Operation Pedestal, the convoy to Malta, in August 1942. Both the IJN and US Navy would have struggled to conduct a comparable operation against an equivalent level of air attack at this time.[225] Overall therefore, while the Royal Navy could not hope to compete with the IJN in late 1941 in either carrier numbers or quantity and quality of embarked aircraft, it would be quite wrong to view it as left behind in the exercise of air power at sea. The Royal Navy carrier force had significant strengths and experience to draw on.

Royal Air Force maritime strike

The 1937 agreement gave the Royal Navy full control of its carrier air arm, but left land-based maritime attack with the Royal Air Force. For the Royal Air Force, this role inevitably took lower priority in the first phase of the war to the air defence of the British homeland, to strategic bombing, and even within the maritime sphere to the anti-submarine effort. The emphasis on strategic bombing reflected long-standing service doctrine and it was the only immediate way of directly attacking Germany.

By late 1940 the Royal Air Force had nevertheless deployed a new torpedo bomber, the Beaufort, for maritime strike. It was broadly equivalent in capability to the IJN land-based torpedo attack bombers, albeit with less range. However, a British equivalent of the IJN 11th Air Fleet would have required a significant diversion of resources from Bomber Command to Coastal Command that was never forthcoming, even in the face of the acute threats in the Battle of the Atlantic and in the Indian Ocean in 1942. The United Kingdom-based Beaufort torpedo force struggled, therefore, to reach four operational squadrons by the end of 1941.[226] The only overseas torpedo force at that time comprised the two Malaya squadrons equipped with obsolete Vildebeest biplanes. The parlous state of Royal Air Force torpedo strike in early 1942 was summarised in a report for the Assistant Chief of Air Staff (Operations). This stated that although torpedo attack was more effective against ships than bombing, the Royal Air Force had neglected it for both technical and tactical reasons. It highlighted lack of high-level commitment, shortage of torpedoes and associated maintenance and support facilities, and inadequate training for this specialised role, given constant diversion of aircraft and crews to other tasks. This presented major difficulties in expanding the force.[227]

The lack of high-level support for torpedo attack partly reflected the scarcity of high-value warship targets accessible to the United Kingdom force, since bombing was seen as adequate for interdiction of commercial traffic. Bombing was also the preferred option for attacking naval targets in port or dockyard. However, it mainly reflected the entrenched belief across most of the Royal Air Force leadership that the strategic bombing of Germany must take primacy and that everything else, with few exceptions, represented a diversion from winning the war. Statistics did not help the Coastal Command case for enhanced surface strike resources. They demonstrated that surface strike was very expensive for only limited benefit. Between April 1940 and March 1943, Coastal Command conducted 3700 attacks which sank 107 vessels (almost all merchant) for the loss of 648 aircraft. Minelaying, primarily by Bomber Command, sank three times the number of ships (369), for about half the losses (329).[228]

The poor Coastal Command surface attack record was painfully underlined by the woeful performance of the Beaufort force during the escape of the German battlecruisers through the Channel in February 1942. By contrast, both *Scharnhorst* and *Gneisenau* were badly damaged by mines dropped along their predicted track, and *Gneisenau* was wrecked by Bomber Command in dock at Kiel a fortnight later.[229] Nevertheless, despite limited resources, the Beaufort force had some notable successes. An attack on 6 April 1941 crippled *Gneisenau* alongside in Brest, and a night operation on 13 June seriously damaged the pocket battleship *Lützow*. This attack on *Lützow* off the Norwegian port of Egersund took place at a range of about 400 miles, only slightly less than the later IJN attack on Force Z.[230] It was the first successful attack by a land-based torpedo force on a capital ship at sea[231] and a harbinger, therefore, for the attack on Force Z.[232] The *Lützow* operation obviously contrasted with the poor performance by all three available United Kingdom Beaufort squadrons against the German battlecruisers six months later, but this reflected incompetent communication, command and control, rather than any deficiency in aircraft performance.

Small size and lack of dedicated expertise in the United Kingdom Beaufort force constrained the development of a torpedo strike force overseas. However, two squadrons were deployed to Egypt via Malta in early 1942 to compensate for the planned departure of the Alexandria battle-fleet. This was destined for the Indian Ocean following the Japanese attack, although the ships were badly damaged by Italian frogmen before they could be released. This planned substitution of Beaufort torpedo bombers for battleships was an almost exact analogy of Yamamoto's use of the 22nd Air Flotilla to counter Force Z.[233] It demonstrated that the Royal Navy leadership recognised the strategic impact that an appropriate land-based strike force could achieve. However, the

Beaufort force was too small, and its crews insufficiently trained, to stand real comparison with its IJN counterpart. The force took some while to achieve operational efficiency in the theatre and there were insufficient resources for an additional force in the Indian Ocean, although one of the Egypt squadrons would be deployed onward to Ceylon at the end of April. The Chief of Air Staff accepted that torpedo bombers were the most pressing need in the Far East, but the only way of providing these was to replace the remaining two Beaufort squadrons in UK with obsolete Hampdens. The remaining Beauforts would then be deployed to the Middle East, releasing the two squadrons already despatched there to go on to India. Clearly, the impact of just two squadrons would have been limited, although still a significant contribution to the defence of Ceylon.[234]

As already noted in Chapter 3, the Far East also suffered problems with the planned production of Beauforts in Australia. Australian Beauforts were to replace the Vildebeests in Malaya by mid-1941 as part of the '336' reinforcement plan. When Brooke-Popham took stock of planned reinforcements following his arrival as Commander-in-Chief Far East at the beginning of 1941, he expected to have two squadrons of Beauforts and reserves, comprising fifty aircraft by the end of the year. However, he was aware, following a visit to Australia, that this reflected an estimated output in Australia of twenty aircraft by October and seventy at the end of the year. Given the embryonic state of the Australian aircraft industry, he should perhaps have anticipated that the targets would slip, even without problems in the American supply chain. Shortages of key parts from the United States meant that only seven aircraft were completed by the end of 1941, when production halted for six months.[235] Even if the original target had been met, the new Beaufort squadrons could not have achieved operational efficiency until well into 1942, not least due to a shortage of suitable torpedoes.[236] The modernisation of the Malaya strike force on which Far East commanders placed much emphasis was, therefore, always compromised although neither the chiefs of staff nor Far East commanders seem to have known this. Following the Japanese attack, they repeatedly pressed the Australian government to expedite the provision of Beauforts to Malaya.[237]

There is no doubt that British maritime air power was quite inadequate to take on the IJN in December 1941. However, this situation cannot be reduced to simple explanations. The Royal Navy's overall record and experience in 1940 and 1941 demonstrates a good grasp of the risks and opportunities presented by modern air power at sea, and often showed remarkable innovation with limited resources. In rebalancing its naval programme in 1940, the Royal Navy cut battleships, not carriers. The Royal Navy knew its Fleet Air Arm aircraft were inadequate. It made reasonable and timely decisions to address this, but fell victim to production priorities in the United Kingdom and United States it could not foresee. The Royal Air Force's Beaufort force had similar potential capability to the IJNAF, but suffered the limitations of small size, multiple roles and inadequate training for the specialised maritime environment. The Royal Air Force could have invested more in the Beaufort force at the expense of bombing. For decision-makers in 1941 that trade-off was hard to justify, but it made it difficult to build up the force when it was urgently needed overseas in 1942. Matters did begin to change from mid-1942 with the decision to develop a variant of the well-proven Beaufighter as a replacement for the Beaufort. This was the Beaufighter TFX, known as the Torbeau, which became a very successful maritime strike aircraft, with the first squadron going operational in the United Kingdom in November that year.[238] The Royal Air Force should, however, have been quicker to spot the problems with the prospective Australian Beaufort force, given its importance to Far East reinforcement.

The lack of adequate maritime air resources to meet the IJN is invariably presented as a consequence of over-stretch. However, the problem was less one of overall capacity than strategic choices. Britain chose to prioritise its air resources in 1941 on Fighter and Bomber Commands at home and in the Middle East, and deliberately to carry risk in the Far East. For a whole series of reasons outside the scope of this book, which included steady attrition, production failings, and the need to re-equip the whole frontline, Bomber Command took a long time to reach a size with which it could have any hope of strategic effect. Air Chief Marshal Sir Arthur Harris stated that, when he took over the command in February 1942, when prospects in the Far East were most grim, immediate strength was 378 aircraft of which only sixty-nine were heavy bombers and fifty were light bombers. His primary force was, therefore, 250 medium bombers, about the same as those in the Middle East and those planned for India by the autumn.[239] Against this background, in the spring of 1942 Pound, with partial support from the new Chief of the Imperial General Staff, Field Marshal Sir Alan Brooke, argued forcefully for air resources to be diverted from bombing to protection of sea communications. Pound's primary concern here was the Atlantic, but he also emphasised the need to improve the defences of the Indian Ocean.[240] He met vigorous opposition from Portal as Chief of Air Staff, and the Harris numbers help to explain why.[241]

The subsequent argument has been described as one of Whitehall's most notorious battles of the war. The debate ran for three months before a compromise position was reached in July, which provided Pound with only a limited part of what he had sought.[242] Four factors have been suggested to explain why Pound substantially conceded:

- The attitude of the prime minister, which was broadly behind Bomber Command;
- Production limitations, which made it impossible for a diversion to maritime air to achieve results in a meaningful timescale;
- Shifting strategic perceptions in favour of bombing U-boat bases and focusing effort on the Bay of Biscay;
- Improved efficiency in Coastal Command by mid-1942.

Portal also had sound reasons for rejecting demands from Attlee, Beaverbrook and Wavell, as well as Pound, for more bombers to be sent overseas at this time beyond those currently planned. These included the obvious constraints in time and shipping space inherent in any move of large air forces; the technical teething problems with the latest aircraft which would raise immense serviceability issues outside United Kingdom infrastructure; the 'strategic immobility' caused by the need to replace Bomber Command's frontline; and the impossibility of adapting heavy bombers to a torpedo strike role. These constraints did not reflect well on previous Royal Air Force planning and procurement, but as 'we are where we are' arguments they were powerful.[243] Also important was the impact of Midway, and the drastic reduction in the threat to the Indian Ocean. In effect, a slow or even minimal air build-up in the East was now tolerable.

The striking point is how little was really changed by this debate. Minimal Admiralty requirements in the Atlantic area were met by the end of 1942, and arguably in the Indian Ocean too, but more from the impact of American production than any shift in British priorities. Figures drawn from the British Official History put the debate in context and underline the limited scope for more diversion from Bomber Command. In September 1942 Royal Air Force strength was allocated as follows:

Command	Squadrons	First line aircraft
Bomber Command	48	468
Fighter Command	76 (day)	1338
Coastal Command	43	532
Army co-operation	20	272
Middle East	62	830
India	27	442

At this time the US Army Air Force also had two bomber groups with ninety-six heavy bombers in the United Kingdom, three squadrons in the Middle East and two in India.[244]

A final perspective is provided in post-war remarks from Dr Noble Frankland, the official historian of Bomber Command, to Admiral Sir

Algernon Willis, Somerville's second in command in the Indian Ocean during 1942.[245] Frankland described Bomber Command during the first part of the war until mid-1943 as a small, undernourished force, which did not grow at all in 1942, partly due to re-equipping the frontline, but also substantial diversions to Coastal Command and overseas.[246] Any further diversion might have led to the collapse of the offensive. Frankland did not believe either Portal or Churchill harboured illusions that bombing alone would win the war, but they did doubt it could be won without it, and they may have been right. Harris may have had illusions that bombing alone would do it, but much of his bombast was also aimed at maximising resource share. Frankland also stressed the need to understand that the strategic air offensive embraced many aims and achievements beyond the general attack on German industry. Initially, reducing the scale of German air attack on the United Kingdom was a priority, while in 1941–43 a large part of its effort went on the Battle of the Atlantic, directly or indirectly. If the results were disappointing, the lesson was not that the strategy was wrong, but that the force was operationally inadequate. That reflected poor Royal Air Force equipment and training decisions before the war. Frankland accepted that by switching more resources to Coastal Command (and by implication wider strategic communications), success at sea might have come a little earlier. But the resulting excess resources could not easily have been switched back later to an effective strategic air campaign. The Battle of the Atlantic had to be won, but winning this was no good on its own.

6

Summer and Autumn 1941:
Reinforcement and Deterrence

B ritish accounts of the final months before the outbreak of war with Japan in December 1941 are dominated by the story of Force Z, comprising the new battleship *Prince of Wales* and the battlecruiser *Repulse*. This is presented as a futile gesture of late and inadequate deterrence leading inexorably to disaster. The loss of the force to Japanese air attack two days after the Far East war began is considered the greatest defeat suffered by the Royal Navy in the Second World War. As a high-profile British naval disaster, the only obvious rivals are the sinking of the battlecruiser *Hood* by the German *Bismarck* earlier in the year, and the destruction of the Arctic convoy PQ17 the following summer. While these two events have received due attention over the years, the loss of Force Z has acquired wider significance.

The loss is portrayed first as the inevitable consequence of a flawed Singapore strategy, where the illusion that a two-hemisphere empire could ever be successfully secured with a one-hemisphere navy led finally to the despatch of a political token. The end, it is suggested, lay in the beginning, echoing the inevitability of classical Greek tragedy. For those coming of age post-war, the sinking of British battleships by aircraft of an upstart Asian power symbolised the wider collapse of British imperial and naval power. It encapsulated not just strategic over-stretch, but failure of will and capability, mixed with professional arrogance and incompetence.

Finally, responsibility for the loss has been pinned firmly on Churchill. He stands accused of pursuing an unrealistic goal of political deterrence, and recklessly disregarding professional naval advice. Force Z, therefore, joins the Dardanelles and Norway in the list of military failures of judgement placed at Churchill's door. In contrast, Pound is cast as the weary First Sea Lord, lacking the political shrewdness, intellect, temperament and constitutional robustness to face down a dominant prime minister. Such is the emphasis placed on the Force Z story that many readers of histories of the Second World War might assume that this deployment was the only occasion when the British leadership thought about and invested resources in the eastern theatre naval problem between 1939 and 1944.

In reality, as we have seen, there never was a single Singapore strategy, certainly not one that promised a single ending. Far East naval defence was never out of British minds for long as the war developed. Nor did the idea of despatching major Royal Navy reinforcements to the Far East suddenly emerge in the late summer of 1941. Such reinforcement reflected the decisions taken at the ABC-1 staff talks and the detailed plans put in place immediately afterward. The traditional story of the genesis of Force Z and the decisions regarding its deployment, virtually unchallenged for sixty years, is flawed. The positions ascribed to Churchill and the Admiralty, now embedded in national memory, are almost the reverse of those they actually adopted.

Force Z was just one strand in a much more ambitious programme of reinforcement planned by the Admiralty in the autumn of 1941. This programme for deploying a full battle-fleet to Singapore, with the intention then of using Manila as a forward operating base, reflected the 'Atlantic substitution' agreement reached with the United States at ABC-1, but also the subsequent American pressure for the Royal Navy to make a greater contribution to the defence of the Malay Barrier, as discussed earlier. These new Admiralty plans were flawed because of the inappropriate composition of the proposed Royal Navy fleet, but they must be judged against the wider American and British strategy to deter and contain Japan which emerged that autumn, which included air and submarine power based in the Philippines. This wider strategy had the potential to check Japan. Failure lay in timing and execution, rather than the concept itself.

The initial debate over Indian Ocean reinforcement

The middle of the year, 1 July 1941, was a watershed for both Britain and the United States in managing the risk from Japan. For both countries, it marked a distinct shift to weighing the threats to their vital security through a global, rather than essentially European, focus. The primary driver for this change in perspective was the German invasion of Russia on 22 June. For Britain, this offered temporary relief from both the threat of invasion and of a major German drive into the Middle East. But Britain was acutely aware that if Russia collapsed quickly, which seemed possible, the nation would then be faced with a much more powerful German challenge, including a northern drive on the Middle East, which it would struggle to meet. American calculations were similar. Both countries anticipated that Japan might exploit the German invasion either by attacking Russia itself in Manchuria, or by taking advantage of Russian preoccupation in the west to drive south into the resource-rich East Indies. A northern attack would provide a breathing space to the hard-pressed British but, as the United States quickly recognised, this would be short-lived if it speeded a Russian collapse.[1]

Magic intercepts gave Britain and the United States valuable and simultaneous insights into Japanese thinking and intentions through the month of July as Tokyo decision-makers wrestled with how best to respond to the opportunity offered by the German attack.[2] They provided forewarning of the decision to move into southern Indochina and, crucially, confirmation that the Japanese leadership viewed this as a stepping stone to a subsequent attack on Malaya, Singapore and the Netherlands East Indies.[3] However, Magic and other sources also pointed to preparations for operations in Manchuria and potential divisions of opinion within the Japanese leadership. As the weeks went by, it became evident that Japan was thinking aggressively and preparing for early military action, but also waiting on events in Russia and keeping her options open. This convinced American and British decision-makers that Japan could yet be dissuaded or deterred.

Japanese sources identify two main factors behind the decision to seek bases first in southern Indochina and then in Thailand: the breakdown in negotiations with the Netherlands East Indies in mid-June over the supply of oil and other strategic resources; and German encouragement to attack Malaya and Singapore, particularly during the visit of Foreign Minister Yosuke Matsuoka to Germany in April.[4] The British knew of the German encouragement regarding Singapore from the GC&CS intercept of a message from Lieutenant General Hiroshi Oshima, the Japanese ambassador in Berlin, on 23 March reporting a conversation with Admiral Raeder.[5] Japanese accounts insist, however, that in July Japan still hoped it could secure oil and other resources by peaceful means, although it was increasingly willing to resort to force if necessary. The IJN, therefore, now began serious contingency planning for operations against both the Netherlands East Indies and the British in Malaya.[6] The German invasion of Russia was a complicating factor because it introduced an attractive 'northern option' for some in the army. However, by August, Japan had decided against intervention in Russia and was pursuing a 'wait and see' policy, ready to exploit opportunities, but not at the expense of its southern interests. As its plans for southern operations developed through the autumn, Japan also recognised that it was desirable to complete these by spring 1942, to avoid having to fight on two fronts if Russia chose to intervene in support of the western powers once the weather permitted.[7]

Against this background, nearly a year after completing the Far East appreciation, and with Japan poised to enter southern Indochina, British plans for Far East naval reinforcement were those agreed by the Admiralty during the ABC-1 staff talks. Immediate phase 1 reinforcement would comprise Force H, redeployed from Gibraltar to protect Indian Ocean communications. If the

United States entered the war, the Royal Navy would mobilise a substantial phase 2 Eastern Fleet centred on five capital ships released by the deployment of US Navy forces in the Atlantic, although three of these would be old and unmodernised and of limited military value. In total this addition would comprise: two *Nelson*s, three 'R' class, ten cruisers, thirty-two destroyers and ten submarines.[8] However, the recent losses of cruisers and destroyers in the Mediterranean, particularly at Crete in May, suggested the Royal Navy would struggle to provide the planned supporting forces in this new Eastern Fleet. In mid-July the strength of the Eastern Mediterranean Fleet had reduced to two battleships, four 6in cruisers, two 5.25in cruisers, two 4in anti-aircraft cruisers, and eighteen destroyers.[9]

At a minimum, therefore, if and when the United States took on active responsibilities in the Atlantic, the Royal Navy could anticipate a stronger holding force in the Indian Ocean than was feasible in 1940. The price of US Navy Atlantic reinforcement was a weakened US Navy Pacific Fleet, now less able to constrain a Japanese southward move because it lacked the strength and mobility to intervene credibly in the western Pacific. As noted previously, the British war leadership underestimated the consequences of this weaker Pacific Fleet and credited it with greater deterrence value than was justified. The limitations to the Pacific Fleet were compounded by the failure to agree an American-Dutch-British joint operating plan that would give practical effect to the Far East defensive strategy established in ABC-1. The defence of the Malay Barrier, on which all parties placed so much emphasis, had no greater naval commitment in mid-1941 than a year earlier, while British air and land reinforcements sent to Malaya remained far below agreed targets. The Admiralty had also done little to address the wider support of an eastern fleet. Some work was done to ensure reserves of fuel and ammunition and identify additional operating bases, such as Port T in the Maldives. But almost nothing was done to improve port defences and protection from air attack in Ceylon, or the provision of long-range air reconnaissance. This attitude reflected the Admiralty response to a 1938 review into fleet support if certain fixed bases, including Singapore, were lost. It ruled then that Singapore should always be available, and that no action was required to ensure reserve support in the Indian Ocean and Far East theatres.[10]

It is traditionally suggested that the decision actually to despatch Royal Navy capital units to the Far East, as opposed to hypothetical planning for this, originated in Churchill's well-known exchange with Pound at the end of August. Two catalysts are identified to explain the prime minister's intervention: the Japanese move into southern Indochina and the United States imposition of sanctions which markedly increased the likelihood of conflict; and pressure from Australia for early naval reinforcement, including a personal message from Prime Minister Robert Menzies.[11] These developments certainly exerted influence on the prime minister, the chiefs of staff and the naval staff, but it is doubtful they were decisive in themselves. The initial reaction to the move into Indochina in the stocktakes prepared for the chiefs by the joint planning staff was surprisingly subdued and argued against substantial early reinforcement.[12] As explained in Chapter 3, this reflected the resource pressures in the Middle East and the prime minister's insistence that Japanese attack remained unlikely.[13] The Australian request was strongly worded, but not substantively different from earlier lobbying, and the Australians had been kept informed on post-ABC-1 plans for an eastern fleet. At the War Cabinet on 8 August, Phillips as VCNS argued forcefully that Britain should not risk conflict with Japan over Thailand, because of the vulnerability of Indian Ocean communications to IJN attack.[14]

The debates within the British leadership over Far East naval reinforcement in the late summer and autumn are better viewed as part of a continuum stretching back to ABC-1. The concept of a new eastern fleet did not suddenly emerge in August; it had been the subject of constant planning from February onward.[15] What had, however, changed by August was the pace and nature of US Navy Atlantic reinforcement. Under ABC-1, it was envisaged that the US Navy would only take over certain Atlantic responsibilities from the Royal Navy after a United States declaration of war. In practice, the US Navy had begun more pro-active escort operations in the western Atlantic as the summer progressed, thereby releasing Royal Navy forces for potential redeployment in peacetime. Admiral Stark underlined American intent at the end of July. With the full agreement of Navy Secretary Knox, he had pressed the president 'to seize the psychological opportunity presented by the Russian-German clash' to implement aggressive Atlantic escort operations and provoke an early clash with Germany.[16]

By August, therefore, the constraint on the build-up of an eastern fleet was less the need for relief by the US Navy and more the need to refit and repair Royal Navy ships subject to war damage, notably at Crete. Phases 1 and 2 of the reinforcement process were also becoming blurred. It was now possible Indian Ocean phase 1 immediate reinforcements could be in place in peacetime by the end of the year. Other units would then join incrementally to achieve the planned phase 2 total, but also in peacetime.[17] These developments were confirmed at the Riviera Atlantic Conference between the British and American leadership at Placentia Bay between 9–12 August. Here the US Navy not only committed to the full relief of Royal Navy escorts in the western Atlantic by mid-September under its Hemisphere Plan 4, but also aggressive anti-U-boat operations designed to provoke confrontation with Germany.[18] It is important therefore to recognise that Churchill's discussion with Pound, initiated on 25 August, was more than a precautionary response to the risk of early attack from Japan, which Churchill insisted was still unlikely. It was also the consequence of long-desired naval reinforcements in the Indian Ocean now becoming available in peacetime. A week earlier, Turner, Director of US Navy War Plans, told Danckwerts, Head of British Admiralty Delegation Washington, he had learnt at Riviera that the 'R'-class battleships were to be withdrawn from Atlantic escort for three-month refits to receive enhanced anti-aircraft armament and protection. They would then be deployed to the Cape area under Phillips, who would move from his present post of VCNS. From the Cape they could cover raider threats in both the South Atlantic and Indian oceans.[19]

This influence of ABC-1 on Royal Navy plans for Far East reinforcement is usually overlooked. It is then difficult to explain why attention suddenly focused on the Indian Ocean in August, and how exchanges at and around the Riviera conference further influenced thinking within British and American decision-making circles. At one level, the plans for Indian Ocean reinforcement and the creation of a new eastern fleet during the first half of 1941 were a consequence of ABC-1 and the American refusal to take primary responsibility for securing British and Dutch interests in the Far East. They marked a resumption of traditional Admiralty Far East war planning, broken into its various phases, and fixed on the ultimate goal of relieving Singapore and protecting the British Far East territories with Royal Navy forces once resources permitted. By August, recent war losses and continuing uncertainty over ultimate American intentions suggested the maximum practical reinforcement goal achievable by the end of the year was a phase 2 concentration in the Indian Ocean. This might protect the reinforcement route to Singapore, but would not in itself guarantee the security of Malaya, Singapore and the Malay Barrier. Pound's response of 28 August to the prime minister maintained the Admiralty's proposed Eastern Fleet composition first agreed in February, but updated previous plans in two respects. It provided the times when capital units were expected to reach the Indian Ocean, half by the end of the year and the rest by end January 1942. This reflected the impact of US Navy peacetime Atlantic relief. It also emphasised that final formation of the Eastern Fleet was now dependent on the availability of cruisers and, above all, destroyers. This reflected the impact of recent war losses.[20]

However, the first half of 1941 had also focused increasing attention on the vulnerability of Indian Ocean communications, including those to the Middle East theatre, to attack from IJN raiders. Such IJN attacks might be co-ordinated with German submarine and raider operations. Admiralty planners recognised that the US Navy could not protect these critical British interests. The Japanese threat, therefore, required a Royal Navy force at Singapore or

Ceylon sufficient to deter them.[21] The raider risk was the primary risk identified by Pound and always uppermost in Churchill's mind.[22] He had highlighted it at the Defence Committee meeting in April and in his exchange with Dill on the relative priority of Middle and Far East at the beginning of May.[23] He underlined it starkly to American Assistant Secretary Sumner Welles at Riviera.[24] It was a risk to which he was prepared to devote valuable resources, such as deployment of a *King George* V-class battleship to the Indian Ocean, in contrast to his reluctance to reinforce Malaya.

Thus, at the mid-point of the year, there was common ground between prime minister and Admiralty on the raider threat, but potential unresolved differences over any wider naval commitment to protection of the Far East territories. Here the prime minister looked to the United States to bear the main burden, while the naval staff remained committed to a fleet at Singapore when possible. The emphasis on the raider threat did not reflect hard intelligence of IJN intent. It was rather a reflection of two things: awareness of the vulnerability of British maritime communications and trade to attack; and 'mirroring' from German raider practice in two wars. The US Navy, by contrast, thought it unlikely the IJN would pursue cruiser operations far from base 'if national characteristics were taken into account'.[25] The US Navy prediction proved the more accurate reading of IJN doctrine. In both pre-war planning and the execution of the war itself, the IJN showed little interest in commerce raiding by either surface or submarine forces.[26] These differences over the Indian Ocean raider threat help explain the difficulty in reaching agreement over the American-Dutch-British (ADB) joint operating plan negotiated at the Singapore conference in April and known as ADB-1. For Britain, the ultimate priority, if resources were limited, was defence of Indian Ocean strategic communications. For the United States, it was forward defence of the Malay Barrier that mattered to keep secure the resources of the Netherlands East Indies and Australasia.

In considering this difference of view, it is worth noting the Allied merchant shipping losses in the Indian Ocean in 1941 and 1942, which were 73,155 tons (twenty ships) and 724,485 tons (205 ships) respectively.[27] Clearly, those in 1941 were due to German surface raiders since no U-boats operated in the Indian Ocean during this year. In 1942 there were minor U-boat operations late in the year, accounting for about 57,000 tons.[28] German raider operations also continued and perhaps contributed a further 100,000 tons loss in this year. This leaves losses of some 567,485 tons in the Indian Ocean in 1942 down to Japanese action. Meanwhile, total Allied losses in the Pacific in 1941 and 1942 were 1,008,876 tons (460 ships). If half these were British-controlled, which seems a reasonable estimate, then total British-controlled merchant losses due to Japanese action in the first year of the Far East war were just over one million tons.[29] Two points follow. First, while it is true the Japanese never pursued a coherent strategy of commerce raiding on a German scale, initial British losses here were still serious. Secondly, Japanese intervention in early 1941 might have increased overall British shipping losses that year by some 25 per cent. Churchill and Pound had good reason to focus on this threat.

In reviewing the impact of the Riviera discussions on Britain's Far East strategy, three points are usually emphasised: the agreement that the US Navy would take over convoy escort in the western Atlantic, thus releasing Royal Navy resources; President Roosevelt's failure to deliver adequately on his promised warning to Japan on the consequences of further aggression; and failure to cut through the ADB impasse. However, there were two other linked threads running through Riviera which were important to the evolution of British, and specifically Royal Navy, Far East strategy. These were the consensus that the survival and military effectiveness of Russia was critical to the security of Britain and the United States, and the perception, especially for the American leadership, that Japan now posed a global as well as regional risk, through the potential damage she could inflict on the wider British and Russian war efforts.[30]

Roosevelt's personal position here is reflected in his remark to Secretary of the Interior Harold Ickes, on 1 July, that it was 'terribly important for the control of the Atlantic to keep peace in the Pacific'. 'I simply have not got enough Navy to go round – and every little episode in the Pacific means fewer ships in the Atlantic'.[31] This led the American leadership to seek a means of deterring Japan. They settled on air power based in the Philippines, alongside new economic sanctions. At Riviera, the United States Chief of Army Staff, General George Marshall, notified the British chiefs of staff of the intent to reinforce the Philippines as a deterrent to further Japanese encroachment to the south. However, American thinking here was still at an early stage, and the British were evidently not convinced such a strategy would have much effect. As the prime minister stated: 'The Americans have, we think, rather exaggerated hopes of the effect of operations, particularly air, from the Philippines against a Japanese expedition to the South China Sea'.[32] Nevertheless, the general concept of 'deterrence' lodged with both the prime minister and chiefs of staff. It explains why the former's minute to Pound later in the month opened with reference to a 'deterrent squadron' in the Indian Ocean.[33]

The exchange between Churchill and Pound from 25 to 29 August on Far East naval reinforcement is important for what it reveals of their respective thinking and intentions at the time, and to understand what happened subsequently.[34] The exchange features in virtually every version of the Force Z story, but some aspects deserve more scrutiny. In addressing Pound, Churchill was aware that the Admiralty Far East reinforcement plans agreed during the

ABC-1 talks had been reviewed at Riviera. Although Far East discussions at Riviera concentrated on resolving the dispute over ADB-1, Stark had reaffirmed Atlantic substitution and emphasised it remained American policy to replace Force H. He would base the new battleships *Washington* and *North Carolina* in the Atlantic and Turner suggested these might go to Force H. Pound had, meanwhile, promised to create the new capital ship force based at the Cape.[35] The prime minister knew that Admiralty reinforcement plans envisaged deployment of Force H as a fast hunting group to deter the IJN Indian Ocean raiders they both feared. Release of this force depended on Atlantic substitution, but early American support here had been reaffirmed. His proposal for 'a deterrent squadron in the Indian Ocean', comprising Force H plus a *King George V* battleship, was therefore a variant of existing Admiralty planning.

The claim that this intervention triggered deployment of an inappropriate force to Singapore is not justified. Churchill's focus was the Indian Ocean, 'the triangle Aden–Singapore–Simonstown', as he underlined to the Australian prime minister on 2 September.[36] The risk he wished to counter was the IJN raider threat he had just highlighted again at Riviera. As we saw in the previous chapter, Churchill simultaneously asked Pound for a full breakdown of IJN strength. The NID response, while generally accurate, included the entirely fictitious 12,000-ton pocket battleship type which was a long-standing Admiralty fixation, but underlined the prime minister's raider fears.[37]

Churchill's proposal that the Force H task force should be joined by a *King George V*-class battleship reflected a similar suggestion put to Pound by the First Lord, A V Alexander, a few days earlier. The context here was a request by Cunningham, as Commander-in-Chief Mediterranean, pressing for early despatch of a carrier to the eastern Mediterranean. Alexander doubted this request could be met because: 'If Japan comes in against us, we ought to have one of the *KGV*s, a carrier and a battlecruiser in the Indian Ocean'. This was a remarkable echo of the prime minister's thinking and it is just possible they had spoken to each other following the prime minister's return from Riviera on the morning of 19 August (although Alexander makes no reference to any prime ministerial views to Pound). An alternative possibility is that Alexander spoke to the prime minister after writing to Pound, in which case the prime minister was rehearsing an Admiralty view, albeit not Pound's! Alexander's note is interesting for other reasons. It demonstrates that, for Alexander at least, the Indian Ocean took priority over the eastern Mediterranean for carriers. It also summarised carrier availability over the next six months. *Victorious* was needed for the Home Fleet, the new *Indomitable* was not expected to be operational until November, and *Illustrious* (under repair in the United States) not until Christmas, with *Formidable* even later. *Ark Royal* and *Furious*, which were both badly in need of refits, would have to cover Gibraltar between them.[38]

In advocating the deployment of a *King George V*, Churchill has been criticised for his analogy between the threats posed by a *King George V* battleship in the Indian Ocean and the German *Tirpitz* in the Atlantic. His critics insist that the two situations were completely different. *Tirpitz* could tie down much superior Royal Navy forces by the threat she posed to British communications at multiple points, all of which had to be defended. By contrast, in the Indian Ocean there were no vital Japanese interests for a *King George V* to threaten. Churchill's point was surely that the presence of a modern fast battleship somewhere in the Indian Ocean would greatly increase the risks for IJN raiders, including battlecruisers. They would either have to deploy disproportionate force, or would be dissuaded from operating at any distance from friendly support. This was a perfectly logical analysis if the raider threat was viewed as real and serious. The new Royal Navy force would retain the high speed of Force H, but have much enhanced gun power.[39] Churchill's criticism of the 'R'-class battleships in his note, able to 'neither fight nor run', was equally valid, and reflected the traditional Admiralty view that they were not suitable for the East, though he was careful not to rule out a 'convoy escort' role 'should we reach that stage'.

The naval staff had anyway raised deployment of a *King George V* to the proposed Eastern Fleet at a meeting held by Pound on 20 August, immediately after his return from Riviera. Churchill may have known this. A full record of this meeting does not seem to have survived, but it seems likely it reviewed all the naval issues discussed at Riviera, including, of course, Far East reinforcement. What is known is that it was agreed a *King George V* might be released for the Far East if the US Navy was willing to provide an equivalent modern battleship to counter the German *Tirpitz*. This possibility of deploying a *King George V* reflected Stark's statement at Riviera that he planned to base the new US Navy battleships *Washington* and *North Carolina* in the Atlantic. If this US Navy deployment went ahead, it would release a *King George V*. (The US Navy did deploy *Washington* to the Home Fleet in early 1942.) Pound's meeting followed a proposal from the naval staff a week earlier that the battlecruiser *Repulse* and the four 'R'-class battleships should be deployed to the Indian Ocean as they became available, with the battleships *Nelson* and *Rodney* to follow later. With the exception of the possible *King George V*, these latest deployment plans merely reaffirmed what had been agreed in principle within the Admiralty since February, but they did suggest transfers to the Indian Ocean would now be accelerated.[40]

Pound's response to Churchill on 28 August maintained the proposed ABC-1 Eastern Fleet composition communicated to overseas commanders in May, with the two *Nelson*s and the 'R' class joining the Force H immediate reinforcement, to achieve the planned phase 2 concentration.[41] He argued that the *Nelson*s remained the best 'backing' to the 'R' class because they were closer in speed and would create a homogeneous battle-fleet. He defended the 'R' class on grounds of availability, 'no longer required in the Atlantic', their value in making up numbers, and of course as escorts. Apart from the last, these arguments for the 'R' class were unconvincing, and drew the Churchill riposte that they were easy prey for the IJN and little more than 'floating coffins', a view fully shared by Admiral Sir James Somerville, as Commander-in-Chief Eastern Fleet, the following year. Indeed, there was a long-standing consensus predating the outbreak of war that they were quite inadequate for modern naval warfare. In his diary entry for 14 March 1939, the Director of Naval Construction, Sir Stanley Goodall, stated: '1st Sea Lord [then Backhouse] sent for me re *Royal Sovereign*s. I said to send them to fight up to date capital ships would be murder. He agreed.'[42]

The specific arguments for deploying the 'R' class to the Indian Ocean were first set out by Director of Plans in February. The naval staff argued that US Navy reinforcement of the Atlantic would make them redundant there; they would be useful as escorts on the Cape–Aden route; the presence of battleships in the Indian Ocean would help keep Japan quiet; and they would be well placed to contribute to an eastern fleet in due course. However, Director of Plans was equally clear that neither the *Nelson* class nor the 'R' class were suitable for raider hunting, owing to their poor speed. In this respect, the prime minister was correct.[43] Meanwhile, Pound's argument that three *King George V*s were required at home was a legitimate professional judgement, but his argument for homogeneity was more dubious. It could equally be argued that a *King George V* would be homogenous with Force H units in the Indian Ocean and create a force more threatening to the IJN. In terms of force structure, the only real point of dispute with the prime minister, as Pound acknowledged, was the trade-off between the two *Nelson*s and a *King George V*. *Nelson* herself was damaged by an Italian torpedo in the Mediterranean just a month later, putting her out of action for six months. The trade-off then narrowed to a *King George V* versus *Rodney*.

Leaving aside force composition, there appeared to be agreement between prime minister and First Sea Lord on deployment. Both were at this time focused on the Indian Ocean, with whatever forces were finally sent based at Ceylon. The only reference to basing capital units at Singapore to enhance 'deterrence' came from Pound. He suggested this might be desirable in peacetime, but the ships must be withdrawn to Ceylon in the event of war. The force he proposed for Singapore comprised the two *Nelson*s, *Renown* and a carrier. These were the most capable vessels and Pound presumably envisaged the four 'R' class would remain in the Indian Ocean on convoy escort duty. The intent to withdraw in the event of war reflected his long-standing belief that any fleet based in Singapore in wartime must be 'adequate' to take on the major part of the IJN fleet.

Stephen Roskill's official history insisted that the Admiralty's proposed Indian Ocean force was to be 'defensive', positioned strategically in the centre of a most important theatre. The prime minister's was 'potentially offensive', based far forward in an area which the enemy threatened to dominate.[44] This was not Churchill's intention in August. He confirmed the position reached after his exchange with Pound to the new Australian prime minister, Arthur Fadden, two days later. The steady reduction of the German and Italian surface fleets made it possible to begin moving heavy ships to the Indian Ocean. The Admiralty was reviewing options, but the aim was to put capital ships, including first-class units, in the triangle Aden–Singapore–Simonstown before the end of the year, without prejudice to the position in the eastern Mediterranean. Churchill also added the usual pledge to come to Australia's assistance in the face of any direct threat.[45]

It has also been claimed that Pound's concept was 'trade defence', while Churchill was concerned with 'deterrence'.[46] Another argument is that Churchill and Pound were both aiming for deterrence, but with different objectives. Churchill wanted a show of strength to prevent Japan entering the war. Pound wanted to deter Japan, in the event of war, from operating in the Indian Ocean.[47] The respective positions were in reality much more blurred. There was no significant difference between Pound and the prime minister over trade defence. Successive naval staff papers over the period February to August show they too thought that battleships in the Indian Ocean would have a general deterrence effect.[48]

The argument was more about means than intent. Churchill undoubtedly believed a modern ship would have more symbolic impact in conveying political will, but he also genuinely believed a modern ship would be militarily more effective in dealing with the raider problem. Pound's immediate priority with the forces likely to be available in the next six months was also to keep the Japanese out of the Indian Ocean. Nevertheless, it is clear, both from Pound's line of argument in the exchange and the whole body of naval staff planning since February, that for the Admiralty this was an interim position. When the Eastern Fleet was finally formed, the intention was to base it at Singapore. The constraint to forming that fleet was not the capital ship composition, based on the *Nelson*s and the 'R' class, which the naval staff now implied were a match for the IJN, nor the availability of a serious carrier force, but shortage of modern cruisers and, above all, destroyers. As regards carriers, it is revealing that Pound planned to deploy no fleet carrier to the East until spring 1942, whereas Churchill noted there were four carriers to divide between Mediterranean and Far East by the end of the year, and clearly expected one or more to go to the latter. This figure reflected an expected net addition of three modern fleet carriers with *Illustrious* and *Formidable* returning from repair in the USA, and *Indomitable* fresh from build. These three would, indeed, all be allocated to the Eastern Fleet in December.

Pound's biographer has insisted that Pound's proposed fleet, 'having a slow speed, but reasonable protection and range of gun', was purely defensive and incapable of threatening the main Japanese fleet which could evade battle if it wished. In reality, Pound's fleet was a heterogeneous mix. The *Nelson*s did, indeed, combine slow speed, reasonable protection and gun range. *Renown* had high speed and good gun range, but limited protection. The 'R' class possessed neither adequate protection nor gun range. Pound's fleet clearly did not pose a credible threat to a major IJN fleet, which could certainly evade it. But nor did it pose credible defence against a major IJN force, which would be able to outmanoeuvre and outrange most of their Royal Navy counterparts.

Stark as Chief of Naval Operations conveyed his understanding of British naval reinforcement plans following these August exchanges to Admiral Husband Kimmel, the Commander-in-Chief US Navy Pacific Fleet, on 23 September. The British would have four 'R'-class battleships on the East Indies Station by the end of December, would retain *Repulse* there until relieved by *Renown* in January, and send one or two modern capital ships to the East Indies early in 1942.[49] These, together with one carrier, four 8in cruisers and thirteen 6in cruisers, including seven modern, ought to make the Japanese task in moving southward considerably more difficult. It should indeed make them think twice if they had taken no action by that time (ie the end of the year).[50] Three points are evident here: nearly a month after the exchanges with the prime minister, the deployments preferred by Pound were still proceeding; the focus of Royal Navy deployment at this time was still the Indian Ocean; and the growing American interest in the contribution of Royal Navy reinforcements as part of a wider deterrence strategy.

The Admiralty shift to an offensive strategy

Most accounts of the naval reinforcement debate in late 1941 insist that the August exchange between Pound and the prime minister ended in stand-off. There was then a hiatus until mid-October when the prime minister brought the issue of capital ship reinforcement to the Defence Committee.[51] Such accounts are wrong in two respects. Their picture of the August exchange as a fundamental clash between Churchill and Pound over Far East strategy overstates a reasonable debate about a force composition not achievable for some months. (The first capital units deployed to the Indian Ocean were, in fact, *Revenge* and the battlecruiser *Repulse*. *Revenge* joined East Indies Command in mid-September and *Repulse* at the beginning of October.[52] None of the other 'R'-class battleships would be available to deploy until November.[53]) More important, there was no hiatus in the Admiralty, who fundamentally changed their Far East plans during the next six weeks.

The trigger here was the need to revise the first attempt at an Allied joint operating plan for the Far East produced at the American-Dutch-British conference at Singapore in April. As explained earlier, the United States chiefs of staff rejected this ADB-1 plan in July. It was therefore agreed at Riviera that Britain would produce a revised draft plan, known as ADB-2, for review at a further conference in Singapore in October.[54] On 26 September Director of Plans, now Captain Gerald Bellars, accordingly produced a draft aide-memoire for use by Far East commanders at this conference, for approval within the Admiralty.[55]

Bellars stated that since ADB-1 the US Navy Fleet had taken on tasks and dispositions originally designed to apply only when it joined the war against Germany. Consequently, it was possible to begin moving capital ships earmarked for the Eastern Fleet into the Indian Ocean earlier than anticipated and movements should complete early in 1942. For political reasons, the implementation of peacetime US Navy convoy escort in the western Atlantic had proceeded more slowly than anticipated at ABC-1. However, by the time Bellars produced his draft, the Americans had taken over battleship cover and escort for the northwest Atlantic, including the western half of the Denmark Strait. This released the 'R' class from the Halifax force, but not yet Force H. However, the availability of three *King George V*s from new build by the end of the year made the two *Nelson*s potentially available too. This meant the Eastern Fleet, first envisaged in February and confirmed by Pound in August, could indeed be deployed by January 1942.[56] Bellars argued that phase 1 forces could now be more powerful than originally planned, available earlier and translate more rapidly into phase 2. This made it feasible to adopt a more offensive strategy towards Japan earlier in a war than previously considered desirable.

Bellars judged that the shortage of destroyers underlined to Pound the previous month still precluded the deployment of capital ships beyond the Malay Barrier.[57] However, capital ships in the Indian Ocean could release cruisers for strike operations forward of the barrier. Rear Admiral Sir Henry Harwood, Assistant Chief of Naval Staff (Foreign), reversing his previous views, now felt Japanese attack would be sudden and the Eastern Fleet should therefore operate offensively from Singapore from the outbreak of hostilities. Destroyers must be found to enable the forward deployment of capital ships. The minimum Royal Navy capital ship strength required depended on pressure exerted by the US Pacific Fleet at Hawaii. The four 'R'-class ships would be an adequate initial force, but must be backed by the two *Nelsons* as soon as possible. Harwood had been advocating the deployment of the 'R' class 'as far east as possible' to threaten Japan since March.[58] His 'reversal of view' meant he now believed a Japanese attack was imminent, rather than implying he had suddenly shifted to supporting forward deployment. Harwood also suggested the best employment for the fleet's proposed striking force of 8in cruisers was the coast of Japan.[59]

This last idea was beyond optimistic, and better described as lunatic. Harwood had made his reputation as the victor of the Battle of the River Plate and he would succeed Cunningham as Commander-in-Chief Mediterranean in April 1942, much to the latter's disgust. His various interventions as ACNS (F), including this one, portray a man of limited intellect, rather out of his depth in the strategic prosecution of a global naval war. Given the inability of his direct boss Phillips, and indeed Pound, to 'suffer fools gladly', it is surprising he survived. The most likely explanation is that he was a term-mate of Phillips and they had both served previously under Pound when the latter was Director of Plans in the early 1920s.[60]

Harwood's proposals for a Royal Navy capital force operating offensively from Singapore further evolved at a meeting chaired by Phillips as VCNS, but also now Commander-in-Chief Eastern Fleet designate, on 30 September. Those present were Harwood, Bellars, Rear Admiral Arthur Palliser (Phillips's chief of staff designate), Captain Ralph Edwards (Director of Operations Home) and Captain John Terry (Director of Operations Foreign). Phillips emphasised the critical dependence on destroyers of any battle-fleet at Singapore, but Edwards advised that there were now options for delivering these. The meeting then agreed that, 'disregarding US prejudices', the Royal Navy preference was a single Allied fleet in the Far East area, with Singapore as its main repair base, but operating from Manila as its advanced operational base, so long as the latter could be adequately defended, especially from air attack. This was a logical evolution of the Bellairs vision for 'Asiatic reinforcement' at ABC-1, with the new Royal Navy battle-fleet now substituting for the US Navy task force. The 'Far East' area referred to was that defined in ABC-1, and broadly comprised the South China Sea, Philippines, Malaya and the Netherlands East Indies. Since the closest Japanese air forces to Manila were 450 miles away in Formosa, the meeting felt that providing adequate air defence should be feasible, and strategically Manila was ideally placed on the flank of Japanese communications to the south.[61]

The proposals agreed at this meeting were incorporated in an updated aide-memoire drafted by Bellars on 2 October and approved successively by Phillips, Pound and the First Lord, Alexander, between 10 and 15 October. There were two key changes in this new draft. First, it directed that plans should anticipate: 'The employment of British forces northward of the Sumatra–Darwin line using British, US or Dutch bases'. Secondly, while not prescribing any final solution, it directed the conference to examine: 'The employment of as powerful a British force from Manila as the destroyer strength will permit, or from other bases if the defences of Manila cannot be considered adequate'.[62] These changes marked a fundamental shift from the British deployment strategy set out in both ADB-1 and the initial ADB-2 draft. The Admiralty had now committed both to defend the Malay Barrier, as the US Navy had constantly pressed, and to deploy north of it with a battle-fleet.

In six weeks, Pound's defensive strategy for the Indian Ocean had translated into an offensive strategy based at Singapore, and ultimately Manila. Its core enabler was a striking force of old unmodernised 'R'-class battleships. Air cover relied on optimistic projections of Japanese strike capability, and whatever fighter cover the Royal Air Force from Malaya and the United States Army Air Force in the Philippines could provide. This Royal Navy Eastern Fleet would be far smaller than any anticipated pre-war, but have a more forward and aggressive role. Its composition ignored the lessons of the European war and known Japanese strength. The plans anticipated significant American support, but how America would intervene remained uncertain.

There are two possible explanations for this dramatic, almost reckless, shift in thinking. The first is Admiralty acceptance, following American rejection of ADB-1 and further insights at Riviera, that effective co-operation with the US Navy in the Far East theatre, and certainly a joint operating plan, was only possible with a far stronger Royal Navy commitment to defending the Malay Barrier, including forward deployment of capital ships. The second is the shift in United States policy towards the Philippines, signposted by Marshall at Riviera. The Admiralty perhaps saw an opportunity in this new American commitment. They could take advantage of the American air umbrella to provide a Royal Navy capital ship force forward in the Philippines, where the US Navy still had no intention of deploying major units. This would neatly counter American complaints over lack of commitment to the Malay Barrier, align with the Royal Navy's pre-war plans for an advanced operating base north of Singapore, and bring the Royal Navy much closer to Pearl Harbor, facilitating joint operations with the Pacific Fleet.[63]

These explanations are consistent with the US Navy position set out by Turner to Danckwerts on 3 October. Turner had already indicated that the United States was unlikely to find the new British ADB-2 draft satisfactory. The chief American criticism was the continuing weakness of British forces earmarked for defence of the Malay Barrier.[64] He now made four important points. First, the US Navy did not regard unified command in the Far East area operating to a single integrated plan as essential. Strategic co-operation would suffice. Secondly, defence of the Malay Barrier must be primarily a British and Dutch responsibility. Thirdly, the overall military position in the Far East had changed considerably since the spring with the United States reinforcement of the Philippines. Finally, the Royal Navy should not fear that the US Navy Pacific Fleet would be inactive in the event of war.[65]

Nevertheless, important questions remain. Did likely United States rejection of ADB-2 really demand such a radical change to British naval policy in order 'to bind the Americans in'? The overarching ABC-1 agreement was still in place and, as Turner acknowledged, strategic co-operation in the Far East would continue with or without a joint operating plan. As regards the Philippines factor, how had the new United States policy for defence of the islands evolved? How far was it communicated to the British war leadership and did they understand the implications? Does the timing of British naval reinforcement planning fit with the shift in American intentions here?

The United States programme to reinforce the Philippines during the autumn of 1941 was vast by any standard, and gathered pace remarkably quickly. As late as June, the islands were still viewed as indefensible. By mid-July, in response to the imminent Japanese move into southern Indochina and the wider shift in the American strategic perspective described earlier, General Marshall was contemplating modest reinforcements, including a small force of B-17 strategic bombers. However, it was at the meeting of the joint chiefs with the president on 7 August to prepare for Riviera that the idea of using the Philippines as a central element in a strategy to contain Japan first got real traction.[66] By early September, the scale of proposed reinforcement had increased significantly and Secretary of War Henry Stimson was an enthusiastic lobbyist for the concept.[67] On 19 September Marshall advised the joint board that the B-17 build-up in the Philippines 'would have a profound strategic effect and might be the decisive element in deterring Japan from undertaking a Pacific War'.[68] By early October, War Department plans anticipated that, by 1 March 1942, Philippines air strength would include 136 first line B-17s with thirty-four in reserve, fifty-seven first line dive-bombers with twenty-nine in reserve and 130 first line modern fighters with sixty-five in reserve.[69] There would also be a significant force of B-24 heavy bombers capable of reaching Japan. The scale of this commitment is underlined by the fact that ninety-five of 128 B-17s and thirty-five of the ninety-five B-24s expected off the production lines by end February 1942, more than 50 per cent of the combined output, were earmarked for the Philippines.[70] By October, the War Department was also planning to extend the reach of the B-17 force by exploiting British and Dutch airbases, including Singapore and Darwin. Ammunition, fuel and spares would be pre-positioned.[71] By this time, Marshall, Stimson and Air

Force chief, General H H Arnold ,viewed the B-17s as a strategic coercive force capable of countering a Japanese attack, not just in the south but also in the event of a move against Russia.[72]

Britain's war leadership, at both the political and military levels, were kept aware of both the details of this build-up and the strategic intent behind it. In addition to numerous contacts through embassy staff in Washington,[73] Stimson personally briefed the ambassador, Lord Halifax, in October, using charts to demonstrate B-17 regional coverage.[74] Halifax's report caused the prime minister to ask Ismay about the background to Philippines reinforcement. Ismay responded that Britain had never pressed for this. It had been a complete surprise when the Americans raised it at Riviera in August. During the ABC-1 staff talks they had insisted such reinforcement was out of the question.[75] The United States commander in the Philippines, General Douglas MacArthur, briefed Brooke-Popham during his visit to Manila, also in October.[76] Brooke-Popham subsequently directed Far East Air Command to make four airfields in Malaya available to operate B-17s, but only one of these was equipped by the outbreak of war.[77] Meanwhile, the chiefs of staff gave their approval to the use of British airbases on 3 October. Those earmarked were Singapore, Rabaul, Port Moresby and Port Darwin. In addition, the United States hoped at least one base suitable for B-17 operations could be developed in North Borneo.[78]

Given this plethora of inputs, it is surprising that no part of the British system conducted an assessment of the implications and effectiveness of this new American strategy. There was relevant background to draw on here. Darvall, as the senior air staff officer for the Far East, made an extensive visit to the Philippines in late May and early June 1941. He emphasised the strategic value of the Philippines as a regional centre for air operations, but also limitations to current airfield infrastructure and operational training.[79] Meanwhile, the Royal Air Force had direct experience of operating B-17s and was critical of its performance.[80] However, the chiefs of staff never discussed Philippines reinforcement in detail; there was no Joint Planning Committee analysis and no significant mention in Joint Intelligence Committee papers. Where reference does appear, for example in the briefing given by Portal as Chief of Air Staff on 12 November to Australian emissary Sir Earle Page, there is little sign the chiefs saw it as a decisive factor in Far East calculations.[81] The British, therefore, never considered the inherent weaknesses and dangers of the strategy, the time lag before the American forces could reach critical mass and operational effectiveness, the logistic implications of supporting a force of this size at long range, or the risk Japan would be provoked into an early strike.

It has been claimed that the new Philippines strategy was entirely owned by the US Army and enjoyed no support from the US Navy, who viewed it as fatally flawed because of the problems in maintaining supply.[82] This claim looks overstated. As early as 31 July, Stark referred positively to Kimmel about the army plans to reinforce the Philippines, which he had advocated for some while.[83] There is no sign of any major disagreement in joint board meetings and the US Navy deployed significant submarine reinforcements to the Philippines through the autumn. Turner, in War Plans, apparently did harbour doubts that the planned United States air reinforcements would be able to provide adequate protection to naval forces based in the Philippines in the face of determined air attack. How far any US Navy reservations over the security of the Philippines were communicated privately to the Royal Navy is not clear, but Stark did warn Pound on the vulnerability of Manila on 13 November.[84] He repeated this message through Vice Admiral Ghormley, his special naval observer in London.[85]

The naval staff, and certainly Phillips, were therefore aware during their discussions at the end of September and in early October of the broad thrust of American plans to reinforce the Philippines. However, they would not have had full detail of scale or timing at that stage, nor known the ultimate ambitions of Marshall and Stimson. None of the documents charting the evolution of the Admiralty's new offensive strategy between late September and mid-November refer specifically to the American air build-up, let alone link it to Royal Navy strategy in a calculated way. So, while the naval staff no doubt had it in mind, it seems it was not a major, let alone decisive, factor in framing their new strategy.

As regards the American criticisms of Royal Navy reluctance to commit forces to defence of the Malay Barrier under ADB-1 and 2, the decision to change to an offensive strategy preceded Turner's letter of 3 October. Phillips had also insisted that this was a British preference, independent of American 'prejudices'. Again, American attitudes no doubt had some influence, but it seems unlikely they were decisive. Stark's message of 23 September to Kimmel judged the presence of Royal Navy reinforcements in the Indian Ocean as sufficient deterrent to Japan. There was no suggestion the Royal Navy should be pushed to move them on to Singapore.[86]

Scrutiny of the various planning papers from late September to late November suggests that, for the naval staff, the offensive strategy was ultimately motivated by two things: that significant forces for the eastern theatre, including potentially destroyers, were now becoming available; and persistence of the long-cherished concept of interdicting Japanese communications into the South China Sea, both from Singapore and an advanced operating base to the north. This advanced base had regularly featured in pre-war planning, although then within restricted scenarios and with much larger forces.[87] The striking point of the papers is that not only is there no direct reference to the arrival of United States air power but, even more important, there is no reference to Japanese strength and what they might do, other than an extraordinary comment by Pound to Stark that the air threat to Manila from Formosa was less than previously feared.[88]

The Admiralty's offensive planning from September must also be placed alongside changing British perceptions of the risk from Japan that autumn. The Japanese move into southern Indochina at the end of July triggered assessments by the Joint Intelligence Committee and joint planning staff through August and early September. The Joint Intelligence Committee recognised that from Indochina, Japan could move rapidly with minimal forces into Thailand, providing a stepping stone for an attack on Malaya. However, the dramatic German successes in Russia also made a Japanese attack on Siberia attractive. It would have insufficient forces for an attack on Malaya, as opposed to Thailand, if it retained a northern attack option. Japan would, therefore, hold back until Russia's situation resolved, although Allied sanctions would ultimately force Japan to choose between concessions and war.[89]

These judgements underestimated how the combination of economic pressure and the influence of the military within the Japanese leadership would encourage her to resort to force sooner rather than later. Once the United States had declared its oil embargo and Britain followed suit, the Japanese military produced an integrated plan to seize Netherlands East Indies oil supplies. To achieve this goal they would first neutralise British and American power to intervene through simultaneous attacks on Pearl Harbor, the Philippines and Malaya. Planning was complete by late September, with the Supreme Command then pressing for a decision for war by 15 October.[90]

There were two unfortunate consequences from this early autumn assessment prepared by the Joint Intelligence Committee. The judgement that the threat to Malaya was not imminent was convenient, because the chiefs of staff could again defer the long-promised air reinforcements for Malaya. Instead, they could meet demands in the Middle East[91] and the new requirement for urgent aid to Russia.[92] It also encouraged a view, endorsed by Far East commanders, that Japan would not risk simultaneous war with four powers (Britain, the United States, Russia and the Netherlands), and was therefore susceptible to pressure.[93] The Foreign Secretary Anthony Eden reflected this thinking to Churchill on 12 September. The combination of Russia, the United States, China, the British Empire and the Dutch was now more than this 'probably over-valued military power' could challenge. He and Churchill favoured increasing the pressure on Japan with a deterrent naval force of one or more modern capital ships and a carrier at Singapore.[94] This was the Force H-plus advocated by Churchill in his earlier exchange with Pound.

These Joint Intelligence Committee, and joint planning staff judgements, of early autumn seriously underestimated the power and flexibility of Japanese strike forces and their ability to project rapidly at long distance once they made their decisions. Rather than injecting urgency and realism into Far East defence, therefore, these flawed assessments encouraged Britain, and especially the Admiralty, down a path of strategic illusion. Eden developed the theme of pressure with the War Cabinet at the end of September. He was optimistic that Britain could achieve a common front against Japan with the United States and the Dutch, and that a display of firmness would deter rather than provoke.[95]

This thinking in London during September coincided with similar views expressed during a Far East conference held in Singapore at the end of the month, attended by all senior British political, diplomatic and military representatives across the region. Brooke-Popham, as Commander-in-Chief Far East, and Layton as Commander-in-Chief China summarised the conclusions for the chiefs of staff. Japan was currently concentrating her forces against Russia in the north and therefore would avoid war in the south in the immediate future, since this would involve conflict with multiple enemies. The bad weather associated with the seasonal monsoon also made southern operations undesirable before February. It followed that Japan would be susceptible to economic pressure and deterred by military reinforcements. The arrival of American bombers and submarines in the Philippines would reduce the risk to Malaya, but a British fleet at Singapore was the only real deterrent, if and when Japan did turn south. Even one or two capital ships at Singapore would have a valuable propaganda effect.[96]

The chiefs of staff response on 9 October, drafted by the joint planning staff, confirmed that transfer of heavy ships to the Indian Ocean was underway and acknowledged the propaganda value of capital ships in eastern waters. Reflecting the latest Admiralty discussions, it added that the build-up of naval forces in the East might allow a more forward policy in the event of war, including use of Manila as an advance base.[97] This exchange included perhaps the first reference outside the Admiralty to basing at Manila and also one of very few papers circulated at chiefs of staff level which specifically highlighted American reinforcement of the Philippines and its potential to reduce the threat to British territories.

The claim by Far East commanders that the northeast monsoon would prevent a Japanese attack on Malaya until February became a significant factor in British assessments through the remaining two months to the outbreak of war. Two authoritative figures associated with Malaya at the time later insisted that although this view became widespread, it never reflected professional military opinion. Major General Ian Playfair, who had just relinquished the post of Director of Military Plans and would shortly become ABDA Chief of Staff, stated that landings on the northeast coast of Malaya, sheltered by the Gulf of Thailand, had always been regarded as 'quite practicable' in the monsoon season. The Japanese were known to be well-trained and effective in landing operations.[98] Layton's secretary, Captain Douglas Doig, endorsed this view. The weather constraint was valid for a seaborne landing on the southeast coast of Malaya, where beaches were exposed to swells generated across the whole South China Sea. It was less true for landings on the northeast coast, exposed only to the Gulf of Siam. Doig claimed there was 'certainly extant and in Service hands' a considered assessment that landings on the northeast coast even during the northeast monsoon were perfectly practicable.[99]

The new thinking on Far East naval reinforcement reflected in these exchanges with Commander-in-Chief Far East and Commander-in-Chief China coincided with a related Admiralty decision communicated to Layton on 3 October.[100] This confirmed Phillips's appointment as Commander-in-Chief Eastern Fleet and stated that he would now arrive in theatre at the end of the year and absorb the responsibilities of Commander-in-Chief China. In a personal signal to Layton, Pound recognised that he would be disappointed by the early termination of his command, but he softened the blow by appointing Layton to the sought-after post of Commander-in-Chief Portsmouth.[101] Previously it had been understood that the creation of an eastern fleet, and therefore Phillips's role, would only follow the outbreak of war with Japan and US Navy relief of Royal Navy ships in the Atlantic.

In a prescient paper prepared for Layton, his secretary, Doig, argued that this formal creation of an eastern fleet before the outbreak of war with Japan represented a major change in Royal Navy policy towards the East, with important implications. A powerful Royal Navy Eastern Fleet, able to count on appropriate American support, would make Japanese attack southward a hazardous undertaking. This aligned directly with Stark's thinking outlined to Commander-in-Chief Pacific Fleet just ten days earlier. The risk was that the Japanese would then act pre-emptively to forestall the effect of the fleet's arrival. Given this risk, the Royal Navy must decide between rapid single assembly of a full fleet or the gradual accumulation of constituent units over an extended period. In the latter case, although deploying a small number of capital ships forward to Singapore could have a useful political or moral effect, such a force might also be a liability, obliging the Royal Navy to risk action with only a partial force. At this point, in early October, Doig had in mind *Revenge* and *Repulse*, which were already in the Indian Ocean, and there had evidently already been informal discussion that they should visit Singapore. On balance, Doig judged major units were best kept in the Indian Ocean, while Singapore would be better served by destroyer and submarine reinforcements.[102] Layton declined to raise these issues with the Admiralty. Doig surmised there were two reasons for Layton's refusal. Layton felt that if he criticised plans for the creation of an eastern fleet, he might be accused of acting out of pique. He was very sensitive to this. He was also aware the Admiralty had to consider the wider strategic picture. When Doig pressed him again to question the plans for the deployment of Force Z in early November, he said – 'No, I am not going to butt in here. They must know what they are doing.'[103]

Two further mysteries surround the Admiralty's offensive planning from the end of September. The first is how far it was communicated outside the Royal Navy and co-ordinated with wider Far East defence measures. As already noted, the chiefs of staff were aware on 9 October. They not only authorised the response to Commander-in-Chief Far East, they also asked the joint staff mission in Washington to brief the American military leadership that additional naval forces were becoming available for the Far East, that their deployment north of the Malay Barrier was now being considered, and that Manila might be required as an advanced base.[104] Meanwhile, on 10 October the Admiralty informed Commander-in-Chief Mediterranean that *Rodney* and four 'R'-class battleships would be sent to the Indian Ocean 'and probably further east as soon as possible'. This signal was picked up by the prime minister who responded: 'This major Fleet movement has not been approved by me or the Defence Committee. No action must be taken pending decision.'[105]

Given this visibility of Admiralty thinking, it is odd that their intent now to base a full battle-fleet at Singapore and deploy it north of the barrier was not explored and tested more fully during the subsequent discussions on Far East naval reinforcement at the Defence Committee meetings held on 17 and 20 October. One suggestion is that the Admiralty deliberately resisted release of *Prince of Wales* for the Far East during these meetings in order to distract the prime minister from questioning their new forward deployment plans, which they feared he would oppose.[106] This depends on Churchill not seeing the earlier chiefs of staff records on Far East naval reinforcement, and deliberate deception by the Admiralty. Both are inherently unlikely, although some of Pound's comments on 20 October did border on the disingenuous.

A more plausible explanation is to assume that potential concentration of a capital ship force at Singapore, rather than Ceylon, as units became available, was now an accepted option for the chiefs of staff and Defence Committee. However, any plans for such forward deployment were viewed as hypothetical until units were released, destroyers were available, and a fleet was actually collecting in the Indian Ocean. The two October meetings focused therefore on the composition and timing of the initial build-up of forces and, from the prime minister's viewpoint, getting a high-profile deterrent force in place quickly. It is nevertheless still puzzling that Phillips made no reference to the new offensive strategy and its implications for Far East naval reinforcement when he briefed Pound on the 17 October meeting from which Pound was absent. Phillips was, after all, reporting just two days after Pound had formally approved the Admiralty's new strategy.[107]

A second mystery is why the numerous accounts of the Force Z story over the years have almost entirely ignored the Admiralty's offensive planning from September. The existence of this planning undermines the argument that the Admiralty was pursuing a defensive strategy centred on defence of the Indian Ocean in comparison to a reckless prime minister. It is conceivable Roskill did not see the relevant Admiralty files when writing his official history, though perhaps less plausible no surviving witness from the naval staff mentioned this planning.[108] A related puzzle is that key naval witnesses who wrote on the Force Z disaster in later memoirs, such as Vice Admiral Godfrey, the Director of Naval Intelligence in 1941, and Captain William Davis, then serving in Admiralty Operations Division, must have known of these plans, yet did not mention them.[109]

The decision to deploy Force Z in its proper context

By early October, two themes were running in parallel. The Admiralty favoured an offensive strategy because it thought it had the necessary resources, it aligned with long-standing strategic principles, and it reinforced American commitment to Far East naval defence. Meanwhile, there was a political conviction that Allied solidarity would dissuade a wavering Japan from further southern adventures. This undoubtedly reflected Washington's new commitment to Philippines defence and determination to resist further Japanese aggression. The fall of the moderate Prince Konoye government in Japan on 16 October now triggered more formal discussion of British naval reinforcement at the Defence Committee.

As with Churchill's August exchanges with Pound, the two Defence Committee meetings on 17 and 20 October which led directly to the despatch of Force Z raise important issues which deserve more attention.[110] (For convenience, the term Force Z is used throughout this book to describe the *Prince of Wales* force. In reality, it was known as Force G from the departure of *Prince of Wales* from the United Kingdom until the morning of 8 December when it assumed the title Force Z. Force G initially comprised *Prince of Wales* and two destroyers until it met *Repulse* off Ceylon on 29 November.) The meetings were undoubtedly driven by the political desire for a more visible commitment of British will to resist further Japanese aggression. The prime minister, the deputy prime minister, Clement Attlee, and Foreign Secretary Eden were all agreed that, from the political perspective, the desired deterrence effect in the Far East was best achieved by deploying a modern battleship. However, for the prime minister, deterrence still fitted neatly with his requirement for a hunting force to tackle raiders in the Indian Ocean. His immediate worry remained an attack on trade, not Malaya. The concern expressed at Riviera persisted. A force could deploy initially to Singapore for political effect, but operate primarily in the Indian Ocean, although no doubt also to protect the Malay Barrier where appropriate.[111]

The Admiralty's offensive ambitions now exerted crucial influence. Pound and Phillips insisted that the 'R'-class battleships and two *Nelson*s (when available) should now base at Singapore, rather than Ceylon. It followed that if *Prince of Wales* deployed she should also base at Singapore. Had Pound maintained his August defensive strategy, he could have insisted that *Prince of Wales* base initially at Ceylon until the full Eastern Fleet was available. Eden would have accepted this, believing that the 'deterrent effect' of *Prince of Wales* began at Cape Town. So would the prime minister. Deployment to Ceylon need not prevent visits to Singapore if war had not broken out. Pound had advocated just such a 'visiting policy' in August.

Because the Admiralty were now committed to basing the *Nelson*s and 'R' class forward at Singapore, the argument reduced, as Eden emphasised, to a trade-off between *Rodney* and *Prince of Wales*. (The choice had narrowed to *Rodney* because *Nelson* was out of action until end March following damage from Italian torpedo attack during the Malta convoy Halberd.) The political and operational value of *Prince of Wales* was compelling. It subsequently transpired that *Rodney* could not deploy to the East before mid-December owing to the need to give leave to her crew, who had been away from the United Kingdom for six months.[112] She also needed her guns changed before she could undertake further operations, requiring a refit to be programmed between February and May 1942.[113] Allowing for work-ups, neither *Nelson* could have reached the Far East before August 1942.[114] If a worked-up operational battleship, other than the 'R' class, was to deploy before the following spring, it had to be *Prince of Wales*.

A striking feature of the October Defence Committee exchanges is not just the Admiralty admission that they planned now to base a battle-fleet at Singapore, but their claim that the ships to be deployed were a match for an IJN battle-fleet. Phillips on 17 October insisted in the face of the prime minister's scepticism that the 'R' class were competitive with the older IJN battleships. Pound on 20 October insisted that numbers would impress the Japanese, while acknowledging this meant relying on the 'R' class. The prime minister's scepticism was justified. He no doubt recalled Phillips's assessment in February 1940, comparing IJN and Royal Navy battleship capability. Phillips then stated that the four IJN *Kongo*-class battlecruisers were equal to the modernised *Renown* (a judgement that probably underrated *Renown*) while the *Fuso-* and *Yamashiro*-class battleships were broadly equivalent to the modernised *Queen Elizabeth*s and superior to the unmodernised *Barham* and *Malaya*, let alone the 'R' class, which he did not bother to rate. Overall, the IJN had ten 'good' ships at that time, while the Royal Navy had only six 'good', and seven 'poor' (meaning four 'R' class, two *Malaya*s, and *Repulse*). This was 'not a very nice position for the British Empire even if we were not fighting Germany'. The contrast between Phillips's previous view of the inadequacies of the 'R' class, and the advice he now tendered eighteen months later was extraordinary.[115]

The claim that Churchill insisted, against professional advice, on a small inappropriate force in place of a 'balanced fleet' is wrong.[116] The positions taken by Churchill and the Admiralty at these two October meetings were essentially the reverse of those traditionally assigned to them. Churchill wanted a small powerful force to double as high-profile deterrent and raider hunter in the Indian Ocean, a logical evolution of his August argument. Basing in Singapore was necessary only if it facilitated this dual objective. It was the Admiralty who wanted a battle-fleet at Singapore operating forward in the South China Sea, obliging Japan to detach a major fleet to cover any southern operation. They pushed this policy, although their fleet would largely comprise slow obsolete vessels, no match for Japanese units. Pound's new position undercut his August argument 'that we could do nothing effective against Japan' without 'a properly balanced fleet' which was 'not achievable until 1942'.[117] Churchill and no doubt others were evidently bemused by the concept of a battle-fleet at Singapore dominated by the ageing 'R' class and the unconvincing defence of this proposal from Phillips and Pound. Indeed, it is surprising Churchill did not challenge their position more robustly.

Force Z is best viewed as the first instalment, or forerunner, of a fleet the Admiralty were now determined to deploy to Singapore anyway between December 1941 and March 1942. Indeed, the Admiralty brief prepared for the First Lord, Alexander, in preparation for his statement to a secret session of the House of Commons on 19 December, stated that Force Z was sent to Singapore 'prior to the concentration of the Eastern Fleet', because 'it was hoped they would act as a deterrent to the Japanese and avert war'.[118]

In assessing the consequences of the October Defence Committee decisions and where responsibility for them lies, it is useful to consider what would have happened if Pound had won the argument. Timing is crucial here. Had Pound won on 20 October, it is probable there would have been no capital units in Singapore when the Japanese attacked, no immediate forces sent there, and therefore no immediate losses. An Eastern Fleet would have gathered in the Indian Ocean in early 1942, as it did in reality, but no doubt strengthened by the Force Z units. By April this would have been a powerful, well-balanced fleet, adequate to safeguard vital communications to the Middle East, India and Australasia, and cover the central Indian Ocean. This picture apparently vindicates Pound, but reflects the consequence of the war breaking out precisely when it did, rather than real Admiralty intent. Had Pound won and the Japanese delayed their attack until mid-February, the end of the monsoon season always viewed by Far East Command as the most credible time for a Japanese attack, four 'R' class and *Repulse* would probably have been in Singapore. Without even one modern carrier this was not a 'balanced fleet'.[119] It might have caused some change to Japanese plans but it is hard to see it intervening successfully or withstanding an IJN attack. It would either have suffered a worse disaster than Force Z, or had to retreat to Ceylon or Darwin. Once it retreated, its composition was unsuited either to helping hold the Malay Barrier, or countering a major IJN raiding force in the Indian Ocean. Churchill's case for a high-quality Indian Ocean hunting group then looks more credible.

Contemporary papers and subsequent accounts of naval reinforcement to the Far East in late 1941 both make rather free use of the term 'balanced fleet' without specifying what this means. It suited some participants in 1941 decisions (and some later historians) to suggest a 'balanced fleet' meant the inclusion of aircraft carriers, thus addressing the criticism that Japanese air power had been deliberately ignored. This is disingenuous. The naval staff never firmly committed to providing fleet carriers for the Eastern Fleet initiated by ABC-1. They only earmarked a single carrier as part of long-term reinforcements. For both the naval staff and Far East commanders at the time, 'balanced fleet' merely referred to an appropriate force of supporting cruisers and destroyers to accompany the much discussed battle-fleet.

The two October Defence Committee meetings had exposed differences between prime minister and naval staff, not just about the composition of a putative Eastern Fleet, but also its role. A key question now is how far these differences had been resolved, if not in the way the naval staff desired. There is a compelling argument that the major differences over Eastern Fleet composition, destination and role all persisted. Churchill believed *Prince of Wales* was bound for Cape Town, the compromise destination agreed on 20 October. The Admiralty already intended her to go to Singapore where their new Eastern Fleet was to concentrate. Churchill believed *Prince of Wales* would spearhead a small deterrent squadron operating from Singapore to support 'R'-class ships protecting vital Indian Ocean communications and trade. The Admiralty, meanwhile, intended to base the 'R' class in Singapore, and ultimately Manila, as the core of a battle-fleet operating north of Singapore against Japanese lines of communication. Churchill had neither understood the Admiralty's new offensive intent, nor the implications arising from their negotiations with the Americans.[120]

However, the divergence between Churchill's focus on the Indian Ocean and the Admiralty's emerging offensive strategy did not initially matter. Debate about the 'R' class and their deployment north of the Malay Barrier was hypothetical until they arrived in theatre. Much would then depend on American and Japanese moves. Singapore was one logical choice to base a fleet, so long as peace prevailed or the Japanese kept their distance. For full logistic support of a fleet, the only other option was Durban. As regards force composition, once it became clear *Rodney* was not available until mid-1942, that point of debate was closed off. It was *Prince of Wales* or nothing.[121]

Evolving Admiralty strategy and its risks

The evolution of Admiralty strategy did not stop with the despatch of Force Z. By the end of October, the Americans had formally rejected the ADB-2 redraft of ADB-1 as still insufficient to deal with the Malay Barrier. Pound, therefore, proposed a fresh start to Stark, drawing on the naval staff thinking of late September and October. Thanks to US Navy Atlantic reinforcement, the Royal Navy was now moving capital ships to the East. By January 1942, six capital ships (*Prince of Wales*, *Repulse* and four 'R' class) should be in the area and they would now operate north of the barrier. Royal Navy forces might base in the Philippines, where Pound noted the air threat 'may not be quite so serious as previously thought'. He sought help with destroyers, which remained the major constraint on Royal Navy deployment. Since ABD-1 and 2 were no longer appropriate, Pound proposed developing fresh plans based on the original principles agreed at ABC-1. Phillips should lead on negotiating new arrangements on arrival in Singapore as Commander-in-Chief Eastern Fleet.[122]

The United States chiefs responded a week later.[123] They welcomed the British naval reinforcements, but hoped that an aircraft carrier could be included. Stark promised that two divisions of destroyers would be allocated to support the Royal Navy Eastern Fleet as soon as the United States was at war. The chiefs emphasised American air reinforcements (clearly a reference to the Philippines) and hoped Britain could provide additional air resources in Malaya, given the reduced German risk to the United Kingdom home territory. Such British air reinforcements would be an additional deterrent to any Japanese move south. They endorsed the idea of reverting to ABC-1 as the basis for joint planning in the theatre, but now identified additional territories to be held by the associated powers (United States, Britain and the Netherlands). Luzon in the Philippines was the most important. Finally, they cautioned against early basing of a Royal Navy battle-fleet in Manila, which was still poorly defended and exposed to attack from multiple directions.[124]

Admiral of the Fleet Sir Ernle Chatfield in 1937, First Sea Lord and chairman of the chiefs of staff from 1933–38, and perhaps the Royal Navy's finest peacetime leader. (© National Portrait Gallery, London, 4602)

Admiral of the Fleet Sir Roger Backhouse, Chatfield's successor as First Sea Lord 1938–39 and sponsor of the more flexible Far East reinforcement strategy described in Chapter 2. He died of a brain tumour after just six months in office. (© National Portrait Gallery, London, x88128)

Admiral Sir Reginald Plunkett-Ernle-Erle-Drax in 1936, widely recognised as a strategic thinker, adviser to Backhouse and Pound, and author of the 'flying squadron' concept. (© National Portrait Gallery, London, x12751)

Vice Admiral Sir Tom Phillips as Deputy Chief of Naval Staff in March 1940. As Director of Plans 1935–38, Deputy (later Vice) Chief of Naval Staff from May 1939–October 1941 and finally Commander-in-Chief Eastern Fleet, he was the dominant influence on the Royal Navy's eastern strategy through most of the period in this book. (© National Portrait Gallery, London, x85377)

Admiral of the Fleet Sir Dudley
Pound. He became First Sea Lord
in June 1939 and held the post until
immediately before his death in
October 1943. He led the Royal
Navy through the most difficult
period of the war until victory was
in sight everywhere. (© Imperial War
Museum, A 20791)

Rear Admiral Roger Bellairs, who led the British
delegation at the first staff talks, known as ABC-1,
with the United States from January–March 1941.
(© National Portrait Gallery, London, x86337)

Admiral Sir Andrew Cunningham, widely regarded as the
outstanding Royal Navy commander of the Second World War, as
Commander-in-Chief Mediterranean in 1940 with the aircraft carrier
Eagle in the background. In April 1939, as Deputy Chief of Naval
Staff, he defined the principles by which the Royal Navy would
prioritise between the eastern Mediterranean and Far East theatres in
the event of global war. He succeeded Pound as First Sea Lord in
October 1943. (© Imperial War Museum, E 488 E)

Right and following pages: In early 1939 the results of the Defence
Requirements Committee rearmament programme described in
Chapter 1 were evident across British shipyards: Vickers-Armstrong
on the Tyne and at Barrow, John Brown and Fairfields on the Clyde,
Cammell Laird at Birkenhead, and Harland and Wolff at Belfast. The
Royal Navy would launch two battleships, three fleet carriers, ten
cruisers, eight fleet destroyers and the first three new Hunt-class
escort destroyers over this calendar year. Three further battleships,
another carrier, two cruisers and nine destroyers would launch before
the end of April 1940.

The photograph on the right depicts the launch of the battleship
Prince of Wales on 5 March 1939 at Cammell Laird's yard in
Birkenhead. *Temeraire*, the second *Lion*-class battleship, was laid
down on the slip vacated by *Prince of Wales* on 1 June. Cammell was
also building the 5.25in cruisers *Dido* and *Charybdis*. The former, the
lead ship of the class, would follow *Prince of Wales* into the water
later in the summer. (R A Burt collection)

eft: Illustrious, the first of the new armoured fleet carriers, is photographed on her building slip at the Vickers-Armstrong yard in Barrow on 1 April 1939. Note the unusual feature of three screws. She will be launched four days later, exactly one month after *Prince of Wales*. Her sister *Indomitable* is building in the adjacent slip and at this stage is about nine months behind. Both carriers will join the Eastern Fleet in the Indian Ocean in early 1942. Immediately the slip vacated by *Illustrious* is clear, work will begin on the Colony-class cruiser *Jamaica*, and the *Dido*-class cruiser *Spartan* will be laid down at Barrow in December. Vickers has also just launched the battleship *King George V* at their Walker Yard on the Tyne and *Illustrious*'s sister carrier *Victorious* will follow there later in the year. The battleship *Lion* will be laid down at Walker in July. (Vickers Photographic Archive, The Dock Museum, Barrow-in-Furness)

Top: A year later, probably in late April 1940, *Illustrious* can be seen in the Buccleuch Dock at Barrow nearing completion. She commissioned on 25 May 1940. Ahead of her is *Indomitable*, launched on 26 March 1940. Note that she still lacks her island superstructure. (Vickers Photographic Archive, The Dock Museum, Barrow-in-Furness)

Prime Minister Winston Churchill on the quarterdeck of the battleship *Prince of Wales* while on passage to the Riviera Atlantic Conference at Placentia Bay in August 1941. (© Imperial War Museum, H12784)

Key figures involved in eastern theatre planning at a meeting in 1942. From left to right: Rear Admiral Alan G Kirk, US naval attaché in London; Admiral Sir Andrew Cunningham, formerly Commander-in-Chief Mediterranean and now appointed head of the British Admiralty Delegation Washington; First Lord A V Alexander; Admiral Harold Stark, former US Navy Chief of Operations, author of Plan Dog and now senior US Navy adviser in London; and First Sea Lord, Admiral of the Fleet Sir Dudley Pound. (© Imperial War Museum, A 8611)

Admiral Sir Tom Phillips, second from the left, watching *Prince of Wales* arrive in Singapore on the afternoon of 2 December 1941. To his right, holding the briefcase behind him, is Commander Michael Goodenough, staff officer operations. Beyond is the chief of staff, Rear Admiral Arthur Palliser. Note Phillips's small stature, which resulted in the nickname 'Tom Thumb'. (© Imperial War Museum, A 6787)

Vice Admiral Sir Geoffrey Layton, Commander-in-Chief China, conferring with his secretary, Captain Douglas Doig, in Singapore sometime in 1941. Layton succeeded Phillips as Commander-in-Chief Eastern Fleet following the latter's death in *Prince of Wales*. He subsequently became Commander-in-Chief Ceylon in early 1942, described by the official naval historian Stephen Roskill as 'one of the best appointments Churchill ever made'. (© Imperial War Museum, K 737)

Vice Admiral Sir James Somerville as commander of Force H, captured in pensive pose in his cabin in the battlecruiser *Renown* in April 1941. He commanded the Eastern Fleet from March 1942 until August 1944. He and Cunningham are ranked as the Royal Navy's outstanding fighting admirals of the war. Somerville was probably the more innovative of the two, and certainly more comfortable with the exploitation of air power and modern technology such as radar. (© Imperial War Museum, A 3747)

The battlecruiser *Renown* and fleet carrier *Ark Royal* photographed from the cruiser *Sheffield* in April 1941. Together they formed the Gibraltar force, Force H, for most of the eighteen-month period after July 1940. Force H was the designated immediate reinforcement for the Indian Ocean in the event of Japanese intervention in the war. *Renown* was perhaps the most successful of the Royal Navy's capital ship reconstructions. (© Imperial War Museum, A 4016)

Operation Halberd, the Mediterranean convoy operation to resupply Malta in September 1941 commanded by Somerville. The Royal Navy here deployed the type of modern task force which should have been viewed as the absolute minimum required for effective intervention against Japanese convoys attacking Malaya. It included three battleships (*Nelson*, *Rodney* and *Prince of Wales*) and the carrier *Ark Royal*. This picture shows the escorting cruiser force. *Hermione*, *Edinburgh* and *Euryalus* are manoeuvring astern of *Sheffield*. These four cruisers were all modern units able to make a substantial contribution to anti-aircraft defence. *Hermione* and *Euryalus*, each mounting ten 5.25in guns, together surpassed the medium range anti-aircraft firepower of *Prince of Wales*. (© Imperial War Museum, A 5746A)

Rear Admiral Kelly Turner, US Navy Director of Plans, in intense conversation with the First Sea Lord, Admiral of the Fleet Sir Dudley Pound, on board the battleship *Prince of Wales* during the Riviera Anglo-American summit at Placentia Bay in August 1941. Turner features prominently in Chapters 4 and 6. Admiral Harold Stark, US Navy Chief of Naval Operations, is in the background to the left leaning towards Prime Minister Winston Churchill seated in the chair. (© Imperial War Museum, A 4818)

The battlecruiser *Repulse* as she appeared in 1941. She did not receive the reconstruction given to her sister *Renown* and her anti-aircraft armament was particularly weak. However she was fast, capable of at least 29 knots, and had been equipped for 'supercharge firing' giving her main armament a range of 27,000yds. (US official)

Prince of Wales leaving Singapore at around 1730 on the afternoon of 8 December for her final operation against the Japanese landings. (© Imperial War Museum, A 29068)

A Martlet of 888 squadron flying over Somerville's flagship *Warspite*. In 1942 the Royal Navy still judged the Martlet (or Wildcat as it was known by the US Navy) the best carrier-borne fighter in the world. (© Imperial War Museum, A 9713)

Fairey Albacore torpedo bombers being prepared on the flight deck of *Indomitable* while operating in the Indian Ocean on 16 June 1942. The biplane airframe may have been primitive, but ASV 2 radar, a good communications it and the excellent Mark XII torpedo made the Albacore an effective overall weapon system. The scene in the late afternoon of 5 April as Somerville prepared for a night attack on the IJN task force off Ceylon would have been similar. (© Imperial War Museum, A 10343)

A Martlet being conveyed to the flight deck on the forward lift of *Illustrious* in the second half of 1942. Note the folding wings which Grumman was so slow to provide, as discussed in Chapter 5. (Phillip Jarrett)

Vice Admiral Chuichi Nagumo, commander of the IJN carrier task force in the attack on Ceylon April 1942. IJN portrait photograph, taken circa 1941/42, when he was commander of the First Air Fleet. (United States Navy Naval History & Heritage Command, NH 63423)

The Japanese aircraft carrier *Akagi* on 26 March 1942 shortly after leaving the Celebes for Operation C, the raid into the Indian Ocean. Her island, unusually, is positioned on the port side of the flight deck where there are B5N Kate torpedo bombers being prepared for take-off. In the background, from left to right are Carrier Division Two, comprising *Soryu* and *Hiryu*, the four battlecruisers, *Hiei*, *Kirishima*, *Haruna* and *Kongo*, and in the far distance the carriers *Zuikaku* and *Shokaku*. (Government of Japan)

IJN aircraft carrier *Hiryu* running speed trials off Tateyama, Chiba, Japan, on 28 April 1939. Her movements during the engagement off Ceylon in 1942 feature prominently in Chapter 8. (United States Navy Naval History & Heritage Command, NH 73063)

Illustrious, Formidable and *Warspite* in the Indian Ocean, 1942. The view might have been similar during Operation C with *Indomitable* substituting for *Illustrious*. (© Imperial War Museum, A13454)

Another view of the IJN task force in the Indian Ocean during Operation C, probably taken on 30 March. Ships shown from left to right are the four battlecruisers, *Hiei*, *Kirishima*, *Haruna* and *Kongo*. Taken from the carrier *Zuikaku*. (Government of Japan)

Zuikaku preparing to launch the strike on Colombo, 5 April 1942. A6M Zeros are in the foreground. (Government of Japan)

A view of the flight deck of *Illustrious* during Eastern Fleet exercises in the Indian Ocean in autumn 1942. In the immediate foreground are five Fulmar fighters of 806 Squadron, Fleet Air Arm. Behind are twelve American Martlet II fighters of 881 Squadron. *Illustrious* carried a total of six Fulmars, twenty-three Martlets and eighteen Swordfish torpedo strike aircraft at this time. In the background, the battleship *Valiant*, repaired after being badly damaged by Italian frogmen in Alexandria harbour, is conducting a practice shoot for her 15in guns. (© Imperial War Museum, A 15152)

This American response of 13 November was assessed by the joint planning staff over the next three weeks.[125] The planners recommended acceptance of the American amendments to ABC-1 and that talks should now proceed in theatre, beginning with an early meeting between Phillips and his opposite number Admiral Thomas Hart, Commander of the US Navy Asiatic Fleet. They advised against early British air reinforcements, quoting the need to supply Russia, preserve adequate strength at home against invasion and the build-up of Bomber Command. The chiefs of staff approved these recommendations on 25 November.[126] They were then widely circulated in Whitehall. By end November, therefore, all the main elements of the British war leadership were aware of the scale of Royal Navy reinforcement in the East, forward basing in Manila and the American attitude on this, and the American air build-up linked to their new commitment to hold the Philippines. Neither the planning staff, nor the chiefs, addressed the fundamental contradiction between no British air reinforcement and their endorsement of a substantial fleet based forward in Singapore and operating northward. If they expected the United States to provide air cover, the feasibility of extending this across the South China Sea and the approaches to Singapore was ignored.

There were also important War Cabinet discussions relating to the role and status of a potential eastern battle-fleet on 5 and 12 November. The Australian emissary, Sir Earle Page, attended both of these. Churchill's comments on 5 November were significant. He told Page it was intended to build up a battle squadron in Singapore to be used for the protection of the vital supply lines between Australia and the Middle East. *Prince of Wales* was now en route to Cape Town and likely to continue to Singapore. Whether she would remain there permanently had yet to be decided, but he hoped she would do so until *Rodney* or *Nelson* was available. In any case, her appearance at Cape Town would have a deterrent effect on Japan. Churchill's reference to building up a battle squadron evidently went beyond Force Z, though he made no reference to operations north of the Malay Barrier.[127] Pound further updated the War Cabinet on the formation of the Eastern Fleet battle-fleet on 12 November, again largely for Page's benefit. Significantly, he implied its six ships would remain in Singapore to contest a Japanese move south, even if the United States remained neutral. He added that the United States was adopting a more forward policy and strengthening its naval forces in the Philippines with nine destroyers and twelve submarines. Portal referred to the Philippines air reinforcements, but downplayed the numbers, and displayed no awareness of the scale of American ambitions. Neither Pound nor Portal suggested the Philippines reinforcements were a major factor in their thinking. Pound emphasised that the defence of the Malay Barrier had still not been resolved with the Americans.[128] The prime minister displayed neither reservations nor anxieties over Pound's dispositions and intentions for the theatre. Prime minister and Admiralty therefore appeared now to have reached a consensus on Eastern Fleet composition and deployment, at least over the next three months. However, the prime minister was still thinking primarily of the defence of the Indian Ocean, while Pound was focusing northward.

Perhaps the best insight into the scale of American ambition for their Philippines forces at this time was the privileged off-the-record press briefing given by Marshall on 15 November, three days after this War Cabinet meeting. Marshall stated that the United States was building up its forces in the Philippines to conduct an offensive war against Japan. If war comes, 'we'll fight mercilessly'. Flying Fortresses would be dispatched immediately to set the paper cities of Japan on fire. Although B-17s could not make the round trip to Japan from the Philippines, they could fly on to Vladivostok to refuel. B-24s, which could do the round trip, would be deployed shortly. Aviation fuel and bombs were being pre-positioned throughout the region. Marshall acknowledged after the war that this strategy had failed due to delay in aircraft deliveries, inadequacies of the Philippines airfields, overestimation of aircraft effective range, and underestimation of the difficulty of hitting ships.[129]

If there was consensus on Far East naval reinforcement by mid-November, other evidence confirms that Pound did not view the outcome of the 20 October Defence Committee meeting as a simple case of the prime minister overriding Admiralty advice. The following March he protested to the prime minister over the rapid promotion of Lord Louis Mountbatten to the rank of vice admiral and membership of the chiefs of staff. The appointment would reinforce a growing belief within senior ranks of the Royal Navy that the prime minister was inclined to 'override' the professional advice of his naval advisers. Pound quoted the appointment of the retired Admiral Sir Roger Keyes as Director of Combined Operations and 'the sending of the *Prince of Wales* and *Repulse* to the Far East' and the 'R class battleships to the Indian Ocean'. He had stated 'quite definitely' that these deployments were 'in accordance with my advice'. This statement is usually discounted as Pound displaying loyalty rather than accuracy. However, his language in a private message implies neither fundamental disagreement nor resentment at being overridden. It is more consistent with Pound's firm commitment from mid-October onwards to pursuing forward deployment at Singapore. As the next chapter demonstrates, Pound would have ample opportunity to hold Force Z in the Indian Ocean during November, but chose not to do so. It is reasonable to take his statement at face value.[130]

A striking feature of the planning to base in Singapore and operate north of the Malay Barrier is the complete absence of reference to the risk of IJN air attack and for the provision of adequate fighter defence, whether land-based or from carriers. Despite the encouragement from the United States chiefs of staff, the Admiralty did not press for additional air reinforcements to Malaya in this period, let alone make this a condition for forward deployment of the Eastern Fleet. Nor did planners view a carrier as essential to operations in the South China Sea. Director of Plans stated at the end of September that, apart from the old light carrier *Hermes* in the Indian Ocean, no carrier was available for the Far East until April 1942. The new *Indomitable* could be moved from Force H where she was due on completion of work-up in November but he did not recommend this.[131] This allocation of *Indomitable* to Force H was in line with the Admiralty dispositions agreed in late August, and notified to the prime minister by Pound. However, it was also conceded that *Indomitable* could be sent east in emergency.

There is a long-standing belief that *Indomitable* was allocated to Force Z after the 20 October Defence Committee meeting, but was prevented from joining by running aground in Jamaica.[132] The evidence does not support this.[133] *Indomitable* never received orders to join Force Z prior to her grounding, and she could never have reached Singapore by early December, even without the grounding, given the timing of her planned work-up. She ran aground in Kingston, Jamaica, on 2 November, right at the start of a three-week work-up. To join Force Z by 8 December, she would have needed to be in Cape Town by 23 November at the latest. Achieving this was possible only if she had not run aground and had completely abandoned the bulk of her work-up. Abandoning the work-up was never contemplated and, indeed, she completed the full three weeks after returning to Kingston in late November, following her repairs at Norfolk. Simple time/distance factors, therefore, absolutely rule out *Indomitable*'s presence off Malaya on 10 December. Frequent speculation on the difference she would have made is pointless.[134]

Furthermore, no Admiralty or joint planning staff papers from early October to mid-December show *Indomitable* allocated to the Eastern Fleet. Phillips gave no indication he anticipated her joining his fleet when he met with Hart on 6 December. The most compelling evidence that *Indomitable* was never allocated to Force Z is the First Lord's secret session speech reporting on the loss of the force to Parliament on 19 December. Alexander spoke in place of the prime minister, who was by then en route to the United States. He stated: 'The question has been raised as to why there was no aircraft carrier with our ships. The simple answer is that none was available.' He added that *Ark Royal* had been sunk, *Illustrious* and *Formidable* were still under repair, *Furious* was in refit, *Eagle* in dock, and *Victorious* required by the Home Fleet. *Indomitable* was not mentioned in the speech, but did feature in the accompanying briefing notes. These stated that there were urgent calls to provide two modern carriers in the eastern Mediterranean and one for Force H. A pencil note stated that the only carrier available here was *Indomitable*, which was working up, but was now (17 December) en route for Durban. The note also stated that (prior to her loss) it was planned to send *Ark Royal* to the Eastern Fleet after completion of her refit in the United States about April 1942. This was again in accord with Pound's August minute to the prime minister.[135]

The most definitive final statement of planned Royal Navy strength in the eastern theatre (the combined Far East, Indian Ocean and Australasia areas) before the outbreak of the Far East war was issued on 7 December, the day before the attack on Malaya. This identified Royal Navy strength by warship category in two columns: planned strength in early 1942, and additional reinforcements that 'may' be sent later. Five battleships were listed in the early 1942 column (*Prince of Wales* and the four 'R' class), one battlecruiser (*Repulse*) and one aircraft carrier (clearly *Hermes*). One carrier was also listed in the 'possible reinforcements' column. This document, approved personally by Pound, confirms that *Indomitable* was not yet formally allocated to the eastern theatre as late as 7 December.[136]

Churchill certainly advocated the inclusion of a fleet carrier with the Force Z package on 17 October, and it is possible this triggered informal discussion within the Admiralty as to whether *Indomitable* might be added. Such discussion would be consistent with post-war claims by both Churchill[137] and Alexander[138] that *Indomitable* was supposed to join Force Z. However, if there was such discussion, it never translated into a firm plan or orders. The Admiralty did inform the prime minister on 17 October that it was intended to allocate *Formidable* and *Illustrious* to the Mediterranean once they completed their repairs in the United States at the end of the year. This may have been the result of a prime minister query over carrier allocation with an eye to the forthcoming Defence Committee meeting.[139] However, five weeks later, and with the Japanese threat ever more imminent, when the prime minister again asked Pound for thoughts on carrier distribution, there was no reference to *Indomitable*'s allocation to Force Z. Indeed, the prime minister said he was reluctant to 'waste' any modern carrier by sending it round the Cape at this stage, or at least until events in the Mediterranean clarified.[140] It is also significant that the First Sea Lord's later report on the loss of Force Z, dated 25 January 1942, made no reference to *Indomitable*. It merely stated that 'there was no aircraft carrier available except *Victorious* which was working up with the Home Fleet'.[141] Given the overwhelming lack of evidence for the formal allocation of *Indomitable* to Force Z, there must be suspicion that the story rests on dubious *post facto* attempts by key participants to suggest they were more proactive in addressing the Japanese air threat than they actually were.

The disregard for the air threat evident in the Admiralty's autumn offensive planning, and their conviction that the 'R' class represented a viable strike force, are hard to explain. In assessing Admiralty thinking, it is useful to compare the challenges posed by operations in the Mediterranean, where the Royal Navy had been heavily engaged for eighteen months, and the vision projected for the South China Sea. There were striking similarities between the two areas. Geographically, they were of similar size. In each sea, the Royal Navy aspired to assert control primarily from bases at each extremity, Singapore and Manila therefore broadly equating to Alexandria and Gibraltar. In each area, the bulk of one long land boundary was under enemy control, such that the enemy could expect, at a minimum, to dominate the central part of the sea. There were parallels too between the size and composition of the Axis air and naval forces in the Mediterranean, and those Japan was likely to make available for the South China Sea. There were also differences. The most obvious was the IJN's carrier capability. The IJN was a more formidable foe than the Italian navy in both capability and fighting efficiency. However, as the Royal Navy considered the problems involved in contesting the South China Sea, there was nothing in the IJN armoury or the way it would be deployed, with the exception perhaps of the Long Lance torpedo, which lay outside Mediterranean experience and could not be reasonably anticipated from available intelligence.

Many would add the long-range land-based torpedo strike aircraft to the list of IJN innovations, arguing that the sinking of Force Z marked a watershed in naval warfare, where the Royal Navy was surprised and overwhelmed by a new phenomenon. Similar points are made regarding the quality of IJN carrier strike aircraft in the Indian Ocean the following April. In reality, neither experience was genuinely new. The Royal Navy had suffered periodic, but very effective, attacks from Italian land-based torpedo aircraft since late 1940. Cunningham described the onset of Italian torpedo attacks using SM79s, which were often conducted in twilight, as 'nerve wracking and dangerous'.[142] Three Mediterranean Fleet heavy cruisers, *Liverpool*, *Glasgow* and *Kent*, were badly damaged by such attacks during the last four months of 1940, and the cruiser *Manchester* the following summer. These Regia Aeronautica aircraft had very similar capability and used broadly similar techniques to the IJNAF torpedo aircraft.[143] The IJNAF dive-bombers deployed at Ceylon were novel only in that they were carrier-launched. The experience at the receiving end was no different from the numerous attacks by German dive-bombers on Royal Navy warships in the Mediterranean during 1941.

The relevance of Mediterranean experience can be taken a stage further. In late September the Royal Navy mounted a major convoy operation, known as Halberd, out of Gibraltar to relieve Malta. To achieve its purpose, the escort had to be strong enough to command the air and sea space around the convoy during its transit. This meant holding off a significant Italian battle-fleet and major air strike forces based in Sardinia and Sicily. During Halberd, the Italians would deploy twenty-nine torpedo bombers, twenty-four high-level bombers, nine dive-bombers and sixty-eight fighters, almost all during the single afternoon of 26 September. The overall scale of attack here was quite close to the Japanese total that would attack Force Z on 10 December, though the Japanese would have no fighters.[144] The largest Italian torpedo attack, with twenty-eight aircraft, was greater than any of the individual Japanese attacks.[145]

The reason Halberd was a success while Force Z would meet disaster lay not in any marked inferiority of Italian performance compared to the IJNAF, but rather in the scale and quality of Royal Navy forces deployed. The Royal Navy convoy escort comprised three battleships, *Rodney*, *Nelson* and *Prince of Wales*, one fleet carrier, *Ark Royal*, with up to twenty-four Fulmar II fighters,[146] five cruisers, including two brand new *Dido*-class anti-aircraft cruisers, and eighteen destroyers. In addition, nine submarines were available to ambush Italian warships, and twenty-seven long-range fighters were available in Malta. The majority of the Royal Navy warships were the most modern and effective in their class, and were experienced and well-trained. This was a modern, balanced task force. It retained significant strike power, but was equipped to defend itself in three dimensions. It is also noteworthy that while a fleet carrier was critical to air defence, it did not rely on this alone.

The Royal Navy (with Royal Air Force support) deployed this scale and quality of force because it judged it the minimum necessary to secure the Halberd corridor against the anticipated Italian air, surface and submarine opposition. It demonstrates, therefore, that by autumn 1941, the Royal Navy would never deploy an unprotected battle-fleet in the central Mediterranean in range of Italian bombers or torpedo aircraft, and certainly not against numbers equivalent to those the Japanese might credibly deploy in the South China Sea.[147] It is equally hard to envisage Home or Mediterranean Fleet commanders being willing to deploy 'R'-class battleships, with their limited gun power, poor protection and low speed, in a scenario such as Halberd, where they might face a surface engagement with modern opponents, or prolonged air attack. Their lack of speed alone, at least 5 knots less than the slowest IJN capital ships, rendered their role as a 'strike force' in the eastern theatre ridiculous.

Previous chapters have shown that intelligence estimates of Japanese air power were accurate enough to discourage any complacency about the potential threat this posed in the South China Sea. The view that the Japanese air forces were on a par with the Italians had certainly gained currency, but Italian air performance at sea during 1941 suggested no comfort could be drawn from this analogy. The Italians had successfully torpedoed the battleship *Nelson* during Halberd. The lesson, surely, was that a weaker force without fighter cover could expect much greater damage. Given what it knew of the IJN and all it had learnt in the Mediterranean, the Royal Navy should have judged a Halberd-type force as the absolute minimum to conduct even the most limited offensive operation north of Singapore, then only if IJN carriers were absent. It is noteworthy that when Admiral Cunningham was briefed on the loss of Force Z by the surviving captain of *Repulse*, William Tennant, he evidently saw nothing new or surprising in the nature of the IJN attack, other than their apparent failure to co-ordinate their torpedo and bombing strikes which, he emphasised, the Italians had certainly learnt.[148]

In the event, there is a surreal quality to the autumn offensive planning. The naval staff, from Pound downward, seem so gripped by the use of a battle-fleet north of the barrier to threaten Japanese communications and bind in the Americans that they put aside all the hard tactical lessons and innovations learned in the European war. They seized on this new strategy with the only resources they could make available, rather than those that all previous experience and calculation from 1937 onward suggested they needed: above all, carriers.[149]

The risks in this new strategy might be explicable, even defensible, if the Admiralty, together with the joint planning staff, Joint Intelligence Committee and chiefs of staff, had carefully assessed the combined impact of their Eastern Fleet, American strategic air power in the Philippines, and the US Navy Pacific Fleet on Japanese intentions. The obvious trigger for such an assessment would have been the United States joint chiefs' message to Pound of 13 November.[150] Such an evaluation was apparently never considered, let alone executed, although the British war leadership had sufficient knowledge of American thinking and capability to produce one.[151] The joint planning staff papers produced in response to the American message of 13 November fell far short of the comprehensive assessment required. They merely endorsed the framework for new discussions between British and American theatre commanders, while providing self-serving arguments for continuing to delay British air reinforcements.

It is illuminating to address the key questions such a comprehensive assessment might have tackled. Most accounts of Far East naval reinforcement in late 1941 make only passing, if any, reference to the exchanges between Pound and the United States chiefs, and to the related discussions on both sides of the Atlantic. Yet these exchanges are fundamental to understanding British and American intentions and calculations in the theatre in the final weeks before the outbreak of war, and of events in the first phase of the war. British accounts have focused almost entirely on Force Z, rather than wider Admiralty planning, and largely ignore the developments in American reinforcement strategy centred on the Philippines. American accounts have looked at events through an exclusively American optic which ignores British developments. Given these gaps, important questions are as follows. Did the United States military and political leadership better identify and understand the risks inherent in their reinforcement strategy than the British? Did British reinforcement have significant influence on United States thinking and calculations? Was the failure of reinforcement and deterrence essentially one of timing? Did the prospect of reinforcement by the associated powers provoke the Japanese to act in December? Would planned reinforcement have altered Japanese calculations by say March 1942? Was the nature of the joint reinforcement package always fatally flawed?

Successive memoranda produced for the president of the United States on 5 and 27 November, under the joint signature of Stark and Marshall, make a substantial contribution to these questions. The 5 November memorandum stated that the US Navy Pacific Fleet was inferior to the Japanese fleet and could not undertake offensive operations in the western Pacific without substantial reinforcement. This was a distinctly bleaker view than Stark had taken with Kimmel at the end of September, even though Pacific Fleet force levels had not changed. Stark had then acknowledged that offensive sweeps by the Pacific Fleet towards the Mandates might not draw substantial IJN forces in their direction. However, he thought they would help pin the IJN to northern waters, or to bases in the western Pacific, diverting them away from the Philippines and Malay Barrier. Now the memorandum argued that reinforcement, including merchant ships needed for supply, was required. This could only come from the Atlantic, and would risk British defeat there. War plans for the Far East must, therefore, be defensive, and based on holding the Philippines and the British and Netherlands East Indies. Present American strength in the Philippines would make a Japanese attack hazardous but by mid-December, United States air and submarine strength would be a positive threat to any Japanese operations south of Formosa. By February/March, when American air strength reached its planned target in the Philippines, it might well be a decisive deterrent to Japanese operations in the south. By that time, British naval and air reinforcements would also have arrived at Singapore. The defensive strength of the entire southern area would have reached impressive proportions.

The memorandum concluded that the ABC-1 principles remained sound. Germany was the primary enemy, and war with Japan must not risk the Atlantic. War should, therefore, be avoided while completing reinforcements, and the United States should respond only to attack on its own territories, or those of Britain and the Netherlands.[152] In a briefing to the joint board two days earlier, Rear Admiral Royal Ingersoll, the Assistant Chief of Naval Operations, emphasised the difficulty of supporting operations in the Far

East, given the threat the Japanese could pose to strategic lines of communication, the limitations to existing facilities at Singapore and Manila, and defences at the latter, and the difficulty of providing more naval support without compromising aid to Britain.[153] The memorandum of 27 November, drafted against the signs of imminent breakdown in the diplomatic negotiations with Japan, again emphasised the need to gain time for military reinforcement to complete.[154]

Turner, as head of US Navy war plans, provided important qualifications to these November briefings in his testimony to the Hart Inquiry into Pearl Harbor. The Navy Department recognised the major military effort of the United States as a whole must be directed at Germany as primary enemy, but believed the principal effort of the US Navy should be directed at the central Pacific. From the outbreak of a war in late 1941, the Pacific Fleet was therefore expected to operate offensively against the IJN in the area of the Marshall and Gilbert Islands, although it would initially lack the resources to seize and hold territory.[155] This focus on the central Pacific differed from the British view that the US Navy should prioritise the Atlantic and Far East area. Turner also confirmed that in the autumn of 1941, the British had promised to establish an eastern fleet, comprising six battleships and two or three carriers. This was to be based in the Indian Ocean, centred on Trincomalee, but using Singapore as an advanced base. In the event, they had moved *Prince of Wales* and *Repulse* forward to Singapore with three further battleships and a carrier to follow shortly after. This eastern commitment by the Royal Navy was a loyal effort to meet the terms of ABC-1. Turner insisted that there was a clear consensus within the Navy Department that in the event of war breaking out with Japan, every effort should be made to trigger simultaneous war with Germany through offensive American action.[156]

The United States strategy for deterring and containing Japan set out in these November memoranda, including the forward role ascribed to the Pacific Fleet by Turner, has intellectual coherence. Furthermore, for the United States leadership, the naval and air reinforcements anticipated from Britain were important in enhancing its credibility. President Roosevelt also linked American and British reinforcements and deterrence. On 7 November, two days after the United States chiefs' first memorandum, he told the prime minister – 'continuing efforts to strengthen our defences in the Philippine Islands, paralleled by similar efforts by you in the Singapore area, will tend to increase Japan's hesitation'.[157]

There remained flaws in this vision. As the United States chiefs recognised, time was required to deploy the forces and make them operationally effective. This would have taken far longer than the March target regularly quoted for the Philippines forces. Linkage between Philippines strategic air power, Pacific Fleet offensive operations, and British reinforcements at Singapore remained aspirational, rather than real. The United States assumed British air reinforcements the British were not willing to make. The Royal Navy made unrealistic assumptions about Manila. Both countries underestimated the sheer ambition of Japanese operations.

It can be argued that the American position in the Philippines would have proved untenable even in the best of circumstances, where war was delayed six months and all air reinforcements were complete, because the IJN could easily cut American supply routes.[158] If this is correct, then by planning to base its new Eastern Fleet in Singapore and operate northwards, the Admiralty was sacrificing the potentially strong defensive position in the Indian Ocean projected by Pound in August to bolster a defensive shield the United States could never deliver. This overlooks important aspects of Japanese perception. By late spring 1942, the American radar-equipped fighter defences in the Philippines would have made the raids the Japanese executed at the start of the Far East war a very risky undertaking. The B-17 force would have been of doubtful effectiveness against IJN forces at sea. However, operating out of the planned regional airbases in Borneo and Malaya, they would have posed a dangerous threat to Japanese airbases and other facilities in Indochina. The modern US Navy submarines in the Philippines, under a good air umbrella, would also have looked menacing. The proposed Royal Navy battle-fleet at Singapore would have had all the limitations discussed in this chapter, but it would have appeared to the Japanese comparable to the threat from the US Navy Pacific Fleet to whose removal they devoted so much effort in mounting the Pearl Harbor raid. To the Japanese, the Allied defences might well have taken on the 'impressive proportions' envisaged in the United States chiefs' 5 November memorandum. They just might have been dissuaded.[159]

The records of the Imperial Conference on 5 November, at which the Japanese decided on war, lend some support to this view. Chief of the Army General Staff, General Hajime Sugiyama, identified four arguments against delay: Japan could not match American war production especially air power; American defences in the Philippines would make rapid progress; defence cooperation between the United States, Britain, the Netherlands East Indies, and Russia would increase, especially their combined power in the southern region; and Russia might intervene in the north in the spring.

Overall, therefore, there is a respectable argument that by late autumn 1941, the associated powers were groping, albeit in a rather haphazard and disconnected way, towards a joint military strategy that had genuine prospects of deterring and containing Japan by mid-1942. However, for the strategy to work, much would have to go right. It required sustained commitment to provide the promised forces and, above all, it needed time, which, as the Allies were about to discover, they did not have.[160]

Emerging American policy explains why, in British minds, both Churchill's deterrence goal and Pound's ambition for a battle-fleet in Singapore looked more credible in November 1941 than in hindsight. Given the scale of future United States commitment, neither deterrence nor the prospects for holding the barrier in the event of war seemed hopeless or unrealistic. Furthermore, the ultimate mid-1942 Eastern Fleet had a modern Force H-plus Halberd-type task force at its core. Given enhanced land-based Allied air power, undertaking limited forays north of Singapore to secure Malaya, the wider barrier, and maintain communications with the Americans was a plausible goal. Embarking on reinforcement with this as the implicit endpoint was reasonable, if the risks in the interim were managed.

In this regard, none of the British decisions to create an Eastern Fleet at Singapore were irrevocable. If circumstances changed, certainly if war looked imminent, plans could be reviewed. Forces could be held short of Singapore, or withdrawn in accordance with Pound's defensive strategy set out in August. The reasons why Force Z ended up in an exposed position in Singapore at the outbreak of war are now explored in the next chapter. Once again, principal responsibility here rested with the Admiralty, not the prime minister.

7

The Deployment of Force Z and its Consequences: Inevitable Disaster?

The previous chapter showed why traditional accounts of the naval reinforcement debate in the autumn of 1941 are flawed. The question now is whether the decision taken by the Defence Committee on 20 October, whatever its merits, to deploy a small advance deterrent force centred on *Prince of Wales*, led inexorably to the subsequent destruction of the force. Most historians have argued that it did.[1] This chapter does not provide a detailed account of the operational sortie by Force Z following the Japanese attack on 8 December or of the final engagement with the IJNAF strike force off Kuantan, which are well documented elsewhere.[2] It concentrates on questions relating to the movement and role of the force prior to its arrival in Singapore, and Admiral Phillips's subsequent decision to deploy north on 8 December to attack the Japanese landings. These have either not been raised at all or not satisfactorily answered. How did the intelligence picture regarding Japanese intentions evolve during the passage of *Prince of Wales* to Singapore? Did it provide a convincing case for holding Force Z in the Indian Ocean? Why did this not happen? Did Phillips and his staff make sufficient use of intelligence on Japanese capability available in Singapore? How far did the Admiralty's recent offensive planning influence Phillips's thinking? What conclusions can be drawn from Phillips's discussions with Admiral Thomas Hart, the commander of the US Asiatic Fleet, on 6 December? We will see that the specific ending off Kuantan reflected judgements and decisions that might have been called differently at several points in the seven weeks after 20 October, and which might then have led to alternative outcomes. The story is more complex than subsequently promoted by both the Admiralty and established history. It is also important to consider the practical consequences for Royal Navy strategy in the East from the loss of the force. Did it matter as much as usually claimed?[3]

Admiralty choices during Force Z's passage east

Despite the Admiralty enthusiasm for placing a battle-fleet at Singapore, it was evident by early November that only two 'R'-class battleships could reach there by the end of the year to join *Prince of Wales* and *Repulse*. *Revenge* was already in the Indian Ocean. *Royal Sovereign* was to sail for the Far East with convoy WS12 on 10 November, allowing her to reach Singapore by end December.[4] *Ramillies* was expected to deploy with WS14 on 30 November and *Resolution* around 21 December. (*Royal Sovereign* did not reach Durban until 17 December, while *Ramillies* and *Resolution* did not leave the United Kingdom for the Indian Ocean until early January 1942.[5]) Prior to departure, all four ships received refits, including improvements to anti-aircraft armament and protection, and a short work-up. *Resolution* and *Royal Sovereign* (though not *Ramillies* and probably not *Revenge*) also had their main armament equipped for supercharge firing, increasing their maximum gun range to about 26,000yds (23,774m) with pre-1938 4crh ammunition and 28,732yds (26,272m) with the latest 6crh shells. On 22 November the Admiralty also announced that the 'R'-class ships would form the 3rd Battle Squadron, under Rear Admiral Bonham-Carter.[6]

It followed that if war came before the end of January, then the initial capital units based at Singapore would not, as Pound had hoped on 20 October, be strong enough (judged by his standards) to meet the forces the IJN could allocate to an attack southward.[7] The Royal Navy force would also be exposed to air attack in harbour, and air or submarine attack in any area north of the Malay Barrier. This called for plans to hold ships in the Indian Ocean, or withdraw them from Singapore in good time if the situation deteriorated, as Pound had advocated to the prime minister in August.[8] Operational caution clashed here with the political need for a visible deterrent. But deterrence rested on Japanese awareness that high-profile reinforcements were in the Far East theatre, not on their specific location in Singapore, as Eden had recognised on 20 October, and Churchill confirmed at the War Cabinet on 5 November.[9]

The 20 October meeting had also agreed only to deploy *Prince of Wales* to Cape Town. Given this decision, it was surprising that the Admiralty sent a signal to relevant overseas commanders the following day, stating that *Prince of Wales* was bound for Singapore via Cape Town. No qualification was placed on the Singapore destination, and key recipients such as Commander-in-Chief China would have taken it as settled. The signal was released by Harwood as ACNS (F).[10] The reason for the Cape Town review was primarily the possibility *Prince of Wales* might be required to meet a Home Fleet emergency while her new sister *Duke of York* was still working up, but it was also an opportunity to review the Far East threat. On 20 October Pound thought the Japanese were more likely to attack northwards against the Soviet

Union. Key questions are, therefore, whether there was intelligence available during the passage of Force Z to justify a reassessment of the deployment and, if so, why no action was taken.

The first point to address is the planned review at Cape Town, where *Prince of Wales* arrived with her two escorting destroyers, *Electra* and *Express*, early on 16 November, and sailed the afternoon of 18 November. Pound confirmed to the prime minister on 2 November during the passage south that he intended to review the situation just before arrival at the Cape.[11] However, this promised review did not happen either prior to arrival at the Cape, or during the visit itself.[12] Pound did not attempt to stall the Force Z deployment as an unwise initiative executed against Admiralty advice. Nor was there pressure from the prime minister to pre-empt a review or rush the force onward to Singapore. During the passage of the force, he asked reasonable questions, but at all times accepted Pound's advice and decisions.[13] Despite Harwood's signal, as late as 5 November the prime minister believed the decision to proceed beyond Cape Town had still to be made.[14]

Pound initially told the prime minister that *Prince of Wales* would stay in Cape Town about a week. This is what Phillips still expected on 6 November. However, Phillips did not doubt his ultimate destination was Singapore, which he anticipated reaching about 13 December, after a further three-day stopover in Ceylon.[15] When he refuelled at Freetown, he confirmed to Vice Admiral Sir Algernon Willis, Commander-in-Chief South Atlantic, that he was definitely headed for Singapore and planned early contact with US Navy commanders in the Far East.[16] However, by 9 November, Pound wanted Phillips in Singapore more quickly. This meant foreshortening *Prince of Wales*'s stay in Cape Town to forty-eight hours.[17] Two days later, on 11 November, the Admiralty issued formal orders for the onward movement of *Prince of Wales* to Ceylon, where she was to rendezvous with *Repulse*, and for both ships then to proceed to Singapore.[18]

The obvious development between Pound's confirmation of the Cape Town review on 2 November and the executive order on 11 November to proceed to Singapore, apparently without the review, was Pound's important message to Stark on the reversion to ABC-1 principles, and the forward deployment of a Royal Navy battle-fleet able to operate north from Singapore.[19] The urgency in pushing *Prince of Wales* on to Singapore was to facilitate the early meeting between Phillips and Hart. The prime minister here questioned the suggestion in Pound's 11 November executive signal that Phillips dispense with his destroyer escort to speed his passage east. 'I should like to talk over with you again the idea of *PoW* being entirely separated from her two destroyers. I do not quite see what all this haste is to arrive at Singapore for a pow wow. This is one of those cases where I am for "Safety First"'.[20]

The famous missing review was not, therefore, a victim of relentless pressure from the prime minister to move the force east. It lapsed due to the Admiralty's new offensive ambitions. Since Pound was now more firmly committed to forward deployment than the prime minister, the only reason to halt the deployment was a new operational requirement in the Atlantic. Without this, Pound saw no reason to persist with a review and the prime minister deferred to his judgement. Its absence, so often remarked, is unsurprising. By now, it was also clear to Pound that *Rodney* could not reach the Far East until the spring at the earliest, and *Nelson* rather later. There was thus now no alternative to *Prince of Wales* to bolster the 'R' class.[21]

Far from the prime minister urging the Force Z elements east without regard for the military risks, it was the Admiralty making the running. Throughout November, therefore, as intelligence increasingly pointed to the risk of early hostile action by Japan, nobody in London was counselling caution over the potential exposure of Force Z, if deterrence were to fail, until too late. However, two people did warn Phillips of the dangers in placing an inferior force in a potentially vulnerable location like Singapore. These were Willis at Freetown and Field Marshal J C Smuts, who Phillips met in South Africa. Willis counselled Phillips to keep his force on the move and avoid being tied to a single base – 'the fleet in being concept'. He believed Phillips agreed.[22] Smuts's warning message to Churchill after Phillips's visit is well known.[23] Less known are his comments to Vice Admiral Sir Philip Vian and his Flag Captain Guy Grantham the following year. Smuts told Phillips that once Force Z reached the East Indies it should hide, ever shifting its location, and making sudden attacks on Japanese targets of opportunity. Once located in a base such as Singapore, the force was as good as sunk.[24]

Even the most authoritative witness has proved unreliable over controversial issues such as the Cape Town review. Phillips's operations officer, Commander Michael Goodenough, later claimed Phillips thought it 'useless to stay in South Africa and desirable to move to Ceylon'. However, he believed Phillips might also have received 'private instructions' from the prime minister urging him on. Phillips certainly did want to press on, but he had received a direct Admiralty order to do so a week earlier, as Goodenough must have known. Goodenough also ignored the implications of Pound's message to Stark, which he must also have seen.[25]

If a review had been conducted immediately prior to *Prince of Wales*'s arrival in Cape Town, what issues might it have raised? A review around 15 November would have found no pressing reason to hold *Prince of Wales* in the Atlantic, matched by a distinct rise in the risk of conflict with Japan. During the first half of November, a steady stream of diplomatic and intelligence reports reached London and Washington describing a rapid build-up of Japanese forces in

Indochina.[26] At the same time, negotiations between Japan and the United States in Washington were reaching a climax. The impact of sanctions meant Japan must cut a deal, which implied concessions, or act to break the stranglehold. This meant risking war with one or more of the associated powers. The Joint Intelligence Committee drew these strands together on 18 November.[27] Its conclusions reflected a growing consensus that invasion of Thailand, including the strategically important Kra Isthmus, would be Japan's most likely move, but that no final decision had yet been taken. In fact, Japan had decided on war at the Imperial Conference held on 5 November.[28]

Deploying *Prince of Wales* as a key element in a deterrent force remained worthwhile. It was also sensible to have her in the Indian Ocean with *Repulse* and *Revenge* as an immediate phase 1 package, to protect vital communications should the situation continue to deteriorate. However, neither of these arguments required the force to be in Singapore. The logical outcome of a Cape Town review would surely have been agreement to concentrate the deterrent force in Ceylon and then review options again. If Phillips had to meet Hart urgently, he could fly from Ceylon, as indeed he did. He did not need a fleet to transport him beyond that point.

The Admiralty did take measures to bring the arrival of *Prince of Wales* at Cape Town and her likely destination to Japanese attention.[29] Tokyo was duly alerted. The Japanese Consul General Cape Town reported the visit on 19 November and specifically stated the ship was bound for Malaya. Director of Naval Intelligence Vice Admiral John Godfrey knew this from a GC&CS intercept on 22 November.[30] Potential deterrence had therefore begun to take effect in Cape Town, as Eden and Churchill anticipated. Tokyo was also alerted by their London embassy to the link with Churchill's Guildhall speech on 10 November. This London message specifically confirmed naval reinforcements, including *Prince of Wales*, were being sent to the East.[31] There were options further to enhance this deterrence potential by publicising the complete Force Z at Ceylon, where *Prince of Wales* met *Repulse* on 29 November.[32] Pound also discussed with Churchill exposing the old battleship *Centurion* which was in the area, disguised as a *King George V*-class battleship.[33] During the passage to Ceylon, confirmation that the Japanese were fully aware of *Prince of Wales* and her destination was matched by continuing indications of the build-up of Japanese military forces in the south. Vice Admiral Nobutake Kondo, naval commander of the IJN southern task force, later claimed he learnt of the arrival of Force Z in Singapore 'towards the end of November'. After consulting combined fleet headquarters, he then moved his covering force from Formosa to Camranh Bay in southern Indochina.[34] Force Z did not reach Singapore until 2 December, so either Kondo only learnt of their arrival then or, more likely, he was alerted well before their arrival.

The Joint Intelligence Committee produced a further assessment on 28 November, concluding that the risks of early Japanese action were increasing.[35] This drew on excellent SIGINT coverage of Japanese force levels in Indochina, but also some important reports on their intentions, including targeting of the Kra Isthmus, from SIS.[36] The committee still expected a step-by-step approach, beginning with a move into Thailand, but from mid-November there was accumulating evidence in the Far East theatre of a more direct and imminent threat to Malaya.[37]

There were also more specific intercepts showing that the Japanese now anticipated imminent hostilities with Britain and the United States. Tokyo advised key overseas posts 'we cannot make any further concessions' and 'the outlook is not bright'.[38] On 25 November GC&CS reported the famous 'Winds Alert' message sent by the Ministry of Foreign Affairs in Tokyo to the chargé d'affaires in London a week earlier. This advised that trigger phrases would be used to denote the imminent breaking of diplomatic relations. The trigger for America was: 'Easterly wind, rain'. For Britain, 'Westerly wind, fine'.[39] This 'Winds Alert' message was subsequently discussed between FECB and the US Station Cast in Corregidor and joint arrangements were made to maximise the chances of picking up an 'Execute' message. Hong Kong intercepted this on the evening of 7 December (6 December in Hawaii).[40] Captain Douglas Doig, secretary to Commander-in-Chief China, later recalled being shown the original 'Winds Alert' intercept by Captain Kenneth Harkness, the Chief of Intelligence Staff (COIS) in Singapore.[41] In addition, on 28 November the US Army War Plans Division advised the British joint planning staff that negotiations with the Japanese were at the point of breakdown, and offensive action against Thailand, the Netherlands East Indies or the Philippines was possible at any time.[42] A similar message simultaneously reached the Admiralty from the US Navy Chief of Naval Operations and was relayed to Far East naval commanders the following day.[43]

By the time Force Z concentrated in Ceylon, therefore, it appeared unlikely that either its own presence in the Far East theatre, or any other British and American measures, would have the desired deterrence effect. Goodenough later stated that 'the situation had worsened considerably by Ceylon', so the deteriorating outlook was a topic within Phillips's staff.[44] On 28 November Pound was sufficiently concerned by the growing sense of crisis to encourage Phillips to fly direct from Ceylon to Singapore, so that he could assume command of the eastern theatre 'should war develop', and to hasten the promised talks with the Americans.[45]

Had Pound or Phillips wanted to exercise caution, there were sufficient grounds here for holding Force Z at least temporarily in Ceylon, on the basis that deterrence applied as much there as Singapore, while the intelligence justified waiting for Japanese intentions to clarify. Godfrey, as DNI, claimed later that this was his view, but it is not clear he stated it at the time.[46] Both Pound and Phillips were aware that all pre-war and more recent contingency planning envisaged concentrating eastern reinforcements in safe waters clear of potential Japanese attack. Once in Singapore, Force Z would not only be exposed, but political and military circumstances would make withdrawal harder. Pound later stated that Force Z could only be considered a raiding force, not 'sufficiently powerful to disrupt enemy communications in the South China Sea'.[47] The situation now equated to that postulated to the prime minister in August, when Pound favoured withdrawal from Singapore prior to war. The hypothetical force considered then comprised *Nelson*, *Rodney*, *Renown*, and a fleet carrier, a significantly more powerful squadron than Force Z.[48]

Vice Admiral Sir Henry Moore, Phillips's successor as Vice Chief of Naval Staff, later claimed that he tried to convince Pound to signal Phillips to lose himself in the Pacific as soon as Force Z had refuelled in Singapore. The reference here to Force Z 'losing itself in the Pacific' is suspiciously similar to ideas aired at the later meeting, recorded by Churchill, at the Admiralty on 9 December, at which Moore was also present. There must be doubt whether he really spoke in these terms to Pound at this time, or whether it was a convenient *post facto* memory, displaying wisdom after the event. In any case, the whole concept of Force Z losing itself in the Pacific was meaningless. It had to base somewhere. There was also limited purpose in going on to Singapore just to refuel if the Japanese were already well aware Royal Navy heavy ships were in the Indian Ocean, as Moore and Pound knew from the intelligence reports that they were. If Moore did tender such advice, then Pound was initially reluctant to second-guess Phillips.[49] Nevertheless, he was sufficiently anxious about the growing exposure of Force Z at Singapore to reconsider the position just a few days later. Successive signals to Phillips on 1 and 3 December asked him to consider sailing the ships away from the base.[50] As far as the prime minister is concerned, his attitude throughout the deployment to date suggests he would have been entirely receptive to arguments for holding Force Z in Ceylon. There is no evidence he pressed for Force Z to push on regardless.

In arguing that the deterrence effect of Force Z applied as much in Ceylon as Singapore, it is important to draw a distinction between British and Japanese perceptions. From the British viewpoint, if deterrence was still judged possible, then exercising it from Ceylon made sense. However, the Japanese had already discounted any force Britain might send in the foreseeable future. Japanese intelligence in the immediate run-up to war assumed the Royal Navy forces in the Indian Ocean comprised six battleships, two carriers, six heavy cruisers, and ten light cruisers.[51] They were not dissuaded and evidently felt this could be managed. Figures provided at the Imperial Conference on 5 November gave an even more accurate estimate of total Royal Navy surface forces expected to be available east of Suez at the end of the month. Force Z was not included here, because its deployment could not yet be known. The Japanese also erroneously credited the Royal Navy with fifteen submarines. Their figures for US Navy strength in the Pacific were, however, significantly overstated.[52]

Pound did not hold Force Z back. Perhaps he judged attack on Malaya, as opposed to Thailand, was not imminent when it left Ceylon on 30 November, and he felt there was time to review options at Singapore.[53] However, the fact that Admiralty thinking was now so firmly fixed on forward deployment at Singapore, following the exchanges with the Americans earlier in the month, must have weighed heavily in the balance. He also later admitted a second deterrence objective. Force Z was sent to Singapore 'prior to the concentration of the Eastern Fleet', because 'it was hoped they would act as a deterrent to the Japanese and avert war'. However, if the Japanese 'decided to take the plunge', two ships at Singapore with the American forces on their flank might cause them 'sufficient anxiety' to prevent an immediate expedition against Malaya.[54] Given the Admiralty intent to operate offensively north of Singapore, it was logical to project this additional deterrence objective on to Force Z.

Personal factors were no doubt influential too. Moore's claim that Pound was reluctant to dictate to Phillips, who knew Admiralty thinking and had been steeped in Far East war planning throughout his career, rings true. Pound was also no doubt sensitive to the point that Phillips would hardly relish taking over in Singapore without a fleet. This underlines the primary argument in Doig's paper to Layton of early October. By creating an Eastern Fleet and a commander-in-chief to lead it in advance of war breaking out, the Admiralty had created momentum that was now hard to check.

Decisions for Phillips at Singapore

Force Z arrived in Singapore on 2 December, six days before the Japanese attack. Events between the sighting of Japanese transports in the Gulf of Siam on 6 December and the subsequent destruction of the force have been closely scrutinised. There is broad agreement that with the force in Singapore when seaborne landings commenced, its commitment to attack was virtually inevitable. There is also agreement that having entered a killing ground, the odds of executing a successful raid on the Japanese landings without being engaged by superior forces, and of then surviving, were, in the words of the Naval Staff History, 'slender in the extreme'.[55] There are, however, important questions relating to the period between Phillips's arrival in Singapore by air from Ceylon on 29 November[56] and his departure to meet Admiral Hart in

Manila on 4 December. Intelligence suggesting an imminent attack on Malaya, derived from multiple sources, was now building up rapidly. As a result, with the agreement of the governor, Sir Shenton Thomas, Brooke-Popham had put Far East forces on war alert on 28 November, the day before Phillips arrived.[57] Extensive air reconnaissance over the South China Sea was initiated next day and Dutch submarines were placed on alert.[58] Phillips, therefore, had to absorb a fast-moving picture in an unfamiliar environment with a new and untested staff. Furthermore, most of the staff were not available until *Prince of Wales* arrived on 2 December. Only the chief of staff, Rear Admiral Arthur Palliser, and Goodenough had flown in with him.[59] It must have been clear to him by the time his small force arrived late on 2 December that it was in an exposed position, with significant reinforcements still weeks away.

Perhaps the best, and certainly the most concise, insight into how the British war leadership assessed the Japanese threat at this stage is the assessment sent by the SIS representative in Manila to his counterpart in Honolulu on 2 December. This repeated one received earlier from the SIS chief, Sir Stewart Menzies. It read:

We have received considerable intelligence confirming following developments in Indo-China.
A. 1. Accelerated Japanese preparation of airfields and railways.
2. Arrival since 10 November of additional 100,000 repeat 100,000 troops and considerable quantities fighters, medium bombers, tanks and guns (75mm).
B. Estimate of specific quantities have already been telegraphed Washington 21 November by American Military Intelligence here.
C. *Our considered opinion concludes that Japan envisages early hostilities with Britain and the US.* Japan does not repeat not intend to attack Russia at present but will act in South.
You may inform Chiefs of American Military and Naval Intelligence Honolulu. [Emphasis added]. [60]

Paragraph A reflected a steady stream of SIS reports on the Japanese military build-up through November, including valuable insights from the French intelligence source Sectude.[61] These reports confirmed those passed on diplomatic channels from the British consul, William Meiklereid, in Saigon.[62] The judgement in paragraph C was influenced by SIGINT reporting, but also reflected the information in paragraph A.[63] 'Our' in paragraph C referred to SIS headquarters. This assessment would have been shared with both the Joint Intelligence Committee, of which Menzies was a member, and the prime minister whom he saw daily. On the same day it was issued, the chiefs of staff instructed the Joint Intelligence Committee, which now judged war likely, to provide a daily intelligence update to Far East commanders, confirming that the chiefs too now accepted that early attack was probable.[64] It is inconceivable C's message was not copied to FECB, who had already received copies of the SIS reports underpinning paragraph A.[65]

The significance of the SIS assessment is that it is sharper and more decisive than the 28 November Joint Intelligence Committee assessment, which kept more options open. It reflected a distinct shift in the weight of evidence pointing to war at the beginning of December. Through November, SIGINT had demonstrated intense Japanese activity in every country that was a potential target for attack. It showed them winding up commitments and perfecting espionage operations with Manila, and Singapore getting particular attention. Meanwhile, the imminence of war was more directly indicated in certain diplomatic traffic, including the 'Winds Alert' on 25 November. This weight of intelligence was 'cumulative' rather than 'sensational' until the beginning of December, when it became rapidly clear hostilities were only days away.[66] This distinct shift in perception explains the tone of the SIS assessment. Its confidence that the Japanese were now committed to attack in the south also, no doubt, reflected a report from SIS Manila to Honolulu dated a week earlier. This cited a secret source (usually reliable) reporting that the Japanese would attack the Kra Isthmus (in southern Thailand) from the sea on 1 December, without any ultimatum or warning, to get between Bangkok and Singapore. Attacking forces would proceed direct from Hainan and Formosa and the main landing point would be in the Songkhla (also known as Singora) area.[67] It is impossible to know whether Phillips saw this SIS material, but FECB would have been negligent if they did not make an exceptional effort to ensure he at least saw C's 2 December assessment.

As already mentioned, signals from a clearly nervous Pound on 1 and 3 December suggested Force Z should be sent away from Singapore.[68] These signals were primarily triggered by concern about the threat from IJN submarines known to be moving south.[69] Although Pound suggested sending the force eastward, the only realistic options were to return to Ceylon or go to Darwin. It is not clear what Pound meant by going 'eastward'. A later meeting in the Cabinet War Room on 9 December discussed the force 'vanishing among the innumerable islands' of the Malay Barrier. As argued earlier, this was a meaningless concept without a base from which to operate.[70] Goodenough claimed that Phillips did plan to get Force Z away before the outbreak of hostilities, if possible, and saw Darwin as the only credible base.[71] The naval facilities available in Darwin at this time were rudimentary, and the port defences even more so, although the airfield had become a vital staging point for the US Army B-17 force in transit to the Philippines.[72] Another option for Force Z was Balikpapan in southern Borneo, where elements of the US Asiatic

Fleet were based at this time. However, this would have offered little more than refuelling, and defences were again rudimentary, although it was beyond the range of Japanese air attack.

Phillips no doubt felt an immediate retreat would be politically awkward and Singapore had the only dock capable of dealing with urgent defects to *Prince of Wales*.[73] However, he must also have been heavily influenced by the offensive strategy of which he was a prime architect. If he sent his ships away, it would be difficult to convince Hart that Britain was now firmly committed to defending the Malay Barrier, let alone to the forward vision which the Admiralty had embraced. (Goodenough later suggested that he personally never supported forward deployment or took it seriously. During the passage out East, he had advised Phillips to deploy the 'R' class on convoy escort in the Indian Ocean, although 'more senior members of the staff' envisaged a combined battle-fleet operating in the South China Sea.[74]) Overall therefore, immediate departure of the force was never likely, though *Repulse* did embark on a courtesy visit to Darwin, before the sighting of Japanese transports provoked her recall.[75] Apart from providing reassurance to the Australians, this visit was presumably intended to explore Darwin's suitability as an operational base. The Admiralty later implied the departure of *Repulse* was a consequence of Pound's warning signals.[76] This seems unlikely. The Commander-in-Chief Eastern Fleet War Diary states that she was to spend only a few days in Darwin and then return to Singapore.[77]

The most important issue influencing a decision either for immediate withdrawal pre-war, or later deployment into the South China Sea, was the effectiveness of Japanese air power. If the Japanese air threat to Singapore, its immediate environs and the southern part of the South China Sea was judged low or at least manageable, perhaps on a par with that of the Italians to Alexandria, then Phillips could initially wait on events and use Force Z and the reinforcements en route to complicate Japanese planning. If the threat was significant, he would be at serious risk as soon as hostilities opened. There is a long-standing belief that 'neither Phillips nor the Singapore intelligence authorities had reliable information on the strength, types, disposition, or efficiency of enemy aircraft in the Indo-China area'.[78] This conclusion reflects the assessment in the Naval Staff History in 1955.[79] It also reflects the assessment in the First Sea Lord's report on the loss of Force Z in early 1942. That stated that, prior to sailing, Force Z had only 'vague information about bomber forces based in Indo-China'.[80]

This view is not consistent with what is now known of British knowledge of Japanese air capability. Phillips's staff had NID intelligence reports issued up to mid-October available in *Prince of Wales* when she left the United Kingdom. Included were weekly intelligence reports covering upgrades to Indochina airbases and the ability of IJNAF heavy bombers to reach Singapore.[81] There was plenty here to stimulate searching questions to FECB on arrival regarding the latest threat picture. However, it appears Phillips was not as well briefed as he could or should have been on what FECB knew. He apparently did not visit FECB, or receive a personal briefing, and it is doubtful his staff had the right contacts either.[82]

The intelligence available to FECB was inevitably incomplete, but quite good enough to demonstrate that the latest estimates of Japanese aircraft numbers and their known capability, especially the IJNAF component, would make any foray north of Singapore a high-risk enterprise. On 2 December FECB reported the total number of aircraft in Indochina was 300, with 180 in the south, including ninety heavy bombers. By 4 December the estimated total had risen to 450 and by 6 December to 500.[83] These FECB estimates compare favourably with the post-war Japanese figure of 564 aircraft committed to operations in Thailand and Malaya at the start of the war. The 564 aircraft split into 447 IJAAF (seventy-two reconnaissance, 168 fighters, 108 light bombers, ninety-nine heavy bombers) and 117 IJNAF (nine reconnaissance aircraft, thirty-six fighters, seventy-two land-based bombers).[84] The primary source for FECB tracking of evolving air strength in Indochina was through radio traffic analysis. A member of the FECB staff recalled after the war the process for identifying air movements in the Saigon area in late 1941: 'By means of Direction Finding (DF) and study of radio traffic, movements and locations of Japanese Air Force squadrons were plotted. Call signs were in the main confirmed by use of Radio Finger Printing equipment and possible sighting reports and known sighting reports and known squadron connections'.[85]

FECB were also aware the aircraft in Indochina now included torpedo bombers. Two sources confirm this: Wing Commander Roy Chappell, the head of the Air Section in FECB, and Doig, who claimed to have discussed this with FECB staff during 1941. Chappell stated in 1978 that he was asked by Brooke-Popham to provide an assessment of the current air threat to Force Z just two hours before its departure on the afternoon of 8 December. He advised that Phillips could expect to be attacked by at least 100 aircraft operating from bases in Indochina around Saigon and comprising high-level bombers and, above all, torpedo bombers. The reference to Saigon is significant. This is indeed where the IJN attack aircraft were based so FECB had located them correctly and it confirms the accuracy of Chappell's memory. However, it appears Phillips and his staff assumed that the aircraft were based at Ca Mau, 150 miles southwest of Saigon, supposedly on the basis of FECB advice.[86] Ca Mau was a reasonable worst-case estimate (bringing the bases closer to Force Z's track), but it also underlines that Phillips's staff had not properly exploited what FECB in fact knew. Chappell insisted he knew that the IJN especially favoured torpedo bombing and were highly trained in it. He emphasised the attackers would be land-based, because of intelligence that there were no carriers in the area.[87] Chappell was well qualified to comment on IJN air capability. He had trained IJN aircrew at Yokohama in 1930/31, and had been air attaché at the embassy in Tokyo from 1935–38.[88] Doig's recollection was that FECB knew that both the IJN land-based attack bombers, the Type 96 Nell and Type 1 Betty, were torpedo-capable, but believed their effective range was limited to 300 miles, whereas in reality it was at least twice that.[89]

It is unlikely that Chappell's intelligence, assuming it was passed on by Brooke-Popham, was properly absorbed and understood by either Phillips or key members of his staff.[90] In his post-action report, drafted within hours on the destroyer *Express*, the Captain of the Fleet, Captain L H Bell, stated that the admiral was well aware of the threat from airbases in Indochina, but expected strikes from there to be hastily organised, and to comprise aircraft armed with fragmentation bombs, rather than anti-ship bombs or torpedoes.[91] They also assumed a maximum range of around 300 miles, similar to Doig, based on Mediterranean experience.[92] The failure of the staff to engage directly with Chappell, who could have provided a wealth of valuable background, was negligent, and demonstrates that the widespread belief that little was known of IJN air capability in the theatre is wrong. In his 1942 despatch, Brooke-Popham said he had been asked by Phillips's chief of staff, Rear Admiral Palliser, for an estimate of the air threat and responded with '50 or 60 bombers five hours after location'.[93] This does not fit with Chappell's testimony. It is likely, therefore, that Brooke-Popham gave Palliser an initial response based on his previous understanding, but then asked Chappell for a more informed view. This underlines that Palliser was dealing with FECB at one remove, and would have gained much more from direct contact. It is also surprising that he did not seek advice from Layton, who as Commander-in-Chief China continued for the present to oversee FECB.

FECB was not the only source of expertise on the air threat. There was the knowledge of Royal Air Force staff to draw on. They had initially underestimated the scale of air attack the Japanese would be able to generate from bases in Indochina, and potentially Thailand, on a sustained basis. Estimates here were based on the number of airfields judged capable of operating heavy bombers and the capacity needed to support adequate reconnaissance and fighter escort.[94] However, the picture was changing rapidly during October and November as the Japanese put major effort into airfield construction, which had been recognised as a key warning indicator. There were also the papers noted previously, confirming that Royal Air Force knowledge of IJAAF and IJNAF aircraft capability was good. They included the brief prepared for Brooke-Popham by Darvall, as his chief of staff, which estimated that heavy bombers could carry a bomb-load of 4000lbs (1800kg) up to 1000 miles, and also noted a long-range fighter capable of reaching 1500 miles.[95] There was enough information here to warn Phillips and his staff to err on the side of caution regarding Japanese strike range.

Given this intelligence available to FECB and Royal Air Force headquarters, Phillips and his staff made three fatal errors in assessing the air risk to Force Z. They failed to recognise the land-based torpedo threat from Indochina. They also failed to appreciate that a significant proportion of the Indochina strike aircraft belonged to the IJNAF, and could therefore be expected to be well-trained and equipped for anti-ship operations. Finally, they underestimated effective strike range from Indochina bases by a factor of half. Only the last of these errors was excusable. This reflects the difficulty in assessing realistic combat range under full war conditions, set against theoretical ranges calculated from aircraft performance data. These three errors were compounded by underestimation of the size of potential attack forces. The accuracy with which FECB monitored the build-up of Japanese air strength and its breakdown by aircraft type in Indochina through November should have allowed no illusions here.

If Force Z could not operate safely against an invasion force and would be at risk anywhere north of Singapore, there was clearly little military purpose in staying there. Would Phillips, therefore, have considered withdrawal if he had been better briefed on the threat during his first days in Singapore? Any view here is hypothetical, but he would probably still have taken comfort in several factors. He would have judged Singapore itself to be too distant from Indochina for the Japanese air groups there to be a serious threat to the ships while in the base, or on passage out, and no doubt counted on the monsoon limiting flying operations. He took immediate steps to ensure fighter cover if the fleet did sortie, including deployment of aircraft to northern airfields. He could not reasonably have anticipated the rapid collapse of British land and air forces in the north of Malaya in the first two days of war.[96] Despite the prospect of imminent Japanese action, he would have felt he had time to consider the options for Force Z.

If assessment of the air threat defined the limits of safe operation north of Singapore, assessment of IJN surface and submarine forces was important in judging whether Force Z had sufficient power to achieve any useful military effect. Because Force Z succumbed to air attack, British knowledge of IJN surface strength, and the implications this posed, has received less attention in the story of Force Z than it merits. By 1 December, coinciding with Phillips' arrival, FECB had identified 'a special Japanese force' created under the command of Commander-in-Chief Second Fleet, Vice Admiral Nobutake Kondo, to undertake operations in the south, probably focused on Thailand, but possibly including a landing on the Kra Isthmus. They estimated the force comprised eight 8in cruisers, twelve 6in cruisers, four aircraft carriers, fifty-two destroyers and eighteen submarines. FECB wrongly assessed that the bulk of the combined fleet remained in Japan. That was true of the battleships, but the carrier fleet, with two of the *Kongo* battlecruisers, was now en route for Pearl Harbor.[97] NID in London also believed the full combined fleet was still in home waters. The NID 4 situation report of 1 December assessed that the IJN First Fleet here comprised all ten battleships, four carriers, four 8in cruisers, four 6in cruisers, forty destroyers and fifteen submarines. Nevertheless, the FECB report was an accurate assessment of the IJN southern task force that had indeed been created to support the attacks on the Philippines and Malaya commencing 8 December.[98] FECB had not at this stage identified the battlecruisers *Kongo* and *Haruna*, which were also included, and they were unaware that the carriers comprised only the light carrier *Ryujo* and seaplane carriers. FECB also underestimated the number of heavy cruisers, because the Royal Navy still believed the *Mogami* class were armed with 6in guns.

The identification and construction of this southern task force order of battle, achieved in close co-operation with the Americans using traffic analysis, was an impressive achievement by FECB.[99] An example of the specific inputs which contributed to this order of battle is the FECB report dated 15 November stating that the 7th Cruiser Squadron had left Japan for Saigon. NID 4 correctly commented that this comprised the four heavy cruisers *Kumano*, *Mogami*, *Mikuma* and *Suzuya*, but repeated the error that they were armed with 6in guns.[100] Japanese records confirm the despatch of the 7th Cruiser Squadron to join what the Japanese called the Malaya force at this time.[101] It was a further signal of Japanese intent to weigh alongside the other war warnings.

Layton would have closely monitored the development of this intelligence, and presumably gave Phillips a headline summary. Phillips would have recognised that this was a substantial IJN force compared to what he had immediately available but if account was taken of his reinforcements en route and the American and Dutch forces, he no doubt judged it need not rule out carefully planned interventions by *Prince of Wales* and *Repulse*, which were superior to any individual IJN units. Nor did it immediately threaten their security in Singapore. The intelligence was also available to Pound and the naval staff in London and it may have provoked his signals of 1 and 3 December suggesting Force Z should move away from Singapore. The second signal showed particular worry over the submarine threat, which worried Phillips too.[102]

In assessing Phillips's understanding and thinking in these initial days at Singapore, especially in regard to Japanese air power, there is another important factor. This is the contribution and attitude of Layton as outgoing Commander-in-Chief China. Layton has been treated kindly by historians, based primarily on his perceived outstanding performance as Commander-in-Chief Ceylon from March 1942 to 1945, an appointment 'without doubt one of the best Churchill ever made'.[103] His performance as Commander-in-Chief Eastern Fleet after the death of Phillips is perhaps less convincing. He wrote a coruscating critique of British performance in the battle for Malaya, where he emphasised the failure of London to allocate the resources known to be necessary to defend the Far East, but also widespread failures of leadership, and a disappointing performance by the US Asiatic Fleet, especially its submarines.[104] However, this posed questions about ambiguity in his attitude to reinforcement through 1941, and his failure to anticipate and address Japanese coastal infiltration, which was a naval responsibility. He also displayed notably poor judgement and poor leadership on at least two specific occasions: his address to the Force Z survivors in Singapore on 11 December, and his 'I'm alright Jack' departure signal when he decided to abandon Singapore for Colombo on 4 January 1942.[105] But it is the silence on his input and influence between Phillips's arrival and the departure of Force Z on its final operation on the evening of 8 December that is striking. Doig said little about this, despite being perfectly placed as Layton's secretary to comment on relations between the two admirals. He did confirm that Phillips arrived in Singapore the evening of 29 November. This meant Phillips had four full days in Singapore prior to his departure by air to Manila on 4 December.[106]

Layton had been in post since September 1940. He knew the Far East area well. He had been chief of staff on the China Station before the war, was familiar with the IJN and had high regard for its capabilities.[107] He had played a key role in the negotiations with the Americans and the Dutch through 1941, and was respected by Hart and his staff. Earlier in the year, Hart noted in his diary: 'Vice Admiral Layton has my people's entire liking and respect – as a fine example of the blue water school of the Royal Navy. He is direct, frank and forceful. In as much as he holds back on anything to do with long range planning, there is the possibility important decisions may not be reached soon enough'. The final sentence reflected the difficulties over practical implementation of the ABC-1 agreement.[108]

Layton made little secret of his disappointment at being superseded by Phillips, whom he viewed as a staff officer ill-prepared for senior operational command. He was not alone in this view. Somerville and Cunningham felt the same. According to Doig, Layton regarded Phillips as a theorist 'who clung to his opinions even when all the facts were against him', and who lacked practical experience.[109] Given Phillips's forceful character and potential sensitivity to being patronised by an admiral of greater seniority in the Navy

List, their relationship and handover would not have been easy at the best of times, let alone under the pressure of imminent war. Goodenough also later expressed views which suggest their handover was unlikely to have been comfortable. Far East commanders had failed to appreciate the fundamental change in the strategic picture brought about by the Japanese occupation of southern Indochina. An attack on Malaya now merely involved a 'ferrying operation', rather than a long sea voyage. This was an outrageous slur, displaying arrogance on the part of Goodenough, and perhaps Phillips, rather than any failings by Layton or Brooke-Popham. Indochina certainly gave Japan a good jumping-off point with much reduced warning of attack, but the most critical problem it brought to the fore was the imbalance of air power, which Far East commanders had constantly stressed and London had ignored. Brooke-Popham had also driven forward Operation Matador, which was designed to counter the new risk to northern Malaya.[110]

The handover was further complicated by the decision made on Phillips's arrival that while he would formally assume the new role of Commander-in-Chief Eastern Fleet on 3 December, Layton should remain in post as Commander-in-Chief China, responsible for 'local command and administration', for a further week until completion of the British naval conference to develop Pound's post-ABD strategy.[111] The China command would then merge into the Eastern Fleet and Layton would depart to be Commander-in-Chief Portsmouth.[112] This temporary division of responsibility meant Layton retained control of FECB, liaison with the Royal Air Force on reconnaissance into the Gulf of Siam, and the Dutch submarines lent to his command, which would be a valuable asset in detecting and then attacking any convoys heading for the Kra Isthmus or Malaya once they were declared hostile. Layton, no doubt with his own axes to grind, later painted a rather chaotic picture of Admiralty decisions regarding the new command arrangements in the Far East. Significantly, he believed, and firmly recommended to the First Sea Lord, that command should be exercised from ashore, because of the sheer size and complexity of the area.[113]

There were three critical issues on which Layton had the expertise and experience, and indeed the duty, to advise and guide Phillips. They were arguably the most important matters for Phillips to address between his arrival in Singapore and his departure for Manila. Yet how far Layton offered, and Phillips accepted, his help is unclear. The silence from contemporary witnesses and records on the level of Phillips's engagement with Layton is matched by an equal silence on his contact with Brooke-Popham. In his 1942 despatch, Brooke-Popham mentions that there was no opportunity for 'full consultation' with Phillips before he departed on Force Z's final voyage.[114] Such consultation should also have been a major priority for Phillips and it is hard to believe it could not be arranged during the four days Phillips spent in Singapore before departing for Manila.

The first issue for discussion with Layton (and indeed Brooke-Popham) was the overall intelligence picture. As Commander-in-Chief China, Layton was the beneficiary of the Royal Navy's long-standing primacy in Far East intelligence. He supervised FECB and visited it regularly, he oversaw the SIGINT relationship with the US Navy at Corregidor in the Philippines, and he received regular reporting from DNI in London and from Washington. As Doig later underlined – 'both Admiral Layton and myself were in regular, almost constant, contact with Harkness (COIS Far East) and FECB'. 'You may take it that Layton had all information on the IJN available in the FECB.'[115] Layton no doubt shared some intelligence insights in private discussion with Phillips, but he apparently did not arrange, let alone insist on, a proper professional briefing for Phillips and his staff from the FECB experts. Harkness was later adamant he did not meet or brief Phillips. He was also unaware of any contacts FECB had with Phillips's staff, although he accepted some informal individual contact could have occurred. Harkness also confirmed that no briefing was set up by Layton which Phillips then declined to take up. Harkness was not even informed that Force Z was sailing on 8 December.[116]

A proper FECB briefing would have tested current assumptions regarding Japanese intentions, and underlined the sheer scale of air, surface, and submarine force the IJN could now potentially bring to bear from Indochina and in the South China Sea. In the event, as noted above, Force Z would deploy on 8 December believing the main air threat was from army bombers in Indochina, when FECB knew they were navy bombers and torpedo-capable.[117] Phillips's failure to engage with FECB is especially odd, because he knew the history of the of the successful SIGINT effort against the IJN from his time as Director of Plans, and he had seen the value of Ultra and Magic at first hand as VCNS. He had also been prepared to back intelligence-driven operations proposed by unconventional figures such as the 21-year-old historian Harry Hinsley from Bletchley Park.[118]

The second issue was the implications the latest intelligence posed for existing Far East war plans and the role of Force Z. The war plans were enshrined in a document known as PLENAPS (Plans for the Employment of Naval and Air Forces of the Associated Powers), which had been updated by Layton as recently as 12 November and defined how the associated powers would respond to Japanese action against the Philippines, Malaya or the Netherlands East Indies. The PLENAPS plans were based on agreement reached by the British and Dutch in April 1941, but also took account of the likely deployment of American forces in the event of United States war with Japan.[119] If deterrence had failed, as seemed all too likely by 1 December, and a Japanese move into Thailand and the Kra Peninsula, and conceivably Malaya, was imminent, did PLENAPS remain a suitable framework for responding, and what were the options for the embryonic Eastern Fleet in the event of conflict?

Doig's paper for Layton in early October, highlighting the potential exposure of a small force in Singapore, was relevant here. Layton later claimed he had never been consulted on the decisions regarding naval reinforcement in autumn 1941, rather implying he disagreed with them.[120] If this was his implication, he was being disingenuous. He had been kept well-informed by the Admiralty of reinforcement plans as they evolved over the course of the year in successive signals, and in a recent letter from Pound in September advising of the intent to move the 'R' class, together with *Rodney* and *Nelson* into the Indian Ocean. As Doig shows, he had chosen not to intervene.[121] While not consulted specifically on the Force Z deterrent concept, given the circumstances in which that deployment was agreed, it aligned closely with the recommendation he and Brooke-Popham had put forward to the chiefs of staff earlier in October.[122] Layton had also played a central role in the ADB negotiations and no obvious differences had emerged during these between him and the naval staff. Where he did perhaps have cause for complaint was over the Admiralty's new offensive strategy. Here, he does not appear to have been properly informed. He was not copied on Pound's signal to Stark of 5 November proposing the post-ABD policy, whereas Phillips as senior officer Force G was. However, the immediate issue for discussion between Layton and Phillips on the latter's arrival was the role and vulnerability of Force Z and the existing China fleet assets if the Japanese triggered hostilities before any further reinforcements arrived.

Layton had been able to monitor the Japanese air build-up in Indochina through FECB during November. He had experienced the impact of German bombing off Norway in 1940, and must have recognised how the growing IJN air strength would curtail operations in the South China Sea. He also had a good picture of the surface forces the IJN could commit to the south and their capability. Against this background, it may be argued that there were only ever three choices for Force Z once it reached Singapore – namely those put by Phillips at his pre-sailing meeting on 8 December. These were to hold fast in Singapore awaiting reinforcements; to retreat to Ceylon or Australia; or to mount judicious raids against Japanese attacking forces.[123] Although this last option was arguably in accord with the principles of PLENAPS, it is tempting to argue that Layton would have seen the hazards it posed for Force Z more clearly than Phillips. Layton was subsequently wont to suggest this, without ever quite committing himself. Thus he would later suggest to his staff, though significantly not to Pound, that he disagreed with Phillips's decision to deploy

Force Z on 8 December.[124] By contrast, he told Pound he would have done exactly the same as Phillips, but only if air cover was definitely available.[125] If Layton was better sighted on the risks of operating from Singapore, then it is tempting to imagine he might have encouraged Phillips to get Force Z back to Ceylon as soon as possible, even though there is no evidence that he did.

Such reasoning overlooks three important things that Layton and Phillips did not know, but with the benefit of hindsight are taken for granted in judging the naval outlook in Singapore in early December. First, the Far East Command would fail to execute Operation Matador, the plan to pre-empt the Japanese by seizing the strategically vital Kra Isthmus before they did.[126] Secondly, the deterrent value of the US Navy Pacific Fleet would be removed by the attack on Pearl Harbor. Thirdly, the substantial modern submarine force of the US Navy Asiatic Fleet, on which Layton clearly set much store, would completely fail to inflict any damage on the IJN.[127] Had Matador been successfully executed, had the Pacific Fleet remained as a deterrent factor on the Japanese flank, however distant, and had the Asiatic Fleet submarines started laying into Japanese convoys, all of which Layton and Phillips could reasonably anticipate as possibilities from their vantage point at the beginning of December, then the case for Force Z holding its position at Singapore, as the nucleus of a 'fleet in being' ready to make judicious interventions, looks more credible. Phillips, with the experience and authority of an ex-Vice Chief of Naval Staff, could indeed reasonably argue that, in terms of capital units, with *Revenge* already in the Indian Ocean and United States forces to throw into the balance, his position in Singapore was little different to that of the Mediterranean Fleet at Alexandria in mid-1941 following the losses at Crete, and no more vulnerable. It is unlikely Layton would have seen matters differently and argued against a Phillips assessment that there was time to consider the options for Force Z once it arrived. There were, indeed, always three options facing Force Z, but the balance of argument between those options looked very different on 1 December from that a week later.

The third area where Layton's advice was important to Phillips was the relationship with the Americans and the forthcoming meeting with Hart to negotiate new post-ABD plans, which had been a key factor in hastening Force Z's passage to Singapore. The Americans had refused to endorse ABD-2 for the same reasons they had rejected ABD-1.[128] They were not convinced the Royal Navy was willing to make a serious commitment to the forward defence of the Malay Barrier. Without this, they believed the whole Far East area would collapse under Japanese attack. In consequence, they had refused to place the Asiatic Fleet under Royal Navy strategic direction, as agreed in the ABC-1 staff talks.[129] The picture had now changed radically following Pound's mid-November exchanges with Stark, but also with British endorsement of the

United States decision to hold the Philippines. The recent developments had, however, created considerable confusion over the role and status of the Asiatic Fleet. In September, Hart was planning in the event of war to fight a defensive battle north of the barrier, operating from Balikpapan in Borneo and Singapore, broadly in accord with ABD-2 principles. By end October, in a dramatic change of plan, he had decided to concentrate all his forces in the Philippines, and was even contemplating more offensive operations under MacArthur's air umbrella, only to have these proposals rejected by Stark.[130] The end of November, therefore, found his fleet evenly divided between Manila and Balikpapan, and no coherent strategy agreed with Washington.[131]

It seems likely that on 1 December neither Layton nor Phillips had a complete picture of recent developments in London, Washington and Manila, since neither had received all the relevant signals. It should, however, have been clear to them, if they pooled their knowledge, that there were three pressing questions to address with Hart if war was now imminent. In the light of the latest intelligence, these questions took priority over Pound's plans for a new ABC-1-based understanding on Far East naval defence, built around all the planned British and American reinforcements available by March 1942. The immediate questions were: whether Hart (and MacArthur) judged it possible to hold the Philippines with existing forces; whether the existing Eastern Fleet of Force Z-plus and the Asiatic Fleet could possibly keep open communications between Singapore and Manila; and, most important of all, confirmation that if the Philippines could not be held, Hart would retire his forces southwest to Singapore. In the event, Hart failed to do this, much to Layton's disappointment and anger.[132]

Phillips's meetings with MacArthur and Hart on 6 December have received little attention in the coverage of the controversies around Far East naval reinforcement in 1941 and the loss of Force Z. This partly reflects the limited records, virtually all on the American side, but more a view that the substance of the talks was completely overtaken by the Japanese attacks the following day, and therefore had little bearing on subsequent events.[133] The meetings deserve more scrutiny for two reasons. First, they represent the culmination of the Admiralty's offensive strategy initiated in Phillips's office on 30 September, and expose the flaws in that strategy. Secondly, they offer a good insight into Phillips's thinking and priorities in these final days of his life.

Phillips's immediate priority, as it appeared to Hart, was to secure the transfer of the two divisions of US Navy destroyers to support the Eastern Fleet promised by Stark the previous month.[134] Phillips argued that the US Navy had promised to provide these destroyers in the event of war with Japan, and this now seemed imminent. If Japan attacked, he intended to take his battle-fleet north from Singapore to counter any landings and needed the destroyers to

protect it. Hart initially hedged on destroyers, and would only make a provisional commitment to release one division from the two currently based at
Balikpapan. Hart did, in fact, release these four destroyers to Phillips before
they parted on the afternoon of 6 December, following the news that a probable
Japanese invasion convoy had been sighted by Royal Air Force reconnaissance
in the Gulf of Siam. The four destroyers reached Singapore on 9 December and
met the surviving Force Z destroyers at sea the following afternoon.[135]

Looking more widely, the admirals agreed the initiative would lie with Japan
in the early stages of a war and this rendered precise Allied planning difficult.
They nevertheless agreed on initial dispositions in the event of imminent
hostilities. These aimed at countering the most likely offensive actions and
preventing IJN movement through the Malay Barrier, which they judged 'of
great importance'. The proposed deployments reflected the framework already
agreed under PLENAPS, but took account of the new Royal Navy reinforcements. The key Royal Navy contribution would now be the Eastern Fleet based
in Singapore, which would operate as a striking force against Japanese moves
into the South China Sea, against the Netherlands East Indies, or through the
barrier. Phillips told Hart he expected to have four capital ships available
before the end of the month, *Revenge* and *Royal Sovereign* joining Force Z, but
no carrier before spring 1942, thus confirming he did not expect
Indomitable.[136] In addition to the Singapore battle-fleet, two other forces
would be deployed to meet the expected Japanese attack: a cruiser group based
at East Borneo and the US Navy submarine fleet, which would remain based
in the Philippines. Further light forces would protect the waters of Australasia
and the Indian Ocean. The admirals also agreed that, as reinforcements
arrived, more offensive operations would become possible. These would be
better conducted from Manila, which should be developed to accommodate
the Royal Navy Eastern Fleet by 1 April.[137] Hart recorded that he was
impressed by Phillips, who seemed offensively minded, and genuinely
determined to contribute serious Royal Navy forces to holding the barrier.
However, he thought the primary Royal Navy goal was still protection of
strategic communications in the Indian Ocean, and the tendency to disperse
forces to achieve this had not disappeared.[138]

The formal report and recommendations from the meeting hardly amounted
to a coherent joint strategy for the Far East naval area. It certainly fell well
short of the elusive 'joint operating plan' which had been pursued since the
conclusion of the ABC-1 staff talks. The outcome is best described as a
commitment to work together, a series of rather broad aspirations, and an
initial distribution of forces which the admirals hoped would achieve these.
There are two striking omissions from the record. The first is any attempt to
set their aspirations and forces against current IJN capability and intent. Given

331

the latest intelligence regarding the southern task force, on which Hart,[139] if not Phillips, was well sighted, was it really possible to contest a seaborne invasion force against either the Philippines or the Kra Isthmus with existing forces, as opposed to those available by March 1942? The second omission was any reference to the air balance which would clearly be crucial to effective operations in the South China Sea. PLENAPS, as a naval and air plan, had made some effort to address this, but recent Japanese reinforcements in Indochina were changing the picture rapidly. A further issue that was either not addressed, or not resolved, was where Hart would withdraw with his remaining forces if the Philippines could not be held. His failure to support Layton at Singapore would prove contentious later.[140] Despite these omissions, the conference recommendations were approved by Stark as Chief of Naval Operations on 7 December as the IJN was moving in on Pearl Harbor. Pound's response would be overtaken by events.

From the British perspective, the conference recommendations gave initial practical effect to the offensive strategy which the Admiralty had been developing since late September. Phillips not only confirmed the Royal Navy was committed to building up a battle-fleet at Singapore capable of operating forward in the South China Sea, but he also emphasised he would remain at Singapore while he awaited reinforcements. His whole stance at the meeting suggests he never seriously contemplated withdrawal to the Indian Ocean, or to Darwin. Despite Pound's earlier caution, his final exchanges with Phillips following the conference and, indeed, the outbreak of war suggest he too remained committed to concentrating the 'R'-class battleships and whatever cruisers could be spared with Force Z at Singapore.[141] Phillips's plea to Hart for the immediate release of US Navy destroyers so that he could intervene against any Japanese landings, by implication even with his current limited force, was also highly significant. It suggests his decision to sortie on 8 December reflected the offensive approach he had favoured since September, and was not just a reaction to immediate events. He confirmed his intention to intervene as the meeting broke up on the afternoon of 6 December, following the news that the Japanese convoys had been sighted.[142]

In the light of subsequent developments, it is difficult to understand how Phillips left the conference on 6 December, as he clearly did, convinced that forward deployment in defence of Malaya and the wider barrier was viable, even with the existing balance of forces. Possibly he was influenced by bombastic guarantees from General Douglas MacArthur, commander of United States land-based forces in the Philippines. He would have taken the containing role of the US Navy Pacific Fleet into account too.[143] However, it is also important to recognise that, on paper, the combined American-Dutch-British forces which the admirals expected to have available by end December looked significant. Excluding the forces committed south and west of the barrier, they comprised three battleships, one battlecruiser, four heavy cruisers, five light cruisers, twenty-four destroyers and forty submarines. These were to be distributed as follows: at Singapore, three battleships, one battlecruiser, one heavy cruiser, four light cruisers, twenty destroyers, four submarines; East Borneo, three heavy cruisers, one light cruiser, four destroyers; Manila: twenty-nine submarines; Netherlands East Indies, seven submarines; Australasia,one heavy cruiser, two light cruisers; Indian Ocean, one heavy cruiser, ten light cruisers. In total, this appeared a credible counterweight to the IJN southern task force, especially when United States air reinforcements in the Philippines were added to the balance.

There were, however, important flaws in a paper balance based on 'bean counting'. First, with the notable exception of *Prince of Wales*, and in theory the US Navy *Tambor*-class submarines, the Allied units were outclassed by their IJN counterparts in both capability and, in some cases, fighting efficiency. Secondly, both the putative Eastern Fleet itself and its American and Dutch Allies were a heterogeneous mix that had not trained together and were thus ill-matched for joint operations. Contesting the barrier against IJN surface forces depended heavily on the credibility of the Singapore battle-fleet strike force. Yet, as discussed earlier, the 'R'-class battleships were quite unsuited to this role and equally unsuited to operating with *Prince of Wales* and *Repulse*, where they had a speed deficit of 10 knots. The designed speed of the 'R'-class was 21 knots, but by this time most of them struggled consistently to achieve 18 knots. *Prince of Wales* and *Repulse* could both comfortably make 28 knots. Thirdly, the US Navy submarine force, of which much was expected by Royal Navy commanders, would prove totally ineffective in its first months of combat, achieving no useful results against the IJN. Finally, and most important, the assessments and dispositions of 6 December woefully underestimated the Japanese ability to achieve rapid air supremacy, and to conduct long-range maritime strike.

As emphasised earlier, Phillips could not know that the US Navy submarine force would prove ineffective, or that the US Navy Pacific Fleet and MacArthur's air force would both be removed from the board in short order by the Japanese. He should, however, have displayed more awareness of the limitations posed by the 'R' class and the lack of modern vessels amongst his cruisers and destroyers. His attitude to the Japanese air threat is examined in more detail below, but he showed little sign in Manila that he saw this as a serious constraint on his ability to operate forward in the South China Sea. It is conceivable that Phillips saw his position and prospects as not dissimilar to that facing Cunningham when he had sortied from Alexandria in July 1940, immediately after the outbreak of war, to challenge Italian communications with Libya in the central Mediterranean. Cunningham had then fought the successful action off Calabria, despite severe Italian bombing. The IJN was a much more formidable opponent, as Phillips would certainly have accepted, but this was, in theory, offset by the overall American contribution. The analogy, therefore, still had some validity at least in bolstering the case to stay in Singapore. In reality, given the speed and scale of the Japanese attack and the limitations of Allied air power after the destruction of MacArthur's air assets, it is impossible to envisage scenarios where Phillips and Hart could ever have successfully challenged a Japanese attack on Malaya or the Philippines. Their only real hope was to secure communications to Australia and the Indian Ocean, and to slow the Japanese advance through judicious raids beyond the reach of their air power, buying time for reinforcements.

The deployment of Force Z against the Japanese landings on 8 December
Hong Kong intercepted the Japanese 'Winds Execute' message advising diplomatic posts of imminent hostilities against the United States and Britain at about 2300 (local) on 7 December. FECB was immediately informed by priority signal and duty staff there informed Harkness and Layton.[144] They had about two hours' advance warning before news arrived of the landings in northern Malaya. Given its presence in Singapore when the Japanese attacked, it would have been immensely difficult for Force Z to stand idly by with a seaborne invasion underway which the Royal Navy had spent two decades planning to counter. It was even harder for Phillips to stand aside, given his commitment to the offensive policy north of the barrier and the attitude he had displayed in his discussions with Hart. As ex-Vice Chief of Naval Staff, he would also have been acutely aware of the potential damage done to Britain's defensive prospects in northern Malaya by the decision not to execute Operation Matador.

There were more personal factors too. Phillips had been relentless during his time as VCNS, along with Churchill and Pound, in hounding senior commanders who were judged to have failed to 'engage the enemy more closely'. Two well-known examples here are the criticism of Somerville for not pursuing the Italian fleet during the action off Cape Spartivento in November 1940, and the criticism of Rear Admiral Frederick Wake-Walker and Captain John Leach of *Prince of Wales* for breaking off the action with *Bismarck* after the sinking of *Hood* on 24 May 1941.[145] Knowing the scepticism in some quarters over his appointment, this was not a charge he would have wished to bring on himself. He would have wanted to prove he was a 'fighting admiral', as well as a highly regarded staff officer.

Much attention has focused on the Admiralty signal to Phillips on 7 December, asking what action might be taken against the Japanese convoys sighted the previous day if they were confirmed to be heading for Thailand,

Malaya or the Netherlands East Indies.[146] This is invariably interpreted as a typical Churchill-inspired 'prodding' signal – 'something must be done' – which Phillips would have read as a spur to action. Despite its attractions to those wedded to an anti-Churchill line, this signal must be placed in the context both of discussions in London and other guidance sent to Phillips. Exchanges between the prime minister and chiefs of staff demonstrate that they were agreed it was militarily advantageous to attack the convoys at sea, but both were also aware of the political risks in any pre-emptive action and the need, above all, to ensure American support.[147]

Following clarification of the United States attitude, the Admiralty sent Phillips updated rules of engagement. These authorised him to respond to any Japanese attack on British, United States, Dutch or Thai territory, but to await further instructions on pre-emptive action at sea.[148] This signal reflected instructions from the prime minister that Phillips should be kept informed of the wider political context and exchanges with the Americans.[149] The promised further instructions on action against convoys at sea were never sent, since the requirement was overtaken by the Japanese landings. As London wrestled with its options, it was perfectly reasonable for the Admiralty to seek Phillips's views on what seemed possible on the ground. The chiefs of staff note of 6.15pm on 6 December shows that Pound was aware *Prince of Wales* was in dock and that *Repulse* was absent from Singapore. There were therefore clear limits on Phillips's immediate ability to act against the convoys.[150] It is also unlikely Phillips needed any 'prodding'. Given his comments in Manila, it seems likely he returned already disposed to intervene against any landings, or against convoys at sea, if he received political clearance.

What the exchanges between the prime minister and chiefs of staff do demonstrate unambiguously is that they assumed action against the convoys was militarily feasible with the existing British naval and air forces based in Malaya, if the political constraints could be addressed. A chiefs of staff note sent to the prime minister on the afternoon of 7 December, but then overtaken by news of the Pearl Harbor attack, included the language: 'from the purely military point of view, we should like to attack a Japanese expedition before it reached its objective', so long as the 'weight of attack is sufficient to make firing the first shot worthwhile'. There is no indication here that either Pound or the other chiefs considered an attack by Force Z on the convoys transiting the Gulf of Siam an unacceptably risky proposition, although they knew they were escorted by powerful IJN surface forces. They should have recognised the convoys would have good air cover too.[151] It followed that once the Japanese landings began early on 8 December, Phillips could reasonably assume London would expect him to retaliate against the expedition if he judged the risk–benefit equation made sense.

Churchill's post-war claim that Phillips's subsequent sortie on 8 December was contrary to the wishes of the Defence Committee was distinctly disingenuous. Besides rejecting the charge of political interference, he insisted that the purpose of Force Z was deterrence, and that on arrival at Singapore, the intention was that the force should 'disappear' in the Malay Archipelago. He added: 'The last thing in the world that the Defence Committee wished was that anything like the movement which Admiral Phillips thought it right to make to intercept a Japanese invasion force should have been made by his two vessels without even air cover'.[152] This was a highly selective account. It was true that the Defence Committee, when it met on the evening of 9 December, favoured 'disappearance', but no final decision was made. Phillips knew nothing of this meeting. What he did believe, quite correctly, was that two days earlier London appeared keen to exploit any opportunity for bold intervention against a Japanese expedition.

It is unlikely that any Royal Navy admiral on the spot, faced with the circumstances on 8 December, would have stayed in port or retreated, and the official Admiralty report into the loss of Force Z recognised this.[153] So did the brief prepared for the First Lord's secret session statement on 19 December, although admittedly this had a defensive purpose politically.[154] Others would probably have adopted a similar plan for intervention to Phillips, although they might have executed it differently. The senior Royal Navy officers who later criticised Phillips were not entirely convincing, because they usually failed to distinguish between the situation on 8 December and different decisions that might have been made before the outbreak of war. Thus Somerville, Godfrey and Willis[155] all suggested they would have avoided being in Singapore in the first place, by halting at Ceylon or going to Darwin.[156] As we have seen, there was indeed a strong case for holding Force Z at Ceylon, but the critics invariably display too much hindsight and ignore the powerful Admiralty momentum built up by November for fleet concentration at Singapore. As Chapter 8 will demonstrate, a strong argument can also be made that Somerville took rather greater risks in his actions off Ceylon in April 1942 than did Phillips off Malaya. Somerville had less excuse, because IJN potential was by then clearer and he had much more at stake, namely the loss of a major fleet, as opposed to a task force. Some senior Royal Navy critics argued that Layton would have halted Force Z short of Singapore, or sent it away. Layton had ample opportunity to present such arguments, but did not do so. Layton said he spoke to Phillips twice about the proposed sortie during the morning of 8 December, but he did not argue against it. He told Phillips that 'if I were in his shoes I should do the same as he was going to do but I should not start on it unless the Royal Air Force would guarantee reconnaissance and fighter protection'.[157]

Phillips knew he was taking a calculated risk in seeking to disrupt the landings. Successful intervention ultimately depended on three things: fighter cover, surprise and bad weather. Arthur Marder explored the balance of argument for intervention and the thinking behind Phillips's plan in exhaustive detail. Subsequent accounts have not added significantly to his analysis, or challenged his interpretation. Is there any new information now to justify revision of Marder's narrative or his judgement of Phillips's decisions? The obvious candidate is the intelligence picture where, as this book shows, there is now more knowledge, especially of the contribution of FECB. If Phillips had known everything FECB did on 8 December, would he have acted differently? He would have been more anxious about the scale of air attack and, above all, the threat of torpedo bombing to Force Z during the long return passage after an engagement at Singora. He was still willing to continue the operation after receiving a signal from Palliser early on 9 December confirming there would be no fighter support. He did so in the belief he still had surprise, and he also had the benefit of bad weather.

Captain L H Bell, the Captain of the Fleet, later claimed that when Phillips received Palliser's signal, he and the staff decided to discard Singora as a target because it would add up to four hours to the time the force was exposed to air attack during its withdrawal. His four hours is probably a significant underestimate. Phillips was still, however, prepared to attack Kota Bharu if he maintained surprise and, ideally, bad weather.[158] If this claim is true, it helps to explain Phillips's willingness to continue. It would also demonstrate careful thought about how the risk of air attack might be managed. However, the signals Phillips transmitted to Force Z during the afternoon of 9 December, more than twelve hours after Palliser's signal, show that Singora was then still the target. Bell also stated that Singora was the target in his immediate post-action report. Perhaps there was some discussion about switching to Kota Bharu, but Bell's claim must be regarded as unreliable. If there was debate over the relative merits of Singora and Kota Bharu, it is worth noting that the landing force at the former was much larger, ten transports compared to three, and the strategic impact of a successful landing there was much greater. However, Phillips and his team are unlikely to have known this.

Once it was clear surprise too was lost, Phillips aborted the operation late on 9 December, because he rightly judged the risk equation had completely turned against him. The landing ships would have gone and he would face concentrated attack from fully alerted air and surface forces. Would access to FECB's full intelligence have caused Phillips to call off the whole operation earlier on receiving Palliser's signal? It is impossible to say with certainty. However, the signal conveyed a bleak picture of a fast deteriorating situation and included the suggestion that Japanese bomber forces were now operating from Thailand. Awareness of the scale of the torpedo threat, even if aircraft range was underestimated, and that he was facing trained IJNAF crews specialising in maritime attack, could well have made the difference here. If it had turned back at this point, Force Z would have been back in Singapore late on 9 December.

Better intelligence on the torpedo threat would probably not have altered Phillips's subsequent decision early on 10 December to divert to investigate a possible landing at Kuantan while en route back to Singapore. Even with better knowledge of potential IJNAF strike range, prevailing war experience from Europe and the Mediterranean would still have argued that Force Z was now too distant, at 450 miles from Indochina, to be at unacceptable risk. The Admiralty briefing paper prepared for the First Lord's secret session statement on 19 December endorsed this assessment.[159] It was not solely an issue of the theoretical strike range of an armed aircraft, as often implied. It also reflected the increasing difficulty, as range increased, of finding and fixing an enemy force sufficiently accurately in the first place to enable the strike to take place. In 1941, in the absence of radio fixing aids or radar, navigating over sea to find a force at 450 miles was a demanding proposition. The IJN search plan on 10 December was well planned and professionally executed, but they did not find Force Z easily. Professionalism was mixed here with a significant dose of luck.[160]

Better understanding of IJN capability might, however, have persuaded Phillips to ask for air cover when he was first sighted on the morning of 10 December. This just might, in turn, have saved his force. There are different views on what would have happened if fighters from Singapore had arrived before the first critical torpedo attack on *Prince of Wales*. Some argue the fighters would have made little difference to the final outcome.[161] Others believe they would have been effective in limiting the damage.[162] The most positive view of the impact of fighter intervention draws a parallel with a US Navy action on 20 February 1942 when fifteen of seventeen IJN Betty bombers were shot down by a force of Wildcats, broadly equivalent to the Royal Air Force Buffalo force deployable off Kuantan.[163] Despite their limitations as fighters, the Buffalos were capable of ripping apart unescorted bombers. One other point deserves mention. The IJN was very short of torpedoes and only had sufficient in Indochina to allocate one weapon per aircraft. They were thus operating to a very fine margin and were effectively committed to a one-shot attack. If the IJN attack squadrons had failed to inflict significant torpedo damage on Force Z as a consequence of fighter interference, adequate anti-aircraft fire, and manoeuvre, there would have been no second chance.[164]

As regards the surface threat, Force Z sailed with a reasonably accurate picture of the IJN forces. This derived from the visual sightings of the troop convoys and their escorts on 6 December, some additions and clarifications through traffic analysis by FECB, and further Royal Air Force reconnaissance on 9 December.[165] The most important FECB addition to the convoy sightings was the battlecruiser *Kongo*. FECB did not, however, spot the presence of her sister ship *Haruna*.[166] The Royal Navy force was heavily outnumbered, but Phillips no doubt judged that speed, radar and superior firepower offered a good chance of inflicting more damage than he would receive in any engagement between warships. Given the available intelligence, such a judgement still looks fair in hindsight. There were nevertheless two important things British intelligence and, therefore Phillips, did not know: the presence of a second *Kongo* battlecruiser, and the existence of the Japanese Long Lance long-range torpedo launched from surface warships. If he had been able to weigh these factors too, alongside the more accurate picture of the air threat, then the risk–benefit equation might well have looked unfavourable, turning him against the operation.

A fair assessment of the arguments for and against the Force Z sortie in the immediate circumstances prevailing on 8 December must balance the possibility of doing significant damage to the Japanese landing operation against an air threat that was recognised by Phillips, but believed to be manageable. Given what Phillips knew, there is a reasonable case for the decision to deploy, and each of his subsequent tactical decisions.[167] If he had properly exploited FECB's knowledge, he would have been more cautious, but the practical impact on his decisions would have been marginal. Most historians have been more critical of Phillips. While sympathising with his predicament, and recognising the pressures to intervene, they have argued in different ways that his actions reflected his persistent tendency to downplay the air threat at sea, and ignore lessons from the war to date.[168] Their judgement here is that other admirals would have weighed the risks differently.

The case that Phillips had a general disregard for the air threat after two years of war from the vantage point of VCNS, and that he did not regard it as a critical factor in conducting naval operations, is not convincing. The claim invariably attributes views to Phillips that were either expressed long before 1941, or have been lifted out of context.[169] Phillips had regularly pressed for Hurricanes to be deployed to Singapore during 1941, against the opposition of the prime minister and Royal Air Force. He also showed keen awareness of the air threat in considering the viability of Manila as a base during his discussions with Hart on 6 December.[170] If an attempt at intervention was virtually obligatory in the circumstances of 8 December, as the Admiralty later agreed, then the only criticism of Phillips that holds up, and it is one Pound acknowledged,[171] is his failure to seek air support off Kuantan on 10 December once he knew he had been located at 1015 that morning. Here Phillips seems to have placed excessive value on continued radio silence, against what he judged was a very low risk of air attack, given his range from Indochina. Other admirals might well have called this differently.[172]

The real charge against Phillips is not what he did between 8 and 10 December, but his central policy role in placing an inadequate force in Singapore in the first place. There were two related failings here, both shared by Pound, who bears ultimate responsibility. The first was the Admiralty decision, taken in early October and strongly promoted by Phillips, to deploy a battle-fleet forward at Singapore, rather than Ceylon, to contest control of the South China Sea, in the same way that the Mediterranean Fleet had guaranteed the eastern Mediterranean during 1940/41. As argued earlier, this decision might have been defensible, if not wise, had it been part of a carefully concerted series of joint moves, involving additional British air reinforcements and co-ordination with the American build-up in the Philippines. This collaboration did not take place. The Admiralty decision was taken in isolation, and pre-empted the other reinforcements required to make the proposed Eastern Fleet either an effective deterrent or operationally capable. The second failing which compounded the first was the inappropriate composition of the planned Eastern Fleet. It was built around the 'R'-class battleships which the Admiralty, and specifically Phillips, had previously judged unsuited to face the Japanese. The plans included no firm commitment to the modern carrier element seen as essential in the Mediterranean, and even more necessary in the East, given what was known of the IJN.

These failings reflected a mindset on the part of Phillips and Pound, borne out in the discussions with Hart, which led directly to the exposed position of Force Z when the Japanese attacked. Taken together, they represented a classic failure of risk management. The risks in pre-emptive forward deployment had no credible benefit to offset them. Such deployment made no practical difference to United States support in the area, the composition of the force was not likely to deter Japan, and it was not capable of engaging the scale of force she would send south. There was sufficient intelligence in London and Singapore throughout the autumn to demonstrate the level of risk in pre-emption and the superiority of force the Japanese could bring to bear.

The Admiralty's strategic response to the loss of Force Z

The fundamental flaws in the autumn strategy come into sharp relief when viewed against the Admiralty's strategic response to the loss of Force Z and the wider Japanese successes in the first days of the war. Following the sinking of *Prince of Wales* and *Repulse*, Britain's immediate naval position in the Far East looked dire. Naval forces east of Cape Town comprised the unmodernised *Revenge*, the rest of the 'R'-class battleships slowly heading for the Indian

Ocean as they came available, the old light carrier *Hermes* of little military value, a significant force of cruisers, albeit widely dispersed across the theatre, a mere handful of destroyers, many old and in a poor state of efficiency, and negligible land-based air support.[173] The Royal Navy could exert minimal influence over the Japanese advance in Southeast Asia, and do little in the short term to stop forays into the Indian Ocean if the IJN chose to make them. Layton, now Acting Commander-in-Chief Eastern Fleet, informed the Admiralty as early as 13 December that Singapore would be untenable as a naval base, and that residual Royal Navy assets should operate from Colombo. Two days later he recommended that naval effort must now focus on holding critical communications in the Indian Ocean and Pacific.[174]

In the face of this grim outlook, the Admiralty refocused its Far East strategy remarkably quickly. Before the loss of Force Z, Pound had already consulted Cunningham on withdrawing all capital ships and carriers from the Mediterranean in order to meet the Japanese attack.[175] Cunningham responded that, so long as Cyrenaica (and its airfields) was firmly held, it might be possible to substitute air power for the capital units. However, the situation would be precarious. The Italian fleet would get a boost; the political impact on Egypt and Turkey was incalculable; interdiction of Axis supply routes to North Africa would be compromised; and there would be no guarantee of denying the enemy access to the eastern Mediterranean.[176] The Vice Chief of Naval Staff, Vice Admiral Sir Henry Moore, now drew up a comprehensive paper, 'Future British Naval Strategy', for the chiefs of staff, which he completed just six days after the outbreak of war.[177] This emphasised that control of sea communications in the Indian Ocean was essential to enable Britain to supply its forces in the Middle East, support Russia through Persia, reinforce Singapore, and protect Australasia. Only the Atlantic lifeline to North America was more important. Although the United States had a vital stake in the security of the Indian Ocean, it could not contribute to its defence, given its overriding need to protect Hawaii and its western coast. No single base could support a combined fleet able to meet the interests of both Britain and the United States. The Indian Ocean and Pacific must therefore be considered separately, with the Royal Navy responsible for the former.

The paper maintained that the best way to protect the Indian Ocean remained a balanced fleet at Singapore able to dispute command of the South China Sea with Japan. This remained the Admiralty's goal. However, it was impossible to provide an adequate fleet to meet Japanese southern forces, comprising perhaps five capital ships and five aircraft carriers, in the foreseeable future. Singapore must depend on land, air and submarine power while a new Eastern Fleet concentrated in the Indian Ocean. After calculating the minimum forces required in the Atlantic, taking account of US Navy support there, and withdrawing the eastern Mediterranean battle-fleet, the paper anticipated up to nine battleships and three fleet carriers were available for this Eastern Fleet. However, apart from the four 'R'-class battleships, most of these could not deploy until February or later. The fleet would initially base at Trincomalee and Port T (Addu Atoll). Both would need improved support facilities and air defence. The paper concluded that under these proposals, three-quarters of Royal Navy strength in major war vessels would be in the Indian Ocean. This might be considered disproportionate. However, the Royal Navy faced greater enemy forces in the East, and the consequences of a Japanese attack on Australasia were incalculable. A drastic change in policy was justified.

This was a remarkable paper, rapidly endorsed by the chiefs of staff and prime minister. The main points were also summarised for Layton on 17 December, in response to his signals of 13 and 15 December. The Admiralty agreed that defence of Indian Ocean communications had overriding priority and defined a timetable for concentrating a new Eastern Fleet, to be based initially at Ceylon. They also emphasised the importance of Abadan, which was essential to successful prosecution of the war.[178]

Moore's paper had admirably defined Britain's vital interests in the eastern theatre, the forces the IJN could send south, including into the Indian Ocean, the limitations to US Navy support, the scale of Royal Navy commitment required to protect the Indian Ocean, and how it could be found. It showed that the Royal Navy had no intention of sacrificing the eastern theatre, or abandoning it to the United States. On the contrary, it demonstrated that, despite its numerous commitments, the Royal Navy still retained sufficient flexibility and resilience to redeploy to protect what mattered most in that theatre. It also demonstrated that for the Royal Navy, meeting a pressing naval threat from Japan in the East would, indeed, take priority over the eastern Mediterranean, as it had always claimed. Here Moore anticipated that the remaining Mediterranean Fleet battleships, *Queen Elizabeth* and *Valiant*, would go to the Indian Ocean. He explained how air power, notably Beaufort torpedo bombers, would be deployed to compensate for the move of the battle-fleet. In the event, both battleships were severely damaged by Italian frogmen in Alexandria Harbour on the morning of 19 December, rendering the move impossible.

Moore's recommendations required time and, as the next chapter shows, not all of them could be executed, but his paper highlights important issues. It underlines why many of the claims regarding the supposed failings of the Singapore strategy, especially those making a direct connection to the deployment and loss of Force Z, are oversimplified. Deploying a substantial fleet to secure the core eastern empire remained an inescapable commitment to safeguard Britain's overall war effort. The real issue, which the Japanese onslaught had brought to the fore, was clarity on what really mattered in the East. Here, the paper had identified three critical strategic factors which would become ever more explicit within the British war leadership in the coming months. First, the human and material resources and access points of the core eastern empire, comprising India and Australasia, were vital in enabling Britain to sustain a global war effort. Secondly, realising that potential depended on the continued availability of Abadan oil. Thirdly, Persia was a key route for delivering aid to Russia. The next chapter shows that in late 1942 and through 1943 it provided the majority of military supplies to Russia, and may have been critical to keeping her in the war. If Britain was to hold its core empire and maintain an effective contribution to the global war now underway, keeping control of the Persian Gulf and key Indian Ocean communications was indeed an essential minimum objective, after defence of the United Kingdom base and Atlantic lifeline.

Essentially, Moore's paper advocated a defensive holding strategy focused on securing these vital interests. It was implicit that the Indian Ocean could be adequately protected from Ceylon and Australia. Singapore remained the preferred base from which to conduct an aggressive forward defence, if resources had permitted. But it was not ultimately necessary to what mattered most in the eastern theatre, as the Americans had argued through the ABC-1 staff talks. The paper, therefore, advocated a distinction between British territories and interests in Southeast and East Asia, which were not ultimately critical to the empire and Allied war effort, and the Indian Ocean and Australasia, which were. Ghormley, as US Special Naval Adviser in London, emphasised this to Stark on 18 December. ACNS (F), presumably Harwood, had stated that Britain now had two commitments in the East: the security of communications round the Cape to the Middle East and Persian oilfields; and the defence of Australia and New Zealand. If forced to choose between these, Britain would prioritise Australia. The British had also stated that if the Netherlands East Indies oilfields were lost, then the oil requirements of Australasia would have to be met from Persia, which would require fifty extra tankers.[179] This distinction between critical and discretionary interests had been broadly accepted by both Pound and the prime minister through the middle six months of 1941, even if they never confronted its full implications.

How the Admiralty presented the loss of Force Z

Stephen Roskill barely mentioned Moore's December strategy paper in his official history. Nevertheless, his summary of Royal Navy eastern strategy between the loss of Force Z and the creation of a new Eastern Fleet in the Indian Ocean has proved influential and long lasting. His first volume concluded that 'under the impact of disaster (ie the loss of Force Z), we reverted to the policy which the Admiralty originally wished to adopt', namely Pound's 'defensive' strategy in the August exchange with the prime minister.[180] His second volume reiterated that the Admiralty's preferred (August 1941) strategy to counter the growing risk from Japan was 'to build up a substantial fleet in Ceylon', to protect the vital Indian Ocean communications. This fleet was to be in place 'by March 1942', and available to move to Singapore when required. The suddenness of Japan's onslaught overtook this graduated strategy, and 'the first reinforcements sent east met with immediate disaster.'[181]

This view was consistent with how the Admiralty presented the Force Z story, both in the formal account of its loss, and through the more informal testimony of key participants. The formal accounting comprised an Admiralty inquiry, initially conducted by Captain John Terry, the Director of Operations Division (Foreign), and Captain William Davis, now Assistant Director of Plans.[182] Bellars was not involved and left the Director of Plans post in early March, after barely six months in the job, to command the cruiser Norfolk.[183] The inquiry conclusions were stark: (i) Since the available force was an 'unbalanced' one, stationing it at Singapore was 'strategically unsound'; (ii) In the circumstances prevailing at Singapore on 8 December, Commander-in-Chief Eastern Fleet was 'left with no alternative', but to attempt a raid on the enemy's sea communications. For this he had to use his ships not as a covering force but as a striking force.[184] These conclusions were considerably tempered in the final report submitted to Pound by Moore as VCNS and Harwood as ACNS (F). They stated: (i) The decision to send an 'unbalanced' force to Singapore was taken in the hope, primarily, of deterring Japan from starting the war or, failing that, of deterring her from sending convoys into the Gulf of Siam. This hope was not fulfilled. (ii) In the circumstances ruling at Singapore on 8 December, drastic and urgent naval action was required since, if successful, it would have presented the army with a good opportunity to defeat the landings, and so possibly have paralysed the invasion of Malaya at its birth.[185] The damning phrases 'strategically unsound' and 'left with no alternative' were therefore excised, but the core conclusion that an 'unbalanced' force had been deliberately despatched to Singapore as a 'deterrent' remained. The report did not assign responsibility for this outcome, but its verdict, and the scale of the overall disaster in the Far East, meant attention would inevitably focus on the respective roles of Pound and the prime minister. The loss of Force Z was already attracting intense scrutiny from both Parliament and press by the time the inquiry was complete, as Pound noted to Cunningham.[186]

In assigning responsibility, the background to the Force Z deployment provided in the inquiry report was bound to be influential. It was a selective and misleading account. It began by referring to an 'original plan' for Far East reinforcement, under which a 'balanced fleet' of seven capital ships, one carrier, ten cruisers and twenty-four destroyers would assemble in the Indian Ocean and proceed to Singapore. This was the eastern fleet plan which emerged from ABC-1 staff talks, following the agreement on 'Atlantic substitution', and discussed in Chapter 4. However, the report did not mention ABC-1, or the vital dependency on US Navy moves in the Atlantic. It merely stated that repair and refit needs would make it impossible to generate the anticipated fleet before March 1942. It then gave a partial and inaccurate summary of the exchange between the prime minister and First Sea Lord in August, without reference to the US Navy Atlantic reinforcement triggered at the Riviera Conference.

The radical shift in Admiralty thinking over the six weeks between end August and mid-October was masked by the single sentence – 'The situation in the Far East had meanwhile still further deteriorated and it became necessary to start forming the Eastern Fleet as ships became available'. There was no reference here to the ADB-2 planning, or to the intention to initiate early deployment of a battle-fleet operating north of Singapore and using Manila as an advanced base which, as we have seen, was formally incorporated by the naval staff in a revised Far East war plan. The exchange at the Defence Committee on 17 and 20 October was reduced to the issue of *Prince of Wales*, with no mention at all of the 'R'-class battleships, and the desire of Pound and Phillips to place them as soon as possible in Singapore. Nor was there any reference to Pound's ongoing discussions with the Americans during early November, and confirmation of his intent to base a battle-fleet at Manila. Finally, the report provided an erroneous summary of the supposed poor state of intelligence on the IJN and, above all, likely IJNAF numbers and capability in southern Indochina.

Overall, the genesis of Force Z set out in this inquiry report represented an extraordinary rewriting of the history of Far East naval planning and reinforcement across the year 1941. The omissions cannot be excused by any requirement for brevity. They created a false picture of what had occurred. It is conceivable that Davis was not immediately aware of all the relevant developments across 1941, since for much of the year he was acting as chief of staff to the Director Combined Operations, Admiral of the Fleet Sir Roger Keyes. However, he still had a duty to track down relevant papers, and Terry as DOD (F) was present at Phillips's meeting on 30 September, which was important in promoting the new offensive strategy. Harwood, as ACNS (F), had been intimately involved in all the developments relating to Far East strategy across the year, so knew he was signing off an incomplete account, as did Pound.

Why these officers reshaped the formal record in this way is hard to explain. It is tempting to suggest that the loss of Force Z, along with the disasters inflicted on the Americans at Pearl Harbor and in the Philippines, rendered the Admiralty's autumn offensive planning based on the 'R'-class battleships so absurd that the naval staff were desperate to bury it to protect Pound and the memory of Phillips. In the midst of a war, containing hostile questioning from both inside and outside the Royal Navy, which might undermine confidence in its leadership, was important. There are, however, objections to this explanation. This was an internal report with limited circulation, which surely permitted more honesty over the background. Cover-ups of the type proposed are notoriously difficult to manage without dissenting voices surfacing sooner or later. Furthermore, as noted in Moore's Future Strategy paper described above, the loss of Force Z did not itself cause the naval staff to abandon the concept of a fleet deployed forward at Singapore as its preferred aspiration. Whatever the explanation, the inquiry report established a narrative which underpinned the post-war Naval Staff History, and was accepted by Roskill as official naval historian, and then by his successors, without challenge.

Davis reinforced the inquiry report in post-war writings.[187] This post-war testimony was significant for two reasons. First, he helped both Roskill and later Marder establish their positions on the Force Z story. Secondly, he achieved high rank in the post-war Royal Navy, becoming Vice Chief of Naval Staff from 1954–57[188] under Admiral of the Fleet Lord Louis Mountbatten as First Sea Lord, then Commander-in-Chief Home Fleet until 1960. He therefore influenced attitudes regarding Force Z in a whole generation of naval officers, helping ensure that the inquiry report became established truth. His naval assistant for part of his time as VCNS was Captain Michael Goodenough, Phillips's former operations officer, with whom Davis noted he had many discussions on Force Z.

In his post-war writing Davis stated that 'various plans were sketched' to establish a 'task force with a core of battleships' at Singapore, but none of these included 'adequate carrier-borne air strength'. It was hoped Royal Air Force cover would suffice, though this was known to be weak.[189] This statement was correct as far as it went, but without more detail of these plans it revealed little. He claimed the naval staff thought it 'most imprudent' to establish a fleet in the Far East which was not 'balanced'. In contrast to the meaning prevalent in 1941, he defined this as carrying its own air cover with it.[190] This may have reflected views at more junior level in the naval staff, but it was not an accurate statement of the formal naval staff position through 1941. He insisted that the primary conclusion of his draft for the inquiry report was that Force Z should never have been sent without its own integral air cover, reiterating here the intent to include *Indomitable* in the force.[191] Chapter 6 has already disputed the allocation of *Indomitable*. Davis's claim does not easily fit with his criticism that wider Far East planning ignored the need for integral air support. Finally, Davis stated that the naval staff were convinced at the beginning of October 1941 that war with Japan would come in eight to ten weeks.[192] Again, that may have reflected opinion at junior level, but formal assessments were more nuanced.

Davis's most important claim was that Plans and Operations (Foreign) were against sending *Prince of Wales* 'almost by herself', as also was the First Sea Lord.[193] The First Sea Lord had argued strongly against despatching a 'wholly unbalanced force into an area where we did not know the strengths or capacities of the potential enemy'. This would make *Prince of Wales* a 'hostage to fortune'.[194] This agrees with Roskill's interpretation, and even echoes Roskill's precise language in his official history, which Davis commended as a faithful account. Roskill may have accurately reflected naval staff perceptions at Davis's level. Equally, Davis may have repeated Roskill here, rather than accurately recorded what was really said at the time. While Force Z can certainly be described as 'unbalanced', Pound was set on sending an even more inappropriate force into an even more exposed position than Singapore. For whatever reason, Davis provided a very partial account.

Other surviving members of the naval staff in late 1941, notably Bellars, Captain Charles Lambe (who was his deputy director and rose to become First Sea Lord in 1959), Moore and Godfrey were all well placed to qualify the view portrayed by Davis and Roskill, but none of them ever did so. Whether this reflected continuing loyalty to the memory of Pound and Phillips, or disinclination to engage in historical battles is impossible now to judge.

The loss of Force Z in perspective

Roskill's portrayal of a wise Admiralty reverting to the sensible strategy it had always favoured, in the face of a prime minister chastened by the loss of Force Z, does not accurately describe the evolution of eastern naval strategy between mid-August and mid-December 1941. There are parallels between the arguments and dispositions in Moore's December paper and those of Pound in August. But those parallels only highlight the lack of realism, and indeed recklessness, evident in the offensive planning during the autumn. Making due allowance for the impact of American losses at Pearl Harbor and the Philippines, Moore's calculation that the Royal Navy might face a potential IJN fleet of five battleships and five carriers in the South China Sea applied just as much in October, when the new offensive strategy was approved by Pound and Alexander, as it did in December. Successive Joint Intelligence Committee reports through 1941 were clear on this. The British War Cabinet decision to prioritise air resources on the Middle East through 1941 and the US Navy decision to adopt a defensive strategy in the Pacific meant it was never feasible for the Royal Navy to confront such an IJN force with the resources available to it in late 1941.

The offensive planning of late autumn may have been reckless, but it continued to cast a long shadow. For all its realism and focus on the critical Indian Ocean interests, Moore's paper still insisted that 'the best means of defending the Indian Ocean was a fleet at Singapore able to contest the South China Sea with Japan'. In accepting a defensive strategy based on Ceylon, the Admiralty therefore suggested it was bowing to a resource imbalance it hoped was temporary, rather than admitting that forward deployment was a flawed strategy. This resurrects the question raised at the end of the last chapter. If the associated powers did have the basis of a credible deterrence strategy in late 1941, and its failure lay in timing and execution rather than the concept itself, was the problem with the Admiralty's forward deployment strategy essentially one of timing?

Here it is necessary to distinguish between deterrence and war fighting. An eastern fleet of the type planned by Pound and Phillips and established in Singapore by March 1942, with Marshall's proposed air reinforcements in the Philippines and some Royal Air Force reinforcement in Malaya, would have looked a more daunting prospect for Japan. It might have been enough to dissuade. But it would still have been ill-suited to actual combat with the IJN in the South China Sea. The 'R'-class battleships would have been useless, lacking mobility and gun range, and highly vulnerable to either submarine or air attack. The remaining fleet would, at best, be in the position of the Mediterranean Fleet trying to contest the central Mediterranean in 1941 and 1942, but facing rather stronger, and more effective, air and surface forces. The prospects of achieving useful military effect would be limited – and of serious losses, high.

The loss of Force Z has frequently attracted apocalyptic language. It has been described as 'a disaster for the Royal Navy, one of the greatest it had ever suffered, and its prestige in consequence tumbled',[195] while 'all the debates about Far Eastern strategy' ended with 'sailors swimming for their lives in a tepid sea 8000 miles from home'.[196] It was a 'catastrophe', which revealed the 'decline, hitherto to a great extent concealed, of Great Britain as a maritime and colonial power'.[197] Such language calls for perspective. Lives lost numbered 840, slightly fewer than in the battleship *Barham*, torpedoed by *U-331* in the Mediterranean two weeks previously.[198] *Repulse* was unmodernised and of limited value for modern naval warfare. *Prince of Wales*, as a new ship, was a more serious loss, but in terms of immediate naval balances, it arguably mattered less than the loss of the battleships *Queen Elizabeth* and *Valiant*, both crippled by Italian human torpedo attack in Alexandria harbour later in the month. The latter barely receives a footnote in history, but these were modernised battleships and valuable units. Following the earlier loss of *Barham*, this Alexandria attack eliminated the entire Royal Navy capital ship force in the eastern Mediterranean. *Prince of Wales* would also be compensated by the completion of two sister ships in mid-1942.

In strategic terms, it is doubtful that the loss of Force Z had any effect on the subsequent fate of Malaya or the Netherlands East Indies, given the comparative scale and quality of Japanese forces immediately available in the Far East theatre. Its foregone value in the defence of the Indian Ocean, where Churchill always wanted to deploy the force, was rather greater. There was certainly reputational damage to the prestige and standing of the Royal Navy, and by extension to Britain as a whole, but this too can be overstated when set against the Royal Navy's overall war record. There is a good case, therefore, that the symbolism surrounding the loss owes more to enthusiasm to expose a flawed Singapore strategy, or to promote the inevitability of British imperial decline, than to objective calculation of long-term political, strategic and military impact.

To put the loss in further perspective, it is useful to consider developments if Phillips had returned to Singapore on 10 December unscathed. The British official history of the war against Japan argues the ships could have played no further role in the defence of Malaya, but could have formed the nucleus of a strong Allied striking force in the southwest Pacific (presumably based at Darwin), which could have disrupted Japanese invasion convoys to the Netherlands East Indies before they had airbases in Borneo and the Celebes.[199] This might have bought enough time to make defence of the Netherlands East Indies viable. That looks unlikely, given the wide options open to the Japanese, and the ability of the IJN to deploy overwhelming carrier power to hunt down any Royal Navy force they judged a serious threat. The IJN carrier force raided Darwin on 19 February almost contemporaneously with the Java Sea action. Had Force Z been available to intervene in the Java Sea, the IJN would merely have redeployed some or all of its carriers to eliminate the threat.[200] Pending serious modern reinforcement, above all carriers, the only sensible employment for Force Z was to act as an initial 'fleet in being' in the Indian Ocean, in accord with the Admiralty's original August defensive strategy.

A classic failure of risk management

The initial decision to deploy Force Z as a deterrent force did not make its destruction inevitable. Churchill can be blamed for misjudging Japanese intentions, for unrealistic expectations of the deterrent value of modern capital ships and, above all, for his major role in the neglect of Far East air strength. But the evidence does not support the popular picture of a prime minister insistent on rushing Force Z onward to Singapore without regard to professional advice. Pound could not easily have resisted the prime minister's desire for a deterrent symbol, but he and Phillips had considerable professional influence and discretion over how that deterrent was applied. The British leadership knew that the deterrence objective had been substantially achieved by the time the force met up at Ceylon. By then, there was compelling intelligence pointing to a high risk of early hostilities. There was sufficient reason therefore to hold the force at Ceylon if the Admiralty wished, and opposition from the prime minister was unlikely. The Admiralty did not do so because it was now firmly committed to an offensive strategy based on a battle-fleet at Singapore. The momentum this created drove the thinking of senior naval commanders, and meant the potential vulnerability of Force Z at Singapore was never seriously addressed. That vulnerability was compounded by the initial Japanese successes, which in turn made it almost impossible to withdraw the force.

The loss of Force Z should not be conflated with the argument that Britain lacked the naval resources to defend its vital maritime interests in the East. As became increasingly clear to the chiefs of staff in early 1942, the vital area the Royal Navy had to control, with Royal Air Force support, was Indian Ocean communications and Ceylon, not the approaches to Singapore and the Malay Barrier. In late 1941 the Royal Navy and Royal Air Force had the potential resources to defend the Indian Ocean, but even with maximum American support in the Atlantic, and a less defensive American stance in the Pacific, they never had the power to hold the barrier at this time, let alone reach beyond it, without a far greater commitment of air resources than the British war leadership was willing to make. The Admiralty's major mistake was to think that it could reach forward into the South China Sea without this. This forward strategy was reckless because it proposed to place an inappropriate capital ship force in an exposed position where the enemy could bring concentrated force to bear, as Moore's December paper underlined. It represented, therefore, a classic failure of risk management. This, more than anything else, doomed Force Z.

It can be argued that the impact of the loss of Force Z was primarily reputational and had little lasting military effect. Singapore would have fallen anyway, and the addition of two capital ships to the Eastern Fleet off Ceylon in April 1942 would have been marginal. That probably understates their value. An intact Force Z, operating in the Indian Ocean and joined shortly by the carrier *Indomitable*, would have created earlier a strong modern nucleus of an Eastern Fleet, complicated IJN planning, and spurred operational efficiency, making the Royal Navy force ultimately available off Ceylon in April more effective. Ironically, Roskill later embraced exactly this view, arguing that had the naval staff preference on strategy prevailed and naval forces been concentrated on Ceylon, then Force Z would probably have been available to help defend the Indian Ocean:

> That could not, of course, have saved Malaya or the Dutch East Indies; but it might well have discouraged the Japanese from sending Nagumo and Ozawa into those waters, it might have saved Rangoon, and it would surely have reduced the time needed for us to regain the initiative at sea.

Unfortunately, this argument rested on a false premise.[201]

PART IV

An Inescapable Commitment:

The Indian Ocean in 1942

8

The Defence of the Indian Ocean in 1942

On the afternoon of 30 March 1942 the Commander-in-Chief of the Royal Navy Eastern Fleet Admiral Sir James Somerville, freshly arrived from the United Kingdom, embarked in his flagship, the modernised battleship *Warspite*, lying off Ceylon. Somerville proceeded to sea to rendezvous with the main part of his new fleet just south of the island. On sighting it, he famously signalled – 'So this is the Eastern Fleet. Never mind. There's many a good tune played on an old fiddle'.[1] This was an apt reference to a motley collection of predominantly ageing warships which had never operated together, and which Somerville's operations officer described as 'a rabble'. Yet Somerville knew that within two days he would probably face a significant modern IJN task force set on attacking Ceylon, and no doubt his fleet too, if they could find it. Whatever the limitations of his 'rabble', he was not a man to shirk a fight and intended 'to have a crack at them'.

The subsequent engagements off Ceylon receive little attention.[2] They are presented as further ignominious defeats for the Royal Navy, underlining its helplessness in the face of the Japanese onslaught and the bankruptcy of its whole eastern strategy. They are also cast as an unimportant footnote in a war now focused elsewhere. What happened off Ceylon was more interesting. Somerville ran reckless risks, but brought his 'rabble' to the edge of an extraordinary victory. The stakes at Ceylon and in the Indian Ocean were also much higher than generally acknowledged. In early 1942 this was, arguably, now the most critical theatre of war for Britain and its new American ally, apart from the Atlantic lifeline. It was vital to Russia's survival too. The fate of Somerville's 'rabble', therefore, mattered. But the term can be stretched too far. Somerville's force was better than that, and it was not indicative of what the Royal Navy was ultimately willing to do to hold the Indian Ocean.

The strategic importance of the Indian Ocean
The Admiralty's paper 'Future British Naval Strategy', completed on 14 December and described in the previous chapter, was incorporated in a wider review of Britain's Far East policy approved by the chiefs of staff just under

a week later.[3] This defined Britain's response to the Japanese attack and the initial defeats suffered by the Allies. It inevitably reiterated Far East defence objectives agreed over the last eighteen months, preventing Japan damaging vital interests and capturing Singapore and other key points essential to future recovery, and the desirability of holding the Lashio–Tonga line.[4] It also established three further principles which underpinned British strategy for the next six months and beyond. The first was the critical importance of the Indian Ocean to the overall British war effort, and the specific priority of securing Ceylon, which was currently virtually undefended.[5] The second was recognition that defence of the Indian Ocean was pre-eminently a naval problem and required a substantial Royal Navy fleet, since American help to Britain would be confined to the Atlantic. The third was the interdependence of the Far East and Middle East. Britain could not relax its grip on either, save in the last resort of invasion of the United Kingdom or Australasia, when the Middle East would be sacrificed.

The decision to deploy three-quarters of the Royal Navy's heavy units to the East was a remarkable change from the August 1940 Far East appreciation and the assumption into the autumn of 1941 that the maximum guaranteed reinforcement for the Indian Ocean was Force H-plus. It was necessary because the Malaya forces were seriously under strength and with the US Navy Pacific Fleet now incapable of intervening, Japan's way south and west was wide open. It was rendered possible, at least in theory, despite the loss of Force Z, by three factors: first, the United States reinforcement of the Atlantic now underway, which even with Pearl Harbor losses, it intended to sustain; secondly, transfer of the battle-fleet from the eastern Mediterranean; and finally, because the new build units from the 1937–39 programmes were now becoming available in significant numbers.

Translating the theory of this commitment to a large Indian Ocean fleet into practice proved more difficult. On 19 December, the same day the chiefs of staff approved the review, a brilliant asymmetric attack by Italian frogmen severely damaged the modernised battleships, *Queen Elizabeth* and *Valiant*, the core capital ships of the planned new fleet, in Alexandria harbour. This Italian achievement, measured by capital ship damage or overall strategic effect, ranked with that of the Royal Navy at Taranto. *Valiant* was out of action for six months and *Queen Elizabeth* for eighteen. Following the losses of the battleship *Barham* and carrier *Ark Royal* to submarine attack the previous month, the Royal Navy Mediterranean Fleet had effectively ceased to exist.[6] The chiefs had agonised over withdrawing the Mediterranean Fleet battleships to the Indian Ocean. By disabling them, the Italians achieved a victory for the Axis with strategic consequences which have been under-recognised.[7]

The three fleet carriers earmarked for the new Eastern Fleet, *Indomitable*, *Formidable* and *Illustrious*, were first-class modern vessels comparable to the latest IJN and US Navy ships in displacement, speed and anti-aircraft protection but, as explained previously, designed to a different concept. Their armoured deck gave the Royal Navy carriers greater protection against high-level and dive-bombing attack, but at the expense of aircraft capacity – at this time still barely two-thirds of US Navy and IJN capacity. Only the new *Indomitable*, following completion of her delayed work-up at the end of November, was immediately available. The other two, under repair in the United States for most of 1941, could not reach the Indian Ocean until March. All three carriers suffered the limitations in aircraft numbers and quality discussed earlier. None was fully worked up and operationally efficient. Modern cruisers and, above all, quality modern destroyers to accompany the capital units remained in desperately short supply. Only the bare minimum was available before mid-1942. A further limitation that hampered the efficiency of the new Eastern Fleet throughout 1942 was the lack of suitable bases and support facilities. At the start of the year neither Trincomalee nor Colombo had repair facilities or docks able to support major fleet units. They offered anchorages and refuelling, but little more.[8] Port T at Addu Atoll in the southern Maldives, 600 miles southwest of Colombo, had been surveyed as an operational fleet base only in autumn 1941. By early 1942 it provided a sheltered anchorage with fuel and water and had rudimentary underwater defences, but still no airfield.[9]

Providing air reinforcements was equally difficult. The chiefs of staff recognised the importance of air power in containing the Japanese and, especially, maintaining control of the Indian Ocean. However, for the first four months of the Far East war, they faced complex and painful trade-offs between three demands: reinforcement of the immediate Far East frontline in Burma, Malaya and the Netherlands East Indies; securing Ceylon, India and other vital points in the Indian Ocean; and sustaining Britain's position in the Middle East. There were complex dependencies here which dominate joint planning staff papers in this period.

The transfer of the huge number of aircraft of all types to achieve and sustain desired force levels in the Middle East and Far East depended on two air bridges, the trans-Mediterranean route through Malta, and the trans-Africa route from Takoradi in the Gold Coast to Sudan. Malta had to be supplied by sea, which depended in part on adequate control of the eastern Mediterranean. To compensate for the loss of the battle-fleet at Alexandria, the chiefs deployed most of the small Beaufort torpedo force described in Chapter 5 from the United Kingdom to Egypt. This made it impossible to deploy Beauforts to the Indian Ocean in the first half of the year.[10] While aircraft could be transferred along the fragile air bridges, they were useless without the ground staff and spares to support them – which could only be deployed by sea. With the Mediterranean closed, the length of the shipping routes and need for convoy protection made this a painfully slow process. Nevertheless, over the next four months the Royal Air Force planned to ship 750 aircraft to India and Ceylon to create and sustain a total force of thirty-seven squadrons by March 1942, with about half being modern fighters. This build-up was comparable to that achieved in the Middle East the previous summer, and came on top of the much increased demands of that theatre in 1942.[11]

Chiefs of staff records for January and February 1942 show few illusions about Japanese potential in the short term, or the prospects of holding them at the Malay Barrier, although they expected the Malaya defence forces to perform better than they did. The Joint Intelligence Committee was generally excellent at assessing both Japanese intent and scale of attack. In an important update on Far East policy on 16 February, immediately after the fall of Singapore, the joint planning staff provided an accurate forecast of likely Japanese moves over the next three months and the critical risks they posed in the Indian Ocean.[12] These risks were simultaneously underlined by Layton, who was still Commander-in-Chief Eastern Fleet. He emphasised the strategic threat to the Middle East supply route and oil supplies from the Persian Gulf but, above all, the vulnerability of troop convoys. The risks to the latter were 'appalling', and the impact of losing twenty thousand Australian troops 'incalculable'. By contrast, Atlantic convoys enjoyed 'blissful security'.[13]

Initial IJN thinking for phase 2 operations, following the phase 1 capture and securing of the 'southern resources area', did indeed closely match these British fears. Their intent can be summarised as: disrupt Allied supply routes; attack and destroy forward bases using mobile air units and the carrier fleet; and, finally, seek opportunities to ambush and destroy the US Navy main fleet or a significant British naval formation. At this time, the IJN consistently advocated cutting reinforcement routes to Australia from both east and west and 'breaking trade' in the Indian Ocean, justifying the fears of Churchill and Pound through 1941.[14]

The planning staff recommended that British effort must now concentrate on holding the 'outer ring' of India, Ceylon, Australia and Fiji. Existing strengths here were inadequate, and reinforcement difficult, owing to the logistic challenges and trade-offs. Any reinforcements now sent beyond this line were likely to be wasted since, once committed, they could not be withdrawn. They stressed that the immediate priority was Ceylon, the loss of which 'will imperil the whole British war effort'. This reflected both its importance in sustaining the Eastern Fleet and the opportunities it would offer the IJN, if captured, to dominate the western Indian Ocean. The chiefs of staff accordingly agreed that air defence of Ceylon must take precedence over reinforcement of Java and that Hurricanes being ferried by *Indomitable* should be offloaded there.[15] Ceylon was the dominant preoccupation of the chiefs in the theatre for the next two months and they monitored defence measures there almost daily. On 13 March they advised eastern theatre commanders that in the last resort, 'the security of the Indian Empire rests on our ability to control sea communications in the Indian Ocean', which in turn depended on holding the naval bases in Ceylon.[16]

As the Japanese consolidated their hold on the Netherlands East Indies during March and moved into Burma to threaten northeast India, British planners recognised that they were now defending a single front from Cyrenaica in the west, through Persia and India, to Australia in the east. The Middle East and Far East were indeed interdependent. The three Axis enemies, operating on more interior lines, could apply more concentrated force at multiple points on this front than Britain, with its immensely long logistic supply routes, could easily defend. This is a more complex version of the strategic over-stretch arguments traditionally emphasised. Britain's problem was only in part overall resources and just as much short-term logistics. This is how the German naval war staff saw matters too. Their paper submitted to Hitler the previous month mirrored the Joint Planning Committee analysis and included a map demonstrating the logistic challenge Britain faced in addressing an Axis pincer directed at the Middle East.[17]

These issues were vividly brought out in early April when the joint planning staff addressed the relationship between the Middle East and India.[18] Both depended on sea communications in the Indian Ocean and air resources through Malta, both covered the southern supply route to Russia, and both protected and were, in the last resort, dependent on Abadan oil. Without this oil, the war effort in the Middle East, India and Australia would fail, because there were no tankers to provide alternative supplies. Britain currently had insufficient resources to launch a Libyan offensive, secure Ceylon and defend Calcutta. Without a Libyan offensive, Malta and its air route could fall. The loss of Ceylon risked the loss of India, but also ultimately Persian oil and the Middle East. Losing Calcutta meant risking India, but probably not Ceylon. The planners judged that first priority must be Ceylon and the security of the Indian Ocean, then Libya. Risk must be carried in northeast India.

As with other contemporary assessments,[19] the planners emphasised three critical strategic factors. First, the human and material resources and access points of the eastern empire were vital to Britain's global war effort. Secondly, realising that potential depended on the continued availability of Abadan oil. Thirdly, maintaining control of the Persian Gulf and key Indian Ocean communications was, therefore, an essential minimum objective after defence of the United Kingdom base and Atlantic lifeline. This depended primarily on an adequate Eastern Fleet, but also on air reinforcement of key points, especially Ceylon. These factors were a major, if not dominant, preoccupation for the British war leadership in the first nine months of 1942, yet they hardly feature in most accounts of this period. Furthermore, during March President Roosevelt and the prime minister endorsed a broad division of global responsibility between the United States and United Kingdom. The American chiefs of staff took responsibility for Pacific strategy and operations, while the United Kingdom chiefs of staff took responsibility for the Middle East and Indian Ocean. The Atlantic and western Europe would be handled on a joint basis.[20]

The importance of Abadan oil to the British war effort is a constant theme in chiefs of staff papers through 1941, but especially in the first half of 1942 when the risks to this supply, from all directions, were at their height. Middle East oil is often dismissed as of little importance, since Britain itself received almost all its supplies from the western hemisphere.[21] The Petroleum Board underlined the significance of Abadan to the chiefs of staff at the end of May. They were responding to concerns raised by the chiefs the previous month as they reviewed the risks to the Indian Ocean.[22] The board stated that for the nine months April to December 1942, the total British Empire oil requirement, including Allies and neutrals for which Britain was responsible, was 24.5 million tons. Current plans anticipated that 41 per cent of this must come from the Middle East; 75 per cent of Middle East supply, and 66 per cent of eastern empire oil needs (including Australasia and South Africa), came from Abadan. If Abadan was lost, an extra 1.5 million tons of deadweight tanker tonnage would be required to replace it. The only possible source was the United States, but other commitments, including the need to rebuild stocks in the United Kingdom, made it impossible for the United States to meet such a demand in the foreseeable future. Drastic economies would therefore be needed to reduce empire oil use, including in the United Kingdom itself, with serious consequences for the overall war effort.[23]

Two months later the Petroleum Board provided a revised assessment. The Middle East was now expected to contribute 14.5 million tons of oil in the year beginning 1 July 1942, 10 per cent higher than the May figure, with 11.5 million tons from the Persian Gulf, although actual production would fall some way short of this target.[24] The higher planned output reflected the new demands of sustaining the eastern war in India and Australasia, and the impact of the supplies now lost to the Japanese in the Netherlands East Indies and Burma. If Abadan was lost, and the threat from German attack in the west or north had now risen significantly, supplies could theoretically be made good from the western hemisphere, but only by deploying 270 additional tankers, which were not available. The consequence would be a reduction in supply of 20 per cent in the West as well as the East. The board concluded that the loss of the Persian fields would therefore be 'calamitous', as it would force a drastic reduction in total war capacity, and probably the abandonment of some operations.[25]

As the First Sea Lord emphasised, without Abadan and the Persian fields it would be impossible to sustain Britain's war effort in the Middle East, but also to provide any significant aid to China through India, or to support the southwest Pacific offensive at Guadalcanal from Australia later in the year.[26] This reflected the fact that, following the loss of the oilfields in the Netherlands East Indies and Burma, Abadan oil underpinned the Indian war effort, including the American forces based there, and aid to China for the rest of the war. Meanwhile, under the Anglo-American joint oil arrangements agreed after Pearl Harbor, Britain and the United States shared responsibility for oil supplies to Australia and New Zealand until autumn 1944, when Britain took over the full commitment. Abadan oil met about half Australia's requirements between early 1942 and late 1944.[27] Although the United States could, in theory, have compensated Australia for the loss of Abadan supplies, the shipping burden would have made this difficult to achieve before mid-1943, with obvious implications for operations.

These Petroleum Board calculations reflected Allied tanker losses to Axis submarines in the first half of 1942, which were worse than in any other period of the war. They sank 152 vessels in this period totalling 1,169,300 tons. This was 11.6 per cent of overall Allied tanker capacity at the start of the year and the net loss, allowing for new build in these six months, was still just over 7 per cent. The bulk of the losses were to German U-boats in American and Caribbean waters.[28] Meanwhile, in the first half of 1942 the additional tanker capacity required to supply oil to the eastern empire territories had already risen by 0.7 million tons, or about 65 per cent, compared to the average for 1941. This rise reflected the increased transit time to make good the loss of the East Indies and Burma supplies, the need to replace stocks lost to the Japanese at Singapore and elsewhere, and the new demands generated by the Japanese war.[29] This increased tanker demand in the Eastern theatre, also 7 per cent of Allied capacity, had to be maintained, just to prevent further Japanese advances in the Indian Ocean or southwest Pacific theatres. This combination of submarine losses and the increased eastern theatre demand had therefore cost the Allies around 14 per cent of their total tanker capacity available in the first half of the year.

The War Cabinet considered the board's report on 5 August. The Chief of Air Staff, speaking for the chiefs of staff, advised that without additional tanker capacity, the loss of the Persian Gulf facilities might reduce Britain's overall war effort by 25 per cent. It was essential to hold Abadan, even at the risk of losing Egypt and the Nile Delta. Simultaneously at the Cairo Conference on 4 August, the Chief of the Imperial General Staff, General Sir Alan Brooke, put the position more starkly. Without Abadan it would be hard to carry on the war.[30]

In underlining the strategic importance of the Indian Ocean, the joint planning staff had emphasised its role in protecting the southern supply route to Russia. The significance of this route in 1942 has been neglected: 23.8 per cent of lend-lease aid to Russia during the whole period 1941 to 1945 used the Persian Gulf route, slightly more than the 22.7 per cent on the north Russia (Arctic convoy) route but only half the deliveries on the Far East route across the Pacific round northern Japan. The overall statistics do not convey the importance of the Persian route in the first half of the Russo-German war.[31] There are two critical points here. First, the Far East route depended on Japanese acquiescence, which relied on the tacit understanding that supplies delivered here were non-military. Secondly, German countermeasures severely curtailed the deliveries possible on the north Russia route between mid-1942 and the end of 1943. Under the Second Protocol, which agreed American/British supplies to Russia over the period July 1942 to June 1943, the Arctic route was meant to deliver 3.3 million tons. In practice, the northern convoys managed little more than one-tenth of this.[32]

As a result, although the Persian route was the longest in mileage and, above all, ship-time, it was relatively safe, was open all year round, could be used for all categories of shipment, and provided relatively easy access to vital military fronts. In 1941 the Persian route supplied only 3.7 per cent of total shipments to Russia, and they barely increased over the first four months of 1942, averaging 4.7 per cent.[33] However, in May shipments were 44.7 per cent, and averaged 40.8 per cent for the whole eight months May to December, about three times deliveries through the Arctic convoys in this period, although the logistic challenges in achieving this build-up, which still fell well short of the desired deliveries to Russia, were formidable.[34]

The proportion of weapons shipments reaching Russia through the Persian Gulf was less than 10 per cent in 1942, but approached 50 per cent in 1943, when weapons shipments here were approximately twice those by the Arctic route. This reflected the fact that Arctic convoys virtually ceased through the summer months that year, as well.[35] Over the fourteen months from 1 November 1942 to 31 December 1943, Russia had a deficit between domestic production of military aircraft and losses of 3794, and a deficit for tanks and self-propelled guns of 2499. Allied aid over this period contributed 9206 aircraft and 3798 tanks and self-propelled guns, more than compensating, therefore, for the deficits, and enabling frontline strength to keep growing, albeit still slowly.[36] Weapons shipments in 1942 were much lower, but

American shipments despatched to Persia this year still included 1500 aircraft, 600 tanks, 1750 guns with ammunition and 55,000 trucks.[37] Meanwhile, Britain delivered 160,000 tons of ammunition and stores to Russia via the Persian route across the whole war. These deliveries included 823 aircraft, 564 tanks, fifty-three guns and 3941 assorted vehicles, with most delivered between autumn 1941 and end 1943.[38] In addition, following new investment at Abadan, it became a vital source of 100-octane aviation spirit for Russia from mid-1943. By the end of that year, Britain was supplying 25,000 tons per month of aviation spirit, a significant proportion of the overall Russian requirement for high specification fuel.[39]

Russian records show the combat weapon shipments through Persia were neither large enough nor fast enough to influence the critical southern front operations in the autumn of 1942. However, the bulk of Persian shipments in the second half of 1942, comprising 350,000 tons of strategic materials including oil, 84,000 tons of food, and the trucks already listed, made a significant contribution to bolstering Russian resistance that winter, and to the mobility and logistic support necessary for the success of the Stalingrad counter-offensive.[40] Overall, lend-lease support in 1942 may well have tipped the balance in enabling Russia to survive, since by all normal rules the Russian economy, and with it their capacity to resist, should have collapsed that year. If this is correct, it underlines the significance of the Persian corridor in the second half of the year, which the Germans certainly recognised.[41]

The Japanese threat in early 1942 and the role of the new Eastern Fleet
Although the chiefs of staff prioritised defence of Indian Ocean communications, they recognised that at the end of March 1942, the developing Eastern Fleet was inferior to the forces the IJN might deploy, especially in carrier air power.[42] They also recognised that Ceylon remained vulnerable, despite improvements in its air defence.[43] The Eastern Fleet must therefore create uncertainty and act as a 'fleet in being', forcing the IJN to deploy major forces to cover any movement.[44] The planning staff thought the IJN would be cautious over penetrating far into the Indian Ocean with a major force if this exposed them to the US Navy in the Pacific. However, they suggested an alternative Japanese view that proved prescient. The IJN might argue that they could deploy a fleet superior to the Royal Navy in speed, offensive power, training and morale before the US Navy could intervene. If they could find and destroy a Royal Navy fleet, India, Ceylon and points west would be wide open to subsequent attacks. If the Royal Navy evaded, the IJN could raid its bases and degrade its ability to operate.[45]

This was an accurate assessment of IJN thinking in mid-March. Earlier proposals were more ambitious. These envisaged an all-out offensive in the

Indian Ocean to take Ceylon, destroy remaining British power in the theatre, and ultimately join up with Germany in the Middle East. A 'Middle East junction' was discussed between Hitler and Ambassador Oshima in Berlin on 14 December, immediately following Japan's entry into the war. Hitler confirmed his intent in the spring to advance into the Caucasus, and from there into Iraq and Iran, partly for their oil, but also to threaten India from the west.[46] In pursuit of this joint vision, the IJN, with Imperial Japanese Army participation, evaluated an operation to capture Ceylon in a war game at the end of February. Planning for a landing did not develop further, because the Japanese army would not allocate the necessary forces, and because a move towards the Middle East was judged premature.[47] The need to retain adequate naval forces to counter the United States in the Pacific and the logistic challenges in operating west of Ceylon were also important factors.[48] Admiral Yamamoto's chief of staff, Rear Admiral Matome Ugaki, stated that although the game achieved a 'landing' on Ceylon, wider conclusions were 'not good'.[49] Admiral Kondo, who as Commander Second Fleet would direct Indian Ocean operations, confirmed that following phase 1 operations, he had initially supported an Indian Ocean offensive to drive Britain out of the war, but subject to two conditions. Germany should penetrate Iraq and Iran, cutting Britain's oil supplies and threatening India from the rear. Sufficient forces must also be deployed to destroy a powerful enemy. This meant withdrawing forces from the primary Pacific theatre, a major disadvantage.[50] In early March Premier Hideki Tojo ruled against a major Indian Ocean offensive for the present.[51]

The IJN accordingly settled for a more limited Indian Ocean raiding operation, designated Operation C, to be executed in early April. Its primary objectives were to find and destroy the Royal Navy Eastern Fleet and to disrupt British trade and communications in the Bay of Bengal in support of operations against Burma, and potentially northeast India.[52] Despite the Japanese army claims, sufficient Japanese land forces to attack Ceylon were available at this time. An all-out offensive in the Indian Ocean to collapse Britain's position in India and the Middle East, and perhaps even drive her out of the war, was credible, and probably represented Japan's best option at this point.[53]

Contrary to the claim made by Brooke, Pound rapidly shared the accurate joint planning staff prediction of aggressive IJN raiding action with his American opposite number Admiral King, in the hope the US Navy could undertake a diversion operation in the Pacific.[54] King confirmed on 8 April through Admiral Ghormley, Special Naval Adviser in London, that suitable action was underway. Although King did not elaborate, this referred to the forthcoming Doolittle raid, which took place on 17 April.[55]

This, then, was the background against which Admiral Sir James Somerville, formerly commander of Force H, arrived in Ceylon to take command of the newly constituted Eastern Fleet at the end of March. None would have questioned this appointment. Somerville was an inspirational leader with an excellent fighting record, an exceptional seaman, and a fine tactician adept at exploiting modern capabilities, especially air power, to operational effect. Of all the Royal Navy's fighting admirals in the first half of the war, he was the most comfortable with modern technology and exploring its potential. He was also a good judge of people. He had rapidly acquired a first-rate deputy, Vice Admiral Sir Algernon Willis, an able chief of staff, Commodore Ralph Edwards, and Staff Officer Plans, Commander Kaye Edden.[56] Edwards had just left the post of Director of Operations (Home) where he was judged by William Davis 'the most outstanding Captain in the Admiralty'.[57]

The fleet, which had so far collected in the central Indian Ocean, divided between Ceylon and Port T, was a reduced version of that envisaged by the Admiralty in December. It comprised only one modernised battleship, *Warspite*, fresh from refit in the United States, which Somerville selected as his flagship, the four 'R'-class battleships, two of the planned modern carriers, *Indomitable* and *Formidable*, eleven assorted cruisers of which few were the most modern, and fourteen destroyers. Somerville was promised a third carrier, *Illustrious*, in April and the modernised battleship *Valiant*, repaired after Alexandria in June.[58] This fleet was more impressive on paper than in reality.[59] The individual units had never operated together and many lacked training.[60] The embarked air group mustered only fifty-seven strike aircraft and thirty-seven fighters,[61] about a third of that in the IJN carrier force it would shortly face, and the air crews lacked experience.[62] The 'R'-class battleships, despite recent refits, were in a poor material state, amply demonstrating how unsuited they were to face the IJN.[63] Somerville did have some advantages. Port T was an alternative base beyond the reach of likely IJN reconnaissance, FECB (now relocated from Singapore to Colombo) provided a distinct intelligence edge, his aircraft could operate at night, and there was now a respectable fighter force of around eighty aircraft in Ceylon.[64]

Somerville arrived in Colombo on 24 March, two days before the IJN task force sailed from their base in the Celebes to execute Operation C. A key question is whether there was an adequate understanding between the Admiralty and Somerville on the role of the Eastern Fleet and his remit as commander. On 11 March Somerville told Pound that the Eastern Fleet should operate as 'a fleet in being', avoiding the risk of engagement with a superior IJN force. If Ceylon was lost, it would be difficult, but not impossible, to retain communications to the Middle East. However, if the Japanese also destroyed the greater part of the Eastern Fleet, the situation would indeed be desperate.[65] Pound endorsed this view in a concise directive for Commander-in-Chief Eastern Fleet despatched on 19 March with the full authority of the chiefs of staff. This set the overall goal of protecting Indian Ocean communications, but stressed the need to act as a fleet in being, and to avoid unnecessary risks, crippling losses, or attrition. It also identified the most likely IJN moves as coastal attacks in the Bay of Bengal and against Burma, and a Pearl Harbor-type raid on Ceylon.[66] This Admiralty instruction was clear and correctly anticipated Japanese moves.[67]

A second question is the intelligence available to Somerville, what he knew about IJN intentions and capabilities, what he knew of a specific attack on Ceylon, and what conclusions he could reasonably draw. Here he could exploit his high-quality staff, the capabilities of FECB relocated from Singapore and now named HMS *Anderson*, and the experience of Vice Admiral Sir Geoffrey Layton, now Commander-in-Chief Ceylon. Both FECB and the US Navy Station Cast based at Corregidor in the Philippines had made further progress on JN 25B, the primary IJN cypher, in the first part of 1942.[68] Around 20 March FECB intercepted JN 25B messages referring to a forthcoming operation by an IJN carrier force, accompanied by another force thought to comprise heavy cruisers, in the 'D' area (assessed to be Ceylon) including an air raid against 'DG' (probably Colombo) on 2 April.[69] FECB also believed the IJN force had concentrated at Staring Bay in the Celebes and would leave there on 21 March.

Somerville therefore called a conference on 29 March between his staff and the head of the FECB SIGINT unit, Paymaster Lieutenant Commander Harry Shaw, to evaluate the reliability of the various intercepts drawn from both British and American SIGINT teams.[70] He accepted Shaw's assessment as accurate.[71] It was characteristic of Somerville to consult the experts directly. By contrast, as we have seen, Phillips failed to do so at Singapore. Somerville summarised the intelligence picture from this meeting for the Admiralty later that day. The intercepts suggested an IJN force, probably comprising two carriers, four cruisers, and twelve destroyers, would leave Staring Bay on 21 March for an attack on Ceylon about 1 April.[72] Although Somerville sourced the intelligence to 'Combined Fleet telegram orders', he added deductions regarding force composition. Here, FECB seriously underestimated the size of the IJN carrier group (which comprised five carriers rather than two) and they included *Kaga*, the one fleet carrier not present. There is an unresolved mystery over how the intelligence identified the date 1 April for the attack. Japanese records show that the initial order to proceed with Operation C was issued by Admiral Yamamoto to Admiral Kondo, the southern force commander, on 9 March.[73] A departure date of 26 March from Staring Bay with a Colombo attack date ('C day') of 5 April was then agreed by the IJN command by 16 March.[74]

After the raids were over, Somerville told the Admiralty that he had expected two carriers with accompanying cruisers and destroyers with the possibility of a battleship covering force in support.[75] He therefore anticipated a 'hit and run' raid which he evidently felt his fleet could manage. However, he misjudged both the numbers and capability of the IJNAF aircraft he would face, even from this supposed smaller force. The first was excusable because NID had consistently underestimated IJN carrier air complements by about a quarter. However, he also expected the IJN carriers to deploy strike aircraft similar to Albacores and showed surprise when they apparently deployed 'fighter bombers' in their air strikes against the cruisers *Dorsetshire* and *Cornwall*.[76] In fact, the IJN had here deployed their standard Type 99 Val dive-bomber on which good intelligence was now available. Somerville's staff should have been well briefed on this.[77]

The intercepts described here were not the only intelligence available. Traffic analysis and direction-finding by both British and US Navy teams had continued to perform impressively since the start of the war. The US Navy Pacific Fleet intelligence organisation transmitted a daily intelligence bulletin providing information on enemy forces and intentions which was shared with the Eastern Fleet through FECB and the Admiralty through the US Navy office in London.[78] NID on 1 March gave a detailed and broadly accurate breakdown of IJN southern forces[79] while successive weekly intelligence reports in mid-March referred specifically to IJN forces likely to be deployed in the Indian Ocean, anticipating at least three fleet carriers, three *Kongo*-class battle-cruisers, and a substantial cruiser force.[80] There were also recent Joint Intelligence Committee assessments[81] and the precedents of Pearl Harbor and the attack on Darwin in February.[82]

The weekly intelligence reports proved an accurate guide to the IJN force actually deployed against Ceylon. Under the command of Vice Admiral Chuichi Nagumo, it comprised five carriers[83] with about 275 aircraft[84], four *Kongo*-class battlecruisers, the only occasion on which the four operated together, and the heavy cruisers *Tone* and *Chikuma*. It left Staring Bay on 26 March, five days later than the date provided to Somerville by Shaw and his team.[85] Overall, there was ample background intelligence here to suggest that, whatever the clues to force composition in the current intercepts, the IJN could deploy a far superior force to the Eastern Fleet, and all previous precedent suggested they would do so. This wider intelligence picture meant the Admiralty was well placed to question whether Somerville's 29 March assessment of the IJN attack force was safe and they had sufficient time to urge caution. They did not do so. This was a major failing. They may have been misled by the NID perception of an apparent lull in Japanese activity and false indications that all IJN carriers were heading back to Japan.[86]

The IJN attack on Ceylon

On the basis of the FECB intelligence and advice from the Royal Air Force Commander in Ceylon, Air Vice Marshal John d'Albiac, Somerville assessed the IJN force would aim for a launch point about 100 miles southeast of Ceylon, convenient for simultaneous strikes on Colombo and Trincomalee.[87] He expected a moonlight launch followed by a dawn recovery.[88] He therefore arranged for air searches using Royal Air Force Catalinas down a wide southeast approach arc out to 420 miles.[89] He himself sailed on 30 March and deployed his fleet in a patrol area centred about 100 miles south of Ceylon, to the southwest of the expected Japanese line of approach.[90] He planned to remain clear of likely IJN reconnaissance sweeps during daylight hours and then close during darkness for a night torpedo attack. He followed this plan for two nights and then late on 2 April retired to Port T, some 600 miles southwest of Ceylon, to refuel.[91] This decision was dictated primarily by the low endurance of the 'R' class, but also growing doubts about the reliability of the intelligence and the value of remaining in the area. Somerville had just reached Port T when the Nagumo force was sighted by a Catalina some 360[92] miles southeast of the southern tip of Ceylon at 1600 on the afternoon of 4 April, four days later than Somerville expected. The Catalina reported the position of the IJN force, but was shot down before giving its composition. Japanese records also suggest the Catalina position was badly out, placing the IJN force some sixty miles west of its true position.[93]

The delay in Nagumo's expected arrival was the first of several lucky escapes for Somerville. Nagumo had indeed approached from the southeast, but his track was well to the west of what Somerville had anticipated and the crucial Catalina sighting at the extreme southern edge of his ordered search arc. Nagumo deliberately held to a westerly course, delaying the turn north to his planned launch point for as long as possible to reduce his exposure to air search from Ceylon. Indeed, he was still on his westerly course of 290 when he was sighted and only turned to his final approach heading of 315 at 1700, an hour later.[94] Nagumo's approach tactic nearly worked and could have had disastrous consequences. Four days earlier it would have taken the IJN force on a heading passing close to the western edge of the Eastern Fleet waiting area.[95]

Historians have suggested several explanations for the apparent delay in Nagumo's arrival compared to the intelligence advice provided to Somerville. These include the desire to hit Colombo on a Sunday, when defences might be more relaxed and there was perhaps a higher chance of catching the Eastern Fleet in harbour, and delay in concentrating the Operation C task force owing to other commitments.[96] However, Japanese sources show that the planned attack date was always 5 April. For whatever reason, the SIGINT interpretation was wrong.[97]

If Nagumo had arrived earlier, he might well have detected Somerville and positioned across the line of retreat to Port T, as illustrated in Map 2.[98] Trapped by a vastly superior force, with overwhelming air power and a significant speed advantage, Somerville would then have suffered heavy losses, if not annihilation. Making due allowance for hindsight, Somerville's choice of waiting area was foolhardy. He expected the IJN force to launch their attack on Ceylon in the dark, well before dawn, and then to recover in daylight.[99] For this to happen, the distance between the two forces in the two hours before sunset the previous evening must be only 150–200 miles, well inside possible IJN reconnaissance sweeps. In the event, the Japanese task force did not sweep ahead on the afternoon of 4 April and a planned reconnaissance of Colombo harbour by cruiser floatplanes was cancelled. Nagumo chose to rely on reconnaissance by the submarines pre-positioned off both Colombo and Trincomalee, although these had limited effectiveness.[100] If the Japanese had followed the same policy on 31 March (for a hypothetical 1 April attack), Somerville would not, therefore, have been sighted prior to nightfall, but he could not reasonably have assumed that.

Avoiding detection before dark would not have ended Somerville's problems. The unique Royal Navy capability to conduct day and night search using airborne radar, supported by the comprehensive modern radar suite in his major units, could, in theory, facilitate the night search and strike he planned, and help evade detection. However, ASV 2 range was only 15 miles for a medium-size warship and perhaps 20 miles for a carrier.[101] His search crews also had limited experience. Night detection and strike in these circumstances, given the obvious uncertainties over the IJN approach track, would be a high-risk enterprise, leaving little margin for successful escape. If Nagumo had closed as expected, and Somerville had failed to find him during the night, then he would have been no more than a hundred miles from the Japanese by dawn.[102] Dawn searches by Nagumo must have found him, with the whole day then available to hunt Somerville down.

Somerville's plan, therefore, made unsafe assumptions about the size of the IJN force and its line of approach, leaving him vulnerable to Japanese detection and counter-strike. To be fair, Somerville had recognised that Nagumo could, in theory, approach Ceylon from any direction from northeast through south to southwest, but it was impossible to cover such a wide area with the limited number of Catalinas. Concentrating search effort to the southeast made sense, but he would still have been wiser to retreat to Port T until he could estimate the size of force he faced from the strength of its attack on Ceylon, or at least positioned his waiting area about 150 miles northeast of Port T. The latter option would make it easier to intervene with a night attack if the intelligence was good enough, while remaining far enough away from Nagumo's worst-case approach route to be relatively safe from discovery. It was an area where the Japanese were unlikely to look, unless they knew about Port T. Post-war investigation shows that they did not, although Somerville could not assume this at the time.[103] Nevertheless, the Japanese did task at least one submarine with reconnaissance of the Maldives during Operation C. Given the size of the island chain, this submarine surveillance would have been lucky to spot Somerville, but it was a further risk to the British force.[104] Another weakness in Somerville's planning was his decision to keep the 'R' class in close proximity to his flagship and fast carriers. He had divided his fleet into a fast Force A, comprising *Warspite*, the carriers and his faster more modern cruisers and destroyers, and a slow Force B focused on the 'R' class. The 'R'-class ships brought him little military value, but were vulnerable and would complicate planning if he had to move quickly. It would have been wiser to leave them training at Port T. The argument for keeping them close to Force A was evidently fear that fast IJN capital ships might close and strike the carrier force in bad weather, or at night.[105]

Somerville made two further decisions which placed all or part of his fleet in danger. His decision late on 2 April to refuel at Port T, rather than Colombo, and keep his fleet concentrated there was sound, and probably saved him from destruction. However, he detached the heavy cruisers *Dorsetshire* and *Cornwall* to Colombo, and *Hermes* to Trincomalee, to resume previous commitments. This reflected his growing belief that the intelligence of imminent attack was wrong. All three ships were consequently then found by Nagumo in the vicinity of Ceylon and sunk.[107] Churchill and others criticised this action, but Somerville was vigorously defended by the Admiralty, who felt he had made reasonable decisions given what he knew at the time.[108] However, in judging the intelligence wrong, Somerville was not ruling out one intercept, but a cumulative weight of evidence. The risk in detaching elements of his force to Ceylon was less justified than he and the Admiralty implied.

The second decision, for which Somerville was heavily criticised by Willis and members of his staff, was to leave Port T and head back towards the IJN force as soon as he learnt of the sighting south of Ceylon on the afternoon of 4 April. This reflected Somerville's continued conviction he faced a relatively small raiding force, which he might catch with a night attack as it retired after striking Colombo. This was a high-risk strategy, exposing the Eastern Fleet to an enemy force whose composition and capability was still unknown.[109] Ironically, the Catalina crew which sighted the Japanese on 4 April saw enough of the task force to have convinced Somerville that he faced a substantial fleet, not a raiding force. Had the crew been able to get this information out before being shot down, Somerville's actions might have been different.[110]

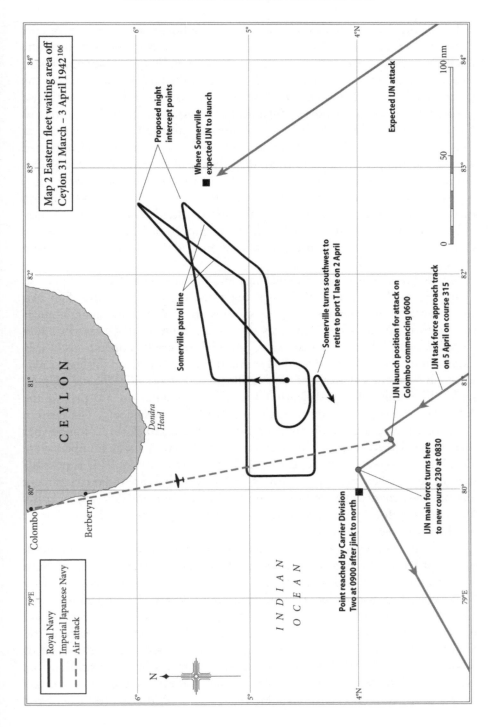

Map 2 Eastern fleet waiting area off
Ceylon 31 March – 3 April 1942 [106]

Proposed night
intercept points

Where Somerville
expected IJN to launch

Expected IJN attack

Somerville patrol line

Somerville turns southwest to
retire to port T late on 2 April

IJN launch position for attack on
Colombo commencing 0600

IJN task force approach track
on 5 April on course 315

CEYLON

Colombo

Berberyn

Dondra
Head

80°

81°

82°

83°

84°

100 nm

50

0

Point reached by Carrier Division
Two at 0900 after jink to north

IJN main force turns here
to new course 230 at 0830

INDIAN
OCEAN

N

Royal Navy
Imperial Japanese Navy
Air attack

79°E

80°

81°

82°

83°

84°

5°

6°

4°N

Taking the fleet to sea was sensible, in case the Japanese were aware of Port T, but Somerville would have been wiser to loiter well to the west until the intelligence picture cleared, especially given the possibility the Japanese might also move west and conduct a rigorous search for the Eastern Fleet. In fact, the Japanese task force did undertake dawn searches on 5 April to the southwest (240–280 degrees to a depth of 200 miles) and northwest (310–320 degrees to a depth of 170 miles). The first search cone found the *Dorsetshire* force at 1000. One of Somerville's Fulmar search planes launched at 0800 also spotted a Japanese searcher about 140 miles directly ahead of Force A at 0855. This aircraft was at the extreme southwest edge of the Japanese southwest cone. Apart from shadowing the *Dorsetshire* force, the Japanese conducted no further searches after the morning aircraft returned. Nagumo apparently judged the morning searches would have picked up any forces leaving Colombo after the alert the previous afternoon, and that no intervention from elsewhere was likely.[111]

Meanwhile, Somerville continued east at 18 knots, even after the attack on Colombo on the morning of 5 April suggested the IJN had more than two carriers, and after observing a large IJN air group on *Warspite*'s radar, 84 miles to the northeast at 1344. This was the strike going in on *Dorsetshire* and *Cornwall*, which both sank just before 1400.[112] Somerville's operations officer, Commander Kaye Edden, described seeing this paint briefly on the large radar screen in *Warspite*'s charthouse. Somerville immediately said – 'That's a Jap air strike.'[113] Somerville's justification for his movements on 5 April to the Admiralty in his post-action report of 11 April is unconvincing. The Eastern Fleet were aware quite soon after the early morning attack on Colombo that seventy-five IJNAF aircraft had been involved.[114] Actual attack numbers were 127, but even seventy-five suggested more than two carriers.[115] It is possible that Somerville believed radar warning and his ability to use radar to intercept any Japanese shadowing aircraft minimised the risk of being taken by surprise. He was, therefore, willing to head towards the Japanese, confident that he would have time to evade if necessary.

The relative movements of the British and Japanese fleets on the afternoon of 5 April raise fascinating questions regarding the performance of both combatants.[116] Detailed analysis reveals the almost reckless risk taken by Somerville, but also shows that he came remarkably close to launching a successful night strike on Nagumo's force that evening. The best visual presentation of what happened is the large-scale map in Admiralty Battle Summary No 15.[117] This shows the movements of British forces, the scope of Somerville's various air searches, and British estimates of the position of the Japanese task force, based on aircraft sightings and other intelligence over the course of the day. Successive Catalina reports from 0700 to 1100 placed the

IJN force about 120 miles south of Ceylon, apparently 'marking time', in Somerville's estimation, as they recovered aircraft.[118] A further Catalina was shot down early on 5 April in the course of this surveillance. There was also some SIGINT from HMS *Anderson* monitoring Japanese air traffic.[119]

The picture provided by Battle Summary 15 excludes the Japanese track, which was unknown when it was published in 1943. However, the Japanese track can be superimposed from post-war records, including a post-action report from the carrier *Hiryu*.[120] Japanese movements on 5 April differ from those shown in most published maps of the Ceylon action.[121] These show a fairly accurate launch position for the attack on Colombo, executed from a point 200 miles to the south at 0600, but then show Nagumo adopting a course of 200 degrees (just west of south) by mid-morning and maintaining this for about 100 miles before turning southeast to retire. In reality, the Japanese force continued to close Ceylon on their mean approach course of 315 for two hours after launch, before turning southwest at 0830.[122] Nagumo's southwest heading of 230 was a more northerly course than that usually represented.[123] It ran some 5 miles south of the 230 bearing drawn on the Battle Summary 15 map which derived from an FECB intercept received by Somerville at 1700.[124] This bearing could not replicate the Japanese track because, although FECB reported the Japanese force steering 230 at 24 knots at 1400, they could not link this with any starting position. The bearing was therefore drawn by Somerville's staff from Catalina positions received during the morning, which were fairly accurate. Although it related to 1400, the information did not get to Somerville until 1700, long after Nagumo had turned southeast to retire.

The new Japanese heading of 230 was probably initially selected to align with the wind direction[125] and facilitate recovery of the Colombo strike force between 0945 and 1030.[126] However, the course was also ideal to close the *Dorsetshire* force, sighted by a search aircraft from the cruiser *Tone* at 1000 and initially reported steering southwest at 24 knots.[127] Throughout the morning the Japanese force moved very fast, maintaining a speed of advance of 24 knots, which increased to 28 knots after the *Dorsetshire* force sighting.[128] There was no 'marking time' off Ceylon waiting to recover aircraft, as Somerville believed. Although neither knew it, Nagumo and Somerville were therefore now steering almost reciprocal courses and closing at almost 50 miles an hour.

The Japanese began launching a strike force against the British cruisers from 1145.[129] Preparations for this did not go smoothly. There were delays in rearming the reserve strike force in Carrier Division Five, *Shokaku* and *Zuikaku*, with torpedoes in exchange for the high-explosive bombs prepared for a second strike on Colombo. Nagumo eventually abandoned a torpedo strike and ordered the dive-bombers, by now available in *Akagi* and Carrier Division Two (*Soryu* and *Hiryu*), to be used instead.[130] The British cruisers were found without difficulty and both sunk by 1400.[131] A Japanese search plane from the cruiser *Tone*, which had been shadowing the British cruisers, searched 50 miles forward of their track and reported nothing to be seen.[132] It was fortunate this plane did not continue. Ten minutes' flying time would have brought the Eastern Fleet Force A into view and Nagumo had a torpedo strike at last ready in Carrier Division Five.

Once he had recovered the *Dorsetshire* strike force by 1445, Nagumo turned southeast to a course of 135, an exact reciprocal of his original approach course for the attack on Colombo. This was the first leg of a wide sweep south of Ceylon to position him for a strike on Trincomalee four days later. Japanese records are unclear whether this turn took place at 1500 or 1530, but the latter seems probable. The location of the turn was approximately 2-35N and 78-24E, about 130 miles northeast of Somerville's then position.[133] Nagumo maintained a speed of advance of at least 20 knots until midnight, before reducing to about 12 knots for the eastward passage round Ceylon. The comparative British and Japanese tracks are shown in Map 3.[134]

Simultaneously with Nagumo's turn southeast, Carrier Division Two, comprising *Hiryu* and *Soryu* and their escorting destroyers, commenced a jink in the opposite direction, starting just after 1500 to a depth of 13 miles, before turning back at about 1545.[135] This jink was conducted at high speed with rapid course changes, including a full figure of eight shortly after 1600, in order to launch fighters to intercept Somerville's incoming Albacore search aircraft. Carrier Division Two eventually passed through the 1530 main force turning point shortly before 1700, travelling at 28 knots to catch up the main force now some 30 miles ahead. The reason for this jink illustrated in Map 4 is not clear. There was a similar jink to the northwest by Carrier Division Two shortly after the 0830 turn to the southwest that morning, although then the deviation was only 6 miles. Possibly the purpose was to check the most exposed flank of the force or, alternatively, to disguise a major course change from any watching eyes. If the latter was the intention, on this second occasion it was successful.[136]

When Nagumo turned to the southeast at 1530, Somerville was still heading east on a mean course of 070, which he would hold until 1726. He had launched four Albacores from *Indomitable* at 1400 to search a 40-degree sector on his port bow (025–065 degrees) out to 200 miles.[138] The location of Nagumo's 1530 turn was at 150 miles on the centre line of the second Albacore search arc from the north, and his new course of 135 would take him through the bottom far corner of the overall search arc about five hours later. This meant the two northerly Albacores were likely to find Carrier Division Two on its jink to the northwest, while the two southerly aircraft should find the main force. In the event, the two northerly aircraft made contact, but the southerly ones did not. The aircraft covering the outer of the two northern sectors sent

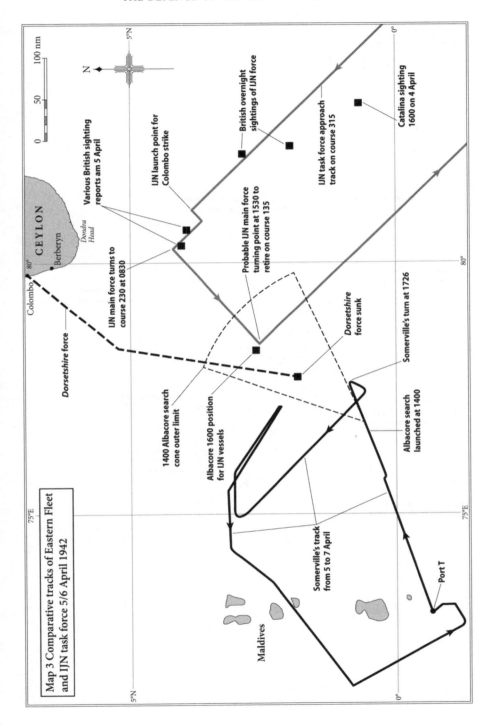

Map 3 Comparative tracks of Eastern Fleet and IJN task force 5/6 April 1942

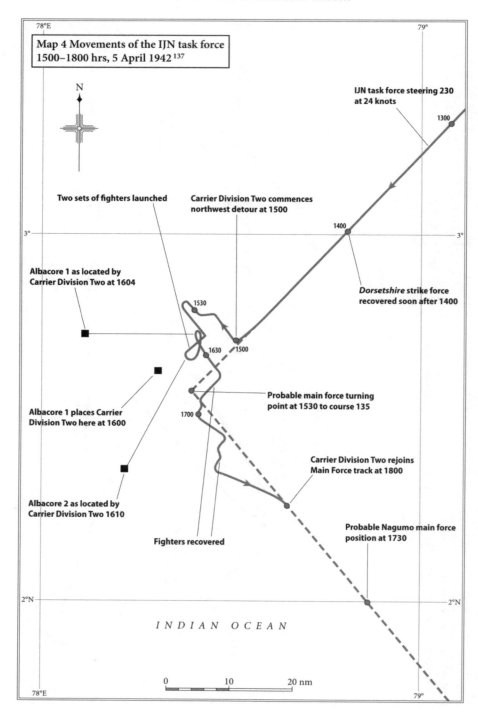

Map 4 Movements of the IJN task force
1500–1800 hrs, 5 April 1942 [137]

N

IJN task force steering 230
at 24 knots

1300

Two sets of fighters launched

Carrier Division Two commences
northwest detour at 1500

1400

Albacore 1 as located by
Carrier Division Two at 1604

Dorsetshire strike force
recovered soon after 1400

1530

1630   1500

Probable main force turning
point at 1530 to course 135

Albacore 1 places Carrier
Division Two here at 1600

1700

Carrier Division Two rejoins
Main Force track at 1800

Albacore 2 as located by
Carrier Division Two 1610

Fighters recovered

Probable Nagumo main force
position at 1730

2°N   2°N

I N D I A N   O C E A N

0   10   20 nm

78°E   79°

an enemy report with a position, but no course or speed or force composition, at 1600, though this did not reach Somerville until 1655.[139] This position was 8 miles southwest of where Japanese records place Carrier Division Two at that time (Map 3). Both positions were estimates, so neither is definitive, although the difficulties of air navigation mean the Japanese one was probably more accurate. This aircraft was subsequently attacked by a Zero fighter launched from *Hiryu* at 1604[140] but successfully evaded, though with some damage. The second aircraft sent no report and was shot down at 1628.[141] *Hiryu*'s action report shows the location of the two Albacore aircraft 25 miles apart, one due west and one to the southwest.[142]

The co-ordinates of the 1600 position transmitted by the first Albacore placed the Japanese force 125 miles from Somerville at that time. Simultaneously with his receipt of this information, at 1655 Somerville now received Colombo's SIGINT report at 1700. The impact of the latter, putting the Japanese on a southwest course at 1400 and thundering towards him at 24 knots, was considerable. It suggested Somerville was rather too close to a force he now judged much superior to his own, and that the Japanese might be heading to attack Port T, which Somerville estimated they could hit at any time after 0400 the following morning.[143] These considerations inevitably dictated Somerville's decisions over the next two hours or so. His immediate response was to turn southwest at 1726 to open the range, or at least keep his distance. As Somerville started this turn, the Nagumo main force was just 120 miles away fine on his port bow and tracking southeast at 20 knots. Carrier Division Two was further round to his northeast, rushing to catch up Nagumo, and even closer to Somerville at barely 100 miles. It was forty minutes to sunset. Both Nagumo and Carrier Division Two were completely oblivious to Somerville's presence on their starboard flank. Nagumo had failed to commission any searches following the appearance of the two Albacores, which he recognised as coming from a carrier, and had taken no look out to the southwest all afternoon. If Somerville had held his easterly heading and speed, Carrier Division Two would have passed directly in front of him at about 2100 at a range of only 20 miles.

Nagumo's behaviour following the appearance of two Albacore search planes is difficult to understand. The Japanese recognised the Albacores as carrier aircraft and, since they were operating 350 miles from Ceylon, accepted that there was a carrier in the vicinity.[144] They maintained an alert that night and planned to search for and attack the carrier at dawn. There are two puzzles here. At 1630 there were still two hours of daylight – enough time to find the supposed carrier, allowing the Japanese to make dispositions for the morning, even if immediate attack was not possible. However, Nagumo maintained an uninterrupted course at 20 knots to the southeast which would take him away from the carrier. He issued no instructions to Carrier Division Two, which also headed away. Apparently, hunting down this carrier was not a priority. Nor, presumably, was it seen as a threat, even to the isolated Division Two. Commander Mitsuo Fuchida, leader of the strike group at both Pearl Harbor and Ceylon, later offered another explanation. During Operation C, search planes often lost their way and the carriers had to send out homing signals. This risked alerting the enemy to the task force's presence, leading to reluctance by Nagumo and his staff to send out search planes, if it could be avoided.[145]

Although he did not know it, Somerville was therefore now superbly placed for a night attack. Not only was a night torpedo strike by his Albacores eminently feasible, but even a night surface attack on Carrier Division Two was possible, when he would enjoy superior gun power and the advantage of radar. He needed one more piece of intelligence to localise the Japanese position – course, speed and, ideally, force composition – sufficiently accurately to enable a night ASV shadowing operation, preparatory to launching a full strike. Thirty Albacores, perhaps attacking in two waves, and ordered to focus on the Division Two carriers, would have a good chance of disabling, and probably sinking, both of them before 2200 when they would rejoin Nagumo's main force. The IJN was superbly trained for night surface operations, but did not expect, and therefore made no provision for countering, night air attack. IJN carriers also conducted maintenance at night, which lowered their damage control status and rendered them more vulnerable.

An attack by Somerville before 2200 would then have left eight hours of darkness to evade and put his force perhaps 300 miles from Nagumo by dawn. (This figure assumes Somerville would have retreated west at 20 knots, giving him 160 miles over eight hours. Even if the attack range was below 100 miles, then 250 miles by dawn is credible.) The standard IJN search range in early 1942 was a single phase radial pattern out to a maximum of 300–350 miles, but often less.[146] None of the searches executed during Operation C exceeded 250 miles.[147] Although most IJN aircrew were night-capable, there was no IJN doctrine for night air attack. Nagumo could not therefore counter-strike in darkness, or do much before dawn to find a Royal Navy force that could have come from almost any direction. Given the strategic importance to Japan of his remaining force, and his distance from support, he would almost certainly have retired, however reluctantly, rather than risk pursuit deeper into the Indian Ocean.[148]

At 1745 the Albacore responsible for the 1600 position, damaged after evading the Zero, landed on *Indomitable* and could amplify its sighting report.[149] With sunset less than half an hour away, it was a dramatic moment. Once the Albacore had cleared the deck, torpedo strike forces were ranged on both Somerville's carriers, with crews standing by in the cockpits while the search crew were debriefed.[150] All Somerville needed was a sufficiently accurate report from this Albacore to initiate a follow-up search in the right direction. Sadly, he did not get it. The debriefing produced two signals from Rear Admiral Aircraft Carriers Denis Boyd. The first received at 1800 provided a position for the Japanese force at 1710, putting them at 020 and 120 miles from Force A at this time and about 10 miles north of the original 1600 position. It was 20 miles north of where the Japanese record places Carrier Division Two.[151] The origin of this 1710 position is a mystery. Somerville's three surviving search aircraft had all landed by 1745. The Albacore's cruising speed of 125 knots meant none of them could, therefore, have sighted the Japanese task force at 1710, then 120 miles away. The position could have been an estimate based on a revised 1600 position which would be transmitted at 1817. But why choose the rather odd time of 1710 for an estimate rather than 1730 or 1800? If it was an estimate, why not say so?[152]

The second signal at 1817 amplified the original 1600 sighting, but without relating it to the newer 1710 position.[153] It had three crucial pieces of information: a revised position for the 1600 sighting about 25 miles north of the original reported co-ordinates; a force composition of two carriers and three unknown vessels; and crucially, a course of northwest. None of these points was immediately helpful to Somerville. The credibility of the original 1600 position, which as we have seen was accurate, was now undermined. The strength of Carrier Division Two had been correctly identified, but Somerville knew by now this was not the whole Japanese force, so it begged as many questions as it answered. The course of northwest was not consistent with the 1710 position, which was about 20 miles southeast of the new 1600 position, and would therefore imply a course of southeast. Neither Boyd nor Somerville addressed this discrepancy.

Possibly Somerville had now lost faith in the reliability of any of these reports.[154] At any rate, he chose to focus on the northwest course in the second signal and brought his force round to parallel it. He still planned a night attack, but judged he must have better intelligence.[155] He therefore ordered an ASV search out to 200 miles, but this initially concentrated on a narrow northern arc with a single aircraft, before additional aircraft extended the arc eastwards.[156] One other piece of intelligence might have helped Somerville at this point. FECB broke a JN 25B message late on 5 April giving the planned movement of the IJN carrier force the next day. This was immediately signalled to Somerville, but through sheer mischance was received garbled.[157] The extended air search proved too late, even to catch Carrier Division Two, now fast opening on a reciprocal course. By 2200, Division Two had rejoined Nagumo some 180 miles due east of Somerville, beyond the southern edge of the new extended search arc, and well beyond effective reach for a night strike, given the limited coverage of ASV 2. Nagumo had commenced the wide circle south and east of Ceylon to position for a strike on Trincomalee on 9 April. Somerville's opportunity was over.

Nagumo did commission a dawn search on 6 April to look for the suspect Royal Navy carrier, but it was not comprehensive, and he did not interrupt his rapid passage east.[158] Somerville now had enough intelligence from SIGINT to convince him the Japanese force, now estimated to include four carriers and three battleships, was beyond his capabilities and that he must err on the side of caution.[159] The need for caution was underlined by the declining serviceability of his fighter strength. On 8 April he informed the Admiralty that this was down to six Martlets, eight Fulmars and eleven Hurricanes.[160]

Royal Navy and IJN performance during the Ceylon operation compared

The operational picture on the afternoon of 5 April illustrates important strengths and weaknesses on both sides. To take the British side first, the traditional picture of the Eastern Fleet off Ceylon in April 1942 is of an ineffective force composed of outdated ships and aircraft, weakened further by limited training and experience. The prospects of a night attack by the Royal Navy have never been adequately assessed, since it is assumed Somerville was never likely to bring one off. It is also assumed that given the disparity of forces, retribution would have been swift and inevitable, rendering the whole concept most unwise. Somerville receives some credit for doing the best he could with a poor hand, but is also viewed as somewhere between naive and over-optimistic, and lucky to escape.

There is much truth in this picture, and this chapter has added further criticisms of Somerville – notably, his failure to exploit all the available intelligence and his poor positioning in the period 31 March to 2 April. The decision to rush eastward from Port T on 5 April, rather than wait for more intelligence of the Japanese composition, bordered on the reckless.[161] However, the afternoon of 5 April demonstrates that this array of negatives is not the whole story. Somerville's concept of maintaining distance during the day, while closing to attack at night, and then retiring without undue risk, was tactically achievable in the right circumstances. Somerville's 1400 search was in exactly the right sector. One further sighting report accurately fixing Carrier Division Two or identifying Nagumo's position and post-1530 southeast course would have made a subsequent night interception feasible. The Eastern Fleet was not, therefore, the helpless bystander usually portrayed. It had the power to do serious damage.

For all their successes on 5 April, and later off Trincomalee, the all-conquering IJN task force showed weaknesses too that day. The most important were rigidity and failure of imagination in their command, and poor aerial reconnaissance. The main Japanese strategic objective was to find and destroy the Royal Navy Eastern Fleet. They had a reasonably accurate picture of its likely composition, although they overestimated British air strength in India and Ceylon.[162] Their prior planning assumed the fleet must be in Colombo or Trincomalee. The attack on the morning of 5 April proved it was not in the former, so Nagumo concluded it must be in the latter. Rigidity of mindset meant other options were not seriously considered.[163] The standard dawn searches had only yielded the *Dorsetshire* force, so the assumption was there was nothing else to be found. Failure of imagination lay in not asking where the *Dorsetshire* force might be going, and in not recognising a link with the appearance of two Albacores just two hours later.[164] Aerial reconnaissance planning and execution throughout the period 4–6 April was weak.[165] Sweeping ahead of the force and on the exposed flanks while in potentially hostile waters was a sensible precaution. Apart from rather limited set-piece searches on the mornings of 5 and 6 April, this was not done.[166]

It is instructive to draw comparisons with the Midway operations just two months later. There are striking parallels. Both IJN operations involved a primary objective of a long-distance carrier strike on a land target, with a secondary objective of engaging an enemy fleet at sea. The rationale for the land strikes was different. At Ceylon, the objective was the elimination of the Eastern Fleet, but the Japanese judged the best means of achieving this was to catch it in harbour. At Midway, the objective was to take the island. There was similar advance intelligence warning of the primary target, which enabled both the Royal Navy and US Navy to plan an ambush on the attacking fleet. The respective Royal Navy and US Navy commanders were both under strict instructions to avoid placing their fleets at serious risk. They should only execute an ambush if they were confident of inflicting significantly greater damage than they might receive. Both commanders ran rather greater risk than superiors would have wished. Both got away with it.[167]

In both cases, the defences at the primary target were strong enough to achieve some attrition on the attacking force. IJN errors at Ceylon were repeated at Midway. Its aerial searches there also proved inadequate[168] and its command again displayed rigidity, a preference to stick to preconceived plans, and a general lack of critical thinking.[169] The Ceylon operations exposed other potential weaknesses in IJN doctrine and capability which reappeared at Midway. Preparations for the *Dorsetshire* attack demonstrated that it was difficult to redeploy and rearm a reserve strike force for a different role at short notice.[170] During the Trincomalee raid on 9 April, nine Royal Air Force Blenheim bombers caught the IJN carrier force by complete surprise and came close to hitting *Akagi*. This revealed that without radar warning an IJN carrier force was highly vulnerable to an unexpected attack, raising questions about the desirability of concentrating the carriers as a single group.[171]

There were differences between the two engagements. At Ceylon, the IJN force was stronger, with five carriers instead of four, while the Royal Navy was much weaker, with far fewer aircraft and no prospect of using them in a day attack. At Midway, the intelligence was more precise, with advantage for force positioning and timing.[172] Given these parallels, were there safer options available to Somerville for inflicting a defeat, or at least significant damage, on the IJN fleet at Ceylon? He achieved an excellent position on the afternoon of 5 April, but by taking a reckless risk, placing his force well within the potential search cone of a much superior enemy. He only survived through Japanese incompetence. With better exploitation of intelligence and better positioning, was it possible to deliver a blow of comparable strategic effect to Midway without unacceptable risk or was the disparity of forces too great?

Somerville was correct that his only viable offensive option was a night strike. Successful execution depended on two things: accurate location of the IJN force and tracking it long enough to get in effective Albacore range, about 125 miles, one hour's flying time; and avoiding counter-detection during the approach, getting no closer than 200 miles before sunset and opening the range beyond 200 miles by dawn. The events of 4 and 5 April demonstrated how difficult this was against an opponent with a constant fighter umbrella able to despatch any shadowing aircraft in short order, at least in daylight,[173] and the ability to mount surveillance over a wide area. For Kaye Edden, Somerville's Staff Officer Plans, combining these different objectives was 'daunting'.[174] The Royal Navy had not faced this challenge before during interceptions in the Atlantic or Mediterranean.

The events of 5 April nevertheless show how, with careful positioning and some luck, Somerville could have achieved a successful attack. If he had loitered 150 miles northeast of Port T, he would have been relatively safe from daytime detection during any likely track taken by the Japanese, other than a direct attack on Port T itself. Successful interdiction then depended on achieving a sufficiently accurate fix of the Japanese position and course to enable a high-speed run in from mid-afternoon keeping just outside Japanese search cones, which would cease before dusk. The afternoon of 5 April illustrated that the desired fix from a combination of Catalina observation, his own searches, and perhaps a lucky JN 25B intercept was possible.

The odds on such a scenario were still long. The Albacores had to localise a fast-moving and probably manoeuvring force with ASV that had a maximum range of 20 miles. The crews evidently believed they could do such an attack, but were inexperienced, there were no real precedents, and Royal Navy doctrine and planning for multi-carrier operations at night was in its infancy.[175] If Somerville had possessed two carriers as operationally efficient as *Ark Royal* in Force H, with which he was wont to compare his present carriers unfavourably, the odds would have been better.[176] With his present force, it was possible, but would have needed more luck. The judgement reached at the end of the previous chapter that an intact Force Z retained in the Indian Ocean from November 1941 would have spurred operational efficiency in the Eastern Fleet is relevant here. Somerville had one other potential asset for a night attack. The two cruisers *Emerald* and *Enterprise* were old, but the fastest in the Royal Navy, with the heaviest torpedo armament and good radar, making them well-suited to a sudden hit and run.[177] We have seen that getting within surface strike range of Carrier Division Two was entirely possible. The Americans had a heavy share of luck at Midway, and Somerville only needed one more lucky break at around 1800 on 5 April. In both cases, luck dovetailed neatly with Japanese incompetence.

How, then, should we rate Somerville's performance off Ceylon? He was regarded by his peers, and by many historians since, as the outstanding Royal Navy admiral of the Second World War, alongside Cunningham. His overall war record as a naval commander and fighting sailor speaks for itself. He deserves great credit for pulling together a scratch force very quickly into the semblance of a viable fleet. He showed characteristic coolness and tactical flair in manoeuvring into a potential attacking position on 5 April, and then in returning the following day to rescue the *Dorsetshire* force survivors, this despite knowing that Nagumo could still be in the area with what Somerville by then knew was a much superior force.[178] But he underestimated the risks he was running at least up to dusk on 5 April. He drew over-optimistic conclusions from the available intelligence, he grossly underestimated IJN air strength, and he hazarded his fleet in direct contravention of his instructions from the chiefs of staff. Ceylon was not his finest hour.

Pound never directly criticised Somerville for his actions, but he was uneasy, demonstrated by the care taken with a naval staff draft on the operation prepared for the prime minister on 3 May. He admitted that 'with the knowledge we have now' (of IJN force composition), it was 'undesirable to engage'.[179] Had Nagumo caught Somerville, as he would have done with a competent search plan on 5 April, or if he had arrived earlier on 1 or 2 April and had exploited Somerville's poor positioning south of Ceylon, the consequences for the Royal Navy and Allied cause would have been catastrophic, as Willis and Layton recognised. The latter famously signalled the Admiralty on 6 April that the Eastern Fleet 'faces immediate annihilation'.[180]

Willis found it hard to explain Somerville's actions, which ran counter to the 'fleet in being' concept they had agreed. He speculated the explanation might lie in the Admiralty accusation in November 1940 that Somerville had been insufficiently aggressive in pursuing a retiring Italian fleet, and that Somerville was determined not to face this charge again.[181] This is possible, but his instructions from the chiefs of staff on 19 March not to run risks were clear enough. Edden dismissed Willis's view, insisting that Somerville took calculated risks on 5 and 6 April and that after the loss of the *Dorsetshire* force, his priority was to rescue 1500 potential survivors, which he achieved.[182] This is probably a fair assessment for 6 April, when it is difficult to see what alternatives Somerville could have adopted, given the information available to him that morning. Returning to Port T or Colombo were both too risky. Positioning to pick up the *Dorsetshire* force survivors, while maintaining a rigorous all-round air search, which he did, was the least bad option.[183]

Somerville survived and kept his core fleet intact, but he had still suffered a strategic defeat. Having already contributed to the loss of the Far East empire, the Royal Navy was now obliged to retreat west and cede control of the bulk of the Indian Ocean for at least a temporary period. The naval losses off Ceylon – *Dorsetshire*, *Cornwall*, and later *Hermes*, along with various minor vessels – were bad enough. Indeed, given their immediate strategic effect and the blow to British confidence, they were a defeat as substantial for the Royal Navy as Matapan for the Italians. The wider balance sheet from Nagumo's raid and the related operations of Vice Admiral Jisaburo Ozawa's Malaya force in the Bay of Bengal also looked grim from the British point of view. The Royal Air Force had suffered badly from the two attacks on Ceylon, losing a third of its fighter strength, and almost all its, admittedly feeble, strike force.[184] Twenty-three merchant vessels had also been lost, almost all to Ozawa, and there was moderate damage to port facilities. The British took some comfort from the aircraft losses they believed they had inflicted on the IJN, but these were exaggerated, and the total loss to the Japanese from their whole Indian Ocean foray was just eighteen aircraft, with about thirty-one damaged.[185]

There is an argument that Operation C was also a strategic failure for the Japanese.[186] At first sight, this seems absurd. Asserting control over the East Indian Ocean and driving Somerville back to East Africa was a major gain by any standard, one which could have been extended through different choices in the coming months. However, Japan probably had sufficient superiority to seize Ceylon in early April, yet had elected not to try. There is a compelling case that by then failing to achieve the primary goal of Operation C, the destruction of the Eastern Fleet, Japan was now tempted on to a path that would rapidly close down its options. As described below, immediate return to the Indian Ocean was not possible but, for a variety of reasons, Japan was then persuaded to give priority to the Pacific theatre instead. By contrast, successful destruction of the Eastern Fleet in early April off Ceylon might have encouraged Japan to resume the idea of an all-out offensive in the Indian Ocean, while remaining on the defensive in the Pacific. With most of its Eastern Fleet gone, Britain would have struggled to prevent Japan from taking Ceylon and severely disrupting communications to the Middle East and Persian Gulf. This might then have had far-reaching consequences for the progress of the whole war. In that sense, missing the Eastern Fleet was more than a lost opportunity. It represents one of the great 'might-have-beens' for the Axis.[187]

Strategic consequences of the Ceylon attack and British reinforcement

The strategic consequences of the IJN attack on Ceylon, and the resulting exposure of the Eastern Fleet, were addressed in two joint planning staff papers dated 18 and 21 April.[188] These drew on an updated Joint Intelligence Committee assessment, which anticipated further IJN raids and the continuing risk of a full-scale invasion of Ceylon as well as simultaneous pressure on northeast India.[189] The key lesson the planning staff drew was that Royal Navy ship-borne air strength was greatly inferior to that of the IJN.[190] The IJN could, therefore, exercise air superiority to command sea communications where it wished, and the Eastern Fleet was powerless to intervene. The planners judged that the first Japanese priority was to consolidate their hold on Southeast Asia and Burma, but a rapid move to drive Britain out of the war by disrupting supplies to the Middle East and India, and of Persian oil, must be tempting. SIGINT seemed to support this judgement. On 13 April, the Japanese foreign minister told the German ambassador in Tokyo that Japan was thrusting towards Ceylon and the area north of it. This thrust would extend 'step by step' into the western Indian Ocean.[191] To achieve this goal, the planning staff argued, the Japanese must take Ceylon and destroy the Eastern Fleet. Safeguarding the fleet was paramount, and took precedence over holding Ceylon. The Eastern Fleet must, therefore, retreat to East Africa until it could be reinforced sufficiently to contest the central Indian Ocean on acceptable terms. The ideal target strength was five modern capital ships and seven fleet carriers, of which five and four were planned by August. In the meantime, defence of Ceylon must rely on air power.

Churchill, meanwhile, highlighted the grave risks in the Indian Ocean in letters to President Roosevelt dated 7 and 15 April.[192] His second letter emphasised that Britain for some months could not match the naval forces the Japanese had demonstrated they were willing to deploy in the Indian Ocean.[193] The loss of Ceylon and invasion of northeast India were real possibilities, but this would only be the beginning. There was little to stop the Japanese dominating the western Indian Ocean and undermining Britain's whole position in the Middle East. He stressed here the consequences of losing Persian oil and the supply line to Russia. Overall, the situation was 'more than we can bear'. He sought United States support through diversionary action in the Pacific, further reinforcement in the Atlantic to release Royal Navy units, or direct naval support in the Indian Ocean itself. This letter reflected discussion at the Defence Committee the previous day, at which General Marshall and Harry Hopkins were present.[194]

The outcome of this Defence Committee meeting has proved controversial. The British endorsed Marshall's proposals for an early invasion of western Europe. However, the prime minister and Brooke insisted that it was still essential to hold the Middle East, India and Australasia. A second front in Europe must not compromise these interests. The justification for their caveat has since been questioned. Brooke is accused of exaggerating the consequences that would follow Japanese control of the Indian Ocean, and demanding an open-ended commitment from the United States to prevent collapse in the Indian Ocean and Middle East. The implication is that the British leadership was engaged in deliberate deception. They had no real intention of committing to a second front at this time, but sought to keep the United States focused on 'Germany first', while they pursued their own interests.[195]

It is important to look dispassionately at the threat to the Indian Ocean as it appeared at the time. Charging Brooke with exaggeration reflects hindsight, rather than a fair appraisal of the risks as Brooke must have seen them. In the wake of Nagumo's raid, a return operation by Japan to seize Ceylon looked entirely credible. So did a concerted IJN effort across the rest of 1942, by raiders, submarines and select use of carrier task forces, to cut effective communication in the western Indian Ocean. If the Japanese pursued this option all-out, there was little the US Navy could do in the Pacific during 1942 to prevent them. From the British perspective, an IJN offensive might, at a minimum, eliminate the prospect of a British Empire material advantage in the North African campaign by the autumn. It could also drastically reduce oil supplies across the eastern theatre, with major consequences for the empire war effort, and for any United States operations mounted from India and Australia. Finally, it would severely disrupt aid on what was becoming the primary military lend-lease route to Russia, with unknowable consequences for Russia's survival. Japan might achieve even more. Countering these risks had to be a top priority.

Nor was Britain seeking an 'open-ended commitment'. Britain wanted American support for a limited period of two and a half months, while sufficient reinforcements were gathered to make the Eastern Fleet reasonably competitive with the maximum force the Japanese were likely to deploy. In effect, Britain's war planners must bridge a period while key Royal Navy units were under repair, or working up, and before new construction became available. *Valiant* was under repair in Durban following her damage at Alexandria in December and expected to complete in June. *Nelson* and *Rodney* were working up after repair and refit. The carriers *Eagle* and *Furious* were in refit. The new battleships *Anson* and *Howe* were expected to be operational in August and October respectively. By the time the Defence Committee met again just a week later on 22 April, a target date of 30 June had been set for assembling the enhanced Eastern Fleet and the relevant forces earmarked.[196] This fleet would have been significantly stronger than the forces available to the US Navy to hold Hawaii.

The British leadership may well have been privately doubtful that Marshall's vision for an early second front reflected realistic understanding of the logistics and the quality of enemy opposition. Hindsight suggests they were right. They inevitably prioritised the protection of the wider empire, because it defined Britain's status as a world power but, more important, because it provided essential war resources. Many in the United States leadership also supported Churchill's emphasis on the Middle East, India and Australasia, for their own reasons.[197]

In response to British pleas, the United States judged it could not help in the Indian Ocean, but it did offer limited support in the Atlantic and, most important, diversionary action was underway in the Pacific. This was the bombing raid on Tokyo led by Lieutenant Colonel James Doolittle. This raid by a small force of B-25 bombers launched from the US Navy carriers *Enterprise* and *Hornet* took place on 18 April. The military impact was negligible, but the psychological effect on the Japanese military leadership was profound. It did not initiate the Midway operation, which had already been approved two weeks previously. However, it underlined Yamamoto's conviction that the US Navy carrier force must be eliminated before other options, including further offensive action in the Indian Ocean, were contemplated. Crucially, it also caused the Japanese to add a second Midway objective – the occupation of the island.[198] The resulting conflict of priorities would have fatal consequences. Pound, meanwhile, underlined British anxieties during a visit to Washington in late April, and received sufficient assurances from Admiral King, the new Chief of Naval Operations, to confirm the feasibility of giving significant reinforcements to Somerville.[199]

The chiefs of staff copied the latest joint planning staff assessment to Somerville on 23 April. Its conclusion encapsulated how London saw the position in the East at this time:

If the Japanese press boldly westwards, without pause for consolidation and are not deterred by offensive activities or threats by the Eastern Fleet or American Fleet, nor by the rapid reinforcement of our air forces in North-East India, then the Indian Empire is in grave danger. The security of the Middle East and its essential supply lines will be threatened. The Middle East and India are inter-dependent.[200]

Somerville, shocked by the ferocity of the IJN strike on the *Dorsetshire* force, and now aware how close he had come to disaster, agreed with the London view.[201] He reinforced the disparity in air power in a sharp exchange with the Admiralty at the beginning of May. For daytime air strike, the Royal Navy was 'completely outclassed' by the Japanese, though Somerville judged that in low cloud or at night it had an advantage. He hoped by now it was appreciated that the Fleet Air Arm, 'suffering from arrested development for many years', could not compete successfully with an IJN carrier arm, 'which had devoted itself to producing aircraft fit for sailors to fly in'.[202] Pending the arrival of better aircraft, he proposed a substantial increase in fighter complement, employing deck parking and outriggers where necessary.[203] The prime minister took a personal interest in Somerville's proposals, which were broadly agreed, though it was recognised that achieving an adequate supply of Martlets would require high-level political lobbying in the United States.[204]

Fleet Air Arm aircraft deficiencies were not easily solved.[205] Despite constant British lobbying at the highest level, the flow of Martlet fighters from the United States remained barely adequate through most of 1942. It was well into 1943 before the first new strike aircraft arrived.[206] In the meantime, Somerville's belief that the IJN had deployed fighter-bombers led the Admiralty briefly to contemplate employing unsuitable Hurricane IIs in a similar role.[207] Some in the Royal Navy leadership, including Pound, still struggled to understand the revolutionary nature of carrier warfare as practised by the IJN, and shortly by the US Navy.[208] This was partly poor intelligence assessment, which continued to underestimate the number and quality of IJN aircraft deployed in their carriers and, therefore, their lead over an equivalent Royal Navy force.[209] It also reflected their persistent belief that the IJN would deploy capital ship raiders against trade on the German Atlantic model. This led to over-emphasis on comparative capital ship strength when measuring the effectiveness of the Eastern Fleet.[210] Churchill also still defaulted to the battleship as the ultimate arbiter of strength.[211]

Nevertheless, it is wrong to imply that the Royal Navy downplayed the role of the carrier in its future force planning, and its importance in bringing the eastern war to a successful conclusion.[212] Its commitment to the carrier as a fleet unit is evident in the extraordinary total of sixteen new light carriers of the Colossus and Majestic classes ordered in the single year 1942, when British war resources, not least shipbuilding capacity, were stretched to the limit. These highly successful ships provided two-thirds of the aircraft capacity at two-thirds of the cost of the latest Illustrious units. More important, by adopting commercial standards of construction and using commercial shipyards, they were completed much more quickly, with the first units commissioned in an average of twenty-seven months.[213] Before the end of the year, the newly appointed Deputy First Sea Lord, Admiral Sir Charles Kennedy-Purvis, was powerfully arguing that carriers represented 'the core of the future fleet', although Pound, still attached to the battleship, preferred the formula, 'the carrier is indispensable'.[214]

The few accounts of the Indian Ocean theatre in 1942 describe the Eastern Fleet, which collected at Kilindini in Kenya during April after the Ceylon raid, as an ineffective force incapable of contesting further serious IJN incursions. Its survival depended on keeping its distance until the US Navy victories at the Coral Sea and Midway rendered its existence largely irrelevant. Its status is seen, therefore, as confirmation of chronic British over-stretch, and Royal Navy inability to meet the demands of modern air warfare at sea.[215] This picture is misleading. Kilindini did, indeed, become the primary base for the Eastern Fleet for the rest of 1942. However, Somerville continued to deploy a fast carrier force, broadly equivalent to the Force A of early April, to the central Indian Ocean on a regular basis over the next six months. He operated from, or around, Ceylon for almost 50 per cent of this period.[216]

Furthermore, during April and May, in line with the joint planning staff recommendations on 18 April and the subsequent Defence Committee discussions, and the promises of indirect support from Washington, the Admiralty redoubled its efforts to send significant reinforcements to the Indian Ocean. By September at the latest, it intended to return an enhanced Eastern Fleet to Ceylon, with six modern or modernised capital ships and four fleet carriers.[217] This was broadly the force planned in Moore's December 1941 paper, but with additions. Three-quarters of the Royal Navy's major units would be in the Indian Ocean. The Home Fleet would be reduced to a minimum, while defence of the Mediterranean would rest on air power and light forces.[218] The Ceylon bases were to be upgraded in the interim, with a Ceylon air group of nine Royal Air Force squadrons, including a Beaufort torpedo force.[219]

These were, by any standard, serious forces, which demonstrated the continuing naval priority accorded to the eastern theatre. Both the initial fast carrier force and the Ceylon air group available in May took time to achieve what Somerville felt was an acceptable operational standard, but the enhanced fleet planned for the autumn could have contested the central Indian Ocean with every prospect of success. The Admiralty also recognised that this enhanced Eastern Fleet would be a sustained commitment with first call on aircraft carriers for the foreseeable future. At the end of 1943, it planned four fleet carriers and six escort carriers deployed in the Indian Ocean, with one fleet carrier and sixteen escort carriers allocated to the Home Fleet, and no carriers at all in the Mediterranean.[220]

The Fleet Air Arm aircraft limitations highlighted by Somerville would have persisted in the enhanced Eastern Fleet carrier force. However, the Royal Navy technological lead in radar and VHF radio, and their exploitation, substantially compensated for the continuing disparity in aircraft numbers and quality. The training and experience shortfall so evident to Somerville in April would also have been addressed. If *Indomitable*, *Formidable* and *Illustrious* had all remained in the Indian Ocean through 1942, these three carriers alone would have deployed some eighty fighters and sixty strike aircraft between them in September. The fighters would have included fifty Martlets. This Royal Navy fighter strength would be comparable to that deployed by the three US Navy carriers at Midway in June, but the Royal Navy had better radar detection and direction. It would have posed a formidable defence to any likely IJN air strike. Sixty ASV-equipped Albacores and Swordfish would have been an equally formidable night strike force.[221] Furthermore, the disparity between IJN and Royal Navy numbers was reducing through 1942, owing to the increasing difficulty the IJN had in maintaining its frontline strength. The IJN Midway strike force only had 151 aircraft.[222]

Proof that the Royal Navy could conduct advanced multi-carrier operations against the most sophisticated air opposition by the second half of 1942 is demonstrated by its performance in Operation Pedestal, the convoy run to relieve Malta in August.[223] Pedestal involved four carriers, including Somerville's *Indomitable*, transferred from the Indian Ocean.[224] The three carriers charged with air defence deployed seventy-two fighters against an estimated Axis force of 650 aircraft employed against the convoy during a three-day running battle between 11 and 14 August. Although convoy losses, both merchant vessels and naval escort, were high, the majority were caused by submarine and E-boat action, not air attack, where the defence proved effective. The two most intense days of air attack on 11 and 12 August only damaged one of the merchant vessels, their primary target, although they achieved minor damage to *Victorious* and more serious damage to *Indomitable*. This reflected excellent fighter defence from the carriers, with sophisticated use of radar and aircraft direction, and intense anti-aircraft fire from a well-constructed screen.[225] Indeed, on the morning of 12 August, 117 Italian aircraft and fifty-eight German achieved just the one ineffective hit on the carrier *Victorious*. Never before had the Axis air forces used so many aircraft for so little result.[226] Despite the losses, the convoy was a strategic success. Enough supplies got through to enable Malta to survive, with important implications for the eastern theatre. As noted previously, it is doubtful whether either the IJN or US Navy could have carried out a comparable operation, and in such a complex multi-threat environment, against an equivalent level of air attack at this time.

While established history has underestimated the true potential of the Royal Navy in the Indian Ocean during 1942, it has overestimated that of the IJN. Joint planning staff assessments of mid-April, arguing that the IJN could achieve air superiority where it wished, at least in the eastern half of the Indian Ocean but potentially further west too, were only true within narrow limits. It was one thing to conduct raids like Operation C. It was another to mount the sustained aerial effort necessary to capture Ceylon, or to provide the logistic back-up required for deep operations to challenge the Eastern Fleet and disrupt communications along the African coast and into the Persian Gulf. The First Air Fleet was not capable of any immediate follow up to Operation C. After six months of intense operations, it required maintenance and replenishment.[227] More seriously, the IJN was struggling to maintain its frontline air strength. Six months into the war, and immediately before the Midway campaign, IJN aircraft complements, especially in the carrier force, were not just 'fraying around the edges', but were 'downright awful'.[228]

On 7 December 1941 aircraft strength within the overall carrier force was 473, with just twenty-two reserves.[229] By the end of May, naval fighter production had kept pace with losses, with a net gain over this period of 121. However, production of the two main carrier attack aircraft, the Nakajima B5N2 Type 97 torpedo bomber and Aichi D3A1 Type 99 dive-bomber, was woeful, with just 143 aircraft built against losses of 273, a net deficit of 130. Incredibly, no Type 99s were produced during the four months December 1941 to March 1942. The available frontline carrier attack force by the time of Midway had therefore declined a staggering 40 per cent. Neither Nakajima nor Aichi had adequately prepared for wartime output, and both companies were focusing their attention on successor aircraft at the expense of existing types.[230] IJN land bomber strength was better. Production almost kept pace with losses over the first six months of the war, with a net deficit of just seventeen, easily covered by reserves. However, total IJN land bomber strength at the start of the war was just 339 aircraft with 106 reserves.[231] This was a small force to cover the numerous commitments the IJN faced in mid-1942.

To mount a successful invasion of Ceylon, the Japanese had to eliminate any British air threat, and generate sufficient air support for their landing forces to overcome a defence force of two Australian brigades. The necessary air effort could only come from a carrier force. Although, in theory, the Japanese could also have deployed land-based bombers from the Andaman Islands, these were 650 miles away. The navigation challenges were formidable, and the aircraft vulnerable to Royal Air Force radar-directed fighters. The Japanese could have attacked Ceylon in place of Midway at the beginning of June and with a similar force. This is the scale of attack the joint planning staff anticipated when preparing the 'Revised Defence Plan for Ceylon' at the end of April. They assumed attack by 250 aircraft, bombardment by a capital ship force, and a large invasion force.[232] The Royal Air Force reinforcements in place by June would have made the outcome much more finely balanced than in April. The

Japanese would have risked unacceptable levels of attrition, leaving them wide open to harassment by the more effective Eastern Fleet, and through American intervention elsewhere.

By June, an IJN carrier force would have faced three Hurricane squadrons, comprising sixty-four aircraft and a further 50 per cent reserves, and three strike squadrons, also with 50 per cent reserves, one of which had Beaufort torpedo bombers. Radar coverage and anti-aircraft defences had significantly improved.[233] Unless the Japanese could use Ceylon as a base, sustained operations in the western Indian Ocean were problematic. Even a limited raid would be difficult. Japan's shortage of aircraft also demonstrates that British fears regarding their use of Madagascar were exaggerated. It might have been possible to base a small submarine force there, but there was little prospect of sparing aircraft to deploy there during 1942. Such aircraft could only have been flown in from carriers with the necessary support personnel coming by ship, all deployed under cover of a substantial task force.

Neither the British nor the Americans had intelligence at this stage to enlighten them on the specific problems faced by the First Air Fleet. However, Churchill's view of prospects in the Indian Ocean underwent a remarkable turnaround within weeks of his gloomy letter of 15 April to the president. As early as 24 April, he advised the president of Eastern Fleet reinforcement plans, which he hoped would complete by the end of June. The Royal Navy would then be capable of dealing with a 'very heavy IJN detachment'.[234] By mid-May he was confident that the capture of Madagascar was beyond Japan's power and that the reinforced Eastern Fleet, comprising four modernised battleships (*Warspite, Valiant, Nelson, Rodney*), the four 'R' class and three carriers (*Indomitable, Formidable, Illustrious*), would be re-established in Ceylon by July.[235] He confirmed these reinforcements to Field Marshal Smuts, who had stressed the critical importance of holding the Indian Ocean, at the end of May.[236] During May he also increasingly badgered the chiefs of staff, joint planning staff, and indirectly Somerville, to consider offensive operations in the eastern Indian Ocean in the autumn.[237]

The prime minister's confidence that the Eastern Fleet with its planned reinforcements, together with the Royal Air Force additions in Ceylon and India, could meet further Japanese attacks went beyond that of the naval staff and, indeed, Somerville.[238] Where did this confidence come from? It was partly no doubt over-simplistic 'bean counting' – his belief that a Royal Navy force of four modernised capital ships and three modern fleet carriers should be able to deal with an equivalent IJN force. The passage of time helped – he intuitively realised the Japanese had a limited window for operations in the west before increasing United States strength made these too risky. This time factor applied to the Germans also. At the end of May the prime minister acknowledged the risk of a German drive southward into the Middle East from the Caucasus, also highlighted by Smuts, but noted: 'The year is advancing and the Germans have a long way to go ...'.[239] Above all, he retained faith in the ability of the US Navy to pose a threat in the Pacific, which the Doolittle raid and Coral Sea action at the beginning of May amply confirmed.

The evolving intelligence picture also probably encouraged the prime minister.[240] NID reported (correctly) on 19 April that the bulk of the IJN forces deployed in the Indian Ocean were returning to Japan, although the carriers *Zuikaku* and *Shokaku* might be redeployed for operations in the southwest Pacific.[241] Successive NID assessments over the next month confirmed the IJN was conducting a major redeployment back to Japan, probably aimed at future operations in the central Pacific. Naval forces in the southern area would be sharply reduced.[242] The Joint Intelligence Committee assessed in mid-May that the bulk of the Japanese fleet was deployed between the Mandates and New Guinea, with no indication that significant forces were being earmarked for the Indian Ocean.[243]

At the end of May 1942, the joint planning staff considered how the war against Japan should be prosecuted.[244] They correctly identified two significant Japanese vulnerabilities, which were relevant to its ability to conduct sustained operations in the Indian Ocean. They judged that Japan's frontline air strength was small in relation to the commitments it had now acquired, and that aircraft production was too low to sustain even this frontline if it undertook major operations. They also emphasised Japan's dependence on Netherlands East Indies oil. In exploiting this, it faced long sea routes, an acute shortage of tankers, and quite inadequate anti-submarine forces. In mid-June the Joint Intelligence Committee produced a more detailed assessment of Japan's air capability after six months of war. Although it admitted its figures for aircraft losses were of variable quality, and it had no precise intelligence on production rates, its estimates for frontline strength were accurate. It correctly forecast that production was struggling to keep up with losses, as the planning staff had already suggested.[245]

In their look ahead, the joint planning staff also reviewed the concept of a joint British-American fleet taking the offensive in the Pacific.[246] Redeploying the bulk of Royal Navy major units to the Pacific meant carrying risk in the Indian Ocean. This transfer could only be considered when retained defences were adequate, when reinforcements had made Australasia secure, and when the arrival of US Navy new build ensured adequate superiority over the IJN. This thinking reflected that conveyed to eastern theatre commanders and Joint Staff Mission Washington some six weeks earlier on 15 April. They had then argued that it was currently impossible to cover Allied interests across two oceans from a single base. It was essential, on the one hand, to cover India, the

Middle East and Persian oil, and, on the other, the United States west coast, Hawaii, and communications across the Pacific to Australasia. The Indian Ocean was critical to the British Empire, but it covered no comparable interests for Japan. It consequently offered no offensive potential. To defeat Japan, a strategic offensive in the Pacific would be necessary, but this was only possible once vital interests elsewhere were secure.[247]

In parallel with the latest joint planning staff deliberations, Pound received requests from Admiral King for more immediate help to the US Navy, which had seen its effective carrier strength cut by half following the Coral Sea action.[248] King would accept a diversion operation by the Eastern Fleet, but would prefer the transfer of one or more Royal Navy carriers to the southwest Pacific. Theoretically, Britain had an opportunity here to take an early stake in the Pacific campaign and buy significant influence for minimal investment. She also risked lasting resentment from King and the US Navy if she refused to help and Midway turned out badly.[249] Pound was reluctant to weaken the Eastern Fleet while a major IJN attack in the Indian Ocean remained possible, and King failed to make a persuasive case that Royal Navy intervention in the Pacific would make sufficient difference to compensate.[250] Time and distance, and the difficulty arranging logistic support, also argued against the transfer, which was not therefore pursued.

The first significant reinforcements reached Somerville at the beginning of May, part of the forces allocated to seize Madagascar (Operation Ironclad).[251] These were a third fleet carrier, *Illustrious*, and the heavy cruiser *Devonshire*. Three other modern cruisers reached him from new build or refit during the next two months.[252] The Eastern Fleet was still planned to reach a strength by the autumn of four modernised battleships, three fleet carriers, one 8in cruiser, five to six modern 6in cruisers, two older 6in cruisers, sixteen modern destroyers, and nine to twelve submarines. In addition, the four 'R' class, with six to seven older cruisers and nine old destroyers, would be retained for trade protection duties. This fleet was comparable in size to the 'maximum Eastern Fleet' of August 1939 discussed in Chapter 2.[253]

In the event, the strength of the Eastern Fleet peaked in early July. By then it had two modernised battleships, *Warspite* and *Valiant* (the latter about to work up, following damage repair at Durban), two fleet carriers *Formidable* and *Illustrious* (*Indomitable* had departed a week earlier for Pedestal), two 'R'-class battleships, *Royal Sovereign* and *Resolution* (*Ramillies* had been damaged by IJN submarine attack), one heavy cruiser, three modern 6in cruisers, six older cruisers and nine destroyers. The fleet now had a more modern core than in April, and was better trained and more cohesive as a fighting force. It remained weak in destroyers, which would constrain Somerville's mobility in the coming months.[254]

The further reinforcements proposed during April and May never arrived. From early July, Eastern Fleet strength rapidly declined. By the autumn, Somerville was down to one modernised battleship and one carrier. He did not recover the mid-1942 strength until early 1944. There were two related reasons for this reduction: the crippling of the IJN carrier arm at Midway on 4 June, and the demands of the Mediterranean. Once the scale of the US Navy achievement at Midway was evident, it appeared to the British that IJN ability to intervene in the western Indian Ocean with anything more than occasional surface raiders or submarines had been eliminated.[255] By early September, the Joint Intelligence Committee judged that Japan now lacked the resources to pursue major new commitments and would adopt a defensive perimeter strategy.[256] The threat to Persian oil would remain a British anxiety into the autumn, but post-Midway, the primary risk was from German attack in the west or north. Ironically, at the moment Midway took place, the Japanese Army general staff revived the idea of major operations in the Indian Ocean, including the seizure of Ceylon, to which they had been distinctly lukewarm in February. Planning continued during June and an Army Directive (No 1196) was produced on 29 June. The reason for this new enthusiasm was the perceived success of the German drive towards Egypt, which resurrected the prospect of an Axis 'junction' in the Middle East, and for knocking Britain out of the war.[257] The IJN endorsed the concept, but had to defer to resource realities, especially as the Guadalcanal campaign got underway.[258]

The British war leadership were clear during the first five months of 1942 that the Indian Ocean took priority over the Mediterranean. Actual and planned naval reinforcements, largely at Mediterranean expense, reflected that. This raised the difficult question of sustaining Malta. Experience demonstrated that supply convoys were only possible with substantial naval cover. If Somerville was to receive his planned reinforcements, such cover was not possible. A proposal was therefore developed during April for a major part of the Eastern Fleet to deploy through the Suez Canal for the two weeks necessary to run a convoy to Malta from Alexandria.[259] This risky plan was put on hold when it was assessed Malta could hold out until August. However, an August convoy was essential if Malta was to survive. It meant either resurrecting the Eastern Fleet option, or running a convoy from the west, which required Somerville to release one of his three carriers to reinforce Force H. The western option was militarily more attractive, and Midway made the release of *Indomitable* in mid-July possible.

By the time this western convoy operation (Pedestal) took place, the wider strategic context had further evolved and the major Anglo-American landing in northwest Africa, codenamed Torch, was planned for November. The political and strategic debates that led to Torch, and the campaign itself, are outside the scope of this book.[260] However, it is important to underline how Torch linked with, and influenced, the naval defence of the eastern empire. The most obvious impact lay in the substantial resources required to execute Torch, for which the Royal Navy provided about two-thirds of the naval forces. They included two battleships, *Rodney* and *Duke of York*, the battlecruiser *Renown*, three fleet carriers (*Victorious*, *Formidable* and *Furious*), the light carrier *Argus*, three escort carriers, nine cruisers and forty-three destroyers.[261] To help generate these forces it was necessary not only to abandon the planned build-up of the Eastern Fleet, but to make substantial further withdrawals from Somerville, including one of his remaining two carriers, *Formidable*. She was required because *Indomitable* had been badly damaged in the Pedestal convoy and was therefore not available for Torch. As the prime minister emphasised to his deputy Clement Attlee, this was neither a permanent withdrawal from the East, nor a sign that the East was unimportant. It was a deliberate strategic choice to apply Britain's scarce naval resources where they had most effect. If the Japanese threat in the Indian Ocean had sharply reduced after Midway, Britain again had options.

Churchill apparently hoped that the reduction of the Eastern Fleet would be for a few months. In the event, in the absence of any new Japanese threat in the Indian Ocean, successive Mediterranean demands following Torch left the Eastern Fleet in a Cinderella state throughout 1943.[262] However, the 1943 Mediterranean campaign was a staged affair, and the successive Royal Navy commitments here were not inevitable. If the Japanese threat had resumed, the Royal Navy could have redeployed to the Indian Ocean earlier than it did. The Royal Navy Torch force, including its three capital ships, three fleet carriers, and three escort carriers, was the force that would have gone to Somerville in place of Torch if the Japanese had pursued a major offensive into the western half of the Indian Ocean in the second half of 1942.

The success of Torch influenced Britain's eastern defence problem in crucial ways.[263] It removed any possibility of the Germans securing new Atlantic bases at a critical stage in the U-boat war. It also secured the eastern empire irrevocably from any Axis threat on its western boundary. These two threats had continued to exercise British planners through the summer, as they contemplated the possibility of Russian defeat. In July the joint planners anticipated that if Russia collapsed, Germany would embark on a strategy to seize Atlantic bases and Middle East oil, which almost exactly mirrored the OKW strategic survey of August 1941 described in Chapter 3.[264] As late as October, the planners judged – 'we are not yet out of the dangerous period of the war: a major false step may still jeopardise our prospects of victory'.[265]

It took longer to clear the Axis from North Africa than the Allies hoped, but after Torch the result was not in doubt. Allied mastery of North Africa then opened up the Mediterranean to Allied shipping, and from there via the Suez Canal to the Indian Ocean, with the first through cargo convoy from Gibraltar to Suez running in May 1943.[266] Reopening Mediterranean transit made it much easier to move reinforcements to secure the Indian front against Japan, and to boost supplies to Russia through the Persian Gulf. In the long run it saved substantial shipping resources.[267] Supplies on the Persian route to Russia in the second half of 1943 were approximately double those in the first half, and more than double those delivered by the Arctic convoys.[268] The Persian route was by far the most important route for supplies delivered to Russia under the Third Protocol from October 1943 to end June 1944, and always had spare capacity if other routes had failed.[269]

Finally, the Torch campaign was catastrophic for the German air force. The Luftwaffe lost 2422 aircraft in the Mediterranean over the seven months from November 1942 to end May 1943. This represented 40 per cent of its overall frontline strength in all theatres at the beginning of November. The Mediterranean losses broadly equalled those on the Russian front in the same period, although in some categories, notably fighters, they were much higher.[270] The German response to Torch also absorbed large numbers of transport aircraft to build up their forces in Tunisia; 320 Ju52s were deployed in November and December, of which half had been lost by end January. The despatch of these precious heavy transport aircraft to the Mediterranean significantly reduced German airlift capacity at Stalingrad. By reducing German air power, Torch therefore made a direct and important contribution to the Stalingrad battle, and then severely hampered German prospects for any lasting recovery in the East.[271] This contribution to Stalingrad and its aftermath must be weighed alongside the simultaneous lend-lease aid delivered through Persia, the impact of which was highlighted earlier. Even if the Germans had achieved a more successful outcome to their 1942 southern offensive in Russia, the air losses suffered in the Torch campaign would have left them insufficient air support to contemplate the early invasion of the Middle East from the north, which the British so feared.[272]

President Roosevelt anticipated these Torch achievements in the instructions he gave to Marshall and King prior to their visit to London in July 1942. He stressed the need to maintain a 'Germany first' strategy, and not to be diverted by Japan. He emphasised his continuing commitment to a cross-channel invasion (Roundup) in 1943, while noting that its feasibility would depend on events in Russia. Less recognised is the importance he placed on holding the Middle East. Losing the Middle East meant losing Egypt and the Suez Canal, and thereafter potentially Syria, Iraq oil and access to Persian oil. This would permit a junction between Germany and Japan, and result in the probable loss of the Indian Ocean. There was also a continuing risk of a German move into northwest Africa, with severe consequences for Atlantic communications. Holding the Middle East required continuing American support on existing fronts, but he commended the advantages of a landing on the Atlantic coast against Germany's back door.[273] Roosevelt's arguments here, notably his stress on the Atlantic trade war, the importance of Persian oil and the Persian supply route, precisely echoed those deployed by Churchill a year earlier in May 1941, and described in Chapter 3.

In the autumn of 1942 the naval defence of the eastern empire had come full circle. The Indian Ocean, so critical not just to Britain's position in the East, but to the whole Allied war effort in the first half of that year, had reverted to a calm backwater. Meanwhile, the need and opportunity to remove the western Axis threat to the Middle East had moved centre stage. Priorities had changed, and Royal Navy resources, in the view of the British war leadership, were now better deployed elsewhere than with Somerville. That meant the Mediterranean during 1943, but it also included deploying the fleet carrier *Victorious* to help the US Navy Pacific Fleet for much of that year, as well.[274]

Royal Navy commitment to the eastern theatre: critical to Allied success

The Royal Navy was over-stretched in 1942, but it faced an inescapable commitment in the eastern theatre for the first half of that year. If the Axis had secured control of the Indian Ocean, denying Britain the resources of India and Australasia, and cutting the supply lines to the Middle East and Russia, while giving Germany potential control of Persian oil, the Allied task would have been immeasurably harder. Indeed, clear victory might have been impossible. The Royal Navy had to counter this risk. It had just enough latent strength in modern ships, modern technology, fighting effectiveness, and global support and experience, to do this, provided it had enough time to redeploy the necessary forces.

The weakness of Royal Navy forces off Ceylon in April 1942 reflected temporary limitations and was not representative of what the Royal Navy could do if required. Its ability, successively through 1942 to deploy a significant Eastern Fleet; plan major reinforcements for that fleet; project a substantial expeditionary force 7000 miles from the United Kingdom to seize Madagascar in May; mount the complex Pedestal operation at the other end of Africa, using some of the same forces, just two months later; and finally to mobilise 160 warships, including seven carriers, for Torch, demonstrates that the picture of Royal Navy power being in decline is overdone. The Royal Navy remained a strong and resilient force with global reach. Somerville undoubtedly hazarded his fleet at Ceylon, but came close to inflicting serious damage on the IJN.

The standard portrayal of a Royal Navy reduced to tokenism in the East, the inevitable consequence of a flawed interwar Singapore strategy, is misplaced. In the ultimate crisis, the British war leadership was prepared to withdraw all major units from the Mediterranean and run significant risks with the Home Fleet in order to secure the East. Despite some limitations, the fleet available to Somerville at the beginning of July 1942, before redeployment to the Mediterranean began, was stronger than any fleet the Royal Navy had deployed in the war to date, and comparable with the US Navy Pacific Fleet at that time. The second quarter of 1942 in the Indian Ocean is best viewed as a window of vulnerability. If the Japanese had made the Indian Ocean their main focus, they had the chance, for a short period, to bring more force to bear than Britain could, and perhaps radically to shift the global strategic balance, with incalculable consequences for the future direction of the war. Given time, Britain still had just enough capacity to close the window off.[275]

Conclusion

Three main arguments lie at the heart of this book. Together, they represent a fundamental reassessment of the part played by Britain's eastern empire in the Second World War and how we think about the overall contribution of the Royal Navy. Indeed, in some respects, we need to view the whole first half of Britain's war in a different way.

The first and most important argument is that through the late 1930s to the summer of 1941, Britain's leadership undertook a 'strategic journey', from the idea of fighting a limited naval trade war with Japan in the Far East, to the need to secure the war potential of the whole area from Egypt, through the Middle East and Indian Ocean, to Australasia. This journey is bounded by two points: Chatfield's concept of a limited Pacific naval war expressed at the 1937 Imperial Conference and described in Chapter 2; and the Joint Planning Committee's justification for holding a forward position in the Middle East in July 1941, summarised in Chapter 3. The latter not only defined the importance of the Middle East, but explained for the first time why control of the Indian Ocean was essential to generate the maximum empire war effort, and therefore ranked second only to the Atlantic lifeline in priority. The implication of this July paper was that Britain could probably secure the United Kingdom homeland so long as it had American support, but it had no prospect of winning a war against Germany, let alone the wider Axis powers, unless it could retain the resources and strategic leverage of this wider eastern space and deny them to its enemies. German calculations were remarkably similar. The naval defence of this wider eastern empire was neither irrelevant nor discretionary. It was an inescapable commitment.

The second argument is that in protecting this eastern empire war potential, Britain, with American support, had sufficient resources to adopt a forward defence position at either end of the empire, but not both. The real British strategic failure in 1941 was to believe that this choice could be avoided or deferred. The failure to rationalise Far East defence by adopting an 'outer ring' position based on the Indian Ocean was reinforced by reckless Admiralty risk-taking in the autumn of 1941. It was the Admiralty's shift to an offensive

400

strategy in late 1941, not political pressure from the prime minister, which was primarily responsible for placing Force Z in an exposed position at Singapore when the Japanese attacked. This contributed significantly to the destruction of the force, and left the Royal Navy weaker in the Indian Ocean in early 1942 than it would otherwise have been.

The final argument is that despite the early disasters at the hands of Japan, the Royal Navy was still strong enough to stabilise the eastern naval theatre by mid-1942. The many critics of the Singapore strategy were only partly right. Singapore fell, as they predicted, but the Royal Navy demonstrated that it could nevertheless still deploy a competitive Eastern Fleet fully capable of securing the Indian Ocean.

Before considering this reassessment further, it is important to underline how this book has qualified traditional explanations for perceived British failure in the East. We have seen in Chapter 1 that from 1935 Britain's defence leadership, represented by the Defence Requirements Committee and Committee of Imperial Defence, recognised the growing possibility of a two-hemisphere naval war. The authorised Royal Navy building plans reflected this. The Royal Navy did not get all the resources it wanted, but it sought to manage the global risks it faced in an optimum way with the resources available at any given time. It recognised it could not take on the full weight of all three Axis navies, but hoped to build sufficient capability to deal with any two of them, while keeping the third in check with a reliable ally, whether France against Italy, or the United States against Japan. This is an important adjustment to the established view of the Royal Navy rearmament programme starting in 1936, which sees it providing too little, too late. By contrast, this book has argued that the programme was sufficiently strong and well-balanced, including in carrier power, to make the long-term aspiration to create sufficient naval power to defend British interests across two hemispheres viable. Larger investment earlier in the 1930s might, paradoxically, have given the Royal Navy less of the capability it most needed in 1941/42.

British assessments of Japanese intentions and the scale of military forces they could deploy were consistently good throughout the period covered. Judged in the round, the intelligence record compares well with that on any other enemy at any other time. That is generally true of the more specific monitoring of IJN strength and movements, which was better than usually suggested. The record was particularly good in the immediate run-up to the Far East war. The argument that the Royal Navy consistently downplayed the IJN's fighting efficiency, as opposed to more legitimate questioning of its maintenance and support, is not convincing. Nevertheless, the Royal Navy's ability to manage the naval risk from Japan suffered from one fundamental strategic miscalculation and one specific intelligence failure. The miscalculation was the consistent belief that American forces in the Pacific were strong enough either to deter Japan from southern expansion, or to reduce an attack to manageable proportions. The intelligence failure was in not recognising the full potential of IJN air power. That failure lay less in judging numbers and performance, and more in not anticipating the scale on which IJN air power could substitute for traditional gun power, and how a concentrated carrier force could now project strategic effect at great distance.

The argument that the Royal Navy suffered a general failure of innovation in the 1930s, compared to the IJN and US Navy, does not stand up. The Royal Navy was technically innovative in the development and deployment of radar, in anti-submarine warfare, and in aircraft communications, all areas which the IJN neglected. It was tactically innovative in the development of the all-arms task force, its emphasis on night fighting, and especially its exploitation of integrated intelligence. It was at least equal to the IJN in the first two areas, and far superior in the last.[1] This book has also challenged the still prevailing view that the Royal Navy failed adequately to recognise the impact of air power at sea and to prepare accordingly. The Royal Navy laid down as many fleet carriers as battleships in the fiscal years 1936–38, more than either the IJN or US Navy. It displayed much innovation in carrier deployment in 1940/41 although it was constrained by the need to deploy across five different theatres, whereas the IJN and US Navy could essentially focus on one. The Royal Navy was also much quicker to invest in anti-aircraft firepower than its competitors, and its assumption that the Mediterranean would be closed to through traffic in wartime showed few illusions about the potential of land-based air power.

The Royal Navy nevertheless faced two weaknesses in managing the air dimension of eastern empire naval defence. First, its carrier aircraft lagged the IJN competition, and indeed the US Navy, in both numbers and performance. This disparity was less when aircraft are judged as overall weapon systems, where limitations in aircraft performance were offset by radar, a good communications fit and excellent torpedoes. Divided responsibility with the Royal Air Force for aircraft procurement was a key factor here, but the American failure to meet contracted obligations, notably in the supply of Martlet fighters, was just as important. The second failing was the lack of an adequate land-based maritime strike capability in overseas theatres prior to mid-1942. This did not reflect lack of a suitable modern aircraft type in the inventory, or failure to recognise the potential of torpedo bombing but, rather, Royal Air Force refusal to give this requirement adequate priority for production and deployment until too late.

Given these qualifications, we return to the central theme, how the Royal Navy adjusted from managing a narrowly defined Japanese threat to Britain's Far East interests in 1935, to crafting a strategy and finding the means to hold the eastern Mediterranean and Indian Ocean through 1941/42 against existential threats at both ends. At one level, the strategic journey was dictated by available resources. Hence the initial response to the growing prospect of a three-enemy war across two hemispheres from late 1938 was to establish a reduced defensive goal for the Far East. This is illustrated in Chamberlain's message to the Dominions the following March, and Cunningham's parallel introduction of flexible reinforcement. But these responses were driven, at least equally, by a changing perception of the risks and opportunities in managing empire security. Thus we have found growing awareness through early 1939 that the potential strategic damage in abandoning the eastern Mediterranean probably matched the damage from any current Japanese move, even if the full stakes in the Middle East were not yet articulated. The prospect of seizing realistic opportunities to damage Italy as the weakest member of the Axis surely made sense.

The key point emphasised in this book is that these 1939 adjustments were not signals of strategic failure, or empty gestures.[2] They were a sensible reaction to the prevailing risks on the two boundaries of the eastern empire before the output of the naval rearmament programme became available. Given French assistance in the western Mediterranean, it was still credible for the Royal Navy to maintain adequate deterrence in the eastern Mediterranean, while deploying sufficient strength to secure the Indian Ocean, and severely disrupt a full-scale Japanese attack on Singapore, which still had to be mounted from long distance, and for which the Japanese had, anyway, yet to do any planning.

It was the collapse of France that drastically reduced Britain's scope to maintain a trade-off between the eastern Mediterranean and Far East, offering adequate security for both. This was not something readily foreseeable before May 1940, and it is easy to forget how different Britain's options in the East might have been had France survived. In the event, Britain now had to find substantial extra resources to secure the western Mediterranean and counter increased German access to the Atlantic. Japanese access to Indochina made an attack on Britain in the Far East a far easier proposition. Meanwhile, over the next fifteen months the damage Britain would suffer if it surrendered a forward defence position in the Middle East became increasingly apparent. The Middle East, therefore, absorbed almost all the air and land resources that Britain could afford to deploy overseas from the United Kingdom.

This book has shown how the justification for this investment used by Britain's war leadership at the time has been largely validated by what is now known of German thinking, and is stronger than usually acknowledged. In explaining the value of both the Middle East and the wider eastern empire to Britain, the book has deployed the term 'war potential'. This term embraces not just resources, human and material, which the book argues added perhaps 25 per cent to British fighting power, but also the strategic leverage exerted by controlling a particular space and denying it to the enemy. Here the book has emphasised four major factors.

First, Persian oil underpinned the whole eastern empire war effort, and from 1942 facilitated American military support to China and, along with other eastern empire resources, made an important contribution to the southwest Pacific campaign from Australia. Without this oil the eastern empire economies faced collapse.

Secondly, British control of the eastern Mediterranean reduced the likelihood that Germany would gain bases in Spain and northwest Africa and transform its prospects in the Atlantic trade war.

Thirdly, the Indian Ocean facilitated delivery of essential aid to Russia through Persia and to China through India. The Persian supply route was important in helping Russia to survive the second half of 1942.

Finally, by controlling this wide eastern space, Britain denied its resources, especially its oil, its communications and its strategic opportunities to the Axis. The use of Iraq oil and secure sea access to Romanian oil would have made a significant contribution to Germany's war effort. The denial of Persian oil to Britain by Germany or Japan would have had a devastating impact on Britain's war effort.

However, the proposition that Britain then effectively sacrificed Far East defence in 1941 for the sake of its position in the Middle East requires crucial qualifications. That is also true of the related and popular argument that if despatch of a fleet to the Far East was improbable by 1939, the fall of France rendered it impossible, demonstrating the fundamental bankruptcy of the whole Singapore strategy. The first qualification is that Britain's Middle East investment brought benefit as well as loss to the security of the eastern empire. It denied access to India and, above all, it protected the Persian oil on which eastern empire war potential depended. The second qualification is that the whole Middle East strategy, and meeting the key strategic goals within it, depended on supplies and manpower delivered through the Indian Ocean. Likewise, the distribution of Persian oil through the eastern empire depended on Indian Ocean security. Defending the Indian Ocean was, therefore, not only an inescapable commitment, but in the last resort, as the chiefs of staff regularly recognised, it was more important than holding a forward position in the Middle East. From the naval point of view, therefore, the strategic trade-off between the eastern Mediterranean and Indian Ocean during 1941 merely reflected the choice identified by Cunningham in April 1939. Britain could always deploy a respectable fleet to meet a major IJN threat to the Indian Ocean during 1940/41, but most of it would have to come from the eastern Mediterranean. The timing and scale of any withdrawal here still depended on an assessment of comparative risk, but the Indian Ocean ultimately mattered most.[3]

If the Indian Ocean was an inescapable commitment, then the real choice facing Britain's war leadership, and above all the Admiralty, was whether its security really required the use of Singapore, and whether its viability as a base was ever achievable with the resources Britain could make available, given potential Japanese access to Indochina, Thailand and the Netherlands East Indies. The 1940 Far East appreciation acknowledged the increased vulnerability of Singapore, but effectively deferred these questions with its adoption of a temporary holding operation based on air power. Deferral was not unreasonable during the winter of 1940/41 while Japanese bases remained at a distance, and Britain harboured hopes of getting the Americans to assume primary responsibility for Far East defence. Indeed, again it may be argued that at this point it was merely a natural evolution of the discretionary reinforcement policy started by Cunningham.

Chapter 4 has shown why British aspirations for the United States to combine a major role in the Atlantic with forward deployment of the Pacific Fleet to cover the South China Sea from Singapore were never realistic, given political constraints in the United States and the limitations of existing American resources. Had the British played their hand better, it might have been possible to create a more modest, but still credible, combined task force which would have bound the United States into defence of the Malay Barrier. This opportunity was fleeting and it is doubtful if the United States would have modified the Atlantic priority which the British did so much to encourage. This American refusal to support forward deployment in the Far East before and during the ABC-1 staff talks should have obliged the British now to address the hard questions about the viability of Singapore. However, the ABC-1 compromise, comprising 'Atlantic substitution' and Pacific Fleet 'distraction operations', effectively offered a means of extending deferral. Even if air reinforcement and modernisation in Malaya was delayed, the potential resurrection of an eastern fleet now made holding Singapore both necessary and apparently feasible. The problem was that the primary forces released by 'Atlantic substitution' (the obsolescent 'R'-class battleships) were quite unsuitable to take on the IJN. The irony, therefore, was that 'Atlantic substitution' made an eastern fleet possible, but it was to be created out of what was available, not what was needed. The Admiralty was willing to embrace a fleet composition here that it would never have contemplated against the Italians in the Mediterranean, and without any of the substantial air and land cover available in that theatre, either.

'Atlantic substitution' still did not in itself make the Far East naval disasters inevitable. Until the end of August, both prime minister and Admiralty were agreed that naval reinforcements should concentrate in the Indian Ocean, even if they disagreed on force composition. This consensus coincided with the separate decision by the British war leadership that the build-up to the Crusader offensive in Egypt must have absolute priority, and that Far East air and land reinforcement should be further delayed. The mismatch between the growing risk of Japanese attack, following their move into southern Indochina at the end of July and the decision to rule against early reinforcement in favour of the Middle East, should have triggered a major chiefs of staff review of Far East defence.

Such a review would surely have anticipated the VCNS paper on future naval strategy produced immediately following the Japanese attack and summarised at the end of Chapter 7. Although this paper followed the initial British losses, its arguments were as valid in September as they would be three months later. It admirably defined Britain's vital interests in the eastern theatre: protecting eastern empire war potential, Persian oil, and the Persian supply route to Russia. It also effectively distinguished between the security of the Indian Ocean and Australasia, which were critical to the empire war effort, and of the British territories and interests in Southeast and East Asia, which were ultimately discretionary. Given the scale of naval forces the IJN could send south and the limitations to American support, it advocated a defensive holding strategy while a balanced fleet of modern units was concentrated at Ceylon. The defence of Singapore, and by implication the Malay Barrier, must rely on air, land and submarine power. Although it did not say so, these were evidently recognised as dispensable, rather as Hong Kong had been in the late 1930s. Judged by ends, ways and means, this was an achievable eastern strategy for Britain in the autumn of 1941, given forthcoming additions to Royal Navy strength from the rearmament programme, ships coming out of repair and units released by the United States in the Atlantic. In essence, it was a more detailed and logically argued exposition of the Admiralty intent, conveyed by Pound to the prime minister at the end of August, to prioritise the defence of the Indian Ocean and to base the new Eastern Fleet at Ceylon for the foreseeable future.

The offensive policy the Admiralty embraced instead was the direct opposite of that claimed by Stephen Roskill and later historians. It was reckless, because it proposed to place an inappropriate capital ship force in an exposed position where the enemy could bring concentrated force to bear. The Royal Navy could no more aspire to meet a potential IJN fleet of five battleships and five carriers in the South China Sea in October than it could when VCNS issued his paper in December. Even with maximum US Navy support in the Atlantic, and a less defensive American stance in the Pacific, Britain could not credibly guarantee to hold the barrier at this time, let alone reach beyond it, without a far greater commitment of air resources than the British war leadership was willing to make. To propose that an intact US Navy fleet at Pearl Harbor and a small United States Army Air Force component in the Philippines justified the risk of deploying an unbalanced fleet of predominantly obsolescent battleships north of the barrier in the face of IJNAF air power was a delusion. It was a classic failure of sensible risk management. It was this policy, more than any other factor, which led to the presence of Force Z in Singapore and its subsequent deployment and loss.

If the popular image of the loss of Force Z as the inevitable consequence of poor political judgement trumping professional advice in a hopeless attempt to rescue a flawed Singapore strategy is wrong, so too is the view that the Royal Navy now became a helpless bystander in the East. In the face of the new Japanese challenge to the Indian Ocean, Britain was not reduced to tokenism. It undertook a drastic redeployment, and the naval and air forces moved to the theatre by mid-1942 were substantial. The Eastern Fleet took time to reach acceptable strength and efficiency, but by July it was not only competitive enough to hold the western Indian Ocean against any force the IJN could send, but broadly comparable to US Navy forces then in the Pacific. The modern carriers laid down in the rearmament programme were at its core. The weakness of Royal Navy forces off Ceylon in April 1942, so frequently emphasised, reflected temporary limitations, and was not representative of what the Royal Navy could do and would do if required. We have seen that Somerville undoubtedly hazarded his fleet in an unacceptable way at Ceylon, but even so came close to inflicting serious damage on the IJN. Ceylon demonstrated Royal Navy potential in the new carrier warfare, as well as the limits to IJN competence. A British Midway here was not impossible.

The reassessment provided in this book matters for three reasons. First, during the period studied, Britain's political and military leaders had a more realistic view of Britain's strategic interests in the East, the competing risks facing the territories and assets under British control, and how limited defence resources could best be deployed to meet those risks and exploit opportunities than is generally accepted. Britain got the most important choices right. Where it made mistakes, as with the Admiralty's forward deployment of late 1941, it demonstrated good ability to adapt and recover. This deserves greater recognition.

Secondly, the widely held perception of the Royal Navy as a declining naval power by 1939, lacking innovation, compromised by industrial and technical weakness, and unable to project serious force beyond the Atlantic and Mediterranean, requires major adjustment.[4] Like other navies, the Royal Navy certainly suffered from the financial stringency of the interwar period. However, it got its investment decisions broadly right and rearmed more quickly and more effectively than its future enemies for the war it would have to fight. With some notable exceptions, it was quick to embrace new technology and markedly improved its fighting quality through the 1930s. The Royal Navy was rapidly overtaken by the pace of US Navy expansion in 1943, when it would also start to lag in key areas of capability, but until the end of 1942 it remained fully competitive in size and performance. It was still a global force to be reckoned with.[5]

It is important to recognise here that by every reasonable measure the Royal Navy was immensely stronger in 1945 than 1939. Construction in every category of warship exceeded losses, with the notable exception of battleships, where new build equalled losses, although even here *Vanguard* was nearing completion. Leaving aside the increases in major fleet units, especially carriers, total destroyer strength had risen to 259, a 57 per cent increase on 1939 strength, with a further 542 escort vessels and 131 submarines.[6] Indeed, this 1945 strength was largely achieved by October 1943, by which date the Royal Navy had suffered more than 90 per cent of its overall war losses.[7] It is also worth noting how vast the Royal Navy commitment (comprising the separate East Indies and Pacific fleets) to the eastern war against Japan became in 1945. It represented an effective fighting capability far surpassing the 1941 IJN. It included six battleships (modern or modernised), six fleet carriers, four brand new light carriers, no less than twenty-five escort carriers, four heavy cruisers, nineteen light cruisers, seventy-three destroyers, and forty-two submarines.[8]

Above all, the contribution of the British Empire and that of the Royal Navy in safeguarding the Middle East and Indian Ocean from the Axis between spring 1941 and winter 1942 has been understated. It has been overshadowed by later American strength, once it was properly mobilised from 1943 onward, and the dominant contribution of the Russian army to breaking German land power. Yet British control of the area from Egypt in the west, through the Indian Ocean to Ceylon, and thence to Australia, was critical in containing Germany's military potential during this period. Britain needed the resources and strategic leverage of this eastern empire to ensure her own survival as an effective fighting power, to wear down Germany and Italy by denying them oil and expending their air power, and later to ensure the survival of her vital Russian ally through the Persian supply route. This empire contribution made while Russia's fate was still in the balance, and before American potential could take effect, was fundamental to future Allied victory.[9] It was the empire's last great gift to Britain. It was delivered by many without much choice, but still in the hope of a better world after the war.

The Royal Navy held prime responsibility for securing the war potential of this space from the existential threats facing it at both ends. The initial British defeats to Japan at sea were not in themselves a sign of imperial failure, nor did they mean that Britain must abandon sea areas previously considered vital. They were temporary, albeit avoidable, setbacks eclipsed by long term strategic success in securing what mattered most in the East. After the protection of the Atlantic lifeline, this was the Royal Navy's greatest achievement in the war.

We now know, of course, that in the spring of 1942 Berlin and Tokyo ultimately lacked both the immediate capability, and certainly the shared insight, to deliver an effective combined strategy to destroy Britain's position in the Middle East, whatever the ambitions of the German naval war staff. But that was not how it appeared at the time. If there ever was a point in the Second World War when joint action by the three Axis powers might have achieved decisive effect, then it surely lay in the vulnerability of the Allies in the Indian Ocean during the first half of 1942. The ability of British leaders from the spring of 1941 onward to recognise the growing risks posed by Axis command of the Indian Ocean and control of Middle East oil, to make credible provision against them, and thereby lessen the risks, deserves acknowledgement.[10]

Annex

Warships Completed by Principal Naval Powers 1930–1942

This annex contains two tables giving information on the warships completed by the principal naval powers between the beginning of 1930 and end of 1942. Table A provides the overall totals for various categories of warship for each power across the whole period. Table B breaks the figures down into individual years.

The selection of 1930 as the start point was for three reasons. First, it marks a transition point in the building cycle of all the naval powers, as they recognised the need to begin addressing the growing obsolescence of ships commissioned during and immediately after the war. Thus both the Royal Navy and the US Navy commenced new destroyer programmes from this date. Secondly, it is the point when the potential of air power begins to exert significant influence on naval thinking and thus to influence procurement decisions. Thirdly, the bulk of the German and Italian navies that would fight in the Second World War were created after this date, as were key elements of the IJN. December 1942 is the chosen end point, partly because it is the widely accepted turning point in the war when the Axis powers moved irrevocably to the defensive. But it is also the point when US industrial strength began to translate into a scale of naval power that within a year would not only overwhelm the combined Axis, but far surpass Royal Navy strength too.

The tables illustrate the overall production achieved by the different powers across the period, their comparative rates of output, and the different choices they made. Because they only list new production, the tables are not in themselves an accurate guide to overall strength at any given time, which would need to take account of pre-1930 production, subsequent modernisation of those units, and war losses. The tables list units by date of completion, not when they were laid down, and therefore omit units ordered but subsequently cancelled. This presentation is more useful than that found in many histories, which do not clarify between orders, completions and previous strength. There are still obvious limitations to tables that rely on raw numbers. Numbers may not reflect quality, and the way warships are allocated between particular categories is inevitably open to debate.

The two tables here underline three conclusions already drawn from Table 5 in Chapter 1, which compared Royal Navy output with that of the three Axis powers from 1935–42. First, they show that, with the exception of capital ships, Royal Navy output over the wider period from 1930 matched the combined Axis total in every category of warship except submarines, and significantly exceeded it in destroyers. If the two *Nelsons* (completed in 1927) are taken into account, the match extends to battleships also. Secondly, they emphasise the weighting of Royal Navy delivery to the period 1940–42, and hence the Admiralty concern that the period 1938–40 would be a window of vulnerability in coping with a two-hemisphere challenge. Finally, they illustrate the impact of the Royal Navy shift to investment in anti-submarine vessels from 1939, and how this anticipated the German decision to concentrate on U-boat output by at least a year, arguably giving Britain a decisive advantage in the Battle of the Atlantic.[1]

The tables illustrate how Royal Navy and US Navy outputs across the period from 1930 were also similar. The US Navy commissioned one more battleship than the Royal Navy, but the Royal Navy compensated by delivering two more fleet carriers. The US Navy produced twice as many heavy cruisers, but the Royal Navy significantly more cruisers overall. Destroyer output was comparable. The Royal Navy built more submarines, but US Navy boats were of better quality. The major difference lies in specialist anti-submarine escort vessels, where US Navy build in this period was negligible, although their output would be vast in 1943. The common perception that the US Navy overtook the Royal Navy in this period is not supported by the figures. The Royal Navy was somewhat smaller than the US Navy in terms of core fleet units by the end of 1942 because of the scale of its war losses. US Navy output was also rising very fast through 1942, with some eighty destroyers delivered that year alone, but its rearmament had generally started later than the Royal Navy. The key point is that taking anti-submarine capability into account, the Royal Navy remained broadly equivalent to the US Navy in both size and fighting capability in most areas through 1942.

Chapter 1 has addressed the argument that the Royal Navy suffered disproportionate damage from the twin effects of the 1930 London naval treaty and the economic depression of 1929–31, that these reduced the size of the Royal Navy below the minimum needed to handle simultaneous threats in two theatres, and reduced British shipbuilding and armament capacity, making future recovery and expansion more difficult.[2] The tables underline that the only credible maritime threat Britain faced in 1930 and, indeed, through to 1935, was that from Japan, and that threat did not seem imminent. Britain must maintain a stronger navy than it needed, or get weaker. Given the significant investment the Royal Navy had made in the late 1920s compared to other powers, including two battleships and thirteen heavy cruisers, the investment recorded here for 1930–35 was broadly in line with that of the other powers and sufficient to maintain its position. It would have been difficult for any British government to justify more. Furthermore, as also discussed in Chapter 1, technology was changing so rapidly through the 1930s that it is doubtful that a higher building rate through the period 1930–35, where treaties permitted, would have worked to the Royal Navy's advantage. The tables confirm that despite the loss of shipbuilding capacity, Royal Navy rearmament from 1936 still matched the combined output of its three potential enemies. More important, the Royal Navy got the balance of investment between fleet units and anti-submarine capacity about right. Its investment strategy was better than either Germany, which was too slow in committing to U-boats, or Japan, which completely ignored the potential submarine threat to its supply lines until 1943. There is a strong argument that where the Royal Navy suffered most in the period 1939–42 was through Britain's lag in building up its overall air power compared to Germany, and its under-investment in land-air capabilities most important to the maritime area.

Table A Total warship completions by the principal naval powers across the period 1930–1942

Warship type	Britain	US	Japan	Germany	Italy	Total Axis
BB	5	6	2	2	3	7
BC	0	0	0	2	0	2
CV	5	3	6[3]	0	0	6
CVL	0	2	3	0	0	3
CVE	6[4]	11	3	0	0	3
CCH	12[5]	25[6]	10	6[7]	5	21
CCL	31	8	4	3	13	20
DD	171[8]	171	68	37	34	139
DE	132[9]	0	4	0	36	40
ASV	269	0	14	13	7	34
SM	109	80	56	545	117	718

Key:
BB   Battleship
BC   Battlecruiser
CV   Fleet aircraft carrier
CVL Light aircraft carrier

CCH Heavy cruiser
CCL Light cruiser
DD   Fleet destroyer
DE   Escort destroyer
ASV Anti-submarine vessel
SM   Submarine

Sources:
The figures in Tables A and B are constructed primarily from the following sources: H T Lenton, *British and Empire Warships of the Second World War* (London: Greenhill Books, 1998); Paul Dull, *A Battle History of the Imperial Japanese Navy* (Annapolis, USA: Naval Institute Press, 1978); S W Roskill, *Naval Policy Between the Wars* (London: Collins, 1968–76), especially appendix C, vol I; US Naval History and Heritage Command website; Robert Mallett, *The Italian Navy and Fascist Expansionism 1935–1940* (London: Frank Cass, 1998); Vincent O'Hara, David Dickson, Richard Worth, *On Seas Contested: The Seven Great Navies of the Second World War*,(Annapolis: Naval Institute Press, 2010); and www.navypedia.org, 'The naval balance 1935' and 'Navies of the world 1940'.

Table B Warship completion by the principal naval powers presented on an annual basis 1930–1942

Year	Type	Britain	US	Japan	Germany	Italy
1930	CCH	1	3	0	0	0
	CCL	0	0	0	1	0
	DD	8	0	4	0	0
	ASV	4	0	0	0	0
	SM	8	2	2	0	7
1931	CCH	1	3	0	0	2
	CCL	0	0	0	1	3
	DD	10 + 2[10]	0	4	0	1
	ASV	4	0	0	0	0
	SM	3	0	0	0	4
1932	CCH	0	1	4	0	2
	CCL	0	0	0	0	1
	DD	5 + 4[11]	0	4	0	7
	ASV	3	0	0	0	0
	SM	3	1	4	0	7
1933	CVL	0	0	1	0	0
	CCH	0	1	0	1[12]	1
	CCL	2	0	0	0	2
	DD	4	0	3	0	0
	ASV	2	0	1	0	0
	SM	4	1	0	0	6

Year	Type					
1934	CVL	0	1	0	0	0
	CCH	0	5	0	1[13]	0
	CCL	2	0	0	0	0
	DD	10	2	2	0	4
	ASV	3	0	5	0	1
	SM	2	1	2	0	11
1935	CCH	0	0	2	0	0
	CCL	3 + 1[14]	0	0	1	3
	DD	8	6	2	0	0
	DE	0	0	0	0	0
	ASV	6	0	0	1	2
	SM	4	2	5	14	5
1936	CCH	0	1	0	1[15]	0
	CCL	1 + 2[16]	0	0	0	1
	DD	17	22	2	0	0
	DE	0	0	0	0	10
	ASV	4	0	3	3	0
	SM	3	4	0	21	13
1937	CVF	0	1	1	0	0
	CCH	5	1	2	0	0
	CCL	1	0	0	0	2
	DD	9	7	12	7	4
	DE	0	0	0	0	0
	ASV	0	0	5	2	4
	SM	3	5	4	1	10
1938	CVF	1	1	0	0	0
	CCH	2	5	1	0	0
	DD	10	5	6	8	5
	DE	0	0	0	0	20
	ASV	3	0	0	1	0
	SM	6	5	4	10	22
1939	BC	0	0	0	2	0
	CVF	0	0	1	0	0
	CCH	3	5	1	2	0
	DD	21 + 1[17]	17	2	7	7
	ASV	2	0	0	4	0
	SM	7	10	0	18	7
1940	BB	1	0	0	1	2
	CVF	2	0	0	0	0
	CVL	0	1	0	0	0
	CCH	0	0	0	1	0
	CCL	7	0	2	0	0
	DD	4 + 5[18]	18	9	1	0
	DE	19 + 50[19]	0	2	0	0

	ASV	$52 + 7^{20}$	0	0	0	0
	SM	15	5	8	50	8
1941	BB	2	2	1	1	0
	CVF	2	1	2	0	0
	CVE	1	0	1	0	0
	CCL	5	0	1	0	0
	DD	16	13	8	7	4
	DE	25	0	2	0	0
	ASV	$76 + 63^{21}$	0	0	0	0
	SM	20	11	8	199	11
1942	BB	2	4	1	0	1
	CVF	0	0	2	0	0
	CVL	0	0	2	0	0
	CVE	5^{22}	11	2	0	0
	CCL	7	8	1	0	1
	DD	$32+3^{23}+2^{24}$	81	10	7	2
	DE	38	0	0	0	6
	ASV	$22 + 18^{25}$	0	0	0	0
	SM	31	33	19	238	6

Notes

Introduction

1. S W Roskill, *The War at Sea* (London: HMSO, 1954–61), vol I: *The Defensive* (1954), vol II: *The Period of Balance* (1956); S Woodburn-Kirby, *The War against Japan* (London, HMSO, 1957–60), vol I: *The Loss of Singapore* (1957), vol II: *India's Most Dangerous Hour* (1958). Both sharpened their criticisms of Prime Minister Winston Churchill in later works: S W Roskill, *Churchill and the Admirals* (London: Collins, 1977); and S Woodburn-Kirby, *Singapore: The Chain of Disaster* (London: Cassell, 1971).

2. The critics' view of the Singapore strategy is summarised in Malcom Murfett's essay, 'Reflections on an Enduring Theme: The "Singapore strategy" at Sixty', in *Sixty Years On: The Fall of Singapore Revisited*, edited by B P Farrell and Sandy Hunter (Singapore: Eastern Universities Press, 2003). Significant works in this genre include Raymond Callahan's article, 'The Illusion of Security: Singapore 1919–1942', *Journal of Contemporary History*, 9:2 (April 1974), pp69–92, expanded as *The Worst Disaster: The Fall of Singapore* (first published 1977 with an updated second edition, Singapore: Cultured Lotus, 2001); Ian Hamill, *The Strategic Illusion* (Singapore, 1981); Paul Haggie, *Britannia at Bay: The Defence of the British Empire against Japan 1931–1941* (Oxford: Clarendon Press, 1981); and more recently, Brian Farrell, *The Defence and Fall of Singapore 1940–1942* (Stroud, UK: Tempus, 2005). Farrell has also produced an excellent overview of British strategy in the Second World War, *The Basis and Making of British Grand Strategy – Was there a Plan* (UK: Edwin Mellen Press, 1998). Roskill's work on the interwar period is also important: *Naval Policy between the Wars* (London: Collins, 1968–1976), esp vol II: *The Period of Reluctant Rearmament, 1930–1939* (1976).

3. The leading exponent of 'declinism' is Correlli Barnett. His case for British economic and military 'decline' across the first half of the twentieth century is his three volume 'Pride and Fall' series. The two volumes relevant to this book are *The Collapse of British Power* (Eyre Methuen, 1972), covering the interwar period, and *The Audit of War: The Illusion and Reality of Britain as a Great Nation* (Basingstoke: Macmillan, 1986), assessing subsequent British performance in the Second World War. Robert Tombs summarises the 'declinist' interpretation of Britain in the twentieth century and its flaws in *The English and their History* (Allen Lane, 2014), esp pp751–6, 759–61.

4. Correlli Barnett, *Engage the Enemy More Closely* (London: Hodder and Stoughton, 1991); Duncan Redford, *A History of the Royal Navy: World War II* (London: IB Tauris, 2014); and, earlier, Paul Kennedy, *The Rise and Fall of British Naval Mastery* (Basingstoke: Macmillan, 1976).

5. For example, Andrew Roberts, *Storm of War* (London: Allen Lane, 2009); Max Hastings, *All Hell Let Loose* (London: Harper Press, 2011); and Anthony Beevor, *The Second World War* (London: Weidenfeld and Nicolson, 2012).

6. Roskill, *The War at Sea*, vol I.

7. The only historian to explore the offensive strategy in detail is Ian Cowman in *Dominion or Decline: Anglo-American Naval Relations in the Pacific 1937–41* (Oxford UK and Dulles (VA) USA: Berg, 1996).

8. This judgement includes seminal works like Michael Howard's *The Mediterranean Strategy in the Second World War* (London: Greenhill Books, 1993). Ashley Jackson explains why the

Mediterranean and Middle East were important to the overall British Empire war effort in *The British Empire and the Second World War* (London: Hambledon Continuum, 2007), chapter 7. However, he does not adequately distinguish between the factors judged most important by the British war leadership at the time, as opposed to those identified by historians with the benefit of hindsight afterwards. Nor does he show how perceptions of relative risk changed over time.

9   If the Mediterranean costs are judged disproportionate, then they certainly fell disproportionately on the Royal Navy. A post-war Admiralty note estimated losses of Royal Navy ships in the Mediterranean theatre, either sunk or damaged beyond recovery, at one battleship, two carriers, seventeen cruisers, sixty-one destroyers, forty-five submarines, thirteen escorts, and 234 minor war vessels: 'Admiralty Notes on the Mediterranean Effort 1939–1945', CAB 106/615, TNA. With the exception of capital ships, this was almost exactly half of all Royal Navy war losses in all theatres. For overall Royal Navy losses, see S W Roskill, *The Navy at War 1939–1945* (London: Collins, 1960), appendix, p449. If Admiralty estimates for ships seriously damaged in the Mediterranean are taken into account (six battleships, four carriers, thirty-one cruisers, sixty-six destroyers), the adverse impact on fighting capability was far higher.

10   Two partial exceptions are Lawrence R Pratt, *East of Malta, West of Suez* (Cambridge University Press, 1975); and Reynolds M Salerno, *Vital Crossroads: Mediterranean Origins of the Second World War, 1935–1940* (New York: Cornell University Press, 2002). Both offer good analysis of Britain's Mediterranean policy over the period 1935–40 and cover similar ground, though Salerno is more wide-ranging and exploits a more extensive research base. Both include aspects of naval policy, but do not cover this in detail. Their work is even more compelling if the Middle East is viewed as part of a wider 'eastern empire', as defined in this book.

11   These include James R Leutze, *Bargaining for Supremacy: Anglo-American Naval Collaboration, 1937–1941* (USA: University of North Carolina Press, 1977); Greg Kennedy, *Anglo-American Strategic Relations in the Far East 1933–1939* (London: Frank Cass, 2002); Malcom Murfett, *Fool Proof Relations: The Search for Anglo-American Naval Co-operation during the Chamberlain Years 1937–1940* (Singapore University Press: 1984); and Cowman, *Dominion or Decline*. Only Cowman covers the period after the ABC-1 staff talks through to the end of 1941 in any detail.

12   The most authoritative works giving a comprehensive overview of the Royal Navy in the Second World War remain Roskill's three-volume *War at Sea* and Correlli Barnett, *Engage the Enemy More Closely*, published thirty years later. Duncan Redford's 2014 book is a much briefer account.

13   Arthur J Marder, *Old Friends, New Enemies: The Royal Navy and the Imperial Japanese Navy, 1936–1945* (Oxford, UK: Clarendon Press 1981–1990). This appeared in two volumes: *Strategic Illusions 1936–1941* (1981); and *The Pacific War 1942–1945* (1990). Marder died in 1980 and *The Pacific War* was completed by three of his students drawing on his notes and records. He had completed drafts of the first six chapters which cover the period of this book. The value of the work lies in its specific focus on the Royal Navy, its wide sweep, and the depth of research. Marder drew on the official British records released in the 1970s, but also exhaustive tapping of surviving witnesses. As a Japanese speaker, he was also one of the first historians to exploit Japanese sources. His account of the Force Z operation is definitive, and much of his excellent and detailed coverage of the Indian Ocean in 1942 is not available elsewhere. He provides an essential yardstick for further research.

14   H P Willmott, *Grave of a Dozen Schemes: British Naval Planning and the War against Japan 1943–1945* (UK: Airlife Publishing, 1996) is a partial exception, although this book does not accept all of Willmott's arguments.

15   One of very few historians to emphasise the centrality of the Indian Ocean to the overall British Empire war effort is Ashley Jackson in *The British Empire and the Second World War*, chapters 10–12. This book is of wider importance in describing the overall empire, as opposed to specific United Kingdom war contribution. Unfortunately, its impact is reduced by an episodic structure, too many factual errors, and poor editing. Jeremy Black also emphasises the strategic significance of the Indian Ocean in 1942 in 'Midway and the Indian Ocean', *US Naval War College Review*, 62:4 (Autumn 2009).

417

16 For example, Max Hastings, *All Hell Let Loose*; Anthony Beevor, The *Second World War*; and Andrew Roberts, The *Storm of War*. Only Roberts suggests Middle East oil was important, but without really explaining why. None of the three comment on the Persian supply route to Russia.

17 There is no biography of Admiral of the Fleet Sir Ernle Chatfield, who was First Sea Lord for most of the 1930s, or of Admiral Sir Tom Phillips, who played a central role in Far East strategy as, successively, Director of Plans (1936–38), Vice Chief of Naval Staff (1939–41) and, finally, Commander-in-Chief Eastern Fleet in late 1941. A recent book by Martin Stephen, *Scapegoat – The Death of the Prince of Wales and Repulse* (Barnsley, UK: Pen & Sword Ltd, 2014), has some new background on Phillips, drawing on family papers, but essentially focuses only on the Force Z story, where it seeks to exonerate him from blame. Robin Brodhurst's biography of Admiral of the Fleet Sir Dudley Pound who was First Sea Lord from 1939–43, *Churchill's Anchor: The Biography of Admiral of the Fleet Sir Dudley Pound OM, GCB, GCVO* (UK: Leo Cooper, 2000), is workmanlike, but selective in its coverage. It does not address Pound's role in promoting the tilt towards the Mediterranean from late 1938, and coverage of the eastern theatre during his time as First Sea Lord is confined to Force Z, where Brodhurst accepts the standard interpretation. The only biography of Admiral of the Fleet Sir James Somerville is Donald MacIntyre's *Fighting Admiral: The Life of Admiral of the Fleet Sir James Somerville* (London: Evans Brothers, 1961). This is now more than fifty years old and drew on limited sources.

18 Cunningham had a central role in the naval defence of the eastern empire as successively Deputy Chief of Naval Staff (1938–39), Commander-in-Chief Mediterranean (1939–42), Chief of Naval Staff in Washington (1942), and, finally, as First Sea Lord (1943–46). There are two modern biographies: John Winton's *Cunningham: The Greatest Admiral since Nelson* (London: John Murray, 1998); and Michael Simpson's *A Life of Admiral of the Fleet Andrew Cunningham: A Twentieth Century Naval Leader* (London: Routledge, 2004). There is an older biography by Oliver Warner, *Cunningham of Hyndhope, Admiral of the Fleet: A Memoir* (London: John Murray, 1967). Cunningham himself produced a substantial autobiography, *Admiral of the Fleet Viscount Cunningham of Hyndhope, A Sailor's Odyssey* (London: Hutchinson, 1957).

Chapter 1 – The Royal Navy 1935–39: The Right Navy for the Right War

1 Paul Kennedy, *The Rise and Fall of British Naval Mastery* (chapter 10 is titled 'The Years of Decay (1919–39)'); Arthur Marder, *From the Dardanelles to Oran: Studies of the Royal Navy in War and Peace 1915–1940* (London: Oxford University Press, 1974), chapters 2 and 3; Correlli Barnett, *Engage the Enemy More Closely*, part I: Britannia Lets the Trident Slip, chapters 1 and 2; and S W Roskill, *Naval Policy between the Wars*.

2 Barnett, *Engage the Enemy More Closely*, p24. Barnett, perhaps the leading proponent of the declinist version of twentieth-century British history, is viewed by many as a divisive figure, partly because he can rarely resist a polemical turn of phrase. This is nevertheless an important work because of its sheer sweep, its command of detail and sources, and because it introduced important new dimensions such as the role of Ultra. Although now twenty years old, it is the most recent one-volume history of the Royal Navy in the Second World War that carries weight, and its judgements have probably shaped perceptions of Royal Navy performance in that war as much as Roskill.

3 Christopher Bell wrote in 2000 that some were challenging this negative view of the interwar Royal Navy. New research suggested the decline of Britain's power in general, and sea power in particular, had been exaggerated. Revisionist studies of the interwar navy portrayed an officer corps more far-sighted and professionally competent than conventional accounts suggested. However, the image of a reactionary, intellectually deficient service remained pervasive. *The Royal Navy, Seapower and Strategy between the Wars* (Basingstoke, UK: Macmillan Press Ltd, 2000), p xvi.

4 George Franklin, *Britain's Anti-Submarine Capability 1919–1939* (London: Routledge, 2003), p2.

5 Roskill, *Naval Policy between the Wars*, vol 1, p536. There were some early challenges. Writing in 1974, in *From the Dardanelles to Oran*, pp38–9, Marder described Roskill as 'off the mark' in a literal sense, but accepted that a general disinterest and disregard for convoy operations was

correct. A more striking reference, suggesting a more complex picture, appeared in Lawrence Pratt's *East of Malta, West of Suez* published in 1975. At p119, Pratt stated: 'Under Pound's supervision, British combined naval and air forces had carried out slow and fast convoy operations in the central Mediterranean and in the Atlantic west of Gibraltar in August 1937 and March 1938. Those exercises had confirmed Pound's pessimism regarding wartime naval movements through the Mediterranean: in the face of hostile Italian air power and submarines, a simple convoy from Malta to Egypt would become a major fleet operation'. Pratt drew on records in ADM 116/3900. Roskill certainly read Pratt because he reviewed the book in *International Affairs*, 52:2 (April 1976), pp274–5. It did not cause him to qualify his original claim.

6 Admiralty figures prepared for the 1937 Naval Estimates put Royal Navy warship tonnage in 1935 at 1.136 million tons compared to 1,019 for the US Navy. The combined tonnage total for the three future Axis powers in 1935 was 1.296 million tons, so the Royal Navy was close to this figure. The Admiralty figures were mainly based on data provided under the various naval treaties and can be considered accurate. The tables show that the US Navy did surpass the Royal Navy briefly in total warship tonnage in 1929. 'Comparative Table of Tonnages and Personnel of Naval Powers', NID paper dated 16 February 1937, for the 1937 Naval Estimates, ADM 116/3596, TNA.

7 Barnett, *Engage the Enemy More Closely*, p24, describes the *Nelson*s as 'a flawed compromise design'. This disparagement is not justified. The ships had their faults, but all battleships involved difficult trade-offs between gun power, protection and speed. The *Nelson*s had the heaviest armament in the world until 1941, most experts agree they were also the best protected until the new generation capital ships of the early 1940s, and they were 2 knots faster than any of the contemporary American battleships, though not the two Japanese *Nagato*s.

8 The Singapore base was not completed until 1940 and even then its capacity for heavy repair remained limited.

9 Joseph A Maiolo, 'Admiralty War Planning, Armaments, Diplomacy, and Intelligence Perceptions of German Sea Power and their influence on British Foreign and Defence Policy 1933–1939' (unpublished doctoral thesis, Department of International History, London School of Economics and Political Science, March 1996), pp22–3, which references a wide range of sources.

10 US Navy General Board to the Secretary of the Navy, Item 37, Michael Simpson, *Anglo-American Relations 1919–1939*, Naval Records Society (Ashgate Publishing, 2010). The text of the Washington Treaty (and subsequent interwar naval limitations treaties) can be found at www.navweaps.com.

11 Bell, *The Royal Navy, Seapower and Strategy between the Wars*, chapter 1.

12 ADM 116/4434, TNA.

13 Andrew Field, *Royal Navy Strategy in the Far East, 1919–1939: Planning for a war against Japan* (London: Frank Cass, 2004), Conclusion; Christopher Bell, *Churchill and Sea power* (OUP, 2012), chapter 4; and John H Maurer, '"Winston has gone mad": Churchill, the British Admiralty and the Rise of Japanese Naval Power', *Journal of Strategic Studies* (2012), pp1–24, first article.

14 Andrew Gordon, *British Seapower and Procurement between the Wars: A Reappraisal of Rearmament* (Annapolis, USA: Naval Institute Press, 1988), pp107–8.

15 Neither the Royal Navy nor others within the British government system ever used the term 'two-power standard excluding the US'.

16 This paragraph and the preceding one draw on the Admiralty historical commentary in 'A New Standard of Naval Strength', D.P. (P.) 3 forwarded to the Committee of Imperial Defence on 29 April 1937. A copy is included in C.P. 316 (37), 'Defence Expenditure in Future Years, December 1937', CAB 24/273, TNA. For an excellent exposition of the interwar one-power standard and the wider history of standards as a measure of Royal Navy strength, see Bell, *The Royal Navy, Seapower and Strategy between the Wars*, chapter 1, and his *Churchill and Sea Power*, chapters 3, 4 and 5.

17 Michael Simpson assesses the four interwar naval limitation conferences (Washington 1922, Geneva 1927, London 1930 and London 1936) in his covering commentaries on the collection of papers on *Anglo-American Naval Relations, 1919–1939*, produced for the Naval Records Society (UK: Ashgate Publishing, 2010). His overall judgement on the treaty process at p160 is:

'In sum, limitation treaties probably prevented Japan from building as large a navy as she would have done otherwise, while, at the last, allowing the democracies just enough scope and time to construct barely enough ships to save the day come Armageddon'. That seems reasonable. The history of the treaty process is also summarised in an Admiralty paper produced as part of the 1937 Estimates package. This provided a rationale for the shift from quantitative to qualitative measures under the 1936 agreement and the perceived advantages to Britain. 'Naval Disarmament since the War', ADM 116/3596, TNA.

18 D K Brown, *Nelson to Vanguard: Warship Design and Development 1923–1945* (London: Chatham Publishing, 2006), chapters 5 and 9.

19 The Washington Treaty assumed capital ships had a life span of twenty years. D K Brown, *Nelson to Vanguard.*

20 Bell states: 'Even in 1929, the Royal Navy was still the strongest navy on earth, more powerful than the US Navy and with a comfortable margin over the IJN and any European navy.' *The Royal Navy, Seapower and Strategy between the Wars*, p25. Professor N A M Rodger sees the Royal Navy through the 1920s consistently outspending other naval powers and 'increasing its lead in both quantity and quality'. 'The Royal Navy in the Era of the World Wars: Was it fit for purpose?', *The Mariner's Mirror*, 97:1 (February 2011), pp272–84, p274.

21 D K Brown judges that 'the rule merely reflected the reality of the times and had little direct effect on budgets'. *Nelson to Vanguard*, Introduction. In support, he quotes G C Peden, *British Rearmament and the Treasury 1932–39* (Edinburgh 1979), pp6–8.

22 Gordon quotes the outgoing First Sea Lord, Admiral of the Fleet Sir Frederick Field, in his pre-retirement 'Review of Naval Policy' in 1932: 'The Ten-Years-No-War formula has mainly effected the reserves of ammunition, torpedoes, mines, fuel and stores for the Fleet, and provision for the auxiliary services such as Armed Merchant Cruisers, Defensively Equipped Merchant Ships, mine-sweepers and all types of anti-submarine measures'. *British Seapower and Procurement between the Wars*, p123. Bell, *Churchill and Sea power*, chapter 4, also assesses the politics and impact of the rule.

23 J R Ferris, '"It is our business in the Navy to command the seas": The Last Decade of British Maritime Supremacy, 1919–1929', in *Far Flung Lines – Essays on Imperial Defence in Honour of Donald Mackenzie Schurman*, ed Greg Kennedy and Keith Neilson (London: Frank Cass, 1997).

24 Ferris. A copy of the London Treaty can be found at www.navweaps.com. The key points were an extension of the ten-year bar on new capital ship construction established at Washington for a further five years and more extensive quantitative limits on cruisers and destroyers.

25 Ferris; and Gordon, *British Seapower and Procurement between the Wars,* chapter 8.

26 Ferris goes further, suggesting that, by the mid-1930s, many German and Italian warships were better than British ones and that either fleet combined with Japan was a match for Britain. His claim that many German and Italian warships were superior is dubious on the basis of both comparative paper specification and subsequent war performance. The six German light cruisers completed between 1925 and 1935 were arguably superior to the Royal Navy light cruisers designed during the First World War (eg 'C' and 'D' classes) which still dominated the Royal Navy light cruiser force in 1935, but inferior to the new *Leander* class commissioning from 1933 onward and vastly outgunned by the fifteen modern heavy cruisers of the County and *Exeter* designs, completed between 1928–31, and the future *Southampton* class which appeared from 1937. The Italian heavy cruisers of the early 1930s were better armoured than the County class because they significantly exceeded the Washington Treaty limits but it is doubtful they were better all-round ships.

27 Ferris.

28 Ferris.

29 The premier post-war historian of the US Navy, Samuel Eliot Morison, claims that the Hoover administration (1929–33) had the sad distinction of being the only one since the eighteenth century in which not a single naval combatant ship was laid down. Morison, *The Two Ocean War: A Short History of the United States Navy in the Second World War* (USA: Little, Brown & Co, 1963). The charge is not literally true since two *Portland*-class cruisers were laid down in 1930, but it is representative of the sad state of US Navy building.

30 The implications of the 1930 London Treaty for all the main naval powers are assessed in *At the Crossroads between Peace and War: The London Naval Conference of 1930*, edited by

John H Maurer and Christopher Bell (Annapolis USA: Naval Institute Press, 2014).

31 Roskill provides relevant figures at appendix D and E in *Naval Policy between the Wars*, vol 1. These appear correct and his exchange calculations to convert US dollars into GBP also seem reasonable.

32 D K Brown, *Nelson to Vanguard*, chapter 9, including footnote 2, and chapter 11.

33 1935 information here from papers prepared as part of the 1937 Naval Estimates, ADM 116/3596, TNA.

34 Ian Johnston and Ian Buxton, *The Battleship Builders: Constructing and Arming British Capital Ships* (Barnsley, UK: Seaforth Publishing, 2013), p239. They were laid down in fiscal year 1922 and completed in fiscal year 1927. It is likely that half the combined cost, ie £6.5 million, fell into the 1925–29 period.

35 Financial calculations here are based on Roskill's figures in appendix D of *Naval Policy between the Wars*, vol 1.

36 Figures from www.ukpublicspending.co.uk.

37 Ferris.

38 'Effect of the London Treaty on British Naval Strength', ADM 116/3373, TNA.

39 Controller's minute dated 26 September 1936, ADM 116/3382, TNA.

40 Included here are the first two German pocket battleships of the *Admiral Scheer* class. Although armed with 11in guns, their displacement and protection fit them better into the heavy cruiser category. In its estimates of comparative strength, the Royal Navy normally counted the three pocket battleships as equivalent to one Royal Navy capital ship.

41 Although armed with 6in guns, the classification 'heavy' is justified by the number of guns and displacement.

42 Under the 1930 London Treaty, the Royal Navy was permitted 91,000 tons of new cruisers by the end of 1936 but only reached this target three months later in March 1937. However, it laid down a further five cruisers prior to the signing of the next limitations treaty in March 1936, on the assumption that its ceiling would be successfully negotiated upward.

43 An important exception is Orest Babij, 'The Royal Navy and the Defence of the British Empire 1928–1934', in Greg Kennedy, *Far Flung Lines*. Babij presents a good defence of the Royal Navy leadership during this period and argues that they won crucial concessions at the London Treaty, sufficient for a steady replacement programme of which the new destroyers were a key part.

44 The Royal Navy had twenty-five destroyers and ten other anti-submarine vessels under construction in 1935, compared with an Axis total of twenty-eight destroyers and eighteen destroyer escorts.

45 Michael Simpson.

46 Expenditure figures from Roskill, *Naval Policy between the Wars*, vol 1, appendix D.

47 R A Burt, *British Battleships*.

48 This calculation reflects the figure of £7.4 million quoted for a *King George V* by 1937 by Ian Johnston and Ian Buxton in *The Battleship Builders*, p239.

49 Jon Sumida states that, in 1933, the Admiralty had reports that the US Navy had spent five times as much as the Royal Navy on battleship modernisation. 'British Naval Procurement and Technological Change, 1919–1939', in *Technology and Naval Combat in the Twentieth Century and Beyond*, ed Phillips Payson O'Brien (London: Routledge, 2007). He does not quote a source but D K Brown refers to a meeting of the Sea Lords in October 1933 at which the Director of Naval Intelligence claimed the US Navy had spent £16 million on modernising their capital ships, Japan had spent £9 million and would probably spend more, and the Royal Navy only £3 million. *Nelson to Vanguard*, chapter 9.

50 'Vessels Modernised', paper prepared with 1937 Naval Estimates, ADM 116/3596, TNA.

51 US naval attaché record, 'Notes on conversation with the First Sea Lord', 19 November 1940, ADM 199/691, TNA.

52 R A Burt, *British Battleships*, p228.

53 Director of Plans minute to First Sea Lord of 29 October 1941, ADM 205/11, TNA. This stated that *Ramillies* would not be modified prior to deployment to the Far East on 30 November, implying the other 'R'-class ships had been modified by that time. Further details on 'supercharge' firing can be found in www.navweaps.com, under the entry for the Royal Navy 15in/42 Mark 1 gun.

54   Anti-submarine warfare was emphasised by Field in his 1932 First Sea Lord Review. A copy
      with subsequent comment from Plans Department is available under 'Review of Naval Policy
      and Investigation of Deficiencies in War Equipment and Stores 1932–35', ADM 116/3434,
      TNA.
55   Minutes by Director of Plans, Captain E L King, on 3 August 1935 and his successor, Captain
      T S V Phillips, on 25 May 1936, on options for modernising capital ships. They address the risks
      of having three ships out of the frontline simultaneously. ADM 116/3382, TNA.
56   D K Brown assesses the whole Royal Navy capital ship modernisation programme in chapter
      9 of *Nelson to Vanguard*. This includes an assessment of value for money, taking account of the
      subsequent operational performance during the war of the relevant vessels.
57   Under the 1930 London Treaty, the Royal Navy was subject to an overall limit of 135,000 tons
      for its carrier force until the end of 1936. Its existing fleet left space for one additional carrier
      of around 23,000 tons which was used for *Ark Royal*, but all existing carriers were classed as
      experimental and could be replaced subject to the overall limit at any time.
58   For a fascinating counterfactual history of the consequences of the Royal Navy reacquiring
      control of its air arm in 1932 as opposed to 1937, see David Row, *The Whale Has Wings*,
      published as an e-book on Amazon in three volumes in 2012–13. It envisages how Fleet Air
      Arm, and wider Royal Navy, history might then have differed over the period 1932–42. Its
      weakness is that, by exploiting the benefit of hindsight, it assumes perfect anticipation and
      decision-making by the Royal Navy leadership, along with trouble-free development of aircraft,
      etc. Nevertheless, it does offer a plausible view of the maximum Fleet Air Arm capability the
      Royal Navy might have achieved within the limits of British economic resources.
59   Ferris. For practical purposes, 'any two' here means Japan and a European power excluding
      France.
60   Chiefs of Staff 1933 Annual Review, CID 1113-B, paras 35–41, and 68–70, CAB 16/109, TNA.
61   Admiral of the Fleet Lord Chatfield speaking as Minister for Defence Co-ordination to the
      Committee of Imperial Defence in 1939. Quoted from D.P. (P.) 60, para 8, in N H Gibbs, *Grand
      Strategy*, vol 1: Rearmament Policy, chapter 10, 'Naval Strategy 1936–39', p378.
62   Director of Plans minute of 25 May 1936 covering 'Modernisation of the Battle fleet', ADM
      116/3382, TNA.
63   Others who have emphasised the comparative decline of the Royal Navy in the 1930s and the
      difficulty in achieving adequate rearmament include Daniel A Baugh, 'Confusions and
      Constraints: The Navy and British Defence Planning 1919–39', and Correlli Barnett, 'The
      Influence of History upon Sea Power: The Royal Navy in the Second World War' (both in *Naval
      Power in the Twentieth Century*, ed N A M Rodger (Basingstoke: Macmillan, 1996)); and
      Duncan Redford's new *World War II* contribution to the *History of the Royal Navy* series
      sponsored by the National Museum of the Royal Navy (London: I B Tauris, 2014). Barnett's
      essay develops themes already evident in *Engage the Enemy More Closely*.
64   Roskill provides the comparative strengths of the six main naval powers at 1 January 1932 at
      appendix B of *Naval Policy between the Wars*, vol 1. If his figures are interpreted alongside
      those in table 1, they confirm that 'two-power equivalence' remained in place three years later.
65   Royal Navy strength in September 1939 from Roskill, *Naval Policy between the Wars*, vol 1,
      appendix B, with completion calculations based on dates in H T Lenton, *British and Empire
      Warships of the Second World War*.
66   Ferris, 'Last Decade of British Maritime Supremacy', Gordon, *British Seapower and
      Procurement*, and Barnett, *Engage the Enemy More Closely*, pp37–8.
67   David Edgerton, *Warfare State* (Cambridge University Press, 2006), pp33–41.
68   Jon Sumida, 'British Naval Procurement and Technological Change, 1919–1939', table 8.2.
      'Major warship' comprised: battleship, carrier and first-class cruiser.
69   August 1939 estimates from Committee of Imperial Defence 361st Meeting, CAB 2/9, TNA.
      Actual completion dates from H T Lenton.
70   Ian Johnston and Ian Buxton, *The Battleship Builders*, p45.
71   N H Gibbs, *Grand Strategy*, vol 1, Rearmament Policy, table 9, New Shipbuilding, p358.
72   ADM 205/5, TNA.
73   R A C Parker, *The Second World War: A Short History* (Oxford University Press, 1989), p135.
74   Figures for merchant ship completions are from the British Shipbuilding Database recorded in

the article 'Measuring Britain's Merchant Shipbuilding Output in the Twentieth Century', by Ian Buxton, Roy Fenton and Hugh Murphy, *The Mariner's Mirror*, 101:3 (August 2015), pp304–22.

75   The origins and initial terms of reference for the DRC are in the introductory paragraphs to its first report dated 28 February 1934, CAB 16/109, TNA. Gordon, p112, provides useful context.

76   N H Gibbs, *Grand Strategy*, vol 1, chapter 10.

77   S W Roskill, *Naval Policy between the Wars* (National Maritime Museum, Maritime Monograph 29, 1978).

78   Gordon, *British Seapower and Procurement*, p111.

79   Quoted from Peter Kemp's DNB entry, OUP 2004.

80   Eric Grove, essay on Chatfield in *The First Sea Lords: From Fisher to Mountbatten* (Westport CT USA: Praeger, 1995), edited by Malcom Murfett. As stated in the Introduction, there is no major biography of Chatfield. He published his autobiography in two volumes between 1942–47 as *The Navy and Defence* (London: William Heinemann, 1942–1947), vol 1: *The Navy and Defence* (1942); vol 2: *It Might Happen Again* (1947). Eric Grove's essay and Peter Kemp's DNB entry both provide good balanced summaries of his contribution as First Sea Lord, his wider career, and his personality and qualities. Gordon is good on his contribution to the DRC and the rearmament programme. Roskill provides much detail in *Naval Policy between the Wars*.

81   Keith Neilson, 'The Defence Requirements Sub-Committee, British Strategic Foreign Policy, Neville Chamberlain and the Path to Appeasement', *English Historical Review*, 118:477 (June 2003), pp651–84.

82   The initial DRC Report, dated 28 February 1934, and the meetings leading up to it are in CAB 16/109, TNA.

83   The record of DRC meetings in 1935 and the Third Report forwarded by Hankey on 21 November 1935 is in CAB 16/112, TNA.

84   The most authoritative and important works here are N H Gibbs, *Grand Strategy*, vol 1: *Rearmament Strategy*; S W Roskill, *Naval Policy between the Wars*, vol II: *The Period of Reluctant Rearmament*; Andrew Gordon, *British Seapower and Procurement between the Wars*; G C Peden, *Arms, Economics, and British Strategy* (Cambridge University Press, 2007); Joseph Maiolo's thesis, 'Admiralty War Planning, Armaments, Diplomacy, and Intelligence Perceptions of German Sea Power and their influence on British Foreign and Defence Policy 1933–1939'; and David Edgerton, *Warfare State*.

85   Maiolo's thesis, 'Admiralty War Planning, Armaments, Diplomacy, and Intelligence Perceptions of German Sea Power and their influence on British Foreign and Defence Policy 1933–1939', and his later book *Cry Havoc: The Arms Race and the Second World War 1931–1941* (London: John Murray, 2011), especially chapter 6.

86   Apart from Maiolo's work on the AGNA, there is valuable analysis by Clare Scammell in her article 'The Royal Navy and the strategic origins of the Anglo-German naval agreement of 1935', *Journal of Strategic Studies*, 20:2 (1997), pp92–118.

87   Maiolo demonstrates that the Royal Navy had a better grasp of German naval thinking and capability than previously supposed. He also convincingly refutes the view established by Wesley Wark that in negotiating the AGNA the Admiralty was the victim of poor intelligence. He shows that it was well informed on German construction and plans. For Wark, see *The Ultimate Enemy: British Intelligence and Nazi Germany, 1933–1939* (USA: Cornell University Press, 1985).

88   Director of Plans minute of 25 September 1936, ADM 1/9729, TNA. The final report, 'A New Standard of Naval Strength', is in DP (P) 3 dated 29 April 1937, CP 316/37, CAB 24/273, TNA.

89   Record of DRC 14th meeting, July 1935, CAB 16/112, TNA.

90   Record of DRC 17th meeting, 10 October 1935.

91   Record of DRC 18th meeting, 14 October 1935.

92   'Forecast of Strategical Situation End 1942. Maximum Attainable Strength?', ADM 116/3631, TNA.

93   CP 170 (38) 'Naval Expenditure' dated 12 July 1938, CAB 24/278, TNA. The Minister for Defence Co-ordination, Sir Thomas Inskip, estimated that over the three fiscal years 1936–38, the Admiralty had received at least 75 per cent of the budget originally proposed for seven years.

94 A summary of projected German and IJN strength in 1942, as anticipated in late 1938, is in C.P. 236 (38) dated 25 October 1938, 'Forecast of British Naval Strength on 31 December 1942, for Transmission to Germany under Terms of the Anglo-German Naval Agreement', CAB 24/279, TNA.

95 Japanese figures from Paul Dull, *A Battle History of the Imperial Japanese Navy* (London: Greenhill Books, 1998). German figures from Roskill, *War at Sea*, vol I. The four battleships were the German *Bismarck* and *Tirpitz* and the IJN super-battleships *Yamato* and *Musashi*. The four carriers were the IJN *Hiryu* (completed 1939), *Shokaku* and *Zuikaku* (both completed 1941), and German *Graf Zeppelin* (never completed). The IJN also converted merchant ships into carriers with two commissioned by end 1941.

96 Barnett, p37, and Haggie, pp121–5.

97 Admiralty Board memorandum, 'New Standard of Naval Strength', dated 26 April 1937, ADM 1/9081, TNA. Included in the Naval Records Society publication, *The Collective Naval Defence of the Empire, 1900–1940*, item 322.

98 Memorandum by Fifth Sea Lord, 'State of the Fleet Air Arm', 4 September 1939, ADM 116/3722, TNA.

99 H T Lenton has the second pair of *Lion*-class battleships (*Conqueror* and *Thunderer*) ordered on 16 August 1939 and the carrier *Indefatigable* on 19 June 1939. Some sources dispute whether the battleships were ever ordered. The Admiralty intent at the end of March was to invite tenders on 9 June and then follow with orders in October and November, although they were also considering replacing the second ship with a new battlecruiser concept – see footnote 100 below. Board Memorandum of 29 March, ADM 205/1, TNA. Ian Johnston and Ian Buxton state tenders for the second two *Lions* were indeed issued on 12 June and the submissions from John Brown and Fairfield accepted at the end of July with orders then placed in August. *The Battleship Builders*, p45. By September 1939, it was evident that technical problems with the new gun mountings of the *Lions* would delay the programme and that work on the hulls could be suspended for up to twelve months without affecting ultimate completion dates. This suspension would create much needed capacity for extra destroyers. The Admiralty Board therefore agreed the suspension on 28 September. ADM 167/103, TNA.

100 ADM 1/10141, TNA. A memorandum for the Admiralty Board at the end of the same month, 29 March, 'Acceleration of Defence Programmes', suggested the new ship could be substituted for the fourth *Lion* in the fiscal year 1939 programme with the latter then joining the fiscal year 1940 programme. The ship would be ordered in November 1939. ADM 205/1, TNA.

101 Minute by Director Naval Air Division dated 11 May 1939. Navy Records Society, vol 159, *The Fleet Air Arm in the Second World War*, vol 1: *1939–1941*, ed Ben Jones (UK: Ashgate Publishing, 2012), paper no 3 taken from ADM 1/10133, TNA.

102 Roskill, *Naval Policy between the Wars*, vol II, p451.

103 ADM 116/3631, TNA.

104 Gordon, *British Seapower and Procurement Between the Wars*, p273, addresses the common criticism that the rearmament programme concentrated on major fleet units to the exclusion of smaller ships.

105 Professor N A M Rodger, 'The Royal Navy in the Era of the World Wars: Was it fit for purpose?', p278.

106 Navy Records Society, vol 137, *The Defeat of the Enemy Attack on Shipping, 1939–1945*, ed Eric J Grove (UK: Ashgate Publishing, 1997), Plan 7 'The rise and decline of the operational U-boat fleet 1939–1945'. There are also useful statistics and background in Clay Blair, *Hitler's U-boat War, The Hunters 1939–1942* (London: Weidenfeld & Nicolson, 1997).

107 *The Defeat of the Enemy Attack on Shipping, 1939–1945*, Plans 7, 10 and 55.

108 Professor N A M Rodger argues that, statistically, the decisive turning point for the Battle of the Atlantic was early 1942 rather than a year later as is usually argued. 'The Royal Navy in the Era of the World Wars: Was it fit for purpose?', pp281–2.

109 Barnett, not noted for his support of British technology, endorses this view for at least the *King George V* battleships and the 1930s cruiser classes. *Engage the Enemy More Closely*, pp41–3.

110 On specific design issues, the research conducted by D K Brown is a good guide. *Nelson to Vanguard: Warship Design and Development 1923–1945*. For the superiority of British armour see also Norman Friedman, *The British Battleship 1906–1946* (UK: Seaforth Publishing, 2015), p47.

111 Roskill, Marder and Barnett all highlighted these failings and the last three were underlined again by Jon Sumida in 'British Naval Procurement and Technological Change, 1919–1939'.

112 Barnett states that 'the RN's responses to the technical and operational puzzles involved in refurbishing British sea power in the late 1930s suggest a narrow professionalism of outlook too much influenced by loyalty to tradition and too little blessed with innovative imagination'. *Engage the Enemy More Closely*, p49.

113 The influence exerted by this theme on the mainstream historiography is summarised by Jon Sumida in '"The Best Laid Plans": The Development of British Battle-Fleet Tactics, 1919–1942', *The International History Review*, 14:4 (1992), pp681–700. He shows how this view pervades the thinking of Roskill, Marder and Barnett.

114 Sumida.

115 David C Evans and Mark R Peattie, *Kaigun: Strategy, Tactics and Technology in the Imperial Japanese Navy* (Annapolis USA, Naval Institute Press, 1997), pp250–63, for IJN investment in 'outranging' as a means of countering a superior enemy force.

116 Cunningham, Admiral of the Fleet Viscount of Hyndhope, *A Sailor's Odyssey* (London: Hutchinson, 1957), pp159–61.

117 Sumida.

118 There are good summaries of these exercises, with some original records, in the following: Navy Records Society, vol 158, *The Mediterranean Fleet 1919–1929*, especially Items 314 and 317, ed Paul Halpern (UK: Ashgate Publishing, 2011); Geoffrey Till, 'The Impact of Air power on the Royal Navy in the 1920s' (unpublished doctoral thesis, University of London, 1976); Philip Anthony Weir, 'The Development of Naval Air Warfare by the Royal Navy and Fleet Air Arm between the two World Wars' (unpublished doctoral thesis, University of Exeter, March 2006); Andrew Field, *Royal Navy Strategy in the Far East, 1919–1939* , especially chapter 6, which covers strategic and tactical exercises relating to a Far East war; and George Franklin, Britain's *Anti-Submarine Capability, 1919–1939*. This has detailed coverage of all interwar anti-submarine warfare exercises, but is especially interesting on convoy exercises which often included fleet cover.

119 'Mission command' has been the dominant command philosophy within the American and British military (and many others as well) for at least the last thirty years. In essence, the overall commander defines his broad intent, or key strategic objective, and then allows his subordinates substantial freedom over how they achieve that intent and respond to enemy counter-moves to disrupt the intent. Mission command is invariably associated with what is known as the 'manoeuvrist approach'. This is not just about outmanoeuvring an enemy but shattering his overall cohesion and will to fight.

120 Field, chapter 6.

121 As noted earlier, the large fast carriers *Glorious* and *Courageous* were not completed until 1929.

122 For early investigation of the potential of an Asdic strike force with air spotting, Report of Fleet Exercise NX dated 7 September 1928, paras 63–66 and 81, from ADM 186/144, Item 314, Navy Records Society, vol 158.

123 Weir's account of Exercise OP in 1930 at pp145–8 of his thesis. He sees the genesis of the future carrier-centred 'task force' concept in ideas tried by Chatfield (as Commander-in-Chief Atlantic Fleet) and Pound (as Commander Battlecruiser Force). Weir stresses that it was not the first time a carrier and battlecruisers worked as a unit but it was the first time the primacy of a capital ship was subordinated to the needs of a carrier.

124 Weir has thoroughly investigated the attitude of individual senior Royal Navy officers in the interwar period to air power at sea. He judges that all commanders-in-chief of the period were 'air converts' and those who went on to become First Sea Lord were both committed to the recovery of the Fleet Air Arm and making the service 'air-minded'. The interest in and commitment to air among the rising generation of junior flag officers and senior captains was even greater. The legend of the 'battleship admiral' utterly unwilling to contemplate the capabilities of aircraft should be firmly put to rest. It is frequently suggested that Vice Admiral Sir James Somerville's success as commander of Force H in 1940/41 came about because he was uniquely air-minded, implying therefore that other flag officers were not. Weir's analysis of individual backgrounds and attitudes as well as the actions of different flag officers in exercises suggests that Somerville was within the mainstream here, rather than an aberration.

True, he was particularly able, but that reflected all-round talent rather than unique awareness of air potential.

125 Barnett states that by the mid-1930s, the Royal Navy had fallen well behind the IJN and US Navy, not only in the number of embarked aircraft, but also their capability, and, most important, in persisting with the belief that carriers were merely an adjunct to the battle-fleet rather than a potential long-range strike force. *Engage the Enemy*, p25. Till in *Air power and the Royal Navy* states that, by 1939, the Royal Navy had 'yielded to the IJN and US Navy in the race to develop air power at sea', but argues it was already falling behind much earlier.

126 Memorandum for the Board, 'Fleet Air Arm Reorganisation and Expansion', ADM 167/103, TNA.

127 Barnett and Till.

128 See Chapter 5 for a full discussion of this.

129 Roskill summarises 'dual control' and the problems it posed for the Royal Navy in chapter 3 of *War at Sea*, vol 1.

130 Till, *Air power and the Royal Navy*.

131 Till first coined the term 'ancillary'. His book drew on his earlier doctoral thesis which focused on the period 1919–29. Some of his judgements were more appropriate to that period than the 1930s.

132 Andrew Gordon, *British Seapower and Procurement between the Wars*, p229.

133 The lack of 'bureaucratic muscle' derives from Caspar John, a junior Fleet Air Arm officer in this period but a future First Sea Lord in the early 1960s. Quoted by Till.

134 Director of Training and Staff Duties minute dated 7 July, 1930, ADM 116/2771, TNA.

135 Weir thesis. Roskill agrees with Till that, during the 1920s, the view that carrier aircraft were 'ancillary' predominated. But he too saw the appointment of Henderson in 1931 as Rear Admiral Carriers, beginning a decisive shift in attitude which gave carriers a more central role. *War at Sea*, vol 1, chapter 3.

136 ADM 116/2771.

137 Norman Friedman, *British Carrier Aviation*, p158.

138 For emerging IJN doctrine, Mark Peattie, *Sunburst: The Rise of Japanese Naval Air power, 1909–1941* (Annapolis, USA: Naval Institute Press, 2001), esp pp72–6, section 'The Emergence of Japanese Carrier Doctrine', which focuses on the late 1930s.

139 For the evolution of US Navy thinking from the late 1930s through the Second World War, Thomas C Hone's article 'Replacing Battleships with Aircraft Carriers in the Pacific in World War II', *US Naval War College Review*, 66:1 (Winter 2013).

140 The most important papers are Director of Plans paper PD 05739/36, 'Carrier Construction', undated but clearly summer 1936, ADM 116/3376, TNA; Director of Plans note for First Sea Lord, 'Aircraft Carrier Strength', dated 14 December 1936, ADM 116/3376; Director of Naval Air Division minute of June 1936, ADM 116/3376; and, the Admiralty submission, 'A New Standard of Naval Strength', to which the above three references clearly contributed. DP (P) 3 dated 29 April 1937, CP 316/37, CAB 24/273, TNA.

141 'Carrier Construction'.

142 Fifth Sea Lord minute dated 4 March 1939, ADM 116/3722, TNA. Eight new carriers by 1943 was an eminently achievable target from the vantage point of 1936.

143 'Carrier Construction'.

144 'Carrier Construction'.

145 'Carrier Construction'.

146 'Carrier Construction'.

147 Dates here from DNB entry by Malcom Murfett, OUP 2004.

148 The post Deputy Chief of Naval Staff (DCNS) became Vice Chief of Naval Staff (VCNS) in April 1940 and Phillips was promoted to acting vice admiral. DNB entry by Malcom Murfett.

149 As an acting admiral, Phillips was the most senior Allied officer killed in action in the Second World War.

150 As noted in footnote 18 of the Introduction, Martin Stephen's recent book, *Scapegoat – The Death of the Prince of Wales and Repulse*, is not a comprehensive biography of Phillips. It focuses primarily on his role in the Force Z story. It says nothing about his role as Director of Plans and little about his time as DCNS/VCNS, certainly offering no definitive judgement of his

contribution in these posts. Stephen does, however, give a balanced assessment of Phillips's view of the air threat at sea. Insights into Phillips's personality based on letters held by the Phillips family are new and valuable.

151 H T Lenton.

152 See Friedman, *British Carrier Aviation*, p158. Also Weir thesis, pp89–97.

153 Norman Friedman, D K Brown and David Hobbs have all examined the balance of argument here.

154 David Hobbs, *British Aircraft Carriers: Design, Development and Service Histories* (UK: Seaforth Publishing, 2013), p108.

155 Douglas Ford, 'British Naval Policy and the War against Japan 1937–1945: Distorted Doctrine, Insufficient Resources, or Inadequate Intelligence', *International Journal of Naval History*, 4:1 (April 2005).

156 Professor N A M Rodger, Lecture given to MA Military History students, University of Buckingham, 17 December, 2012.

157 Nicholas E Sarantakes, 'One Last Crusade: The British Pacific Fleet and its Impact on the Anglo-American Alliance', *The English Historical Review*, 121:491 (April 2006), pp429–66.

158 N A M Rodger has coined the term 'dead end' while acknowledging the Royal Navy had good reasons for taking this path. David Hobbs, *British Aircraft Carriers: Design, Development and Service Histories*, p89.

159 David Weir thesis, pp105–40.

160 In July 1939 the Fifth Sea Lord expected the first 250 Barracudas (the successor torpedo bomber to the Albacore) to reach the frontline during 1941. 'Progress report on the Fleet Air Arm', 26 July 1939, ADM 116/3722, TNA. The reasons this did not happen are described in chapter 5.

161 Norman Friedman, *British Carrier Aviation*.

162 Roskill, *Naval Policy between the Wars*, vol II, p333. As a former gunnery officer, Roskill had strong views on this subject.

163 Jonathan Parshall and Anthony Tully in *Shattered Sword: The Untold Story of the Battle of Midway* (Washington, USA: Potomac Books, 2007), chapter 8, claim the IJN Type 94 was a tachymetric system comparable to the Mark 37 though they also admit it was slow and therefore ineffective against dive-bombers.

164 Barnett, *Engage the Enemy More Closely*, pp46–7. His judgements, while trenchantly expressed, and in line with his well-known prejudices regarding the backwardness of British industry, rely heavily on Roskill's sources and correspondence.

165 Sumida, 'British Naval Procurement and Technological Change, 1919–1939', draws on Roskill's comparative budget figures at appendix E of *Naval Policy Between the Wars*, vol I, to argue that the United States 'spent 50 percent more on its navy than Britain in the 1920s and more than a third more in the 1930s', hence having much more funding for research. This chapter demonstrates that these figures are misleading and that expenditure on the surface navies was about the same.

166 Philip Pugh, 'Managing the Aerial Threat: Provisions for anti-aircraft warfare during the 1930s', in Richard Harding, The *Royal Navy, 1930–2000, Innovation and Defence* (London and New York: Frank Cass, 2004).

167 See Allan G Bromley, British Mechanical Gunnery Computers of WWII, 1984.

168 Letter to Admiral Sir Roger Backhouse, dated 8 October 1937, CHT/4/1, NMM.

169 An excellent well sourced paper, 'The British High Angle Control System (HACS)', dated 10 May 2009, by Tony D Giuliani, is available under the Naval Technical Board section of the website www.navweaps.com. It includes a comparison with the US Mark 37 system. The paper describes the evolution of HACS through six successive variants ending with the Mark VI in 1942.

170 Giuliani.

171 Norman Friedman in his definitive study of anti-aircraft gunnery published in 2014 argues that the Royal Navy, so often criticised for lack of air-mindedness, was actually the naval power most alert to the threat. Its systems were inadequate not because they were too primitive, but because they tried to achieve too much. Norman Friedman, *Naval Anti-Aircraft Guns and Gunnery* (UK: Seaforth Publishing, 2014).

172 US Navy Anti-Aircraft Action Summary WWII, dated 8 October 1945, issued HQ Commander-in-Chief Fleet, Navy Department Library.

173 Martin Middlebrook and Patrick Mahoney, *Battleship: The Loss of the Prince of Wales and the Repulse* (London: Allen Lane, 1977), pp176–7, 230.

174 This report was produced by Admiral Sir Sidney Bailey as part of his package of reports prepared for use with the Americans (see Chapter 4 for more context on the Bailey report). Bailey minute PD 06939/40 of 10 August, 1940, approved by First Sea Lord the same day, ADM 199/691, TNA.

175 D K Brown, *Nelson to Vanguard: Warship Design and Development 1923–1945*, pp207–9, agrees with Friedman that Royal Navy deficiencies were a consequence of trying to do too much too early before the technology was good enough and before key threats such as the Luftwaffe dive-bomber were foreseeable. Professor N A M Rodger sees one possible exception here, the Dutch navy Hazemeyer system. This not only provided a stabilised tachymetric anti-aircraft director but, uniquely, the gun mounting was slaved to the director. It could track modern high-performance aircraft in three dimensions, even at close range, and was light enough for installation in small ships. 'The Royal Navy in the Era of the World Wars: Was it fit for purpose?', p275.

176 US Navy Anti-Aircraft Action Summary.

177 For Royal Navy ships, see H T Lenton and R A Burt. For *Yamato*, Evans and Peattie, *Kaigun*, p376.

178 The improvement in anti-aircraft outfit was not confined to new build and modernised vessels. A statement on naval deficiencies prepared for the Committee of Imperial Defence in October 1938 reports that anti-aircraft rearmament had been completed for nine battleships, one carrier, ten heavy cruisers, six light cruisers and five anti-aircraft cruisers by that time. The programme had extended to most remaining major units by the outbreak of war. Statement on CID Questions, October 1938, ADM 167/103, TNA.

179 'Progress in Tactics', ADM 239/142, TNA, and Friedman, p94.

180 Friedman, chapters 4 and 8.

181 George Franklin summarises the prevailing historical consensus in the introduction to *Britain's Anti-Submarine Capability, 1919–1939*.

182 Franklin, p2. Compare Barnett's scathing comment on the interwar Royal Navy referred to earlier.

183 Franklin's separate article on this topic: 'The origins of the Royal Navy's vulnerability to surfaced night U-boat attack 1939–40', *The Mariner's Mirror*, 90:1 (February 2004), pp73–84).

184 Franklin.

185 Barnett, *Engage the Enemy More Closely*, pp44–6.

186 COS 535 (JP) of 15 December 1936, 'Protection of Seaborne Trade, part 1, War with Germany', CAB 53/29, TNA. This updated an earlier paper prepared in July. Barnett acknowledges the establishment of the multi-department Shipping Defence Advisory Committee in early 1937, though he suggests this came rather late. Since the Germans only started building submarines in 1935, and had just ten oceangoing boats at that time, his view seems over-critical.

187 COS 640 of 26 November 1937, 'The Protection of Seaborne Trade', CAB 53/34, TNA.

188 See the chart of U-boat sinkings in the first nine months of the war, Plan 16 (1) in *The Defeat of the Enemy Attack on Shipping, 1939–1945*, ed Eric J Grove. Here this period is called 'phase 1' of the Atlantic Campaign. Virtually all of these sinkings did indeed take place in the Admiralty's Home Waters area.

189 This is illustrated in Plan 16 (2) in *The Defeat of the Enemy Attack on Shipping*, showing U-boat sinkings during phase 2 of the Atlantic Campaign from 1 June 1940 to 31 March 1941. In this period about half of sinkings took place to the west and south of the Admiralty's pre-war Home Waters area.

190 Recent articles by Professor N A M Rodger and Joseph Maiolo endorse this overall judgement, although on specific issues their interpretations differ from this chapter. Rodger states that, by all reasonable measures, throughout the interwar years, the Royal Navy remained 'certainly the greatest naval power'. For Maiolo, the interwar period for the Royal Navy is 'not a story of inevitable decline' but rather of 'astonishing ingenuity and audacity in the face of mounting challenges'. N A M Rodger, 'The Royal Navy in the era of the World Wars: Was it fit for purpose?'; and Joseph A Maiolo, 'Did the Royal Navy decline between the two World Wars?', *The RUSI Journal*, 159:4 (August/September 2014), pp18–24.

Chapter 2 – The Naval Defence of the Eastern Empire 1935–40: Managing Competing Risks

1 These were territories ceded or leased to Britain (and many other western powers) by China during the nineteenth century. By the 1930s, the main British concessions were Hong Kong, and parts of Shanghai and Tientsin. These had slightly different legal status with Hong Kong effectively a Crown colony. Britain had troops based in all three locations.

2 COS 209th meeting of 1 June 1937, CAB 53/7, TNA.

3 The reasons for selecting Singapore are covered in David W McIntyre, *The Rise and Fall of the Singapore Naval Base 1919–1942* (London: Macmillan, 1979) and James Neidpath, *The Singapore Naval Base and the Defence of Britain's Eastern Empire 1919–1941* (Oxford, UK: Clarendon Press, 1981). Both provide a more balanced view of the Singapore strategy than other histories published in the 1970s and 1980s.

4 Quoted by Alan Warren, *Singapore 1942: Britain's Greatest Defeat* (Hambledon & London, 2002), p289. Also, Haggie, *Britannia at Bay*, p11.

5 Malcom Murfett's essay, 'Reflections on an Enduring Theme: The "Singapore Strategy" at Sixty', has a good summary of the evolution of the Singapore strategy and the critiques by successive historians. In *Sixty Years On: The Fall of Singapore Revisited*, ed Brian Farrell and Sandy Hunter (Singapore: Eastern Universities Press, 2003).

6 Christopher M Bell, *The Royal Navy, Seapower and Strategy between the Wars*, chapter 3 'Far Eastern War Plans'. This chapter begins with a list of the main works critical of the Singapore strategy. Andrew Field's *Royal Navy Strategy in the Far East, 1919–1939: Planning for a war against Japan* (London: Frank Cass, 2004), broadly endorses Bell's view.

7 This paragraph draws mainly on Bell, pp59–60 and 93–4.

8 The term 'risk' is widely used and abused. This book adopts the modern definition which defines 'risk' as a combination of 'threat', 'probability' and 'impact'. 'Threat' in turn comprises 'intent' and 'capability'. Cm 7953, *A Strong Britain in an Age of Uncertainty: The National Security Strategy* (London: HMSO, 2010).

9 COS 368 of 16 March 1935, 'The Situation in the Far East', CAB 53/24, TNA.

10 For the Japanese perspective, JM 146, Political Strategy Prior to the Outbreak of War, part II, United States Army Center for Military History, USA.

11 COS 370 of 6 April 1935, 'The Situation in the Far East', CAB 53/24, TNA. Bell provides a summary of earlier Royal Navy views of the threat posed by Japan at pp61–2 of *The Royal Navy, Seapower and Strategy*.

12 COS 372 of 29 April 1935, CAB 53/24.

13 COS 295 of 23 February 1932, 'Annual Review of Imperial Defence Policy 1932', para 13, CAB 53/22, TNA. An annex 'Situation in the Far East', prepared by the deputy chiefs looked at the defence deficiencies here in more detail.

14 COS 305 of 31 March 1933, 'Situation in the Far East', CAB 53/23, TNA.

15 COS 310 of 12 October 1933, 'Imperial Defence Policy, Annual Review (1933)', CAB 53/23, TNA.

16 COS 314 of 14 October 1933 provides Chief of Air Staff views on the prospects of a four carrier air strike. COS 317 of 11 January 1934 by the First Sea Lord explores the issue further. COS 327 of 20 April 1934 summarises 'Air Requirements for Defence of Singapore'. All CAB 53/23, TNA.

17 Dreyer to Chatfield, 12 December 1933. Chatfield responded in letters of 2 February and 7 August 1934. CHT/4/4/, NMM.

18 COS 357 of 30 November 1934, 'Annual Review of Imperial Defence 1934', CAB 53/24, TNA.

19 COS 372 of 29 April 1935, 'Annual Review of Imperial Defence 1935', CAB 53/24, TNA.

20 Annex 3 of review. Following submission of the DRC First Report, it was agreed in 1934 that work on these defences would proceed in two stages. In mid-1935, the chiefs of staff expected stage I to complete by end 1936 and were finalising proposals for stage II. COS 386, of 9 July 1935, 'Singapore: Acceleration of Provision of Defences'. In October, the Defence Policy and Requirements Committee of the Cabinet approved part of Stage II following receipt of £500,000 from the Sultan of Johore. JDC 222 of 1 October 1935, 'Singapore Defences'. Both in CAB 53/25, TNA.

21 COS 347 of 29 October 1934, 'Strategic Position in the Far East with particular reference to Hong Kong and air requirements for the Far East', CAB 53/24, TNA.

22 Annex 5 of 1935 Review of Imperial Defence Policy contains comparative naval strengths in 1935. COS 372 of 29 April 1935, CAB 53/24, TNA.
23 COS Memo 392 of 9 August 1935, 'Italo-Abyssinian Dispute', provides naval forces originally planned. CAB 53/25, TNA. For actual strength achieved by late September, Arthur Marder, *From the Dardanelles to Oran*, p78.
24 COS 442 of 18 March 1936, 'The Condition of our Forces to meet the Possibility of War with Germany', CAB 53/27, TNA.
25 COS 460 JP of 27 April 1936, 'Situation in the event of unprovoked aggression by Germany arising out of the present crisis (March – April 1936)', CAB 53/27, TNA.
26 Roskill quotes COS 442 in *Hankey, Man of Secrets*, vol III: *1931–1963*(London: Collins, 1974), p224, to argue that the naval picture here was 'depressing in the extreme'. He does not mention the more balanced view in COS 460.
27 The British estimate of IJN strength at the start of 1935 is in appendix 5 of the Chiefs of Staff 1935 Review. This quoted nine capital ships, four carriers, fourteen heavy cruisers, twenty light cruisers, one hundred and four destroyers, and fifty-seven submarines. However, only seven capital ships were immediately available (two in modernisation) and only two of the carriers were large fleet units – 75 per cent would be a reasonable figure for maximum availability of the other forces.
28 Chapter 1, table 3. The calculation here was based on the estimated strength of the IJN in 1942 not the IJN of 1936 which was significantly smaller.
29 COS 347 of 29 October 1934, 'Strategic Position in the Far East with particular reference to Hong Kong and Air Requirements for the Far East', CAB 53/24, TNA.
30 COS 579 of 7 May 1937, 'Chiefs of Staff Far East Appreciation', CAB 53/31, TNA.
31 COS 305 of 31 March 1933, 'The Situation in the Far East', CAB 53/23, TNA. Chatfield's view of the risk to the Suez Canal is in his letter to Commander-in-Chief Mediterranean, Admiral Sir William Fisher, dated 24 January 1935. CHT/4/5/, NMM.
32 COS 305 of 31 March 1933.
33 COS 344 of 30 July 1934, 'Hong Kong: Plans for Defence, Relief or Recapture', CAB 53/24, TNA. The paper does not address recapture but suggests this would be a formidable operation probably requiring the landing of a substantial expeditionary force.
34 Chiefs of Staff 209th meeting dated 1 June 1937, CAB 53/7, TNA.
35 Bell summarises the evolution of Admiralty planning for a Far East war across the whole interwar period in chapter 3 of *The Royal Navy, Seapower and Strategy*. He emphasises the importance of economic coercion at the core of Royal Navy thinking. While he addresses the distinction between an 'offensive' and 'defensive' strategy, his analysis focuses on 'ways' and 'means' rather than 'ends'. He does not sufficiently describe the consequences and limitations of pursuing a defensive strategy.
36 Chatfield letter to Sir Warren Fisher, Permanent Under Secretary Treasury, dated 4 June 1934, CHT/3/1, NMM.
37 Anthony Best, *Britain, Japan and Pearl Harbor: Avoiding War in East Asia, 1936–1941*(London: Routledge, 1995), p7.
38 COS 523 of 3 November 1936, 'Vulnerability of Burma in a Far Eastern War', CAB 53/29, TNA.
39 COS 588 of 28 May 1937, CAB 53/31, TNA.
40 COS 1935 review.
41 JM 146, Political Strategy Prior to the Outbreak of War, part II.
42 Christopher Thorne, *Allies of a Kind: The United States, Britain and the War Against Japan, 1937–1945* (London: Hamish Hamilton, 1978), pp36–7.
43 In his memoirs, Chatfield stated: 'Collective security inflicted on the COS impossible responsibilities. No-one could tell us who to fight against'. *The Navy and Defence*, vol II: *It Might Happen Again* (London: William Heinemann, 1947), p87.
44 Notes by Chatfield on Sir Robert Vansittart's 'Memorandum on the World Situation' and Hankey's subsequent comments, dated 5 January 1937, CHT/3/1, NMM. These notes were shared with Hankey.
45 Imperial conferences were gatherings of government leaders of the Dominions and self-governing territories of the empire. They took place approximately every five years. The

previous full conference was in London in 1930 but there was an Imperial Economic Conference in Ottawa in 1932.

46 COS 560 of 22 February 1937, 'Imperial Conference, 1937, Review of Imperial Defence', CAB 53/30, TNA. Paragraphs relevant to the Far East are: 25–28, 37–39, and 55–64.

47 COS 596 of 14 June 1937, 'Appreciation of the Situation in the Far East, 1937', CAB 53/32, TNA.

48 COS 570 of 24 March 1937, 'Naval Appendix to the Chiefs of Staff Review of Imperial Defence', CAB 53/30, TNA.

49 COS 576 of late April 1937, letter from First Sea Lord to Secretary of the Committee of Imperial Defence, CAB 53/31, TNA.

50 Minutes of Imperial Conference 7th meeting, 26 May 1937, AIR 8/220, TNA.

51 Minutes of Committee of Imperial Defence 348th meeting, CAB 2/8, TNA.

52 Chiefs of Staff 209th meeting, 1 June 1937, CAB 53/7, TNA.

53 Paragraph 84 of review.

54 The Imperial Review formally ranked British security interests as:
   (i) Security of Imperial communications throughout the world;
   (ii) Security of the UK homeland against German aggression;
   (iii) Security of Empire interests in the Far East against Japanese aggression;
   (iv) Security of interests in the Mediterranean and Middle East;
   (v) Security of India against Soviet aggression.
The chiefs of staff would continue to rank the Far East above the Middle East in theory, if not in practice, until 1942.

55 E (PD) 37, 7th Meeting of Principal Delegates, 26 May 1937, AIR 8/220, TNA.

56 Hoare had also underlined this point on 26 May.

57 Bell, *The Royal Navy, Seapower and Strategy*, pp63–5.

58 COS 587 of 28 May 1937, 'Protection of Sea Routes in Waters Adjacent to India', CAB 53/31, TNA. This memorandum responded to a government of India request for guidance on the level of Royal Navy protection available in the Indian Ocean in the case of a 'world war'. It reflected concern over the protection of Indian Army troops earmarked to reinforce Singapore.

59 Strategic Appreciation Committee First Meeting, 1 March 1939, CAB 16/209, TNA.

60 Chatfield was especially committed to the wider empire perspective.

61 Paragraphs 12, 14 and 79 of Chiefs of Staff Review.

62 Paragraph 83 of Chiefs of Staff Review.

63 JM 146.

64 Paragraphs 83–88 of Chiefs of Staff Review.

65 COS 731 of 26 May and COS 740 of 15 July 1938, both CAB 53/39, TNA.

66 Paragraph 330 of Far East appreciation.

67 Appendix A to Far East appreciation, COS 596.

68 Alastair Mars, *Submarines at War 1939–1945* (London: William Kimber, 1971), chapter 3 for 'The Influence of British Submarine Power in the Far East', and appendix 1 for the war game. Mars subsequently became one of the most successful submarine commanders of the Second World War and staff operations officer at submarine headquarters. His assessment therefore commands credibility.

69 Backhouse letter dated 11 October 1938 to Commander-in-Chief China, ADM 205/3.

70 For this definition and a wider debate about the meaning of strategy: Cm 7953, *A Strong Britain in an Age of Uncertainty: The National Security Strategy*, Introduction 0.14 and HC 435, House of Commons Public Administration Select Committee, *Who does UK National Strategy?* (London: HMSO, 2010), 2 Defining Strategy, paras 9–16.

71 Backhouse minute dated 24 March 1939, ADM 1/9909, TNA.

72 'Core eastern empire' here means India and Australasia.

73 Chatfield letter to Fisher of 4 June 1934, CHT/3/1, NMM.

74 Imperial conference, Minutes of 7th Meeting, AIR 8/220, TNA.

75 Greg Kennedy, 'Symbol of Imperial Defence: The Role of Singapore in British and American Far Eastern Strategic Relations, 1933–1941', in *Sixty Years On: The Fall of Singapore Revisited*.

76 JM 146.

77 COS 603 of 26 July 1937, 'Mediterranean and Middle East Appreciation Interim Draft', CAB

53/32, TNA. Hankey subsequently confirmed that this was part I of a wider appreciation. There would be a part II covering the situation where Britain and France were opposed to Germany and Italy, and a part III with Japan also an enemy. The full paper would be updated to present the situation anticipated on 1 April 1938. COS 619 of 22 September 1937, CAB 53/33, TNA.

78 COS 646 of 24 November 1937, 'Defence of Egypt', CAB 53/34, TNA, examined this in detail.
79 Chatfield letter dated 5 August, CHT/4/10, NMM.
80 CAB 50/5–8, TNA.
81 Chatfield's letter to Pound of 30 December 1937 discusses the possibility that Pound may need to deploy to Singapore following the crisis provoked by Japanese attacks on the gunboats HMS *Ladybird* and USS *Panay*. CHT/4/10, NMM.
82 Steven Morewood, *The British Defence of Egypt 1935–1940: Conflict and Crisis in the Mediterranean* (London: Frank Cass, 2005), p182.
83 *The Navy and Defence*, vol II: *It Might Happen Again*, p89.
84 'Artery of Empire' is a widely used term for the Mediterranean through route and Suez Canal. Michael Simpson later coined a more modern phrase: 'superhighway to the world-wide web'. 'Superhighway to the World Wide Web: The Mediterranean in British Imperial Strategy, 1900 – 1945', in *Naval Strategy and Policy in the Mediterranean*, ed John B Hattendorf (London: Frank Cass, 2000).
85 Director of Plans minute dated 23 March 1939, ADM 1/9909, TNA.
86 COS 651 of 13 December 1937, enclosing telegram to the Permanent Under Secretary Foreign Office, Sir Robert Vansittart, dated 30 November 1937, CAB 53/34, TNA.
87 COS 691 of 21 February1938, CAB 53/37, TNA.
88 Anthony Best, *Britain, Japan and Pearl Harbor*, pp36–7, judges the outbreak of the Sino-Japanese war had a profoundly detrimental impact on Anglo-Japanese relations.
89 Haggie, *Britannia at Bay*, pp115–19.
90 COS 639 of 12 November 1937, 'Comparison of the Strength of Great Britain with certain other Nations as at January 1938', CAB 53/34, TNA, paragraph 42.
91 COS 755 of 5 August, 'Appreciation of the Situation in the Event of War against Germany in April 1939', CAB 53/40, TNA.
92 Chatfield comments at the Chiefs of Staff 227th meeting of 19 January 1938 and memorandum he circulated prior to this meeting, 'Military Preparations in relation to Imperial Defence Policy'. CAB 53/8, TNA.
93 COS 686, 'Defence of Egypt', dated 14 February 1938, CAB 53/36, TNA.
94 Lawrence Pratt, *East of Malta, West of Suez*, pp131–2.
95 315th Meeting, CAB 2/7, TNA.
96 COS 691 of 21 February 1938, 'Mediterranean, Middle East and North East Africa Appreciation', CAB 53/37, TNA.
97 COS 755 of 5 August 1938, 'Appreciation of the Situation in the Event of War Against Germany in April 1939', CAB 53/40, COS 765 of 4 October 1938, 'Appreciation of the Situation in the Event of War Against Germany', CAB 53/41, COS 843 of 20 February 1939, 'European Appreciation 1939–1940', CAB 53/45, all papers in TNA.
98 Pratt, p 132–133.
99 Chatfield at the Chiefs of Staff 228th meeting on 28 January 1938, CAB 53/8, TNA.
100 COS 680 of 4 February 1938, 'Staff Conversations with France and Belgium', CAB 53/36, TNA. This reflected discussion at the Chiefs of Staff 228th meeting on 28 January, CAB 53/8.
101 COS 795 of 18 November 1938, 'Staff Conversations with France', CAB 53/42, TNA. This memorandum gives a full account of staff contacts by all three services following the Cabinet directive of April.
102 Chatfield comments at Chiefs of Staff 224th meeting on 9 December 1937 and 228th meeting on 28 January, both in CAB 53/8.
103 Pound letter to the Admiralty dated 14 November 1938, ADM 116/3900, TNA.
104 COS 737 of 2 July 1938, 'Defence of India', CAB 53/39, TNA. The review dated 28 May was produced by Major General H R Pownall who served on the Committee of Imperial Defence staff from 1933–38 and was later Vice Chief of the Imperial General Staff in 1941.
105 COS 846, 'European Appreciation', paragraph 228. The appreciation specifically noted that the intervention of Japan could threaten communications to Egypt and the Middle East.

106 COS 843.
107 Chiefs of Staff 276th meeting dated 15 February, CAB 53/10, TNA.
108 European Appreciation Appendix I. 'Political Review April 1939'.
109 JM 146.
110 European Appreciation Appendix IV, 'Probable British Naval Dispositions April 1939'.
111 European Appreciation paragraphs 269–270.
112 European Appreciation paragraphs 39–140 and 258. It also included wider offensive options against Italy using land and air as well as naval power 'as our strength develops'. Paras 265–266.
113 European Appreciation, para 237. The Committee of Imperial Defence meeting was the 348th and the minutes are in CAB 2/8, TNA. Also Pratt, *East of Malta West of Suez*, p171.
114 Eg, Pratt, Salerno and Michael Simpson; Haggie, Murfett, Farrell and Bell.
115 Malcom Murfett in his chapter on Backhouse in *The First Sea Lords: From Fisher to Mountbatten*; Michael Simpson, 'Superhighway to the World Wide Web: The Mediterranean in British Imperial Strategy, 1900–1945'; and Reynolds Salerno, *Vital Crossroads*, pp97–8.
116 This assurance came at a meeting with the Australian High Commissioner Stanley Bruce on 1 November. Lord Stanhope, the First Lord, was also present. Backhouse reaffirmed that, in a war with Japan, the Royal Navy would send a minimum fleet of seven capital ships to Singapore. Contemporary records show that he remained fully committed to sending a fleet to counter a threat to Australia but he judged, quite reasonably, that the risk to Australia at this time was remote. His only significant caveat was that, if war in Europe was underway, force redistribution would take time and the existing seventy days' period before relief at Singapore might not be met. This was no different from the line taken by Chatfield in 1937. COS Memos, 813 of 22 December 1938, CAB 53/43, and COS 837 of 7 February 1939, CAB 53/44, and the COS meetings on 13 January and 15 February, both CAB 53/10, all CAB references in TNA.
117 The last meeting of the chiefs of staff which Backhouse attended was the 281st meeting on 15 March. CAB 53/10 and CAB 53/11, TNA. His tenure was therefore little more than six months. Cunningham, as Deputy Chief of Naval Staff, was Acting First Sea Lord from end March until the beginning of June when Pound took over.
118 Backhouse minute to First Lord dated 30 March 1939, ADM 1/9909, TNA.
119 Backhouse set out the capital ship position in 1939 in a note for the Strategic Appreciation Committee dated 28 February. SAC 4, CAB 16/209, TNA.
120 COS 596, CAB 53/32, TNA. Chatfield in his memoirs claims the Controller (Henderson) under-estimated the time needed for these reconstructions. *The Navy and Defence*, vol II, pp122–3.
121 Chiefs of Staff 263rd meeting on 23 November 1938, CAB 53/10, TNA. Also Admiralty paper at SAC 4.
122 The best guides to Backhouse's thinking on Far East reinforcement are his comments at the first meeting of the Strategic Appreciation Committee on 1 March 1939, CAB 16/209 TNA, and his minute dated 24 March which addressed Foreign Office proposals for a stronger Royal Navy commitment to the Mediterranean reported by Director of Plans. The Foreign Office note was written by Victor Cavendish-Bentinck, recently returned from Egypt to become chairman of the Joint Intelligence Committee, a post he retained throughout the war. He argued that abandoning the eastern Mediterranean might be more disastrous for the British Empire than accepting a temporary loss of trade in the East or a small risk of attack on Australia. Given his future role this attitude was significant. ADM 1/9909, TNA.
123 The first meeting was on 1 March and the second on 13 March. The minutes are in CAB 16/209, TNA.
124 At the Chiefs of Staff 266th meeting on 5 January 1939, Backhouse expressed concern about growing hostility to Britain in the Arab world and the need for a Joint Planning Staff assessment. CAB 53/10, TNA.
125 Lawrence Pratt, *East of Malta, West of Suez*, and Reynolds Salerno, *Vital Crossroads: Mediterranean Origins of the Second World War*. Both chart the conflicting calculations and ambiguities that marked British policy towards Italy and the Mediterranean from 1935 through to the outbreak of the European war, and in Salerno's case to June 1940. Pratt's later chapter headings record a journey from 'acquiescence and appeasement', through 'containment' to

'England's first battlefield', and then back to partial acquiescence to preserve Italian neutrality, partly in response to renewed crisis in the Far East.

126 Backhouse letter to Drax dated 15 October 1938, DRAX 2/10, CCA.

127 Michael Simpson, 'Superhighway to the World Wide Web: The Mediterranean in British Imperial Strategy, 1900–1945'.

128 Pratt, *East of Malta West of Suez*, pp167–8. The main papers relevant to these exchanges are in ADM 116/3900, TNA.

129 There is a biographical summary for Drax at pp12–14 of *Dreadnought to Daring: 100 Years of Comment, Controversy and Debate in The Naval Review* (Barnsley: Seaforth Publishing, 2012), ed Peter Hore.

130 Joseph Maiolo, 'Admiralty War Planning, Armaments, Diplomacy, and Intelligence Perceptions of German Sea Power and their influence on British Foreign and Defence Policy 1933–1939', pp196–9. Chatfield's letter to Drax is in CHT/3/1, NMM.

131 Robert Lynn Davison, 'Admiral Sir Reginald Drax and British Strategic Policy: Festina Lente' (unpublished MA thesis, Wilfred Laurier University, Ontario, Canada, 1994), pp110–16. Roskill, *Churchill and the Admirals*, pp93,146.

132 Drax developed his strategy ideas in a series of papers over the winter concluding with a final summary dated 16 March 1939. Drax Memo OPC 11, ADM 1/9897, TNA. His earlier papers and associated correspondence are in the Drax Papers, Box 2, CCA.

133 Bell, *The Royal Navy and Seapower*, pp86–90.

134 Notable examples here are Haggie in *Britannia at Bay*, pp139–41; Murfett in his Backhouse chapter in *The First Sea Lords*; and Brian Farrell in *The Defence and Fall of Singapore* (Tempus Publishing, 2005), pp46–7.

135 Salerno, *Vital Crossroads*, pp98–101, 118–21, and Pratt, *East of Malta West of Suez*, p173.

136 Davison, pp111–12.

137 Drax Memo OPC 11.

138 Strategic Appreciation Committee first and second meetings, CAB 16/209.

139 Bell, *The Royal Navy and Seapower*, p88.

140 Backhouse minutes dated 30 March and 2 April, ADM 1/9897, TNA.

141 AT to overseas commanders, transmitting revised Section XVII to Naval War Memorandum Eastern, dated 15 June 1939, ADM 116/3863, TNA.

142 Bell provides a thoughtful and well balanced summary of the Backhouse and Drax inputs to Far East naval strategy at pp86–90 of *The Royal Navy and Seapower*.

143 SAC 13 of 13 April, CAB 16/209, TNA.

144 Backhouse's telegram was despatched on 17 March to the Australian First Naval Member, Vice Admiral Sir R Colvin. ADM 1/9831, TNA.

145 Backhouse letter to Colvin of 9 January 1939, ADM 205/3, TNA.

146 James Neidpath, *The Singapore Naval Base*, p150.

147 261st meeting on 10 November 1938 and 273rd and 278th meetings, CAB 53/10, TNA.

148 COS 850 (JP) of 28 February 1939, CAB 53/45, TNA.

149 This version omitted sensitive national passages. COS 850 (JP).

150 Salerno disputes this arguing that the French dictated Mediterranean policy at the staff talks. *Vital Crossroads*, p120.

151 COS 915 of 25 May 1939, 'Covering Memorandum to the Chiefs of Staff European Appreciation, 1939–40', CAB 53/49, TNA.

152 COS 799 of 21 November 1938, 'Franco-British Co-operation in the Organisation of National Defence', CAB 53/42, TNA.

153 COS 891 of 24 April 1939, covering paper AFC (J) 17, 'Anglo-French Staff Conversations, 1939, Intervention of Japan', paragraphs 24 and 26.

154 Salerno.

155 Cunningham's memorandum 'Despatch of a Fleet to the Far East', dated 4 April 1939, met a request at the Strategic Appreciations Committee second meeting on 13 March for clarification of the Admiralty view of Far East naval reinforcement. Director of Plans prepared enclosures A, B, C and D to support the memorandum. His preferred draft response was B, advocating the traditional view that the only effective counter to Japan was deployment of a competitive fleet. On 2 April Backhouse, writing to Cunningham from his

hospital bed, described Director of Plans' paper as 'purely defensive', offering no prospect of winning a wider war. Cunningham's final memorandum was more flexible than Director of Plans' recommendations and drew on Backhouse's thinking. All papers are in ADM 1/9897, TNA.

156 Cunningham's memorandum was submitted to the Strategic Appreciations Committee as SAC Paper No 16 at its sixth meeting on 17 April before going to the Committee of Imperial Defence. CAB 16/209, TNA.

157 Minutes of Committee of Imperial Defence 355th meeting, CAB 2/8, TNA.

158 Haggie, *Britannia at Bay*, p143. Hampton's records of his meetings are in ADM 116/3922, TNA.

159 Neidpath, pp150–5.

160 Haggie, p145.

161 B P Farrell, *The Defence and Fall of Singapore 1940–1942*, pp46–7.

162 Farrell, pp46–7.

163 Murfett, 'Reflections on an Enduring Theme', pp15–17.

164 ADM 1/9909, TNA.

165 COS 863 of 27 March 1939, 'Allied Plans Against Italy', CAB 53/46, TNA.

166 Minute to Cunningham dated 2 April 1939, ADM 1/9897, TNA.

167 Cunningham's comment was made at the Chiefs of Staff 290th meeting on 19 April, CAB 53/11, TNA. The guidance to Mediterranean commanders-in-chief is included as annex II to the minutes of this meeting.

168 COS 946 of 10 July 1939, CAB 53/51, TNA.

169 Chatfield's comments on ministers being misled were made at the Chiefs of Staff 309th meeting dated 19 July 1939, CAB 53/11, TNA.

170 Cunningham Papers, MS 52560, BL.

171 This is the first reference to the concept of 'strategic depth' in Middle East defence which would resonate through 1941 and 1942.

172 COS 146 of 5 December 1939, 'Middle East: Review of Military Policy', CAB 80/6, TNA.

173 COS 914 of 25 May, 'Staff Conversations with the French', CAB 53/49, TNA, covering AFC 25 Report on stage II. See: annex II, Intervention of Japan. This draws on a joint paper agreed between the two delegations, AFC (J) 65.

174 Minutes of Chiefs of Staff 303rd meeting on 19 June 1939, CAB 53/11, TNA.

175 These papers are in PREM 1/345, TNA.

176 Pratt, *East of Malta West of Suez*, pp174–5.

177 The draft Section XVII of the war plan, Director of Plans' covering minute dated 5 May 1939, with Cunningham's subsequent approval, and successive drafts of the signal to Commander-in-Chief China are in ADM 116/3863, TNA. The new section XVII adopts a more flexible approach to Far East reinforcement than Director of Plans' earlier 'Enclosure B' produced for inclusion in Cunningham's memorandum at the end of March. This may reflect the influence of the Drax papers which Director of Plans probably only saw during the first half of April. Certainly the term 'flying squadron' must have come from Drax.

178 Also in ADM 116/3863.

179 Phillips comments at Chiefs of Staff 298th meeting on 25 May, Item 2, New Zealand Defence Conference 1939, CAB 53/11, TNA.

180 See p89.

181 Minutes of 355th Committee of Imperial Defence, CAB 2/8, TNA.

182 Anthony Best provides a good summary of the Tientsin crisis in *Britain, Japan and Pearl Harbor: Avoiding War in East Asia 1936–41*, pp71–4.

183 The most important 'Tientsin papers' are COS 931 of 24 June 1939, 'The Situation in the Far East', which draws on an earlier First Sea Lord draft circulated as COS 930, and the previous Joint Planning paper 'The Situation in the Far East' circulated as COS 927 on 16 June. All these are in CAB 53/50, TNA.

184 COS 927 of 16 June 1939, CAB 53/50, TNA

185 David McIntyre provides a good summary of the Committee of Imperial Defence debate in *The Rise and Fall of the Singapore Naval Base*, p157, drawing on the records of the 362nd meeting of the CID on 26 June in CAB 2/9, TNA. The records of the prime minister's subsequent meeting

with Dominion representatives on 28 June and the follow-up meeting at the Dominions Office on 11 July are also in CAB 2/9.

186 Phillips was junior to get this post and the appointment aroused resentment among more senior officers. It reflected a longstanding working relationship with Pound. Phillips had served under him when Pound was Director of Plans in the early 1920s and then as Staff Officer Operations when Pound moved to become chief of staff in the Mediterranean Fleet. Pound had the highest regard for his abilities and completely trusted him. Robin Brodhurst, *Churchill's Anchor*, pp123–5.

187 The title DCNS changed to VCNS for Vice Chief of Naval Staff in April 1940.

188 Christopher Bell, 'The "Singapore Strategy" and the Deterrence of Japan: Winston Churchill, the Admiralty and the Dispatch of Force Z', *English Historical Review*, 116:467 (June 2001), pp604–634, pp613–14. Bell states that Pound 'was uncomfortable with his predecessor's plans'; 'required little prompting from Chatfield to revert to a more orthodox line'; and that by June the chiefs of staff had 'rejected the idea of a 'flying squadron''. Also *Royal Navy, Seapower and Strategy*, p90.

189 ADM 1/9767, TNA.

190 Phillips as the incoming DCNS stood in for the absent First Sea Lord at the 298th meeting of the chiefs of staff on 25 May and was the senior Royal Navy representative in Whitehall until Pound arrived on 7 June. The first chiefs of staff meeting attended by Pound was the 300th on 16 June. CAB 53/11, TNA.

191 Item 3 of Chiefs of Staff 298th meeting on 25 May, CAB 53/11, TNA. The update was issued and forwarded to the Committee of Imperial Defence as 'Covering Memorandum to the Chiefs of Staff European Appreciation 1939–40', COS 915 of 25 May 1939.

192 Item 5 of the Chiefs of Staff 299th meeting on 1 June, CAB 53/11, TNA. Issued and forwarded to the Committee of Imperial Defence as COS 914 of 25 May 1939.

193 COS 920 of 6 June 1939, 'Malaya: Period Before Relief', CAB 53/50, TNA.

194 CAB 2/9, TNA.

195 Admiralty Circular Telegram dated 4 August 1939, Amendments to Naval War Memorandum (European), ADM 1/9767, TNA. The new sections were numbers XVI and XVII.

196 There is a manuscript minute by an unknown author dated 10 July stating that Director of Plans had indicated Section XVII of War Memorandum (Eastern) was to be cancelled. This is linked to Director of Plans' minute of 31 May covering a draft for DCNS (Phillips) to send to the Committee of Imperial Defence on the communication of changes in Far East reinforcement policy to the Dominions. ADM 116/3863, TNA.

197 Cunningham Papers, MS 52560, BL.

198 ADM 116/3863, TNA.

199 Discussion between Cabinet Office historians and Japanese War History Institute September 1966, 'The Malaya campaign and the fall of Singapore 1941–42', CAB 106/180, TNA.

200 Professor Tomoyuki Ishizu and Professor Raymond Callahan, chapter 3, The Rising Sun Strikes: The Japanese Invasions, in *The Pacific War Companion* edited by Daniel Marston (Osprey Publishing, 2011). This chapter draws on the Japanese official *War History: The Malayan Campaign* (Tokyo, 1966).

201 ADM 1/9767, TNA.

202 In November, Churchill as First Lord would point out that the distance from Japan to Singapore (in reality about 2400 miles) was 'as great as that from Southampton to New York'. Transporting and maintaining an army sufficient to besiege Singapore over that distance would be a 'forlorn undertaking' given the risk of Royal Navy interdiction. WP (39) 135 of 21 November 1939, 'Australian and New Zealand Naval Defence', CAB 66/3/35, TNA. Churchill overstated the distance here. The Japanese could have gathered an attack force at a base like Hainan in Southern China which was only 1100 miles, but the basic argument is valid.

203 D W McIntyre, *Rise and Fall*, p136.

204 To have the full confidence of the Royal Navy, a First Sea Lord at any time, but especially when war looked imminent, had to come from one of the two major sea commands, Home or Mediterranean. The only realistic choice for Chatfield in mid-1938 was Backhouse or Pound. With Backhouse out of the picture, it had to be Pound. Charles Forbes, Backhouse's successor as Commander-in-Chief Home Fleet was too new and untested.

205 This was broadly the view taken by Roskill and then followed by Barnett and many others. Robin Brodhurst, Pound's biographer, demonstrates that not only were there no other credible candidates in mid-1939, but that Pound was eminently well qualified. *Churchill's Anchor*, pp115–16.

206 Barnett, *Engage the Enemy More Closely*, pp51–2. A key witness, influential in establishing views on Pound, was Vice Admiral John Godfrey, who as DNI had a central view of the Admiralty leadership throughout 1939–42. Godfrey's view of Pound, and indeed Phillips, and their interaction with Churchill, is valuable, but must be weighed with care. His dismissal by Pound in 1942 rankled and he harboured grievances against Churchill. He was not therefore a detached and objective observer. *Naval Memoirs*, vol V: *1939–1942*, NMM.

207 Roskill in particular argued, especially in *Churchill and the Admirals*, that Pound's poor health rendered him medically unfit to be First Sea Lord in 1939 and that physical and mental exhaustion increasingly affected his decision-making and performance. Marder vigorously disputed this in *Old Friends, New Enemies*, vol I, pp233–8, provoking a long-running dispute between the two historians. Robin Brodhurst provides a balanced summary of the evidence in his biography of Pound and broadly endorses Marder's view. *Churchill's Anchor*, pp113–15.

208 Brodhurst, pp279–80.

209 Brodhurst, pp120.

210 Andrew Gordon, *The Rules of the Game: Jutland and British Naval Command* (London: John Murray, 1996), p576.

211 Roskill did acknowledge this in *War at Sea*, vol I, chapter 2, where he stated that although Pound 'made occasional mistakes in the direction of maritime operations, the true measure of his accomplishment lies in the turn of the tide at sea in 1943'.

212 WP (39) 135 of 21 November 1939. Paul Haggie describes the paper itself, the War Cabinet concern that it went beyond Chamberlain's guarantee of 20 March, and subsequent discussion with Australian representatives. *Britannia at Bay*, pp164–6. The War Cabinet debate is in WM 39, 89th Conclusions dated 20 November 1939, item 7, CAB 65/2/23.

213 Haggie, p165.

214 Callahan, *The Worst Disaster*, p26.

215 Farrell, *Defence and Fall*, p47.

216 Marder stated: 'All the thinking (by the Royal Navy) about the IJN's strategy (through the 1930s) was a grand exercise in futility – and a waste of countless man hours – since IJN operational planning paid scant attention to Great Britain before 1940–41, and even then its plans bore little relation to the cogitations of Whitehall planners'. *Old Friends, New Enemies*, vol 1, p65. Although Marder acknowledged this outcome was in the nature of contingency planning, his judgement is still unfair. Military risk assessment must address possibilities as well as certainties and the future as well as the present. British assessments of the Japanese threat, as it evolved through the 1930s, were realistic and balanced.

Chapter 3 – Securing Eastern Empire War Potential after the Fall of France

1 Roskill and Barnett and the main historians of the 'Singapore strategy'.

2 David Brown, *The Road to Oran: Anglo-French Naval Relations September 1939–July 1940* (London: Frank Cass, 2004), chapter 1.

3 The complex negotiations, and subsequent French and British actions, to prevent French naval units falling into German hands, are outside the scope of this book. They are covered by David Brown in *The Road to Oran*. This also provides an excellent overview of Anglo-French naval relations over the first nine months of the war.

4 Angelo N Caravaggio, 'The Attack at Taranto: Tactical Success, Operational Failure', *US Naval War College Review*, 59:3 (Summer 2006).

5 Admiral Dönitz describes the advantages gained by deploying U-boats from France in his memoir, *Ten Years and Twenty Days* (Frontline Books edition, 2012), chapter 8.

6 JM 146, 'Political Strategy Prior to the Outbreak of War, Part II', pp7–12.

7 JM 146, pp13–18.

8 JM 146, p30.

9 Brian Farrell claims the fall of France, more than any other single event, compromised Singapore. *The Defence and Fall of Singapore 1940–1942*, p56. Christopher Bell states that it

was the event that finally precluded the despatch of a substantial fleet to the Far East. *The Royal Navy, Strategy and Seapower*, p94.

10   COS 639 of 12 November 1937, paragraph 41.

11   COS 754 of 2 September 1938, 'Planning for War with Germany', CAB 53/40, TNA. This included the Joint Planning Staff appreciation 'Situation in the event of war with Germany in April 1939'.

12   COS 827 (JP) of 25 January 1939, 'The Strategic Position of France in a European War', CAB 53/44, TNA. This included reports from the Paris Embassy, including the military attaché, that the French military leadership did not now believe France could defend itself against Germany without direct military assistance from Britain.

13   COS 827 of 25 January 1939, 'State of Preparedness of the Army in relation to its Role', CAB 53/44, TNA.

14   COS 843 of 20 February, 'European Appreciation', para 123.

15   COS 914 of 25 May, 'Staff Conversations with the French', CAB 53/49, TNA. Allied naval co-operation is detailed at Annex V, pp14–16.

16   COS 915 of 25 May, 'Covering Memorandum to the Chiefs of Staff European Appreciation', 1939–1940, paras 55–58, CAB 53/49, TNA.

17   COS 915, paras 17–26.

18   WP (40) of 26 March 1940, 'Certain Aspects of the Present Situation', CAB 66/6/41; and COS (40) 320 of 4 May 1940, 'Review of the Strategical Situation on the assumption that Germany has decided to seek a decision in 1940', CAB 80/10, both in TNA.

19   WP (40) of 26 March.

20   COS 148th meeting on 19 May 1940, CAB 79/4, TNA.

21   COS (40) 390 of 25 May, 'British Strategy in a Certain Eventuality', CAB 80/11, TNA.

22   Adam Tooze covers this well in *The Wages of Destruction: The Making and Breaking of the Nazi Economy* (London: Penguin Books, 2007), chapter 11, especially pp370–80.

23   'Future Strategy', W.P. 362 of 4 September, CAB 66/11/42, TNA.

24   COS 629 (JP) of 14 August, 'Anglo-American Standardisation of Arms Committee', CAB 80/16, TNA, and, COS 675 of 28 August, 'Anglo-American Standardisation of Arms Committee', CAB 80/17, TNA.

25   Brian Farrell, *The Basis and Making of Grand Strategy – Was there a Plan?* (UK: Edwin Mellen Press, 1998), pp21–3.

26   True figures from Horst Boog and others, *Germany and the Second World War*, vol VI, table III.iii.i, p348.

27   COS (40) 390 of 25 May 1940, 'British Strategy in a Certain Eventuality', CAB 80/11, TNA.

28   Geirr Haarr, *The German Invasion of Norway April 1940* (UK: Seaforth Publishing, 2011).

29   *Second World War*, vol II, pp385–7.

30   *The Defeat of the Enemy Attack on Shipping, 1939–1945*, ed Eric J Grove, Introduction, appendix C, p xlvii.

31   Dönitz, *Ten Years and Twenty Days*, chapter 5.

32   There are authoritative figures for monthly U-boat strength in *Germany and the Second World War*, vol VI: *The Global War* (OUP, 2001) by Horst Boog, Werner Rahn and Bernd Wegner. Table III.iii.i. Their figures are consistent with those in *The Defeat of the Enemy Attack on Shipping, 1939–1945*, ed Eric J Grove, at plan 7 'Rise and Decline of the Operational U-boat fleet'. John Ellis also has similar figures, drawn from earlier sources in Table 37 of his *Brute Force: Allied Strategy and Tactics in the Second World War* (London: Andre Deutsch, 1990).

33   *The Defeat of the Enemy Attack on Shipping, 1939–1945*, at plan 10 'The build-up of the main anti-submarine forces under British operational control 1939 – 1945', also chapter 1, table 4.

34   The text of this Directive is available at www.ww2db.com.

35   Halder Diaries, vol IV, part 2, US Army Archives, Fort Leavenworth.

36   For a good assessment of the strategic influence exerted by Force H during the period 1940–42 both in discouraging Spanish intervention and pro-Axis action by French naval forces, Michael Simpson, 'Force H and British Strategy in the Western Mediterranean 1939–42', *The Mariner's Mirror*, 83:1 (1997), pp62–75.

37   *Germany and the Second World War*, vol III: *The Mediterranean, South-East Europe and North Africa 1939–1941* (UK English edition: Clarendon Press, 1998), by Gerhard Schreiber and

Bernd Stegemann, esp pp145–52, 187–93, provides an excellent analysis of German aspirations in the southwest, as well as the competing German and British pressures acting on Spain.

38 David Stafford, *Churchill and Secret Service* (UK: Overlook Press, 1997), pp236–8.

39 COS (40) 469 of 17 June, 'Military Implications of the Withdrawal of the Eastern Mediterranean Fleet', CAB 80/13, TNA.

40 Director of Plans' paper setting out the naval arguments for withdrawal is attached to the minutes of the Chiefs of Staff 183rd meeting on 17 June 1940, CAB 79/5, TNA.

41 COS (40) 521 of 3 July, 'Military Policy in Egypt and the Middle East', CAB 80/14, TNA.

42 Stalin attached particular importance to Britain's ability to control the eastern Mediterranean through naval power and saw this as a key factor both in weighing Russia's options in the Balkans and in judging Britain's war prospects against Germany. Gabriel Gorodetsky, *Grand Delusion: Stalin and the German Invasion of Russia* (Yale University Press, 1999), esp pp13, 58–9.

43 General Sir Archibald Wavell as Commander-in-Chief Middle East fully recognised the importance of oil in the successful prosecution of the war. He highlighted Britain's enormous comparative advantage here over Germany and the importance of maintaining it, in a paper for Field Marshal Sir John Dill as Chief of the Imperial General Staff at the end of May. Harold E Raugh, *Wavell in the Middle East 1939–1941* (London: Brassey's, 1993), pp61–3, contains relevant papers. Michael Howard also quotes Wavell's biographer John Connell recording Wavell's view that 'the prime task of Middle East Command should be to prevent Rumanian oil reaching Germany'. Michael Howard, *The Mediterranean Strategy in the Second World War* (London: Greenhill Books, 1993), p10. Setting such a goal meant not only denying transport of Romanian oil by sea but acquiring airbases in the Balkans to interdict Romanian oil infrastructure and land transport routes.

44 Gerhard Schreiber and others, *Germany and the Second World War*, vol III: *The Mediterranean, South-East Europe and North Africa 1939–1941*. Section III, 'The Strategic Dilemma of the Summer and Autumn of 1940: An Alternative or Interim Strategy?', contains an authoritative account, drawing on primary German sources, of the various discussions relating to a Mediterranean initiative.

45 *Germany and the Second World War*, vol III, p133, states Hitler announced his decision on 31 July 1940.

46 *Germany and the Second World War*, vol III. Raeder's proposals and various meetings with Hitler on 6 and 26 September and 14 November are described at pp212–35. See also German Naval History Series, 'Axis Naval Policy and Operations in the Mediterranean 1939–1943', by Vice Admiral Eberhard Weichold, German Admiral in Rome 1940–1943, para 62, ADM 199/2518, TNA.

47 *Germany and the Second World War*, vol III.

48 Extract from Chiefs of Staff Study – A O (46) 1 (8 March 1946): 'Oil as a factor in the German war effort', CAB 146/382, TNA.

49 *Germany and the Second World War*, vol III, pp853–4.

50 Enemy Documents Section letter dated 25 July 1968, CAB 146/382, TNA.

51 *Germany and the Second World War*, vol III, p764. In reality, an effective air attack against Ploesti, mounted from east Mediterranean bases, was well beyond Royal Air Force bombing capability at this time. The first major attack would not be mounted until August 1943 by the United States Air Force from Benghazi. This was a disaster with 40 per cent losses and little impact on oil output. Only in mid-1944 were the Allies able to mount a serious and ultimately effective campaign out of Italy. Richard Overy, *The Bombing War: Europe 1939–1945* (London: Allen Lane, 2013), part 2, chapter 9.

52 The texts of these Führer Directives can be found on the website www.ww2db.com.

53 John Winton, *Cunningham: The Greatest Admiral since Nelson* (London: John Murray, 1998).

54 COS (40) 592 of 31 July, 'The Situation in the Far East in the Event of Japanese Intervention against Us', p 23, CAB 66/10/33, TNA.

55 There is a good summary of the main critics and their case by Douglas Porch in the preface and introduction of *The Path to Victory; The Mediterranean Theatre in World War II* (New York: Farrar, Straus and Giroux, 2004).

56 This was the Future Strategy 'last resort' line.

57   J M A Gwyer, *Grand Strategy*, vol III: *June 1941–August 1942*, part 2 (London: HMSO, 1964), pp5–7.

58   The best account of these wider issues is given by Klaus Schmider in his article, 'The Mediterranean in 1940–1941: Crossroads of Lost Opportunities', *War and Society*, 15:2 (October 1997).

59   Even Michael Howard makes only brief mention. *The Mediterranean Strategy in the Second World War*, pp7–10.

60   Major General I S O Playfair, *The Mediterranean and Middle East*, vol I: *The Early Successes against Italy* (HMSO, 1954), Review of the Desert Campaign, p362.

61   Horst Boog and others, *Germany and the Second World War*, vol VI, pp1038–48.

62   Bernhard R Kroener, Rolf Dieter Muller and Hans Umbreit provide the basic figures for German oil consumption and output during the first half of the war at pp472–5 of *Germany and the Second World War*, vol V: *Organisation and Mobilisation in the German Sphere of Power*, part 2: Wartime Administration, Economy and Manpower Resources 1942–1944/45 (UK English edition: Clarendon Press, 2006).

63   For another good summary of the dire consequences that shortage of oil had for the German and Italian war effort, Adam Tooze, *The Wages of Destruction: The Making and Breaking of the Nazi Economy*, esp pp411–13.

64   *Germany and the Second World War*, vol V.

65   OCB (41) 27 of 20 March 1941, 'Oil and Tanker Position 1941', CAB 77/4, TNA.

66   Michael Howard draws the parallel between the importance of Romanian oil to Germany and Iranian oil to Britain. Denial of either would be a critical blow. *The Mediterranean Strategy in the Second World War*, p10. However, both sides exaggerated the potential of air power to achieve serious effect against oil infrastructure with the capabilities available in the first half of the war.

67   D J Payton-Smith, *Oil: A Study of Wartime Policy and Administration* (London: HMSO, 1971), table 14, p233, table 46, p454, and table 48.

68   OCB (40) 95 of 22 November 1940, CAB 77/3; and OCB (41) 27 of 20 March 1941, CAB 77/4, both TNA.

69   Payton-Smith, p 49.

70   Payton-Smith, table 45, p453, and table 46, p454.

71   This argument is explored further in Chapter 8. Charles More provides a good account of the role of Middle East oil in the Second World War, and especially its contribution to Britain's war effort, in chapter 4 of *Black Gold: Britain and Oil in the Twentieth Century* (London: Continuum, 2009).

72   The survey had the title 'Brief strategic survey of the continuation of the war after the campaign in Russia'. EDS Appreciation 8, 'The War in the Mediterranean February to November 1941', pp61–4, CAB 146/9, TNA.

73   The diary of Colonel General Franz Halder, Chief of the German General Staff, for 13 September 1941 contains a summary of this survey. This is one of very few genuinely 'strategic' papers included in Halder's diary. The entry appears in vol VII, The Campaign in Russia, part 2, and is available from the US Army Historical Division at Fort Leavenworth.

74   *Germany and the Second World War*, vol III, p 639, states that the 28 August survey which they give the title 'The strategic situation in the late summer 1941 as a basis for further political and military plans' was the last representation of the operational sequence that Hitler had envisaged from late autumn 1940: deal with Russia first, drive from the Caucasus into the Middle East, and then complete the conquest of North Africa. In a conference of the Assistant Chief of Staff Operations on 24 October 1941, it was noted: 'Because of the course of the campaign in the east, the development of the supply situation in Africa, and the still unclear attitude of Turkey, of the three possible operational directions for attack on the Middle East (Egypt, Anatolia, Caucasus), at the present time the Caucasus is the obvious choice'. Thereafter, the authors judge that 'the dogma that a decisive success against the USSR would solve all Germany's problems came to dominate the thinking of the German military'.

75   The authors of *Germany and the Second World War*, vol III, recognise that the OKW survey is an important insight into German thinking, but do not underline, or indeed mention, the Mediterranean/Atlantic connection.

76   Andrew Roberts, *Masters and Commanders: The Military Geniuses who led the West to Victory in World War II* (London: Allen Lane, 2008), p69. There is a copy of WW1 in three parts included with the First Sea Lord's Personal Papers 1939–1941, ADM 178/322, TNA.

77   COS (40) 592 of 31 July 1940, 'The Situation in the Far East in the event of Japanese Intervention against us', CAB 66/10/33, TNA. The covering note for the War Cabinet described this as a 'Far East Appreciation'.

78   COS (40) 488 (JP) of 24 June 1940, 'Immediate Measures Required in the Far East', CAB 80/13, TNA.

79   JM 146, 'Political Strategy Prior to the Outbreak of War, Part II', pp13–18 provides a good summary of Japanese leadership discussions on southern expansion from June to September. There was no concerted strategy at this time and there were major differences between army and navy.

80   COS 579 (JP) of 7 May 1937, 'Far East Appreciation 1937', CAB 53/31, TNA.

81   The parallel paper, COS (40) 308 of 7 August, 'Assistance to the Dutch in Event of Japanese Aggression in the Netherlands East Indies', CAB 66/10/39, TNA, did explore the scope for American naval intervention and highlighted the value of a US Navy fleet basing in Singapore.

82   There is a detailed and fascinating account of the Automedon incident in Eiji Seki's book, *Mrs Ferguson's Tea Set: Japan and the Second World War: The Global Consequences Following Germany's Sinking of the SS Automedon in 1940* (Global Oriental, 2006). *Atlantis* was subsequently sunk in the South Atlantic en route home by the cruiser *Devonshire* in early 1941.

83   Ken Kotani, *Japanese Intelligence in World War II* (UK: Osprey Publishing, 2009), pp141–2, records that the Japanese naval attaché in Berlin, Captain Tadao Yokoi, sent a summary of the documents to the Navy Ministry in Tokyo. Meanwhile the German naval attaché in Tokyo, Rear Admiral Paul Wenneker, handed selected documents to Admiral Nobutake Kondo, then Vice Chief of Naval Staff, on 12 December. This was four months after the Far East appreciation had been drafted. Kotani states that the *Automedon* affair subsequently influenced IJN strategy in favour of a southward move. He offers no authoritative Japanese source for this statement, referring only to rather questionable secondary British sources. He does add that the appreciation stated that Britain would not go to war against Japan even if they invaded Indochina and that Admiral Koshiro Oikawa referred specifically to this insight in December. However, the Japanese had been in effective control of northern Indochina since September, so the judgement was only relevant to southern Indochina, where the Japanese could surely already calculate likely British acquiescence. United States attitudes were another matter.

84   Haggie, pp179–81.

85   The Admiralty's view of what now constituted an 'adequate' fleet was defined in WP (40) 308, 'Assistance to the Dutch in Event of Japanese Aggression in the Netherlands East Indies'.

86   WP (40) 308.

87   The conclusions of this meeting contain Churchill's draft telegram subsequently despatched to Dominion premiers on 11 August. Churchill used language here almost identical to that of November 1939. WM (40) 222nd War Cabinet Conclusions, Minute 4, CAB 65/14/20, TNA. The telegram is also given at pp385–7 of Churchill's *Second World War*, vol II. Major General Hastings Ismay, Military Secretary to the Prime Minister and War Cabinet, provided earlier reassurance in a letter to the Australian High Commissioner S M Bruce on 3 July 1940 in response to Australian anxiety that despatch of a fleet to the Far East was now impossible. This letter is attached to the record of COS (40) 209th meeting on 5 July 1940. Item 3 covered 'Defence of Singapore'. CAB 79/5, TNA.

88   Haggie, pp179–80.

89   See Chapters 7 and 8.

90   James Neidpath, *The Singapore Naval Base*, p179.

91   Roskill, *Churchill and the Admirals*, p209, quotes Vice Admiral Sir Geoffrey Layton, Commander-in-Chief China, briefing his staff in Singapore in September 1941 on Admiralty intent to deploy a powerful fleet to the Far East. While he accepts Layton was faithfully repeating an Admiralty signal, Roskill treats this possibility with incredulity while noting how long-lived the concept of a 'main fleet to Singapore' was. The dismissive tone is surprising. As Chapter 4 demonstrates, contingency planning for an eastern fleet never entirely lapsed. It resumed in earnest following decisions taken at the ABC-1 staff talks with the Americans in

February and March 1941. The September signal was just one of a regular stream of preparatory signals and papers on planning for an eastern fleet which followed these talks.

92 Two powerful recent reiterations of the view that the Far East appreciation marked a fundamental shift in the prospects for Far East defence are Malcom Murfett, 'Reflections on an Enduring Theme', in *Sixty Years On: The Fall of Singapore Revisited*, pp21–2; and Brian Farrell, *The Defence and Fall of Singapore 1940–1942*, pp63–4.

93 The likelihood that Japan would choose to execute an attack on Singapore via an invasion mounted through Northern Malaya had received increasing recognition in British military circles since late 1937. Ong Chit Chung, *Operation Matador: World War II: Britain's attempt to foil the Japanese invasion of Malaya and Singapore* (London: Times Academic Press, 1997), chapter 3 'The Defence of Malaya', for a detailed account.

94 JP (41) 338 of 29 April 1941, 'Air Threat to the Mediterranean Fleet', CAB 79/11, TNA.

95 WP (39) 135 of 21 November 1939.

96 COS (41) 152 (O) of 28 July 1941, 'Far East Defence Arrangements', CAB 80/59, TNA.

97 WP (40) 308, 'Assistance to the Dutch in Event of Japanese Aggression in the Netherlands East Indies'.

98 Edward Miller argues that the same problem applied to the much more ambitious American plans in late 1941 to use airpower to defend the Philippines, *War Plan Orange* (Annapolis, USA: Naval Institute Press, 1991), p63.

99 JP (41) 103 of 7 February, 'Implications of a Japanese Southward Move', attached to COS 46th meeting minutes of 8 February, CAB 79/9, TNA.

100 Almost every document from 1940 to 1942 measured Royal Navy effectiveness against Japan in terms of comparative battleship strength. For example: WP (40) 95: War Cabinet Memorandum from First Lord, 'Comparison of British and Japanese Fleets', 12 March, 1940, CAB 66/6/25, TNA; WP (40) 308 of 7 August 1940, 'Assistance to the Dutch in Event of Japanese Aggression in the Netherlands East Indies', Annex 1, p 5-6; COS (40) 893 of 2 November 1940, 'Allied Strategy in the Far East', CAB 80/21, TNA; and minutes between prime minister and naval staff on comparative strength of Allied and Axis capital ships in early 1942 in PREM 3/324/14, TNA.

101 Vice Admiral Sir Algernon Willis, Mediterranean Fleet Chief of Staff in 1940, identified Calabria (also known as Punto Stilo) as a defining moment. 'It was apparent from our experiences with the Italian Air Force that, without a carrier with modern fighters, sorties into the central Mediterranean would sooner or later lead to damage or loss of important fleet units.' Memoirs, pp28–9, IWM. Cunningham's reaction was similar and reflected in a note to Pound on return to Alexandria. John Winton, *Cunningham, The Greatest Admiral since Nelson*, pp96–8.

102 Comments made at COS (40) 374th meeting of 5 November, Item 4, CAB 79/7, TNA.

103 Report by Vice Admiral Sir Geoffrey Layton, Commander-in-Chief China 1940/41 and Acting Commander-in-Chief Eastern Fleet from 10 December 1941, 'Remarks on the Operations in Malaya and the Defence of Singapore', pp2 and 3, ADM 199/1472A, TNA; and 'Despatch on the Far East' by Air Chief Marshall Sir Robert Brooke-Popham, W.P. (42) 403 of 8 September 1942, CAB 66/28/33, TNA.

104 Christopher Shores, *Bloody Shambles*, vol I (London: Grub Street, 1992), pp57–8.

105 This predicted scale of attack proved accurate, though in the event it would be entirely land-based, as opposed to including an expected 40 per cent carrier borne element. Shores, pp52–3.

106 In the run-up to war in autumn 1941, Royal Air Force Far East Command formally saw its role as follows: find the enemy at sea as far away from Malaya as possible; strike hard and often at invasion convoys; disrupt any subsequent landings; and, finally, support the army by delaying any onward enemy advance from the landing grounds. Despatch of Air Vice Marshal Sir Paul Maltby on Air Operations in Malaya and NEI 1941–1942, para 135, Supplement to the London Gazette 26 February 1948, CAB 106/86, TNA.

107 When the Far East appreciation issued, it was reasonable to assume the quality of many Japanese aircraft, especially fighters, lagged behind their Royal Air Force counterparts. The standard Japanese naval fighter in mid-1940 was the Type 96 or Claude, a fixed undercarriage aircraft far inferior to the Hurricane, let alone the Spitfire. The famous A6M Zero did not become operational until autumn 1940 and the first intelligence on its performance did not appear until early 1941. The standard carrier dive-bomber until late 1940 was the Type 96

'Susie' equivalent to the Swordfish. The G3M 'Betty' was an excellent state-of-the-art long-range naval bomber, but it was highly vulnerable to modern fighters. Peattie, *Sunburst*, chapter 4 and appendix 6.

108 The Royal Air Force believed, from observation of Japanese air performance in China, that the efficiency and effectiveness of both the Imperial Japanese Army Air Force (IJAAF) and Imperial Japanese Naval Air Force (IJNAF) was low by western standards, although it judged the IJNAF the better of the two. John Ferris, 'Student and Master: The United Kingdom, Japan, Airpower, and the Fall of Singapore, 1920–1941', pp109–13, in *Sixty Years On: The Fall of Singapore Revisited*. Also, Henry Probert, *The Forgotten Air Force: The Royal Air Force in the War against Japan 1941–45* (London: Brassey's, 1995), pp25–7. This includes reference to various Air Ministry Weekly Intelligence Summaries from 1940.

109 Shores, *Bloody Shambles*, vol I, pp57–8, has sixty-four Buffalo fighters, fifty-five Blenheim I and IV, and twenty-six Vildebeest torpedo bombers, deployed in operational squadrons in December. A further Buffalo squadron was forming but this still left about 100 per cent reserves from a total delivery during 1941 of 170. There were, however, few Blenheim or Vildebeest reserves. The Buffaloes and Blenheims could be viewed as 'modern', if inferior to their Japanese equivalents. The Vildebeests were certainly completely obsolete. There were in addition twenty-four Hudson aircraft, also modern, formally tasked on reconnaissance but capable of a bombing role.

110 Future Strategy paper, para 271.

111 JM 146.

112 Miller, *War Plan Orange*, p265, and Ian Cowman, *Dominion or Decline*, p190. Also paper prepared for the chiefs of staff by Rear Admiral Roger Bellairs, COS (40) 893 of 2 November, 'Allied Strategy in the Far East', CAB 80/21, TNA. Bellairs noted that at the end of October the deficit between current aircraft strength in Malaya and the target strength in the August appreciation was 166 aircraft with no fighters yet available.

113 Miller, *War Plan Orange*, p265.

114 Minute by Director of Dockyards, ADM 1/11855, TNA. H P Willmott, *Empires in the Balance* (Annapolis, Naval Institute Press, 1982), p218, claims the value of Singapore as a naval base was undermined by its inability to repair Royal Navy warships damaged off Crete in May 1941, though he does not quote sources for this claim.

115 Haggie, p188.

116 Quoted by Cowman, *Dominion or Decline*, pp194–5.

117 Various figures have been quoted for the overall cost of the Singapore base. Many are poorly sourced, and some are clearly exaggerated and designed to highlight the resources wasted on a flawed strategy. Raymond Callahan quoted £60m at p80 of his 1974 article, 'The Illusion of Security: Singapore 1919–1942', *Journal of Contemporary History*, 9:2 (April 1974), pp69–92. This was repeated by James Morris in *Farewell the Trumpets* (Penguin Books, 1979) and widely replayed. Malcom Murfett offers £25m in the introductory chapter of *Sixty Years On* (ed Brian Farrell). An official figure of £15m (of which £4m was provided by the Dominions, the Malay States, and the Sultan of Johore) was given by Ismay in a minute to the prime minister dated 9 January 1942, PREM 3/156/6, TNA. The Ismay figure seems consistent with a statement by the First Lord recorded in Hansard for 15 February 1933 that expenditure to date at that time (covering initial excavations and preparation etc and some armament) was £3.5m. If the 1942 figure of £15m was correct, and it looks the most authoritative, then the cost equated to two *King George V* battleships.

118 Pound as Director of Plans 1923–25 had supervised much of the early planning to create the Singapore strategy, while Phillips as Director of Plans from 1935–38 had, as described in Chapter 2, sought to keep the strategy viable in the new circumstances posed by the rising 'triple threat'.

119 Ismay's letter to Bruce, noted previously, is revealing here. He summarised the chiefs of staff view as follows: Japan cannot undertake a serious invasion of Australia so long as: a) The British fleet (wherever it may be) is in being; and b) Singapore is secure.

120 As Chapter 4 demonstrates, the concept of Singapore as essential foothold from which eventual recovery could be mounted, even if there were heavy initial losses in the Far East, was a major theme running through the British position at the ABC-1 staff talks.

121 H P Willmott, *Empires in the Balance*, chapter 8. Ong Chit Chung, *Operation Matador*, gives an exhaustive account of the Matador strategy and its problems. It failed because Britain would not authorise invasion of a neutral country until it was too late.

122 'Some Personal Reflections on the Malaya Campaign July 1941–January 1942', CAB 106/193, TNA.

123 Prime Minister to Ismay, 10 September 1940, Churchill, *The Second World War*, vol II, pp591–2.

124 COS (40) 317th meeting of 19 September 1940, CAB 79/6, TNA.

125 JM 146.

126 Kirby argues that Churchill's view of Singapore as a 'fortress', capable of surviving an all-round siege for a significant period, was genuine. He also emphasises the prime minister's consistent belief that American naval power would shield Singapore and contain the consequences of a Japanese attack. Had the chiefs of staff disabused the prime minister of this picture, he would have given the Far East theatre more priority in the second half of 1941. *Singapore: The Chain of Disaster*, Epilogue, pp254–5.

127 COS (40) 1053 of 19 December, 'Far East Tactical Appreciation', and COS (40) 1054 of 19 December, 'Far East Singapore Defence Conference', both in CAB 80/24, TNA.

128 John Ferris, pp114–15, quotes figures for proposed Royal Air Force fighter strength in these assessments which are not correct. He states that Singapore commanders were arguing seventy-two fighters could defeat 175/195 Japanese at odds of 2.4 to 2.7. In fact commanders were asking for twice that strength and not far from fighter parity.

129 The 100 per cent increase is valid if comparison is made with the Far East appreciation strike allocation based in Malaya. However, the appreciation also allocated thirty-two bombers to Borneo which the Far East commanders now argued would be better covered from Malaya. The increase within the overall Far East theatre was therefore closer to 50 per cent for strike aircraft.

130 Letter from Commander-in-Chief Far East designate, Air Chief Marshal Sir Robert Brooke-Popham to the chiefs of staff dated 27 October contained in COS (40) 873 of 27 October, 'Defence of Singapore', CAB 80/21, TNA.

131 The Japanese attacked Borneo in late December, the Celebes in early January, and commenced operations against Sumatra on 14 February. H P Willmott, *Empires in the Balance*, map p288.

132 This of course was a similar argument to the 'pre-positioning' debate relating to Egypt in 1937–38. See Chapter 2.

133 Item 6, COS (41) 13th meeting of 8 January 1941 and attached papers, CAB 79/8, TNA.

134 *Cunningham*, pp95–6.

135 JIC (41) 11 of 6 January, 'Scale of Attack on Malaya', CAB 81/99, TNA.

136 DDMI (I) minute of 2 January 1942 covering MI2 paper 'Note on JIC Papers on Japan', WO 208/871, TNA.

137 Prime Minister to Ismay dated 13 January. JP (41) 56 of 22 January, papers associated with: 'Allocation of PBY Output and Reinforcements for the Far Eastern Air Forces', CAB 79/8, TNA.

138 Brian Farrell, *The Defence and Fall of Singapore*, chapter 3, provides a good account of this.

139 COS (40) 899 (JP) of 4 November, 'Period of Warning of an Attack on Singapore', CAB 80/21, TNA. Phillips as VCNS rejected this view as unconvincing. Item 2. COS (40) 377th meeting of 6 November, CAB 79/7, TNA.

140 G2 Minute dated 20 February 1941, Brooke-Popham Papers 6/1/8, and tel to Air Ministry of 1 March 1941, Brooke-Popham Papers 6/1/11, both in LHC.

141 Daniel Ford, *The Sorry Saga of the Brewster Buffalo* (USA: Warbird Books, 2011).

142 Playfair, *The Mediterranean and Middle East*, vol I: *The Early Successes against Italy*, p254.

143 'Draft Interim Reply to Mr Menzies', dated 28 April 1941, attached to minutes of Chiefs of Staff 152nd meeting, CAB 79/11, TNA.

144 JP (41) 565 of 20 July, CAB 79/13, TNA.

145 Ferris, 'Student and Master', p115. Ferris acknowledges that, even with the 336 strength, the disparity would have been more than 2:1 and that, while air power was important, it was only one of several factors causing defeat. A D Harvey argues convincingly that Japanese aircraft did not enjoy any significant advantage over the modern Allied aircraft deployed in theatre in late 1941. Their latest fighters, the Zero and KI43, lagged well behind the latest aircraft in the

European theatre such as the Spitfire VB. He emphasises that they did have an enormous advantage in the quality and experience of their pilots and their ability to achieve concentration of force at decisive points. These factors, which broadly agree with Ferris, were decisive. See 'Army Air Force and Navy Air Force: Japanese Aviation and the opening phase of the war in the Far East', *War in History*, 6:2 (1999), pp174–204.

146 Discussion between Cabinet Office historians and the War History Institute Tokyo September 1966, 'Why no attack on Britain in 1940?', CAB 106/180, TNA.

147 JM 150, 'Political Strategy Prior to the Outbreak of War, Part IV', pp6–7.

148 1966 discussion between historians, 'Why no attack on Britain in 1940?'.

149 JM 146, p 17–18.

150 Kirby, as official Far East historian, was one of the first to emphasise this. *Singapore: The Chain of Disaster*, Epilogue pp254–5.

151 Richard Overy, The *Bombing War: Europe 1939–1945*, chapter 2. In chapter 5 he also describes the problems with bomber production during 1940–42 and the problems this posed in balancing overseas needs with the build-up of Bomber Command as a credible strike force at home.

152 Roskill argued that the substantial reinforcements rushed out after the Japanese attack in December 1941 'gave the lie' to Churchill's claim that it was impossible to spare more resources for the Far East given the overall demands facing Britain in 1941. He also accused Churchill of consistently underrating Japanese prowess and efficiency. *Churchill and the Admirals*, pp196–7.

153 Two good studies here are: James Neidpath, *The Singapore Naval Base and the Defence of Britain's Eastern Empire*, and Raymond Callahan, *The Worst Disaster: The Fall of Singapore* (2nd edn, Singapore: Cultured Lotus, 2001).

154 JP (41) 335, 'Draft Interim Reply to Mr Menzies', dated 28 April 1941. The note was approved by the chiefs of staff at their 152nd meeting on 29 April, and is attached to the minutes. CAB 79/11, TNA.

155 At their 152nd meeting, the chiefs of staff approved a telegraphic report on the Middle East primarily for HM Ambassador Washington to draw on with the American president. Halifax had informed the chiefs in Washington 1764 of 23 April that the president wanted to discuss the Middle East, following reports from his own advisers that Britain would have difficulty holding Egypt. CAB 79/11, TNA. The final text is in COS (41) 271 of 29 April, 'Situation in the Middle East: Memorandum by the COS', CAB 80/27, TNA. It covered the same ground as the Menzies assessment, but without the Japan angle and was shared with the Dominions. The first draft, considered by the chiefs at their 150th meeting the previous day concluded with the passage: 'Malaya has always been regarded as second only in importance to the UK as a base for the security of the Empire. Important though the Middle East is politically and from the point of view of exercising economic pressure, it must be realised that neither in the UK nor in Malaya have full defence requirements been met'. This passage was removed probably because the chiefs had now received the prime minister's 28 April directive.

156 'Directive by the Prime Minister and Minister of Defence', dated 28 April 1941, AIR 8/919, TNA. The catalyst for this was not the Joint Planning Committee assessment, but comments by the Director of Military Operations, Major General John Kennedy, at dinner at Chequers on 27 April, when he revealed contingency plans had been prepared to evacuate Egypt. Kennedy's own account is in his memoir, *The Business of War: The War Narrative of Major General Sir John Kennedy* (London: Hutchinson, 1957), pp104–8. There is a full account in Martin Gilbert, *Winston S Churchill*, vol VI: *Finest Hour 1939–1941*, vol VII: *Road to Victory 1941–1945* (London: William Heinemann, 1983 and 1986), p1071. It also features in the Brooke diaries, Field Marshal Lord Alanbrooke (ed Alex Danchev and Daniel Todman) *War Diaries 1939–1945* (London: Weidenfeld and Nicolson, 2001), p154.

157 These views are illustrated in the initial chiefs of staff draft response to the prime minister dated 5 May, AIR 8/919, TNA. This was proposed by Dill, but Kennedy claimed to be the originator. *Business of War*, p110–12.

158 Ismay produced his redraft on 5 May which the chiefs of staff adopted for their final response on 7 May, AIR 8/919.

159 Chief of Imperial General Staff to Prime Minister dated 6 May, WO 216/5, TNA.

160 Prime Minister response to Chief of Imperial General Staff dated 13 May, WO 216/5.

161 This letter dated 4 May is quoted in *The Second World War*, vol III: *The Grand Alliance*,

pp208–9. The full correspondence is in PREM 3/469, TNA. The incoming Roosevelt message reflected the advice he had received, relayed to the chiefs of staff by Halifax on 23 April that Egypt might fall.

162 Churchill conversation with Ismay, Jock Colville, his private secretary, and US Presidential Envoy Averell Harriman, recounted by Martin Gilbert in *Finest Hour*, p1079.

163 CAB 69/2, TNA.

164 COS (41) 79 (O) of 15 May, 'Air Reinforcements for the Middle East', CAB 80/57, TNA. The Chief of Air Staff plan was approved by the Defence Committee the same evening. Minutes of 30th Meeting, CAB 69/2, TNA.

165 COS (41) 125 (O) of 3 July, 'Air Reinforcements for the Middle East', CAB 80/58, TNA.

166 COS (41) 154 (O) of 31July 1941, 'Strategic Situation in the Middle East', TNA.

167 This was not only evident in the chiefs of staff initial draft response to the prime minister's directive, prepared by Dill, but in a record of the discussion held at the 161st meeting on 5 May available in AIR 8/919, TNA. This states that the relative importance of Egypt has to be weighed against other theatres when considering reinforcements; the Joint Planning Committee will demonstrate this in their forthcoming Strategic Appreciation and show that the loss of Malaya would be a bigger disaster than the loss of Egypt; and that there must be no risk of denuding the United Kingdom of essential forces.

168 Raymond Callahan, *The Worst Disaster*, pp92–3. Lieutenant General Sir Henry Pownall, at this time VCIGS, stated in his diary for 20 December 1941 that Dill, who remained CIGS throughout 1941, had always placed the Far East second in importance to home defence and therefore above the Middle East. Pownall, however, felt the prime minister placed the Middle East above the Far East. *Chief of Staff: The Diaries of Lieutenant General Sir Henry Pownall*, vol II: *1940–44*, ed Brian Bond (London: Leo Cooper, 1974), p66.

169 The chiefs of staff commissioned this appreciation at their 150th meeting on 28 April. It was designed to take a more comprehensive look at the Middle East situation, expanding on the report prepared for HM Ambassador Washington. The first draft was JP (41) 364 of 10 May, 'Situation in the Mediterranean and Middle East', CAB 79/11, TNA. The final version was a telegram to Dominion prime ministers and is in COS (41) 92 (O) of 31 May, CAB 80/57, TNA.

170 JP (41) 444 of 13 June, 'Future Strategy', attached to COS (41) 213th of 16 June, CAB 79/12, TNA.

171 With this paper, the Joint Planning Committee began to refer to 'Singapore' as the key interest in the Far East in place of 'Malaya' which they had been using for the past month or so.

172 JIC (41) 175 of 1 May, 'Japan's Future Strategy'.

173 COS (41) 82 (O) of 21 May 1941, 'The General Situation with particular reference to the Mediterranean and Middle East', CAB 80/57, TNA.

174 COS (41) 92 (O) of 31 May.

175 He used almost identical language with Australian Prime Minister John Curtin in January 1942: 'To try to be safe everywhere is to be strong nowhere'. *The Second World War*, vol IV, p14.

176 Prime Minister minute to First Sea Lord and First Lord of 17 February 1941, ADM 116/4877, TNA.

177 The secretary to the chiefs of staff provided a 'commentary' collating individual comments by the chiefs on the original Joint Planning Committee 'Future Strategy' draft on 22 June. COS (41) 115 (O) of 22 June, CAB 80/58, TNA. There is no evidence the chiefs disagreed with the original Far East sections drafted by the Planning Committee. The original paper, JP 444, was forwarded with the Planning Committee commentary to the prime minister on 24 June and Pound, as chairman of the chiefs of staff, subsequently congratulated the Planning Committee on the quality of their work. COS 225th meeting of 26 June, item 4, CAB 79/12.

178 The paper was considered at the 44th meeting of the Defence Committee on 25 June. Pound commended it as a valuable overview but, without being specific, suggested there were issues that merited more discussion. The prime minister evidently regarded the paper as too hypothetical for his taste and effectively side-lined it. CAB 69/2, TNA.

179 COS (40) 285th meeting, 29 August 1940, CAB 79/6, TNA.

180 Kennedy, *The Business of War*, p190.

181 Prime Minister minute to Chief of Imperial General Staff dated 13 May 1941 and response, WO 216/5, TNA.

182 Richard Aldrich, *Intelligence and the War against Japan* (Cambridge UK: Cambridge University Press, 2000), pp52–67.
183 Michael Goodman, *The Official History of the Joint Intelligence Committee*, vol I: *From the Approach of the Second World War to the Suez Crisis* (London: Routledge, 2014), pp102–7. He agrees with Aldrich that Joint Intelligence Committee performance was 'rarely wide of the mark' and that 'strategically its assessments were accurate'. However, he also argues that awareness of Japanese capability at the tactical level was poor, although he fails to support this judgement with hard evidence.
184 The intelligence assessments which informed this risk, and the likelihood of it being realised, are described by F H Hinsley, with others, in *British Intelligence in the Second World War: Its Influence on Strategy and Operations*, vol II (London: HMSO, 1977–84), pp277–9. Hinsley also describes how the northern risk influenced the timing of an offensive into Libya and the differences of view between London and Commander-in-Chief Middle East, now General Sir Claude Auchinleck.
185 Kennedy, *The Business of War*, pp152–3, records a note he wrote on 21 July stating that there was still time for the Germans to finish the Russian campaign and turn on either the United Kingdom or the Middle East before the winter. If they chose the latter, they would have the whole winter suitable for operations.
186 Hinsley, *British Intelligence*, pp290–1.
187 JP (41) 565 of 20 July 1941, 'Far East: Action in view of Japanese Intentions', CAB 79/13, TNA.
188 'Prime Minister's Personal Minute, Serial No M 745/1', Annex I to JPS (41) 565 of 20 July, 'Far East – Action in view of Japanese Intentions', attachment to COS (41) 254th meeting of 21 July, CAB 79/13, TNA.
189 Note to the prime minister from US presidential adviser Harry Hopkins, considered at chiefs of staff 254th meeting on 21 July, CAB 79/13.
190 Quoted by Kennedy. He adds background and colour to US criticisms in chapters 16 and 17 of *The Business of War*. Kennedy thought American criticism was helpful in promoting a sense of balance in the allocation of resources. He also noted at this time that Japanese action might prove a determining factor on Middle East policy. If they entered the war, effort might have to be reduced in the Middle East to hold Malaya.
191 JP (41) 580 of 23 July, 'The Strategic Necessity of Holding our Present Middle East Position', CAB 79/13, TNA.
192 The chiefs of staff were still unclear precisely why Persian oil was so important when the matter was raised on 31 July and decided to ask the Oil Board to clarify. COS 270th Meeting, CAB 79/13, TNA.
193 Robert Mallett, *The Italian Navy and Fascist Expansionism 1935–1940* (London: Frank Cass, 1998), chapters 4 and 5.
194 Minutes of 260th Meeting, CAB 79/13, TNA.
195 The 1941 estimate draws on figures in Hinsley, *British Intelligence in the Second World War*, vol II, p291, and John Ellis, *Brute Force*, table 42, drawing on Webster and Frankland. 1942/43 estimate is from Ellis, Preface, xx.
196 Phillips Payson O'Brien, *How the War was Won: Air–Sea Power and Allied Victory in World War II* (Cambridge University Press: 2015), chapter 5. The figures for comparative German air deployment on 27 December 1941, drawn from AIR 40/1207, TNA, are at Table 21.
197 256th meeting on 22 July, CAB 79/13, TNA.
198 COS (41) 154 (O) of 31 July, 'Strategic Situation in the Middle East', CAB 80/59, TNA.
199 COS (41) 155 (O) of 31 July, 'General Strategy', CAB 80/59, TNA.
200 Srinath Raghavan, *India's War: The Making of Modern South Asia 1939–1945* (London: Penguin, 2016), chapter 4.
201 Figures from Brian Farrell, *The Basis and Making of Grand Strategy – Was there a Plan?*, book 2, appendix B, and I C B Dear and M R D Foot, *The Oxford Companion to World War II* (Oxford University Press, paperback edition, 2001).
202 Raghavan, *India's War*, chapter 14.
203 Footnote 69 refers.
204 Raghavan, chapter 14.

205 G C Peden explores the pluses and minuses of the wider empire contribution to Britain's war potential in 'The Burden of Imperial Defence and the Continental Commitment Reconsidered', *Historical Journal*, 27:2 (1984), pp405–23.

206 An equivalent title to JP (41) 580 substituting 'Far East' for 'Middle East'.

207 COS (41) 152 (O) of 28 July, 'Far East Defence Arrangements', CAB 80/59, TNA.

208 Within six weeks, the chiefs of staff formally confirmed there would be no further air reinforcements for the Far East until 1942. COS (41) 324th of 16 September, CAB 79/14, TNA.

209 The impact of aircraft shipments to Russia is evident in COS (41) 301st of 28 August, CAB 79/14, TNA, which discussed the consequences of supplying 200 Hurricanes, and COS (41) 207 (O) of 17 September, 'Allocations of Aircraft to Russia from American Production and the effect on RAF Expansion', CAB 50/89, TNA.

210 Roskill letter to Admiral Sir William Davis, dated 11 April 1975, ROSK 4/79, CCA.

211 JP (41) 664 of 12 August, 'Improvement of our position in the Far East', CAB 79/13, TNA.

212 *Business of War*, p183.

213 Dr Stephen Bullard, *Japanese Army Operations in the South Pacific Area: New Britain and Papua Campaigns 1942–1943*, translation from Japanese Official History of World War II, Senshi Sosho, Introduction p4, quoting Japanese planning documents (Australian War Memorial, 2007).

214 JP (42) 147 of 16 February, 'Far East Policy', attached to COS (42) 54th meeting of 17 February, CAB 79/18, TNA. Kennedy produced a note for Brooke, the new CIGS, on 14 December, just one week into the Far East war, which suggested Malaya might be beyond saving and that effort should focus on holding Burma, Ceylon and the Indian Ocean. *The Business of War*, 'Note on the Situation 14.12.41', pp185–9. Such an 'outer ring' defence was of course analogous with the contingency 'outer ring' for the Middle East based on the line from Kenya to the Persian Gulf.

215 COS (41) 310th meeting of 3 September, CAB 79/14, TNA.

216 JP (41) 1093 of 25 December, 'Far East and Middle East', CAB 79/16, TNA.

217 COS (42) 107 (O) of 19 April, 'Proposed Air Reinforcements for India, Burma and Ceylon', CAB 80/62, TNA.

218 General Sir Archibald Wavell, who took over the 'ABDA' Southeast Asia Command in January 1942, argued that holding out an extra month in Malaya would have been sufficient to inject sufficient forces to stabilise the theatre. Wavell note dated 17 February to chiefs of staff quoted in Kennedy, *Business of War*, pp197–8.

219 JM 152, 'Political Strategy Prior to the Outbreak of War, Part V', p10.

220 Figures from James Neidpath, *The Singapore Naval Base*, p199, one of the few historians to examine the trade-off between reinforcement of Malaya in autumn 1941 and the impact on Crusader.

221 Discussion between Cabinet Office historians and War History Institute Tokyo, September 1966, 'The Malaya campaign and fall of Singapore 1941–42', CAB 106/180, TNA.

222 Defence Committee 53rd Meeting, CAB 69/2, TNA.

223 Hinsley, *British Intelligence*, vol II, pp290–1.

224 AT 666 to Commander-in-Chief China of 4 April 1941, ADM 116/4877, TNA.

225 Minute from First Sea Lord to Prime Minister of 16 February dealing with the implications of a guarantee to the Netherlands East Indies, ADM 205/10, TNA; First Sea Lord views at Defence Committee 12th meeting on 9 April, CAB 69/2, TNA; and VCNS views at Defence Committee 56th meeting on 8 August, CAB 69/2, TNA.

226 VCNS views at Defence Committee 56th meeting on 8 August, CAB 69/2, TNA.

227 Cunningham signal to the Admiralty of 25 April 1941, ADD MS 52567, Cunningham Papers, British Library.

Chapter 4 – The American Relationship, ABC-1 and the Resurrection of an Eastern Fleet

1 Roskill gave the first volume of his *Naval Policy between the Wars* the title *The Period of Anglo-American Antagonism, 1919–1929*.

2 Key works covering the relationship in the 1930s are James R Leutze, *Bargaining for Supremacy: Anglo-American Naval Collaboration, 1937–1941*; Greg Kennedy, *Anglo-American Strategic Relations in the Far East 1933–1939*; Malcom Murfett, *Fool Proof Relations: The*

Search for Anglo-American Naval Co-operation during the Chamberlain Years 1937–1940; Ian Cowman, Dominion or Decline: Anglo-American Naval Relations in the Pacific 1937–41; and Arthur Marder, Old Friends, New Enemies, chapter 2, part 6. There are also useful primary documents in the Navy Records Society, vol 155, Anglo-American Naval Relations, 1919–1939 (ed Michael Simpson), especially part 6, 'Edging towards an Alliance, 1937–1939'.

3   Anglo-American Naval Relations, 1919–1939 and John Maurer and Christopher Bell, At the Crossroads between Peace and War: The London Naval Conference of 1930 (USA, Annapolis: Naval Institute Press, 2014). Maurer's opening essay emphasises London 1930 as a turning point, arguing 'the foundation for the grand alliance of the Second World War can be found in the fine print of the correspondence leading up to and the language of the London Naval Treaty'.

4   Haggie, Britannia at Bay, p119; and Cowman, Dominion or Decline, p137. Cowman repeats Haggie's language here, although without acknowledgement.

5   As recorded in chapter 2, Commander T C Hampton briefed the US Navy leadership on the impact of the Cunningham Strategy on Royal Navy Far East reinforcement. Hampton met the Chief of Naval Operations, Admiral William Leahy, and Director of Plans, Rear Admiral Robert Ghormley.

6   Cowman, pp153–4, and chapter 3. Lawrence Pratt is more positive than Cowman on the impact of the Ingersoll talks. He judges that the talks convinced the two navies that they had common interests and established the trust that promoted strategic co-operation in 1940. 'The Anglo-American Naval Conversations on the Far East of January 1938', International Affairs (Royal Institute of International Affairs 1944–), 47:4 (1971), pp745–63.

7   Kennedy, Anglo-American Strategic Relations, p3. He emphasises that the deepening relationship in the late 1930s reflected personal contacts, and willingness to share information and views, across multiple geographic locations (Tokyo and China as well as London and Washington), and institutions (Foreign Office and State Department as much as Admiralty and US Navy Department).

8   Haggie, Leutze, Cowman and Murfett all provide useful accounts with varying levels of detail.

9   Records of the Ingersoll and Hampton meetings are in ADM 116/3922, TNA.

10 Hampton record of 14 June meeting, ADM 116/3922, TNA.

11 Hampton record. Also Leutze, Bargaining for Supremacy, pp38–40.

12 Cowman describes the history of Admiralty interest in the Philippines as a base in 'Defence of the Malay Barrier? The Place of the Philippines in Admiralty Naval War Planning 1925–1941', War in History, 3:4 (November 1996), pp398–417. He demonstrates that interest preceded the Ingersoll meeting and explores how it was resurrected in late 1941.

13 ADM 116/4302, TNA. The evolution of naval technology and intelligence sharing in the first nine months after the outbreak of the European war is described by Leutze at chapter 5 of Bargaining for Supremacy.

14 Cowman, Dominion or Decline, p171.

15 James Leutze, Bargaining for Supremacy. Some 80 per cent of this book covers this period compared with just thirty pages by Cowman in Dominion or Decline, who focuses more on the period after ABC-1. Marder covers this period briefly in Old Friends, New Enemies, vol 1, chapter 5, part 2, but includes material not available elsewhere.

16 Neither Leutze (pp134–5) nor Cowman (pp170–1) distinguishes these three roles. Neither gives the original terms of reference, nor do they explain why only one section (out of twelve) and five pages (out of 115) dealt with 'Operational Assistance' in the final report dated 11 September. Apart from sections on 'Liaison' (ie management of the relationship) and 'Communications' (ie between the two parties), there were nine devoted to the third role, ie the 'knowledge pool'. ADM 199/1159, TNA.

17 ADM 199/691, TNA.

18 Bailey Committee note dated 20 September 1940, ADM 199/1159, TNA.

19 Bailey's initial report on 'Form of Operational Assistance desired from the US' was submitted to the First Sea Lord on 24 June with comments from Director of Plans. A revised version dated 9 July was approved by the First Sea Lord on 18 July as a good baseline for discussion with the US Navy. The 9 July redraft shows greater emphasis on the need for a maximum American contribution in the Atlantic. ADM 199/691, TNA. The final 'Bailey report' addressing all three requirements mentioned in these paragraphs is in ADM 199/1159, TNA.

20 'Redistribution of the fleet in the event of war with Japan', dated 2 August 1940, ADM 205/6, TNA.

21 COS 390 of 25 May 1940, 'British Strategy in a Certain Eventuality', CAB 80/11, TNA.

22 COS 496 of 27 June, 'Staff Conversations with the United States', CAB 80/13, TNA.

23 Report of first meeting dated 24 June, ADM 199/691, TNA.

24 Phillips's minute of 16 April 1940, FO 371/24716, TNA.

25 *The Second World War*, vol II: *Finest Hour*, pp22–4.

26 The chiefs of staff briefing for Ghormley took place over two meetings, the 285th on 29 August and 289th on 31 August. The Far East briefing and discussion took place on the 31st. CAB 79/6, TNA.

27 Bailey Committee First Meeting, 17 September, ADM 199/1159, TNA.

28 COS (40) 796 of 2 October 1940, 'The Far East: Policy with regard to the NEI', CAB 80/19, TNA.

29 COS (40) 798 of 3 October, 'British-American-Dutch Technical Conversations', CAB 80/19, TNA. HM Ambassador Washington's account of his conversation with Hull in Washington tel 2146 of 30 September is attached to this memorandum, as is an assessment of Japanese intent from HM Ambassador Tokyo. Hull suggested the talks should embrace Britain, the United States, Australia and the Dutch.

30 COS (40) 831 of 14 October, 'Anglo-Dutch-American Technical Conversations', CAB 80/20, TNA.

31 COS (40) 833 of 15 October 1940, 'Anglo-Dutch-American Technical Military Conversations', CAB 80/20, TNA.

32 AT 562 to Commander-in-Chief China of 15 October 1940, ADM 199/1232, TNA.

33 ADA (J) (40) 2, 'British United States Netherlands Technical Conversations, Précis of Naval Eastern War Memorandum', ADM 199/1232, TNA.

34 Chiefs of Staff 357th meeting on 23 October 1940, Item 6, CAB 79/7, TNA. The suggestion that the Joint Planning Committee might need to prepare a completely new appreciation was made in COS (40) 856 of 22 October, 'British-United States-Dutch Technical Conversations – Strategical Basis for Conversations', CAB 80/21, TNA.

35 COS (40) 856 of 22 October.

36 Ghormley's letter of 25 October and British response are in ADM 199/1232, TNA.

37 The chiefs of staff tasked Bellairs with producing this at their 359th meeting on 23 October, Item 6, CAB 79/7, TNA.

38 Paragraph 17 of 1940 Far East appreciation.

39 Annex III of WP (40) 308 of 7 August.

40 'Allied Naval Dispositions in the event of Japan joining the Axis and the United States entering the war on our side', dated 30 October 1940, ADM 205/6, TNA.

41 Director of Plans minute for VCNS, 'Commitment of our Naval Forces', dated 11 November 1940, ADM 199/1159, and Naval Staff briefing prepared for the First Sea Lord's meeting with Ghormley on 19 November, 'Memorandum A – Our inability to provide forces for the W Atlantic', ADM 199/691, both in TNA.

42 'Memorandum B – Reasons for our present policy', ADM 199/691, TNA.

43 Naval Staff briefing for First Sea Lord for meeting with Ghormley on 19 November, 'Memorandum B – Reasons for our present policy'.

44 'Notes on Conversation with the First Sea Lord', 19 November 1940, drafted by the US naval attaché, Captain Alan Kirk, ADM 199/691, TNA.

45 Bailey's agenda and record of the 22 November meeting are in ADM 199/1159, TNA.

46 Leutze, *Bargaining for Supremacy*, chapter 9, footnote 38, p290. Miller is equally disparaging in *War Plan Orange*, pp264–5.

47 David Reynolds, *The Creation of the Anglo-American Alliance 1937–41: A Study in Competitive Co-operation* (Europe Publications, 1981), p224.

48 Haggie, *Britannia at Bay*, p188. Cowman, *Dominion or Decline*, pp185–92.

49 'Allied' means British Empire, American and Dutch interests.

50 Rainbow 2 is described by Edward Miller in *War Plan Orange*, pp255–9, with a map of the proposed US Navy deployment at p258. Miller stresses that the plan was never formally approved and would never have the support of Commander-in-Chief Pacific Fleet. Leutze provides a briefer description in *Bargaining for Supremacy*, pp40–1, as does Cowman in

Dominion or Decline, pp178–9. None of them notes the remarkable similarity between Bellairs's November 1940 strategy and Rainbow 2 dating from exactly a year earlier.

51 Leutze, A *Different Kind of Victory: A Biography of Admiral Thomas C Hart* (Annapolis, USA: Naval Institute Press, 1981), pp186–7. Miller, *War Plan Orange*, pp262–3.

52 Paragraph 9 of Pound redraft for United States President of 30 October, 'Allied Naval Dispositions in the event of Japan joining the Axis and the United States joining the war on our side', ADM 205/6. Paragraph 5 of COS 921 used similar language: 'It follows therefore that the main military effort must be made in the West and there should only be diverted to the East the minimum force which will be sufficient to neutralise the Japanese armed forces and thereby safeguard our general strategic position in the Pacific'.

53 Ghormley comments in 22 November meeting with Bellairs and Bailey, ADM 199/1159, TNA.

54 'Meeting between Lord Lothian, the First Lord and Naval Staff', 9 November 1940, ADM 199/1159, TNA.

55 Chiefs of Staff 374th meeting of 5 November, CAB 79/7, TNA.

56 Washington tels 2762 of 22 November and 2778 of 23 November, ADM 199/1232, TNA. Marshal of the Royal Air Force, Sir John Slessor, who was in Washington as an air commodore and Director of Air Plans at this time, was one of Hornbeck's interlocutors. He adds additional colour on these conversations in his autobiography *The Central Blue: Recollections and Reflections by Marshal of the Royal Air Force Sir John Slessor* (London: Cassell & Co, 1956), pp346–7.

57 Pound redraft for the US President of 30 October, 'Allied Naval Dispositions in the event of Japan joining the Axis and the United States entering the war on our side'.

58 'Memorandum B: Reasons for our Present Policy', briefing paper prepared for First Sea Lord meeting with Ghormley on 19 November 1940, ADM 199/691, TNA.

59 Cowman, *Dominion or Decline*, p179.

60 Chiefs of Staff 383rd meeting of 8 November 1940, CAB 79/7, TNA.

61 Director of Plans Minute PD 09239/40 for VCNS dated 11 November 1940, ADM 199/1159, TNA.

62 The origins and content of the Plan Dog memorandum are described in Leutze, *Bargaining for Supremacy*, chapter 12.

63 The memorandum is available online from the Franklin D Roosevelt Library.

64 John Lukacs, *The Legacy of the Second World War* (New Haven, USA and London: Yale University Press, 2010), chapter 6, 'Rainbow Five', describes the evolution of US strategic thinking across 1940.

65 Edward Miller's *War Plan Orange* and Cowman, *Dominion or Decline*, pp178–9. *War Plan Orange* is the definitive history of American planning for a Pacific war from 1918–41 though Miller includes some coverage of the periods before and after. The book is important for the range of its coverage and command of detail and sources. It has two failings. The structure lacks logic and coherence. It is neither chronological, nor built around consistent themes. This often makes Miller's core arguments hard to follow and less powerful than they deserve. He also adopts a dismissive, even frivolous, style, which sometimes overcomes proper historical analysis. This applies especially to aspects of the American-British engagement through 1940/41, so is particularly irritating to British readers.

66 Clarke was appointed Special Naval Liaison Officer to Washington in July 1940 at the suggestion of the Bailey Committee. Leutze summarises his background and the genesis of the appointment at pp135–9 of *Bargaining for Supremacy*.

67 Leutze, *Bargaining for Supremacy*, pp186–7.

68 Washington tel 2400 of 31 October 1940, ADM 199/691, TNA.

69 Director of Plans minute on Clarke telegram of 31 October dated 12 November 1940, ADM 199/691, TNA.

70 Ghormley letter to Pound of 13 November 1940, ADM 199/691, TNA.

71 Director of Plans minute of 14 November 1940, commenting on Ghormley letter to First Sea Lord dated the previous day, ADM 199/691, TNA.

72 Washington tel 2750 of 20 November, FO 371/24243, TNA.

73 Washington tel 2750 of 20 November.

74 Washington tel 2750.

75 Washington tel 2952 of 6 December 1940, FO 371/24243, TNA.
76 Washington tel 2952 of 6 December, FO 371/24243, TNA.
77 Washington tel 2869 of 30 November, FO 371/24243, TNA.
78 Leutze, *Bargaining for Supremacy*, chapter 13, footnote 26, p297.
79 Washington tel 2851 of 29 November 1940, copy attached to COS 940) 1014 of 5 December 1940, CAB 80/24, TNA. The story behind the American decision to proceed with staff talks is summarised by Leutze in *Bargaining for Supremacy*, pp202–5.
80 Washington tel 2952 of 6 December 1940, ADM 199/1232, TNA.
81 Ghormley letter to Bailey dated 9 December 1940, ADM 199/1232, TNA.
82 Prime Minister minute to First Sea Lord, dated 22 November 1940, CAB 84/24, TNA.
83 Prime Minister minute on Washington tel 2952, CAB 84/24, TNA.
84 First Sea Lord letter to Ghormley of 10 December and his tel to Washington of 12 December, ADM 199/1232, TNA.
85 *Bargaining for Supremacy*, p200.
86 Marder describes this meeting in *Old Friends, New Enemies*, vol 1, p150, and Cowman refers to it in *Dominion or Decline*, p191. Neither addresses its full significance. Leutze does not mention it at all.
87 'Staff Discussions with the USA', 'Minutes of Meeting held in Director of Plans' Room on 10 December', ADM 199/1232, TNA.
88 Leutze, *Bargaining for Supremacy*, p217.
89 COS (40) 1052 of 19 December 1940, 'British – United States Technical Conversations', CAB 80/24, TNA. The evolution of these instructions can be tracked through successive Joint Planning Committee drafts over the previous week.
90 DO (40) 51st Meeting of 17 December 1940, TNA.
91 There is more detail on the rationale for these changes in the Joint Planning Committee draft response to American questions relating to the forthcoming ABC-1 talks sent by Ghormley on 4 December 1940. The response and original questions are in COS (40) 1038 of 13 December 1940, CAB 80/24, TNA. The response was approved by the Defence Committee on 17 December. It is striking that Ghormley's questions related only to Atlantic reinforcement and assumed that the United States was either not at war with Japan or, if it was, would restrict operations to the central Pacific. This assumption dated 4 December preceded Turner's rejection of Singapore basing on 7 December.
92 Samuel Eliot Morison, *The Two Ocean War* (USA: Little, Brown & Co, 1963), p39.
93 Miller, *War Plan Orange*, table 24.1, Principal US Naval Forces, Disposition, 1940–1941, p278. By December 1941, with the commissioning of *Hornet* as a seventh carrier, the US Navy had four carriers in the Atlantic and three in the Pacific.
94 COS (40) 48 (O) of 13 December 1940, 'British – United States Technical Conversations', CAB 80/106, TNA. This survey met a request from the US military attaché Brigadier General Raymond Lee. The chiefs of staff agreed the response at their 423rd meeting on 11 December. They agreed to be as frank as possible, omitting only details of future operations. CAB 79/8, TNA. The survey included as Annex 1, a current order of battle for the Royal Navy, 'State of His Majesty's Fleet – Mid December 1940', broken down into 'Effective' and 'Repairs/Refit' columns. Two points are worth noting. First, the 'Western Approaches Command' escort force covering the Atlantic convoys now had an effective escort strength of 126 vessels with forty-eight more in repair/refit. This faced a frontline U-boat force at this time of twenty-two boats. *Germany and the Second World War*, vol VI, table III.iii.i. Secondly, total Royal Navy and Dominion forces east of Suez at this time were seven heavy cruisers, seven light cruisers, eight destroyers and twelve escort vessels. Because of the sensitivity of the survey, it was only released to the Americans on board *King George V*, which transported both ABC-1 delegations to the United States, leaving Scapa Flow on 15 January 1941. COS (41) 4th Meeting of 2 January 1941, CAB 79/8, TNA.
95 Mark Skinner Watson, *US Army in World War II, Chief of Staff: Pre-war Plans and Preparations* (Washington: US Government Printing Office, 1950), chapter 12, p368. According to Roskill, total Allied shipping losses for 1940 (all types of vessel from all causes) were 3,991,641 tons. Losses of British controlled shipping were less, but it was clearly the current rate of loss that mattered, and Stark's figure was about right for the end of the year. Roskill figures from *War at Sea*, vol 3, part 2, appendix ZZ.

96 The survey was formally approved by the Defence Committee on 17 December and its content was not questioned. DO (40) 51st Meeting of 17 December 1940, CAB 69/1, TNA. W K Hancock and Margaret M Gowing quote the prime minister writing separately in the same month at p254 of *The British War Economy* (British Official History Civil Series) (London: HMSO, 1949): 'The decision for 1941 lies upon the seas. Unless we establish our ability to feed this Island, to import the munitions of all kinds we need ... we may fall by the way. It is in shipping and in the power to transport across the oceans, particularly the Atlantic Ocean, that in 1941 the crunch of the whole war will be found'.

97 Merchant ship losses from W K Hancock and Margaret M Gowing, *The British War Economy*, part 3 Statistical Summary, item d, 'Shipping Gains and Losses'. U-boat inflicted losses from Clay Blair, *Hitler's U-boat War, The Hunters 1939–1942*, appendix 18.

98 Roskill, *War at Sea*, vol I, chapter 25.

99 British plans and dispositions to deal with large German surface raiders are explored in two papers drafted by Director of Plans. The first, in two parts A and B, was prepared in response to minute PD 09225/40 from the First Sea Lord on 6 November 1940. The second, 'Heavy Ship Enemy Raids on Trade', is dated 2 March 1941. Both are in ADM 116/4324, TNA. They are excellent background for understanding the composition of the forces, including carrier 'hunting groups' sought for the Atlantic from the US Navy during ABC-1.

100 Roskill, *The War at Sea*, part I, chapter 25. Figures from vol III, part 2, appendix ZZ.

101 Roskill, *War at Sea*, vol III, part 2, appendix ZZ.

102 Net loss comprised losses from all causes (war and marine losses and capture) set against gains (new vessels, captures and acquisition of foreign tonnage).

103 The impact of the one-off shipping windfall through requisitions and captures over the first year of the war is shown in Clay Blair's figures which draw on Hancock and Gowing. British controlled shipping comprising vessels over 1600grt was 17,784 thousand tons at the start of the war in September 1939 but reached 21,373 thousand tons by 30 September 1940. The limited net loss over 1941 meant total stock was still 20,693 thousand tons on 31 December 1941. *Hitler's U-Boat War*, vol I, plate 6, p99.

104 Hancock and Gowing, *The British War Economy*, part 3 Statistical Summary. They provide details of the main sources of the tonnage windfall through one-off captures and acquisitions in 1940/41 at pp255–6 of the main text.

105 Leutze, *Bargaining for Supremacy*, chapter 13, p213 and footnote 41, quoting a letter from Ghormley to Stark recording a meeting with Pound on 7 January. There appears to be no British record of this meeting.

106 Leutze, *Bargaining for Supremacy*, chapter 13, p213 and footnote 41.

107 This figure represents column 3 minus column 4.

108 Clay Blair, *Hitler's U-boat War*, vol I, p434.

109 Only half of this total would be modern.

110 Roskill, *The War at Sea*, vol II, appendix L.

111 Samuel Eliot Morison, *The Two Ocean War*, p38.

112 Leutze, Marder and Cowman have provided detailed accounts. Others have summarised what they see as key issues, including David Reynolds, *The Creation of the Anglo-American Alliance*, chapters 7 and 8; and Waldo Heinrichs, *Threshold of War: Franklin D Roosevelt and American Entry into World War II* (Oxford UK: Oxford University Press, 1988), chapter 2. Some, notably Roskill and Barnett, barely mention ABC-1.

113 Leutze heads chapter 14 of *Bargaining for Supremacy* '"Heavy Weather" at ABC'. Cowman heads a section with an almost identical title 'Heavy Weather at ABC-1', *Dominion or Decline*, p192. The term 'heavy weather' derives from the prime minister minute to the First Sea Lord of 12 February. ADM 116/4877, TNA. Marder too quotes this at length.

114 Leutze, *Bargaining for Supremacy*, p249.

115 The conference began with an exchange of 'Opening Statements' that established the respective 'national military positions'. The British statement was a précis of the Instructions to Delegates in COS (40) 1052 and is recorded in the Conference Papers as B.U.S. (J) (41) 2 of 29 January 1941. The US paper is B.U.S. (J) (41) 2. Both are in CAB 99/5, TNA.

116 The final ABC-1 Report is recorded as B.U.S. (J) (41) of 27 March 1941, CAB 99/5, TNA. There is also a copy under COS (41) 255 of 22 April 1941, CAB 80/27, TNA.

117 Watson, *US Army in World War II, Chief of Staff: Pre-war Plans and Preparations*, p380, quoting an undated memo prepared in US Army War Planning Department for a conference on 16 April 1941, WPD 4402-9.

118 Most historians, including Leutze, at least imply that in stressing the importance of Singapore to their war effort, the British continued to promote US basing. Some, eg David Reynolds, go further. At p185 of *The Creation of the Anglo-American Alliance* he states: 'The Admiralty delegates continued to press the USA to send a fleet to Singapore'. The record is clear that they did not.

119 B.U.S. (J) (41) 6 of 31 January, Annex 1, 'Relative Importance of Middle and Far East Theatres', CAB 99/5, TNA. In suggesting that the Far East took ultimate priority over the Middle East, the annex was reflecting the 'last resort' pledges re-affirmed to the Dominions by Churchill in August: ie in the event of a direct and immediate threat to Australasia, the Mediterranean Fleet would be withdrawn and sent to their rescue. The annex did not emphasise this quite specific prime minister qualification.

120 B.U.S. (J) (41) of 3 February, Record of 3rd Meeting, Section V, CAB 99/5, TNA.

121 ADM 178/322, TNA.

122 B.U.S. (J) (41) 6 of 31 January, para 16, answers to questions raised by Lee and Ghormley, CAB 99/5, TNA.

123 Record of 6th meeting, CAB 99/5, TNA.

124 Washington tel Gleam 6 of 11 February 1941, Bellairs for Chiefs of Staff, ADM 116/4877, TNA. This tel reflected discussion at the 6th ABC-1 meeting held the previous day, 10 February.

125 Prime Minister minute to Chiefs of Staff, First Lord and First Sea Lord, dated 12 February, ADM 116/4877, TNA.

126 Minute from First Sea Lord to Prime Minister of 13 February, ADM 205/10, TNA. Leutze does not refer to this minute. Cowman and Marder do mention it but perhaps understate its significance.

127 Director of Plans minute, paper on 'Far East', and draft response to Bellairs, dated 15 February, ADM 116/4877, TNA.

128 Admiralty circular tel dated 4 August 1939, ADM 1/9767, TNA.

129 The Far East appreciation sent to the Americans by Bellairs on 11 February, in response to their request at the 6th ABC-1 meeting the previous day, accepted the Pacific Fleet would remain at Hawaii and advocated only the detachment of a carrier and four heavy cruisers to the Asiatic theatre. He suggested these might be based at Singapore, but the British had made it clear that Manila was a reasonable alternative. B.U.S. (J) (41) 13 of 11 February, 'Far East: Appreciation by the UK Delegation', CAB 99/5, TNA.

130 As claimed by Leutze, Cowman, Marder and Reynolds.

131 Bellairs summarised his appreciation in Gleam No 8 of 15 February not circulated in London until am of 16 February. Both the appreciation and the prime minister's minute dated 17 February are in ADM 116/4877, TNA. Leutze quotes the prime minister's minute in full at pp241–2 of *Bargaining for Supremacy*. The full appreciation, as shared with the Americans, is in B.U.S. (J) (41) 13 of 11 February, CAB 99/5, TNA. There are significant omissions in the version telegraphed to London. Leutze is representative of most historical opinion here. He states: 'Although Churchill's reaction made his intent of embroiling the US in the war more explicit than ever before, it offered no new route round the strategic stumbling block in the Far East. Thus, even though the Chiefs of Staff shared Bellairs' sentiments, Churchill's view would have to prevail or there would be a major confrontation (with the US). The only course seemed to be to act as if there were no strategic stumbling block and move on to other subjects'. *Bargaining for Supremacy*, p242.

132 First Sea Lord minute of 18 February, ADM 116/4877, TNA. David Reynolds agrees both that the basis of a compromise agreement on the Far East was achieved with the chiefs of staff instructions of 19 February, and that Leutze fails to recognise this. Reynolds, however, suggests that the main factor driving agreement was the renewed insistence by the prime minister that Britain concede to the Americans on Hawaii basing. This was never really in dispute across the British leadership. It was the American offer of Atlantic substitution that made an acceptable compromise possible. *The Creation of the Anglo-American Alliance*, p226.

133 Director of Plans minute to VCNS and ACNS (F) of 17 February. This stated that, while basing

the US Navy Pacific Fleet at Singapore remained the best way 'to check the Japanese', it was not practicable for the Americans who would naturally reject any splitting of their fleet between Honolulu and Singapore. Director of Plans therefore agreed that the prime minister had 'the only practicable answer': ie accept the American dispositions and hope better options would emerge when they faced reality. Meanwhile, their offer to relieve Royal Navy forces in the Atlantic for the Far East should be taken up.

134 The prime minister offered a draft reply to Bellairs in his minute of 16 February, which went through successive amendments in the Admiralty, not least to incorporate Royal Navy commitment to a capital ship force. The final outcome was therefore significantly different. See Director of Plans minute to VCNS and ACNS (F) of 17 February, ADM 116/4877, TNA.

135 Tel Boxes No 5 dated 19 February 1941, ADM 116/4877, TNA. This again illustrates the primacy Britain gave to Atlantic security at this time.

136 Paragraph 13 (d), B.U.S. (J) (41) 30 of 27 March 1941, 'United States – British Staff Conversations – Report', CAB 99/5, TNA.

137 *Bargaining for Supremacy*, chapter 15, esp pp249–50.

138 David Reynolds, *The Creation of the Anglo-American Alliance*, pp226–7.

139 Director of Plans minute dated 23 February 1941. The details were also communicated to Far East naval commanders in AT 1135 of 24 February. ADM 116/4877, TNA.

140 AT 417 to Commander-in-Chief China of 25 February 1941, ADM 116/4877, TNA.

141 DO (41) 12th meeting of 9 April, CAB 69/2, TNA.

142 Director of Plans minute dated 6 March 1941, ADM 116/4877, TNA. Details were also shared with Australian Prime Minister Robert Menzies at the end of this month. COS (41) 217 of 2 April, CAB 80/27, TNA.

143 AT 666 to Commander-in-Chief China of 4 April 1941, ADM 116/4877, TNA.

144 AT 1904B of 13 May 1941, ADM 116/4877, TNA. This communicated the division of responsibilities and force dispositions, following American entry into the war, which had been agreed at ABC-1, to all Royal Navy commanders-in-chief. Dispositions for the Far East were unchanged from the April tel to Commander-in-Chief China.

145 Annex II of COS (41) 727 of 7 December, 'Far East: United States – British – Dutch Staff Conversations', CAB 80/32, TNA. This identifies Royal Navy strength by warship category in two columns: planned strength in early 1942; and additional reinforcements that 'may' be sent later. Five battleships are listed in the early 1942 column (clearly *Prince of Wales* and the four 'R' class), one battlecruiser (*Repulse*) and one aircraft carrier (clearly *Hermes*), nine modern cruisers and thirteen destroyers. A further carrier, five cruisers, eight destroyers and ten submarines were earmarked as reinforcements. The overall total is virtually identical to the combined phase 1 and phase 2 force defined in February.

146 Cowman is the only historian who has previously recognised the continuum in Admiralty planning for Far East reinforcement, from ABC-1 to the autumn. *Dominion or Decline*, pp233–4. Even he does not adequately bring out how comprehensive and consistent it was. Nor does he adequately explain the ABC-1 origins. Leutze does not cover the period after ABC-1 apart from a brief epilogue. Marder notes the plans for a new eastern fleet evolved at ABC-1, but does not address their subsequent implementation and certainly does not recognise a continuum. *Old Friends, New Enemies*, vol I, pp197–200. Roskill and Barnett ignore ABC-1 and its aftermath, only picking up the story with the debate between the prime minister and Admiralty in August.

147 AT 666 to Commander-in-Chief China of 4 April 1941.

148 'The Situation if the US enters the War and Japan remains neutral', circulated by Director of Plans on 6 March, ADM 116/4877, TNA.

149 Marder, *Old Friends, New Enemies*, vol I, p200.

150 Cowman, *Dominion or Decline*, p197. His view here explains the title of his book.

151 James Leutze, *Bargaining for Supremacy*. This accounts for his title. He provides a useful summary of the key developments in British-American naval relations during the nine months between the signing of ABC-1 and United States entry into the war, including the implementation of pre-war Atlantic escort, in his 'Epilogue' at Chapter 16. However, he does not address the full impact and value of ABC-1 on the British war effort during this period.

152 Miller, *War Plan Orange*, pp264–6.

153 It is important to emphasise that there is no evidence in chiefs of staff or War Cabinet records that the overall ABC-1 agreement was viewed by the British war leadership as unsatisfactory or a setback. It was approved successively by the chiefs on 5 May and Defence Committee, chaired by the prime minister, on 15 May with little comment. COS (41) 161st meeting of 5 May, CAB 79/11; COS (41) 304 0f 12 May, CAB 80/28, containing Chiefs of Staff presentation to the Defence Committee; and DO (41) 30th meeting of 15 May, CAB 69/2. All in TNA.

154 David Reynolds, *The Creation of the Anglo-American Alliance*, p184.

155 COS (41) 250 of 2 April 1941, 'British – US Staff Conversations, Report by the UK Delegation', para 12, CAB 80/27, TNA.

156 JP 444 of 14 June 1941, 'Draft Future Strategy: Review', attached to minutes of COS 213th meeting on 16 June, CAB 79/12, TNA.

157 Figures and calculations drawn from Clay Blair, *Hitler's U-Boat War*, vol I, appendix 18 and other data in this volume.

158 F H Hinsley, 'The influence of Ultra in the Second World War', in F H Hinsley and Alan Stripp, *Code Breakers* (Oxford University Press, 1993), p6.

159 Clay Blair, appendix 18.

160 Roskill, *War at Sea*, vol III, part 2, Appendix ZZ.

161 One of the best expositions of this view, and indeed one of the best summaries of the ABC-1 agreement as a whole, is by Marshal of the Royal Air Force Sir John Slessor who, as an air commodore and Director of Air Plans, represented the Royal Air Force at the ABC-1 talks. Slessor insists that the American refusal to commit to forward naval deployment in the Far East theatre was a mistake. However, he also emphasises how important the United States Atlantic commitment was to Britain and that this was not a foregone conclusion. His testimony is perhaps unique in combining the perspective of a witness and senior strategic planner at the time, with the benefit of post-war hindsight, drawing on a range of senior military positions through the war and after. Marshal of the Royal Air Force Sir John Slessor, The *Central Blue: Recollections and Reflections by Marshal of the Royal Air Force Sir John Slessor*, pp343–7.

162 Likewise, there is no criticism in the various Admiralty planning papers relating to the implementation of 'Atlantic substitution' in ADM 116/4877.

163 Willmott, *Empires in the Balance*, pp437–8.

164 The Churchill view reflects his minute of 17 February to the First Sea Lord and First Lord where he stated Australia could be adequately defended by a fleet based at Darwin. ADM 116/4877, TNA.

165 Paper 'Far East' attached to Director of Plans' minute of 15 February, ADM 116/4877, TNA.

166 It was in Pound's mind at this time, ie mid-February, because the British believed a Japanese attack might be imminent. This is known as the 'February crisis'. Haggie, *Britannia at Bay*, pp190–1.

167 Minute from First Sea Lord to Prime Minister of 16 February on the implications of a guarantee to the Netherlands East Indies. ADM 205/10, TNA.

168 B.U.S. (J) (41) 16 of 19 February 1941, 'Statement by the US Staff Committee: US Military Position in the Far East', CAB 99/5, TNA.

169 First Sea Lord statement in DO (41) 31st of 19 May, CAB 69/2, TNA.

170 AT 666 of 4 April 1941, ADM 116/4877, TNA.

171 Steven Morewood, *The British Defence of Egypt 1935–1940*, p182.

172 Peter Doling, *From Port T to RAF Gan* (UK: Woodfield Publishing, 2003), p14.

173 JP (41) 291 of 16 April 1941, 'Far East – Effect of US and Japanese Intervention', attached to COS (41) 137th of 17 April, CAB 79/10, TNA.

174 Captain John F O'Connell, *Submarine Operational Effectiveness in the 20th Century: Part Two 1939–1945* (USA: iUniverse Inc, 2011), chapters 4 and 8. Also: Layton paper, 'Remarks on the operations in Malaya and the defence of Singapore', ADM 199/1472A, TNA.

175 Danckwerts letter to VCNS dated 23 June, CAB 122/4, TNA.

176 COS (41) 504 of 20 August 1941, 'Riviera', COS (R) 7, CAB 99/18, TNA.

177 B.U.S. (J) (41) 30 of 27 March 1941, Report, paragraphs 29–32, CAB 99/5, TNA.

178 The ADB-1 report is contained in COS (41) 387 of 21 June 1941, 'Report of the American – Dutch – British Conversations held at Singapore April 1941', CAB 80/28, TNA.

179 COS (41) 160 (O) of 6 August 1941, 'American-Dutch-British Conference', CAB 80/59, TNA.

Danckwerts, as Head of British Admiralty Delegation in Washington, was briefed on the contents of this letter by Turner on 1 July. Washington Embassy memorandum M M 41 75 of 1 July. However it was not formally signed off by the American chiefs of staff until 23 July. Washington memorandum M M 41 106 of 29 July. Both memoranda are in CAB 122/8, TNA.
180 Haggie, *Britannia at Bay*, p187. Commander-in-Chief Far East, Air Chief Marshal Sir Robert Brooke-Popham, would acknowledge the interdependence of Singapore and the Netherlands East Indies after the Japanese attack. In a telegram to the chiefs of staff on 29 December he stated: 'Protracted defence of Singapore means defence of Southern Malaya, Sumatra and Java'. 'Far East – Strategic Appreciation by the Commander-in-Chief', JP (42) 10 of 2 January 1942, CAB 79/17, TNA.
181 Herman T Bussemaker, 'Paradise in Peril: The Netherlands, Great Britain and the Defence of the Netherlands East Indies, 1940–41, *Journal of Southeast Asian Studies*, 31:1 (Mar 2000), pp115–36.
182 Cowman, Dominion *or Decline*, p228.
183 COS (R) 9, 'Informal discussion between First Sea Lord and Chief of Naval Operations', dated 11 August, CAB 99/18, TNA.
184 Washington tel 1883 of 29 April 1941, CAB 105/36, TNA.
185 DO (41) 31st meeting of 19 May, CAB 69/2, TNA. Exchanges between London and the Washington Embassy on the issue are in CAB 122/4, TNA.
186 Director of Plans minute of 30 April, ADM 116/4877, TNA.
187 David Reynolds provides an overview of thinking in both Washington and London in *The Creation of the Anglo-American Alliance*, pp227–8.
188 Miller, *War Plan Orange*, pp284–5 and Cowman, *Dominion or Decline*, pp217–24.
189 Miller is frank about the limitations faced by the Pacific Fleet at pp276–9 and again at pp286–8 of *War Plan Orange*. However, in his chapter 25 he demonstrates that Commander-in-Chief Pacific Fleet, Admiral Husband Kimmel, who took command in February 1941, remained committed to offensive operations and would have sortied to put these into effect if the Japanese had not pre-empted him with their attack on Pearl Harbor.
190 COS (41) 308 of 14 May, 'Visit of Rear Admiral V H Danckwerts and Captain A W Clarke RN to the United States Commander-in-Chief Pacific Fleet', CAB 80/28, TNA. Danckwerts' personal covering letter to the First Sea Lord, dated 17 April, and the telegraphic summary of his report, dated 19 April, are in CAB 122/294, TNA. His personal letter also notes that, according to Royal Navy officers seconded to the Pacific Fleet, US Navy long range anti-aircraft fire was 'years ahead of our own'.
191 WM (41) 48th meeting, dated 8 May 1941, Conclusions, Item 5, CAB 65/22/18, TNA.
192 VCNS comment dated 10 March on Director of Plans minute dated 6 March 1941, ADM 116/4877, TNA. At the end of May, he endorsed the view of ACNS (F) (Harwood) that US Navy transfers to the Atlantic would facilitate earlier release of Royal Navy capital ships for an Eastern Fleet.
193 ADM 116/4877.
194 COS (41) 80 (O) of 18 May 1941, 'Despatch of a Fleet to the Far East', CAB 80/57, TNA.
195 See Haggie, *Britannia at Bay*, pp194–5, for a good summary of Australian lobbying here and the British response.

Chapter 5 – Royal Navy Readiness for a War with Japan in Mid-1941: Intelligence and Capability
1 'Fine tradition' featured in JIC (41) 175 of 1 May, 'Japan Future Strategy', and would have reflected NID thinking. This paper noted that the IJN had little experience of modern warfare, though in China they had demonstrated excellence in combined operations.
2 The *Kongo*-class battlecruisers (1913) and *Nagato*-class battleships (1920) were superior to their foreign contemporaries when they first appeared. This was recognised by both the Royal Navy and US Navy. The *Nagatos* were the first battleships to mount 16in guns. The Royal Navy was sufficiently impressed by the *Kongos* to try and negotiate their loan in 1915 albeit without success. Evans and Peattie, pp159–75.
3 Evans and Peattie, p226; H T Lenton, pp33–7, 46–52, 60–4, 212–15; Peter Padfield, *War Beneath the Sea* (London: John Murray, 1995), pp18–19.
4 Wesley Wark, 'In Search of a Suitable Japan: British Naval Intelligence in the Pacific before the

Second World War', *Intelligence and National Security* 1:2 (1986), pp189–211. Douglas Ford reached a similar view fifteen years later. His assessment is broader both in areas covered, dealing with intelligence performance on the IJA as well as IJN, and time. Douglas Eric Ford, 'Climbing the Learning Curve: British Intelligence on Japanese Strategy and Military Capabilities during the Second World War in Asia and the Pacific, July 1937 to August 1945' (unpublished doctoral thesis, Department of International History, London School of Economics and Political Science, 2002).

5   John Ferris, 'Intelligence and the Origins of World War II', in *Intelligence and Strategy* (Oxon UK: Routledge, 2005), p123.
6   Bell, *The Royal Navy, Seapower and Strategy between the Wars*, pp63–5. Also his essay, 'The Royal Navy, war planning, and intelligence assessments of Japan, 1921–1941', in *Intelligence and Statecraft – Use and Limits of Intelligence in International Security*, ed Peter Jackson and Jennifer Siegel (Westport, CT, USA: Praeger, 2005).
7   First Sea Lord minute to Prime Minister, covering NID 4 minute, dated 26 August, PREM 3/252/4, TNA. This met a request from the prime minister the previous day. The prime minister had also the previous day sent his first minute proposing the despatch of *Prince of Wales* to the Far East. The NID minute expanded on a report on IJN strength circulated in Weekly Intelligence Report No 74 dated 8 August. ADM 223/151, TNA.
8   The minute did not provide details of fleet organisation though a separate NID note, NID 02344/41, produced two months earlier on 19 June, set out squadron allocations which, while not comprehensive, were broadly correct compared with post-war reports.
9   Japanese Monograph 160, *Naval Production – Immediate Preparations for War 1940–41*, p35, provided official Japanese totals of 112 and sixty-five. Roskill's post-war figures at appendix L of *War at Sea*, vol II, were 113 and sixty-three.
10 NID 4 quoted 10,000 tons for *Hiryu* and *Soryu*, and 7000 tons for *Ryujo*. True figures, taken from Peattie, *Sunburst*, appendix 4, were *Hiryu* 17,300, *Soryu* 15,900 and *Ryujo* 10,600.
11 The official Japanese figure for the embarked carrier complement at the outbreak of war in December, in JM 160, Chart 6, p37, is 473. Peattie, p152, estimates around 464 at this time following the formation of the First Air Fleet. *Zuikaku* did not commission until 25 September.
12 Evans and Peattie, chapter 8.
13 NID report, 'Disposition of the Japanese Fleet', dated 5 July 1942, ADM 223/497, TNA.
14 JIC (41) 175 of 1 May.
15 Weekly Intelligence Report No 74 of 8 August 1941, ADM 223/151, TNA.
16 Air Ministry Weekly Intelligence Summary No 120 of 17 December 1941, AIR 22/75, TNA.
17 Figures from JM 160, *Naval Production – Immediate Preparations for War 1940–1941*, Chart 6, p37. The *Naval Staff History, War with Japan*, vol I, pp79–80 gave a total strength at the outbreak of war of 1737, comprising 660 fighters, 330 carrier strike aircraft, and 240 land-based bombers. This is too high for fighters (even with reserves) and too low for the other categories. Three other post-war estimates of IJNAF strength at the outbreak of war are Masatake Okumiya and Jiro Horikoshi, *Zero* (USA: Bantam, 1991), p34; Christopher Shores and Brian Cull, *Bloody Shambles*, vol II (London: Grub Street, 1993), appendix IV, p470; and Ikuhiko Hata, Yasuho Izawa and Christopher Shores, *Japanese Naval Air Force Fighter Units and their Aces 1932–1945* (London: Grub Street, 2011), p14. *Zero* gives a frontline strength of 1384 with 691 deployable by carrier, Shores gives an overall strength of 1565, while Hata and Izawa have the lowest first line strength of 1216 with around 500 ship-borne.
18 This is the Weekly Intelligence Report 120 17 December figure but NID 4 had given the figure of 362 carrier aircraft in their August minute to the prime minister.
19 Ismay minute to Prime Minister dated 7 March 1942, PREM 3/252/3, TNA.
20 JM 160, Chart 6.
21 These figures are from Japanese Monograph 160, Chart 6 and Japanese Monograph 172, *Naval Production 1942–44*, Chart 4, pp50–1. Also, Peattie, p166.
22 Hinsley, *British Intelligence*, vol I, p75, for pre-war German estimates, and pp227–8 for 1940 estimates.
23 'Performance Tables, Japanese Army and Naval Air Services', circulated under covering minute by Air Ministry (A.I.2.©) on 20 May 1941, AIR 40/241, TNA. This included a note at the front with recent headline intelligence on the new Zero fighter. Specifications and performance data

were correct, including a possible endurance of 6–8 hours. A.I.2.© also circulated detailed and accurate assessments of the three primary IJN carrier aircraft, the Zero fighter, Type 97 torpedo bomber, and Type 99 dive-bomber, on 13 December 1941. These are in AIR 40/33 and AIR 40/35, both TNA. Although circulated after the outbreak of war, this data had clearly been in the intelligence community for some months. All papers were copied to NID. It seems likely that NID's accurate assessment of the Type 96 Nell naval heavy bomber, published in Weekly Intelligence Report No 105 of 13 March 1942, drew on this earlier data. Performance data in these 1941 papers has been compared with that given in Peattie, appendix 6.

24   Details of the Zero are given in the covering letter circulating the Tables. A D Harvey notes that details of the Zero were also printed in a booklet 'Japanese Service Aircraft' issued by the general staff in India at the time of Pearl Harbor. A D Harvey, 'Army Air Force and Navy Air Force: Japanese Aviation and the opening phase of the war in the Far East', *War in History*, 6:2 (1999), pp174–204, p178.

25   Weekly Intelligence Summary No 120 of 17 December. The three main bombs were: 250kg (550lbs), 500kg, and 800kg (1800lbs). This report correctly stated that the Type 99 D3A1 Val dive-bomber was normally armed with the 250kg while the Type 97 B5N2 torpedo bomber could carry the 800kg. It also referred to the Type 91 Mod 2 which had only entered service in mid-1941 and recorded generally accurate dimensions, overall weight, and warhead weight. It gave a release height of 80m (260ft).

26   Type 91 performance data from US Strategic Bombing Survey, Military Analysis Division, Japanese Air Weapons, pp55–56. Comments on operational deployment from USSBS, NAV No 77, Operations of 22nd Air Flotilla in Malaya.

27   Group Captain Lawrence Darvall, senior Air Staff Officer Far East, sent a note to Brooke-Popham, undated but from the content probably September, on the Japanese air threat. AIR 23/1970, TNA. He quoted Japanese light bombers carrying 1000lbs (450kg) to 800 miles and heavy bombers 4000lbs (1800kg) to 600–1000 miles. A D Harvey gives figures for Japanese Army light bombers at p182 of his article. The Mitsubishi K 21 (Sally) had a capacity of 1653lbs (750kg) and operating radius of about 800 miles. The Nakajima K 49 (Helen) could carry 1653lbs to about 900 miles. Peattie gives equivalent figures for the IJNAF heavy bombers in Appendix 6. The Type 96 Nell could carry 2000lbs (900kg) to 1200 miles and the Type 1 G4M Betty 2000lbs to 1600 miles. Darvall's figures were therefore in the right order. For the heavy bomber he overstated payload and understated maximum range, though his maximum of 1000 miles was probably reasonable under operational conditions. Darvall also stated that the long range fighter, ie Zero, had a range of 1500 miles which, as a maximum, was right.

28   Weekly Intelligence Report No 76 of 2 August 1941, ADM 223/151, TNA.

29   WIR, No 77 dated 29 August, ADM 223/151, TNA.

30   Despatch of Air Vice Marshal Sir Paul Maltby on Air Operations in Malaya and NEI 1941–1942, paragraphs 68 and 104, Supplement to *London Gazette* 26 February 1948, CAB 106/86, TNA.

31   W.P. (40) 95, 'Comparison of British and Japanese Fleets', 12 March 1940, CAB 66/6/25, TNA. Some of the comparative data that contributed to W.P. (40) 95 is in a paper, 'British Equivalent to Japanese Capital Ships', attached to a Director of Plans minute of 26 February 1940, ADM 116/5757, TNA. A paper prepared by the DCNS, Vice Admiral Sir Tom Phillips, earlier in February also stressed the current superiority of IJN capital ships. Minute to Pound as First Sea Lord and Churchill as First Lord dated 6 February 1940 in ADM 205/5, TNA. The minute was part of a trenchant, indeed almost intemperate, case put forward by Phillips to resume construction of the four *Lion*-class battleships which had been halted to meet other more pressing priorities, notably escort vessels. Despite his romantic attachment to battleships, Churchill did not accept Phillips's argument.

32   'Future Strategy', paragraph 25, CAB 66/11/42, TNA.

33   NID 4 repeated the details provided in February 1940 but with additions. They noted (correctly) that the new anti-aircraft armament comprised 5in guns and that catapults had been provided to allow ships to carry up to three aircraft. NID 4 note of 28 August 1941, PREM 3/252/4, TNA.

34   Minute to First Sea Lord from Director of Gunnery and Anti-Aircraft Warfare Division of Naval Staff, dated 13 March 1942, ADM 205/13, TNA.

35   Evans and Peattie, pp250–63 and footnote 69, p595.

36 DNI minute of 11 March 1944, 'Comparison of British and Japanese capital ships in South East Asia', ADM 223/495, TNA.

37 Marder, vol I, pp355–62; Ong Chit Chung, chapter 8 especially pp215–20; and John Ferris, '"Consistent with an Intention": The Far East Combined Bureau and the Outbreak of the Pacific War, 1940–41', *Intelligence and National Security*, 27:1 (February 2012), pp5–26.

38 Beesly, *Very Special Admiral: The Life of Admiral J H Godfrey CB* (London: Hamish Hamilton, 1980).

39 Ian Pfennigwerth has a description of the Pacific Naval Intelligence Organisation in his biography, *A Man of Intelligence: The Life of Captain Eric Nave, Australian Codebreaker Extraordinary* (Rosenberg Publishing, 2006), p140.

40 'NID Vol 40, Far East and Pacific', ADM 223/297, TNA.

41 Relevant SIS reporting was passed to FECB but the Joint Intelligence Committee also recommended in May 1941 that an SIS representative 'should become a member'. Minutes of 14th JIC Meeting 1941, CAB 81/88, TNA.

42 Ferris, 'The Far East Combined Bureau and the Pacific War', pp15–16. Pfennigwerth also has a description of radio fingerprinting at pp140–1.

43 Lieutenant Commander E G Sandwith, who joined FECB in August 1941, had a low opinion of D/F. He claimed bearings were often highly inaccurate and identifying call-signs too often out of date. Quoted in monograph, 'Loss of Singapore, February 1942 and its Lessons for NID', p3, included in papers of Vice Admiral J H Godfrey, DNI 1939–42, GOD/92, NMM, Greenwich.

44 Paper prepared for Professor A J Marder by Lieutenant Commander S W Francis, dated May 1979, Arthur J Marder Papers, MS-F02, Special Collections and Archives, The University of California Irvine Libraries, Irvine, California.

45 Frederick D Parker, *Pearl Harbor Revisited: US Navy Communications Intelligence 1924–1941* (Center for Cryptologic History, US National Security Agency, 1993), pp37–8.

46 Ralph Erskine and Michael Smith, *The Bletchley Park Codebreakers* (Biteback, 2011), chapter 8. Robin Denniston, in his biography of his father A G Denniston, head of GC & CS throughout the interwar period, confirms that in early 1939 GC &CS had full control of diplomatic and attaché traffic, were reasonably fluent in reading all main naval cyphers, and also knew a lot about the army cyphers in use in China. *Thirty Secret Years: A G Denniston's work in Signals Intelligence 1914–1944* (UK: Polperro Heritage Press, 2007), p106.

47 *The Bletchley Park Codebreakers*, chapter 8.

48 John Prados, *Combined Fleet Decoded: The Secret History of American Intelligence and the Japanese Navy in World War II* (New York: Random House, 1995), pp163–6.

49 The most authoritative sources on this visit are, on the British side, GCHQ's post-war assessment of 'war warning' intelligence in HW 50/52, TNA, and, on the American side, the summary given in Robert Louis Benson, *A History of US Communications during World War II: Policy and Administration* (Center for Cryptologic History, US National Security Agency, 1997), p19, which draws on NSA records. Both sources state that GC&CS provided full details of their work to date on German Enigma in exchange for Purple. Michael Smith, *The Emperor's Codes*, chapter 6, also provides an accurate account.

50 Prados, p165.

51 Smith, *The Emperor's Codes*, pp86–8.

52 There is a readily accessible and comprehensive set of Magic intercepts during 1941 in the five-volume *Magic Background of Pearl Harbor* published by the US Department of Defence in 1978. British intercepts of Japanese Purple messages from July to December that year are in HW 12/266–HW 12/271, TNA.

53 These are contained in HW/1, TNA.

54 HW 50/52, TNA.

55 Benson, *A History of US Communications during World War II*, p20. He does not give a date for despatch to Singapore but it was late in the year.

56 Smith, *The Emperor's Codes*, pp105–6.

57 The British draft FECB history, p9, states that by mid-1941 about 75 per cent of IJN traffic used JN 25B. HW 50/88, TNA.

58 NID vol 42, 'Far East and Pacific III, Special Collaboration of British and US Radio Intelligence', ADM 223/297, TNA, and 'History of Far East Sigint', HW 4/25, TNA. Benson also states that

an encrypted radio link was provided between FECB and Station Cast from April 1941.

59   Benson, *A History of US Communications during World War II*, p20.
60   See the post-war GCHQ summary of 'war warning' intelligence, HW 50/52, TNA.
61   Smith, *Emperor's Codes*, p80.
62   Peter Donovan and John Mack, *Codebreaking in the Pacific* (New York: Springer International, 2014). They also confirm that by mid-1941 there was a full exchange on JN 25 between FECB and Station Cast.
63   Pfennigwerth, in his biography of Eric Nave, at p146, states that GC&CS had 'read 1000 (JN 25A) messages' by end 1940. If this means partial readability, it is possibly correct, since the draft history of FECB refers to 20 per cent readability of JN 25B in May 1941. However, all official British (and American) records seem clear that there was no operational intelligence, ie full decryption of key signals, until December 1941. See HW 50/88, TNA; Frederick D Parker, *Pearl Harbor Revisited: US Navy Communications Intelligence 1924–1941*, pp22–3; Donovan and Mack, *Codebreaking in the Pacific*; Captain Duane L Whitlock, 'The Silent War against the Japanese Navy', *US Naval War College Review*, 48:4 (Autumn 1995), p43. The latter states that the US Navy was able to decrypt a few JN 25 messages between 1939 and December 1941, but these provided no insights to the current intelligence picture. He offers a good layman's summary of the structure of JN 25.
64   Draft history of FECB, pp7–9, HW 50/88, TNA.
65   Ibid.
66   *The Bletchley Park Codebreakers*, chapter 10, table 10.1.
67   Benson, *A History of US Communications during World War II*, p4. Michael Smith, chapter 8, for a balanced summary of the Purple and JN 25 contribution. He confirms that the British were at this stage generally ahead of the Americans on JN 25.
68   Keith Jeffery, *MI6: The History of the Secret Intelligence Service 1909–1949* (London: Bloomsbury, 2010), pp262–6.
69   'Japanese Naval Shipbuilding', dated 17 April 1939, ADM 223/885, TNA.
70   Craigie tel 2017 to FO of 17 October, FO 371/27964, TNA.
71   Ralph Lee Defalco III, 'Blind to the Sun: US Intelligence Failures Before the War with Japan', *International Journal of Intelligence and Counter-Intelligence*, 16:1 (2003), pp95–107.
72   Arthur Marder, *Old Friends, New Enemies*, vol I, p356. Marder believed the patrol occurred in October 1940, a year later than the true date. By autumn 1940 *Regulus* was in the Mediterranean.
73   Log of HMS *Regulus* covering October 1939, ADM 173/15986, TNA. It has not proved possible to locate the relevant patrol report, although the report for *Regulus*'s next patrol to Vladivostok in December, which involved close surveillance of the Russian naval units there, is in ADM 199/1833, TNA.
74   Alastair Mars, *Submarines at War 1939–1945*, pp57–8. As noted in Chapter 2, Mars's chapters 3 and 4 give a wider account of British submarine operations in the Far East in the late 1930s.
75   Private papers of Commander J H Bartlett, HMS *Perseus* March 1939 – July 1940, p10. Item 1459, IWM.
76   Marder.
77   Mars, chapters 3 and 4.
78   Captain John F Connell, *Submarine Operational Effectiveness in the 20th Century, Part Two (1939–1945)*, chapter 3 (British submarines) and chapter 8 (American submarines).
79   FECB Intelligence Summary No 1822, 'Warning of attack by Japan', December 1940, WO 208/888, TNA.
80   FECB 1822, p4.
81   JIC (41) 175 of 1 May, 'Japan's Future Strategy'.
82   AIR 23/1865, TNA.
83   JM 107, Malaya Invasion Naval Operations, Office of US Military History, p6.
84   In a separate note dated 28 July, 'Some Notes on the Present Situation', Darvall suggested three possible Japanese motives for their move into southern Indochina: a stepping stone for further moves on Malaya; to secure their southern position prior to attacking Russia; or to increase their economic control in the region as a bargaining counter with western powers. AIR 23/1970, TNA. Eri Hotta's recent work, *Japan 1941: Countdown to Infamy* (New York: Knopf, 2013),

chapter 6, suggests this was quite a good summary of the thinking within the Japanese leadership at this time.

85 JM 107.

86 This reference is a further indicator that the arrival of the Zero had been noted, at least in FECB and Far East Air HQ, many months before the outbreak of war.

87 August comments in AIR 23/1865, TNA.

88 Darvall note dated 8 September. AIR 23/1970, TNA.

89 Commander-in-Chief Far East tel to Chiefs of Staff of 16 September 1941, Brooke-Popham Papers, 6/1/31, LHCMA.

90 This judgement differs from Douglas Ford in chapter 1 of his thesis 'Climbing the Learning Curve'.

91 For the status of Meiklereid, see Martin Thomas, 'Disaster Foreseen? France and the Fall of Singapore', in *Sixty years On*, p83.

92 Jeffery, *MI6*, pp574–5 for a summary of intelligence provided in late 1941 by the French liaison contact in Indochina codenamed Sectude.

93 For examples of Meiklereid's reporting: Ong Chit Chung, *Operation Matador*, pp219, 224, 227, 229. SIS claimed in March 1942 that it had issued twenty-one reports on Japan's 'preparations for southward move' during the week 30 November–7 December alone.

94 Commander-in-Chief Far East tel to Air Ministry for Chiefs of Staff, dated 6 January 1941, WO 193/920, TNA.

95 Jeffery, *MI6*, pp574–5.

96 Derek Wood & Derek Dempster, *The Narrow Margin: The Battle of Britain and the Rise of Air Power 1930–1940* (London: Tri-Service Press, 1990), appendices 17 and 20.

97 Air Vice Marshal Sir Paul Maltby, in his 'Despatch on Air Operations in Malaya and NEI 1941–1942', at para 227, stated that, during the first three days of the war, Japanese deployment over Northern Malaya averaged 120 aircraft. It is not clear whether this figure refers to total aircraft deployed or sorties, but was probably the former, in which case the initial sortie rate was likely to be at least twice that. Supplement to *London Gazette* 26 February 1948, CAB 106/86, TNA.

98 Ferris states that Darvall often expressed disdain for his intelligence staff, but does not provide a source for this. 'Consistent with Intention', p9. He may have been drawing on Aldrich, who states that Darvall rejected FECB projections about the strength of Japanese air power in southern Indochina as 'alarmist and defeatist'. Aldrich, *Intelligence and the War against Japan*, p63. Aldrich apparently drew on Peter Elphick, *Far Eastern File*, p167. The exchanges described in the text suggest a more positive and collegiate relationship. However, Admiral Thomas Hart, Commander-in-Chief US Navy Asiatic Fleet, claimed that Darvall had made 'a far from good impression on my observers' during contacts in the autumn of 1941, by which time Darvall was acting as Brooke-Popham's chief of staff. Leutze, *A Different Kind of Victory*, pp195–6.

99 Director of Plans and DNI minutes dated 22 December 1937, file PD 06563/37, ADM 116/3735, TNA. For more background on the SIS report, Keith Jeffery, *MI6*, p266.

100 W.P. (40) 95, 'Comparison of British and Japanese Fleets'.

101 DNI minute of 22 December 1937 in file PD 06563/37, ADM 116/3735, TNA. D K Brown quotes the diary entry of DNC Sir Stanley Goodall dated 3 March 1939: 'First Sea Lord (Backhouse) talking about *Hood*. Believes Japan building 12in battlecruisers. I said that was an argument against laying up *Hood*'. *Nelson to Vanguard*, chapter 9, footnote 12.

102 Evans and Peattie, p294.

103 SIS report 'Japanese Naval Shipbuilding', dated 17 April 1939, ADM 223/885, TNA.

104 These began with an exhaustive review conducted by Commander Hilken of NID. Relevant papers are in ADM 116/5757, TNA.

105 FECB Intelligence Summary, 'Japan: Warship Construction Programme', Index No: 911, dated 1 August 1941, ADM 223/347, TNA. The distribution list shows this was shared with DNI.

106 Japanese figures from JM 160, p35.

107 'Comparison of British and Japanese Fleets'.

108 'Air Requirements for the successful prosecution of the War at Sea'.

109 First Lord note for the Prime Minister dated 16 March 1942, PREM 3/324/14, TNA.

110 Hinsley, *British Intelligence*, vol I, appendix 4.

111 Weekly Intelligence Report No 81 of 26 September, ADM 223/151, TNA.

112 NID 4 report of 7 October 1941, 'Disposition of Japanese Fleet', FO 371/27964, TNA.
113 ADM 223/152, TNA.
114 MEW produced weekly reports on Japanese shipping intelligence under reference T 33/57/Z. Examples are in FO 371/27964. Ferris, 'Consistent with Intention', p25, drawing on FECB sources, states that FECB traffic analysis showed that, by early November, all Japanese merchant traffic had withdrawn northward, suggesting danger at the end of the month. This then triggered the air searches which found the Japanese invasion convoys. Although FECB certainly contributed to shipping intelligence, the process was directed by MEW and drew on many other sources, eg, Lloyd's. The MEW reports were circulated to the Foreign Office, the Admiralty and Ministry of War Transport.
115 NID 4 Note 4/20 dated 8 October, FO 371/27964.
116 Captain Duane L Whitlock, 'The Silent War against the Japanese Navy', *US Naval War College Review*.
117 The assessment of British knowledge of the IJN provided in this paragraph is more positive than that offered by Douglas Ford in chapter 1 of his thesis 'Climbing the Learning Curve'.
118 John Ferris, '"Consistent with an Intention": The Far East Combined Bureau and the Outbreak of the Pacific War, 1940-41'. For the quotes, see p26. Ferris accepts, p17, that FECB offered 'fairly accurate accounts of the characteristics and quality of Japanese forces'. He also states these were often largely ignored by local commanders and that FECB staff were also isolated from the intelligence departments in London. Sources on both these points conflict although Richard Aldrich broadly supports Ferris. *Intelligence and the War against Japan*, especially chapter 4.
119 FO 371/27884, TNA.
120 Ong Chit Chung, *Operation Matador*, p222-223.
121 WO 208/1080 and MI2c and DDMI comments dated 16 November in WO 208/653, both TNA.
122 This point is demonstrated by comparing one of the best examples of FECB political reporting that has survived, 'Japan at the Crossroads: May 1941', released on 5 June 1941, and available in WO 208/902, TNA, with contemporary reports from HMA Tokyo. 'Japan at the Crossroads' essentially draws up a balance sheet. On the one hand, Japan is better placed militarily for a move south than in 1940. On the other, it faces more determined opposition from the United States and some strengthening of British and Dutch forces. Most of its judgements are reasonable, though it grossly exaggerates German technical assistance. But it is essentially a speculative piece, lacking either hard information or penetrating insight.
123 It is worth comparing the picture provided by Ferris in 'Consistent with Intention' with that provided by Ong Chit Chung in chapter 8 of *Operation Matador*. Ong Chit Chung brings out the wide range and diversity of inputs feeding the intelligence picture through October and November. By end October it was clear something was probable in the southern theatre, but the more definitive warning indicators were only triggered in the last half of November. The British system actually did pretty well picking these up. WO 208/1080, TNA, has many representative reports at this time, including some from American sources via BAD Washington.
124 War Office to Commander-in-Chief Far East of 7 June 1941, WO 193/607, TNA.
125 JM 107, p2 has 225.
126 Ong Chit Chung, p229 provides more detail on British estimates and sources.
127 Again, the judgement on 'war warning' reached here differs from Douglas Ford in chapter 1 of his thesis 'Climbing the Learning Curve'.
128 Aldrich, pp60-5, looks more widely at British intelligence on Japanese capability and is generally fair in his judgements.
129 Commander-in-Chief Eastern Fleet signal 1227z to Admiralty of 13 February 1942, ADM 223/867, TNA. Layton's view was incorporated in Weekly Intelligence Report No 102 circulated a week later on 20 February. This stated that pre-war impressions here now appeared to be confirmed by wartime experience. ADM 223/153, TNA. Also Marder, vol II, p45.
130 For an account of this latter action, see Jeffrey R Cox, *Rising Sun, Falling Skies: The Disastrous Java Sea Campaign of World War II* (Osprey Publishing, 2014), chapter 17.
131 'Far East Appreciation 1937', p84, CAB 53/31, TNA.
132 DNI minute NID 3515/39 of 19 February 1940, ADM 116/5757, TNA.

NOTES TO PAGES 246–251

133 Admiralty *History of Naval Aviation 1919–1945*, vol II, appendix VII, ADM 234/374, TNA.
134 Two out of three IJN fleet carriers were listed as 'modernised' in appendix 1 to Committee of Imperial Defence paper 1366-B, 'Comparison of the Strength Of Great Britain with that of certain other Nations as at January 1938', CAB 24/273, TNA. These would be *Akagi* and *Kaga*, with the newly completed *Soryu* being the third. The Royal Navy does not appear to have learnt the scale of these modernisations as it continued to list them with their original displacement of 27,000 tons until at least 1941, whereas it had actually increased by some 30 per cent in each case. See Peattie, appendix 4 for a detailed account. *Akagi* and *Kaga* were completely reconstructed between 1934/35 and 1935–38 respectively, finishing at 36,500 and 38,200 tons. The light carrier *Ryujo* was also reconstructed in this period. None of the older Royal Navy carriers received comparable investment.
135 Cunningham signals to the Admiralty dated 25 April, 29 April, 27 May, 2 June, and 2 November. Cunningham Papers, ADD MS 52567, British Library. Cunningham's views on the centrality of carriers in modern naval warfare were shared by Somerville at Force H and Admiral Sir John Tovey as Commander-in-Chief Home Fleet.
136 Fifth Sea Lord minute to fellow Admiralty Board members, dated 27 December 1941, ADM 1/11971, TNA.
137 Peattie, pp147–53.
138 Jonathan Parshall and Michael Wenger, 'Pearl Harbor's Overlooked Answer', *Naval History Magazine*, 25:6 (December 2011).
139 Alan Zimm, *The Attack on Pearl Harbor*, chapter 10.
140 Parshall and Wenger.
141 Lyster's minute of 27 December 1941 arguably did offer an equivalent vision of the way air power would ultimately impact at sea.
142 Peattie, pp147–53.
143 Cunningham, *A Sailor's Odyssey*, p396.
144 Marder, vol I, p491. Quote from a personal letter dated February 1942.
145 Marder, vol I, p352. Quote from a letter to Marder in 1976.
146 Vice Admiral J H Godfrey, 'Afterthoughts', ADM 223/619, TNA. Godfrey was writing in the 1960s.
147 Vice Admiral Sir Geoffrey Layton, 'Remarks on the operations in Malaya and the Defence of Singapore', ADM 199/1472A, TNA.
148 'Some Personal Reflections on the Malayan Campaign July 1941–January 1942', CAB 106/193, TNA.
149 Godfrey's biographer did not agree with Godfrey's negative assessment of intelligence on the IJN. Addressing the question, 'Was faulty intelligence to blame for the disasters of 1941/42?', he answered with an emphatic 'No'. Beesly's view is in line with the assessment in this chapter. Patrick Beesly, *Very Special Admiral: The Life of Admiral J H Godfrey CB* (London: Hamish Hamilton, 1980). Beesly corresponded extensively with Marder and surviving members of NID4 and FECB in 1978/9. Correspondence in MLBE 3/2, CCA, Cambridge. Michael Goodman in his *Official History of the Joint Intelligence Committee* states at p106 that, when reviewing Joint Intelligence Committee reporting during 1941, Godfrey concluded that 'the War Cabinet and Chiefs of Staff were fully and accurately advised as to Japanese intentions and preparations'. This is sourced to an NID paper in ADM 223/494, 'JIC Appreciations in 1941 of Japanese Intentions'. This paper does indeed reach this judgement, which accords with a separate assessment conducted in early 1942 by DMI. However, the NID paper was written post-war by Captain Alan Hillgarth in 1945/6 when Godfrey was long gone. It did not therefore necessarily reflect Godfrey's personal assessment, and there is no certainty he even saw it.
150 H P Willmott, *Empires in the Balance*, pp82–3. Osamu Tagaya, *Imperial Japanese Aviator* (Osprey, 2003), makes an identical point regarding the IJNAF. In his view, the IJNAF at the start of the war was immensely skilled but fragile and lacking in depth.
151 Alan Zimm, *The Attack on Pearl Harbor*, chapter 4.
152 H P Willmott, *The Second World War in the Far East* (London: Cassell, 1999), p71.
153 *The Defeat of the Enemy Attack on Shipping, 1939–1945*, plan 9.
154 H P Willmott.
155 Phillips Payson O'Brien, *How the War was Won*, chapter 1. O'Brien also provides figures to

demonstrate that the profiles of Japanese and British naval production between 1942 and 1944 were similar. Here he credits Japan with one *Yamato* battleship, thirteen carriers, five cruisers, fifty-five destroyers and ninety-nine submarines against a Royal Navy total of two battleships (combined tonnage equal to *Yamato* class), six carriers, fifteen cruisers, 141 destroyers and 111 submarines. In reality, these figures flatter Japan. The IJN carrier figures include escort carriers, where the Royal Navy also built six, plus the maintenance carrier *Unicorn*. If these are added to the Royal Navy total, the discrepancy in this category is less stark, and the Royal Navy had a further ten light carriers nearing completion in spring 1945. His IJN destroyer total also includes twenty-seven escort destroyers. These were similar to the 150 anti-submarine escorts which the Royal Navy completed alongside the destroyer total given by O'Brien, and which he omits from his figures. Leaving carriers and submarines aside, British naval production was probably three times that of Japan over these years.

156 Vivian's paper and subsequent Admiralty comments are in ADM 116/3862, TNA. There is a detailed discussion by Marder, who discovered the paper, in vol I, pp346–52.

157 COS 931, 'Situation in the Far East', paragraph 10, CAB 53/50, TNA. This stated that fighting equipment in the IJN was believed to be at a lower standard due to lack of training among specialist staff. In consequence the relative state of efficiency compared to the Royal Navy had been arbitrarily set at 80 per cent, but could be higher. The impact of this judgement on post Tientsin adjustments to Far East war plans was discussed at the end of Chapter 2. See also Director of Plans paper dated 4 August 1939, 'The Situation if Japan intervened when we are already at war with Germany and Italy', ADM 1/9767, TNA.

158 COS (41) 13th meeting of 8 January 1941 and attached papers, CAB 79/8, TNA.

159 Evans and Peattie, pp240–5.

160 Letter from Admiral Sir William Davis to Roskill, dated 16 April 1975, ROSK 4/79, CCA, Cambridge.

161 Evans and Peattie, chapter 11, especially pp401–5.

162 The ships concerned were *Kent* on 17 September, a night attack conducted in moonlight; *Liverpool*, a dusk attack on 14 October; *Glasgow* on 3 December; and *Manchester* during the convoy operation 'Substance' on 23 July when a destroyer was also hit and sunk. Peter C Smith, *Images of War: The Story of the Torpedo Bomber* (Pen & Sword, 2007).

163 Middlebrook and Mahoney, pp51–2 and Barnett, p370.

164 *A Sailor's Odyssey*, pp258–9.

165 James J Sadkovich has provided an important reassessment of Italian military capability, arguing it has been consistently underestimated by British and American historians. He confirms that in most aspects of naval and maritime air capability their equipment and techniques were competitive with the Royal Navy in the first years of the war. Indeed, he argues that the Italians effectively 'stalemated' the Royal Navy in the Mediterranean up to 1943 with minimal German help. He also notes that their thirty-two submarines operating from Bordeaux sank 586,673 tons of Allied shipping, more than German surface raiders, and with a higher kill rate per boat than the German U-boats achieved. 'Understanding Defeat: Reappraising Italy's Role in World War II', *Journal of Contemporary History*, 24:1 (January 1989), pp27–61.

166 *Churchill and the Admirals*, p196.

167 Churchill's minute of 11 February 1940, ADM 116/5757, TNA.

168 Marder notes this quote and judges that both Churchill and the naval staff were 'culpable' of underestimating the IJN, vol I, p352, footnote 30.

169 Ian Johnston and Ian Buxton in *The Battleship Builders*, Table 'Labour employed on warships by type 1940–45', p262.

170 H T Lenton.

171 Memorandum by Fifth Sea Lord, 'State of the Fleet Air Arm, 4 September 1939', ADM 116/3722, TNA.

172 'Future Strategy', September 1940.

173 Calculations are based on the data in H T Lenton.

174 First Sea Lord note on the destroyer shortage dated 23 August 1941, ADM 178/322, TNA.

175 Compare Table 8 column 1 figures with those in parenthesis in column 3.

176 Roskill, *War at Sea*, vol III, part II, appendix XX.

177 *The Defeat of the Enemy Attack on Shipping*, appendix 2.

178 *War at Sea*, vol III, part I, appendix G. These losses can then be compared with the German and Italian build figures in tables A and B of the Annex.
179 Total losses from Roskill, *War at Sea*, vol III, part II, appendix ZZ. However, the net loss (after taking account the gains from build and requisition, etc) for vessels over 1600grt in this period was only 0.9 million tons. Hancock and Gowing, *The British War Economy*, part III, Statistical Summary, table 3 (d).
180 Clay Blair, *Hitler's U-Boat War*, vol I, plate 6, p99, drawing on the figures provided by Hancock and Gowing.
181 D J Payton-Smith, *Oil: A Study of Wartime Policy and Administration*, table 16, p244.
182 See the Annex.
183 'Future Strategy'.
184 COS (40) 48 (O) of 13 December 1941.
185 Churchill, The Grand Alliance, pp768–74.
186 This was an entrenched Admiralty belief backed by many historians, not least Roskill. However, it was (perhaps inevitably) disputed by Beaverbrook as Minister of Aircraft Production who claimed in mid-1942 that the prioritisation issue had little practical effect. Minute by Minister of Aircraft Production circulated under DC (S) (42) 60 of 10 July 1942, TNA.
187 Norman Friedman, *British Carrier Aviation: The Evolution of the Ships and their Aircraft* (London: Conway Maritime Press, 1988), chapter 10; and David Hobbs, *The British Pacific Fleet: The Royal Navy's Most Powerful Strike Force* (UK, Barnsley Yorkshire: Seaforth Publishing, 2011), p22.
188 Specification N 11/40.
189 Minute to Prime Minister of 6 February 1941covering First Sea Lord brief on Fleet Air Arm Fighters dated 30 January, PREM 3/171/4, TNA, and Friedman, pp208–9. Also: www.fleetairarmarchive.net/Aircraft/Firebrand.
190 JSM Washington Memorandum of 19 September 1941, 'Strategic Importance of Single Seater Fighters to the Navy', CAB 122/142, TNA.
191 Minute to Prime Minister of 6 February 1941 copying brief prepared by First Sea Lord on Fleet Air Arm fighter position dated 30 January. PREM 3/171/4, TNA.
192 First Sea Lord note prepared for US Special Adviser Averell Harriman, 25 November 1941, ADM 205/9, TNA.
193 Friedman, p210.
194 First Sea Lord note for Averell Harriman.
195 Minute to the Prime Minister of 6 February 1941 PREM 3/171/4, TNA.
196 First Sea Lord note for United States Special Adviser Averell Harriman. David Hobbs points out that the Royal Navy not only commissioned the folding wing Wildcat but deployed it before the US Navy. The 250 aircraft ordered in 1940 predated lend-lease and were paid for. *The British Pacific Fleet*, p14 and footnote 29.
197 Minute to Prime Minister of 6 February 1941 copying First Sea Lord brief of 30 January, PREM 3/171/4 and Prime Minister Minute of 16 August 1941, ADM 205/10, both in TNA.
198 COS (41) 593 of 30 September, which followed a visit by the prime minister to the new carrier *Indomitable*, CAB 80/30, TNA.
199 Letter to First Sea Lord from US naval attaché London, dated 3 October 1941, ADM 205/9, TNA and letter to BAD Washington from CNO Admiral Stark dated 9 October 1941, CAB 122/142, TNA. BAD commentary on Stark's position and the difficult politics involved in resolving competing Royal Navy and US Navy demands for Wildcats is in BAD signal to First Sea Lord of 12 November 1941, PREM 3/171/4, TNA.
200 Friedman, p210.
201 Letter from Vice Admiral Naval Air Stations to Secretary of the Admiralty dated 21 September 1941, ADM 1/13522, TNA.
202 First Lord minute to Prime Minister dated 4 December and circulated under DC (S) (41) 151 of 6 December, CAB 70/4, TNA.
203 Minute by Minister of Aircraft Production circulated under DC (S) (42) 60 of 10 July 1942, CAB 70/5, TNA. Also: COS (41) 613 of 8 October 1941, 'Aircraft for Aircraft Carriers', CAB 80/30, TNA, and COS (41) 666 of 8 November 1941, 'Spitfires for use in Aircraft Carriers, Priority for Development', CAB 80/31, TNA.

204 First Lord minute circulated under DC (S) (42) 61 of 10 July 1942 and Minister of Aircraft Production minute circulated under DC (S) (42) 76 of 24 August, CAB 70/5, TNA.

205 Professor N A M Rodger, Lecture given at University of Buckingham, 17 December 2012.

206 Peattie, p157.

207 David Brown, *Carrier Fighters* (London: Macdonald and Jane's, 1975), chapter 2.

208 ADM 234/374, Naval Aviation 1919–45, vol 1, p169.

209 ADM 234/374, Naval Aviation 1919–45, vol 1, pp210–12, TNA.

210 Derek Howse, *Radar at Sea: The Royal Navy in World War II* (Basingstoke: Macmillan, 1993), appendix F, pp307–8.

211 A D Harvey, 'Army Air Force and Navy Air Force: Japanese Aviation and the opening phase of the war in the Far East', *War in History*, 6:2 (1999), pp174–204.

212 ADM 234/374, Naval Aviation 1919-45 vol I, appendix VII, TNA.

213 Admiralty Board memorandum, ADM 167/112, TNA.

214 Chapter 1 records how Rear Admiral Reginald Henderson, the first flag officer given specific responsibility for Royal Navy carriers in 1933, conducted the first experiments with multi-carrier operations before either the IJN or US Navy. See also Friedman, p158, and Hobbs, p21.

215 Jonathan Parshall, *Shattered Sword*, chapter 5, for a detailed discussion of this.

216 Professor N A M Rodger, Buckingham Lecture, December 2012.

217 Somerville Papers, ed Michael Simpson (Navy Records Society, 1996).

218 *Ark Royal* was an exception here in never receiving radar. However, for much of her operational life she operated in consort with ships, eg the cruiser *Sheffield* in Force H, that were radar-fitted and could pass her air warning data, etc.

219 David Brown, *Carrier Fighters*, chapter 4, for a good summary of the evolution of Fleet Air Arm fighter operations and early experiments with radar control. Taylor's testimony can be found in the 1944 Hart Inquiry on Pearl Harbor, day 30 proceedings, p367.

220 David Hobbs, p16.

221 Jonathan Parshall, *Shattered Sword*, chapter 8, for a very thorough analysis of IJN carrier air defence arrangements and capability. Also Mark Peattie, p156.

222 ADM 234/374, Naval Aviation 1919–45, vol I, pp65–6 for a useful summary of the development of night attack capability. The Bailey Committee report on Royal Navy strength and capability prepared for the Americans and dated 11 September 1940 includes useful material on the Fleet Air Arm including night torpedo techniques. ADM 199/1159, TNA. There is an interesting blog from emason on the Taranto attack, under 'Operation Judgement' in the World Naval Ships Forum/Battles and Events. This has several original records, including a report from an American observer present in *Illustrious*, Lieutenant Commander John Newton Opie USN. Opie offers more valuable detail on how Fleet Air Arm night operations were executed.

223 Letter from the Secretary to the Admiralty to Rear Admiral Naval Air Stations, dated 15 November 1941, 'HMS Victorious Operations against the Bismarck', ADM 199/1187, TNA.

224 Friedman, p156.

225 Milan Vego, 'Major Convoy Operation to Malta, 10–15 August 1942 (Operation Pedestal)', *US Naval War College Review*, 63:1 (Winter 2010).

226 For the development of the Beaufort force, Ralph Barker, *Shipbusters: The story of the RAF torpedo bombers* (London: Chatto & Windus, 1957).

227 Minute to ACAS (O) of 25 May 1942, AIR 20/887, TNA. Also earlier DCAS minute to Sir Henry Tizard of 9 December 1941, AIR 20/887, TNA. This emphasises the torpedo is the most effective weapon for maritime attack but highlights shortcomings in the Beaufort, lack of dedicated crews and torpedo shortage.

228 John Terraine, *The Right of the Line* (London: Hodder and Stoughton, 1985), p422.

229 John Deane Potter, *Fiasco: The break-out of the German Battleships* (London: William Heinemann, 1970).

230 Peter C Smith, *Images of War: The Story of the Torpedo Bomber* (Pen & Sword, 2007).

231 Ralph Barker, pp16, 59.

232 Martin Middlebrook and Patrick Mahoney, pp302–3.

233 JP (41) 1072, 'Far East Policy', attached to COS (41) 428th of 19 December 1941, CAB 79/16, TNA.

234 COS (42) 109th meeting of 7 April, CAB 79/20, TNA.
235 COS (42) 7 of 6 January 1942, 'Provision of Beauforts for Malaya from Australia', CAB 80/33, TNA.
236 Brooke-Popham letters to Street, Permanent Under Secretary Air Ministry, dated 22 February and 28 October 1941, Brooke-Popham Papers 6/3 and G2 minute of 20 February 1941, Brooke-Popham Papers 6/1, all in LHCMA. Air Staff minute dated 29 May 1941, 'Should Australian Beauforts be equipped with torpedoes?, AIR 20/887, TNA.
237 COS (41) 435th of 26 December, item 5, CAB 79/16, TNA.
238 Beaufighter, *Flypast Special* (Key Publishing, 2012).
239 Terraine, *The Right of the Line*, p461.
240 DO (42) 23 of 6 March, minute by First Lord covering memorandum by First Sea Lord, dated 6 March 1942, 'Air Requirements for the successful prosecution of the War at Sea', PREM 3/324/14, TNA. This contains the famous opening paragraph: 'If we lose the war at sea, we lose the war'. Also: COS (42) 71 (O) of 21 March 1942, 'Future Strategy', CAB 80/61, TNA and COS (42) 171 (O) of 16 June, 'The Bombing of Germany', CAB 80/63, TNA.
241 COS (42) 183 (O) of 23 June, 'The Bombing of Germany', CAB 80/63, TNA.
242 COS (42) 204 (O) of 18 July, 'Provision of Aircraft for the War at Sea', CAB 80/63, TNA. This reflected a report negotiated by the ACNS (Home) and ACAS (P).
243 Brian Farrell, *The Basis and Making of British Grand Strategy: Was there a Plan?*, book 2, pp376–80.
244 Farrell, p388.
245 Willis sent a paper to Frankland, which he had written for Marder in 1966, setting out the classic partisan naval view that much of Bomber Command effort was wasted and would have been better spent on air support at sea. Frankland's letter in reply is dated 10 December 1966. Both are with the Willis papers in the IWM.
246 Frankland quoted frontline strengths for Bomber Command of 506 in November 1941, 417 in May 1942, and 515 in January 1943. The May 1942 figure is consistent with that of Harris.

Chapter 6 – Summer and Autumn 1941: Reinforcement and Deterrence
1 Waldo Heinrichs, *Threshold of War: Franklin D Roosevelt and American Entry into World War II* (New York: Oxford University Press, 1988), chapters 5 and 6, summarises these calculations.
2 Magic refers to American and British intercept of the Japanese Purple diplomatic cypher. Exhibit No 1 located in vol 12 of the 'Joint Investigation into Pearl Harbor' contains a selection of Magic intercepts from 1 July to 8 December 1941. There is a more comprehensive set of Magic intercepts in the five-volume 'Magic Background of Pearl Harbor' published by the US Department of Defence in 1978. British intercepts of Japanese Purple messages in July are in HW 12/266 and those for August to November in HW 12/267 – 12/270, TNA.
3 Magic intercept of Purple message Canton to Tokyo of 14 July 1941, decrypted by the United States on 19 July. This is at page 2 of Exhibit No 1, vol 12, 'Joint Investigation into Pearl Harbor'. The British version is in HW 12/266, TNA.
4 The evolution of Japanese thinking on an advance southward is described in JM 147, Political Strategy Prior to the Outbreak of War, Part III, esp pp27–34, and JM 150, Political Strategy Prior to the Outbreak of War, Part IV, esp pp6–7.
5 F H Hinsley, *British Intelligence in the Second World War*, vol 1, p454.
6 Chapter 1 of Willem Remmelink's translation of Senshi Sosho, Japanese War History Series, volume III, *The Invasion of the Dutch East Indies*, originally published by the War History Office of the National Defence College of Japan in 1967 (Holland: Leiden University, 2015).
7 JM 152, Political Strategy Prior to the Outbreak of War, Part V, p12.
8 AT 523 of 13 May to Commander-in-Chief Home Fleet, copied to all overseas commanders, ADM 116/4877, TNA.
9 Naval Staff minute DOD (H) to ACNS (F) of 18 July, ADM 205/11. A note from the First Sea Lord to the prime minister, a month later on 24 August, demonstrates the acute shortage of cruisers and destroyers against potential commitments at this time. ADM 178/322, TNA.
10 Roskill summarises the history of mobile support for the Royal Navy in *War at Sea*, vol III, part II, appendix P, 'The History of the Royal Navy's Fleet Train'.

11 Cowman, *Dominion or Decline,* p231.
12 'Far East – Action in view of Japanese Intentions', attachment to COS (41) 254th meeting.
13 COS (41) 139 (O) of 16 July, 'Japanese Intentions', CAB 80/58, TNA.
14 DO (41) 56th meeting of 8 August, CAB 69/2, TNA.
15 Director of Plans minute of 15 February 1941 providing the rationale for a Royal Navy Eastern Fleet in the context of the ABC-1 talks; Director of Plans minutes beginning 6 March ending with VCNS minute of 29 May considering options if the United States enters the war and Japan remains neutral; AT 523 of 13 May. ADM 116/4877, TNA.
16 Letter to Commander-in-Chief Pacific Fleet (Kimmel) dated 31 July 1941, Joint Committee on Investigation of Pearl Harbor Attack, Part 16, Exhibit 110, US Library of Congress.
17 Cowman, *Dominion or Decline,* pp233–4.
18 Cowman, *Dominion or Decline,* p235 and Haggie, *Britannia at Bay,* p203.
19 Danckwerts note circulated within British Embassy on 19 August, CAB 122/577, TNA. Turner had just returned from Riviera.
20 Phase 2 concentration in the Indian Ocean using Trincomalee or Port T as primary operating base was first defined in AT 666 to Commander-in-Chief China of 4 April 1941, ADM 116/4877, TNA. Pound's minute is in Churchill, *The Second World War,* vol III, appendix K.
21 Director of Plans minute dated 15 February 1941, ADM 116/4877, TNA.
22 Minute to Prime Minister of 13 February, ADM 205/10.
23 Defence Committee, minutes of 12th Meeting, CAB 69/2, TNA. Prime Minister to CIGS dated 13 May, WO 216/5, TNA.
24 Page 5 of memorandum by US Assistant Secretary of State Sumner Welles drafted at Placentia Bay, 10 August 1941, Exhibit 22B, Joint Committee on the Investigation of the Pearl Harbor Attack, Part 14.
25 AT BAD Washington to Admiralty of 24 November 1941 quoting US Naval Staff. CAB 122/9, TNA.
26 Evans and Peattie, *Kaigun, Strategy, Tactics and Technology in the Imperial Japanese Navy 1887–1941,* especially chapters 12 and 14, for background on IJN attitudes here.
27 Roskill, *War at Sea,* vol III, part II, appendix ZZ. The figures here do not distinguish between German and Japanese action.
28 Michael Wilson, *A Submariner's War: The Indian Ocean 1939–1945* (UK: Spellmount, 2008), chapter 8, for an account of U-boat operations in the Indian Ocean.
29 *The Defeat of the Enemy Attack on Shipping, 1939–1945,* ed Eric J Grove, plan 14, has slightly different figures to Roskill. It puts the losses in the Pacific in 1941 and 1942 at 849,000 tons. If these are used, then British losses in the first year of the Far East war were about 900,000 tons.
30 The best accounts of Riviera, as regards Far East strategy and American and British planning for reinforcement are Theodore A Wilson, *The First Summit, Roosevelt and Churchill at Placentia Bay, 1941* (revised version, University Press of Kansas, 1991), and Heinrichs, *Threshold of War,* chapter 6.
31 Quoted in Eri Hotta, *Japan 1941: Countdown to Infamy* (New York: Knopf, 2013), chapter 7.
32 COS (41) 504 of 20 August 1941, 'Summarised records of meetings between British and US Chiefs of Staff' on 9 August, page 4, CAB 80/30, TNA; and Prime Minister's memorandum to the Cabinet on Riviera discussions, page 11, WP (41) 202 of 20 August 1941, CAB 66/18/25, TNA. Britain's ambassador, Lord Halifax, was also alerted by the president to the despatch of strategic bombers to the Philippines prior to Riviera – AT Gleam 102 of 2 August from BAD Washington, CAB 122/120, TNA. Washington Embassy military staff also received briefings on Philippines reinforcements during the first half of August – internal memorandum circulated by Minister Balfour on 19 August, CAB 122/72, TNA.
33 John Costello claims that at Riviera the British chiefs of staff agreed to dispense with their share of future B-17 bomber production so that it could be diverted to the Philippines. The quid quo pro was a secret agreement that the Philippines B-17 force would then be used to defend British territories in the Far East. Costello believes the B-17s, 'which the United States War Department had initially regarded as a quick fix to bolster MacArthur's defence of the Philippines, were to emerge from the Churchill-Roosevelt summit as the "big stick" of an Anglo-American strategy that they mistakenly believed would be a powerful threat to curb Japan from further encroachment'. He argues that this 'secret agreement' then directly drove Churchill to pursue

forward naval reinforcement against Admiralty advice. This is not convincing. There is no direct documentary evidence for such an agreement. The claim of an American promise to protect British territories ignores the political constraints facing Roosevelt. Nor does the concept of such an agreement at Riviera fit with the timeline under which United States plans to reinforce the Philippines were agreed. Most of the key decisions here were not taken until September. John Costello, *Days of Infamy* (New York, USA: Nimbus Communications, 1994), chapter 3.

34 Churchill, vol III, appendix K.

35 Riviera records (R) 9 and (R) 15, CAB 99/18, TNA; and Turner's account to Danckwerts, of 19 August, CAB 122/577, TNA. Herbert Feis, at p256, footnote 2, of his classic work *The Road to Pearl Harbor* (Princeton University Press, 1950), states that at Riviera 'The British agreed to send stronger forces to the Far East than had been contemplated before'. He sources this to a report by Commander Goodenough from the minutes of an Admiralty liaison meeting of 22 August which it has not been possible to locate. There is no evidence elsewhere that the Admiralty planned stronger forces than those agreed in February and regularly reviewed since but, as Turner indicates, Pound did promise acceleration. It seems likely Feis mistook acceleration for an increase in strength.

36 PREM 3/163/3, TNA.

37 Prime Minister memo to First Sea Lord of 25 August and NID reply of 28 August, PREM 3/252/4, TNA.

38 Minute from First Lord to First Sea Lord dated 21 August 1941, PREM 3/171/4, TNA. Cunningham's request was dated the previous day.

39 For a typical example of the critics' view see the letter from Commander Michael Goodenough, Staff Officer Operations to Commander-in-Chief Eastern Fleet in 1941, to Roskill dated 8 May 1951, ROSK 4/79, CCA.

40 References to this meeting are included in the Report on the Loss of HMS *Prince of Wales* and HMS *Repulse*, ADM 199/1149, TNA. These potential Indian Ocean naval reinforcements were incorporated in the Joint Planning Committee note prepared for the chiefs of staff following the Japanese move into southern Indochina. This recorded existing force levels for each service in the Far East, then identified reinforcements that could be provided in thirty days, and additional forces for 'later' despatch. JP (41) 664 of 12 August, 'Improvement of our position in the Far East', CAB 79/13, TNA. Alexander does not refer to this 20 August meeting when writing to Pound the following day and possibly was not aware of it.

41 AT 1904B of 13 May, ADM 116/4877, TNA.

42 Quoted by D K Brown, *Nelson to Vanguard: Warship Design and Development 1923–1945*, chapter 9, footnote 6.

43 ADM 116/4877, TNA.

44 Roskill, *War at Sea*, vol I, pp555–6. Marder broadly follows Roskill. He states: 'There was patently a clash between the Prime Minister's conception of a small but "high class" squadron that would through a show of strength act as a deterrent to Japanese aggression, and the Admiralty's, which envisaged two larger forces of older capital ships to deter the Japanese Navy'. Vol II, pp222–3.

45 Prime Minister letter of 31 August, PREM 3/156/6, TNA.

46 Robin Brodhurst, *Churchill's Anchor*, p 194.

47 J M A Gwyer, *Grand Strategy*, vol III, part I, pp270–1.

48 ADM 116/4877.

49 Stark drew here on a briefing from British Admiralty Delegation Washington. BAD received an Admiralty telegram the previous day, 22 September, providing exactly these details. CAB 122/8, TNA. Stark was evidently aware that *Revenge* and *Repulse* were already in the Indian Ocean. 'Modern capital ship' is the term used in the Admiralty telegram. It could imply a *King George V* but is more likely to refer to the preferred Admiralty option of one or both *Nelsons*.

50 Stark letter to Commander-in-Chief Pacific Fleet (Kimmel) dated 23 September 1941, Joint Committee on Investigation of Pearl Harbor Attack, Part 16, Exhibit 110, US Library of Congress. Stark's figures for the Royal Navy forces planned for the Indian Ocean at this time are consistent with those communicated to Commander-in-Chief China in AT 0337 of 22 September, ADM 116/4877, TNA.

51 Roskill stated: 'It proved impossible to reconcile the two points of view and the matter was not

discussed again until mid-October', vol I, p556. Marder stated: 'for the time being no decision was reached', vol I, pp222–3. Brodhurst, Pound's biographer, also states that 'little happened for six weeks on the naval front, until matters moved on the political front'. Brodhurst, *Churchill's Anchor*, p195.

52 Burt, *British Battleships 1919–1945*, pp196, 238.

53 Director of Plans note for First Sea Lord dated 29 October 1941, ADM 205/11, TNA.

54 The promised draft of ABD-2, 'Draft Agreement on the outline plan for the employment of American, Dutch and British Forces in the Far East Area in the event of war with Japan', was completed by end August. A copy showing the amendments to ABD-1 is in CAB 122/8, TNA.

55 Director of Plans minute of 26 September 1941, ADM 116/4877, TNA.

56 For summaries of the implementation of US Navy Atlantic escort post ABC-1, Leutze, *Bargaining for Supremacy*, chapter 16, and Clay Blair, *Hitler's U-Boat War*, vol I, pp351–5.

57 Paper for First Sea Lord dated 23 August 1941, ADM 178/322, TNA. Pound would have had these figures in mind during his end August exchange with Churchill.

58 ACNS (F) minutes of 6 March and 18 May 1941, ADM 116/4877, TNA.

59 ACNS (F) minute of 29 September, ADM 116/4877, TNA.

60 See the view of the DNI Vice Admiral J H Godfrey in chapter 7, p64, of his Afterthoughts, ADM 223/619, TNA.

61 Director of Plans record of VCNS meeting dated 1 October 1941, ADM 116/4877, TNA.

62 Director of Plans minute of 2 October, VCNS of 10 October, First Sea Lord and First Lord of 15 October and accompanying draft aide-memoire, ADM 116/4877, TNA.

63 Cowman, *Dominion or Decline*, pp244–6. Cowman is the only historian to investigate the Admiralty's offensive planning. Christopher Bell acknowledged this work in his article 'The "Singapore Strategy" and the Deterrence of Japan: Winston Churchill, the Admiralty and the Dispatch of Force Z'. However, he did not address its implications and has since held to the conventional narrative on Far East naval reinforcement in autumn 1941, notably in *Churchill and Seapower*. Ashley Jackson has acknowledged that Cowman has provided 'an alternative explanation' of the naval debate that autumn that 'reverses' the roles traditionally ascribed to Pound and Churchill. However, his exposition of the Cowman alternative is somewhat muddled, and consequently has had little impact on mainstream naval historians. *The British Empire and the Second World War*, pp290–1.

64 AT 618 from BAD of 2 October, CAB 122/8, TNA. BAD reiterated American objections in Gleam 150 of 12 October. This was seen by the prime minister. PREM 3/156/6, TNA.

65 Letter from Turner dated 3 October, CAB 122/8, TNA.

66 Waldo Heinrichs, *Threshold of War*, p148.

67 Heinrichs, p176.

68 William H Bartsch, *December 8, 1941: MacArthur's Pearl Harbor* (Texas A & M University Press, 2003), p98.

69 Daniel F Harrington, 'A Careless Hope: American Air Power and Japan, 1941', *Pacific Historical Review*, 16:2 (May 1979), p224.

70 Marshall to Stimson on 8 October. Bartsch, p102.

71 Bartsch, pp145–6.

72 Heinrichs, chapter 6.

73 The earliest briefing to British Embassy staff was probably that given to the military attaché Colonel Vogel by the Director of US War Plans, Brigadier Leonard Gerow, on 14 August. Note by Vogel dated 14 August, CAB 122/30, TNA.

74 Halifax letter to Prime Minister of 11 October 1941, PREM 4/27/9, TNA.

75 Ismay minute to Prime Minister dated 14 August 1941, PREM 3/156/6, TNA.

76 Bartsch, p101.

77 Despatch of Air Vice Marshal Sir Paul Maltby 'Air Operations in Malaya and Netherlands East Indies', para 34, Supplement to *London Gazette* 26 February 1948, CAB 106/86, TNA.

78 Letter from US Army Brigadier General Joseph T McNarney dated 1 October 1941 seeking agreement for the use of British airbases in the Far East area by United States heavy bombardment and reconnaissance aircraft. COS (41) 223 (O) of 1 October, CAB 80/59, TNA. The chiefs of staff approved these arrangements two days later. Item 4 of 341st meeting on 3 October, CAB 79/14, TNA.

79 'Report on visit to Philippine Islands 29 May–6 June 1941' and 'Notes on Defence Problem of Luzon', AIR 23/1869, TNA.
80 Letters to Air Ministry by Commander-in-Chief Bomber Command, Air Marshal Richard Pierse, dated 8 October and 3 November, AIR 14/629, TNA.
81 WM (41) 112th Conclusions, Minute 1, CAB 65/24/4, TNA. This represents further evidence against the Costello thesis of a secret agreement at Riviera. Footnote 33.
82 Miller, *War Plan Orange*, p62. Miller accepts the Royal Navy planned to do what the US Navy would not, and deploy a battle-fleet in Manila, but regards Royal Navy ambitions as deluded.
83 Stark letter to Commander-in-Chief Pacific (Kimmel) dated 31 July 1941, Joint Committee on Investigation of Pearl Harbor Attack, Part 16, Exhibit 110, US Library of Congress.
84 Tel BAD to ADM of 13 November 1941, CAB 105/36, TNA.
85 Ghormley letter to Pound of 7 November, ADM 205/9, TNA.
86 Exhibit 110, Part 16, Joint Committee on Pearl Harbor.
87 This is broadly Cowman's view. It features in his 1996 article 'Defence of the Malay Barrier? The Place of the Philippines in Admiralty Naval War Planning 1925–1941', published almost contemporaneously with *Dominion or Decline*. This concludes: 'Throughout the interwar period the "Main Fleet to Singapore" concept was part of a wider scheme devoted to the rescue and relief of all British Far Eastern possessions. Operations to the north of the Malay Barrier, ultimately leading to naval penetration of the waters surrounding the Japanese home islands, were the key. Because of its strategic and geographic location, Manila was intended to play a pivotal, if not vital, role in these plans. When the Admiralty decided to base the Eastern Fleet on Manila in mid-October 1941, that decision was not an adhoc gesture emerging from a strategic vacuum, but rather the product of intent and of years of planning based firmly on pre-war principles and practices'. Cowman overstates the offensive ambitions in pre-war planning, which were always constrained by the limits of resource and time, but the idea of exploiting a forward base to sever IJN communications well north of Singapore did retain a powerful hold on Admiralty thinking.
88 Paragraph D of AT 1559A of 5 November 1941 to BAD Washington, ADM 116/4877, TNA.
89 JIC (41) 320 of 11 August, 'A Simultaneous Move by Japan against Siberia and Thailand', CAB 79/13, TNA. For the reduction of Japanese air forces available for Malaya, approximately 50 per cent down on those estimated in January and May, see JIC (41) 327 of 13 August, 'Probable Scale of Japanese Attack on Malaya', CAB 79/13, TNA. JIC (41) 362 of 13 September, 'Japan's Intentions', CAB 79/14, TNA.
90 JM 150, Political Strategy Prior to the Outbreak of War, Part IV, pp8–16.
91 COS (41) 324th of 16 September, CAB 79/14, TNA.
92 The impact of aircraft shipments to Russia can be seen at the COS (41) 301st meeting of 28 August which discussed the impact of supplying 200 Hurricanes, CAB 79/14, TNA, and in COS (41) 207 (O) of 17 September, 'Allocations of Aircraft to Russia from American Production and the effect on RAF Expansion', CAB 80/59, TNA. The latter paper estimated that, over the nine months October 1941–June 1942, the Royal Air Force would lose 1800 fighters from United Kingdom production and 1800 assorted aircraft from American production. United Kingdom fighter squadrons would need to be capped and upgrades to the Middle East and Far East put on hold.
93 JP (41) 816 of 7 October, 'Japan: Our Future Policy', CAB 79/14, TNA.
94 Christopher M Bell, 'The "Singapore Strategy" and the Deterrence of Japan: Winston Churchill, the Admiralty and the Dispatch of Force Z', pp622–3. Bell, quoting Eden's memoirs, suggests the agreed force was: fast battleship, battlecruiser, and carrier. Also Marder, vol I, p223.
95 WP (41) 230 of 30 September, 'Far East Policy', CAB 66/19/3, TNA.
96 Commander-in-Chief Far East telegram of 1 October, JP (41) 816 of 7 October, 'Japan – Our Future Policy', attached to COS (41) 348th of 9 October, CAB 79/14, TNA.
97 Tel attached to JP (41) 816 of 7 October.
98 'Some Personal Reflections on the Malayan Campaign July 1941–January 1942', written by Playfair in 1943, CAB 106/193, TNA.
99 Doig paper, 'Misfortune off Malaya', p3, Doig Papers, National Museum of the Royal Navy Library, Portsmouth.
100 AT 1151 of 3 October 1941.

101 Doig, 'Misfortune off Malaya', p5.
102 Doig told Marder in a letter dated 16 May 1979 that his paper was drafted immediately after the receipt of AT 1151. The content of the paper feels consistent with this claim, but the document is an undated draft with no definite proof of time of origin. There is thus some risk it was drafted later and reflects hindsight. If it is genuine, it brings out exactly the questions the Admiralty should have been addressing through October and November as the plan to deploy an eastern fleet, with Force Z as forerunner, took shape. Doig's paper and his correspondence with Marder are with the Doig collection at the National Museum of the Royal Navy Library, Portsmouth.
103 As conveyed to Marder in 1979. Doig papers.
104 Tel also attached to JP (41) 816 of 7 October.
105 Cowman, *Dominion or Decline*, p246.
106 Cowman, *Dominion or Decline*, p255.
107 ADM 178/322, TNA.
108 For the limitations on Roskill's access to Admiralty records, see Barry Gough, *Historical Dreadnoughts: Arthur Marder, Stephen Roskill and Battles for Naval History* (Barnsley, UK: Seaforth Publishing, 2010), p145. The most authoritative surviving witness from the naval staff with whom Roskill corresponded over twenty-five years was Admiral Sir William Davis, a captain in Operations Division in 1941. Another potential witness was Phillips's Staff Operations Officer, Commander Michael Goodenough. Prior to joining the staff of Commander-in-Chief Eastern Fleet, Goodenough was in Naval Plans and attended the Riviera Conference in this capacity, giving him a central view of naval strategic planning. He makes a passing, and disparaging, reference in his letter to Roskill, dated 8 May 1951, that 'more senior members' of Phillips's staff wished to deploy the 'R' class to Singapore, but that is all. Yet Goodenough was also with Phillips when he met Hart at Manila on 6 December, so he was witness there to all the discussions around forward basing. See ROSK 4/79, CCA, Cambridge. Arthur Marder records seeing the most important Admiralty file in *Old Friends, New Enemies*, vol I, p398. Paul Haggie confirms he did not find the papers when researching *Britannia at Bay*, but agrees they are important, 'modifying our view of one of the significant turning points of the war'. Email to author dated 10 July 2013.
109 Vice Admiral J H Godfrey, 'Afterthoughts', ADM 223/619, TNA; 'Loss of Prince of Wales and Repulse, 10 December 1941, Recollections of Captain William Davis, Deputy Director of Plans, Admiralty'. ROSK 4/79, CCA, Cambridge. The First Sea Lord's report on the loss of Force Z, submitted on 25 January 1942, summarised the seven weeks between the August exchange with the prime minister and the Defence Committee meeting on 17 October as follows: 'The situation in the Far East meanwhile had further deteriorated and it became necessary to start forming the Eastern Fleet as ships became available'. ADM 199/1149, TNA.
110 The record of the 17 October meeting is item 1 in DO (41) 65th of 17 October 1941, CAB 69/2, TNA. The record of the second meeting on 20 October is in the Defence Committee Standing File at CAB 69/8, TNA. The reason there were two separate discussions was because the First Sea Lord was absent on 17 October. Robin Brodhurst, Pound's biographer, states that the main discussion on 20 October took place at the COS 360th meeting in the morning chaired by the prime minister with the Defence Committee then ratifying the chiefs of staff decision to deploy *Prince of Wales* in the afternoon. However, the quotations Brodhurst ascribes to the chiefs of staff meeting all come from the Defence Committee meeting. The record of the COS 360th has no reference to discussion of Far East naval reinforcement, the prime minister did not chair it, and the First Sea Lord was not present either. Brodhurst also gives a file reference CAB 79/24 for the COS 360th meeting whereas it is actually contained in CAB 79/15. The claim that there was a separate chiefs of staff discussion seems to be an error. Brodhurst, *Churchill's Anchor*, pp196–7.
111 What Churchill really meant by 'deterrence' during these Defence Committee exchanges and the earlier August exchange with Pound is a crucial question. Christopher Bell credits Churchill with a much wider political goal than set out here. This goal comprised two elements: to signal to the Japanese specific British resolve to defend its Far East possessions, and to demonstrate British alignment with the increasingly robust United States attitude to Japan, including Philippines reinforcement. His argument has intellectual appeal, but it gives the deterrence

concept from August onward more coherence than was in reality the case. Bell's two motives were undoubtedly present, but they were two factors within a much more pragmatic and evolutionary approach to managing the risk posed by Japan as the autumn progressed. Churchill's intentions must be viewed against a more complicated Admiralty position than Bell portrays and, indeed, a fast-evolving intelligence picture in the Far East theatre. *Churchill and Sea Power*, chapter 8.

112 Brief for First Sea Lord dated 29 October 1941, ADM 205/11, TNA.

113 R A Burt, *British Battleships 1919-1945*, p413.

114 EPS (41) 242 (Also JP (41) 1088) of 22 December, CAB 79/16, TNA.

115 Phillips's minute of 6 February 1940 to Pound as First Sea Lord and Churchill as First Lord, ADM 205/5, TNA. The context for this minute is given in Chapter 5, footnote 30. Roskill makes no comment on the role proposed for the 'R' class at the two Defence Committee meetings, but certainly doubted their fighting value. In a post-war letter to Cunningham dated 22 July 1959, he stated: 'Everyone who had the *Royal Sovereign*s, especially James Somerville, called them a liability rather than an asset!'. Cunningham Papers, Add MS 52563, British Library.

116 Marder claims that Pound was so concerned at the prospect of sending a 'completely unbalanced force' to Singapore that he summoned a meeting of 'the Sea Lords and other professional members of the Board' to discuss their position. 'Their unanimous opinion against the strategically unsound disposition was then expressed in a memorandum to the First Lord.' Marder's sources here were a 1975 letter from Rear Admiral Sir Rowland Jerram, secretary to ACNS (Home) in 1941, and a 1979 letter from Admiral Brockman, Pound's secretary in 1941. Marder found no documentary record for this meeting, which apparently happened between the two Defence Committee meetings. No other historian refers to it. Marder's account looks dubious for at least four reasons. First, there would be no justification for such a formal démarche before the second meeting on 20 October. The prime minister had stated categorically he would take no decision without hearing the First Sea Lord's views. Secondly, the supposed forceful objections to an unbalanced fleet were hardly consistent with the Admiralty's own plans for forward basing at Singapore. As described, the argument had effectively reduced to *Prince of Wales* v *Rodney*. Thirdly, such a démarche ignores the scope for compromise, eg, the initial deployment to Cape Town which was agreed, or deployment to Ceylon. Finally, such a démarche seems totally at odds with the way political/military differences had been resolved during the war to date, often when the strategic stakes were much higher. It is perhaps revealing that another potential witness who Marder consulted, Admiral of the Fleet Lord Fraser, who was Controller in 1941, had no recollection of this meeting. What seems more plausible is that Pound called an informal meeting of the naval staff following his return from leave to hear what had transpired on 17 October and discuss tactics for the 20th. It is also plausible that this produced a briefing note for Alexander as First Lord who would be joining Pound and Phillips at the Defence Committee. But it was not the formal démarche described by Jerram.

117 Gwyer, *Grand Strategy*, III, part I, p272.

118 ADM 1/11043, TNA. Admiral J H Godfrey, DNI 1939–42, described Force Z as 'the forerunner' of a large 'Pacific Fleet' [sic] in his unpublished memoir, 'Afterthoughts', ADM 223/619, TNA.

119 It is unlikely *Rodney* would have been there, footnote 118.

120 Cowman, *Dominion or Decline*, p251.

121 The briefing note prepared for the First Lord dated 17 December, following the loss of Force Z, in preparation for his statement to a secret session of Parliament, states that a key reason for deploying *Prince of Wales* to the Far East was the non-availability of *Rodney*. ADM 1/11043, TNA.

122 AT 253 of 5 November, ADM 116/4877, TNA.

123 In fact, Pound received an informal response conveying Stark's views in a letter from the US Navy Special Observer in London, Vice Admiral R L Ghormley, on 7 November. Ghormley was responding to soundings from Director of Plans at the end of October conveying the Admiralty's new thinking on forward deployment north of the barrier. ADM 205/9, TNA.

124 Telegram Gleam 163 from BAD Washington of 13 November 1941, copy attached to JP (41) 991 of 21 November, CAB 84/37, TNA. Hart had also communicated reservations regarding

Manila to the US Navy Delegation in London on 6 November, OPNAV to SPENAVO of 6 November, CAB 122/9, TNA.

125 JP (41) 971 of 16 November and JP (41) 991 of 21 November 1941, both in CAB 84/37 TNA and COS (41) 727 of 7 December 1941, CAB 80/32, TNA.

126 COS 397th meeting of 25 November, CAB 79/15, TNA.

127 WM (41) 109th Conclusions, Minute 2, Confidential Annex, CAB 65/24/2, TNA.

128 WM (41) 112th Conclusions, Minute 1, Confidential Annex, CAB 65/25/4, TNA.

129 *Papers of George Catlett Marshall*, ed Larry I Bland, Sharon Ritenour Stevens and Clarence E Wunderlin, Jr (Lexington, Va: George C Marshall Foundation, 1981–). Electronic version based on the *Papers of George Catlett Marshall*, vol II: *'We Cannot Delay,' July 1, 1939–December 6, 1941* (Baltimore and London: Johns Hopkins University Press, 1986), pp676–81.

130 Pound's letter of 7 March 1942 is in PREM 3/119/6, TNA. Brodhurst quotes the full letter in *Churchill's Anchor* at pp214–15. He states that 'Pound's comment that he did not believe he had been over-ruled is surprising, particularly given what had occurred over *Force Z*, and certainly shows a greater degree of loyalty than accuracy'. Roskill wrote to Cunningham regarding the letter in December 1957 while researching *The War at Sea*. 'Many of Dudley Pound's letters as First Sea Lord are missing. I found one in the PM's papers of which there is no copy in the Admiralty. Dudley Pound accepts responsibility for the loss of Prince of Wales and Repulse. Why? It wasn't true! Excessive loyalty to the PM I think! God knows, Dudley Pound had a difficult task but I am forced to the reluctant conclusion that my old CinC and FSL was not always quite straight in his dealings with men of our service'. Roskill letter of 30 December 1957, ADD 52563, Cunningham Papers, BL. Roskill's copy of the Pound letter is in ROSK 4/79, CCA. Roskill apparently did not know that Cunningham had burnt most of Pound's letters on taking over as First Sea Lord in October 1943. Brodhurst, Introduction, ix. So Cunningham was not being straight either!

131 Director of Plans minute of 29 September, ADM 116/4877, TNA.

132 This is also the line in the Naval Staff History. It states (p 2): 'It had originally been intended to include an aircraft carrier in the squadron but owing to the recent grounding of *Indomitable* none was available'. Battle Summary No 14, Loss of HM Ships *Prince of Wales* and *Repulse*, ADM 234/330, TNA. This is oddly phrased. *Prince of Wales* sailed from the United Kingdom on 25 October, but *Indomitable* did not go aground until nine days later on 3 November. If she was to join the force there was ample time to issue the relevant orders but this never happened. The History goes on to say that 'only the extreme urgency of the political situation' could justify continuing without a carrier. This is a blatant piece of *post facto* justification.

133 Arthur Nicholson, the most recent historian of Force Z, provides a good summary of the evidence here. *Hostages to Fortune, Winston Churchill and the Loss of the Prince of Wales and Repulse* (UK: Sutton Publishing Ltd, 2005), pp41–4.

134 Nicholson, quoting the Fleet Air Arm historian, David Hobbs, states *Indomitable* was originally due to complete work-up by 22 November and was then programmed to arrive at Gibraltar on 29 November. Nicholson, p41. For two first-hand accounts of *Indomitable*'s time in Kingston, the grounding and the work-up see Hugh Popham, *Sea Flight* (Seaforth Publishing, 2010), pp70–83 and Gordon Wallace, *Carrier Observer* (Airlife, 1993), pp44–50. For Marder's comments, see *Old Friends, New Enemies*, vol I, pp229–30.

135 Hansard records a secret session took place on 19 December but not the content. The text of the First Lord's statement and the prior Admiralty briefing notes are in ADM 1/11043, TNA. The carrier issue is dealt with at pp12 and 13 of the statement.

136 Annex II of COS (41) 727 of 7 December, 'Far East: United States – British – Dutch Staff Conversations', CAB 80/32, TNA.

137 PM minute M 265/53 dated 11 August 1953, ROSK 6/26, CCA.

138 Alexander wrote to the official historian Professor J R M Butler on 14 November 1952 responding to queries raised on behalf of Roskill. He stated: 'There was some difficulty because we had great arguments with the PM about air cover and Pound and I stood out against sending a squadron without a carrier. On [sic] pressure we agreed to try and speed up the "working up" of a new carrier just completed and on the understanding that after working up in the West Indies she would rendezvous with *Prince of Wales* in Cape Town. Unfortunately the carrier was stranded on a reef in the West Indies during fog and it was too late to go back on the promise

made to Australia and New Zealand'. In a postscript, Alexander suggested the carrier was *Indomitable*. This testimony supports the idea of informal soundings over *Indomitable*, but his other claims look dubious. Pound did not raise air cover as an issue, either during his August exchanges with the prime minister or at the Defence Committee sessions in October. No other Admiralty papers suggest either concern about carrier support for an eastern fleet or much determination to prioritise this. It is possible there was consideration given to expediting *Indomitable*'s work-up, but unless it was abandoned altogether she could never have reached Cape Town in time to join *Prince of Wales*. ROSK 6/26, CCA.

139 PREM 3/171/4, TNA.

140 Prime Minister minute to First Sea Lord of 23 November 1941, ADM 205/10, TNA.

141 Paragraph 10 of report, ADM 199/1149, TNA.

142 Cunningham, *A Sailor's Odyssey*, p279.

143 The primary Italian torpedo bomber was the Savoia-Marchetti tri-motor SM 79 Sparviero which had a maximum speed in 1941 of about 270mph and a range of around 1150 miles. The IJNAF G3M 'Nell' had a lower speed at 232mph but much greater range – up to 2365 miles.

144 Marder estimates a total of seventy-one IJNAF strike aircraft attacked the Force Z battleships on 10 December, *Old Friends, New Enemies*, vol I, pp467–74.

145 For a good description of Halberd, and comparative Royal Navy and Italian strengths, see Jack Greene and Alessandro Massignani, *The Naval War in the Mediterranean 1940–1943* (UK: Chatham Publishing, 2002), pp181–91.

146 H T Lenton. *Ark Royal* was probably the most operationally efficient carrier in the Royal Navy inventory at this time.

147 Middlebrook and Mahoney note the potential relevance of Halberd to the subsequent loss of Force Z at pp51–2 of their book *Battleship* partly because of the coincidental presence of *Prince of Wales*. However, they miss the point of a comparison between the two operations. While accepting the presence of a strong escort and a carrier were important factors in the defence, they suggest it demonstrated that the well-fought battleship still had little to fear from air attack. The real lesson was rather different. It was that a well-balanced task force, including integral fighter support and layered defence, could defend itself against quite heavy levels of air attack, but that without such layered defence, it would be at heavy risk.

148 Tennant saw Cunningham in Alexandria while en route back to the United Kingdom to report to the Admiralty on the Force Z disaster. Cunningham then recorded his views to Pound on 28 December. ADD 52561, Cunningham Papers, BL. Marder notes that, while there was much truth in Cunningham's judgement here, the IJN had, in fact, managed one co-ordinated attack. He could have added that they were also operating at much greater range than was customary in the Mediterranean and had experienced considerable difficulty in finding Force Z. *Old Friends, New Enemies*, vol I, p513. Cunningham's more general assessment of the high quality of Italian maritime air capability was quoted in chapter 5.

149 The reassessment of Italian naval capability provided by James Sadkovich, and already noted in Chapter 5, is relevant to the argument here. 'Understanding Defeat: Reappraising Italy's Role in World War II'.

150 See footnote 127 above.

151 For example, ATs Gleam 164 of 14 November and Gleam 166 of 19 November, both from BAD Washington, CAB 105/36, TNA, gave detailed and accurate summaries of current American strength in the Philippines and the timetable of planned reinforcements. Air strength was given as follows:
B-17: thirty-five in place, thirty-five to be delivered December, thirty in January and sixty-five in February.
P40 fighters: sixty-one in place, sixty-four en route and further ninety-five planned.
A-24 dive-bombers: fifty-two to be in place by 30 November.
Older aircraft: 135 in place.
B-24 bombers – to follow in early 1942.

152 Memorandum for the President dated 5 November 1941, Exhibit 16, Joint Committee on Investigation of Pearl Harbor, vol 14, p1061.

153 Minutes of the Joint Board Meeting of 3 November, Exhibit 16, Joint Committee of Investigation of Pearl Harbor Attack, vol 14, p1062.

154 Memorandum for the President of 27 November, Exhibit 17, Joint Committee of Investigation of Pearl Harbor Attack, vol 14, p1083.
155 This view perhaps reconciles Stark's letter of 23 September with the Joint Board view on 5 November.
156 Turner testimony, Hart Inquiry, Joint Committee of Investigation into Pearl Harbor, vol 26, pp263–87.
157 PREM 3/469, TNA.
158 Miller, p63.
159 JM 152, Political Strategy Prior to the Outbreak of War, part V, p12.
160 The conclusion to Marder's *Old Friends, New Enemies*, vol II, p548, has a variant of this argument. It states that, however feeble a deterrent Force Z represented, its despatch to Singapore was in part intended to create the nucleus of a multinational fleet to control the South China Sea and protect the Indies. Its power lay not only in its ability to operate independently, but also in its scope to rally the disparate forces, British, Dutch, and American, not least the substantial modern submarine striking power, already in the region. The Admiralty were indeed reaching towards this idea with their putative Eastern Fleet based forward at Singapore, even if it was never formally articulated.

Chapter 7 – The Deployment of Force Z and its Consequences: Inevitable Disaster?

1 For example, Haggie, Barnett, Murfett, Farrell and Willmott. Christopher Bell is a notable exception here. In both his article, 'The "Singapore Strategy" and the Deterrence of Japan: Winston Churchill, the Admiralty and the Dispatch of Force Z', and chapter 8 of his *Churchill and Sea Power*, he argues that a distinction should be drawn between 'Churchill's decision to place two capital ships at Singapore on the eve of war', and 'the subsequent decision, taken thousands of miles away', that resulted in the ships being caught off the coast of Malaya. He states that Churchill undeniably made their destruction possible, even probable, but not necessarily inevitable.
2 The best accounts here remain those in Marder, *Old Friends, New Enemies*, vol I, and Martin Middlebrook and Patrick Mahoney, *Battleship: The Loss of the Prince of Wales and the Repulse*. The latest research which demonstrates in detail why the first IJN torpedo hit proved fatal to *Prince of Wales* is by William H Garzke, Robert O Dulin and Kevin V Denlay, in 'Death of a Battleship: The Loss of HMS *Prince of Wales*, December 10 1941, A Marine Forensics Analysis of the Sinking'. Paper originally presented at the Royal Institute of Naval Architects in September 2009, updated in 2010 and 2012, and placed on www.pacificwrecks.com website.
3 For example, the views of Haggie, Marder and Barnett recorded at the end of this Chapter.
4 Brief for First Sea Lord dated 29 October, ADM 205/11, TNA.
5 Burt, *British Battleships*, p413.
6 AT to SO Force G of 22 November, CAB 122/9, TNA.
7 Record of 20 October meeting, CAB 69/8.
8 Pound minute of 28 August, Churchill, *The Grand Alliance*, appendix K.
9 CAB 65/24/2.
10 There is a copy in ROSK 4/79, CCA. The Naval Staff History, perhaps not entirely convincingly, explains this signal as follows: 'This went beyond the decision reached at the Defence Committee Meeting but was probably intended mainly to ensure that adequate administrative preparations were made for a not improbable move'. Battle Summary 14 (revised), Loss of HM Ships *Prince of Wales* and *Repulse*, p2, ADM 234/330, TNA.
11 First Sea Lord minute of 2 November, ADM 205/10, TNA.
12 ROSK 4/79, CCA, Cambridge. Roskill became obsessed with this issue. In a letter to Cunningham, dated 30 March 1953, he wrote: 'I have tried very hard to get WSC to come clean about ordering *Prince of Wales* and *Repulse* to Singapore against DP's repeated opposition. I am sure he approved the order but the Admiralty gave it.' Cunningham Papers, Add MS 52563, British Library.
13 ADM 205/10.
14 Record of the War Cabinet meeting that day in CAB 65/24/2, TNA.
15 Phillips signal to Admiralty of 6 November setting out proposed movements. Battle Summary No 14, 1955 version, appendix D, ADM 234/330.

16 Willis letter to Roskill dated 16 May 1953, ROSK 4/79, CCA. The brief refuelling stop in Freetown was on 5 November.
17 AT First Sea Lord to NOIC Simonstown, ADM 234/330, TNA.
18 AT Admiralty to SO Force G of 11 November, ADM 234/330, TNA.
19 Chapter 6.
20 Minute to Pound of 11 November, ADM 205/10, TNA.
21 Brief for First Sea Lord dated 29 October.
22 Willis letter to Roskill of 16 May 1953.
23 Middlebrook and Mahoney, *Battleship*, p68.
24 Letter, Grantham to Roskill of 3 February 1953, ROSK 4/79, CCA.
25 Goodenough letter to Roskill dated 8 May 1951, ROSK 4/79, CCA.
26 This is summarised by Ong Chit Chung, *Operation Matador*, pp224–8.
27 JIC (41) 439 of 18 November 1941, 'Japanese Intentions', CAB 81/105, TNA.
28 Ian Kershaw, *Fateful Choices: Ten Decisions that changed the World 1940–1941*, pp364–6 (London, Allen Lane, 2007).
29 First Sea Lord minute to Prime Minister of 18 November 1941, ADM 205/10, TNA.
30 Issued by GC&CS as report 098017 on 22 November. A second intercept was circulated as 098052 the following day. HW 12/270, TNA. Also NID report 00421 of 23 November, ADM 223/321, TNA.
31 Circulated by GC&CS as report 998240 on 27 November, also in HW 12/270.
32 Marder, vol I, pp391–2.
33 First Sea Lord minute to Prime Minister of 2 November, ADM 205/10, TNA.
34 'Some Opinions Concerning the War', summary of interviews given to American historian Gordon Prange in 1948, included in Donald M Goldstein and Katherine V Dillon, *The Pacific War Papers: Japanese Documents of World War II* (Washington: Potomac Books, 2004).
35 JIC (41) 439 of 18 November, 'Japan's Intentions', and JIC (41) 449 of 28 November, 'Possible Japanese Action', CAB 81/105, TNA.
36 A summary of the latest intelligence pointing to an attack on Thailand was sent by Commander-in-Chief Far East and Commander-in-Chief China on 30 November and is in ADM 199/1477, TNA. It is representative of the material available in FECB which the Joint Intelligence Committee could draw on. Keith Jeffery, *MI6*, pp574–5.
37 Ong Chit Chung, p228; Jeffery, p575.
38 Circulated as GC&CS report 095151, HW 12/270, TNA.
39 GC&CS report 098127, HW 12/270 and also NID 00429 of 25 November, ADM 223/321, both TNA.
40 GCHQ's post-war official history of HMS Anderson, HW 50/52, TNA.
41 Doig letter to Marder dated 20 October 1978, Doig papers, National Museum of the Royal Navy, Portsmouth.
42 Caesar 560 from Joint Military Staff in Washington of 28 November, CAB 122/73, TNA.
43 AT to Commander-in-Chief China of 29 November, ADM 199/1477, TNA.
44 Letter Goodenough to Roskill dated 8 May 1951, ROSK 4/79, CCA.
45 AT to SO Force G of 28 November, ADM 234/330, TNA.
46 Marder, vol I, p 499, quoting Godfrey's unpublished memoirs.
47 First Sea Lord report on loss of HM ships *Prince of Wales* and *Repulse*, ADM 199/1149, TNA.
48 First Sea Lord minute to Prime Minister of 28 August, appendix K of Churchill, *The Grand Alliance*.
49 Marder, *Old Friends, New Enemies*, vol I, p402, quoting a letter from Moore dated 23 June 1976.
50 AT First Sea Lord to SO Force G of 1 December and AT First Sea Lord to SO Force G of 3 December, both ADM 234/330, TNA.
51 JM 107, Malaya Invasion Naval Operations.
52 JM 152, Political Strategy Prior to the Outbreak of War, Part V, pp13–15.
53 Commander-in-Chief Eastern Fleet War Diary, ADM 223/494, TNA.
54 The first reference to this second deterrence goal seems to be the Admiralty briefing note prepared for the First Lord A V Alexander prior to his statement on Force Z at the secret session of Parliament on 19 December 1941. The briefing note and record of the speech are in ADM

1/11043, TNA. The two deterrence goals also appear in the First Sea Lord report on the loss of Force Z to the prime minister on 25 January 1942. ADM 199/1149, TNA. Several historians have quoted the deterrence goal in full from the First Sea Lord report, but none have suggested the second dimension was significant.

55 Battle Summary No 14, 1955 version, p9.

56 This is the date given by Layton in paragraph 21 of his 'Supplementary Report on Events in the Far East 1940-45', ADM 199/1472B, TNA.

57 Ong Chit Chung, pp228–31.

58 Commander-in-Chief Eastern Fleet War Diary, ADM 223/494, TNA.

59 This is demonstrated by the famous photograph showing these officers waiting with Phillips on the dockside for *Prince of Wales*'s arrival.

60 For background on this message, drawn from SIS archives, Keith Jeffery, *MI6*, pp576–7, and Henry C Clausen, *Pearl Harbor Final Judgement* (USA: Da Capo Press, 2001), pp113–14.

61 Jeffery, *MI6*, pp574–5.

62 Ong Chit Chung, pp228–9.

63 The National Security Agency monograph by Robert J Hanyok and David P Mowry, *West Wind Clear: Cryptology and the Winds Message Controversy – A Documentary History* (Center for Cryptologic History: US National Security Agency, 2008), p84, describes Clausen's efforts to clarify the sourcing of paragraph C. GC&CS acknowledged in 1945 that the primary source for this statement was a SIGINT report. The monograph concluded that the SIGINT report was a Japanese diplomatic message of 1 December from Tokyo to Hsinking China stating 'great care shall be taken not to antagonise Russia'.

64 COS 405th meeting of 2 December, Items 1 and 2, CAB 79/16, TNA. Michael Goodman in his official history agrees that, by end November, Joint Intelligence Committee papers conveyed 'the inevitability of war'. *The Official History of the Joint Intelligence Committee*, vol I, p104.

65 Jeffery, *MI6*, p 574, confirms this SIS material was copied to FECB.

66 GCHQ's post war assessment of 'war warning' intelligence, HW 50/52, TNA.

67 This earlier message from SIS Manila to Honolulu which survives in the SIS archives is dated 26 November. Jeffery, *MI6*, pp576–7.

68 Text of Admiralty signals given by Nicholson, *Hostages to Fortune*, p198.

69 Briefing for First Lord's 'secret session' statement on 19 December, ADM 1/11043, TNA.

70 Marder, vol I, pp404–5.

71 Goodenough letter to Roskill dated 8 May 1951, ROSK 4/79, CCA, Cambridge.

72 Dr Tom Lewis and Peter Ingman, *Carrier Attack Darwin 1942* (Avonmore Books, 2013).

73 *Prince of Wales* underwent a three-day docking on 4 December, Nicholson, *Hostages to Fortune*, p54. The nearest battleship dock otherwise was at Durban.

74 Letter to Roskill dated 8 May 1951. Goodenough ended this sentence with an exclamation mark conveying his incredulity.

75 Marder, vol I, p396.

76 Briefing for First Lord's 'secret session' statement on 19 December, ADM 1/11043, TNA.

77 ADM 223/494, TNA.

78 Marder, vol I, p413.

79 'Loss of HM Ships *Prince of Wales* and *Repulse*', Battle Summary 14, p8, ADM 234/330, TNA. Marder's judgement is almost a precise transliteration of the Staff History judgement.

80 'Loss of HMS *Prince of Wales* and HMS *Repulse*', Appendix, 25 January 1942, ADM 199/1149, TNA.

81 WIRs 76 of 2 August and 77 of 29 August. Chapter 5 refers.

82 Captain Kenneth Harkness, Chief of Intelligence Staff (COIS) FECB, told Marder in 1978 that he had no contact with either Phillips or his staff before the sailing of Force Z. Harkness, letter to Marder dated 11 July 1978. Arthur J Marder Papers, MS-F02, Special Collections and Archives, The UC Irvine Libraries, Irvine, California. Harkness also confirmed this in correspondence with Doig the same year. Doig papers. A separate letter in the Marder papers from the Head of the Air Section in FECB, Wing Commander R Chappell, to Harkness, dated 14 October 1978, states that the Royal Air Force Section were not consulted about the air threat by either Phillips or his staff until a request came from Brooke-Popham shortly before sailing. Marder referenced this correspondence in *Old Friends, New Enemies*, vol I, but also appears

to go against this evidence in footnote 73, p413, where he suggests Goodenough did meet Harkness, although he gives no source for this.

83 Ong Chit Chung, p229, quoting numerous documentary sources.
84 JM 107, p6.
85 Paper prepared for Marder, 'History of the Special Intelligence Organisation in the Far East' by Lt Cdr S W Francis, Marder papers.
86 Marder, footnote 75, p416.
87 Letters from Chappell, FECB Air Section to Harkness, COIS Singapore, dated 14 October 1978 and to Marder dated 6 December 1978. Marder papers. Chappell passed his assessment to Brooke-Popham before Force Z sailed and assumed it had been forwarded but could not confirm this. Chappell was eighty-one when he wrote to Marder and his health was failing. There is a risk his memory was failing also, but his information to Harkness and Marder was consistent and looks authentic. Harkness also claimed to recall the number of aircraft quoted by Chappell.
88 Letter to Marder of 23 November 1978.
89 Doig's claims are in note 2 of his paper 'Misfortune off Malaya' with his papers at the National Museum of the Royal Navy, Portsmouth. There are doubts over the accuracy of his account. It is not clear he understood the difference between the Type 96 and Betty or Type 1. He states that estimates of the performance of IJN torpedo aircraft were based on the assumption they would carry the 24in Long Lance torpedo. The Long Lance was never adapted to aerial use and its weight would have ruled this out as a practical proposition. The IJN aerial torpedo was the 18in Type 91. It is also doubtful the Royal Navy had any intelligence on the Long Lance at this stage of the war. There must be suspicion, therefore, that Doig's comments reflect later knowledge and hindsight.
90 Marder judges Chappell's intelligence was probably not passed on. Footnote 105, pp433–434, vol I. Middlebrook and Mahoney, p304, note 'hearsay evidence' that the 'Intelligence Officer' on Phillips's staff found, on his return to Singapore after the sinkings, that the naval staff ashore had known of the presence of Japanese torpedo bombers in Indochina while Force Z had been at sea, but had not thought it necessary to send a warning signal. They could not follow this up because the officer concerned was dead. Phillips's SO (I) was Commander J R M Laird. He would have been the natural link to FECB. However, Marder claims, though without giving a source, that Goodenough insisted to Laird that he would deal with FECB. Marder, footnote 73, p413, vol I. Marder suggests Goodenough did see Harkness the COIS. Harkness is adamant he did not.
91 Captain Bell post-action report dated 10 December, ADM 199/1149, TNA.
92 Marder, pp415–17, for discussion of the range of attacking aircraft. Goodenough told Roskill in his letter of 8 May 1951 that Kuantan, where Force Z was ultimately attacked, was judged, at 450 miles from Indochina, to be out of effective air strike range. ROSK 4/79, CCA.
93 'Despatch on the Far East by Air Chief Marshal Sir Robert Brooke-Popham', dated 8 September 1942, para 110, WP (42) 403, CAB 66/28/33, TNA.
94 Chapter 5.
95 The relevant paper carries Darvall's initials but is undated. It must, however, post-date the move into Indochina so was probably written in September or October. The fighter was clearly the Zero. Chapter 5.
96 Goodenough to Roskill.
97 The NID 4 version of this report, NID 4/23 – 'Naval Situation in the Far East: Situation up to 1 December' – is in WO 208/1080, TNA. Further background on British knowledge of IJN dispositions in the immediate pre-war period is in the NID history prepared in 1946 by Hillgarth and Barrett. This includes a detailed picture of the respective estimates in NID 4 and FECB and the interaction between them. Hillgarth and Barrett memorandum, 'History of the Far East and Pacific War', 'Pearl Harbor and the Loss of Prince of Wales and Repulse', ADM 223/494, TNA.
98 Roskill gives the composition of the Southern Force at appendix L of War at Sea, vol II.
99 For the American input, see Smith, The Emperor's Codes, p96.
100 WO 208/653, TNA.
101 JM 107, p 4 and 12.
102 Marder, p418, quoting Captain of the Fleet L H Bell.

103 Roskill, *Churchill and the Admirals*, p203. For Marder's positive view of Layton, see 'An Unconventional Officer: Layton', *Old Friends, New Enemies*, vol II, pp6–10. Marder relied heavily on a portrait of Layton prepared for him by Doig, who was Layton's secretary for a total of nine years, including all his time in the Far East. His note 'Geoffrey Layton' is in the Doig papers at the National Museum of the Royal Navy, Portsmouth.

104 'Remarks on the Operations in Malaya and the Defence of Singapore', written in early 1942, which is in ADM 199/1472A. He later expanded on some points in his 'Supplementary Report on Events in the Far East 1940–45', dated 25 April 1947, which is in ADM 199/1472B. Both in TNA.

105 Marder, vol I, p488, and vol II, p20.

106 Doig papers.

107 Doig's 'Geoffrey Layton', section II, and Marder, vol II, p8.

108 James Leutze, *A Different Kind of Victory*, p196.

109 Marder, pp393–4.

110 Goodenough's letter to Roskill of 8 May 1951.

111 AT Senior Officer Force G to Admiralty of 1 December, ADM 234/330, TNA, and Marder, p 393.

112 Marder, p393.

113 Paragraphs 13–19 of his 'Supplementary Report'.

114 Brooke-Popham despatch, paragraph 107, CAB 66/28/33.

115 Doig letter to Marder dated 20 October 1978, Doig papers, Royal Naval Museum, Portsmouth.

116 Harkness letter to Marder dated 11 July 1978. Harkness confirmed these points to Doig during their correspondence in 1978, Doig papers.

117 Report of Captain L Bell, Captain of the Fleet, ADM 199/1149, TNA.

118 Hugh Sebag-Montefiore, *Enigma: The Battle for the Code* (London: Weidenfeld and Nicolson, 2000), chapter 12.

119 AIR 23/1873 and ADM 1/11926, TNA.

120 Layton, 'Remarks on the operations in Malaya and defence of Singapore', paragraph 14.

121 Pound letter dated 15 September 1941, and earlier in signals such as AT 927 of 13 May and AT 666 of 4 April, both from Admiralty to Commander-in-Chief China. ADM 116/4877, TNA.

122 Commander-in-Chief Far East tel of 1 October, JP (41) 816 of 7 October.

123 Middlebrook and Mahoney, *Battleship*, pp105–6, and Marder, vol I, p414.

124 Marder, pp423, 488.

125 Letter of 18 December 1941 to Pound, Layton papers, British Library.

126 The concept for Matador, the reasons it was not finally implemented, and the lost opportunity it represented, is discussed exhaustively by Ong Chit Chung.

127 Layton's expectations of the US Navy Asiatic Fleet and his subsequent disappointment are set out in paragraphs 25 and 26 of his 'Supplementary Report' in ADM 199/1472B, TNA. Doig also emphasises this in his 'Geoffrey Layton', Section II.

128 The text of ADB-2 is in CAB 122/8.

129 Naval Staff History, ADM 234/384, TNA.

130 Leutze, *A Different Kind of Victory*, pp211–21, for an account of these shifts in policy and plans.

131 AT BAD to Admiralty 373 of 1 December, CAB 122/9, TNA.

132 Layton 'Supplementary Report', ADM 199/1472B.

133 Hart completed a detailed record 'Report of the Conference in Manila 6 December 1941', which is in the Hart Papers at the US Navy Operational Archives. His summary signal to Stark and Stark's reply are in the Joint Committee on the Investigation of the Pearl Harbor Attack, part 4, pp1930–36. This was presented to the committee during their session with Turner as Head of War Plans at the time. Turner provided some additional and useful context. Leutze includes relevant extracts from Hart's diary in his account at pp224–5 of his biography. Marder, Cowman, and Leutze provide the best accounts of the conference, but none are comprehensive.

134 Ghormley letter to Pound of 7 November, ADM 205/9.

135 Leutze, *A Different Kind of Victory*, p225.

136 Chapter 6 refers.

137 Admiral Hart's summary telegram of this meeting sent to Admiral Stark and passed by him to

Pound is in the *Joint Committee on the Investigation of the Pearl Harbor Attack*, vol IV, pp1930–6.

138 Leutze, *A Different Kind of Victory*, p225.

139 For Hart's interest in and handling of intelligence, Leutze, p207.

140 Leutze describes the controversy here at pp236–7. For Doig's view, 'Geoffrey Layton', section II, p1.

141 Text of signals in Nicholson, *Hostages to Fortune*, p208 (no 37), and p213 (no 46).

142 Leutze, p226.

143 For MacArthur's attitude, see Bartsch, *December 8 1941, MacArthur's Pearl Harbor*, p193. Also Costello, *Days of Infamy*, p148.

144 GCHQ's post-war assessment of 'war warning' intelligence, HW 50/52, TNA.

145 For the Somerville incident, Roskill, *Churchill and the Admirals*, pp169–70. For Wake-Walker, Ludovic Kennedy, *Pursuit: The Sinking of the Bismarck* (London: William Collins, 1974), p224.

146 Nicholson, *Hostages to Fortune*, p202, no 19.

147 Chiefs of Staff note to the Prime Minister of 6.15pm on 6 December and the Prime Minister's note clarifying potential rules of engagement after consultation with the Americans of 12.30pm on 7 December. PREM 3/158/6, TNA.

148 Nicholson, *Hostages to Fortune*, p206, no 28.

149 Prime Minister note of 12.30pm on 7 December, PREM 3/158/6.

150 PREM 3/158/6.

151 Chiefs of Staff note of 7 December returned without being shown to the Prime Minister, PREM 3/158/6, TNA.

152 Prime Minister minute M 265/53 dated 11 August 1953 to naval assistant Commodore Allen, ROSK 6/26, CCA. This minute responded to Roskill's initial draft of the *War at Sea*, vol I, which claimed Churchill had overruled the Admiralty in demanding the deployment of *Prince of Wales* to Singapore.

153 ADM 199/1149, TNA.

154 ADM 1/11043, TNA.

155 Willis was Commander-in-Chief South Atlantic at this time and became deputy to Somerville as Commander-in-Chief Eastern Fleet in early 1942. As noted in footnote 22, he met Phillips at Freetown during *Prince of Wales*'s passage out. Marder states (vol I, p499) that Willis advised Phillips to withdraw westward to Ceylon in the event of war. Willis's account written in 1966/67 stated that he told Phillips 'he must avoid getting caught' at Singapore since it was 'not a fleet's job to defend its base'. He should therefore 'disappear among the islands'. The phrase 'disappear among the islands' is convenient, especially with hindsight, but also meaningless. Force Z had to base somewhere and if not Singapore, that meant Ceylon or Darwin. Willis papers, IWM.

156 Marder summarises the various positions taken by the critics and the wider arguments around Phillips's decision to intervene on 8 December at pp498–504 of vol I.

157 Letter to Pound dated 18 December, Layton papers, British Library.

158 Marder, *Old Friends, New Enemies*, vol I, pp429–30, quoting a 1978 letter from Bell.

159 ADM 1/11043, TNA.

160 Marder, vol I, pp462–3.

161 Marder, vol I, pp480–1.

162 Middlebrook and Mahoney.

163 Nicholson, pp150–1.

164 Masatake Okumiya and Jiro Horikoshi, *Zero* (USA: Ballantine, 1957), p79; Middlebrook and Mahoney, p143.

165 There is a summary in the appendix to the First Sea Lord's report on the loss of Force Z, ADM 199/1149.

166 Hillgarth and Barrett memorandum, ADM 223/494.

167 Marder, vol I, pp494–506.

168 Roskill, *Churchill and the Admirals*, pp198–201, and *The Navy at War 1939–1945*. Roskill was not consistent in his view of Phillips. Writing to Phillips's son in 1962, he stood by the claim that had played down the dangers of air attack during the Norwegian campaign, but accepted that 'by the time he got to Singapore, he was fully alive to the realities of the air threat'. ROSK 4/79, CCA. Also, Middlebrook and Mahoney, pp304–5; Barnett, pp411–12.

169 Marder gave a detailed and balanced picture of the evolution of Phillips's views on the air threat at sea in vol I, pp386–8. He drew on key witnesses such as Goodenough and Willis to demonstrate that by 1941, Phillips held no illusions about the serious risk posed by air attack. Martin Stephen in *Scapegoat*, chapter 3, also insists Phillips was realistic about the air threat. Although a distinctly partisan supporter of Phillips, his summary here is fair, although he does not add significantly to Marder.

170 Bartsch, p193.

171 ADM 199/1149 and Marder, vol I, p503.

172 Middlebrook and Mahoney, p306, argue that if Phillips had called for air support immediately after the 1015 sighting, fighters would have arrived before the first fatal torpedo attack on *Prince of Wales*.

173 See AT Admiralty to BAD Washington of 16 December, CAB 122/164, TNA, for status of all British Empire naval forces at Singapore and east of Cape Town on that date. They comprised battleships, *Revenge* and *Royal Sovereign*, five heavy cruisers, six modern 6in cruisers, nine older cruisers suitable only for trade protection, and nine destroyers. Roskill provides a summary of ships available in December, *War at Sea*, vol I, p562.

174 CAB 105/20, TNA.

175 Personal signal First Sea Lord to Commander-in-Chief Mediterranean dated 0112A of 10 December 1941.

176 ADD MS 52567, Cunningham Papers, BL.

177 'Future British Naval Strategy', COS (41) 277 (O) of 14 December 1941, CAB 80/60, TNA.

178 CAB 105/20, TNA.

179 SPENAVO to OPNAV of 18 December, CAB 122/164, TNA.

180 Roskill, *War at Sea*, vol I, p569.

181 Roskill, *War at Sea*, vol II, pp2–22.

182 Davis had been deputy director to Terry in Operations Division during the autumn. In February 1942 Plans Division was still headed by Captain Gerald Bellars. The deputy director was now Captain D H Everett. Davis was one of four assistant directors. Charles Lambe, the previous deputy director, would shortly succeed Bellars. Navy Lists for 1941/42.

183 Bellars confidential report, ADM 196/92/202, TNA.

184 Marder, *Old Friends, New Enemies*, vol I, p498. Marder claims the DOD (F) was Captain A D Nicholl. This is not correct. He was serving at sea in the Mediterranean as captain of the light cruiser *Penelope* between April 1941 and June 1942 and only became DOD (F) on 27 August 1942. Terry was DOD (F) from 24 March 1941 until August 1942. www.unithistories.com/officersRN.

185 The inquiry reports, along with Pound's covering note for the Admiralty Board dated 25 January 1942, are in ADM 199/1149, TNA.

186 Pound letter to Cunningham of 29 January 1942, ADD 52561, Cunningham Papers, BL.

187 These writings by Davis comprise three elements. First, his correspondence with Roskill where three letters are relevant, one dated 1962, and two from 1975 in ROSK 4/79, CCA. Secondly, a paper Davis prepared in retirement 'Loss of *Prince of Wales* and *Repulse* 10th December 1941' which he sent to Roskill with his letter to him of 7 April 1975, and which is also available in ROSK 4/79, CCA. Finally, there is Davis's unpublished autobiography included with his papers deposited with CCA under WDVS 1-3. This autobiography focuses heavily on his period with the naval staff.

188 Autobiography, p271.

189 Davis, Loss of *Prince of Wales* paper, p1.

190 Davis autobiography, p258.

191 Davis autobiography, p273.

192 Davis autobiography, p255.

193 Davis was deputy director of Operations (Foreign) in autumn 1941, moving to assistant director in Plans around the turn of the year. Navy Lists 1941/42.

194 Davis, Loss of *Prince of Wales* paper, pp1–2. Davis's phrase here 'hostage to fortune' provided the title for Arthur Nicholson's recent book on Force Z.

195 Marder, vol I, p520.

196 Barnett, *Engage the Enemy More Closely*, p421.

197 Haggie, p208.
198 John Winton, *Cunningham*, pp239–40.
199 Stanley Woodburn Kirby, *The War Against Japan*, vol I, chapter 27, 'Retrospect'.
200 This is Marder's view, vol I, p506.
201 Roskill, *The Navy at War 1939–1945* (London: Collins, 1960), p189.

Chapter 8 – The Defence of the Indian Ocean in 1942

1 War Memoirs of Admiral Sir Algernon Willis, IWM. Willis was at this time second in command to Somerville.
2 Arthur Marder, *Old Friends, New Enemies*, vol II, chapters 4 and 5, is the notable exception.
3 JP (41) 1072, 'Far East Policy', attached to COS (41) 428th of 19 December, CAB 79/16, TNA.
4 August 1940 Far East appreciation and COS (41) 152 (O) of 28 July, 'Far East Defence Arrangements'.
5 COS (41) 280 (O) of 20 December, 'Far East Policy', CAB 80/60, TNA.
6 Vincent O'Hara and Enrico Cernuschi, 'Frogmen against a Fleet: The Italian Attack on Alexandria 18/19 December 1941', *US Naval War College Review*, 68:3 (Summer 2015). Also Barnett, *Engage the Enemy More Closely*, pp376–7.
7 James Sadkovich, 'Understanding Defeat: Reappraising Italy's Role in World War II', p49.
8 Both Colombo and Trincomalee had docks able to accommodate cruisers, but with the loss of Singapore, there was no dock capable of taking battleships or carriers east of Durban. Colombo received an Admiralty floating dock to support capital ships, newly constructed in Bombay and designated AFD 39, in spring 1944. Sydney received a capital ship dock in 1945. D K Brown provides details of the large docks available to the Royal Navy in *Nelson to Vanguard*, appendix 9. Also Marder, *Old Friends, New Enemies*, vol II, p141.
9 Peter Doling, *From Port T to RAF Gan*, chapters 3 and 4.
10 Although the chiefs of staff agreed this transfer in December, only twenty Beauforts were available in the Middle East on 12 March, COS (42) 81st of 12 March, CAB 79/19, TNA.
11 COS (42) 66 (O) of 18 March, 'Reinforcements for India and Ceylon', CAB 80/61, TNA.
12 JP (42) 147 of 16 February, 'Far East Policy', CAB 79/18, TNA.
13 Commander-in-Chief Eastern Fleet to Admiralty of 17 February 1942, CAB 121/729, TNA.
14 Dr Stephen Bullard, *Japanese Army Operations in the South Pacific Area: New Britain and Papua Campaigns 1942–1943*. Chapter 3 summarises the debates within imperial general headquarters between December 1941 and April 1942 on the goals of phase 2 operations.
15 COS (42) 56th of 19 February and 63rd of 25th February, CAB 79/18, TNA. AT 1228A of 6 March to Commander-in-Chief Eastern Fleet relayed subsequent instructions that all Hurricanes were to be off-loaded. ADM 223/867, TNA. Marder claimed that Vice Admiral Sir Geoffrey Layton, now Commander-in-Chief Ceylon, unloaded the Hurricanes on his own initiative but this is not correct, vol II, p126.
16 AT 1749A of 13 March 1942 to Commander-in-Chief Eastern Fleet. ADM 223/867, TNA.
17 *Germany and the Second World War*, vol VI, pp121–2.
18 JP (42) 376 of 8 April, 'Relation of Strategy in the Middle East and India', CAB 79/20, TNA.
19 JP (42) 413 of 18 April, 'Indian Ocean: Strategy in Certain Eventualities', CAB 79/20, and JIC (42) 141 of 18 April, 'Japan's Intentions', CAB 79/20, both in TNA.
20 Letter from Commander Coleridge, JSM Washington, to Joint Planning Staff dated 9 September 1942, CAB 122/218, TNA.
21 See three recent high-profile one-volume histories of the Second World War: Andrew Roberts, *Storm of War*; Max Hastings, *All Hell Let Loose*, and Anthony Beevor, *The Second World War*. All mention Middle East oil in passing. Roberts admits it was 'critical'. None of them explains precisely why it was important, why it was such a preoccupation for the British chiefs of staff, and whether their concerns were valid.
22 COS (42) 105th meeting, item 10, CAB 79/20, TNA.
23 COS (42) 281 of 28 May 1942, CAB 80/36, TNA.
24 Production from the Middle East oilfields was 11.6 million tons in calendar year 1942 and 12.9 million tons in 1943. D J Payton-Smith, *Oil: A Study of Wartime Policy and Administration* (London: HMSO, 1971), table 46, p454.

25   COS (42) 352 of 21 July 1942, circulated to the War Cabinet as WP (42) 338 of 4 August, CAB 66/27/8, TNA.
26   COS (42) 199 (O) of 8 July 1942, Memorandum by the First Sea Lord, 'Oil Denial Schemes in the Middle East and Persia', CAB 121/658, TNA.
27   D J Payton-Smith, chapter 11, p249.
28   Clay Blair, *Hitler's U-boat War*, vol I, appendix 17. Blair notes that these losses would be easily recovered the following year. Not only did tanker sinkings fall steadily from the mid-point of 1942, but American and British shipyards together completed 245 new tankers, totalling 2,031,000 tons, in 1943.
29   D J Payton-Smith, pp343–7 and table 28.
30   WP (42) 372 of 23 August, PREM 3/76A/12, TNA.
31   The information and statistics in this paragraph are drawn from the *US Official History of the US Army in World War II, The Middle East Theater, The Persian Corridor and Aid to Russia*, by T H Vail Motter (US Army Center of Military History, Library of Congress, 1952), especially appendix A. Figures for deliveries through Persia in 1942 are from the United States. The total tonnage of United States aid via this route for that year (all categories) was 705,259 tons, while the United Kingdom and Canada contributed just 19,759 tons, ie about 2.8 per cent. It is not clear how much of their tonnage was weapons.
32   Joan Beaumont, *Comrades in Arms: British Aid to Russia, 1941–1945* (London: Davis-Poynter, 1980), p140.
33   The first United States shipment on the Persian route arrived in November 1941. US Army History, *Persian Corridor*, p5.
34   These challenges are described in the companion volume of the US Army History – *Global Logistics and Strategy 1940–1943*, by Richard M Leighton and Robert W Coakley, pp566–87. 128 ships arrived in Russia via the Arctic route in the first half of 1942. Following the PQ17 disaster in July, there was only a single convoy PQ18 over the next five months, which delivered twenty-seven ships in September after losing thirteen from forty sailed. Two convoys in December delivered a further thirty ships without loss. Traffic therefore virtually halted for a critical period. Roskill, *War at Sea*, vol III, part II, appendix R, Statistics of the Arctic Convoys 1941–1945, table A, 'Eastbound'.
35   Alexander Hill, *The Great Patriotic War of the Soviet Union, 1941–45* (London: Routledge, 2009), chapter 8, table 8.5, quoting figures from the Russian State Archives. Weapons shipments through Persia were approximately twice those by the Arctic route in 1943. This reflected the suspension of Arctic convoys in the summer months that year as well.
36   I C B Dear and M R D Foot, *The Oxford Companion to World War II*, p951, USSR, table 2.
37   Figures interpolated from shipment data at p484 of the US Army History, Persian Corridor. They have been crosschecked with those provided by Hubert Van Tuyll, in *Feeding the Bear: American Aid to the Soviet Union, 1941–1945* (Connecticut, USA: Greenwood Press, 1989), table 30, pp52–6, 171. The figures relate to supplies despatched. A significant proportion would not have reached the Russians for actual deployment until well into 1943.
38   Admiralty Notes on the Mediterranean Effort 1939–1945, CAB 106/615, TNA. The United States Army History figures mention British and Canadian shipments via Persia but give no details.
39   David Edgerton, *Britain's War Machine: Weapons, Resources and Experts in the Second World War* (London: Allen Lane, 2011), chapter 6; Beaumont, *Comrades in Arms*, p153.
40   Van Tuyll, *Feeding the Bear*, p56.
41   Chris Bellamy, *Absolute War: Soviet Russia in the Second World War* (London: Macmillan, 2007), pp420–3, 468–73. He argues that, although lend-lease only added about 5 per cent to Soviet resources in 1942 and perhaps 10 per cent in 1943, it may still have been crucial in enabling Russia to hold on. Interestingly, he downplays the significance of the Persia route (p422), suggesting it was much less important than the north Russia route. This paragraph shows that the opposite was the case. Mark Harrison's figures for Soviet production suggest the contribution of lend-lease to the specific military sector in 1942 was higher than 5 per cent. 'The USSR and Total War: Why didn't the Soviet Economy collapse in 1942?', Warwick Economic Research Papers, No 603 (University of Warwick, 2001). A report from the

Commander-in-Chief German Navy to the Führer dated 13 April 1942 highlighted the potential significance of the Persian supply route. Supplies here would go to the southern front and would make operations in the Caucasus more difficult. Quoted at p5 of US Army History.

42 JP (42) 338 of 30 March, 'Defence of Australia', CAB 79/20, TNA.

43 On 26 March the Chief of Air Staff believed there were sixty-eight fighters available in Ceylon, mainly Hurricanes, but some Fleet Air Arm Fulmars, COS (42) 96th of 26 March, CAB 79/19, TNA.

44 COS tel to Commander-in-Chief India and SO Force V of 18 March, COS (42) 66 (O) of 18 March, CAB 80/61, TNA.

45 JP (42) 338.

46 EDS Appreciation 10, pp42-3, CAB 146/18, TNA.

47 Discussion on 'Ceylon' between Cabinet Office Historical Section and Japanese War History Institute in Tokyo in September 1966. CAB 106/180, TNA.

48 For a summary of the debates within the Japanese military leadership over possible 'second phase' operations (ie, follow up to the successful occupation of the Netherlands East Indies), including specific options for the Indian Ocean and Ceylon: Marder, vol II, pp86-7; John B Lundstrom, *The First South Pacific Campaign* (Annapolis, USA: Naval Institute Press, 2014), chapter 6; H P Willmott, *The Barrier and the Javelin*, pp46-53; Captain Toshikazu Ohmae, 'Japanese Operations in the Indian Ocean', in David C Evans, *The Japanese Navy in World War II* (Annapolis: Naval Institute Press, 1986), p109; Hiroyuki Agawa, *The Reluctant Admiral: Yamamoto and the Imperial Japanese Navy* (Kodansha International Ltd, 2000); and Gordon Prange, *Miracle at Midway* (McGraw Hill, 1982), pp14-16. Lundstrom, whose first edition was published in 1976, with the updated paperback version in 2014, was the first historian to draw on the Japanese official war history Senshi Sosho. Willmott provides the most detailed account and analysis but has limited information on sources. The evolution of Japanese thinking regarding phase 2 operations is also described in chapter 3 of Dr Stephen Bullard's Senshi Sosho translation, *Japanese Army Operations in the South Pacific Area: New Britain and Papua Campaigns 1942-1943*, referenced earlier.

49 *Fading Victory: The Diary of Admiral Matome Ugaki*, ed Donald M Goldstein and Katherine V Dillon (Annapolis USA: Naval Institute Press, 1991), entries for 20-22 February 1942.

50 1948 interview with Gordon Prange, mentioned in 'Some Opinions Concerning the War', in Goldstein and Dillon, *The Pacific War Papers*.

51 Prange, p16.

52 Japanese Monograph 113, 'Task Force Operations' describes the objectives and conduct of Operation C. It was produced by the US Office of Military History immediately after the war, drawing on captured Japanese records and interviews with Japanese personnel, including Captain Toshikazu Ohmae. Ohmae states that the combined fleet had already decided on a limited fleet operation in the Indian Ocean, centred on a mass carrier strike on Ceylon, when it was war-gamed between 20-22 February. The executive order to proceed followed on 9 March. However, Willmott and Prange, the latter drawing on 1964 interviews with two of the key IJN planners involved, Captain Kameto Kurishima and Captain Yasuji Watanabe, insist that the war games, which included senior IJA representatives, were still focused on a more ambitious scheme, including a landing on Ceylon.

53 H P Willmott, *The Barrier and the Javelin*.

54 Personal signal First Sea Lord to King of 3 April, PREM 3/163/8, TNA. Brooke's claim is in his diary entry for 6 April. Alanbrooke, Field Marshall Lord, edited by Alex Danchev and Daniel Todman, *War Diaries 1939-1945*, (London: Weidenfeld and Nicolson, 2001).

55 ADM 223/259, TNA.

56 Marder provided a comprehensive, often vivid, account of Somerville's qualities, his reaction to the appointment, the limitations of his fleet and thoughts about how he should operate in *Old Friends, New Enemies*, vol II, chapter 4.

57 Davis memoir, p246.

58 Details of the fleet at this date are in COS (42) 66 (O) of 18 March, CAB 80/61, TNA. *Valiant* was not in reality ready until August.

59 For example, Roskill, Marder, Barnett, Murfett and Willmott.

60 Vice Admiral Sir Kaye Edden, in his paper written for Marder in 1977, described the Eastern

Fleet as little more than a 'rabble' when Somerville took over. Edden, paragraph 51, SMVL 8, CCA, Cambridge.

61 Marder, vol II, p113. The fifty-seven strike aircraft included eleven Swordfish in *Hermes*. The remainder were Albacores.

62 The lack of experience of the aircrews and low operational efficiency of the carriers is explained in an Admiralty minute to the prime minister of mid-April, PREM 3/163/8, TNA.

63 Marder, vol II, p113. Marder drew on the testimony of Vice Admiral Sir Algernon Willis, who commanded the battle-fleet for Somerville.

64 COS (42) 66 (O) of 18 March, 'Reinforcements for India and Ceylon', has an overall fighter strength of sixty-eight Hurricanes and seventeen Fleet Air Arm Fulmars, and a strike/recce force of twenty-four Blenheims, twenty-four Swordfish/Albacore, and nine Catalinas. Combinedfleet.com (posting 'Operation C' started by Rob Stuart on 1 December 2008, under forum 'Battles') has slightly different figures for the end of March sourced from Royal Navy and Royal Air Force station and squadron records. It summarises the land-based forces as comprising forty-seven Hurricane IIs, forty Fulmar II, two Martlets, fourteen Blenheims, sixteen Swordfish, and twelve Catalinas. Not all were serviceable. The Catalinas were a mix of Royal Air Force, Royal Canadian Air Force and Dutch. Overall fighter strength is about the same, at least eighty-five aircraft, but the strike component is smaller than in the chiefs of staff memorandum.

65 Somerville letter to First Sea Lord of 11 March, SMVL/8, CCA, Cambridge.

66 AT to Commander-in-Chief Ceylon and SO Force V of 19 March, REDW 2/8, CCA, Cambridge. SO (Senior Officer) Force V was Somerville en route to the Indian Ocean in the carrier *Formidable*.

67 The captain of *Dorsetshire*, Augustus Agar VC, described Somerville showing him 'a personal cypher message' from the First Sea Lord, in which the latter strongly advised that Somerville was not to allow his fleet to become engaged with anything except inferior forces until the Eastern Fleet could be reinforced. Agar's autobiography quoted in Michael Tomlinson, *The Most Dangerous Moment* (London: William Kimber, 1976), pp81–2.

68 History of HMS *Anderson*, chapter 4, p5, HW 4/25, TNA. This states that the first British decrypts of JN 25B operational messages were achieved by FECB on 4 January 1942 before departure from Singapore. Once re-established at Colombo, further progress was made with JN 25B recoveries, in co-operation with the US Navy Station Cast team at Corregidor, until the latter was evacuated to Melbourne in Australia. The official GC&CS post-war history, 'Organisation and Evolution of Japanese Naval Sigint Part VI, Production and Use of Sigint in the Early Part of the War, December 1941–1942', p6, in HW 50/59, TNA, confirms that FECB achieved some decryption of JN 25B operational messages during the six months it was in use from December 1941 to May 1942. John Prados, *Combined Fleet Decoded*, p215, states that Station Cast achieved their first decrypt of a JN 25B operational message on 8 December 1941. This may be correct but p20 of the more authoritative work by Frederick Parker, *A Priceless Advantage: US Navy Communications and the Battles of Coral Sea, Midway and the Aleutians* (Center for Cryptologic History, US National Security Agency, 1993), drawing on National Security Agency records, has the main American breakthrough into JN 25B in early February. Prados states that the US Navy could decrypt about 10 per cent of JN 25B messages by the beginning of May 1942 (p305). Parker does not give a figure, but suggests that by April it was higher than this, with decrypted messages often circulated within six hours of receipt. In his *Naval War College Review* article 'The Silent War against the Japanese Navy', Captain Duane D Whitlock states that by late May, when JN 25B coverage was lost, the US Navy was intercepting 60 per cent of JN 25B traffic and reading 40 per cent. However, for traffic read, content actually recovered only averaged 10–15 per cent. Furthermore, the IJN never despatched complete operational plans by radio. The Anderson history acknowledges that the United States achieved a higher volume of decrypts than the British. The GC&CS history, Parker and Prados all agree that all JN 25 coverage was lost when the Japanese switched to JN 25C on 25 May.

69 GC&CS official history 'Organisation and Evolution of Japanese Naval Sigint Part VI', HW 50/59, TNA.

70 John Prados, p274, describes a wider range of intercepts than HW 50/59. The picture presented to Somerville on 28 March drew on several decrypts relating to forthcoming Indian Ocean

operations from both FECB, the US Navy SIGINT team at Station Hypo in Pearl Harbor, and the new Cast organisation in Melbourne now renamed Belconnen. By this time Anderson, Hypo and Melbourne were linked by a dedicated communications network for sharing intercept material and decryption techniques. Parker, *A Priceless Advantage*, p12.

71 'Organisation and Evolution of Japanese Naval Sigint', p5. Somerville Pocket Diary entry for 29 March, item 229, The Somerville Papers, Navy Records Society, 1995.

72 Commander-in-Chief Eastern Fleet Zymotic signal 0626Z (probably 1226 Ceylon time) to Admiralty of 29 March 1941, ADM 223/867, TNA. 'Zymotic' was a security classification indicating sensitive SIGINT material.

73 Discussion between Cabinet Office and Japanese historians, Tokyo September 1966, 'Ceylon', CAB 106/180, TNA.

74 JM 113, pp64, 68.

75 The presence of the 'battleship covering force' proved correct but is not mentioned in the 29 March Zymotic signal.

76 Commander-in-Chief Eastern Fleet to Admiralty of 11 April, REDW 2/8, CCA, Cambridge. Also Battle Summary No 15, ADM 234/331; Commander-in-Chief Eastern Fleet Report of Proceedings dated 13 April, ADM 199/429; both in TNA, and Marder, vol II, pp117–18. Copies of the Reports of Proceedings for the Eastern Fleet for most of 1942 are at www.naval-history.net.

77 Chapter 5, footnotes 23 and 25, show that accurate performance data for the three primary IJN carrier aircraft, and their armament, was available to NID by December 1941. Somerville and his staff had ample time to absorb this material before *Formidable* sailed from the United Kingdom in mid-February, and copies of relevant intelligence publications would have been held on board. Details of the IJN carrier aircraft were available to the Royal Air Force squadrons defending Ceylon. The logbook of Flying Officer Robert Mayes, a pilot with 261 Hurricane squadron, based at China Bay, states that Trincomalee was raided on 9 April by '50+ Navy 97s and 50+ Navy O's'. Japanese records (JM 113, p77) confirm that these aircraft identifications were correct, although the actual numbers deployed were ninety-one Type 97s and thirty-eight Zero fighters. Mayes's logbook kindly provided by his daughter, Mrs Felicity Stribley.

78 John B Lundstrom, *The First South Pacific Campaign* (Annapolis, USA: Naval Institute Press, 2014), chapter 9.

79 NID LC Report No 136 of 1 March 1942, ADM 205/13, TNA.

80 WIRs No 105 of 13 March and 106 of 20 March, ADM 223/153, TNA. These reports did not get the composition quite right, but their estimate of overall strength was good. WIR 106 also reported (presumably from traffic analysis) that either *Kaga* or *Akagi* was returning to Japan. This was *Kaga*, which had engine trouble.

81 The most recent relevant Joint Intelligence Committee assessment was JIC (42) 70 (O) of 3 March, 'Defence of Ceylon', CAB 79/19, TNA. This anticipated Pearl Harbor-type raids and judged the Japanese could deploy three *Kongo*-type battlecruisers, three to four carriers, and four 8in cruisers. This was close to the force actually deployed in April, and consistent with the NID assessment.

82 Four carriers, *Kaga*, *Akagi*, *Hiryu* and *Soryu*, took part in the Darwin raid, launching a total of 188 aircraft. The raid is described by Tom Lewis and Peter Ingman in *Carrier Attack Darwin 1942*. This appears to be the only time the IJN carriers conducted a 'full deck load' strike, ie, a single continuous launch of the maximum strike force, as opposed to breaking it into two waves. Also Dull, *A Battle History of the Imperial Japanese Navy*, p54.

83 *Akagi*, *Hiryu*, *Soryu*, *Shokaku* and *Zuikaku*.

84 Marder, vol II, p94, suggests the IJN carriers had 400 aircraft. That aligns with the maximum aircraft complement figures quoted by Peattie in *Sunburst*, appendix 4. However, even at Pearl Harbor, with maximum effort, and six carriers, Jonathan Parshall in *Shattered Sword* states that the IJN only achieved 412 aircraft. Alan Zimm has the slightly higher figure of 417 at Pearl Harbor. *The Attack on Pearl Harbor*, chapter 4. The combination of attrition in the first six months of the war and low production rates steadily reduced carrier complements, so that the four carriers at Midway only carried 225 aircraft, compared to 267 at Pearl Harbor. A maximum of 300 for the five carriers in the Indian Ocean is therefore a more realistic estimate. A blog on the website 'combinedfleet.com' ('Operation C' under 'Battles' forum, initiated on 1

December 2008 by Rob Stuart) quoting Japanese Carrier Group records, gives a precise total of 273 aircraft allocated as follows: *Akagi* 54; *Soryu* 54; *Hiryu* 54; *Shokaku* 56; and *Zuikaku* 55. The Admiralty minute to the prime minister after the Ceylon action stated that the five IJN carriers had 228 aircraft. This quoted a lower displacement for *Zuikaku* of only 16,000 tons, suggesting NID no longer assessed her to be a sister ship of *Shokaku*. PREM 3/163/8.

85 JM 113, p65, has a detailed breakdown of the IJN force. This includes details of the separate 'Malay Force' under Vice Admiral Ozawa operating in the Bay of Bengal and centred on the light carrier *Ryujo* and five heavy cruisers. Also, Prados, p274.

86 WIR No 107 of 27 March 1942, ADM 223/153, confirmed in WIR No 108 of 3 April based on intelligence received up to 29 March, ADM 223/154, both in TNA. It is not clear how NID reached this assessment which conflicted with the developing FECB view in Ceylon. Possibly these two WIRs predated the main JN 25B intercepts and there was an absence of radio traffic while the Nagumo force was in Staring Bay, and certainly after their departure. Absence of call signs for major units in the southern theatre was then interpreted as evidence they had left for Japan or the Pacific theatre.

87 Somerville's anticipated launch point for the Japanese force is shown on the map at p21 of BS 15. JM 113, p68, shows that this was an accurate reflection of the original Japanese intention. Their initial plans anticipated that the task force would proceed to either a Point C at 6N 84E or Point D at 6-20N 82-40 E. These positions were indeed off the southeast corner of the island and Point D was about 50 miles north of Somerville's estimate, with Point C further away to the east. The actual Japanese launching point on the morning of 5 April was about 140 miles southwest of Point D. Captain Agar, again quoted in Tomlinson, pp63–4, stated that Somerville's assessment of the likely Japanese launch point was influenced by d'Albiac, who gave a prescient reading of Japanese intentions at a briefing to Somerville's captains on 26 March.

88 There was a full moon on 1 April and dawn was about 0600 hours. JM 113 shows the task force always planned a dawn launch at 0600.

89 Only six Catalinas were available from a possible maximum of twelve for this search. Rob Stuart, 'Leonard Birchall and the Japanese Raid on Colombo', *Canadian Military History Journal*, 7:4, footnote 12 for sources.

90 The eastern edge of Somerville's patrol area was just to the southwest of the likely Japanese approach course if they had selected Point D as their launch point. Point C was further away to the east.

91 Admiralty Battle Summary No 15, Naval Operations off Ceylon, 20 March–10 April 1942, pp2–4, ADM 234/331, TNA.

92 Battle Summary No 15, p4. The episode is described in Rob Stuart's article and in Michael Tomlinson, *The Most Dangerous Moment*, pp84–8, 94–8, and David A Thomas, *Japan's War at Sea* (London: Andre Deutsch, 1978), p105.

93 The Catalina position was 0-40N, 83-10E, or 360 miles from Dondra Head on a bearing of 155, Battle Summary No 15, p4. Japanese records all agree their estimated position at this time was about 0-40N, 84-10E. See Japan Center for Asian Historical Records of the National Archives of Japan (JACAR), Detailed engagement report from March 26 to April 22, 1942, Warship *Hiryu*, National Institute of Defence Studies, reference, C08030581700, image 39; extrapolation back from Colombo attack launch position shown on image 41; and JM 113 map on p92. Sergeant Bruce Catlin, the flight engineer of the Catalina, later confirmed severe difficulty with navigation during the sortie but insisted there was a good fix immediately prior to sighting the task force. Arthur Banks, *Wings of the Dawning: The Battle for the Indian Ocean 1939–1945* (Malvern: HMR, 1997), p53.

94 JACAR Hiryu engagement report, reference, C08030581700, image 39.

95 BS 15, maps pp20, 22.

96 Rob Stuart.

97 JM 113.

98 Map 1 is based on the map on p21 of Battle Summary No 15 with the actual Japanese flying-off position taken from the co-ordinates shown in the map at p92 of Japanese Monograph 113.

99 Somerville's Report of Proceedings, and Battle Summary No 15, ADM 234/331, TNA.

100 JM 113, p66.

101 Derek Howse, *Radar at Sea*, appendix F, p308.
102 Map at p 21 of Battle Summary No 15.
103 Roskill, vol II, p25.
104 JM 113, p65.
105 Somerville's Report of Proceedings, para 27.
106 This map is based on that at p21 of Battle Summary No 15 showing Somerville's movements from 2–4 April. The IJN track on 5 April is superimposed, drawing on the information in the *Hiryu* engagement report, JACAR reference C08030581700, image 41.
107 *Dorsetshire* and *Cornwall* were sunk to the west of Ceylon on the afternoon of 5 April while on fast transit from Colombo to rejoin Somerville. *Hermes* was sunk south of Trincomalee on 9 April after Nagumo raided that port.
108 Churchill's criticism of Somerville is in Marder, vol II, pp171–2. The First Lord's reply on behalf of the Admiralty on 10 June is in PREM 3/163/8, TNA.
109 War Memoirs of Admiral Sir Algernon Willis, pp33–5, IWM.
110 Testimony of the Catalina crew recorded by Rob Stuart, Tomlinson and others.
111 JM 113, p72.
112 Battle Summary No 15, p11.
113 Para 74, Edden paper for Marder dated 24 February 1977, SMVL8, CCA, Cambridge.
114 Both in REDW 2/8, CCA.
115 *Japanese Naval Air Force Fighter Units and their Aces 1932–1945*, p431.
116 Marder does not cover these movements on 5 April in his otherwise comprehensive account.
117 Battle Summary No 15, p22.
118 Battle Summary No 15, p11 and Michael Tomlinson, pp88, 122.
119 History of HMS *Anderson*, chapter 4, p6.
120 JACAR, *Hiryu* report, images 39, 41, 42, 43, 45, 46 and 47. Japanese Monograph 113 also includes a map at p92 setting out the movements of the IJN Operation C task force with timings for key events and course changes.
121 Roskill's map is in vol II, p25. Marder's map is in vol II, p120.
122 JACAR, *Hiryu* report, image 41.
123 A better map than those of Roskill and Marder, although still with some errors, is provided by Gordon Wallace, an observer who was serving during the Ceylon operation with 831 Squadron in *Indomitable*. He correctly presents Nagumo's 230 course and illustrates how this related to the attack on the *Dorsetshire* force, but he has him turning southeast at 1400, ninety minutes earlier than he in fact did. Gordon Wallace, *Carrier Observer* (Shrewsbury UK: Airlife Publishing, 1993), p82.
124 Battle Summary 15, p11.
125 Lieutenant Commander Egusa, commanding the *Dorsetshire* strike force, assessed the wind as 230 degrees 6 metres (ie, about 12.5 knots) at the start of the attack. Osamu Tagaya, *Aichi 99 Kanbaku 'Val' Units 1937–42* (Oxford: Osprey Publishing, 2011), chapter 6.
126 JACAR, *Hiryu* report, image 41.
127 JM 113, p74. Parshall and Tully describe this sighting and subsequent developments in *Shattered Sword*, chapter 7. According to Battle Summary No 15, p7, *Cornwall* sighted an unknown aircraft at 1100.
128 JACAR, *Hiryu* report, image 42.
129 JM 113, p74.
130 Parshall and Tully, chapter 7.
131 JACAR, *Hiryu* report, image 47.
132 Tagaya, chapter 6.
133 The map on p90 of JM 113 suggests this turn was at 1530, whereas the large scale track chart included with the JACAR *Hiryu* report at image 39 suggests 1500. The JM 113 time looks more precise and the later Carrier Division Two track which is shown in detail at image 43 of the Hiryu report seems consistent with a 1530 turn.
134 Map 2 is a copy of the map on p22 of Battle Summary No 15 with the Japanese track then superimposed. The Japanese track is based on the information in the map at p92 of Japanese Monograph 113 and the JACAR *Hiryu* report, images 39, 41, 42 and 43.
135 The evidence for this jink is the *Hiryu* report, image 43. Although this only provides a track

chart for the carrier *Hiryu*, it is inconceivable that *Hiryu* alone would have made such a detour. It is possible that the whole task force followed the same track as *Hiryu*, but that is not consistent with the other records, which have the task force turning southeast at either 1500 or 1530. If the whole task force had made a jink to the northwest, then logically the turn southeast from the 230 heading would have been marked as taking place at 1700. The balance of probability is that Carrier Division Two plus its escort made the detour northwest, while the main force turned southeast at the same time.

136 Gordon Wallace, p85, states that Nagumo turned southeast with the bulk of his force at about 1400, while the *Dorsetshire* strike force was still in the air, and left two carriers with their escort to recover it and follow on. Michael Tomlinson, p124, appears to agree Nagumo began to retire southeastward before the strike force had been recovered. Both authors are correct in suggesting the force split at the time of the turn southeast, although the turn was later than Wallace states. However, they are wrong about the reason. The JACAR *Hiryu* report is clear that recovery was complete before the turn. Following their destruction of the *Dorsetshire* force by about 1350, the Japanese strike force required no more than forty minutes to cover the 100 miles or so to reach the carriers which were rushing towards them. Tagaya, chapter 6, confirms the strike force had all returned to the carriers by 1445.

137 This map has been constructed primarily from the JACAR *Hiryu* report, images 42 and 43, with the British 1600 position superimposed from Battle Summary map at p22. The Japanese times shown in the *Hiryu* track chart are three hours ahead of the British times quoted in this chapter.

138 The search sector is shown on the Battle Summary 15 map at p22. The aircraft would have flown courses 10 degrees apart to 200 miles and then turned to cover 10 degrees of perimeter before reversing course back to the carrier. Gordon Wallace, p85, suggests it might have been wiser to deploy Fulmars, as used for the morning search, which were less vulnerable to Japanese fighters. He recognises there was also a case to conserve all available fighters to protect the carriers.

139 Battle Summary 15, p11. There is a discrepancy over the co-ordinates of this initial 1600 position. Both the Battle Summary 15 text at p11 and Somerville's separate Report of Proceedings, para 37, give the position of the 1600 Albacore sighting as 3-38 N and 78-18E. Yet the accompanying Battle Summary map at p22 plots the sighting at 2-38N, 78-18E, which is 60 miles to the south. Somebody therefore, at some stage, misread the latitude and substituted '2' for '3' or '3' for '2' in recording the position. It is most unlikely that the Battle Summary 15 map, which was almost certainly copied from the original operations plot in Somerville's flagship, is wrong. Not only does this position fit with where the Japanese force actually was, but a position 60 miles to the north would be outside the planned search arc. It is probable, therefore, that somebody made a simple error in preparing the Report of Proceedings using positions read off the plot.

140 JACAR, *Hiryu* report, image 43.

141 JM 113, p74.

142 JACAR, *Hiryu* report, image 43.

143 Somerville describes his reaction to this report at paragraph 40 of his Report of Proceedings.

144 JM 113, p74.

145 Quoted in Mitsuo Fuchida and Masatake Okumiya, 'The Battle of Midway', at p139, in David C Evans, *The Japanese Navy in World War II*.

146 Mark Peattie, *Sunburst*, pp153–5.

147 JM 113.

148 The aviation historian Mark E Horan has commented on the feasibility of a night attack by Somerville's carriers on the night of 5/6 April in the website www.j-aircraft.com. Search under Message Boards/Archives/Everything else archive/Admiral Somerville v's Kido Butai 1942 initiated by Jim Oxley on 31 January 2010. For background on Horan, see Jonathan Parshall, *Shattered Sword*, Acknowledgements.

149 Gordon Wallace, p86. The pilot of this aircraft was Sub Lieutenant Grant-Sturgis and it was the most westerly of Somerville's four search planes. The aircraft got off a position on sighting the IJN force of 126 miles bearing 026 from the Eastern Fleet, but was jumped by a Zero fighter before he could provide any clarifying detail, including force composition, course and speed. He

evaded with minor damage, but his communicator was wounded. In these circumstances, the difficulty the crew had in giving a precise account of what they had seen when they landed is unsurprising.

150 Gordon Wallace, pp69, 86. He does not provide any detail of squadron strength for these attacks. Marder, vol II, p113, states that *Indomitable* had twenty-four Albacores and *Formidable* twenty-two. Each carrier had two Albacore squadrons. Most sources suggest these totals are about right, but actual operational availability of aircraft would have been lower. Edden refers to serious serviceability problems, Edden, para 66, CCA. A maximum potential attack force of, say, thirty, perhaps released in two waves, therefore looks reasonable. Wallace states that the Albacore squadrons of both carriers 'were capable, if inadequately practised, in the execution of a night torpedo attack', but the only ASV 2-fitted aircraft were in *Formidable*, which would have complicated planning. *Carrier Observer*, p66. Derek Howse claims the ASV 2-fitted aircraft were in *Indomitable* rather than *Formidable*. *Radar at Sea*, p308. However, Wallace is adamant all the night ASV searches were flown by *Formidable*. As a direct witness, it seems inconceivable he could get this wrong. Mark Horan also insists the ASV aircraft were in *Formidable*, but may here have been drawing on Wallace's testimony.

151 JACAR, *Hiryu* report, image 43.

152 Battle Summary No 15.

153 This second signal is also summarised in Battle Summary No 15, p11. Gordon Wallace provided additional information from his personal recollection of that afternoon and subsequent researches. He stated that the reporting aircraft, flown by Grant-Sturgis of 827 squadron (the other *Indomitable* Albacore squadron to his own), landed on at 1745. The damage from the Zero attack had burst a tyre and the aircraft almost went overboard. It was also immediately obvious the communicator was badly wounded. Grant-Sturgis did, indeed, report the force steering northwest, but Wallace claimed that after reconstructing events, it seemed more likely the course was southeast, and that a corrective signal to Somerville was sent. None of the obvious records refer to this. If it is true, Somerville does not seem to have been convinced, because he continued to operate on the basis the Japanese were going north. Gordon Wallace, p86.

154 Wallace, pp68–9, 85–6, suggests the Grant-Sturgis Albacore was able to make only a fleeting sighting of the Japanese force 'in the distance' (so perhaps 20 miles away) before it was attacked. The crew were, no doubt, disorientated, and would have struggled to give any reliable position. Willis stated in his unpublished memoir that one Albacore had sighted the enemy force, but both pilot and observer were wounded, and unable to give a coherent account of the enemy composition. Willis was probably here reflecting his memory of what Somerville and Boyd told him on return to Addu Atoll on 8 April. The inability to give a coherent account sounds all too likely given the circumstances. Willis Memoirs, IWM, pp33–4.

155 Somerville's continued commitment to a night attack is recorded at para 43 of his Report of Proceedings and his letter to his wife dated 4–6 April 1942, item 232, Somerville Papers.

156 These search arcs are shown in the map, p22 of Battle Summary No 15.

157 GC & CS History, 'Organisation and Evolution of Japanese Naval Sigint Part VI', p6, HW 50/59.

158 JM 113, p75. Nagumo searched a wide western sector from 215–305 degrees out to 230 miles, but at the start of the search Somerville was some 450 miles to the northwest.

159 Commander-in-Chief Ceylon's signal of 0334Z of 6 April estimated the IJN task force comprised at least four carriers and three battleships, and was still located somewhere between Port T and Ceylon. The force composition was about right, but by now Nagumo was southeast of Ceylon, rather than between the island and Port T. Somerville Report of Proceedings, para 52, and ADM 223/259, TNA. Pound relayed the Ceylon report to King in Washington, adding that the battleships were now (correctly) believed to be *Kongo* class. He also forwarded an accurate assessment of Ozawa's force in the Bay of Bengal. First Sea Lord to Chief of Naval Operations of 6 April, ADM 223/259, TNA.

160 Commander-in-Chief Eastern Fleet to Admiralty of 1056Z of 8 April, REDW 2/9, CCA.

161 Somerville stated afterwards that it was not until 1700 on 5 April that he realised he faced a substantial carrier force, much closer than he had expected. Somerville signal 0644Z of 11 April, ADM 223/259, TNA.

162 JM 113, p64, defined the strategic objective of Operation C as to 'surprise and annihilate the enemy forces in the Ceylon Island area and secure the sea lanes supporting the Burma operation'. At p68, the priority naval targets were identified as carriers, battleships and cruisers in that order. British naval strength in the Indian Ocean was assessed at a minimum of two carriers, three battleships, four heavy cruisers, and eleven light cruisers. A further six battleships and two carriers were potentially available as reinforcements. Specific identifications included *Warspite*, three named 'R' class, *Indomitable*, *Eagle* and *Hermes*. With the exception of *Eagle*, these were all correct. British air strength in the Indian Ocean theatre was put at 500 aircraft. JM 113, p61.

163 The lack of flexibility in Japanese planning at the operational level is analysed in Alan Zimm's book *The Attack on Pearl Harbor*, especially in chapter 4 and the concluding chapter 10. He contends that Pearl Harbor was not the 'brilliantly conceived and meticulously planned' operation usually presented, but one beset by major flaws in both planning and execution. He emphasises the failure to respond to changing requirements and circumstances, and suggests this was a Japanese weakness throughout the war.

164 Marder noted this lapse at vol II, p145, and could identify no satisfactory explanation for it. He interviewed one of Nagumo's staff officers, Commander Nakajima Chikataka, who confirmed Nagumo chose to ignore the sighting and stated that he also commissioned very little scouting. Rob Stuart makes a valid comparison between the IJN failure here and the initiative taken by the commander of the dive-bomber group from USS *Enterprise* at Midway, who faced an analogous situation when he spotted the IJN destroyer *Arashi* and followed her to find Nagumo's carriers. Willmott, *The Barrier and the Javelin*, pp419–20.

165 Anthony Tully and Lu Yu have provided a new perspective on IJN aerial reconnaissance practice during the first nine months of the war, including Operation C. 'A Question of Estimates: How Faulty Intelligence Drove Scouting at the Battle of Midway', *US Naval War College Review*, 68:2 (Spring 2015).

166 Malcom Murfett scathingly notes of Nagumo that 'he might have discovered Somerville's Eastern Fleet had he devoted a little effort, rather than none at all, to even the most rudimentary of reconnaissance duties'. This is an overstatement, but not by much. *Naval Warfare 1919– 1945: An Operational History of the Volatile War at Sea* (Abingdon: Routledge, 2009), pp161–3, 491.

167 Somerville certainly disobeyed the chiefs of staff directive 'to act as a Fleet in being, avoid unnecessary risks, crippling losses and attrition'. Footnote 66 refers. The directive issued by Admiral Chester Nimitz, Commander-in-Chief US Navy Pacific Fleet, to his Midway task force commanders read: 'In carrying out the task assigned in operation plan 29-42, you will be governed by the principle of calculated risk, which you shall interpret to mean the avoidance of exposure of your force to attack by superior enemy forces without good prospect of inflicting, as a result of such exposure, greater damage to the enemy'. Robert C Rubel, 'Deconstructing Nimitz's principle of calculated risk: Lessons for today', *US Naval War College Review*, 68:1 (Winter 2015), pp31–45.

168 Parshall and Tully, *Shattered Sword*, chapter 6, assesses IJN air search doctrine and its weaknesses. The IJN generally preferred to rely on floatplanes launched from the battleships and cruisers accompanying a carrier task force for search duties, rather than the carriers. This enabled the maximum number of carrier aircraft to be available for strike operations. However, the number of floatplanes was often insufficient to achieve adequate coverage. In addition, some older floatplanes still in use in early 1942, such as the Type 95, had inadequate search range – barely 200 miles.

169 Parshall and Tully explore the IJN weaknesses displayed at Midway, and the reasons behind them, in *Shattered Sword*. James Levy defends IJN planning for Midway, disputing several key points in *Shattered Sword*. However, he acknowledges both the reconnaissance weakness and the difficulty IJN carrier doctrine had in tackling more than one objective. 'Was there something unique to the Japanese that lost them the Battle of Midway', *US Naval War College Review*, 67:1 (Winter 2014).

170 When the *Dorsetshire* force was first sighted around 1000 on 5 April, Nagumo ordered a torpedo strike. IJN doctrine decreed torpedoes should be used to guarantee the destruction of

capital units or heavy cruisers. This required the reserve strike force on Carrier Division Five, *Shokaku* and *Zuikaku*, to be re-armed. This took so long that dive-bombers from Carrier Division Two, *Hiryu* and *Soryu*, had to be used instead. Jonathan Parshall, p131.

171 Marder, vol II, pp134–5, and Parshall, p145.
172 The British appear to have had as good an advance picture of Japanese plans for Midway as the Americans. NID report 00976 of 2 June, ADM 223/322, TNA.
173 The Nagumo force destroyed two out of three Catalinas which sighted it and intercepted both Albacores destroying one and damaging the other.
174 Para 65, Edden memoir, SMVL 8, CCA.
175 Staff paper on night flying operations, probably dated 4 June 1942, REDW 2/9, CCA, Cambridge. Also Somerville letter to First Sea Lord of 4 July, SMVL/8, CCA, Cambridge.
176 For comparison with *Ark Royal*, see Somerville personal letter to First Sea Lord of 11 March, SMVL 8, CCA, Cambridge.
177 H T Lenton, pp45–6. They carried sixteen 21in torpedo tubes, whereas most other Royal Navy cruisers had six or eight. Speed was 33 knots.
178 Marder, vol II, p132.
179 ADM 205/13, TNA.
180 Marder, p132.
181 Marder, vol II, p125.
182 Edden letter to John Somerville of 24 July 1990, SMVL 8, CCA.
183 The only major historians to offer serious criticism of Somerville's performance during Operation C are H P Willmott in *Empires in the Balance*, p444, and Malcom Murfett in *Naval Warfare 1919–1945: An Operational History*, pp161–3, 491. Willmott's case is presented more as assertion than reasoned, evidence-based argument. Murfett looks more clinically at Somerville's performance, judging he was 'not at his best' in coping with the Ceylon raid with decision-making 'flawed, irresponsible and costly'. Murfett was even more critical of Nagumo.
184 The losses were seventeen Hurricanes, six Fulmars, six Swordfish, five Blenheims and three Catalinas. Tomlinson, p176. However, there were enough reserves of fighters immediately available on the island to bring those squadrons up to strength.
185 Tomlinson gives a broadly accurate summary of the balance of losses at pp175–7. He suggests seventeen aircraft were lost. A much more detailed analysis in the website Combinedfleet.com puts the losses at eighteen (two B5N2 bombers, ten D3A1 dive-bombers, and six A6M2 Zero fighters) with thirty-one damaged (almost all B5N2s and D3A1s). See Rob Stuart posting, 'Operation C' under forum 'Battles'.
186 Ashley Jackson, *The British Empire and the Second World War*, p348.
187 Ashley Jackson.
188 JP (42) 413 of 18 April, 'Indian Ocean: Strategy in Certain Eventualities'; and, JP (42) 429 of 21 April, 'Indian Ocean Area – Appreciation for Commanders-in-Chief'. Both CAB 79/20, TNA.
189 JIC (42) 141 of 18 April, 'Japan's Intentions'. This assessment was updated a week later in JIC (42) 152 of 25 April. Both CAB 79/20, TNA.
190 By this time, more intelligence was available on the precise composition of the IJN forces that had operated against Ceylon and in the Bay of Bengal, and on their subsequent movements. NID 00866A of 19 April, ADM 223/322, TNA.
191 Reported by NID on 17 April as report 00860, ADM 223/322, TNA.
192 PREM 3/163/8, TNA.
193 NID's initial post-attack assessment was that the IJN Ceylon force probably comprised five battleships (three *Kongo*s and two *Nagato*s), four carriers (*Hiryu*, *Soryu*, *Shokaku* and *Zuikaku*) and six heavy cruisers. WIR No 109 of 10 April, ADM 223/154, TNA. A week later, drawing on intelligence up to 12 April, they were still struggling to confirm the battleship force (now thought to comprise two *Nagato*s, two *Yamashiro*s, and possibly two *Kongo*s), while *Akagi* had been added to the carrier force though (wrongly) she was not thought to have joined until after the raid on Ceylon. The number of heavy cruisers present had reduced to three, but ship identifications were incorrect. NID also rightly concluded that a separate force had operated in the Bay of Bengal and here they correctly identified the carrier *Ryujo* and three of five heavy cruisers. WIR No 110 of 17 April, ADM 223/154, TNA.

194 DO (42) 10th Meeting of 14 April 1942, CAB 69/4, TNA.

195 Andrew Roberts, *Masters and Commanders: The Military Geniuses who led the West to Victory in WWII*, pp153–63.

196 DO (42) 12th meeting of 22 April, CAB 69/4, TNA.

197 For example, King and Stark. On 5 March King wrote to the president with his views on war priorities. He stated that the Middle East was an important line of effort for the British, 'but also for us, and one we cannot afford to let go'. He also stressed the need to support British effort on the India–Burma–China line. And he emphasised the importance of Australia and New Zealand, which were 'white men's countries' we cannot afford to lose to Japan because of the repercussions elsewhere. King to Roosevelt of 5 March, FDR Library. At the combined chiefs of staff 11th meeting, five days later on 10 March, Stark stated that the loss of the Middle East would be more serious to the United Nations cause than the loss of the Far East. It was the only place Germany could currently be engaged, and was critical to perceptions across the Muslim world. King endorsed the importance of the Middle East. Marshall was not present. CCS 11th of 10 March, CAB 88/1, TNA.

198 Discussion between Cabinet Office and Japanese historians, Tokyo, September 1966, 'Effect of the Doolittle raid', CAB 106/180, TNA.

199 Minutes CCS 16th Meeting on 21 April, CAB 88/1, TNA. Stark, newly appointed as Commander United States Naval Forces in Europe, made two significant comments. He saw the Russian army as a critical ally, and every effort must be made to prevent its defeat, which would be a catastrophe. He also stressed the importance of the Middle East. If it fell the blockade of Germany would be broken. Also J R M Butler, *Grand Strategy*, vol III, part 2 (HMSO, 1964), p502.

200 COS (42) 128th meeting of 23 April, CAB 79/20, TNA.

201 Marder, vol II, p131.

202 AT of 1 May and Commander-in-Chief Eastern Fleet response of 2 May, REDW 2/9, CCA, Cambridge. Somerville also commented on the current limitations of his carriers as regards aircraft complements, state of training and general performance in his signal to the First Sea Lord of 1 May 1942 advising against temporary diversion of the Eastern Fleet to the eastern Mediterranean. PREM 3/171/4, TNA.

203 Commander-in-Chief Eastern Fleet signal to Admiralty of 17 April 1942.

204 First Lord minute to Prime Minister dated 3 May 1942, PREM 3/171/4, TNA.

205 The sad history of Fleet Air Arm fighter procurement is summarised in a memo by the prime minister to the Defence Committee in mid-June 1942. DO (42) 40 of 16 June 1942, 'Fleet Air Arm Fighters', CAB 69/4, TNA.

206 For the lobbying, First Lord minute to Prime Minister of 3 May, Prime Minister letter to United States President of 12 May, Fifth Sea Lord minute to First Sea Lord of 13 May, all in ADM 205/13, TNA. On 10 July, the First Lord expected eighty-six Martlets to be delivered by end July and a further 133 by end September, but no more until early 1943. First Lord minute under DC (S) (42) 61 of 10 July 1942, CAB 70/5, TNA.

207 First Sea Lord minute to First Lord, ADM 205/13, TNA.

208 Pound initially thought the American success at Midway was primarily due to land-based aircraft operating from the island. First Sea Lord minute to Prime Minister of 10 June 1942, ADM 205/14, TNA.

209 Paper for prime minister on IJN carriers in response to prime minister minute M. 136/2 of 14 April, PREM 3/163/8, TNA.

210 First Sea Lord comment and corrections on note of 3 May probably from Director of Plans, ADM 205/13, TNA. Pound reiterated here the value of the 'R' class.

211 D K Brown quotes the diary entry of Goodall dated 25 January 1944 here: 'Winston all out for battleships. There is now a pro-battleship set back in the Admiralty'. According to Goodall, this included Cunningham as the new First Sea Lord. *Nelson to Vanguard*, chapter 1, with Churchill reference at footnote 55.

212 Barnett, for example, states: 'In retrospect it is remarkable that Britain did not order and complete a single fleet carrier, the new arbiter of seapower, within the compass of the Second World War'. *Engage the Enemy More Closely*, p438. This statement is literally true, but perhaps misleading. Britain still completed six heavy fleet carriers and six light carriers between

September 1939 and September 1945. The comparable US Navy figures, with the much greater American economic resources, were eighteen and nine. The Royal Navy also had a further six fleet carriers and ten light carriers under construction at the end of the war.

213 The first three carriers were ordered on 14 March 1942, so before the Ceylon operation, with a further ten in August and three more at the end of the year. Six ships were complete by the end of the Japanese war, with four deployed operationally with the British Pacific Fleet, although just too late to participate in actual combat. The displacement of these carriers was about 15,000 tons, comparable to the IJN *Hiryu* and *Soryu*. Each of the four carriers operational in 1945 typically deployed forty-two aircraft, eighteen Barracudas and twenty-four Corsairs. These carriers were originally designed for a very limited life expectancy. In the event, they proved so adaptable and effective that they formed the core of the Royal Navy carrier force for ten years after the war, when they were preferred to the heavy *Illustrious* class. Many were sold overseas after 1945, where at least one was still operational fifty years later. D K Brown, *Nelson to Vanguard*, chapter 3, and H T Lenton, pp107–9.

214 Deputy First Sea Lord minute to First Sea Lord dated 18 November 1942, ADM 205/20, TNA. Also additional comments on this debate by D K Brown in *Nelson to Vanguard*, chapter 1.

215 Barnett, *Engage the Enemy More Closely*, pp863–4; and Douglas Ford, 'British Naval Policy and the War against Japan 1937–1945: Distorted Doctrine, Insufficient Resources, or Inadequate Intelligence', *International Journal of Naval History*, 4:1 (April 2005).

216 Eastern Fleet Reports of Proceeding between May and October.

217 Vice Chief of Naval Staff to First Sea Lord of 22 April proposing deployment of battleship *Duke of York*, new sister to *Prince of Wales*, and battlecruiser *Renown* to Eastern Fleet, ADM 205/19, TNA. Also, Director of Plans minute of 18 May proposing deployment of fleet carrier *Victorious* or *Furious* with Escort carriers, ADM 205/13, TNA.

218 The only major units left at home would be two *King George V*s (*King George V* herself and the new *Anson*) and either the carrier *Victorious* or *Furious*. Force H would have the old battleship *Malaya* and old carrier *Eagle*. Commander-in-Chief Home Fleet expressed strong objections to these reductions in a submission to the chiefs of staff and Defence Committee which appears as Annex 1 to DO (42) 12th meeting of 22 April, CAB 69/4, TNA. The plan to deploy *Duke of York* to the Eastern Fleet was abandoned when *King George V* was damaged in a collision with the destroyer *Punjabi* on 1 May and was under repair until late July.

219 COS (42) 236 of 26 April, 'Revised Defence Plan for Ceylon', CAB 80/36; and COS (42) 156 (O) of 2 June 1942, 'The Indian Ocean', CAB 80/63, both in TNA. A Beaufort squadron was to be deployed by the end of April.

220 AT to BAD Washington of 11 April. In addition, the old carrier *Eagle* and six further escort carriers would be allocated to Atlantic escort. PREM 3/492/2, TNA. The Royal Navy received thirty-five escort carriers between April 1942 and December 1943, almost all built or converted in the United States, so the total force was a realistic projection. H T Lenton.

221 HT Lenton, pp126–7; and JP 42 466 of 1 May, 'Counter-offensive v Japan', CAB 79/20, TNA. The latter anticipated that the Royal Navy would have three or four carriers in the Indian Ocean by end August with 140–180 aircraft. For US Navy Midway figures, see H P Willmott, *The Barrier and the Javelin*, pp340–1.

222 Jonathan Parshall, *Shattered Sword*, chapter 5.

223 There are good accounts of Pedestal in Jack Greene and Alessandro Massignani, *The Naval War in the Mediterranean*, chapter 19; and Peter C Smith, *Pedestal – The Convoy that saved Malta* (London: William Kimber, 1970).

224 The others were *Victorious* (sister to *Indomitable*), *Eagle* and *Furious*. The latter was used to fly forty Spitfires to Malta.

225 Smith.

226 Greene and Massignani.

227 Parshall, *Shattered Sword*, chapter 1.

228 Parshall, *Shattered Sword*, chapter 5.

229 Japanese Monograph 160, Outline of Naval Armaments and Preparations for War, part 3, chart 6, Air Strength at time of the outbreak of war, p 7, Office of the Chief of Military History, US Army.

230 Parshall.

231 Japanese Monograph 172, Outline of Naval Armaments and Preparations for War, part 5, chart 4, Actual Aircraft Production 1941–44, p49. Parshall, *Shattered Sword*, chapter 5, states Japan produced only fifty-six 'carrier attack aircraft' (by which he presumably means Type 97s) during all of 1942. It is not clear what his source was and the figure is not correct. JM 172 has 271 aircraft built over FY 1942 and a further eighty-one between December 1941 and March 1942.

232 COS (42) 236 of 26 April, CAB 80/36, TNA.

233 COS (42) 107 (O) of 19 April provides details of Royal Air Force strength in Ceylon on 16 April, a week after the Nagumo raid, and the reinforcements expected by 30 April. This demonstrates not only the rapid Royal Air Force recovery, but also arrival of significant reinforcements. CAB 80/62, TNA.

234 J R M Butler, *Grand Strategy III*, p502. This letter drew on a memo he circulated for the Defence Committee on 22 April. Annex II to DO (42) 12th meeting of 22 April, CAB 69/4, TNA.

235 Personal signal to the Operation Ironclad commander, Vice Admiral Neville Syfret, of 14 May. Annex VI to COS (42) 287 of 1 June 1942, CAB 80/36.

236 PREM 3/158/6.

237 JP (42) 466 of 1 May, 'Counter-Offensive Against Japan', commenting on proposals from the prime minister over the previous two weeks. CAB 79/20, TNA.

238 At the beginning of May, the joint planning staff remained distinctly cautious about the balance of forces in the Indian Ocean for the rest of 1942, JP (42) 466 of 1 May, 'Counter-offensive against Japan', CAB 79/20, TNA.

239 PREM 3/158/6, TNA.

240 The prime minister asked Ismay for an estimate of Japanese wartime losses to date on 28 February. The response from the Joint Intelligence Committee, taking account of American figures, was broadly accurate for aircraft losses, but overstated naval losses. The committee already doubted that Japanese aircraft production was sufficient to maintain their frontline. While this was true for specific categories, such as carrier attack aircraft, it was not yet true overall. Indeed in fiscal year 1942, overall aircraft production would exceed overall losses by a small margin, despite deficits in specific areas. Prime Minister minutes of 28 February and 13 March and Ismay replies on 7 and 25 March, PREM 3/252/3, TNA.

241 NID report 00866A of 19 April, ADM 223/322, TNA. This probably drew on JN 25B intercepts.

242 WIR 111 of 24 April, WIR 112 of 1 May, and WIR 113 of 8 May. ADM 223/154, TNA. By 8 May NID assessed that all fleet carriers had left the southern area along with most of the battleships, leaving only *Hiei* and several heavy cruisers. WIR 116 of 29 May, which drew on intelligence up to 24 May, confirmed that virtually the whole IJN fleet was now concentrated in Japanese home waters.

243 JIC (42) 189 of 19 May, 'Situation in the Far East from the Japanese Point of View', CAB 79/21, TNA.

244 JP (42) 537 of 30 May, 'Appreciation of the War Against Japan', CAB 79/21, TNA.

245 JIC (42) 231 of 15 June 1942, 'Japanese Air Situation', CAB 79/21, TNA. The figures have been compared with the official Japanese production data in JM 172 and aircraft loss figures in NAV No 50, USSBS No 202.

246 The prime minister first raised this concept in part 4 of his 'Memorandum on the Future Conduct of the War', drafted on 20 December 1941 for the chiefs of staff, and formally circulated as Annex 1 to DO (42) 6 of 22 January 1942, CAB 69/4, TNA. The Australian prime minister raised the idea of a 'superior' combined British-American fleet based in the Pacific in his letter to the prime minister of 29 December, PREM 3/163/8, TNA.

247 PREM 3/492/2, TNA.

248 The sinking of *Lexington* and serious damage to *Yorktown* reduced the Pacific Fleet to two operational carriers (*Enterprise* and *Hornet*), though *Yorktown* was repaired in time for Midway.

249 H P Willmott, *The Barrier and the Javelin*, pp331–5. Somerville advised the Admiralty on 20 May that the United States believed Japan was planning an imminent attack on Midway, Alaska or Hawaii. His source was clearly FECB, who were in contact with the US Navy SIGINT stations in Melbourne and Pearl Harbor. This may have been the first pointer to Midway

received in London. Commander-in-Chief Eastern Fleet Zymotic signal to Admiralty 1436z of 20 May, ADM 223/867, TNA. Prados states that King and Nimitz concluded the Japanese target was Midway three days earlier on 17 May. *Combined Fleet Decoded*, p318.

250 King did not inform the British of the loss of *Lexington* until 22 May, two weeks after the event. He also implied to Admiral Charles Little, Head of BAD in Washington, that the request came more from a panicky General MacArthur than from him. Letter from Little to Pound of 22 May, ADM 178/323, TNA.

251 An assessment of Ironclad is outside the scope of this chapter. There are good summaries in Marder, *Old Friends, New Enemies*, vol II, and Barnett, *Engage the Enemy More Closely*, chapter 28. The joint planning staff produced a final balance of argument for and against the operation in JP (42) 435 of 23 April, CAB 79/20, TNA. By late April, the Joint Intelligence Committee judged a full-scale landing by the Japanese was unlikely. The main threat was that the Vichy French leadership might collaborate in providing the IJN with a refuelling base. JIC (42) 152 of 25 April.

252 *Birmingham, Mauritius* and *Gambia*.

253 The last document which anticipates an eastern fleet with the strength planned during April and May is probably JP (42) 586 of 12 June, 'Appreciation of the Problem of Re-opening the Burma Road in the Autumn of 1942', CAB 79/21, TNA. This includes force levels expected in the eastern theatre by 1 October.

254 Pound note giving Eastern Fleet strength on 14 July. PREM 3/163/8, TNA.

255 Exchange between prime minister and Pound on 10 June 1942. The prime minister noted that the loss of four carriers by the Japanese would impose a severe restraint on their movements in the Indian Ocean. Pound agreed. ADM 205/14, TNA.

256 JIC (42) 339 of 9 September 1942, 'Japan's Intentions', CAB 121/748, TNA.

257 Discussion between Cabinet Office and Japanese historians, Tokyo September 1966, 'Plan 21 (Burma) and cooperation with Germany', CAB 106/180, TNA.

258 Toshikazu Ohmae essay, pp113–17; and Marder, vol II, pp185–9.

259 DO (42) 12th meeting dated 22 April and related DO (42) 44 record, both CAB 69/4, TNA.

260 The most recent account of Torch and a good starting point for both the course of the campaign and its consequences is by Vincent O'Hara, *Torch: North Africa and the Allied Path to Victory* (Annapolis: Naval Institute Press, 2015).

261 Roskill, *War at Sea*, vol II, chapter 13, table 25. O'Hara, *Torch*, appendix 3.

262 The prime minister summarised the history of the Eastern Fleet in 1942 in a letter to the deputy prime minister, Clement Attlee, dated 29 October. He had anticipated bringing the fleet back up to strength after Torch but other priorities had intervened. PREM 3/163/8, TNA.

263 This dimension is largely ignored by O'Hara.

264 JP (42) 639 of 17 July 1942, 'Strategy in certain circumstances', CAB 119/56, TNA.

265 JP (42) 849 of 3 October 1942, 'The War against Germany in 1943', CAB 119/56, TNA.

266 US Army Official History, *Global Logistics and Strategy 1940–1943*, p720.

267 Whether, and how far, Torch saved Allied shipping resources remains controversial. There is a case now reiterated by O'Hara that, judged by raw numbers, shipping gains from Mediterranean transit in 1943 and 1944 were outweighed by the supply demands generated by the Mediterranean campaigns in those years, making a cross-channel invasion logistically impossible before mid-1944. However, numbers are only part of the story. The strategic factors discussed in this paragraph, the impact of aid to Russia, and flexibility of Indian Ocean reinforcement, must be weighed too. For the logistics argument, see Kevin Smith, *Conflict over Convoys: Anglo-American logistics diplomacy in World War II* (Cambridge University Press, 1996).

268 US Army Official History, *The Middle East Theater, The Persian Corridor and Aid to Russia*, appendix A, tables 1 and 2.

269 Joan Beaumont, p168.

270 Williamson Murray, *The Luftwaffe 1933–1945: Strategy for Defeat* (London: Brassey's, 1996), pp159–66 and tables XXX and XXXI.

271 Murray, ibid, p160. Also Joel S A Hayward, *Stopped at Stalingrad: The Luftwaffe and Hitler's Defeat in the East 1942–1943* (University Press of Kansas, 1998).

272 O'Hara dissents from the judgements in this paragraph, arguing that Torch made little

contribution to wearing down German power generally, and had no significant impact on the Russian theatre. *Torch*, Conclusion, pp287–90.

273 FDR Library, President's Secretary's File (PSF) 1933–1945, Box 3, Ernest J King, Roosevelt Memorandum for General Marshall, Admiral King and Harry Hopkins, 'Instructions for London Conference – July 1942', dated 15 July 1942.

274 Hobbs, p15.

275 H P Willmott and Ashley Jackson are two of very few historians to highlight the strategic stakes in the Indian Ocean in the first half of 1942. Willmott provides an excellent summary of what the Japanese might have achieved with an all-out effort in this theatre, set against a sound appraisal of the logistic limitations they faced. He concludes that Japan's overall strategic position was all but impossible, but that the adoption of an Indian Ocean strategy could not have produced worse results than the ones the Japanese actually registered in the period March – July 1942. Willmott does not, however, take sufficient account of British determination to reinforce the Indian Ocean at the expense of other theatres in the way brought out in this chapter. H P Willmott, *Empires in the Balance*, pp437–8. Jackson, *The British Empire and the Second World War*, chapters 10 and 11.

Conclusion

1 Ken Kotani, *Japanese Intelligence in World War II* (Oxford: Osprey Publishing, 2009), describes the strengths and weaknesses of IJN intelligence and Japanese intelligence in general.

2 Steven Morewood, *The British Defence of Egypt 1935–1940*, p206; and Brian Farrell, *The Defence and Fall of Singapore 1940–1942*, pp46–8.

3 Jon Robb-Webb adopts a different argument in *The British Pacific Fleet Experience and Legacy, 1944–50* (UK: Ashgate, 2013), pp28–9. He insists the Mediterranean always had primacy and that significant forces could only be released for the war against Japan once it was secured. This argument fails to recognise the ultimate dependence of the Middle East theatre on the Indian Ocean until early 1943.

4 The most forthright exponent of this view is Correlli Barnett, especially in 'The Influence of History upon Sea Power: The Royal Navy in the Second World War', in *Naval Power in the Twentieth Century*.

5 Useful correctives to Barnett's negative view of Royal Navy potential and which stress the relative success of late 1930s rearmament include David Edgerton, *Warfare State*, and *Britain's War Machine*; G A H Gordon, *British Seapower and Procurement Between the Wars*; and J R Ferris, 'The Fulcrum of Power: Britain, Japan and the Asia-Pacific Region: 1880–1945', in *Maritime Strategy and National Security in Japan and Britain*, ed Alessio Patalano (Leiden, Netherlands: Koninklijke Brill NV, 2012).

6 Roskill, *War at Sea*, vol III, part 2, appendix S.

7 *War at Sea*, vol III, part 1, chapter 1, table 1.

8 H P Willmott, *Grave of a Dozen Schemes: British Naval Planning and the War against Japan 1943–45*.

9 This argument was first suggested by Anthony Clayton in *The British Empire as a Superpower 1919–39* (Basingstoke: Macmillan, 1986), pp513–17. It is also consistent with the important reappraisal of Britain's contribution to Allied success in World War II provided by Robert Tombs in *The English and Their History* (Allen Lane, 2014), p752.

10 *Germany and the Second World War*, vol 6, pp181–3, 848–50.

Annex – Warships Completed by Principal Naval Powers 1930–1942

1 Dönitz's memoirs, *Ten Years and Twenty Days*, chapter 5, gives details of the ambitious Z Plan for a major surface navy and its suspension to concentrate on U-boat production.

2 John R Ferris, 'It is our business in the Navy to command the seas: The last decade of British maritime supremacy' and 'The Fulcrum of Power: Britain, Japan and the Asia–Pacific Region: 1880–1945', in *Maritime Strategy and National Security in Japan and Britain*, ed Alessio Patalano (Leiden, Netherlands: Koninklijke Brill NV, 2012).

3 Two of these carriers were converted merchant vessels not built to full warship standards.

4 Five of these carriers were provided by the United States under lend-lease in 1942.

5 This total includes the ten *Southampton* class completed from 1937–39. They qualify as heavy cruisers on the basis of displacement, number of guns and level of protection.
6 Totals include *Brooklyn* and *St Louis* classes which merit heavy cruiser status on the same basis as the *Southampton* class.
7 This total includes the three pocket battleships of the *Admiral Scheer* class.
8 Total includes seventeen vessels either built in Australia or Canada or requisitioned at the start of the war.
9 Includes fifty old destroyers acquired from the United States under the destroyers for bases deal of August 1940. The remainder are variants of the Hunt class but include five vessels built overseas.
10 The two additional ships here were ordered by the Royal Canadian Navy.
11 The four ships here were again ordered by the Royal Canadian Navy.
12 This was a pocket battleship.
13 This was a pocket battleship.
14 This unit was handed to the Royal Australian Navy.
15 This unit was a pocket battleship.
16 These two vessels also went to the Royal Australian Navy.
17 This unit was requisitioned from a Brazilian order.
18 These five vessels were also requisitioned from Brazil.
19 These are fifty old US destroyers acquired under the August 1940 destroyers for bases deal.
20 These seven vessels were built in Canada.
21 These vessels were built in Canada.
22 These five carriers were supplied by the United States.
23 These three vessels were built in Canada.
24 These two vessels were requisitioned from Turkey.
25 These units were built in Canada.

Bibliography

Primary sources

National Archives

Cabinet Office papers
CAB 2: Committee of Imperial Defence and Standing Sub Committee Minutes
CAB 16: Committee of Imperial Defence, Ad Hoc Sub Committees
CAB 24: War Cabinet and Cabinet Memoranda
CAB 50: Oil Board Minutes and Memoranda
CAB 53: Chiefs of Staff Minutes and Memoranda 1923–1939
CAB 55: Joint Planning Committee Minutes and Memoranda 1923–1939
CAB 65: War Cabinet and Cabinet Minutes (WM and CM Series) 1939–1942
CAB 66: War Cabinet and Cabinet Memoranda (WP and CP Series) 1939–1942
CAB 69: Defence Committee Operations Minutes and Papers 1940–1942
CAB 70: Defence Committee Supply 1941–1942
CAB 77: Oil Policy Minutes and Papers 1939–1942
CAB 79: Chiefs of Staff Minutes 1940–1942
CAB 80: Chiefs of Staff Memoranda (O) 1940–1942
CAB 81: JIC Minutes and Reports 1941–1942
CAB 84: Joint Planning Committee Papers 1940–1942
CAB 88: Combined Chiefs of Staff Meetings 1942
CAB 99: US and UK Summit Conferences 1941–1942
CAB 105: War Cabinet and Cabinet Office Telegrams
CAB 106: Historical Section: Archivist and Librarian Files
CAB 119: Joint Planning Staff: Correspondence and Papers
CAB 120: Minister of Defence Secretariat Records
CAB 121: Cabinet Office: Special Secret Information Centre: Files
CAB 122: Records of British Joint Staff and Joint Services Missions Washington
CAB 146: Historical Section, Enemy Documents Section: Files and Papers

Premier files
PREM 1: Prime Minister's Office: Correspondence and papers 1916–1940
PREM 3: Prime Minister's Office: Operational correspondence 1937–1946
PREM 4: Prime Minister's Office: Confidential correspondence 1934–1946

Foreign Office records
FO 371: Foreign Office: Political Developments: General correspondence
from 1906–1966

Intelligence records
HW1: Government Code and Cypher School: Signals Intelligence passed to
the Prime Minister, messages and correspondence
HW 4: Government Code and Cypher School: Far East Combined Bureau,
Signals Intelligence Centre in the Far East (HMS Anderson): Records
HW 12: Government Code and Cypher School: Diplomatic Section and
predecessors: Decrypts of intercepted diplomatic communications (BJ
Series)
HW 50: Government Code and Cypher School: Records relating to the
writing of the history of British signals intelligence in the Second World
War.

Records of the fighting services
Admiralty
ADM 1: Admiralty: Correspondence and Papers
ADM 116: Admiralty: Record Office: Cases
ADM 167: Board of Admiralty: Minutes and Memoranda
ADM 173: Admiralty: Submarine Logs
ADM 178: Admiralty: Naval Courts Martial Cases, Boards of Enquiry
Reports, and other papers
ADM 199: Admiralty: War History Cases and Papers, Second World War
ADM 205: Admiralty: Office of the First Sea Lord, correspondence and
papers
ADM 223: Admiralty: Naval Intelligence Division and Operational
Intelligence Centre: Intelligence Reports and Papers
ADM 234: Admiralty: Reference Books (BR Series)

War office
WO 193: Directorate of Military Operations and Plans: Planning and
Intelligence
WO 208: Records of Directorate of Military Intelligence 1940–1942
WO 216: Office of the Chief of the Imperial General Staff: Papers

Air Ministry
AIR 2: Air Ministry records comprising policy, case and committee reports
AIR 8: Records of the Chief of Air Staff
AIR 14: Bomber Command operational and technical matters
AIR 20: Papers accumulated by the Air Historical Branch
AIR 22: Air Intelligence Summaries
AIR 23: Royal Air Force Overseas Commands
AIR 40: Air Ministry: Directorate of Intelligence: reports and papers

Japan
*Japan Center for Asian Historical Records, National Archives of Japan,
National Institute for Defence Studies*
C08030581700: Detailed engagement report from March 26 to April 22,
1942, Warship *Hiryu*

Published official records

United Kingdom
Navy Records Society, vol 136: *The Collective Naval Defence of the Empire
1900–1940*, ed Nicholas Tracy (UK: Ashgate Publishing, 1997)
Navy Records Society, vol 137: *The Defeat of the Enemy Attack on
Shipping, 1939–1945*, ed Eric J Grove (UK: Ashgate Publishing, 1997)
Navy Records Society, vol 139: *The Battle of the Atlantic and Signals
Intelligence: U-boat Situations and Trends, 1941–1945*, ed David Syrett
(UK: Ashgate Publishing, 1998)
Navy Records Society, vol 155: *Anglo-American Naval Relations, 1919–
1939*, ed Michael Simpson (UK: Ashgate Publishing, 2010)
Navy Records Society, vol 158: *The Mediterranean Fleet 1919–1929*, ed
Paul Halpern (UK: Ashgate Publishing, 2011)
Navy Records Society, vol 159: *The Fleet Air Arm in the Second World War,
vol II: 1939–1941*, ed Ben Jones (UK: Ashgate Publishing, 2012)

United States
Franklin D Roosevelt Presidential Library
US Congress, Joint Committee on the Investigation of the Pearl Harbor
Attack, *Report* (Washington DC: US Government Printing Office, 1946)
US Congress, Joint Committee on the Investigation of the Pearl Harbor
Attack, *Hearings before the Joint Committee,* vols 1–39 (Washington,
DC: US Government Printing Office, 1946)
The 'Magic' Background to Pearl Harbor, vols 1–8 (US Department of
Defence, 1977)

US Strategic Bombing Survey (Pacific), Naval Analysis Division, *Interrogation of Japanese Officials*, OPNAV-P-03-100

Military History Section Headquarters, US Army Forces Far East, *Japanese Monographs*, distributed by the Office of the Chief of Military History, Department of the Army, 1946–1960. Most of these monographs can be accessed at: www.ibiblio.org/hyperwar/Japan/Monos/index.html; and www.milspecmanuals.com.

Reports of General MacArthur: Japanese Operations in the Southwest Pacific Area, vol II, part 1. Compiled from Japanese Demobilisation Bureau Records (US Centre for Military History, 1994 edition)

Private papers

Alexander, Viscount A V, Churchill College, Cambridge

Beesly, Patrick, Churchill College, Cambridge

Brooke-Popham, Air Chief Marshal Sir Robert, Liddell-Hart Centre, Kings College, London

Chatfield, Admiral of the Fleet, Lord, National Maritime Museum, Greenwich

Cunningham, Admiral of the Fleet Viscount of Hyndhope, British Library

Davis, Admiral Sir William, Churchill College, Cambridge

Doig, Captain D H, Royal Naval Museum Library, Portsmouth

Drax, Admiral Sir Reginald P E, Churchill College, Cambridge

Godfrey, Vice Admiral J H, National Maritime Museum

Grimsdale, Major General G E, Personal Memoir, Imperial War Museum

Halder, Generaloberst Franz, War Journal, US Army Historical Division, Fort Leavenworth, Kansas

Layton, Admiral Sir Geoffrey, British Library

Marder, Professor Arthur J, University of California Irvine Libraries, Special Collections

Marshall, General George C, Marshall Papers, Marshall Research Library, Lexington, Virginia

Roskill, Captain S W, Churchill College, Cambridge

Somerville, Admiral of the Fleet Sir James, Churchill College, Cambridge

Willis, Admiral of the Fleet Sir Algernon, 'War Memoirs', Imperial War Museum

Published memoirs

Alanbrooke, Field Marshal Lord, ed Alex Danchev and Daniel Todman, *War Diaries 1939–1945* (London: Weidenfeld and Nicolson, 2001)

Avon, The Right Honourable Earl of, *The Eden Memoirs* (London: Cassell, 1962–1968): *Facing the Dictators* (1962); *The Reckoning* (1965)

Chatfield, Admiral of the Fleet Lord, *The Navy and Defence* (London: William Heinemann, 1942–1947), vol I: *The Navy and Defence* (1942); vol II: *It Might Happen Again* (1947)

Churchill, Winston S, *The Second World War* (London: Cassell, 1948–1954): *The Gathering Storm* (1948); *Their Finest Hour* (1949); *The Grand Alliance* (1950); *The Hinge of Fate* (1951)

Crosely, Commander R M, *They Gave Me a Seafire* (Barnsley: Pen & Sword Aviation, 2014)

Cunningham, Admiral of the Fleet Viscount of Hyndhope, *A Sailor's Odyssey* (London: Hutchinson, 1957)

——————, *The Cunningham papers, Selections from the Private and Official Correspondence*, ed Michael Simpson (Navy Records Society, 1999)

Dönitz, Admiral Karl, *Memoirs: Ten Years and Twenty Days* (Frontline Books edition, 2012)

Ismay, General the Lord, *Memoirs* (London: William Heinemann, 1960)

Kennedy, Major General Sir John, *The Business of War: The War Narrative of Major General Sir John Kennedy* (London: Hutchinson, 1957)

Popham, Hugh, *Sea Flight: The Wartime Memoirs of a Fleet Air Arm Pilot* (London: William Kimber, 1954)

Pownall, Lieutenant General Sir Henry, *Chief of Staff: The Diaries of Lieutenant General Sir Henry Pownall*, vol II: 1940–44, ed Brian Bond (London: Leo Cooper, 1974)

Slessor, Marshal of the Royal Air Force Sir John, *The Central Blue: Recollections and Reflections by Marshal of the Royal Air Force Sir John Slessor* (London: Cassell & Co, 1956)

Somerville, Admiral of the Fleet Sir James, *The Somerville Papers, Selections from Private and Official Correspondence*, ed Michael Simpson (Navy Records Society, 1995)

Ugaki, Admiral Matome, *Fading Victory: The Diary of Admiral Matome Ugaki*, ed Donald M Goldstein and Katherine V Dillon (Annapolis USA: Naval Institute Press, 1991)

Secondary works

Books

Aldrich, Richard, *Intelligence and the War against Japan: Britain, America, and the Politics of Secret Service* (Cambridge University Press, 2000)

Agawa, Hiroyuki, *The Reluctant Admiral: Yamamoto and the Imperial Japanese Navy* (Kodansha International Ltd, 2000)

Ball, Simon, *The Bitter Sea* (London: Harper Press, 2009)

Banks, Arthur, *Wings of the Dawning: The Battle for the Indian Ocean 1939–1945* (Malvern UK: Images Publishing, 1996)

Barber, Noel, *Sinister Twilight: The Fall of Singapore* (London: Collins, 1968)

Barker, Ralph, *Shipbusters: The story of the RAF torpedo bombers* (London: Chatto & Windus, 1957)

Barnett, Correlli, *Engage the Enemy More Closely* (London: Hodder and Stoughton, 1991)

——————, *The Audit of War: The Illusion and Reality of Britain as a Great Nation* (Basingstoke: Macmillan, 1986)

——————, *The Collapse of British Power* (Eyre Methuen, 1972)

Bartsch, William H, *December 8, 1941: MacArthur's Pearl Harbor* (USA: Texas A & M University Press, 2003)

Bath, Alan Harris, *Tracking the Axis Enemy: The Triumph of Anglo-American Naval Intelligence* (USA: Kansas University Press, 1998)

Bayly, Christopher, and Tim Harper, *Forgotten Armies: Britain's Asian Empire and the War with Japan* (London: Allen Lane, 2004)

Beaumont, Joan, *Comrades in Arms: British Aid to Russia 1941–1945* (London: Davis-Poynter, 1980)

Beesly, Patrick, *Very Special Admiral: The Life of Admiral J H Godfrey* (London: Hamish Hamilton, 1980)

Beevor, Anthony, *The Second World War* (London: Weidenfeld and Nicolson, 2012)

Bell, Christopher, *Churchill and Seapower* (Oxford University Press, 2012)

Bell, Christopher M, *The Royal Navy, Seapower and Strategy between the Wars* (Basingstoke, UK: Macmillan Press Ltd, 2000)

Bellamy, Chris, *Absolute War: Soviet Russia in the Second World War* (London: Macmillan, 2007)

Benbow, Tim, *British Naval Aviation: The First 100 Years* (UK: Ashgate Publishing, 2011)

Benson, Robert L, *A History of US Communications Intelligence in World War II: Policy and Administration* (USA: Center for Cryptological History, National Security Agency, 1997)

Best, Anthony, *British Intelligence and the Japanese Challenge in Asia 1914–1941* (London: Palgrave Macmillan, 2002)

——————, *Britain, Japan and Pearl Harbor: Avoiding War in East Asia 1936–41* (London: Routledge, 1995)

Black, Jeremy, *The Politics of World War Two* (London: The Social Affairs Unit, 2009)

Blair, Clay, *Hitler's U-boat War, The Hunters 1939–1942* (London: Weidenfeld & Nicolson, 1997)

Boog, Horst, Werner Rahn, and Bernd Wegner, *Germany and the Second World War*, vol VI: *The Global War* (OUP, 2001)

Brodhurst, Robin, *Churchill's Anchor: The Biography of Admiral of the Fleet Sir Dudley Pound OM, GCB, GCVO* (UK: Leo Cooper, 2000)

Brown, D K, *Nelson to Vanguard: Warship Design and Development 1923–1945* (London: Chatham Publishing, 2006)

———, *The Road to Oran: Anglo-French Naval Relations September 1939–July 1940* (London: Frank Cass, 2004)

Budiansky, Stephen, *Battle of Wits: The Complete Story of Codebreaking in World War II* (London: Viking, 2000)

Bullard, Dr Stephen, *Japanese Army Operations in the South Pacific Area: New Britain and Papua Campaigns 1942–1943*, translation of Senshi Sosho, Japanese War History Series, War History Office of the National Defence College of Japan, edited extracts from several volumes (Australian War Memorial, 2007)

Burt, R A, *British Battleships 1919–1945* (UK: Seaforth Publishing, 2012)

Butler, Professor J R M, *Grand Strategy*, vol III: *June 1941–August 1942, Part II* (London: HMSO, 1964)

———, *Grand Strategy*, vol II: *September 1939–June 1941* (London: HMSO, 1957)

Callahan, Raymond, *The Worst Disaster: The Fall of Singapore*, 2nd ed (Singapore: Cultured Lotus, 2001)

Clausen, Henry C, and Bruce Lee, *Pearl Harbor: Final Judgement* (USA: Da Capo Press, 2001)

Clayton, Anthony, *The British Empire as a Superpower 1919–39* (Basingstoke: Macmillan, 1986)

Costello, John, *Days of Infamy* (New York, USA: Nimbus Communications, 1994)

Cowman, Ian, *Dominion or Decline: Anglo-American Naval Relations in the Pacific 1937–41* (Oxford UK and Dulles (VA) USA: Berg, 1996)

Cox, Jeffrey, *Rising Sun, Falling Skies: The Disastrous Java Sea Campaign of World War II* (Osprey Publishing, 2014)

Cradock, Percy, *Know Your Enemy: How the Joint Intelligence Committee saw the World* (London: John Murray, 2002)

Dear, I C B, and M R D Foot, *The Oxford Companion to World War II*, paperback edn (Oxford University Press, 2001)

Denniston, Robin, *Thirty Secret Years: A G Denniston's work in Signals Intelligence 1914–1944* (UK: Polperro Heritage Press, 2007)

Dimbleby, Jonathan, *The Battle of the Atlantic: How the Allies won the War* (Penguin, 2015)

Doling, Peter, *From Port T to RAF Gan* (UK: Woodfield Publishing, 2003)

Donovan, Peter, and John Mack, *Codebreaking in the Pacific* (New York: Springer International, 2014)

Dreifort, John E, *Myopic Grandeur, The Ambivalence of French Foreign Policy toward the Far East, 1919–1945* (Ohio, USA: Kent State University Press, 1991)

Dull, Paul S, *A Battle History of the Imperial Japanese Navy* (Annapolis USA: Naval Institute Press, 1978)

Edgerton, David, *England and the Aeroplane: Militarism, Modernity and Machines* (London: Penguin Books, 2013)

——————, *Britain's War Machine: Weapons, Resources and Experts in the Second World War* (London: Allen Lane, 2011)

——————, *Warfare State: Britain, 1920–1970* (Cambridge University Press, 2006)

Ellis, John, *Brute Force: Allied Strategy and Tactics in the Second World War* (London: Andre Deutsch, 1990)

Elphick, Peter, *Far Eastern File: The Intelligence War in the Far East 1930–45* (London: Hodder & Stoughton, 1997)

Erskine, Ralph and Smith, Michael, *The Bletchley Park Codebreakers* (Biteback, 2011)

Evans, David C, *The Japanese Navy in World War II* (Annapolis USA: Naval Institute Press, 1986)

——————, and Mark R Peattie, *Kaigun: Strategy, Tactics, and Technology in the Imperial Japanese Navy* (Annapolis USA: Naval Institute Press, 1997)

Evans, Richard J, *The Third Reich at War* (London: Penguin, 2009)

Farrell, Brian, *The Defence and Fall of Singapore 1940–1942* (Stroud, UK: Tempus, 2005)

——————, *The Basis and Making of Grand Strategy – Was there a Plan?* (UK: Edwin Mellen Press, 1998)

——————, and Sandy Hunter (eds), *Singapore, Sixty Years On: The Fall of Singapore Revisited* (Singapore: Eastern Universities Press, 2002)

Faulkner, Marcus, *A Naval Atlas 1939–1945* (UK: Seaforth Publishing, 2012)

Feis, Herbert, *The Road to Pearl Harbor* (USA: Princeton University Press, 1950)

Ferris, John R, *Intelligence and Strategy* (London, Routledge: 2005)

Field, Andrew, *Royal Navy Strategy in the Far East, 1919–1939: Planning for a war against Japan* (London: Frank Cass, 2004)

Ford, Daniel, *The Sorry Saga of the Brewster Buffalo* (USA: Warbird Books, 2011)

——————, *The Pacific War: Clash of Empires in World War II* (London: Continuum International Publishing, 2012)

Ford, Douglas, *Britain's Secret War Against Japan 1937–1945* (Abingdon, UK: Routledge, 2006)

Franklin, George, *Britain's Anti-Submarine Capability, 1919–1939* (London: Routledge, 2003)

Frey, John W, and H Chandler Ide, *A History of the Petroleum Administration for War, 1941–1945* (Hawaii: University Press of the Pacific, 2005)

Friedman, Norman, *The British Battleship 1906–1946* (UK: Seaforth Publishing, 2015)

—————, *Naval Anti-Aircraft Guns and Gunnery* (UK: Seaforth Publishing, 2014)

—————, *British Carrier Aviation: The Evolution of the Ships and their Aircraft* (Conway Maritime Press, 1988)

Fuchida, Mitsuo, and Masatake Okumiya, *Midway: The Japanese Story* (USA: Naval Institute Press, 1955)

Gibbs, Professor N H, *Grand Strategy*, vol I (HMSO, 1976)

Gilbert, Martin, *The Churchill War Papers*, vol III: *The ever-widening war* (London: William Heinemann, 2000)

—————, *Winston S Churchill*, vol VI: *Finest Hour 1939–1941* and vol VII: *Road to Victory 1941–1945* (London: William Heinemann, 1983 and 1986)

Glancey, Jonathan, *Spitfire: The Biography* (London: Atlantic Books, 2006)

Goodman, Michael S, *The Official History of the Joint Intelligence Committee*, vol I: *From the Approach of the Second World War to the Suez Crisis* (London: Routledge, 2014)

Gordon, G A H, *The Rules of the Game: Jutland and British Naval Command* (London: John Murray, 1996)

—————, *British Seapower and Procurement between the Wars* (Annapolis, USA: Naval Institute Press, 1988)

Goldstein, Donald M, and Katherine V Dillon, *The Pacific War Papers: Japanese Documents of World War II* (Washington, USA: Brassey's, 2004)

—————, *The Pearl Harbor Papers: Inside the Japanese Plans* (Virginia, USA: Brassey's, 1993)

Gorodetsky, Gabriel, *Grand Delusion: Stalin and the German Invasion of Russia* (Yale University Press, 1999)

Gough, Barry, *Historical Dreadnoughts: Arthur Marder, Stephen Roskill and Battles for Naval History* (Barnsley UK: Seaforth Publishing, 2010)

Greene, Jack, and Alessandro Massignani, *The Naval War in the Mediterranean 1940–1943* (UK: Chatham Publishing, 2002)

Grove, Eric, *The Royal Navy* (Basingstoke, UK: Palgrave Macmillan, 2005)

Gwyer, J M A, *Grand Strategy*, vol III: *June 1941–August 1942*, part 1 (London: HMSO, 1964)

Haarr, Geirr H, *The German Invasion of Norway April 1940* (UK: Seaforth Publishing, 2011)

Haggie, Paul, *Britannia at Bay: The Defence of the British Empire against Japan 1931–1941* (Oxford: Clarendon Press, 1981)

Hancock, W K, and M M Gowing, *The British War Economy* (British Official History Civil Series) (London: HMSO, 1949)

Harding, Richard, *The Royal Navy, 1930–2000, Innovation and Defence* (London and New York: Frank Cass, 2004)

Harvey, A D, *Collision of Empires: Britain in Three World Wars 1793–1945* (London: Hambledon Press, 1992)

Haslop, Dennis, *Britain, Germany and the Battle of the Atlantic* (London: Bloomsbury Academic, 2013)

Hastings, Max, *The Secret War: Spies, Codes and Guerillas 1939–1945* (London: William Collins, 2015)

——————, *All Hell Let Loose: The World at War 1939–45* (London: Harper Press, 2011)

Hata, Ikuhiko, Yasuho Izawa, and Christopher Shores, *Japanese Naval Air Force Fighter Units and their Aces 1932–1945* (London: Grub Street, 2011)

Hattendorf, John B, *Naval Strategy and Power in the Mediterranean: Past, Present and Future* (London: Frank Cass, 2000)

Hayward, Joel S A, *Stopped at Stalingrad: The Luftwaffe and Hitler's Defeat in the East* (USA: University Press of Kansas, 1998)

Heinrichs, Waldo, *Threshold of War: Franklin D Roosevelt and American Entry into World War II* (Oxford University Press, 1988)

Hill, Alexander, *The Great Patriotic War of the Soviet Union, 1941–45* (London: Routledge, 2009)

Hinsley, F H, with E E Thomas, C F G Ransom, and R C Knight, *British Intelligence in the Second World War. Its Influence on Strategy and Operations*, 3 vols (London: HMSO, 1977–1984)

Hinsley, F H, and Alan Stripp, *Code Breakers: The Inside Story of Bletchley Park* (Oxford University Press, 1993)

Hobbs, David, *British Aircraft Carriers: Design, Development and Service Histories* (UK: Seaforth Publishing, 2013)

——————, *The British Pacific Fleet: The Royal Navy's Most Powerful Strike Force* (UK, Barnsley Yorkshire: Seaforth Publishing, 2011)

Holland, James, *Together We Stand: North Africa 1942–1943: Turning the Tide in the West* (London: Harper Collins, 2005)

Holley, Irving Brinton, *US Army in World War II, Buying Aircraft: Material Procurement for the Army Air Forces* (Washington USA: US Government Printing Office, 1964)

Hopkins, William B, *The Pacific War* (USA: Zenith Press, 2008)

Hore, Peter (ed), *Dreadnought to Daring: 100 Years of Comment, Controversy and Debate in The Naval Review* (Barnsley: Seaforth Publishing, 2012)

Hotta, Eri, *Japan 1941, Countdown to Infamy* (New York: Knopf Publishing, 2013)

Hough, Richard, *The Hunting of Force Z* (Glasgow: William Collins, 1963)

Howard, Michael, *The Mediterranean Strategy in the Second World War* (London: Greenhill Books, 1993)

Howarth, Stephen, *Morning Glory: A history of the Imperial Japanese Navy* (London: Hamish Hamilton, 1983)

Howse, Derek, *Radar at Sea: The Royal Navy in World War II* (Basingstoke: Macmillan, 1993)

Huston, John W, *American Airpower Comes of Age: General Henry H 'Hap' Arnold's World War II Diaries*, vol 1 (Alabama USA: Air University Press: 2002)

Jackson, Ashley, *The British Empire and the Second World War* (London: Hambledon Continuum, 2006)

Jackson, Julian, *The Fall of France: The Nazi Invasion of 1940* (OUP, 2003)

James, Lawrence, *Churchill and Empire: Portrait of an Imperialist* (London: Weidenfeld & Nicolson, 2013)

—————, *The Rise and Fall of the British Empire*, paperback edn (Abacus, 1998)

Jeffery, Keith, *MI6: The History of the Secret Intelligence Service 1909–1949* (London: Bloomsbury, 2010)

Johnston, Ian, and Ian Buxton, *The Battleship Builders: Constructing and Arming British Capital Ships* (Barnsley, UK: Seaforth Publishing, 2013)

Kennedy, Greg, *Anglo-American Strategic Relations in the Far East 1933–1939* (London: Frank Cass, 2002)

Kennedy, Paul, *Engineers of Victory: The Problem Solvers Who Turned the Tide in the Second World War* (London: Allen Lane, 2013)

Kennedy, Paul M, *The Rise and Fall of the Great Powers* (London: Unwin Hyman, 1988)

—————, *The Rise and Fall of British Naval Mastery* (London: Allen Lane, 1976)

Kershaw, Ian, *Fateful Choices: Ten Decisions That Changed The World* (London: Penguin Group, 2007)

King, Dan, *The Last Zero Fighter* (USA: Pacific Press, 2012)

King, William Donald, *The Stick and the Stars* (London: Hutchinson, 1958)

Kitchen, Martin, *Rommel's Desert War: Waging World War II in North Africa 1941–43* (Cambridge University Press, 2009)

Kolinsky, Martin, *Britain's War in the Middle East, Strategy and Diplomacy, 1936–42* (Basingstoke: Macmillan, 1999)

Kotani, Ken, *Japanese Intelligence in World War II* (Oxford, UK: Osprey Publishing, 2009)

Kroener, Bernhard R, Rolf Dieter Muller, and Hans Umbreit, *Germany and the Second World War*, vol V: *Organisation and Mobilisation in the German Sphere of Power: Part 1 Wartime Administration, Economy and Manpower Resources 1939–1941*, English edn (UK: Clarendon Press, 2006)

————, *Germany and the Second World War*, vol V: *Organisation and Mobilisation in the German Sphere of Power Part 2: Wartime Administration, Economy and Manpower Resources 1942–1944/45*, English edn (UK: Clarendon Press, 2006)

Leighton, Richard M, and Robert W Coakley, *United States Army in World War II, Global Logistics and Strategy 1940–1943* (Washington DC: US Government Printing Office, 1955)

Lenton, H T, *British and Empire Warships in the Second World War* (London: Greenhill Books, 1998)

Leutze, James R, *A Different Kind of Victory: A Biography of Admiral Thomas C Hart* (Annapolis, USA: Naval Institute Press, 1981)

————, *Bargaining for Supremacy: Anglo-American Naval Collaboration, 1937–1941* (USA: University of North Carolina Press, 1977)

Lewis, Tom, and Peter Ingman, *Carrier Attack Darwin 1942* (Australia: Avonmore Books, 2013)

Lukacs, John, *The Legacy of the Second World War* (New Haven, USA and London: Yale University Press, 2010)

Lundstrom, John B, *The First South Pacific Campaign: Pacific Fleet Strategy December 1941–June 1942* (Annapolis, USA: Naval Institute Press, 2014)

Lyman, Robert, *First Victory: Britain's Forgotten Struggle in the Middle East, 1941* (London: Constable, 2006)

————, *Slim, Master of War: Burma and the Birth of Modern Warfare* (London: Constable and Robinson, 2004)

McBeth, B S, *British Oil Policy 1919–1939* (London: Frank Cass, 1985)

McDonough, Frank, *The Origins of the Second World War: An International Perspective* (London and New York: Continuum International Publishing, 2011)

McIntyre, David W, *The Rise and Fall of the Singapore Naval Base 1919–1942* (London: Macmillan, 1979)

MacIntyre, Captain Donald, *Fighting Admiral: The Life of Admiral of the Fleet Sir James Somerville* (London: Evans brothers, 1961)

McKinstry, Leo, *Hurricane: Victor of the Battle of Britain* (London: John Murray, 2010)

McLachlan, Donald, *Room 39, Naval Intelligence in Action 1939–45* (London: Weidenfeld and Nicolson, 1968)

Maiolo, Joe, *Cry Havoc: The Arms Race and the Second World War 1931–1941* (London: John Murray, 2011)

Mallett, Robert, *The Italian Navy and Fascist Expansionism 1935–1940* (London: Frank Cass, 1998)

Manchester, William, *American Caesar: Douglas MacArthur 1880–1964* (New York, USA: Dell Publishing, 1978)

Marder, Arthur J, *From the Dardanelles to Oran: Studies of the Royal Navy in War and Peace, 1915–1940* (London: Oxford University Press, 1974)

———, *Old Friends, New Enemies: the Royal Navy and the Imperial Japanese Navy, 1936–1945* (London and New York: Oxford University Press, 1981–1990), vol I: *Strategic Illusions 1936–1941* (1981); vol II: *The Pacific War 1942–1945* (1990)

Mars, Alastair, *Submarines at War 1939–1945* (UK: William Kimber, 1971)

Marston, Daniel, *The Pacific War Companion: From Pearl Harbor to Hiroshima* (Osprey Publishing, 2011)

Matloff, Maurice, and Edwin M Snell, *Strategic Planning for Coalition Warfare 1941–1942* (USA: Centre of Military History, US Army, 1990)

Maurer, John H, and Christopher M Bell, *At the Crossroads between Peace and War: The London Naval Conference of 1930* (Annapolis, USA: Naval Institute Press, 2014)

Middlebrook, Martin, and Patrick Mahoney, *Battleship: The loss of the Prince of Wales and the Repulse* (London: Allen Lane, 1977)

Miller, Edward S, *War Plan Orange: The US Strategy to Defeat Japan 1897–1945* (Annapolis USA: Naval Institute Press, 1991)

Millett, Allan R, and Williamson Murray, *Military Effectiveness*, vol II: *The Interwar Period* (Cambridge University Press, 2010)

———, *A War To Be Won: Fighting the Second World War* (USA: Harvard University Press, 2000)

More, Charles, *Black Gold: Britain and Oil in the Twentieth Century* (London: Continuum, 2009)

Morewood, Steven, *The British Defence of Egypt 1935–1940: Conflict and Crisis in the Eastern Mediterranean* (London: Frank Cass, 2005)

Morton, Louis, *United States Army in World War II, The War in the Pacific: Strategy and Command: The First Two Years* (Washington DC: US Government Printing Office, 1962)

——, *United States Army in World War II, The War in the Pacific: The Fall of the Philippines* (Washington DC: US Government Printing Office, 1953)

Morison, Samuel Eliot, *The Two Ocean War* (USA: Little, Brown & Co, 1963)

Murfett, Malcom H, *Naval Warfare 1919–1945: An operational history of the volatile war at sea,* (Oxford: Routledge, 2009)

——, *The First Sea Lords: From Fisher to Mountbatten* (Westport CT USA: Praeger, 1995)

——, *Fool Proof Relations: The Search for Anglo-American Naval Co-operation during the Chamberlain Years 1937–1940* (Singapore University Press: 1984)

Murray, Williamson, *The Luftwaffe 1933–45: Strategy for Defeat* (London: Brassey's, 1996)

Neidpath, James, *The Singapore Naval Base and the Defence of Britain's Eastern Empire, 1919–1941* (Oxford University Press, 1981)

Nicholson, Arthur, *Hostage to Fortune: Winston Churchill and the Loss of the Prince of Wales and Repulse* (Stroud, UK: Sutton Publishing, 2005)

O'Brien, Phillips Payson, *How the War was Won: Air-Sea Power and Allied Victory in World War II* (Cambridge University Press: 2015)

O'Connell, John F, *Submarine Operational Effectiveness in the 20th Century: Part Two 1939–1945* (USA: iUniverse Inc, 2011)

O'Hara, Vincent P, *Torch: North Africa and the Allied Path to Victory* (Annapolis: Naval Institute Press, 2015)

——, David Dickson, and Richard Worth, *On Seas Contested: The Seven Great Navies of the Second World War* (Annapolis: Naval Institute Press, 2010)

Okumiya, Masatake, and Horikoshi, Jiro, *Zero* (USA: Ballantine, 1957)

Ong, Chit Chung, *Operation Matador: World War II: Britain's attempt to foil the Japanese invasion of Malaya and Singapore* (London: Times Academic Press, 1997)

Overy, Richard, *The Bombing War: Europe 1939–1945* (London: Allen Lane, 2013)

——, *Why the Allies Won,* (London: Pimlico, 2006)

——, and Andrew Wheatcroft, *The Road to War: The Origins of World War II* (London: Vintage, 2009)

Padfield, Peter, *War Beneath the Sea* (London: John Murray, 1995)

Parker, R A C, *The Second World War: A Short History* (Oxford University Press, 1989)

514

Parshall, Jonathan B, and Anthony Tully, *Shattered Sword: The Untold Story of the Battle of Midway* (Washington, USA: Potomac Books, 2007)

Payton-Smith, D J, *Oil: A Study of Wartime Policy and Administration* (London: HMSO, 1971)

Peattie, Mark, *Sunburst: The Rise of Japanese Naval Airpower, 1909–1941* (Annapolis, USA: Naval Institute Press, 2001)

Peden, G C, *Arms, Economics and British Strategy: From Dreadnoughts to Hydrogen Bombs* (Cambridge University Press, 2007)

Pfennigwerth, Ian, *A Man of Intelligence: The Life of Captain Eric Nave Australian Codebreaker Extraordinary* (Rosenberg Publishing, 2006)

Pike, Francis, *Hirohito's War: The Pacific War, 1941–1945* (London: Bloomsbury, 2015)

Playfair, Major General I S O, *The Mediterranean and Middle East*, vol I: *The Early Successes against Italy* (HMSO, 1954)

Polmar, Norman, with Minoru Genda, Eric Brown, and Robert M Langdon, *Aircraft Carriers: A Graphic History of Carrier Aviation and Its Influence on World Events* (London: MacDonald & Co, 1969)

Porch, Douglas, *The Path to Victory; The Mediterranean Theatre in World War II* (New York: Farrar, Straus and Giroux, 2004)

Postan, Professor M M, *British War Production*, History of the Second World War, United Kingdom Civil Series (London: HMSO, 1952)

Potter, John Deane, *Fiasco: The Break-out of the German Battleships* (London: William Heinemann, 1970)

Prados, John, *Combined Fleet Decoded: The Secret History of American Intelligence and the Japanese Navy in World War II* (New York: Random House, 1995)

Prange, Gordon W, *Miracle at Midway* (USA: McGraw-Hill Book Co., 1982)

Pratt, Lawrence R, *East of Malta, West of Suez* (Cambridge University Press, 1975)

Preston, Anthony, *Aircraft Carriers* (London: Hamlyn, 1979)

Probert, Henry, *The Forgotten Air Force: The Royal Air Force in the War Against Japan 1941–45* (London: Brassey's, 1995)

Raghavan, Srinath, *India's War: The Making of Modern South Asia 1939–1945* (London: Penguin, 2016)

Raugh, Harold E, *Wavell in the Middle East 1939–1941* (London: Brassey's, 1993)

Redford, Duncan, *A History of the Royal Navy, World War II* (London: I B Tauris, 2014)

Remmelink, Willem, *The Invasion of the Dutch East Indies*, translation of Senshi Sosho, Japanese War History Series, vol III, War History Office of the National Defence College of Japan 1967 (Holland: Leiden University, 2015)

Reynolds, David, *From Munich to Pearl Harbor: Roosevelt's America and the Origins of the Second World War* (Chicago: Ivan Dee, 2001)

——————, *In Command of History: Churchill Fighting and Writing the Second World War* (London: Allen Lane, 2004)

——————, *The Creation of the Anglo-American Alliance 1937–41: A Study in Competitive Co-operation*, (Europe Publications, 1981)

Robb-Webb, Jon, *The British Pacific Fleet Experience and Legacy, 1944–50* (UK: Ashgate, 2013)

Roberts, Andrew, *The Storm of War: A New History of the Second World War* (London: Allen Lane, 2009)

——————, *Masters and Commanders: The Military Geniuses who led the West to Victory in World War II* (London: Allen Lane, 2008)

——————, *The Holy Fox: A Life of Lord Halifax* (London: Weidenfeld and Nicolson, 1991)

Roberts, John, *British Warships of the Second World War* (London: Chatham Publishing, 2000)

Romanus, Charles F, and Riley Sunderland, *US Army in World War II, China – India – Burma Theater, Stilwell's Mission to China* (Washington USA: US Government Printing Office, 1953)

Roskill, S W, *Naval Policy between the Wars* (National Maritime Museum, Maritime Monograph 29, 1978)

Roskill, S W, *Churchill and the Admirals* (London: Collins, 1977)

——————, *Naval Policy Between the Wars* (London: Collins, 1968–1976), vol I: *The Period of Anglo-American Antagonism*, 1919–1929 (1968); vol II: *The Period of Reluctant Rearmament*, 1930–1939 (1976)

——————, *The Navy At War 1939–1945* (London; Collins, 1960)

——————, *The War at Sea* (London: HMSO, 1954–1961), vol I: *The Defensive* (1954); vol II: *The Period of Balance* (1956); vol III: *The Offensive* (1961)

Salerno, Reynolds M, *Vital Crossroads: Mediterranean Origins of the Second World War, 1935–1940* (New York: Cornell University Press, 2002)

Schreiber, Gerhardt, and Bernd Stegemann, *Germany and the Second World War*, vol III: *The Mediterranean, South-East Europe and North Africa 1939–1941*, English edn (UK: Clarendon Press, 1998)

Sebag-Montefiore, Hugh, *Enigma: The Battle for the Code* (London: Weidenfeld and Nicolson, 2000)

Seki, Eiji, *Mrs Ferguson's Tea Set: Japan and the Second World War: The Global Consequences Following Germany's Sinking of the SS Automedon in 1940* (Global Oriental, 2006)

Shores, Christopher, with Brian Cull, and Yasuho Izawa, *Bloody Shambles*, vol II: *The Defence of Sumatra to the Fall of Burma* (London: Grub Street, 1993)

———, *Bloody Shambles*, vol I: *The Drift to War to the Fall of Singapore* (London: Grub Street, 1992)

Sokolov, Boris, *The Role of the Soviet Union in World War II: A Re-examination* (Solihull, UK: Helion, 2013)

Smith, Bradley F, *The Ultra-Magic Deals and the Most Secret Special Relationship 1940–1946* (UK: Airlife Publishing, 1993)

Smith, Colin, *England's Last War Against France: Fighting Vichy 1940–1942* (London: Weidenfeld and Nicolson, 2009)

———, *Singapore Burning: Heroism and Surrender in World War II* (London: Viking, 2005)

Smith, Kevin, *Conflict over Convoys: Anglo-American logistics diplomacy in the Second World War* (Cambridge University Press, 1996)

Smith, Michael, *The Emperor's Codes: Bletchley Park's role in breaking Japan's secret ciphers* (London, Bantam Press, 2000)

Smith, Peter C, *Pedestal: The Convoy that saved Malta* (UK: Crecy, 1999)

———, *The Story of the Torpedo Bomber* (London: Pen & Sword, 2007)

———, *Aichi D3A1/2 Val* (UK: Crowood Press, 1999)

Soybell, Phyllis L, *A Necessary Relationship: The Development of Anglo-American Co-operation in Naval Intelligence* (USA: Praeger, 2005)

Stafford, David, *Churchill and Secret Service* (UK: Overlook Press, 1997)

Stephen, Martin, *Scapegoat – The Death of the Prince of Wales and Repulse* (Barnsley, UK: Pen & Sword Ltd, 2014)

———, *The Fighting Admirals* (London: Leo Cooper, 1991)

Stewart, Graham, *Burying Caesar: Churchill, Chamberlain and the Battle for the Tory Party* (London: Weidenfeld and Nicolson, 1999)

Stoler, Mark, *Allies in War: Britain and America Against the Axis Powers 1940–1945* (London: Hodder Education, 2005)

Stone, Norman, *World War II: A Short History* (London: Allen Lane, 2013)

Tagaya, Osamu, *Aichi 99 Kanbaku 'Val' Units 1937–42* (UK: Osprey Publishing, 2010)

———, *Imperial Japanese Aviator 1937–1945* (UK: Osprey Publishing, 2003)

Taliaferro, Jeffrey W, Norrin M Ripsman, and Steven E Lobell, *The Challenge of Grand Strategy: The Great Powers and the Broken Balance between the Wars* (Cambridge University Press, 2012)

Terraine, John, *The Right of the Line* (London, Hodder and Stoughton, 1985)

Thomas, David A, *Japan's War at Sea: To the Coral Sea* (London: Andre Deutsch, 1978)

Thorne, Christopher, *Allies of a Kind: The United States, Britain and the War Against Japan, 1937–1945* (London: Hamish Hamilton, 1978)

Till, Geoffrey, *Air Power and the Royal Navy, 1914–1945: A Historical Survey* (London: Janis, 1979)

Tomlinson, Michael, *The Most Dangerous Moment: The Japanese Assault on Ceylon* (London: William Kimber, 1976)

Tombs, Robert, *The English and Their History* (Allen Lane, 2014)

Tooze, Adam, *The Deluge: The Great War and the Remaking of Global Order 1916–1931* (London: Allen Lane, 2014)

——————, *The Wages of Destruction: The Making and Breaking of the Nazi Economy* (UK: Allen Lane, 2006)

Toye, Richard, *Churchill's Empire: The World that Made Him and the World He Made* (London: Macmillan, 2010)

Vail Motter, T H, *US Army in World War II, The Persian Corridor and Aid to Russia* (Washington USA: US Government Printing Office, 1952)

Van Tuyll, Hubert, *Feeding the Bear: American Aid to the Soviet Union, 1941–1945* (Connecticut, USA: Greenwood Press, 1989)

Warren, Alan, *Singapore 1942: Britain's Greatest Defeat* (London: Hambledon and London, 2002)

Wallace, Gordon, *Carrier Observer* (Shrewsbury, UK: Airlife Publishing, 1993)

Wark, Wesley, *The Ultimate Enemy: British Intelligence and Nazi Germany, 1933–1939* (USA: Cornell University Press, 1985)

Watson, Mark Skinner, *US Army in World War II, Chief of Staff: Prewar Plans and Preparations* (Washington: US Government Printing Office, 1950)

Williford, Glen, *Racing the Sunrise: Reinforcing America's Pacific Outposts, 1941–1942* (Annapolis, USA: Naval Institute Press, 2010)

Willmott, H P, *The Second World War in the Far East* (London: Cassell, 1999)

——————, *Grave of a Dozen Schemes: British Naval Planning and the War Against Japan 1943–1945* (UK: Airlife Publishing, 1996)

——————, *The Barrier and the Javelin: Japanese and Allied Pacific Strategies February to June 1942* (Annapolis USA: Naval Institute Press, 1983)

——————, *Empires in the Balance: Japanese and Allied Pacific Strategies to April 1942* (Annapolis USA: Naval Institute Press, 1982)

Wills, Matthew B, *In the Highest Traditions of the Royal Navy: The Life of Captain John Leach MVO DSO* (UK: Spellmount, 2013)

Wilson, Ben, *Empire of the Deep: The Rise and Fall of the British Navy* (London: Weidenfeld & Nicolson, 2013)

Wilson, Michael, *A Submariners' War: The Indian Ocean 1939–45* (UK: Spellmount Ltd, 2008)

Wilson, Theodore A, *The First Summit: Roosevelt and Churchill at Placentia Bay, 1941* (University Press of Kansas: 1991)

Winton, John, *Cunningham: The Greatest Admiral since Nelson* (London: John Murray, 1998)

———, *Ultra in the Pacific: how breaking Japanese codes and ciphers affected naval operations against Japan 1941–1945* (Annapolis USA, Naval Institute Press, 1993)

Wood, Derek, and Derek Dempster, *The Narrow Margin: The Battle of Britain and the Rise of Air Power 1930–1940* (London: Tri-Service Press, 1990)

Woodburn-Kirby, S, *Singapore: The Chain of Disaster* (London: Cassell, 1971)

———, *The War against Japan*: (London, HMSO, 1957–60), vol I: *The Loss of Singapore* (1957); vol II: *India's Most Dangerous Hour* (1958)

Worth, Roland H, *Secret Allies in the Pacific: covert intelligence and codebreaking between the United States, Great Britain and other nations prior to Pearl Harbor* (North Carolina, USA: McFarland & Co, 2001)

Wragg, David, *The Fleet Air Arm Handbook 1939–1945* (UK: Sutton Publishing, 2001)

Zimm, Alan D, *The Attack on Pearl Harbor: Strategy, Combat, Myths, Deception* (Newbury UK: Casemate Publishers, 2011)

Articles and monographs

Alvarez, David, 'Left in the Dust: Italian Signals Intelligence, 1915–1943', *International Journal of Intelligence and CounterIntelligence*, 14:3 (2001), pp388–408,

Barnett, Correlli, 'The Influence of History upon Sea Power: The Royal Navy in the Second World War', in *Naval Power in the Twentieth Century*, ed N A M Rodger (Basingstoke: Macmillan, 1996)

Baugh, Daniel A, 'Confusions and Constraints: The Navy and British Defence Planning 1919–39', in *Naval Power in the Twentieth Century*, ed N A M Rodger (Basingstoke: Macmillan, 1996)

Beesly, Patrick, 'Godfrey, Vice Admiral John Henry (1888–1971)', *Dictionary of National Biography* (OUP, 2004)

Bell, Christopher M, 'The Royal Navy, war planning, and intelligence assessments of Japan', in *Intelligence and Statecraft: Use and Limits of*

Intelligence in International Security, ed Peter Jackson and Jennifer Siegel (Westport, CT, USA: Praeger, 2005)

——————, 'The "Singapore Strategy" and the Deterrence of Japan: Winston Churchill, the Admiralty and the Dispatch of Force Z', *English Historical Review*, 116:467 (June 2001), pp604–34

Best, Anthony, 'Intelligence, diplomacy and the Japanese threat to British interests, 1914–1941', *Intelligence and National Security*, 17:1 (2002)

——————, 'This probably overvalued military power: British Intelligence and Whitehall's view of Japan', *Intelligence and National Security*, 12:3 (1997), pp67–94

Black, Jeremy, 'Midway and the Indian Ocean', *US Naval War College Review*, 62:4 (Autumn 2009)

Bussemaker, Herman T, 'Paradise in Peril: The Netherlands, Great Britain and the Defence of the Netherlands East Indies, 1940–41', *Journal of Southeast Asian Studies*, 31:1 (Mar 2000), pp115–36

Buxton, Ian, Roy Fenton, and Hugh Murphy, 'Measuring Britain's Merchant Shipbuilding Output in the Twentieth Century', *The Mariner's Mirror*, 101:3 (August 2015), pp304–22

Callahan, Raymond, 'The Illusion of Security: Singapore 1919–1942', *Journal of Contemporary History*, 9:2 (April 1974), pp69–92

Caravaggio, Angelo N, '"Winning" the Pacific War: The masterful strategy of Commander Minoru Genda', *US Naval War College Review*, 67:1 (Winter 2014)

——————, 'The Attack at Taranto: Tactical Success, Operational Failure', *US Naval War College Review*, 59:3 (Summer 2006)

Charrier, Philip, 'British Assessments of Japanese Naval Tactics and Strategy 1941–45', in *The History of Anglo-Japanese Relations 1600–2000*, vol III: *The Military Dimension* (Basingstoke, Palgrave Macmillan, 2003)

Cowman, Ian, 'Defence of the Malay Barrier? The Place of the Philippines in Admiralty Naval War Planning 1925–1941', *War in History*, 3:4 (November 1996), pp398–417

——————, 'Pearl Harbor: Fleet Planning and Fleet Bases', *Australian Defence Journal*, 109 (November/December 1994), pp45–51

Davison, Robert L, 'Striking a Balance between Dissent and Discipline: Admiral Sir Reginald Drax', *The Northern Mariner*, 13:2 (April 2003), pp43–57,

Defalco III, Ralph Lee, 'Blind to the Sun: US Intelligence Failures before the War with Japan', *International Journal of Intelligence and Counter-Intelligence*, 16 (2003), pp95–107

Dunlop, C G H, 'Ebb and Flow: The British at War with the Japanese', in

Japan and Britain at War and Peace, ed Hugo Dobson and Kosuge Nobuko (Routledge, 2009)

Edgerton, David, 'Liberalism, Militarism and the British State', *New Left Review*, 1/185 (Jan–Feb 1991)

Ferris, John, 'The Fulcrum of Power: Britain, Japan and the Asia-Pacific Region: 1880–1945', in *Maritime Strategy and National Security in Japan and Britain*, ed Alessio Patalano (Leiden, Netherlands: Koninklijke Brill NV, 2012)

——————, '"Consistent with an Intention": The Far East Combined Bureau and the Outbreak of the Pacific War, 1940–41', *Intelligence and National Security*, 27:1 (February 2012), pp5–26

——————, 'The road to Bletchley Park: The British experience with Signals Intelligence, 1892–1945', *Intelligence and National Security*, 17:1 (March 2002), pp53–84,

——————, '"It is our business in the Navy to command the Seas": The Last Decade of British Maritime Supremacy, 1919–1929', in *Far Flung Lines – Essays on Imperial Defence in honour of Donald Mackenzie Schurman*, ed Greg Kennedy and Keith Neilson (London: Frank Cass, 1997)

——————, '"Worthy of Some Better Enemy?" The British Assessment of the Imperial Japanese Army , 1919–1941, and the Fall of Singapore', *Canadian Journal of History*, 28 (August 1993)

Ford, Douglas, 'A Statement of Hopes? The effectiveness of US and British naval war plans against Japan, 1920–1941', *The Mariner's Mirror*, 101:1 (February 2015), pp63–80

——————, 'British Naval Policy and the War against Japan 1937–1945: Distorted Doctrine, Insufficient Resources, or Inadequate Intelligence', *International Journal of Naval History*, 4:1 (April 2005)

Franklin, G D, 'The origins of the Royal Navy's vulnerability to surfaced night U-boat attack 1939–40', *The Mariner's Mirror*, 90:1 (February 2004), pp3–84

Garzke, William H, Robert O Dulin, and Kevin V Denlay, *Death of a Battleship: The Loss of HMS Prince of Wales, December 10 1941, A Marine Forensics Analysis of the Sinking.* (Paper originally presented at the Royal Institute of Naval Architects in September 2009, updated in 2010 and 2012, and placed on www.pacificwrecks.com website.)

Goodman, Michael S, 'Learning to Walk: The Origins of the UK's Joint Intelligence Committee', *International Journal of Intelligence and CounterIntelligence*, 21:1 (2008), pp40–56

Gordon, Andrew, 'The Admiralty and Imperial Overstretch 1902–1940', *Journal of Strategic Studies*, 17:1 (1994), pp63–85

Gow, Ian T M, 'The Royal Navy and Japan', in *The History of Anglo-Japanese Relations 1600–2000*, vol III: *The Military Dimension* (Basingstoke, Palgrave Macmillan, 2003)

Grove, Eric, 'A War Fleet built for Peace: British Naval Rearmament in the 1930s and the dilemma of Deterrence versus Defence', *US Naval War College Review*, 44:2 (Spring 1991)

Hanyok, Robert J, and David P Mowry, 'West Wind Clear: Cryptology and the Winds Message Controversy – A Documentary History' (Center for Cryptologic History, US National Security Agency, 2008)

Harrington, Daniel F, 'A Careless Hope: American Air Power and Japan, 1941', *Pacific Historical Review*, 48:2 (May 1979), pp217–38

Harvey, A D, 'Army Air Force and Navy Air Force: Japanese Aviation and the opening phase of the war in the Far East', *War in History*, 6:2 (1999), pp174–204,

Hirama, Yoichi, 'Japanese Naval Preparations for World War II', *US Naval War College Review*, 44:2 (Spring 1991)

Hone, Thomas C, 'Replacing Battleships with Aircraft Carriers in the Pacific in World War II', *US Naval War College Review*, 66:1 (Winter 2013)

Horner, D M, 'Australian Estimates of the Japanese Threat, 1905–1941', in *Estimating Foreign Military Power*, ed Philip Towle (London: Croom Helm, 1982)

Kemp, Peter, 'Chatfield, Admiral of the Fleet Lord Alfred Ernle Montacute (1873–1967)', *Dictionary of National Biography* (OUP, 2004)

Kennedy, Greg, 'Anglo-American Strategic Relations and Intelligence Assessments of Japanese Airpower 1934–1941', *Journal of Military History*, 7:4 (July 2010), pp737–73

———, 'What Worth the Americans? The British Strategic Foreign Policy-Making Elite's View of American Maritime Power in the Far East, 1933–1941', in *British Naval Strategy East of Suez, 1900–2000*, ed Greg Kennedy (UK: Frank Cass, 2005)

Levy, James, 'Was there something unique to the Japanese that lost them the Battle of Midway', *US Naval War College Review*, 67:1 (Winter 2014)

———, 'Race for the decisive Weapon: British, American, and Japanese Carrier Fleets, 1942–43', *US Naval War College Review*, 58:1 (Winter 2005)

Lowe, Peter, 'Britain, the Commonwealth and Pacific Security', in *From Pearl Harbor to Hiroshima: The Second World War in Asia and the Pacific, 1941–45*, ed Saki Dockrill (UK: Macmillan, 1994)

Mahnken, Thomas G, 'Gazing at the sun: The Office of Naval Intelligence and Japanese naval innovation, 1918–1941', *Intelligence and National Security*, 11:3 (1996), pp424–46,

Maiolo, Joseph A, 'Did the Royal Navy decline between the two World Wars?', *The RUSI Journal*, 159:4 (August/September 2014), pp8–24

Martin, Bernd, 'The German-Japanese Alliance in the Second World War', in *From Pearl Harbor to Hiroshima: The Second World War in Asia and the Pacific, 1941–45*, ed Saki Dockrill (UK: Macmillan, 1994)

Maurer John H, '"Winston has gone mad": Churchill, the British Admiralty and the Rise of Japanese Naval Power', *Journal of Strategic Studies* (2012), pp1–24

Murfett, Malcom H, 'Phillips, Admiral Sir Tom Spencer Vaughan (1888–1941)', *Dictionary of National Biography* (OUP, 2004)

Neilson, Keith, "Unbroken Thread': Japan, Maritime Power and British Imperial Defence, 1920–32', in *British Naval Strategy East of Suez 1900–2000*, ed Greg Kennedy (UK: Frank Cass, 2005)

Neilson, Keith, 'The Defence Requirements Sub-Committee, British Strategic Foreign Policy, Neville Chamberlain and the Path to Appeasement', *English Historical Review*, 118: 477 (June 2003), pp651–84

O'Hara, Vincent P, and Enrico Cernuschi, 'Frogmen against a Fleet: The Italian Attack on Alexandria 18/19 December 1941', *US Naval War College Review*, 68:3 (Summer 2015)

Parshall, Jonathan B, with David D Dickson, and Anthony P Tully, 'Doctrine Matters: Why the Japanese Lost at Midway', *US Naval War College Review*, 54:3 (Summer 2001)

Parker, Frederick D, 'Pearl Harbor Revisited: US Navy Communications Intelligence 1924–1941' (Center for Cryptologic History, US National Security Agency, 1993)

——————, 'A Priceless Advantage: US Navy Communications Intelligence and the Battles of Coral Sea, Midway and the Aleutians' (Center for Cryptologic History, US National Security Agency, 1993)

Peattie, Mark R, 'Japanese Naval Construction, 1919–41', in *Technology and Naval Combat in the Twentieth Century and Beyond*, ed Phillips Payson O'Brien (London: Routledge, 2007)

Peden, G C, 'The Burden of Imperial Defence and the Continental Commitment Reconsidered', *Historical Journal* 27:2 (1984), pp405–23

Pratt, Lawrence, 'The Anglo-American Naval Conversations on the Far East of January 1938', *International Affairs (Royal Institute of International Affairs 1944–)*, 47:4 (1971), pp745–63

Pritchard, John, 'Winston Churchill, the Military, and Imperial Defence in East Asia', in *From Pearl Harbor to Hiroshima: The Second World War in Asia and the Pacific, 1941–45*, ed Saki Dockrill (UK: Macmillan, 1994)

Rahn, Werner, 'German Naval Strategy and Armament, 1919–39', in

Technology and Naval Combat in the Twentieth Century and Beyond, ed
Phillips Payson O'Brien (London: Routledge, 2007)

Rodger, N A M, 'The Royal Navy in the Era of the World Wars: Was it fit
for purpose?', *The Mariner's Mirror*, 97:1 (February 2011), pp272–84

Rubel, Robert C, 'Deconstructing Nimitz's principle of calculated risk:
Lessons for today', *US Naval War College Review*, 68:1 (Winter 2015),
pp31–45

Sadkovich, James J, 'Understanding Defeat: Reappraising Italy's Role in
World War II', *Journal of Contemporary History*, 24:1 (January 1989),
pp27–61

Sarantakes, Nicholas E, 'One Last Crusade: The British Pacific Fleet and its
Impact on the Anglo-American Alliance', *The English Historical Review*,
121:491 (April 2006), pp429–66

Scammell, Clare M, 'The Royal Navy and the strategic origins of the Anglo-
German naval agreement of 1935', *Journal of Strategic Studies*, 20:2
(1997), pp92–118,

Schmider, Klaus, 'The Mediterranean in 1940–1941: Crossroads of Lost
Opportunities', *War and Society*, 15:2 (October 1997)

Simpson, Michael, 'Force H and British Strategy in the Western
Mediterranean 1939–42', *The Mariner's Mirror*, 83:1 (1997), pp62–75

Stuart, Rob, 'Leonard Birchall and the Japanese Raid on Colombo',
Canadian Military Journal, 7:4 (Winter 2006–2007)

Sumida, Jon Tetsuro, 'British Naval Procurement and Technological Change,
1919–1939', in *Technology and Naval Combat in the Twentieth Century
and Beyond*, ed Phillips Payson O'Brien (London: Routledge, 2007)

——————, '"The Best Laid Plans": The Development of British Battle-Fleet
Tactics, 1919–1942', *The International History Review*, 14:4 (1992),
pp681–700

Thomas, Martin, 'Imperial Defence or Diversionary Attack: Anglo-French
Strategic Planning in the Near East 1936–1940', in *Anglo-French
Defence Relations between the Wars*, ed Martin S Alexander and William
J Philpott (Basingstoke: Palgrave Macmillan, 2002)

Till, Geoffrey, 'Adopting the Aircraft Carrier: The British, American and
Japanese Case Studies', in *Military Innovation in the Interwar Period*, ed
Williamson Murray & Allan Millett (Cambridge University Press, 1996)

——————, 'Perceptions of Naval Power between the Wars', in *Estimating
Foreign Military Power*, ed Philip Towle (London: Croom Helm, 1982)

Towle, Philip, 'Britain's Strategy in World War II and Reconciliation with
former Enemies', in *Japan and Britain at War and Peace*, ed Hugo
Dobson and Kosuge Nobuko (Routledge 2009)

Tully, Anthony, and Lu Yu, 'A Question of Estimates: How Faulty

Intelligence Drove Scouting at the Battle of Midway', *US Naval War College Review*, 68:2 (Spring 2015)

Vego, Milan, 'Major Convoy Operation to Malta, 10–15 August 1942' (Operation Pedestal), *US Naval War College Review*, 63:1 (Winter 2010)

Wark, Wesley, 'In search of a suitable Japan: British naval intelligence in the Pacific before the Second World War', *Intelligence and National Security*, 1:2 (1986), pp189–211,

Whitlock, Captain Duane L, 'The Silent War against the Japanese Navy', *US Naval War College Review*, 48:4 (Autumn 1995), p43

Wildenberg, Thomas, 'Midway: Sheer luck or better doctrine', *US Naval War College Review*, 58:1 (Winter 2005)

Wilford, Timothy, 'Watching the North Pacific: British and Commonwealth Intelligence before Pearl Harbor', *Intelligence and National Security*, 17:4 (2002), pp131–64

Winter, Captain P D, 'Comparing the "Singapore Strategy" and "Fortress Australia"', *Australian Defence Journal*, 65 (July/August 1987), pp29–40

Zimm, Alan D, 'A strategy has to be able to work to be masterful', *US Naval War College Review*, 68:1 (Winter 2015)

Unpublished theses

Austin, Douglas, 'The Place of Malta in British Strategic Policy 1925–1943' (unpublished doctoral thesis, University of London, 2001)

Davison, Robert Lynn, 'Admiral Sir Reginald Drax and British Strategic Policy: Festina Lente' (unpublished MA thesis, Wilfred Laurier University, Ontario, Canada, 1994)

Ford, Douglas Eric, 'Climbing the Learning Curve: British Intelligence on Japanese Strategy and Military Capabilities during the Second World War in Asia and the Pacific, July 1937 to August 1945' (unpublished doctoral thesis, London School of Economics and Political Science, 2002)

Haggie, Paul, 'The Royal Navy and the Far Eastern Problem 1931–1941' (unpublished doctoral thesis, Victoria University of Manchester, 1974)

Maiolo, Joseph A, 'Admiralty War Planning, Armaments, Diplomacy, and Intelligence Perceptions of German Sea Power and their influence on British Foreign and Defence Policy 1933–1939' (unpublished doctoral thesis, Department of International History, London School of Economics and Political Science, 1996)

Mee, Richard Charles, 'The Foreign Policy of the Chamberlain Wartime Administration September 1939–May 1940' (unpublished doctoral thesis, University of Birmingham, 1998)

Millar, Russell D, 'The Development of Anglo-American Naval Strategy in

the Period of the Second World War, 1938–1941' (unpublished doctoral
thesis, Kings College, University of London, 1988)

Moretz, Joseph Alan, 'The Royal Navy and the Capital Ship Controversy of
the Interwar Period: An Operational and Tactical Assessment'
(unpublished doctoral thesis, Kings College, University of London, 1999)

Murfett, Malcom H, 'Anglo-American Relations in the Period of the
Chamberlain Premiership May 1937–May 1940: The Relationship
between Naval Strategy and Foreign Policy' (unpublished doctoral thesis,
University of Oxford, 1980)

Thornhill, Paula G, 'Catalyst for Coalition: The Anglo-American Supply
Relationship 1939–1941' (unpublished doctoral thesis, University of
Oxford, 1991)

Thynne, John Francis, 'British Policy on Oil Resources 1936–1951 with
particular reference to the defence of British controlled oil in Mexico,
Venezuela and Persia' (unpublished doctoral thesis, London School of
Economics and Political Science, 1987)

Till, Geoffrey, 'The Impact of Airpower on the Royal Navy in the 1920s'
(unpublished doctoral thesis, University of London, 1976)

Weir, Philip Anthony, 'The Development of Naval Air Warfare by the Royal
Navy and Fleet Air Arm between the two World Wars' (unpublished
doctoral thesis, University of Exeter, 2006)

Wells, Anthony Roland, 'Studies in British Naval Intelligence 1880–1945'
(unpublished doctoral thesis, University of London, 1972)

Websites

The following have provided valuable information and in some cases access to
primary documents. Where appropriate they are referenced in the footnotes.

forum.axishistory.com: Forum primarily devoted to the military operations
and capabilities of the Axis states but much Allied material too. Covers
all major war theatres.

www.britishempireatwar.org: Forum for scholars interested in all aspects of
the British Empire's war history.

www.combinedfleet.org: Ed Jonathan Parshall. Contains useful reference
material and comment on all aspects of the IJN and its operations during
the Second World War.

www.fleetairarmarchive.net: Excellent source of material on the Fleet Air Arm.

www.history.army.mil: Website for the US Army Centre of Military History.
Contains a range of US Army publications and some documents in digital
form relevant to the Second World War. Includes a full digital collection
of the US Army's Official History of the Second World War.

www.ibiblio.org/hyperwar: Contains a useful selection of digitised original political, military and diplomatic documents relating to the Second World War. Includes some digitised official histories including volumes from the British Official History series.

www.intellit.muskingum.edu: Ed J Ransom Clark, this is an excellent bibliography of published works on intelligence history.

www.jacar.go.jp/english: Japan Center for Asian Historical records. Operated by the National Archives of Japan and provides digital access to a wide range of Japanese official documents relating to the Second World War originating with the Cabinet, Ministry of Foreign Affairs, Army and Navy. It facilitates searching in English but the documents themselves remain in the original Japanese.

www.j-aircraft.com: Primarily a site devoted to IJNAF and IJAAF aircraft capability, deployment and operations. However, it includes much information on wider naval operations in the eastern and Pacific theatres complementing that in www.combinedfleet.com.

www.milspecmanuals.com: Contains a large range of digitised military and intelligence documents relating to the Second World War. The emphasis is primarily on American sources. Especially useful for sourcing Japanese monographs and similar material. Includes a good searchable database.

www.naval-history.net: Includes copies of various Royal Navy reports and documents from the Second World War including most of the Reports of Proceedings of the Eastern Fleet in 1942.

www.navweaps.com: Naval Technology section has useful papers on technical topics, eg naval weaponry of all types, armoured flight decks and the Royal Navy High Altitude Control System (HACS) for anti-aircraft defence.

www.navypedia.org: Reference site providing construction data and basic order of battle of the main naval powers in the twentieth century.

www.nsa.gov/about/cryptologic_heritage/center_crypt: The historical section in the US National Security Agency website. Contains publications relating to the Second World War which can be downloaded in pdf format.

www.pacificwrecks.com: Database contains much valuable information on all naval and air forces involved in the Pacific war.

www.unithistories.com: Database providing a breakdown of individual units and biographical details of key individuals involved in the Second World War. Useful for checking appointments held by Royal Navy officers.

www.worldnavalships.com/forums: Searchable database and vast series of blogs covering every aspect of naval capabilities and operations in the Second World War.

www.ww2db.com: Database with useful reference material relating to the Second World War including copies of original documents.

Index

Abadan: 129, 132; and British war effort 165–7, 342–3; impact of loss 359–62; aviation spirit for Russia 363

ABC-1 staff talks: historical importance xviii–xix; approval 191–2; British preparations 195,198; respective national objectives 202–3; progress 203–9; consequences 210–15; results less flexible than British hope 217–8; American pressure to defend Malay Barrier 219, 220, 272, 274, 276; and Admiralty offensive strategy 285–7, 298

ABDA (American-British-Dutch-Australian joint Far East command) 150, 250, 292

Abyssinian Crisis 60–1, 72, 74–5

Action Information Organisation (AIO) 263

ADB (American-Dutch-British): Singapore conference 218; Americans criticise ADB-1 219–20, 277–9, 284, 286; ADB-2 286–7, American rejection 289, 298; and Layton 328

Admiral Scheer (Ge) 14, 126, 197

Aichi 391

Akagi (Ja) 16, 373, 381

Albacore (Br): 229, 258, 260; as overall weapon system 261; 367, 374; night attack at Ceylon 377–9, 381–2; 390

Alexander, A V: IJN strength 241,253; Fleet Air Arm 260; carrier availability 279; Far East offensive planning 285–6, 347; secret session statement 296, 301; *Indomitable* 301

Alexandria: Abyssinian crisis 72, 74; Italian threat 80, 82; limitations overstated 128; 135; German air threat 143–5; 149, 159, 173, 253, 266, 303, 320, 329, 333; Italian frogmen attack 342, 348–9, 356–7, 365, 386; first through convoy 395

Anderson, HMS 366, 373

Anglo-American naval relationship 175–6

Anglo-Dutch staff discussions 181–2

Anglo-French staff talks 81, 90–1, 93, 98, 105, 123

Anglo-German Naval Agreement (AGNA) 24, 29, 65

Anti-Aircraft Gunnery Committee 46

Anti-Submarine Warfare (ASW) 50–1

Appeasement 22

Ark Royal, HMS 16, 33, 42, 44, and Force H 141, 178, 206, 209, 259, 261, 264, 279, 301, 302, Halberd 304, loss 356, Somerville praises 382

Armoured carriers 27, 45

Arnold, General Henry H 288

Asdic (anti-submarine detection system) 15, 23, 37, 39, 50–51

ASV (Air to Surface Vessel) radar 261, 264, 369, 378–9, 382, 390

Atlantic, Battle of 50, 159, 162, 256–7, 265, 270, 411

Atlantic Conference, see Riviera

Atlantis (Ge) 140

Attlee, Clement 269, 294, 396

Australia: xv, 11, 63–5, 68, 70, 84; SAC debate 89; Chamberlain guidance 89, 95, 104, 107; Churchill sea power memorandum 99; Drax flying squadron 106; Churchill guarantee 114; and German Navy weakness 126; Far East appreciation assurances 141; Beaufort production 154, 267; and balance between Middle and Far East 158, 160, 162, 170, 184; and Empire war effort 167–8; US dismisses Japanese threat to 203; and Pacific Fleet reductions 222; lobbying for Far East naval reinforcement 275, 279; War Cabinet briefings 288, 299; and Phillips/Hart exchanges 334; and VCNS paper 342–3; threat to troop convoys 358; and outer ring defence 358–9; dependence on Abadan 359–61, 404

Automedon (Br) 140

Avenger (US) 260

Axis powers xx, 56, 83, 98, 121, 123, 176, 181, 184, 186, 190, 194, 205, 400

B-17 (US) 287–8, 300, 308

B-24 (US) 300

Backhouse, Admiral of the Fleet Sir Roger: 66–7; and 4th Submarine Squadron 71; loss of Singapore 72; and European appreciation 83; revisionist views on Far East 84–6; at SAC 86–8; and Drax 86–8; reassurance to Australians 89; tilt towards Mediterranean 92–6, 104, 112, 142; and 'R'-class 281

Backhouse/Drax school 88

Bailey, Admiral Sir Sydney 177–180, 185, 187, 191–192, 194, 198–199

Bailey Committee 177–178, 180, 190

Bailey report 180, 184

Baldwin, Stanley 65

Balikpapan 245, 319, 330–1

Baltimore (US) 154–5, 160, 170

Barham, HMS 14, 15, 109, 296, 348–9, 356
Barracuda (Br) 258, 260
Battlecruisers: managing German threat 17, 69; disposition in two-hemisphere war 33; carrier/battlecruiser combination 39; and Drax 'flying squadron' 88; battlecruiser/carrier Indian Ocean deployment 127, 183; IJN battlecruiser threat 210, 230–1; fictitious IJN battlecruiser programme 235, 240–1
Battle of Britain 153, 239, 258
Beaufort (Br) 154–5, 160, 170, 265–8, 342, 357, 389, 392
Bell, Captain L H 322, 337
Bellairs, Rear Admiral Roger: importance of Singapore 149; leader at ABC-1 staff talks 182; and British Far East requirements 182–8, 192–3; and Ghormley 185, 190–1; at ABC-1 203–9; Churchill criticises 205, 207; 215–6, 285
Bellars, Captain Gerald 284–5, 344, 347
Bismarck (Ge) 4, 69, 113, 125, 197, 242; ASV2 and 261, 264; 262, 271, 334
Blenheim (Br) 152, 381
Bletchley Park 327
Bofors anti-aircraft gun 49
Bomber Command 160, 265–6, 268–270, 299
Borneo 147, 150, 154, 245, 288, 308, 319, 330–1, 333, 349
Brauchitsch, Field Marshal Walter von 136
British Empire: xv, 4, 9, 20, 53, 55, 68, 79, 133–5, 139, 159, 192, 209, 216, 255, 290, 296, 386, 394, 408; oil requirements 134–5, 360; war potential 167
British Pacific Fleet 408
Brooke, Field Marshal Sir Alan: as strategist 113; supports Pound over air resources 268; and Abadan 362; and defence of eastern theatre 386
Brooke-Popham, Air Chief Marshal Sir Robert: and Japanese air threat 238; critical of FECB 244; and Japanese air strength in Indo-China 244, 322, 326; and British air reinforcements 267; and B-17 force 288; Japan susceptible to deterrence 291, 308; puts Far East on war alert 318; and air threat to Force Z 321–2; and Operation Matador 326; no consultation with Phillips 326
Bruce, Stanley M 107, 114
Buffalo (Br) 154–5, 160, 259, 338
Burma: oilfields 135, 360–1; and Far East appreciation 144, 146; and air route to Far East 153; and British defence line 168, 357; Japanese move into 359, 364, 366, 385
Burma Road 139, 144, 244

Camranh Bay 154, 314
Cape Town 295, 297, 299, 301, 311–14, 340
Capetown, HMS 27
Ceres, HMS 27
Ceylon: 72, 95, 110–1, 113, 141, 149, 170, 173, 183, 210, 214, 267; and debate over Far East reinforcement 274, 277, 281, 293, 297, 303; and Force Z 312–17; as alternative to Singapore 319, 325, 328–9, 336, 340, 342–4, 348, 350–1; strategic importance 355–60; IJN attack on 363–74, 377–8, 380–86; defence improvements 389, 391–2, 395, 398; strategic status in retrospect 406–8
Chamberlain, Sir Neville 65; and new eastern empire

defence objectives 89–90; 93, 95, 98; Tientsin crisis 101–4; assurances to Dominions 106–9; 142, 144, 173, 215, 403
Chatfield, Admiral of the Fleet Sir Ernle: qualities as First Sea Lord 21; and new naval arms race 23–25; and DRC proposals for two-power standard 25–26; and 'New Standard' 26–27; and air threat 47; arguments against permanent Far East fleet 56; Royal Navy has time to improve 59; rejects direct attack on Japan 62–3; and League of Nations 'unlimited liability' 64; British strategy for 'Pacific war' 65–6, 400; role of Singapore 73, 127, 143, 150; importance of Egypt 74–5; reluctance to see war over Abyssinia 75–6; triple threat not insoluble 78–9; resists cooperation with France 80–1; advocates continuing primacy for Far East 83; and SAC 83, 85–6; clashes with Drax 86–7; 'knock-out blow' against Italy 96; Churchill's 1939 memorandum 98–9; and Tientsin crisis 103–6; and succession planning for First Sea Lord 112
Chiefs of Staff 1932 Annual Review 58
Chiefs of Staff 1933 Annual Review 17, 20 59
Chiefs of Staff 1934 Annual Review 59
Chiefs of Staff 1935 Annual Review 59–60
China: British concessions 55; Japan's ambitions 57–8; and economic action against Japan 60; British interests in 61–3; and their defence 62–3; and 1937 Far East appreciation 69; interests discretionary 72–3; consequences of Sino-Japanese war 77–8; Japan's preoccupation with 82; Backhouse views 84–5; Churchill's view 99; and Tientsin crisis 102–6; Japanese pressure to cut aid 121; tension over Burma road 139; brake on Japanese move south 156, 236; aid through India and Abadan oil 361, 404
China Fleet, also China squadron: poor state in 1933 59; and Abyssinian crisis 61; ability to counter 1937 IJN attack 71; complement to 'flying squadron' 103; and 1939 war plans 109; 1940 reductions 131; proposals for US Navy command 181; 1941 strength 200–1; 230, 328
Churchill, Winston: historic responsibility for Force Z xiv, xvi, 271–2; and 'fleet in being concept' 73; and Drax 87; memorandum on sea power 98–9; relationship with Pound 112; 'kith and kin' reassurances to Dominions 114, 141; and German naval weakness after Norway 126; and OKW survey 138; challenges Far East appreciation 151; and strategic importance of Middle East 159; loss of confidence in Dill 159–61; scepticism over Singapore as 'keystone' 162; and Plan Dog 192; interventions at ABC-1 193–4, 205–7; defers to Admiralty on Netherlands East Indies 219; and US Navy transfers from Pacific 220; and capital ship inferiority versus Japan 230, 242; and NID exaggeration of IJN strength 253–4; Fleet Air Arm fighter problems 259; argument over maritime air resources 269–70; and triggers for Far East naval reinforcement 274–6; exchange with Pound 278–82; Riviera summit 277–9; discusses deterrence of Japan with Eden 290; Defence Committee debate 294–7; divergences of view with Admiralty 297–8; War Cabinet discussions 299; *Indomitable* 302; exchange with Roosevelt on deterrence 307; Cape Town review 312–3; holding Force Z at Ceylon 316; guidance to Phillips on outbreak of war 334–

6; responsibility for loss of Force Z 349–50; criticism of Somerville at Ceylon 370; highlights risks in Indian Ocean to Roosevelt 375; caveats over 'second front' 386–7; more optimistic on Indian Ocean 392; drawdown of Eastern Fleet for Torch 396

Clarke, Captain Arthur 190–2, 199–201, 221

Coastal Command 246, 249, 265–6, 269–70

Colombo 149, 325, 341, 357, 365–6, 368–70, 372–4, 377, 381, 384

Colossus-class (Br) construction and qualities 388

Committee of Imperial Defence: 21; and New Standard 24; and naval deficiencies 49; and 1935 Far East position 57; and risk management 1937–8 78–9; and 1937 Mediterranean appreciation 80; opposition to French staff talks 80; and European appreciation 83; and SAC 85; and Chamberlain's 1939 message to Dominions 89; and Cunningham memorandum 70, 91–3, 101–2; and early action against Italy 96, 99; and Tientsin crisis 103–7; 401

Compass 133

Cornwall, HMS 367, 370, 372, 384

Corregidor 233–4, 315, 327, 366

County-Class (Br) 7–8, 10, 226

Courageous, HMS 16, 33

Craigie, Sir Robert 12, 243

Crete 130, 136, 160, 249, 274–5, 329

Crusader 164, 168, 170–2, 406

Cunningham, Admiral Sir Andrew: biographical coverage xix; endorses night-fighting 38; and increased priority for Mediterranean 86–9; and flexible Far East reinforcement 92–5, 403–4; and knock-out blow against Italy 96–7; and new Far East war plans 100–1, 109; relations with Pound 113; and effectiveness of Italian air capability 153, 253, 303; role of air power in Mediterranean 173, 246–7, 249, 279; and loss of Force Z 305, 344; view of Phillips 325; and withdrawal of Mediterranean capital units to meet Japanese attack 341

'Cunningham factors' 92–5, 108, 142, 158

Curlew, HMS 258

Curzon-Howe, Captain L C A 178

Cyrenaica 133, 341, 359

Czechoslovakia 122

Danckwerts, Rear Admiral Victor: Suez Canal pointless without Singapore 76, 95; and revised Far East war plan 99–101; moves Far East into new European war plan 105–7; preparation for ABC-1 staff talks 192; warns Phillips Americans litigious over ABC-1 217; angers Churchill 220; visits US Pacific Fleet 221–2; Riviera discussions 276; Turner warns on ADB-2 286

Daniel, Captain Charles 190, 192, 205–6, 210

Darvall, Group Captain Lawrence: Indo-China airbases as warning factor 237–8; Japanese sortie generation against Malaya 239; visit to Philippines 288; briefs Brooke-Popham on Japanese air capability 322–3

Darwin 149, 286–8, 297, 319–20, 332, 336, 349, 367

Davis, Captain William: and IJN capability 252; and offensive planning for Far East 294; and inquiry into loss of Force Z 344–7

Defence Committee 159, 172, 193–4, 205, 214, 220,

277, 283, 293–7, 300–2, 310, 336, 345, 386, 389

Defence Requirements Committee (DRC), see also DRC fleet under Standards: origin and composition 20–1; expanding role 21–2; deficiencies programme and Third Report 22–4; and DRC fleet versus New Standard 25–28; anti-submarine sloops 53; 64, 67, 79, 85, 401

Delhi, HMS 47

Deutschland (Ge) 14, 30, 91

Devastator (US) 260

Dido-class (Br) 304

Dill, General Sir John: 113; clashes with Churchill over priority of Malaya 159; prime minister's loss of confidence in 160–1; 163, 169, 180, 277

Divisional tactics 38–9

Doig, Captain Douglas: seaborne landings in Malaya during Monsoon 292; warns of new eastern fleet deploying piecemeal 292, 317, 328; and Layton refusal to query 293; and 'Winds Alert' 315; FECB and IJN torpedo bombers 321–2; silent on Layton-Phillips handover 325; Layton's poor opinion of Phillips 325; relations with FECB 327

Doolittle raid 193, 364, 393

Dorsetshire, HMS 367, 370, 372–6, 381, 383–4, 387

Drax, Admiral Sir Reginald: background 86–87; Royal Navy deployment in global war and 'flying squadron' 87; influence 87–88; attitude of historians to 95; 100, 104; valued by Pound and Phillips 106; 109, 126, 141, 200

'DRC Fleet' 26–8, 53

DRC Third Report 22, 24, 26–8, 67

Dreyer, Admiral Sir Frederick, 59

Dunkerque (Fr) 12, 91, 98, 121

Dutch, see ABDA, ADB, Anglo-Dutch staff conversations, Dutch Navy, Holland and Netherlands East Indies

Dutch Navy: 201; submarines in Netherlands East Indies 214, 217, 318, 326; contribution to Allied force 332–3

Eagle, HMS 16, 111, 131, 211, 301, 386

Eastern Empire: definitions xvii–xviii; risks to 74, 86, 131; defence of 75–6, 83, 97–8, 110; oil supplies to 75, 120, 135–6, 165, 359–61; isolation in wartime 81–2; concept of core 84, 89, 95, 114–5, 215; war potential of 137, 166–8, 343, 359

Eastern Fleet: pre-war role 67, 82; and commitment to Australia 141; and 'Atlantic substitution' 156, 175, 202, 204–6, 209–10, 213–20, 275–6, 284; composition of 274, 276, 280–1, 297–8, 307–9, 365, 389, 392–4; air capability of 247, 301, 357; basing of 282, 284, 295, 299, 341–2, 389; role of 284–6, 297, 340, 348, 350, 360, 363, 365, 385; Phillips appointed C-in-C 292, 298; and Somerville 355, 365; and Ceylon action 368–80

Eden, Sir Anthony 290–1, 294–5, 311, 314

Edwards, Captain Ralph 285, 365

Egypt: Chatfield and Italian threat 74–6; reduced value if Singapore lost 76; Lampson stresses importance 76; reinforcement of 79–80; and 1937 Mediterranean appreciation 81–2; Pound proposes offensive from 86; and European appreciation 91; and SAC 93; and strategic depth 97–8; risk of 1940 German attack 127–30; prime minister prioritises over Singapore 159; influence on Spain, Vichy and Turkey 173; and Plan Dog 189;

Beauforts deployed to 266; Abadan has precedence over 362; Roosevelt and importance of 397; 406, 408

Enigma 213, 233

Essex-class (US) 45

European appreciation: 80, 82–4; version shared with French 90–1; 97, 102, 105, 109, 122–3, 142, 162

Exe engine 258

Fadden, Arthur 282

Far East appreciation 1937 64, 68–71, 74, 120, 246

Far East appreciation 1940 120, 138, 142, 145, 147–52, 154–6, 163–4, 168, 178–9, 182–4, 215, 226, 236, 246, 252, 255, 273, 356, 405

Far East Combined Bureau (FECB): 230; origin, composition and role 231–2; relationship with NID 232; Noble views on 232; SIGINT and relationship with GC&CS 232; cooperation with US Station Cast 233; and loss of Purple machine 233; and JN 25 234; liaison with Dutch 234; 'war warning' indicators 236–7; and Indo-China airbases 237–9; and IJN new construction 241; overall performance and influence 242–4, 245, 249; and 'Winds Alert' 315; and SIS reports 319; does not brief Phillips 321; intelligence picture immediately prior to war and IJN torpedo capability 321–2; and IJN southern task force 323–4; relationship with Layton 326–8; and Japanese landings 334; impact on Phillips's decisions 337, 339; relocation to Colombo 365; IJN attack on Ceylon 366–8; 373, 379

Firebrand (Br) 258–60

Firefly (Br) 258

Fisher, Admiral of the Fleet, Sir John 21

Fisher, Sir Warren 21, 25, 62

Fleet Air Arm: DRC and increased investment 15, 22, 24; 1938 review 39; comparison with US Navy and IJN 40, 42, 246; consequences of dual control 40–1; pre-war equipment 44–5; Dakar 121; Taranto 193; torpedoes 229, 261; strength, performance and procurement 1940–41 257–64, 267–8; Somerville's view 388–9

Flower-class (Br) 53, 256

Flying Squadron 87–9, 95, 100–7, 109, 141, 200, 216

Force G 328

Force H: concept anticipated pre-war 39; influence of 'flying squadron' 88–9; impact on Spain 128; 1941 composition 141; Indian Ocean contingency force 141–2, 193, 209–10, 257, 273, 279–81; possible deployment to Singapore 199, 201, 214–5; relief by US Navy 201, 205–6, 213, 279, 284; Somerville's innovative operations 263–4; and *Indomitable* 301; reinforcement for Torch 395

Force Z, also *Prince of Wales* and *Repulse*: historical resonance 271–2; and relationship between Pound and Churchill 112, 300; and Royal Air Force strength in Malaya 146–7, 171; and ABC-1 209–10; FECB and risks to 232, 321–3 ; and *Lützow* attack 266; Layton views on 293, 336; Admiralty offensive planning and genesis of 294–7; Defence Committee meetings 294–7; as deterrent 278, 281, 294–5, 309, 311, 314–5, 317; *Indomitable* and 301–2; decisions during passage east 311–17; Japanese knowledge of 314; and choices at Singapore 317–33; case for attacking landings

334–40; Admiralty inquiry into loss 344–9

Foreign Office 21, 57–8, 82, 219, 244

Formidable, HMS 33, 44; modified for Wildcats 261; 279, 283, 301–2; at Ceylon 357, 365; 390, 392, 394; part of Torch force 396

Formosa 60, 62, 218, 236, 238, 285, 290, 306, 314, 319

4th Submarine Flotilla 71, 131 236

France: 4, 5, 12, 18: and naval arms race 23; implications of alliance with 59, 65, 68, 70, 78–83, 98, 104; staff talks with 90–1, 93; impact of fall of 36, 40, 53, 55, 57, 97, 110, 114, 120–2, 138, 150, 177, 179; British anticipation of fall 122–4; consequences of hostility 121, 125; German pressure on 137

Frankland, Dr Noble 269–270

Fraser, Rear Admiral Bruce 20

'Freak navy' 24, 71

Fubuki-class (Ja) 252

Führer Directives 127, 130, 136–7, 158

Fulmar (Br) 258, 260–61, 304, 372, 380

Furious, HMS 16, 27, 33, 280, 301, 386, 396

'Future strategy' paper 125, 127–8, 131, 133, 138, 147–8, 163, 178–9, 196, 230, 255, 257

Future strategy review 161-2, 218

German air force (Luftwaffe): 50, 145, 239, 397

German navy (Kriegsmarine): 1935 strength 17; British estimate of 1939 strength 52; comparison with 1937 Royal Navy forces in East 71; Norway losses 126

German rearmament 21, 64

Germany: 3, 4, 6, 9, 20–3; AGNA 24, 65; and New Standard 24–7, 29; threat to trade pre-war 52–3; occupation of Rhineland 60–1; implications for Far East in war with 66–8, 70, 78–9; alignment with Italy 80; and European appreciation 82; and French staff talks 90; views on Singapore 110, 273; and fall of France 119–21; British views of threat to France 122–4; 'Future Strategy' blueprint for victory over 125; 1940 risk to Middle East 127–30; and Middle East oil 133–5; August 1941 OKW survey and Middle East and North Africa in overall strategy 136–8, 158, 396, 398; air strength in Mediterranean 166; 1940–41 effort to defeat Britain at sea 196–7; implications of attack on Russia 272–3; Middle East 'junction' with Japan 364; consequences of Torch for 396–7

Ghormley, Rear Admiral Robert: background 179; and American fact finding mission 125, 163, 179–80; Bailey report and meetings 180; and abortive staff talks 181; and Far East exchanges 181–2, 184; and Singapore basing 184–7, 189, 191–2; unsighted on Plan Dog 191; Pound meeting before ABC-1 198; believes Britain cannot hold Atlantic without assistance 198; and Atlantic substitution 204; warning on vulnerability of Manila 289; and 1942 British priorities 343; and American diversion action in Pacific 364

Gibraltar: 74; Axis threat to 123, 127, 130, 158, 196; establishment of Force H 128, 141; control of access to Atlantic 178; Halberd operation 253; 280, 303, 397

Giulio Cesare (It) 126

Glorious, HMS 16, 33

Gneisenau (Ge) 13, 17, 126, 197, 266

Godfrey, Vice Admiral John H 250, 294, 314, 316, 336, 347
Goodenough, Commander Michael 313, 315, 318–20, 326, 346
Göring, Reichsmarschall Hermann, 130, 136
Government Code & Cypher School (GC&CS): relationship with FECB and coverage of Japanese cyphers 232–4; German encouragement of Japanese to attack Singapore 273; Japanese knowledge of Force Z 314; 'Winds Alert' 315
Great Depression 6, 9, 53, 189
Grumman 259

Haifa 80 127, 132–3, 135
Hainan 150, 236–8, 319
Halberd 253, 295, 303–5, 309
Halder, Colonel General Franz 127
Halifax, Lord Edward: shows ABC-1 paper to Hull 208; Stimson briefs on B-17 regional coverage 288
Hampden (Br) 267
Hampton, Commander T 94, 176–179, 186
Hankey, Sir Maurice: chairman of DRC 21, 25; Chatfield tells imperial security policy 'drifting' 64
Harkness, Captain Kenneth: background 231; and 'Winds Alert' 315; access to C-in-C China 327; failure to meet Phillips 327; Japanese landings in Malaya 334
Harris, Air Chief Marshal Sir Arthur 268, 270
Hart, Admiral Thomas: Rainbow 3 186; meeting with Phillips 299, 301, 310, 312, 314, 317, 320, 329–32, 334, 339–40; and Pearl Harbor inquiry 307; and Layton 325, 330; and war plans 330
Harwood, Rear Admiral Sir Henry 113, 192, 222, 284–285, 311–312, 343–345
Hawaii 172, 183, 185, 187–8, 191, 194–5, 199, 203–9, 211, 215–16, 221–2, 285, 315, 341, 387, 394
Henderson, Rear Admiral Reginald 41
Hermes, HMS 44, 211, 301–2, 341, 370, 384
High Altitude Control System (HACS) 46–48, 50
Hinsley, Harry 327
Hipper (Ge) 35, 125–6, 197
Hiryu (Ja) 42, 111, 227, 236, 373–4, 377
Hitler, Adolf 129–30, 136, 159, 359, 364
Hoare, Sir Samuel 64–5, 73
Holland 53
Home Fleet 33, 38, 43, 47, 108, 113, 141–2, 145, 206, 279–80, 301–2, 311, 346, 389, 399
Home terminals 27, 57, 62
Home Waters area 53
Hong Kong: constitutional and military status 58, 61–3, difficulty defending 68, 72, 78; Backhouse doubts strategic value 85; Churchill sees as expendable 99; 1939 putative eastern fleet cannot protect 104; 156, 176–7, 181, 235, 315, 334, 406
Hood, HMS 4, 7, 14, 84, 108, 230, 271, 334
Hopkins, Harry 165–6, 386
Hornbeck, Stanley K 187
Hornet (US) 47, 201, 387
Horton, Admiral Sir Max 113
Houston (US) 245
Hull, Cordell 181, 187, 208–209, 221
Hunt-class (Br) 254, 256
Hurricane (Br): Buffalo compared to 154; provision for Middle East 154, 160; and Russia 168; ruled out for Malaya 160; and shipping limitations 169; and Wildcat 259; adapted for carrier use 260–1;

and Phillips 339; and Ceylon 359, 380; 388, 392

Iceland 212
Ickes, Harold 278
IFF (Identification Friend or Foe) 45, 264
Illustrious, HMS 33, 42, 44, 45, 261, 264, 279, 283, 301–2, 357, 365, 390, 392, 394
Illustrious-class (Br) 18, 28, 32, 35, 42, 44, 254, 257, 259, 388
Imperial Conference 1937 56, 64, 67–8, 73–4, 76–7, 79, 83, 89, 127, 162, 400
Imperial Defence Review 1937 64–5
Imperial Japanese Army (IJA) 110, 151, 156, 228, 235, 364, 395
Imperial Japanese Navy (IJN): super-battleship programme 12, 49, 240–1; capital ship modernisation 14–15, 38, 59, 88, 230–1; aircraft carriers 16, 42, 246–9, 262; comparative quality of ships 36; air capability 40–43, 45, 59, 229–30, 245, 248–9, 262–3, 265; operational effectiveness 66, 245–9, 249–54, 303; and 1939 threat to Singapore 110-11; planning for war against Britain 121, 156, 273; 1940 threat to Malaya 153; strength on outbreak of Far East war 195, 237; Royal Navy views of 225–7; mid-1941 order of battle 227–9; and JN 25 234; fictitious battlecruiser programme 240–1; formation of 1st Air Fleet 248–9; land-based 11th Air Fleet 249; underestimation by Royal Navy 249–54; strengths and weaknesses 250–1; attitude to commerce warfare 277; comparison with Italians 303; air deployment to Indo-China 321; southern task force 324; phase 2 operations 358, 363–4; and Operation C 364, 366–7, 368–80; strengths and weaknesses in Operation C 380–3; strategic consequences of Operation C 384–5; decline in carrier aircraft frontline 391; June 1942 plan to attack Ceylon 395
Implacable, HMS 32–3, 35, 45, 254–5
Indefatigable, HMS 32–3, 35, 45, 254–5
India: defence priority of 58, 65, 71–2, 89, 149, 358–9; dependence on naval security 68, 73, 139–40, 161, 211, 359, 363; 1938 defence review and 82; oil supplies to 135, 359–60; war potential of 139, 167–8, 343; air reinforcements for 358
Indiana (US) 264
Indian Army general staff 63
Indian Ocean: strategic importance 82, 89, 98, 120, 122, 133–4, 148, 165–6, 277, 341–3, 350, 356, 359, 362, 394, 398, 400, 404–6; resources to secure 87–9, 103, 106, 127, 141–2, 158, 209–10, 257, 341–2, 356–7, 385, 389–90, 392; risks to 62, 67, 103, 127, 141, 161–2, 164–5, 214, 216, 275, 341, 358, 363–4, 385–6, 396; British responsibility for 206, 342, 356, 360; reinforcement of 275–6, 279–82, 295–8, 307, 365; IJN raider threat 277–9; defensive strategy for 282, 286, 294, 344
Indo-China: Japanese moves into 121, 160–1, 273, 290, 326, 406; threat from Japanese bases 145–6, 150, 152, 170, 229, 238, 244, 253, 315, 321–3, 327, 345, 403
Indomitable, HMS 33, 34, 261, 279, 283; and allocation to Force Z 301–2; 331, 346, 350, 357, 359; at Ceylon 365, 374, 378; Pedestal 390; 392, 394–6

Ingersoll, Captain Royal E: visit to London 176–77; 186; briefs US Joint Board on Far East 306–7
Inskip report into Fleet Air Arm 17
Inskip, Sir Thomas 29, 33
Invergordon mutiny 21
Iran, also Persia: security of oilfields 97, 129, 132–3, 160, 165; German threat to 130, 134–5, 165, 364; oil output 134; and Eastern Mediterranean Fleet 135; and Russia 137, 165–6; and British war potential 173
Iraq 76, 97, 130–1, 135, 158, 160, 165, 364; oil from 80, 91, 120, 129–30, 132–5, 159, 167, 397, 404
Ironclad 394
Ismay, Major General Sir Hastings, 151, 159–61, 228, 288
Italian air force (Regia Aeronautica): control of central Mediterranean 88; comparator for Japanese 253; Cunningham praises quality of maritime operations 253; Halberd 304; Pedestal 390
Italian Navy (Regia Marina): new construction 9; new capital ships 12; and naval arms race 23; and Abyssinian crisis 60; early British successes against 126; oil shortage 134; losses to end 1941 256; and comparison with IJN 60, 303
Italy: DRC makes no provision against 21; Chatfield concern over 25, 65, 67, 74–5; and Abyssinian crisis 60–1; and 1937 Mediterranean and Middle East appreciation 74–5, 80–1; and chiefs of staff end 1937 78; threat to eastern Mediterranean 80; ability to close Mediterranean in war 82; and European appreciation 83–4; knockout blow against 86–97, 131, 133, 165, 202; and Churchill memorandum on sea power 99; initial neutrality 123; Britain establishes early supremacy over 126; importance of Mediterranean Fleet in containing 128; tensions with Germany 129; access to Indian Ocean 134, 165

Japan: pre-1932 threat 4–6, 9; primary naval threat to Britain 12, 21, 26; withdrawal from 1936 London Treaty 29; growing threat from 1935 55–58, 61–3, 68, 77–8, 102; no military planning against Britain before 1941 74, 82, 110, 121, 156; move into northern Indochina 121; tensions over Burma Road 139; plans step by step expansion southward 139; and Automedon capture 140; threats against oil may cause war 156; sees Anglo-American military cooperation as threat 156; move into southern Indochina 160; but avoids early commitment to war 164; expects attack on Malaya to make slow progress 170; overestimates British and Dutch air strength 171; ambition of immediate war goals overlooks setbacks 171–2; resource limitations in war with western powers 251; intentions after German attack on Russia 273; oil embargo initiates integrated plan to seize Netherlands East Indies supplies 290; fall of Konoye government 294; increases forces in Indochina as talks with United States stall 314; Imperial conference decides on war 314; hostilities with Britain and United States imminent 315; intentions for phase 2 operations 358; discussions with Germany on Middle East 'junction' 364; strategic consequences of Operation C 384–5

Japanese Imperial Conference 5 November 1941 308, 314, 317
Jean Bart (Fr) 121
Joint Intelligence Committee (JIC): status, role and composition 51–2; performance on Far East excellent 163–4, 250, 358
Joint Intelligence Committee assessments: of threat to Malaya 139, 143, 153, 161, 163, 237; Japanese strength and capability 228, 347, 393; and Magic 233; war warning 243; rates Japanese on par with Italians 252–3; and Philippines 288; Japanese intentions late 1941 290–1, 305, 314–5, 318–9; 1942 threat to Indian Ocean 367, 385, 393, 395
Joint Planning Committee (JPC): status, role and composition 51–2
JN 25 233–6, 366, 379, 382
Jutland, Battle of 3, 37–8, 56

Kaga (Ja) 16, 366
Kamer 14 234
Kate B5N2 (Ja) 40, 228, 262, 391
Kilindini 389
Kimmel, Admiral Husband E 283, 289, 306
King, Admiral Ernest: 364, 387, 394
King George V, HMS 18–19, 206
King George V-class (1914) (Br) 11
King George V-class (1936) (Br) 12, 18–19, 28, 33–4, 42, 141, 230, 240, 257, 277, 279–81, 284, 314
Knox, Frank: avoiding war with Japan 186; and Plan Dog 189; and naval transfers to Atlantic 221; endorses early clash with Germany 275
Kondo, Vice Admiral Nobutake: tells Emperor no plans for war with Britain 121; alerted to arrival of Force Z 314; dispositions for attack on Malaya 323; supports Indian Ocean offensive 364; and Operation C 366
Kongo (Ja) 324, 339
Kongo-class (Ja) 88, 231, 295, 324, 339, 367
Konoye, Prince Fumimaro, 243, 294
Kra Isthmus 145, 172, 314–5, 319, 324, 326, 329, 332

Lampson, Sir Miles 76
Lashio 144, 168, 356; Lashio-Tonga line 356
Layton, Vice Admiral Sir Geoffrey: and advanced deployment to Far East 109; and Allied submarines in Far East 217; claims IJN dislike night-fighting 245; and underestimation of IJN 250; argues for deterrence force 291; replaced by Phillips and appointed C-in-C Portsmouth 292; and questions over Far East reinforcement 293, 317; Palliser fails to consult 322; and FECB 324, 327; career and reputation 325; relationship with Phillips 325–30; notified of Japanese attack 334; attitude to Force Z deployment 336; advises Singapore untenable 341; and Indian Ocean risks 358; advice to Somerville 366; warns of Eastern Fleet annihilation 383
Leahy, Admiral William 94, 176–7, 179
Lee, Brigadier General Raymond 204
Lexington (US) 16
Lion-class (Br) 12, 19, 28, 32, 33, 35, 42, 240, 254
London Naval Conference 1930 8, 10, 11–13, 24, 59, 176
London Naval Conference 1936 24, 29, 176
Lothian, Philip Kerr, Lord: lobbies for American

naval support 184; briefed by naval staff on British priorities 187; and risk to US Navy communications across Pacific 188; authorisation of staff talks 191

Lützow (Ge) 126, 266

MacArthur, General Douglas: briefs Brooke-Popham on B-17 force 288; and Asiatic Fleet dispositions 330; meeting with Phillips 330, 332–4

Madagascar: threat from Japan 392; British operation to seize (Ironclad) 394; 398

Magic, see also Purple 233, 243–4, 273, 327

Majestic-class (Br) construction and qualities 388

Malacca Strait 39, 230

Malay Barrier: 71–2, 120, 144, 146, 148, 150–1, 163; and Rainbow 2 186; and Anglo-American planning 195, 201, 208, 214–5, 218–21, 272, 274, 276–7, 287, 289, 298, 329; and Admiralty offensive strategy 285–6, 293, 298–9, 320

Malaya: and 1937 Far East appreciation 69, 71–3; and Japanese plans to attack 74, 110, 226, 237–9, 273, 290; and 1940 Fae East appreciation 120, 139–49; and plans for defence 149–55; and priority compared to Middle East 158–72, 290; and American assistance 182–3, 185, 187–8, 191, 203–4, 208; and importance to American economy 209; and impact of monsoon 291–2; and warning of imminent attack 318

Malaya, HMS 14–15, 61, 296

Maldives 210, 217, 274, 357, 370

Malta: sacrificed for Far East 65; and Mediterranean Fleet move to Alexandria 72, 149; and 1937 Middle East appreciation 74–5; and Mediterranean transit 82; and Middle East strategy 133; and Halberd 253, 303–4; and Pedestal 265, 390; air reinforcement to East 266, 357, 359; 395

Manchuria 57–8, 272–3

Manila: as potential base for Royal Navy eastern fleet 156, 181, 183, 186, 188, 272, 285–6, 291, 293, 297,345; and US Navy Asiatic Fleet 193, 199, 330; and Brooke-Popham visit 288; Pound warned on vulnerability 289, 298; Pound relaxed about air threat to 290, 308; Phillips visit 318, 325, 330, 332–3, 335, 339; and Force Z inquiry 345

Marder, Arthur: describes Royal Navy engagement with Japan xix; definitive account of Force Z sortie 337; collaboration with Davis 346

Mark 37 anti-aircraft fire control system 46–47

Marshall, General George C: and reinforcement of Philippines 278, 286–7, 289, 300; United States planning prior to Japanese attack 306–7, 348; Defence Committee meeting on invasion western Europe 386–7; Roosevelt's instructions for London visit 397

Martlet (Br), also Wildcat, 258–9, 380, 388, 390, 402

Matapan, Battle of 38, 262, 264, 384

Matsuoka, Yosuke 273

McCrea, Commander John 186

Mediterranean: historiography of British strategy in xvii; Italian threat to 17, 57, 60, 64, 74, 123; balance with Far East 23, 65, 67–8, 70, 74, 79–80, 90, 92–5, 97–8; anticipated closure in war 74–7, 82; and France 80–1, 90–1, 121–2; British strategic risks and opportunities 83–6, 132–5, 165–6, 395, 403–4; and German strategy 127–30,

136–7, 158; lessons for Far East 145, 149, 173, 246–7, 303, 348, 405; and Plan Dog 189; and US Navy support 194, 202, 208, 212; and Torch 396–7

Mediterranean and Middle East appreciation 1937 74–76, 79–80

Mediterranean and Middle East appreciation 1941 161–2

Mediterranean Fleet: night-fighting 38; move to Alexandria 72; role in Far East war 75, 80, 151; as guarantor 86, 135–6, 329, 340; case against 1940 withdrawal 128–30, 136, 216; strength 131, 142, 274, 356; Italian performance against 153, 253, 303–4; commitment to Dominions 141, 172; transfers to Indian Ocean 342, 356

Meiklereid, William 238, 244, 318

Menzies, Robert: seeks assurances from Chamberlain 107; Joint Planning Committee assessment for 158; presses Churchill for Far East reinforcement 275

Menzies, Sir Stewart: war warning message 318

Middle East: historiography I Second World War xvii; strategic status pre-war 74, 76–7, 86, 97, 403; strategic importance in 1940–41 119, 133–8, 165–6, 168, 403–4; and Future strategy paper 128–9; and Churchill directive 158–9; interdependence with Far East 356, 359; and Axis junction 364; Roosevelt's view of 397–8

Midway, battle of 47, 227, 229, 263, 269, 381–3, 387, 389–391, 394–6, 407

Midway-class (US) 45

Minister for Defence Co-ordination, see under Inskip and Chatfield

Ministerial subcommittee on defence policy and requirements 27

Ministry of Aircraft Production 257–8

Mission command 39

Mogami-class (Ja) 226–7, 252, 324

Moore, Vice Admiral Sir Henry: on underestimation of Japanese capability 250; and Force Z disappearing in Pacific 316–7; and 'Future British Naval Strategy' 341–2; and report on loss of Force Z 344, 346–50; 389

Nagato (Ja) 206

Nagumo, Vice Admiral Chuichi 351, 367–70, 372–4, 377–81, 383–4, 386

Nakajima 391

Naval appendix to 1937 Imperial Defence Review 64

Naval Intelligence Division (NID): on IJN strength 227; on IJNAF 228–9; on IJN capital ship modernisation 230–1; and FECB 231–2; and submarine surveillance 235–6; on IJN build plans 240–2; and war warning 242; underestimation of IJN 245; exaggeration of IJN 253–4; 320, 324, 367, 393

Nelson, HMS 4, 7, 11, 205–6, 253, 280–1, 295, 299, 304, 313, 316, 328, 386, 392

Nelson-class (Br) 4, 7–8, 10, 14, 19, 33–4, 69, 87, 108, 141–2, 206, 211, 230, 274, 281–5, 295, 411

Netherlands East Indies: vital to British Far East security 63; Japanese contemplate seizing 121, 156; oil output 135; and Far East appreciation 140, 143–7, 150–1; and Far East commanders' assumptions 152; British need credible policy towards 180–1; United States prepared for loss

190, 203; Admiralty resists guarantee 219; and
Dutch policy of 'aloofness' 219–20; Magic
illuminates Japanese plan to attack 273; Dutch-
Japanese relations break down 273; Japanese
integrated plan to seize oil 290; American plan to
secure with Philippines reinforcement 306; and
final war warning 315; PLENAPS and 327; Hart-
Phillips plans to shield 331–3; impact of lost oil on
Allies 360–1
New Standard Fleet, see under Standards
New Zealand xv, 11, 64–5, 68, 70, 104, 109, 126,
  162, 167–8, 178, 194, 201, 218, 222, 343, 361
Noble, Admiral Sir Percy 71, 100, 113, 232
North Africa: and Axis access if Spain enters war
  123, 127; and tension between Germany and Italy
  129; and Compass 133; and strategic impact on
  war 135–8; 158, 164, 202; and wearing down
  Germany 165–6; and Crusader 172; and IJN
  interdiction 386; and Torch 396
North Carolina (US) 19, 49, 264, 279–80

O'Connor, Lieutenant General Sir Richard 133
Oerlikon anti-aircraft gun 49
Oil, see also Iraq and Persia: xvii – xviii; Japan's
  access to 58–9, 156, 161, 273, 290, 393; and
  closure of Mediterranean in war 75, 77, 82; and
  French supplies 80, 91; and bombarding Italian
  storage facilities 96; as factor in defence of Middle
  East 97, 120, 127–8, 132–5, 158–9, 165–8, 173–
  4; Germany's limited supplies 128–30, 134–5, 216,
  396–8; supplies to Spain 128; IJN failure to secure
  supply lines 251; importance of Persian fields and
  Abadan 343, 358–61, 363–4, 385–6, 394–5, 404,
  406
Oil Board 75
OKW (Oberkommando der Wehrmacht, German
  Supreme Command) strategic survey 136–7, 396
Okinawa 45
One-power standard, see standards
Operational Intelligence Centre (OIC) 232
Oran 121
Oshima, Lieutenant General Hiroshi 233, 273, 364
Ozawa, Vice Admiral Jisaburo 351, 384

Pacific Naval Intelligence Organisation, see also
  Operational Intelligence Centre, 232
Pacific war, xix; as defined by Chatfield 65; 287
Page, Sir Earle 288. 299
Palliser, Rear Admiral Arthur 285, 318, 322, 337
Pearl Harbor (American spelling) 45, 156, 179, 183,
  186, 201, 213, 221, 233, 245, 247–8, 262, 286,
  290, 307–8, 324, 329, 332, 335, 346–7, 356, 361,
  366–7, 378, 407
Pedestal 265, 390, 394–6, 398
Perseus HMS/M 236
Persia: 359, 404; and oil supplies xv, xix, 120, 128,
  132, 166–8, 343, 359, 361, 385, 394–5, 397–8,
  404, 406; and supplies to Russia xv, xix, 343,
  362–3, 385, 397–8, 404, 406, 408
Persian Gulf 108, 111, 127, 131–3, 158, 343, 358–
  62, 385, 391, 397
Perth (Aus) 209, 245
Petroleum Board 360–1
Philippines: 157; as advanced base for Royal Navy
  169, 177, 286, 298; as barrier to Japanese
  southward advance 180, 183, 218, 272, 278, 306–

8; American air reinforcement of 278, 287–9, 291,
294, 300; Japanese decision to attack 171, 290,
324; and PLENAPS 327; and US Navy Asiatic
Fleet 330–2
Phillips, Admiral Sir Tom: and one-power standard
  5–6; and balance between Germany and Japan 27;
  and carrier building rate 42; and comparison of
  Royal Navy and IJN air capability 42–4; career,
  personal qualities and achievements 43; approves
  new Far East war plans and ' flying squadron'
  101–2; Tientsin planning and Far East 'flexible
  reinforcement' 105–7, 109; relations with Pound
  111–113; authorship of Singapore strategy 149;
  and threat to Indian Ocean communications 172,
  275; meeting with Ingersoll 176–7; and US Navy
  use of Singapore 179; and Bellairs paper 182–3;
  and preparation for ABC-1 staff talks 192;
  Danckwerts warning over American attitudes to
  ABC-1 217–8; large US Pacific Fleet a 'waste' 222;
  proposed for 'Cape' command 276; relationship
  with Harwood 285; and offensive deployment
  north of Singapore 285, 289, 294; awareness of
  American reinforcement of Philippines 289;
  appointed C-in-C Eastern Fleet 292; Defence
  Committee meetings 294–6; nominated to lead Far
  East negotiations with Americans 298–9; and
  Indomitable 301, 331; and Force Z questions 310;
  and Force Z movements 312–4; and warnings
  from Willis and Smuts 313; and holding Force Z at
  Ceylon 315–7; decisions on arrival at Singapore
  317–8; and SIS warning 319; and options for
  moving Force Z from Singapore 319–20; failure to
  exploit FECB intelligence 321–4, 327, 366;
  relationship with Layton 325–6, 328–9; and
  Brooke-Popham 326–7; and pre-war options for
  Force Z 329–30; meetings with MacArthur and
  Hart 330–3; case for intervention after Japanese
  attack and personal motivations 334–5;
  understanding of attitudes in London 335–6;
  position of later critics 336; decisions during Force
  Z deployment 337–40; attitude to air threat at sea
  339–40; responsibility for offensive strategy 340,
  345–6, 349–50
Placentia Bay, see Riviera
Plan Dog 175, 188–91, 196, 201
Playfair, Major General Ian 150, 250, 291
PLENAPS (Plans for the Employment of Naval and
  Air Forces of the Associated Powers) 327–8, 331–
  2
Portal, Marshal of the Royal Air Force, Sir Charles:
  plans to double Middle East air strength 160;
  hopes to engage 30 percent of German air strength
  in Mediterranean 166; argument with Pound over
  maritime air resources 268–9; attitude to bombing
  campaign 270; briefing to Page 288; and
  Philippines reinforcement 299
Port T, Maldives 210, origins 217, 274, 342, 357,
  365, 368–71, 377, 380, 382, 384
Pound, Admiral of the Fleet Sir Dudley: and Phillips
  43, 112–13; and 1937 Mediterranean and Middle
  East appreciation 74–5; stresses problem of
  Mediterranean transit in war 81–2; promotes
  offensive against Libya 86, 96–7; and 'knock-out
  blow' against Italy 92, 96–7; endorsement of new
  Far East war plan and 'flying squadron' 101;
  Tientsin and implications for Far East

reinforcement 104–7, 109; qualities and achievements as First Sea Lord 111–13; and creation of Singapore strategy 149–50; and Japanese threat to Indian Ocean 169, 172, 178, 216, 358; advocates increased fighter strength for Far East 170; and Hampton report 177; and Bailey committee 177; and balance between Mediterranean and Far East 180; gives Bailey report to Ghormley 180; brief for US President 184; and Ambassador Lord Lothian 184, 188; and US Navy deployment to Singapore 185, 188, 192, 194, 200; emphasises priority of Atlantic 186, 190, 198; and ABC-1 negotiations 203, 205, 207, 216; instructions for new eastern fleet 205–6; warned on limitations of US Navy Pacific Fleet 221; and consequences of US Navy transfers to Atlantic 222; underestimation of IJN 249–50; and transfer of air resources to meet naval priorities 268–9; and historic presentation of Force Z 271; exchange with prime minister on Far East naval reinforcement 230, 274, 276–83; development of Far East forward deployment strategy 284, 286; and air threat to Manila 289–90, 298; appointment of Phillips as C-in-C Eastern Fleet 292; October Defence Committee meetings 293–97; proposal to Stark for 'fresh start' on Far East 298; War Cabinet discussion on Far East reinforcement 299–300; and prime minister over-riding advice of naval advisers 300; and *Indomitable* 302; and flaws in Admiralty offensive planning 305–6, 309; and deployment of Force Z 311–17; and moving Force Z from Singapore 319–20, 324; exchanges with Layton 328–9; commitment to battle-fleet at Singapore after outbreak of war 332; attitude to Force Z intervention 335, 339; and responsibility for loss of Force Z 340, 350; and Force Z inquiry 344–5, 347; shares prediction of aggressive IJN raiding action in Indian Ocean with King 364, 387; directs Somerville to avoid unnecessary risks 365–6; uneasy with Somerville's conduct at Ceylon 383; slow to grasp carrier warfare 388; and US Navy request for help in southwest Pacific 394; reluctance to weaken Eastern Fleet 394; 406

Prince of Wales, HMS xiv, xvi, 19, 43, 47–8, 253, 262, 293–5, 297–9, 302, 304, 307, 310–14, 318, 320, 324, 333–4, 338, 347, 349

Prinz Eugen (Ge) 197

Purple, see also Magic, 233–5, 242, 244

Queen Elizabeth, HMS 14, 15, 69, 84, 230, 255, 342, 348, 356

Queen Elizabeth-class (Br) 33, 69, 87–8, 142, 230–1, 265, 296

Radar (also RDF): 23, 27, 37; and transformation of fighter defence 44–5; and anti-aircraft fire control 47, 49; and U-boat night surface attack 51; 155; IJN lack of for fire control 231; 239, 251; Fleet Air Arm development for fighter direction 258, 261, 263; and ASV 261, 264; and Somerville radar pickets 263; 308, 338–9; at Ceylon 369, 372, 378, 381, 383; 389–92, 402

RDF (see radar)

Raeder, Großadmiral (Grand Admiral) Erich 129, 136, 273

Rainbow war plans: Rainbow 2 186, 188, 190; Rainbow 3 186, 190, 198, 200–1; Rainbow 5 196, 198, 200–1, 220

Ramillies, HMS 311, 394

Ranger (US) 16, 201

Rearmament 14, 16, 18, 22–3, 25, 29, 34, 37, 46, 64, 68, 79, 81, 124, 411–2

Red cypher 234–5

Regulus, HMS/M 235–236

Renown, HMS 14, 49, 69, 84, 108, 141, 178, 205–6, 209, 230–1, 281, 283, 296, 316, 396

Repulse, HMS viii, xiv, xvi, 14–15, 48, 61, 108, 262, 271, 280, 283–4, 292, 294, 296–8, 300, 302, 305, 307, 311–12, 314, 320, 324, 333, 335, 340, 348

Resolution, HMS 15, 311, 394

Revenge, HMS 84, 108, 284, 292, 311, 314, 329, 331, 340

Richelieu (Fr) 121, 262

Richmond, Admiral Herbert 56

Riviera summit meeting at Placentia Bay, Newfoundland, also Atlantic conference 218, 220, 275–280, 284, 286–8, 295, 345

Rodney, HMS 4, 7, 11, 205–6, 280–1, 293, trade-off with *Prince of Wales* for Far East reinforcement 295, 298–9, 304, 313, 316, 328, 386, 392, 396

Romania and Romanian oil 129–130, 132, 134, 404

Roosevelt, President Franklin: and new naval investment 10; and strategic withdrawal from Middle East 159, 165–6; and Singapore basing 179; orders US Navy Fleet to remain at Pearl Harbor 179; message to Hart 186; authorises staff talks with Britain 191–2; and Japan warnings at Riviera 278; and overstretch between Atlantic and Pacific 278; and Philippines reinforcement 287; Joint Board memoranda and American-British deterrence of Japan 306–7; and American-British division of responsibility 360; and threat to Indian Ocean 385; and Torch and impact on Middle East 397

Roskill, Stephen W 3, 112, 282, 294, 343, 346–7, 350, 406

Royal Air Force: relationship with Fleet Air Arm 10, 16, 40, 402; and pre-war pressures on defence budget 29, 124; and pre-war plans for trade protection 52; inferior to Italian forces facing Egypt 80; and consequences of fall of France 121; 1940 Far East appreciation and strength in Malaya 146–7, 155, 239, 246; commitment in Middle East 158; impact on of aid to Russia 168; and potential trade-offs between Far East and Middle East 171–2; and ranking Japanese with Italians 253; maritime strike capability 265–70; and intelligence on Japanese air capability 322–3; reconnaissance in Gulf of Siam 326, 331, 339; cover for Force Z 336, 338; reinforcement of India and Ceylon 358; aerial surveillance of IJN raid on Ceylon 368; Blenheim strike on IJN task force 381; losses at Ceylon 384; and upgrade of Ceylon defences 389, 391–2

Royal Navy: rearmament programme xx, 4, 13, 21–4, 42–3, 54, 71, 124, 189, 225, 242, 401–7

Royal Oak, HMS 14, 15, 61

Royal Sovereign, HMS 15, 311, 331, 394

'R'-class (*Royal Sovereign* class) battleships (Br) 108–9, 141; join new Eastern Fleet following 'Atlantic substitution' 206; 211, 257; refits for service in

East 276; Churchill criticises capability 280–1; Admiralty plans for deployment to Singapore 283–6, 293, 295, 297; limitations in fighting the IJN 304; to form 3rd Battle Squadron 311; Admiralty place at core of Singapore battle-fleet despite poor quality 332–3, 340; delay in deploying to the East 342, 345–6; 348; part of Somerville's fleet off Ceylon 365, 370, 394; and 'Atlantic substitution' 405

Russia, also Soviet Union: Japanese attitudes to threat from 57–8, 93, 156, 273, 308; German encouragement to attack Persian Gulf 127; German plans against and implications for Middle East 129–30, 132, 134, 136–8, 162, 164, 396; and Persian supply route 137, 165–6, 343, 362–3, 385–6, 397, 404, 408; impact of British lend-lease supplies on 166, 168–9; impact of German invasion on British prospects 272–3, 278; and autumn 1941 assessments of threat to Malaya 290–1; and impact of Torch on 397

Ryujo (Ja) 16, 42, 227, 235, 324

Saratoga (US) 16

Scharnhorst (Ge) 13, 17, 33, 69, 126, 197, 242, 266

Secret Intelligence Service (SIS) 52; unable to provide war warning for Malaya 154; administration of GC&CS 232; unable to cover IJN building programme 235–6; exploitation of French liaison sources in Indo-China 238–9; reporting on IJN super battleships and battlecruisers 240; 242, 244, 315; war warning report to Manila 318–9

Shanghai 62

Shaw, Paymaster Lieutenant Commander Harry 366–7

Shokaku (Ja) 228, 241, 248, 373, 393

SIGINT (Signals Intelligence): contribution to FECB 232–3; liaison with Dutch 234; limitations 235; 238, 242–4, 315, 318–9, 327; contribution during attack on Ceylon 366–8, 373, 377, 380: 385

Singapore base: 4, 8, 15; selection of 56; as 'pivot of naval strategic position in Far East' 62; as 'keystone' 68, 78, 95, 148, 162; symbolic status 73; distance via Suez 75; ability to withstand attack 110–11, 144–5; as foothold for recovery 127; why strategic status not challenged 149–50; cost of 149; Churchill's views as 'fortress' 151–2; American scepticism over 204–4, 214; Admiralty assumes always available 274

Singapore strategy: historical status xiv, xvii, xix; and New Standard 31; definition and origins 56; critics of 56; 1937 Far East review as stocktake 64; and 1937 Imperial conference debates 70, 73; and 1937 China crisis; and 1939 British strategic adjustments 94, 95; and Tientsin crisis 102–3; and fall of France 122; and personalities 149; and loss of Force Z 271–2, 342, 349; the strategy in perspective 399, 401, 404, 407

Singora aka Songkhla 319, 337

Sinkov-Rosen mission 233

Smuts, Field Marshal J C 313, 392–3

Somerville, Admiral Sir James: respects Italian air capability 253; and multi-task air operations 263; and deficiencies of 'R'-class 281; critical of Phillips 325, 336; and Spartivento inquiry 334, 383; meets Eastern Fleet 355; qualities as leader and naval commander 365; and composition of initial

Eastern Fleet 365; Admiralty directive to 365–6; and FECB 366–7; and IJN attack on Ceylon 368–80; performance at Ceylon 380, 382–4; views on Fleet Air Arm 388; operates off Ceylon through mid-1942 389; and rise and decline of Eastern Fleet 394–5

Soryu (Ja) 16, 42, 227, 373–4

Southampton-class (Br) 13, 226

Soviet Union, also Russia: and defence of India 58; and consequences of German attack from northern Iraq 135; and British oil supplies 135; comparative performance of wartime aircraft industry with Japan 251

Spain: Admiralty alert to alliance with Axis 123; German effort to bring into war and threat to Gibraltar 127–9, 137, 158, 196–7; influence of British position in Middle East on 159, 165, 173; impact of American entry into war on 221; and Atlantic trade war 404

Spitfire (Br) 154, 160, modification for carrier deployment 260

Stalingrad 363, 397

Standards, measures of comparative naval strength: one-power standard 5–6, 10, 56, 59; two-power standard 5–6, 9, 22, 24–25, 27; 1932 standard 6, 26–27, 60; new standard 22–29, 31–34, 44, 53, 61, 64, 67, 254

Stanhope, Viscount, First Lord 1938–39 83–86, 88, 92–93, 97

Stark, Admiral Harold: and keeping US Navy Fleet in Pearl Harbor 179; tells Hart no backing down with Japan 186; produces Plan Dog 188–91; and British 1940 ship losses 196; favours early clash with Germany 275; reaffirms Atlantic substitution at Riviera 279–80; briefs Kimmel on Royal Navy Far East reinforcement 283, 289, 292; favours Philippines reinforcement 289; warns Pound on vulnerability of Manila 289; agrees 'fresh start' with Pound on Far East reinforcement 298, 312–13, 328; and Joint Board discussions 306; rejects Hart's offensive plans 330; approves Hart-Phillips conference recommendations 332

Stimson, Henry: favours maximum naval transfers to the Atlantic 221; lobbyist for Philippines bomber force 287; briefs British ambassador Lord Halifax on B-17 regional coverage 288; 289

Strasbourg (Fr) 121

Strategic Appreciations Committee 83, 85, 88–90, 92–3, 96, 99, 105, 128

Sudan 158, 357

Suez Canal: risk of Japanese sabotage 62; and 1937 Mediterranean and Middle East appreciation 74–5; defence requires strategic depth 97; German plans to seize 127, 130; value to Germany 133, 135; and 1941 briefing of Australian prime minister 158; and 1941 Middle East defence review 165; disruptive mining by Italians 253; and deployment of Eastern fleet for Malta convoy 395; re-opening to through traffic 397; Roosevelt's views on 397–8

Swordfish (Br) 258, 260, capability as part of overall weapon system 261, at Taranto 262, 390

Tachymetric anti-aircraft system 46–47, 50

Takoradi air route 169, 357

Tambor-class (US) 333

Taylor, Commander E G USN, 263
Tennant, Captain William 305
Ten-year rule 8, 22
Terry, Captain John 285, 344–5
Thomas, Major General Georg, German chief of war
  economy 130
Tientsin 62; 1939 crisis and consequences for naval
  strategy 99, 102–9, 111, 141, 183, 252
Tirpitz (Ge) 125, 197, 280
Tojo, General Hideki 364
Tokyo: Royal Navy proposes attack by US Navy
  carrier aircraft 193; decision-makers consider
  response to German attack on Russia 273; alert to
  eastward deployment of *Prince of Wales* 314; war
  warnings to overseas missions 315; Doolittle raid
  387; lack of combined strategy with Berlin 409
Tone (Ja) 367, 373–4; *Tone*-class 227
Torbeau (Br) 268
Torch 395–8
Torpedo: problems in US and German submarines 37,
  217; inadequacies of US Navy aerial torpedoes
  260; Fleet Air Arm Mark XII with duplex warhead
  121, 229, excellence of 260–1; Royal Air Force
  shortages for Beaufort force 267; IJNAF Type 91
  229, 261; IJN Long Lance 245, 303, 339; Italian
  human torpedo 348
Torpedo Strike Reconnaissance (TSR) 39
Treasury 5, 6, 8, 21, 25
Tribal-class (Br) 87
Trincomalee: alternative to Singapore 149, 217;
  Pound judges best base to protect Indian Ocean
  178, 307, 342; lacks repair facilities 357;
  Somerville anticipates IJN strike against 368, 370,
  374, 380–1.
Tripartite pact 181
Triple threat xiv, 55, 56, 70, 77, 78, 115
Tripoli, Lebanon 80 133–4
Turing, Alan 234
Turkey 86, 93, 97, 128–30, 132, 137, 158–9, 164–5,
  173, 341
Turner, Rear Admiral Richmond Kelly: influence on
  US Navy thinking pre-war 41; and Plan Dog 190–
  1; rejects Singapore basing 192; and Asiatic Fleet
  reinforcement 199–201; and 'Atlantic substitution'
  204; protective of ABC-1 principles 218; considers
  ADB-1 unsound 220; and Pacific Fleet reductions
  220–1; and redeployment of 'R'-class to Cape 276;
  and relief of Force H 279; US finds ADB-2
  unsatisfactory 286; plays down joint operating
  plan 287; doubts air defence in Philippines 289;
  and Hart inquiry 307
Two-hemisphere war xv, 33, 42, 53, 64, 66
Two-power standard, see standards

U-boats: production 1935–42 35; 1939 strength and
  build rate 36; Royal Navy anticipation of

campaign 51–3; and implications of fall of France
  123, 125–6; and December 1940 Admiralty survey
  196–7; and reduced shipping losses second half
  1941 212–13; losses to August 1941 256; and
  Indian Ocean 277; and losses of tankers early
  1942 361; 396, 411
Ugaki, Rear Admiral Matome 364
Ultimate enemy, Germany as 22, 26, 202
Ultra intelligence 162, 198, 213, 327
Unicorn, HMS 28, 32, 44
United States Army War Plans Division 315

Val Type 99 D3A (Ja) 391
Valiant, HMS 14–15, 49, 69, 84, 230, 342, 348, 356,
  365, 386, 392, 394
Vanguard, HMS 33, 254, 408
Vansittart, Sir Robert 21
VHF (Very High Frequency) 45, 251, 258, 264, 339
Vichy France 134, 159, 173, 238
Victorious, HMS 33, 44; *Bismarck* operation 261,
  263–4; 279, 301–2; Pedestal 390; Torch 396;
  deployed to US Navy Pacific Fleet 398
Vildebeest (Br) 265, 267
Vittorio Veneto (It) 12, 262
Vivian, Captain J P G 252

War Cabinet 114, 138, 141, 167–8, 170, 181, 221,
  230, 243, 275, 291, 299–300, 311, 347, 361
War Memorandum Eastern (Eastern naval war plan)
  99–101, 105, 107–8, 182
War Memorandum European (European naval war
  plan) 104–5, 107–9
War Office 244
War potential of eastern empire xx, 120, 134, 137,
  166–8, 173, 400, 403–4, 406, 408
Warspite, HMS: modernisation 14; 61, 69; hits
  Italian *Giulio Cesare* at Calabria 126; 230;
  Somerville's flagship at Ceylon 1942 355, 365,
  370, 372; remains with Eastern Fleet 392, 394
Washington Naval Limitations Treaty 4–5, 7, 9–10,
  12–13, 226
Welles, Sumner 277
Wildcat (US), also Martlet, 40, 258–61, 263, 338
Willis, Vice Admiral Sir Algernon 269–70, 312–13,
  336, 365, 370, 383–4
'Winds Alert' messages 315, 319, 334
WW1 138

Yamamoto, Admiral Isoruku 248–9, 266, 366, 387
Yamato (Ja) 12, 36, 49, 240–1
Yorktown (US) 16, 47, 201

Zero A6M (Ja): 40, 228; numbers at start of war
  229; intelligence on 229, 238, 249; comparison
  with Fulmar 261; at Ceylon 377–8
Zuikaku (Ja) 228, 241, 248, 373, 393